THE
BOOK OF
KEY FACTS

POLITICS
WARS
SCIENCE
LITERATURE
THE ARTS

The Queensbury Group

**PADDINGTON
PRESS LTD**
NEW YORK & LONDON

Library of Congress Cataloging in Publication Data
Queensbury Design Group.
   The book of key facts.

   Includes index.
   1.   Encyclopedias and dictionaries. I. Title.
AG6.Q43   1978   031   77-16267
ISBN 0-448-22896-3

Copyright © 1978 Paddington Press (U.K.) Ltd.
All rights reserved
Compiled for The Queensbury Group
by David Lambert MA (Cantab),
Maurice Chandler and Bernard Moore FRSA
Edited by Peter Presence
Index: Joodi Lynch
Filmset in England by
SX Composing, Rayleigh, Essex.

IN THE UNITED STATES
PADDINGTON PRESS
Distributed by
GROSSET & DUNLAP

IN THE UNITED KINGDOM
PADDINGTON PRESS

IN CANADA
Distributed by
RANDOM HOUSE OF CANADA LTD.

IN SOUTHERN AFRICA
Distributed by
ERNEST STANTON (PUBLISHERS) (PTY) LTD.

INTRODUCTION

Here at last is the essential family reference book for everyone who needs and enjoys the authority of facts. *The Book of Key Facts* is a comprehensive, easy-to-use guide to what, when and where it all happened. The 30,000 key facts of world politics, science, discovery, wars, religion, literature and the arts give you instant history—in perspective.

How To Use Your Book of Key Facts

To get an immediate sense of all the major happenings of any one year or period, turn to the Timetable section of the book. Look at 1867, for example. You will see that among other important events, the US bought Alaska from Russia; the Dominion of Canada was created; Garibaldi failed to capture Rome; Strauss composed "The Blue Danube" waltz; Lister introduced antiseptic surgery; and Marx penned the first volume of "Das Kapital."

If you wish to look up a particular event or character, turn to the Index. Take "New Orleans, battle of," for example. At a glance you will see that it was fought in 1815. Turn to "Brown, John," and you will find two dates against his name. Look up the first, 1856, in the Timetable section and you can see that John Brown headed a massacre at Pottawatomie Creek in the "Bleeding Kansas" war over slavery. Then look up the second date, 1859, and you will find that he led the attack on Harper's Ferry for which he was hanged.

This ingeniously designed time-saver of a book shows you what influences were at work in the world at any one time. Any event must be put into perspective, and *The Book of Key Facts* does it.

30,000-5001 BC

Last Ice Age in progress, 30,000 BC • Ice sheets cover much of Northern Hemisphere • Sea level lowered by the quantity of water held on land as ice • First men to enter North America arrive 30,000 BC or earlier from northeastern Asia by land bridge across the Bering Strait • All continents except Antarctica and South America are now peopled • In Europe, Cro-Magnon hunters establish last and richest phase of Paleolithic (Old Stone Age) culture by 30,000 BC • Earliest known cave paintings executed in France and Spain 30,000 BC • Earth mother statuette made in Austria c. 30,000 BC • Oldest known ceramic (bear's head) fashioned in Moravia (now part of Czechoslovakia), c. 25,000 BC • Earliest known rafts used in southeastern Asia, c. 24,000 BC • Earliest known Asian sculpture of a face executed, c. 18,000 BC • Bone sewing needles used in France by 18,000 BC • Oldest musical instrument (bone pipe) used in Pyrenees, 16,000 BC • Spear-throwing device used in Europe, 13,000 BC • Man reaches southern South America by 10,500 BC • Ice sheets in retreat by 10,000 BC • Mesolithic (Middle Stone Age) hunting cultures emerge c. 10,000 BC • Bow and arrow in use by 9000 BC • Dog domesticated by 9000 BC • Neolithic (New Stone Age) agricultural cultures emerging in southwestern Asia by 9000 BC • Sheep domesticated by Iraq 8000 BC • Pottery appears in Japan c. 8000 BC • Paleolithic hunters prey on bison in North America, 8000 BC • Copper first used 8000 BC • Jericho (now in Jordan), oldest known city, settled by 8000 BC • Dwellings are built of bricks in Middle East by 7000 BC • Wheat cultivated in Middle East, 7000 BC • Loom used for weaving in Middle East, c. 6000 BC

5000-3501 BC

Sumerians established in lower Mesopotamia by 5000 BC • Boomerang used in Australia, 5000 BC • Irrigation canals built in Iraq by 5000 BC • Corn cultivated in Mexico by 5000 BC • Copper spear points made near America's Great Lakes, 5000 BC • Honeybee domesticated in Eurasia and Africa by 4500 BC • Neolithic Jomon culture flourishes in Japan by 4500 BC • Rock paintings made in Sahara Desert, 4500 BC • Collapsible huts are built in Central Asia • Neolithic culture replaces Mesolithic culture along the Mediterranean Sea coast • Sailing boats are built in Egypt • City-states begin evolving in Sumeria (southern Mesopotamia), for example at Al Ubaid • Grapes are grown for winemaking in the Middle East • Painted pottery appears in southeastern Europe • Sledges come into use in northern Eurasia • Earliest known map, showing Euphrates River, inscribed on clay tablet, c. 3800 BC • Jewish calendar starts at 3760 BC • Bronze alloy in limited use by Sumerians and Egyptians, about 3750 BC • Painted fabric made in Egypt about the same time • Cretan ships active in eastern Mediterranean • Harps and flutes are played in Egypt • Sumerians settle on site of Babylon between 4000 BC and 3500 BC • Colored ceramics from the Ukraine reach China

3500-3001 BC

Sumerian civilization, based on city-states, developing by 3500 BC • Neolithic culture now spreading from the eastern Mediterranean through Europe • Elamite script inscribed on tablets in southeast Iran, c. 3500 BC • Wheeled vehicles first appear in Sumeria, c. 3500 BC • Sumerian temples built at Eridu, Al Ubaid, Uruk and Tepe Gawra (now in Iraq) • In Egypt and Sumeria, food surplus produced by improved farming methods sustains an increasing variety of full-time specialist craftsmen, including smiths and masons • Egyptian vessels trade in the Mediterranean Sea • Potatoes are grown in South America by 3500 BC • Egyptians develop the *mastaba*, a burial pit covered by a brick platform and forerunner of pyramids • Flax is grown for linen-making in the Middle East • Egyptians develop earliest known numerals and a hieroglyphic script • 3372 BC is first date of the Mayan chronology • Egypt's so-called Gerzean culture is established by 3200 BC • Clay tablets are inscribed with pictographic precursor of Sumerian cuneiform (wedge-shaped) script at a temple in Uruk, just before 3000 BC • Sumerians use the arch principle of building construction by the end of this period • Egypt is not yet politically united, but consists of two kingdoms: the Upper Kingdom in the north, and the Lower Kingdom in the south around the Nile River delta

3000–2701 BC

Bronze Age well established in southwestern Asia by 3000 BC • Bronze Age begins in southeastern Europe after 3000 BC • Semitic tribes occupy Assyria and Akkad in Mesopotamia, c. 3000 BC, living side by side with the already-established Sumerians • Semitic Phoenicians establish themselves on Syrian coast, notably at Tyre and Sidon • Merchant trading ships active off Egyptian coast by 3000 BC • Sumerians build *ziggurats*, stepped brick pyramids topped by temples • Mediterranean ships first venture into the Atlantic Ocean, c. 3000 BC • Sumerians begin using drums and lyres to make music • Wrestling is shown on wall-paintings in Egypt and Iraq • Sumerians use oil lamps • Beehive-shaped huts are built in central Africa by 3000 BC • Asses used as beasts of burden in the Middle East, c. 3000 BC • Inflated skin rafts used in Middle East c. 3000 BC • Trepanning is practiced • Plow is in use in Mesopotamia • Wheel-thrown pottery made in Mesopotamia • Neolithic (New Stone Age) culture reaches Britain c. 3000 BC • Neolithic culture at its peak in the Danube River region, c. 2900 BC • Egyptians use standard measures by 2900 BC • According to tradition Menes, King of Upper Egypt, unites Upper and Lower Egypt, founding the first dynasty of pharaohs, c. 2850 BC • China enters a golden age under the legendary Sage Kings, c. 2850 BC • Chinese musicians use bamboo pipes • Egyptians make metal mirrors by 2850 BC • Sumerians at Ur produce clay tablets inscribed with writing, 2800 BC • Early Bronze Age cultures flourish in and near the Aegean Sea by c. 2800 BC • Dams being built in Egypt by 2750 BC • Silbury Hill, Wiltshire, largest manmade mound in Europe, built in England c. 2745 BC

2700–2401 BC

Gilgamesh (Sumerian hero of one of the world's first epics) rules at Uruk in Sumeria, c. 2700 BC • Egypt's Old Kingdom period (under dynasties III–IV) starts 2615 BC • Memphis becomes Egyptian capital • Physician Imhotep designs the Step Pyramid of Saqqara (first Egyptian pyramid) for Pharaoh Zoser, c. 2615–2565 BC • First true pyramid is built at Meidum for Pharaoh Sneferu, c. 2550 BC • Khufu (Greek version of name, Cheops) erects the Great Pyramid at Gizeh, c. 2500 BC • Khafre (Chephren) follows with another great pyramid and the Sphinx • Soon after, Menkaure (Mycerinus) erects the third pyramid of Gizeh • Lime kilns are used in Mesopotamia by about 2500 BC • Cowries are used in Asia as one of the first forms of currency by 2500 BC • In what is now Pakistan, Indus Valley civilization emerges c. 2500 BC, with Harappa and Mohenjo-Daro as major centers • Semitic Canaanite tribes are now in Palestine • Early Minoan Bronze Age culture thrives in Crete, 2500–2200 BC • Peruvians grow beans, chili, cotton and squash by 2500 BC • Skis are used in Scandinavia by end of this period • Long-barrows (Neolithic burials) are constructed in Britain • Egyptians use papyrus to write on • Neolithic (New Stone Age) culture reaches Scandinavia by 2500 BC • Neolithic Scandinavians at first bury their dead in pits, later dig graves with passages leading to many-sided chambers • Sumerian royal tombs at Ur constructed, probably after 2500 BC • Earliest known major collection of literature assembled at Ebla, Syria, c. 2450 BC • Egyptian priests gain power during Dynasty V, 2440–2315 BC

2400–2201 BC

Lugalzaggisi, ruler of the Sumerian city-state of Uruk, c. 2400–2350 BC, conquers Lagash and seizes all Sumeria • Sargon, ruler of Akkad, north of Sumeria, crushes Lugalzaggisi, seizes all Mesopotamia and builds world's first empire, ranging from Syria east to Iran, c. 2360 BC • The talent, a Sumerian measure of weight, is now in use • World's first observatory is built in Mesopotamia by 2300 BC • Egyptian religious writings known as *Pyramid Texts* are made, c. 2300 BC • Akkadian Empire reaches its peak under Sargon's grandson Naramsin, 2280–2244 BC, first Mesopotamian ruler to style himself "divine" • Trade develops between cities of Mesopotamia and Indus Valley (now in Pakistan) • Pharaoh Teti founds Dynasty VI in Egypt, c. 2315 BC; it lasts to 2175 BC • Authority of pharoahs weakens during the reign of Pepi II, c. 2270–2180 BC; viziers (chief ministers) gain power during this period • According to tradition, Chinese astronomers work out the times of solstices and equinoxes before 2200 BC • First works on astronomy are written in Mesopotamia, c. 2230 BC • China's semilegendary Hsia Dynasty traditionally begins 2205 BC • Resurrection cult of Isis and Osiris develops in Egypt at this time • Ishtar is established as the supreme goddess of Sumeria and Akkad • In Mesopotamia Semitic writing (right to left, vertical) replaces the Sumerian style (left to right, horizontal) • Chinese music develops a five-tone scale • Egyptian ships import gold from African lands in the south • Crete's Early Minoan culture uses the bull and snake as religious symbols

2200-2001

Barbarians from further north in Europe begin to colonize Greece *c.* 2200 BC, overthrowing existing Bonze Age civilizations; early form of Greek is spoken there • Painted pottery is made in northwestern China about now • Middle Minoan (middle Bronze Age) culture flourishes in Crete from *c.* 2200 BC • Minoan pottery reaches Greece • Middle Bronze Age cultures thrive in the Aegean Sea area • Farming develops in Malaya, where Indonesian peoples replace Melanesians • Akkadian rule collapses in Mesopotamia by 2180 BC • Feudalism develops in Egypt and destroys central authority • Egypt's Old Kingdom effectively ends by *c.* 2175 BC • Civil strife between rival dynasties creates an intermediate dynastic period (Dynasties VIII–XI) in Egypt, 2175–1991 BC • Egypt is divided until reunited under Mentuhotep II of Dynasty XI, 2133–1992 BC, who makes Thebes his capital • Egyptians, who believe that royalty have a life after death, begin to think that people not of royal birth may also have an afterlife • Athotes writes a history of Egypt, *c.* 2124 BC • Temple of Mentuhotep is built near Thebes, *c.* 2065 BC • Kings of the Third Dynasty of Ur revive Sumerian power and dominate Mesopotamia, 2060–1950 BC • King Urnammu of Ur, *c.* 2060–2043 BC, establishes the oldest known code of laws, and builds a *ziggurat* faced with kiln-fired bricks and crowned by a temple • Empire of Ur is at its peak under Urnammu's son Shulgi, 2042–1995 BC; his lands include Elam and Assyria

2000-1801 BC

Bronze Age culture reaches Spain, *c,* 2000 BC • Crete's Middle Minoan period continues • Megalithic (huge stone) structures are built in western Mediterranean region and Brittany, *c.* 2000 BC • Egyptians influence Crete • Elephants and chickens are domesticated in Indus Valley by 2000 BC • Earliest extant dyed cloth (mummy linen) dates from *c.* 2000 BC • Rice is cultivated in Asia by 2000 BC • First Chinese maps appear, *c.* 2000 BC • Pile houses are built in southeastern Asia, *c.* 2000 BC • Crete exports copper, ceramics, timber and olives and imports gold, marble, silver • Carpenters develop joinery techniques • Tripod cooking pots appear in northeastern China • Horses are domesticated in central Asia, *c.* 2000 BC • Locks and latches are used in Egypt • Signs of the Zodiac are established in Mesopotamia • Tobacco is grown in Mexico and Amazon region of South America by 2000 BC • Despite political disunion, Egyptian literature flourishes: *Story of Sinuhe,* earliest known novel • Egypt's Middle Kingdom (Dynasty XII), 1991–1786 BC; centralized rule is restored, bringing fresh stability, prosperity and cultural growth • Pharaoh Amenemhet I begins Egyptian wars of conquest • Sesostris I of Egypt leads a task force into Canaan (Palestine), 1950 BC • Assyrians build a great temple and palace at Mari in western Mesopotamia, *c.* 1950 BC • Ancient Britons begin building Stonehenge in southern England, *c.* 1900 BC • Sesostris II of Egypt (1878–1843 BC) starts land reclamation in Fayyum region (south of modern Cairo) • First Dynasty of Babylon rulers (1830–1531 BC) makes this city-state the nucleus of a new Mesopotamian empire to succeed Assyria

1800-1601 BC

Europe is now entering its Bronze Age, *c.* 1800–750 BC • Cretan kings rule from palaces at Knossos, Phaistos and Mallia; Cretans use the script Linear A • Rhind Papyrus of Egypt (before 1800 BC) contains algebraic equations • Stonehenge in southern England becomes late Neolithic cult center • Oldest known musical notation is produced in Sumeria, now southern Iraq • Aryans (Indo-European peoples) invade the Iranian Plateau from northeast • Nomadic Amorites (a Semitic people) settle in Syria-Palestine • According to ancient Chinese histories, Shang Dynasty starts its reign in northern China, *c.* 1766–1050 BC • King Hammurabi (1728–1686 BC) conquers Mari on the Euphrates River and establishes the Babylonian Empire • Hammurabi formulates a law code based on "an eye for an eye" • The chinese develop a system of writing by 1700 BC • Hurrians (Biblical Horites) migrate into southwestern Asia from the Caucasus • Phonetic alphabet replaces pictograms in Sinai after 1700 BC • Egyptian royal rule declines; Hyksos "shepherd kings" (Syro-Palestinian rulers) dominate the Nile Delta, *c.* 1678–1570 BC • Horse-drawn chariots introduced to Egypt from southwestern Asia

1600–1401 BC

Mycenae becomes power center in Bronze-Age Greece • Labarnas I reputedly founds Hittite kingdom in Anatolia • Bronze Age people of southern England raise the major stones at Stonehenge • Asmosis of Egypt drives out the Hyksos and starts the New Kingdom Period, c. 1570–332 BC • Amenophis I (c. 1545–1525 BC) secures Egypt's borders with Nubia (northern Sudan) and Libya, and launches phase of expansion • Hittites invade northern Syria and crush Babylonia, c. 1531 BC • Barbarian Kassites rule Babylonia, c. 1531–1150 BC • Tuthmosis III of Egypt (1504–1450 BC) wins lands in southwestern Asia reaching to Euphrates River; Egypt at peak of imperial power • Egyptians make glass vessels and shadow clocks and know of mercury • Hurrians found kingdom of Mitanni in northern Mesopotamia • Mexican Indians grow corn • Bronze Age civilization of Indus Valley collapses • Aryan invaders (from southern Russia?) begin to colonize northern India • Devastation caused by explosion of the Aegean volcano Thira, c. 1470 BC, may explain decline of Crete's Minoan civilization • Amenophis III (c. 1417–1379 BC) builds a vast temple at Luxor, and the Colossi of Memnon • Chinese begin to evolve a distinctive culture

1400–1201 BC

Mycenaean culture dominates much of the Aegean area • Aryans strengthen their hold in northern India • Shang Dynasty craftsmen make fine bronze vessels in China • Iron extensively used in southwestern Asia; iron tools reach India • Canaanite Bronze-Age culture flourishes at Ugarit and elsewhere • Suppiluliumas, c. 1380–1346 BC, makes Hittite Empire the most powerful force in southwestern Asia • Mitanni declines and collapses, 1380–1250 BC • Egypt's Amenophis IV (1379–1362 BC) founds monotheist religion based on the Sun god, Aton, and calls himself Akhenaton • New, naturalistic art styles appear at Akhenaton's new capital, El-Amarna; Egyptian power weakens as Hittites invade Syria • Under Tutankhamun, c. 1361–1351 BC, priests restore the worship of Egypt's old gods, notably Amun • Seti I and Ramesses II fail to dislodge Hittites in the north (c. 1319–1237 BC) • Assyria gains power in northern Mesopotamia under Shalmaneser I, 1275–1246 BC • East Mediterranean invaders ("Sea Peoples") topple the Hittite Empire, c. 1260–1200 BC • Peruvian peoples grow corn by c. 1250 BC • Assyrians repeatedly attack the kingdom of Van (Urartu), Armenia, from c. 1245 BC • Egypt defeats Mediterranean coalition of enemies 1233 BC • Moses leads captive Israelites from Egypt; by 1232 BC, they hold part of Palestine

1200–1001 BC

Phrygians colonize central Anatolia from Thrace • Aryans in northern India practice cattle raising and farming, and worship nature gods Indra, Agni, Varuno • Mycenaean Greeks supposedly destroy Troy • Celtic peoples speaking Indo-European tongues enter Britain • Ramesses III (c. 1188–1156 BC) saves Egypt from combined attacks of the Sea Peoples • Philistines, a group of the Sea Peoples, settle in Palestine, c. 1180 BC, and subdue Iraelites • Tiglath-pileser I (1116–1078 BC) enlarges Assyrian Empire • Dorians conquer Greek Peloponnesus, c. 1104 BC, smash Mycenaean Bronze-Age culture, and start a Greek dark age • Chinese scholars produce what is thought to be first Chinese dictionary, c. 1100 BC • Aeolians and Ionians colonize western Asia Minor, 100–900 BC • Aramaeans and Chaldeans overrun Mesopotamia, 1078–935 BC, and begin a dark age • Egyptian imperial power declines in late dynastic period, c. 1065–332 BC • Egypt splits into two kingdoms during Dynasty XXI, 1065–935 BC • Western Chou Dynasty reigns in northern China, c. 1050–771 BC • Israelite tribes combine for defense under a king, Saul, 1020–1000 BC • Aramaean states emerge in Syria from late 11th century BC • Iron is used in Austria by end of this period

1000–851 BC

Israelite power reaches its height under David, 1000–961 BC • Phoenicians (known as Canaanites before 1200 BC) trade from ports including Sidon and Tyre, and become great Mediterranean merchants and colonists • The Villanova culture flourishes in Italy, c. 1000–600 BC • Chinese make sophisticated silk looms, and probably use coal as fuel • The Rigveda hymns of India are written from c. 1000 BC • Solomon (961–922 BC) begins building the Temple at Jerusalem • A new Assyrian empire emerges (935–860 BC) under Assurnasirapli and his successors, practicing ruthless warfare, massacre and deportation • Sesonchis (935–914 BC) reunifies Egypt and overruns Palestine • Solomon's kingdom splits on his death, into Israel in the north and Judah in the south, 922 BC • Etruscans appear in Italy, c. 900 BC • Damascus is a major Aramaean power, 900–850 BC • Greek pottery features the Geometric style, c. 900–700 BC • Greek culture slowly recovers after the Dorian invasions

850–701 BC

The Chavin culture flourishes in Peru, c. 850–500 BC • Phoenicians from Tyre found colony of Carthage 814 BC, and Phoenician colonies thrive in Spain and Sicily • Aryans expand eastward in northern India; Brahmanism and the caste system develop, 800–c. 550 BC • Olmecs raise the earliest New World pyramid at La Venta in southeastern Mexico, c. 800 BC • Agriculture reaches what is now the USA before 800 BC • Greek city-states under aristocracies emerge • The Greek poet Hesiod flourishes, c. 800 BC • First Olympic Games are held, 776 BC • The weak Eastern Chou Dynasty reigns in China, 770–256 BC • Greeks colonize Mediterranean and Black sea coasts, c. 760–550 BC • Rome is founded, c. 753 BC, as a Latin outpost against the Etruscans; according to tradition, Romulus becomes Rome's first king • Greeks adopt and adapt the Phoenician alphabet • Celts and Illyrians develop iron technology in Central Europe from c. 750 BC • Sparta wins the first Messenian War, c. 736–716 BC • Tiglath-pileser III of Assyria crushes Urartu (eastern Turkey), 735 BC • Damascus falls to Assyria, 732 BC • Media comes under Assyrian rule, c. 715 BC • Shalmaneser V of Assyria destroys Israel, 722 BC; 27,000 Israelites are sent into exile • Southern invaders establish an Ethiopian dynasty (Dynasty XXV) in Egypt, c. 715–656 BC • Midas rules Phrygia, c. 715 BC • Sennacherib (705–682 BC) makes Nineveh the splendid new Assyrian capital • Assyria subdues Judah, 701 BC • Scythian culture reaches central Europe • Homer composes the *Iliad* and the *Odyssey*, before 700 BC

700–651 BC

Etruscan art thrives in Tuscany, Italy, throughout this period • Rome is ruled by elective kings and develops an advisory senate and a weak council of the people, the *comitia curiata* • Scythian culture persists north of the Black Sea • Almost all Attica, Greece, is united • Manasseh, king of Judah, 691–638 BC, encourages worship of Assyrian gods by the Jews • Cimmerians from southern Russia ravage Phrygia, 690 BC • Sennacherib of Assyria destroys Babylon, 689 BC • Attica abolishes hereditary kingship in 683 BC and establishes rule by *archons*, selected from the aristocracy by a nobles' council, the *areopagus* • Sennacherib of Assyria is assassinated by his elder sons, 681 BC; Esarhaddon, a young son, succeeds him, 680–669 BC • Under its king, Pheidon, Greek city-state of Argos becomes powerful, c. 680 BC • Gyges of Lydia in western Asia Minor, 680–652 BC, issues earliest-known dated coins • Assurbanapal, 669–c. 627 BC, the last great Assyrian king, forms a huge library of tablets which preserves much Babylonian literature • Assyrians crush Egypt's Ethiopian rulers, 663 BC • According to ancient chronicles, Jimmu, first emperor of Japan, comes to the throne 660 BC • Psammetichus I, Assyrian governor of Saïs and Memphis, rebels against Assyria 652 BC, and founds Egypt's Dynasty XXVI, with its capital at Saïs; he revives Old Kingdom art forms • Shamash-shumukin, viceroy of Babylonia, rebels against his half-brother, Assurbanapal; civil war rages 652–648 BC, until Shamash-shumukin commits suicide • Cimmerians sack Lydian capital Sardis and kill Gyges, 652 BC

650–601 BC

Sparta wins the Second Messenian War, c. 650–630 BC • Ambitious men overthrow aristocracies to rule Greek city-states as tyrants (dictators), c. 650–500 BC • Assyria crushes Elam on the Iranian plateau, c. 640 BC • Assyria dominates Phoenicia until 627 BC; Phoenician influence declines • Nabopolassar founds a Chaldean dynasty in Babylon, 626 BC, in defiance of Assyria • Civil war begins to destroy Assyria, 626 BC • Cyaxares founds a Median Empire, 625 BC • Paracas culture flourishes in Peru, lasting to the first century AD • The archon Draco publishes Athens' first written laws, notable for their harshness, 620 BC • The tyrant Thrasybulus rules Miletus in Asia Minor, c. 620 BC • Lydian kings strengthen their hold on Greek coastal cities during this period • In Greece, Oriental-style pottery gradually replaces Geometric style • King Josiah of Judah leads a religious revival and bans foreign cults from c. 620 BC to his death, 609 BC • Tarquinius Priscus becomes the first Etruscan king to rule Rome, 616 BC • Medes conquer Urartu 612 BC, and that nation ceases to exist • After 612 BC, Armenians gradually occupy the former area of Urartu • Cyaxares of Media and Nabopolassar of Babylon capture Nineveh, 612 BC, and complete Assyria's collapse • Sparta becomes a strong military state, c. 610 BC • Necho II of Egypt defeats Judah at Megiddo, 609 BC, killing King Josiah • Necho II attempts to build canal linking Nile River and Red Sea, c. 609 BC • Prince Nebuchadrezzar of Babylon defeats Necho II of Egypt at Carchemish, 605 BC, and drives Egyptians out of Syria–Palestine • Nebuchadrezzar becomes king of Babylon, 605 BC • Adena culture flourishes in what is now southeastern USA, lasting to the first century AD

600–576 BC

Black-figured pottery is made in Greece • Chinese philosopher Lao-tzu is born, c. 600 BC • Phoenician ships in Egyptian service reported to circumnavigate Africa, c. 600 BC • Achaemenian kings rule Anzan in Elam (now southwestern Iran) • In India, c. 600–550 BC, the *Upanishads* (confidential teachings) proclaim the doctrine of repeated reincarnation • Greek lyric poet Sappho of Lesbos is active • Greeks from Phocaea found Massilia (Marseille), c. 600 BC • Thebes forms the Boeotian League, c. 600–550 BC • Greek tyrants Cleisthenes and Periander respectively rule Sicyon and Corinth • *Cloaca Maxima*, great drain, built in Rome • Solon is made sole archon of Athens, 594 BC and introduces economic and social reforms • Nebuchadrezzar of Babylon begins 13-year siege of Tyre, 587 BC • Nebuchadrezzar devastates rebellious Jerusalem, 586 BC, and carries off many Jewish captives to Babylon, leaving Judah without leadership • Babylon, splendidly rebuilt by Nebuchadrezzar, emerges as one of finest cities of ancient world: it features great encircling walls, the richly-decorated Ishtar Gate, a processional way, a massive *ziggurat* (the so-called Tower of Babel) and the Hanging Gardens • Thales of Miletus develops the world's first school of philosophy and predicts the solar eclipse of 585 BC • Jews exiled in Babylon write down some hitherto orally-preserved books of the Old Testament • Philosophers Anaximander and Anaximenes of Miletus develop theories of how the universe is constructed • Anaximander makes first Greek map of the known world • The Doric column, earliest order in Greek architecture, comes into use • Greek sculpture becomes increasingly natural • Servius Tullius (578–534 BC) brings Rome into the Latin League

575–551 BC

Writing material papyrus reaches Greece from Egypt • Tyre in Asia Minor surrenders to Nebuchadrezzar, 573 BC • Death of Nebuchadrezzar in 561 BC effectively marks end of Babylonian power • Greeks of Cyrene in North Africa defeat Apries of Egypt, 568 BC • Pharaoh Amasis (568–526 BC) overthrows Apries, adopts some part of Greek culture, and expands trade with Greeks • Peisistratus conquers Salamis for Athens, c. 565 BC • Peisistratus becomes tyrant of Athens, 561 BC, but is expelled almost at once by Lycurgus and Megacles • Siddhartha Gautama, founder of Buddhism, is born in what is now Nepal, c. 563 BC • Attic black-figured vases are made at this time • Celtic peoples are established in Scotland and Ireland • Peisistratus regains power in Athens, c. 560 BC, develops industry and trade, and introduces the cult of Dionysus which derived from Thrace in what is now Bulgaria • Nabonidus (555–539 BC) briefly revives declining Babylon • Confucius (K'ung Fu-tsu) is born in China, 551 BC

550–526 BC

Carthaginian armies campaign in Sicily, 550 BC • The Greek colony of Massilia (Marseille) is trading with rulers of barbarian Celts living in Burgundy, Baden and Wurttemberg • Cyrus II, the Great (550–530 BC), Achaemenid king of Anzan, founds the first Persian Empire • Northern India is ruled by 16 petty kings • Cyrus the Great deposes his overlord, Astyages of Media, 549 BC • Lydia and its king Croesus (c. 560–547 BC) fall to Persia, 547 BC; almost all Asia Minor is under Persian rule, and autocratic government begins to stifle creative thought in the Greek city-states • Sparta strengthens its power in the Peloponnesus, 546 BC, and forges the Peloponnesian League • Peisistratus continues to dominate affairs in Athens • Cyrus the Great conquers Babylonia and makes Phoenician kings his vassals, 539 BC; Cyrus's Persian empire now runs from Mediterranean Sea to Indus Valley and south from Caucasus to Arabian Sea • Jews freed by Cyrus from Babylonian captivity begin returning home, 539 BC, but Judah is now a Persian province • Thespis establishes tragic drama at Athens, 539 BC • Carthaginians and Etruscans defeat Phocaean Greek settlers on Corsica in the sea battle of Alalia, 535 BC • Massilia (Marseille) soon afterwards defeats Carthage and curbs its influence in Corsica • Tarquinius Superbus becomes the last king of Rome, 534 BC • Tyrant Polycrates of Samos dominates the Aegean with his fleet, c. 530 BC • Cambyses becomes the ruler of Persia, 530 BC • Peisratus's sons Hippias and Hipparchus succeed to his dictatorship of Athens, 527 BC

525–501 BC

Red-figured ware replaces the black-figured style in Athens, c. 525 BC • Cambyses defeats Psammetichus III, 525 BC, and Egypt comes under Persian rule, until 404 BC • Darius I (521–486 BC) succeeds Cambyses as ruler of Persia • Persia's conquests of Greek cities in Asia Minor help to shift the Greeks' cultural center westward to mainland Greece and Sicily • Jews, urged on by the prophet Haggai, rebuild the temple at Jerusalem 520–515 BC • In India, the founders of Jainism and Buddhism develop their alternatives to Brahmanism • Cleomenes I of Sparta leads an abortive thrust against Attica, c. 520 BC • Darius I of Persia crushes the revolt of Smerdis, thrusts his boundaries east beyond the Indus by 519 BC, and divides his empire into 20 *satrapies* or provinces • Darius I rules from palaces at Babylon, Ecbatana, Susa and his chief capital (from 518 BC), Persepolis • Map by Hecataeus shows the world as a disk, 517 BC • Darius I takes Gandhara in India and sends the Greek admiral Skylax to investigate the Indus Valley, 517–509 BC • Harmodius and Aristogeiton kill Hipparchus, dictator of Athens, 514 BC • Athenians expel Hipparchus's brother Hippias, thus ending the Peisitratid tyranny, 510 BC • Romans expel their last king, Tarquinius Superbus, 510 BC • The Roman Republic is founded 509 BC, and ruled by two consuls annually elected by the *comitia centuriata* assembly • Cleisthenes introduces extensive democratic reforms in Athens, 508 BC • The Etruscan Lars Porsena briefly restores Etruscans dominian over Rome, 508 BC, and Rome breaks with the Latin League • Greek and Carthaginian colonies appear in Spain before 500 BC • Mines at Mount Laurion are a valuable source of Athenian silver, iron, lead and zinc

500–476 BC

Ionian Greeks in Asia Minor revolt against Persian rule, 500 BC • Greek poets Pindar and Anacreon are active • Athens sends ships to aid the Ionians against Persia, 498 BC • Roman dictator Postumius defeats the Latins at Lake Regillus, 496 BC • Rome's oppressed plebeians win concessions from governing patricians, 494 BC • Persian troops sack Miletus and crush other Ionian rebels, 494 BC • Rome reenters the Latin League, 493 BC • The archon Themistocles fortifies the Piraeus, 493 BC • Persian vessels sailing to punish Athens are shipwrecked off Mount Athos, 492 BC • Rome banishes dissident general Coriolanus, 491 BC • Miltiades leads an Athenian victory at Marathon, crushing Persia's second attempt to invade Greece, 490 BC • Athens is at war with Aegina, 489–c. 483 BC • Athens introduces the punishment of ostracism (banishment), 487 BC, to keep would-be tyrants from power • Darius I of Persia dies, 486 BC • Persian power declines under Xerxes I (486–465 BC) • Soon after the Buddha's death, c. 483 BC, disciples start to spread his beliefs • Athenians banish the statesman Aristides, 483 BC; Themistocles becomes head of state and builds a fleet of warships, making Athens a great naval power • Persian forces under Xerxes I crush Spartans under Leonidas at Thermopylae, 480 BC • Xerxes burns Athens, 480 BC • Athenian navy smashes Persian fleet at Battle of Salamis, 480 BC • Gelo of Syracuse defeats Carthaginians under Hamilcar Barca at Himera, Sicily, 480 BC • Athenian artist Polygnotus paints large masterpieces, c. 480 BC • Greeks led by Pausanias defeat Persians at Plataea, 479 BC, and Persia abandons its invasion of mainland Greece • Aristides helps to establish the Delian League of Greek states, c. 478 BC

Hieron of Syracuse defeats Etruscans off Cumae, 474 BC • Statesman Themistocles is banished from Athens, 471 BC • Athens becomes the leading member of Delian League and subdues dissident members, starting with Naxos, 467 BC • Athenian general Cimon defeats Persian forces at Eurymedon River in Asia Minor, 466 BC • Xerxes I of Persia is murdered, 465 BC, and is succeeded by son Artaxerxes I • Syracuse in Sicily gains democratic government, 465 BC • Spartans win the Third Messenian War, 464–461 BC • Ephialtes strengthens popular power in Athens when Cimon is ostracized, 461 BC • Greek pottery is in its classical phase • Greek scholars Empedocles, Anaxagoras and Leucippus develop atomic theories during this period • Ephialtes is murdered, c. 461 BC, and Pericles comes to power in Athens as leader of the popular party • First Peloponnesian War between Athens and the Peloponnesus, 460 BC • Athens defeats hostile Peloponnesian fleet at Aegina, 458 BC • Cincinnatus becomes dictator to save Rome from neighboring Aequi, 458 BC • Sparta joins in war against Athens, 457 BC • Athenians aid anti-Persian revolt in Egypt, 456–454 BC • Pericles introduces pay for jurors in popular courts, 451 BC, so that poor may serve • The Twelve Tables, reputedly adaptation of Solon's laws, become the basis of Roman law, 451 BC

Celtic peoples develop La Tène Iron-Age culture on the Middle Rhine by 450 BC • Defeated by an Athenian force in Cyprus, Persia agrees the Peace of Callias, acknowledging the Greek cities' independence, 449 BC • Rome's Valerio-Horatian laws curb patrician powers, 448 BC • Boeotian League emerges as hostile rival to Athenian League, 447 BC • Parthenon in Athens is built, 447–432 BC • First Peloponnesian War ends, 446 BC • Rome creates military tribunes with consuls' powers, 444 BC • Syracuse becomes chief power in Sicily, c. 443 BC • Myron develops Greek classical sculpture • In China, Han Wei and Chao partition the state of Chin, 458–424 BC • Greek playwright Sophocles writes Antigone (443 BC) • Athens subdues Samos, 440 BC, leaving Chios and Lesbos as last independent members of Athenian League • Nehemiah rebuilds walls of Jerusalem, 439 BC • Athens founds city of Amphipolis to control Thracian mines, 437 BC • Athenian ruler Pericles sends emissaries to grain producers in Black Sea area, c. 437 BC • Corcyra (Corfu) crushes Corinthian fleet at Leucinne, 435 BC • Potidaeans revolt against Athens, 432 BC • The Parthenon and Propylaea are completed at Athens, 432 BC • Rome expands against the Aequi and Volsci, 431 BC • The Archidamian War (431–421 BC) marks start of Second Peloponnesian War (431–404 BC) involving most Greek city-states • A devastating "plague," possibly smallpox, reaches Athens, 430 BC • Pericles dies, 429 BC, and Cleon and Nicias succeed him in Athens • General war starts in Sicily, 427 BC

Xerxes II of Persia is assassinated by Sogdianus, 424 BC • Darius II kills Sogdianus and rules Persia, 424–404 BC • Plague at Athens ends, 423 BC • Cleon of Athens is killed, 422 BC • Rome makes plebeians eligible to become quaestors—judges who are destined to become financial comptrollers—421 BC • Athens and Sparta agree the Peace of Nicias, 421 BC • Sparta breaks the Peace of Nicias by making treaty with Boeotia, 420 BC • Sparta invades Argos, and defeats Athenians, Argives and Mantineans at Mantinea, 418 BC • Athens captures island of Melos, 416 BC • Athens decides on military expedition to Sicily under Alcibiades, Lamachus and Nicias, 416 BC • Athenians accuse Alcibiades of sacrilege and withdraw him from Sicilian expedition, 415 BC • With the Decelean or Ionian War (414–404 BC), Peloponnesian War enters its decisive phase • Athenians try to besiege Syracuse, 414 BC; Syracusans crush besieging Athenians, and Athens loses vital land and sea forces in Sicily, 413 BC • Spartans seize Attic stronghold of Decelea, 413 BC • Peloponnesian ships force Athens to end siege of Miletus, 412 BC • Athenians led by Alcibiades smash Peloponnesian fleet at Cyzicus, 410 BC • Medes unsuccessfully rebel against Persia, 408 BC • Plato becomes a pupil of the philosopher Socrates, 407 BC • Athenians win naval battle of Arginusae against Spartans, 405 BC • Athens submits to Sparta and Peloponnesian War ends, 404 BC • The Thirty Tyrants rule Athens, 404–403 BC • Artaxerxes II of Persia (404–358 BC) kills his rebellious brother Cyrus at Cunaxa, 401 BC

400–376 BC

Iron Age proper starts in England, c. 400 BC • Celts spread through Bohemia, the Carpathians and the Ukraine • Xenophon's "Ten Thousand" Greek mercenaries, defeated at Cunaxa, reach Black Sea, 400 BC • In India, Panini produces first Sanskrit grammar, c. 400 BC • Athens condemns Socrates to death for atheism, 399 BC • Rome captures neighboring town of Veii, 396 BC • In Corinthian War (395–387 BC), Persia backs allied Greek states, including Athens, against Sparta • Spartan attacks weaken Persia's hold on Asia Minor and Ionians set up democracies, 394 BC • Persia smashes Sparta's navy at Cnidus, 394 BC • Athenian imperialist leaders rebuild Athenian power in Aegean, 392 BC • Roman dictator Camillus brings all Etruria under Roman rule, 392 BC • Gauls—a Celtic people—sack Rome, 390 BC, but are bought off and withdraw • Athenian navy regains control of parts of Aegean Sea, 389 BC • Camillus rebuilds Rome, c. 387 BC • In 387 BC, Sparta and Persia agree on a Greek settlement, "the King's Peace," which declares Greek cities independent except for those of Asia Minor, now restored to Persian control • Catapults are in use as weapons • The Hopewell culture of ancient Amerindians (named for a farm in Ohio) flourishes (to c. AD 500) in what is now the southeastern USA • Epic poem *Mahabharata* takes form in India about this period • *Pentateuch* (first five books of the Bible) organized in final form • Egypt's last native dynasty begins, 380 BC • Plato's *Phaedo* supports belief in immortality, 379 BC • Greek city-state Thebes, largely led by Epaminondas, establishes a democracy, 378 BC • Thebes and other states join Athens in new Athenian League against Sparta, 377 BC

375–351 BC

Egypt repulses a Persian attack, 373 BC • General peace is made with Sparta, 371 BC • Epaminondas of Thebes destroys Sparta's prestige at Battle of Leuctra, 371 BC • Greek city-state of Thebes founds Arcadian League to balance the power of Sparta, and frees Messenia from Spartan control, 370 BC • Thebans found cities of Messene and Megalopolis, and unify almost all Thessaly, after 369 BC • Roman tribunes Licinius and Sextius put through reform measures that open one consulship to plebeians, 367 BC • Rome at war with the Gauls, 367–349 BC • Aristotle joins Plato at Athens, c. 367 BC • Temple of Concordia is constructed in Rome, 366 BC • Insurrections break out in Persian-controlled Asia Minor, 366–360 BC • First drama produced in Rome, 365 BC • Roman dictator Camillus dies, 365 BC • Arcadian League is dissolved, 362 BC • Epaminondas is killed at Mantinea, fighting coalition including Athens and Sparta, 362 BC • Rome subdues Latins in a revolt, 362–345 BC, and Rome continues subduing its hostile neighbors • Iron Age emerges in Africa south of the Sahara • The Ch'in minister Shang Yang develops centralized rule, 359–338 BC • Philip becomes regent of Macedonia, 359 BC • Persian King Artaxerxes III (358–338 BC) strengthens royal power over his provinces • Philip of Macedonia conquers Amphipolis, with army reorganized using infantry phalanx, 357 BC • Refusal of Byzantium, Chios, Cos and Rhodes to pay Athens protection money leads to the Social War, 357–355 BC • Philip II becomes King of Macedonia, 356 BC • Athens loses Social War, 355 BC • Phocis and Thebes dispute guardianship of temple at Delphi and start the Sacred War, 355 BC

350–326 BC

Completed Mausoleum (tomb of Mausolus of Caria in Asia Minor) becomes one of the wonders of ancient world, c. 350 BC • Splendid Greek theater at Epidaurus is built, c. 350 BC • Athenian statesman Demosthenes, fearing Philip II of Macedonia's expansionist plans, draws Athens into war against Philip, 349 BC • Philip of Macedonia razes Olynthus, 348 BC • Athens and Macedonia agree Peace of Philocrates, 346 BC • Philip II conquers Phocis, 346 BC • Rome fights Samnites in the inconclusive first Samnite War, 343–341 BC • Philip II of Macedonia defeats Greeks at Chaeronea, 338 BC, making Macedonia supreme state in Greece • Rome wins Latin War, 340–338 BC, ends Latin League, and subordinates its members • Philip II is murdered, and his son, Alexander III, the Great, becomes king of Macedonia, 336 BC • Alexander smashes revolt of Greek states, 335 BC • Greek philosopher Aristotle, former tutor of Alexander the Great, founds Peripatetic school of philosophy in Athens, 335 BC • Alexander's Greco–Madeconian invasion force enters Asia Minor, 334 BC • Alexander defeats Persians at the Granicus River, 334 BC • Ch'u kingdom in China annexes Yueh state, 334 BC • Alexander wins Battle of Issus, 333 BC • Phoenicia and Palestine fall to Alexander, 332 BC • Alexander enters Egypt and founds Alexandria, 332–331 BC • Alexander crushes Persians at Guagamela, 331 BC, and takes Mesopotamia • Darius III of Persia is murdered, 330 BC • Greek traveler Pytheas circumnavigates Britain • Alexander invades Bactria, 329 BC • Alexander invades India, 327 BC • Second Samnite War starts in Italy, 326 BC • Greek navigator Nearchus explores Persian Gulf, 326–324 BC

325-301 BC

Alexander the Great dies of fever at Babylon, 323 BC, and his empire begins to break up • Greek general Ptolemy becomes governor of Egypt, 323 BC • In Wars of the Diadochi (322–275 BC) Alexander's generals Antipater, Antigonus, Craterus and Ptolemy refuse allegiance to Perdiccas, regent for King Philip III of Macedonia, and fight over Alexander's empire • Athenian statesman Demosthenes dies, 322 BC • Macedonia destroys Athenian fleet at Amorgos, 322 BC • Chandragupta Maurya founds India's Maurya Dynasty, c. 321–184 BC • Antipater, regent of Asia from 320 BC, dies, 319 BC • Ptolemy of Egypt annexes Syria, 319 BC • Antigonus, ruler of Macedonia, takes Lydia and Phrygia, 319 BC • Ardvates (317–284 BC) founds an independent Armenian dynasty, 317–211 BC • Cassander, son of Antipater, establishes Salonika and rebuilds Thebes, 316 BC • Ptolemy, Cassander and Lysimachus combine against Antigonus, 315 BC • Seleucus takes Babylon from Antigonus, c. 312 BC • Roman censor Appius Claudius starts building Appian Way, 312 BC • Cassander secures Macedonia and Lysimachus controls Thrace, 311 BC • Hamilcar of Carthage defeats Agathocles of Syracuse, Sicily, 311 BC • Antigonus of Macedonia and his son Demetrius I declare themselves kings in succession to Alexander the Great, 307 BC • After defeat at the Caudine Forks, 321 BC, Rome crushes the Samnites, 305 BC • Ptolemy declares himself king, 305 BC, and founds Egypt's Ptolemaic Dynasty, 305–30 BC • Seleucus declares himself king in Syria, 305 BC, and founds the Seleucid Dynasty, 305–64 BC, centered on Babylon and Syria

300-276 BC

Wars of the Diadochi continue throughout this period • Alexandria now emerges as center of Western learning • Greek scientific thinker Theophrastus writes earliest surviving study of minerals and fossils, c. 300 BC • Pharos (lighthouse) of Alexandria—one of the Seven Wonders of the ancient world—is built, c. 300 BC • Alexandrian physician Herophilus investigates the brain and conducts pioneer post-mortem studies, c. 300 BC • Cassander of Macedonia dies, 298 BC • Chandragupta Maurya, founder of India's Maurya Empire, dies, c. 297 BC: he is succeeded by his son Samudragupta (to c. 375 BC) • Demetrius, exiled King of Macedonia, wins back Macedonia and much of mainland Greece by 294 BC • Aetolian League is formed in western Greece, 290 BC • Samnites, Gauls and Etruscans lose the third Samnite War against Rome, 298–290 BC • Lysimachus and Pyrrhus of Epirus attack Demetrius of Macedonia, 288 BC • Roman dictator Quintus Hortensius passes a law, the *Lex Hortensia*, making plebeians theoretically legal equals of the patricians, 287 BC • Ptolemy II (Philadelphus) inherits Egypt from his father Ptolemy I, 285 BC • Seleucus of Syria seizes Demetrius of Macedonia, 285 BC • Library of Alexandria is established, c. 284 BC • Demetrius dies, 283 BC • Rome defeats Gauls, Etruscans and Greeks, 285–282 BC, and occupies Thurii and other Greek cities in Italy, except Tarentum • Tarentum attacks Thurii, 282 BC, and starts Rome's war with Pyrrhus of Epirus • Seleucus kills Lysimachus, 281 BC, and masters much of Asia Minor • Antiochus I (280–261 BC) succeeds Seleucus I as ruler of Syria • Pyrrhus of Epirus defeats Rome at Heraclea, 280 BC • Achaean League formed in northern Peloponnessus, 280 BC. •

275-251 BC

Antigonus II founds Macedonia's Antigonid Dynasty (276–167 BC) • Celts establish Galatia in Asia Minor, 275 BC • Rome defeats Pyrrhus of Epirus at Beneventum, 275 BC, and he returns to Greece • Asoka (c. 274–236 BC) rules northern two-thirds of Indian subcontinent, and proclaims Buddhist ideology • Antigonus II fights off Pyrrhus, 273 BC • Pyrrhus dies, 272 BC • Ptolemy II of Egypt wins lands from Antiochus I of Syria, 279–272 BC • Rome captures Tarentum, 272 BC • Greek philosopher Aristarchus declares that the Earth revolves around the Sun, c. 270 BC • The Syracusan poet Theocritus writes sensitive pastoral verse, c. 270 BC • Hiero II is tyrant of Syracuse (269–216 BC) • Rome absorbs Calabria, 266 BC • Rome clashes with Carthage in first Punic War, 264–241 BC • Pergamum in Asia Minor breaks away from Antiochus I of Syria, and Eumenes I founds Pergamum's Attalid Dynasty (263–1339 BC) • Athens and Sparta fight Antigonus in Chremonidean War, which leaves Athens under Macedonian control, 262 BC • Antiochus II rules Seleucid Empire 261–246 BC • Ptolemaic influence has extended from Egypt down the Red Sea and into Arabia • Rome defeats Carthage in naval battle off Mylae in northwestern Sicily, 260 BC • Antiochus II recovers some lost land in Asia Minor in Second Syrian War (260–255 BC) against Ptolemy II of Egypt • Rome wins naval battle of Ecnomus, 256 BC, and Roman general Regillus lands an invasion force in Africa near Carthage itself • Xanthippus, Spartan general fighting for Carthage, captures Regillus near Carthage, 255 BC • Cornelius Scipio's new Roman fleet wins the fine harbor of Panormus in Sicily, 254 BC • Rome defeats Hasdrubal of Carthage, 251 BC

250-226 BC

Diodotus I becomes king of an independent Bactria, 250 BC • Pergamum in Asia Minor begins to develop parchment as writing material, 250 BC • Greek scientist Ctesibius makes water-clocks and a water-organ, *c.* 250 BC • Ptolemy III (Euergetes) reigns in Egypt (246–221 BC) • Seleucus II becomes Syrian ruler, 246 BC, but proceeds to lose east Mediterranean coast to Ptolemy III in Third Syrian War (246–241 BC) • Aratus of Sicyon captures Corinth, 243 BC • Attalus I becomes king of Pergamum, 241 BC • Roman literature begins, 241 BC, with Latin play translated from Greek by the Greek Livius Andronicus • Romans destroy Carthaginian fleet off Lilybaeum in Sicily, 241 BC, and Sicily becomes a Roman province • Buddhism reaches Ceylon about this period • Demetrius II of Macedonia succeeds Antigonus II, 239 BC, but war and rebellion weaken Demetrius's hold on mainland Greece, 239–229 BC • Rome seizes Sardinia, 238 BC • Carthaginian general Hamilcar Barca starts conquest of Spain, 238 BC • After Asoka's death, *c.* 236 BC, India's Maurya Empire begins to decline • Chinese philosopher Han Feitzu dies, 233 BC; authoritarian precepts taught by his Legalist school of philosophy influence Ch'in rulers in China, paving way for strong centralized rule from which Chinese nation is to emerge • Attalus I makes Pergamum master of western Asia Minor, *c.* 230 BC • Ch'in state conquers all its rivals, 230–221 BC • Carthage rules southern Spain by 229 BC • Antigonus III of Macedonia succeeds Demetrius II, 229 BC • Roman fleet suppresses pirates in first Illyrian War, 229–228 BC • Rome creates a province from Sardinia and Corsica, 227 BC

225-201 BC

Romans crush Celtic invaders and build forts in north Italy, 225–222 BC • Antiochus III of Syria (223–187 BC) begins reconquest of lands taken by Pergamum • Antigonus III of Macedonia wins Sparta, 222 BC • Philip V becomes king of Macedonia 221 BC • Ptolemy IV (Philopater) succeeds his father Ptolemy III as ruler of Egypt, 221 BC • Ptolemy IV and Antiochus III fight fourth Syrian War, 221–217 BC • Ch'in ruler Shih Huang-ti becomes China's "First Emperor," 221 BC • Under Ch'in Dynasty (221–207 BC), China gains standardized laws, weights and measures • Macedonia fights War of the Allies (219–217 BC) against piratical Aetolians • Rome fights Carthage in Second Punic War (218–201 BC) • Carthaginian general Hannibal crosses Alps and invades Italy, 218 BC, winning victories at the Ticinus and Trebbia rivers • Roman forces campaign against Carthage in Spain from 218 BC • Hannibal crushes Romans at Lake Trasimene, 217 BC • Quintus Fabius Maximus, appointed dictator of Rome, harries Hannibal but avoids set battles, 217 BC • Hannibal defeats Romans at Cannae, 216 BC • In first Macedonian War (215–205 BC) Rome's Greek allies prevent Philip V of Macedonia from helping Hannibal • Great Wall of China constructed, *c.* 214 BC • Roman troops defeat Carthaginians at Metaurus River in Italy, 207 BC • Publius Cornelius Scipio (later called Scipio Africanus) drives Carthaginians from Spain, 206 BC • Scipio defeats Carthaginian force in Africa, 203 BC, and Carthage recalls Hannibal from Italy • Romans destroy Carthaginian army at Zama in Africa, 202 BC, ending the second Punic War • Carthage surrenders all its Mediterranean lands to Rome, 201 BC • The Western Han Dynasty rules China (202 BC–AD 9)

200-176 BC

Waterwheels are used for irrigation by 200 BC • Asked for help against Philip V of Macedonia, Rome joins Greek states in second Macedonian War, 200–196 BC • Eumenes II (*c.* 197–160 BC) makes Pergamum a center of Hellenistic art • Flaminius of Rome, helped by Achaean and Aetolian leagues, defeats Philip V of Macedonia at Cynoscephalae, 197 BC • Rome declares Greek city-states independent, 196 BC • Antiochus III of Syria wins fifth Syrian War, 195 BC, which leaves Egypt's Ptolemy V (Epiphanes), ruler from 205 BC, shorn of all Asian lands except Cyprus • Antiochus III invades Greece and with the Aetolians fights Rome, which is backed by Macedonia and the Achaeans, 192 BC • Romans crush Antiochus III at Thermopylae and drive him from mainland Greece, 191 BC • Romans defeat Antiochus III at Magnesia in Asia Minor, 190 BC; Greek rulers in Armenia and Bactria break away from Syrian control • By peace settlement of 189 BC, Rome makes Antiochus III hand over Asia Minor to Rhodes and Pergamum • Rome helps Pergamum against the Galatians, 189 BC • Seleucid power in Syria begins reviving under Seleucus IV (187–175 BC) • Demetrius of Bactria takes the Punjab (*c.* 185 BC) • Sunga Dynasty emerges, *c.* 184 BC in Ganges Valley of India • Ptolemy VI (Philomater) succeeds Ptolemy V in Egypt, 181 BC • Confucianism and Taoism become established in China • Chinese discover how to make porcelain about this time • First Roman stone bridge is built, *c.* 179 BC • Philip V of Macedonia dies, 179 BC • Perseus rules Macedonia (179–167 BC), and is hostile to Rome

175–151 BC

First known Roman pavement is laid, *c.* 175 BC • Seleucus IV of Syria is murdered, 175 BC, and Antiochus IV rules the Seleucid Empire (175–163 BC) • Mithridates I, founder of Parthian Empire, comes to the throne in Parthia, *c.* 171 BC • Rome and Macedonia clash in third Macedonian War, 171–167 BC, after Eumenes II of Pergamum (hailed as champion of Greek independence) persuades Rome to take action • Roman forces under Paullus crush Macedonian army at Pydna, 168 BC; Rome imprisons Macedonian ruler, Perseus, subordinates Macedonia and Illyria, and ravages Epirus • Ptolemy VII (Euergetes) becomes joint ruler of Egypt with his brother Ptolemy VI, 168 BC • Antiochus IV of Syria desecrates the temple at Jerusalem, 168 BC; Jews led by the Maccabees—Judas, Jonathan and Simon—revolt against Seleucid rule, 168–165 BC • Rome stops Antiochus IV capturing Alexandria, 168 BC • Macedonia's Antigonid Dynasty ends with the death of Perseus, 167 BC • Rome takes Greek hostages to Italy, among them the historian Polybius, 167 BC • Jews win religious freedom, 164 BC • Seleucid Empire is ruled by Antiochus V (163–162 BC) and Demetrius I (162–150 BC) • Mithridates I of Parthia seizes Media by 161 BC • Rome has public libraries • Judas Maccabeus dies, 160 BC, while fighting the Seleucids • Chinese prince Liu Teh (155–130 BC) forms library of ancient writings; Lou An, his cousin, compiles Chinese works of philosophy • Revolt in Spain, 153 BC, forces Roman consuls to take office on January 1 and not March 15 as usual; thus January 1 becomes first day of Rome's civil year • Rome introduces a new law forbidding the reelection of consuls, 151 BC

150–126 BC

Roman tribune Lucius Calpurnius Piso enacts a law, the *Lex Calpurnia*, giving the Senate greater control over Rome's provincial governors, 149 BC • Alarm at resurgent Carthaginian power leads Rome to start third Punic War, 149–146 BC • Rome wins fourth Macedonian War, 149–148 BC, and makes Macedonia a Roman province • Achaean League attacks Sparta; defeated by Roman troops under Mummius, 146 BC; most Greek states come under Roman rule • Roman troops under Scipio Aemilianus raze Carthage 146 BC, and Rome founds an African province • Demetrius II rules Seleucia, 145–139 BC • On the death of Ptolemy VI, 145 BC, Ptolemy VII becomes sole ruler of Egypt, 145–116 BC • Jews win political independence in Judaea, 142 BC, under Simon Maccabeus, founder of the Hasmonean Dynasty • Mithridates I of Parthia captures Babylon, *c.* 141 BC • China's Han Empire attains its greatest extent under Emperor Wu Ti, *c.* 140–87 BC • Venus de Milo is sculpted, *c.* 140 BC • Seleucid ruler Demetrius II defeats Mithridates I of Parthia, 140 BC • Mithridates I captures Demetrius II, 139 BC • Antiochus VII (139–127 BC), brother of Demetrius II, helps to restore Seleucid fortunes • Scythians invade Bactria, *c.* 139 BC • Attalus III (138–133 BC) bequeaths Pergamum to Rome • Sicilian slaves rebel against Rome in first Servile War, 135–132 BC • Rome subdues all Spain, except for the northwest, by 133 BC • Reactionary nobles murder tribune Tiberius Gracchus to halt his sweeping social reforms, 133 BC • Rome crushes Sicilian slave revolt, 132 BC • Attalus III of Pergamum (now part of Turkey) dies and leaves his lands to Rome; Pergamum becomes a Roman province named Asia, 129 BC; Rome now controls nearly all civilized Mediterranean lands

125–101 BC

Antiochus VIII, younger son of Demetrius II, rules Seleucid Empire, 125–96 BC • Astronomer Hipparchus produces a star catalog, 125 BC • Under Mithridates II, the Great (124–88 BC), Parthia crushes Scythians • Caius Gracchus becomes a tribune, 123 BC, and plans vast social reforms • Rome occupies the Balearic Islands, 123 BC • Southern Gaul becomes Roman province • Caius Gracchus dies in riot, 121 BC, and his reforms largely lapse • Overland silk trade between Rome and China develops • Peru's Nazca culture is developing at this time • Chinese drive the nomadic Hsiung-nu (Huns) into the Gobi Desert, 119 BC • Ptolemy VIII (Soter) reigns in Egypt, 116–108 BC • Sadducees and Pharisees become prominent in Judaea, *c.* 112 BC; their rivalry weakens kingdom built up by Hasmonean ruler John Hyrcanus (134–104 BC) • Rome wages Jugurthine War in Africa, 111–105 BC, against Numidian usurper Jugurtha • Antiochus VIII of Syria divides the Seleucid realm with his half-brother Antiochus IX, 111 BC • Beginning 111 BC, Han forces pacify China's southwest and southern coasts • Korea comes under Chinese control by 108 BC • Ptolemy IX (Alexander) expels his brother Ptolemy VIII and reigns over Egypt, 108–88 BC • Roman general and politician Gaius Marius becomes consul for the first time, 107 BC • Marius and fellow-general Lucius Cornelius Sulla capture Jugurtha and divide his kingdom among other North African states, 105 BC • Celtic tribe the Cimbri expand west, crushing Roman armies at Arausio on Rhône River, 105 BC; Cimbri and Teutons advance on northwestern Italy • Emperor Wu Ti's Chinese forces push beyond the Tarim Basin in western China, 104 BC, and reach outposts of Western culture

17

La Tène peoples invade England from Continental Europe, bringing new Iron Age culture • Great stupa (Buddhist shrine) at Sanchi in India built • Greek physician Asclepiades differentiates between acute and chronic diseases • Roman politician Marius becomes consul for sixth time and murders his political opponents, 100 BC • Roman forces win second Servile War in Sicily, 99 BC • Antiochus VIII of Seleucia is murdered, 96 BC; his half-brother Antiochus IX is killed in battle, 95 BC; civil and other wars weaken Seleucid realm, 95–64 BC • Mithridates II of Parthia makes a treaty with Rome, 92 BC • Livius Drusus unsuccessfully proposes Roman citizenship for all Italians, 91 BC, and much of Italy revolts • Marius subdues northern Italy, 91–89 BC • Alexandrians kill Ptolemy IX of Egypt, 88 BC, and restore Ptolemy VIII • Roman general Lucius Cornelius Sulla pacifies south Italy by 88 BC, but Rome is forced to open Roman citizenship to all Italians • Mithridates VI of Pontus clashes with Roman-backed Bithynia, 88 BC, and overruns Roman province of Asia • Civil war in Rome: Marius flees from Sulla, 88 BC • Chinese emperor Wu Ti dies, 87 BC • Ssu-ma Ch'ien compiles the first comprehensive history of China before 87 BC • Marius returns to Rome and rules with Lucius Cornelius Cinna, 86 BC, but soon dies • Sulla subdues Mithridates VI, 84 BC • Rome and Pontus wage second Mithridatic War, 83–81 BC • Sulla returns to Rome and makes himself dictator, 82 BC • Sulla retires, 79 BC, after introducing reforms largely aimed at restoring senatorial powers • Roman generals Quintus Lutatius Catulus and Gnaeus Pompeius (Pompey) smash revolt by Marcus Aemilius Lepidus, opponent of Sulla's reforms, 78–77 BC

Cyrene in North Africa becomes Roman province, 74 BC • Pontus and Armenia seize Cappadocia and Syria, provoking Third Mithridatic War, 74 BC • Roman general Lucius Licinius Lucullus takes Pontus for Rome, 73 BC • Spartacus and other Thracian gladiators rally slaves in third Servile War, 73 BC • Pompey crushes revolt in Spain, 72 BC • Spartacus is defeated, 71 BC • Roman generals Marcus Licipius Crassus and Gnaeus Pompeius (Pompey) use their troops to make themselves consuls, 70 BC • Lucullus invades Armenia, 69 BC • Romans capture Cretan bases of Mediterranean pirates, 68 BC • Pompey crushes Mediterranean pirates, 67 BC, and Crete becomes a Roman province • Roman lyric poet Gaius Valerius Catullus is active by the mid-60s BC • Pompey pursues Mithridates VI of Pontus, who kills himself, 65 BC • Pompey makes Syria a Roman province, ending Seleucid rule, 64 BC • Pompey conquers Palestine, 63 BC • Peru's Nazca culture is emerging • Roman statesmen Gaius Julius Caesar, Marcus Crassus, and Gnaeus Pompeius form a Triumvirate to rule Rome, 60 BC • Caesar masters middle and upper Rhine, 58 BC, crushing Helvetii and Sueves and starting conquest of Gaul • Caesar subdues the Belgae, 57 BC • Caesar conquers Brittany and southwestern Gaul, 56 BC • Caesar briefly invades Britain, 55 BC • Pompey and Crassus become consuls, 55 BC– Crassus rules Suria, Pompey rules Spain • Caesar invades Britain again, 54 BC, crushing south British king Cassivellaunus • Parthians kill Crassus and rout his army in Mesopotamia, 53 BC • Caesar ends Gallic chief Vercingetorix's revolt in Gaul, 52 BC • Pompey becomes sole consul and virtual dictator in Rome; Caesar and Pompey jockey for power

Roman Senate backs Gnaeus Pompeius (Pompey) against Julius Caesar and expels Caesar's supporter, Marcus Antonius, 49 BC • Caesar's troops cross Rubicon River into Italy, thus opening civil war, 49 BC • Caesar defeats Pompey at Pharsalus in Greece, 48 BC • Caesar pursues Pompey to Egypt; Pompey is murdered and Egyptian ruler Ptolemy XII dies in battle • Ptolemy's sister and co-ruler Cleopatra VII continues to rule with another brother, Ptolemy XIII, 47 BC • Cleopatra becomes Caesar's mistress • Rome adopts the Julian calendar, 46 BC • Caesar becomes dictator of Rome for life, 44 BC • Patriots Marcus Junius Brutus and Gaius Cassius lead group which assassinates Caesar, 44 BC • Marcus Antonius, Marcus Lepidas, and Gaius Octavius form Second Triumvirate, 43 BC • Octavius and Antonius defeat Cassius and Brutus at Philippi, 42 BC • Antonius settles in Egypt, 41 BC • Parthians establish Antigonus as the last Hasmonean King of Judaea, 40 BC • Marcus Antonius marries Octavia, sister of Caesar's heir Gaius Octavius, 40 BC • Hasmonean Dynasty ends when Marcus Antonius executes Antigonus, 37 BC • Herod the Great is made King of Judaea by Rome • Herod takes Jerusalem, 37 BC • Octavius seizes lands in Africa controlled by his fellow Roman ruler, Marcus Lepidus, after Lepidus tries to grab Sicily, 36 BC • Parthians defeat Antonius, 36 BC • Antonius bigamously marries Cleopatra VII of Egypt, 36 BC • Antonius gives Cleopatra's children Roman provinces, 34 BC • Dalmatia becomes a Roman province, 34 BC • Octavius defeats fleet of Antonius and Cleopatra at Battle of Actium, 31 BC • Antonius and Cleopatra commit suicide, 30 BC • Octavius closes Temple of Janus, 29 BC, signifying peace

Octavius becomes the Emperor Augustus, 27 BC, and proceeds to reform criminal law, tighten citizenship requirements, improve moral standards and strengthen institution of marriage; Roman Republic is now replaced by the Roman Empire; imperial civil service evolves • Augustus's assistant, Marcus Agrippa, starts building Pantheon temple at Rome, 27 BC, and aqueduct near Nîmes, France • Greco-Asian Gandhara school of sculpture thrives in northwestern India • Greek-influenced Roman art is by now established • Roman engineer Marcus Vitruvius writes De Architectura, after 27 BC • Pahlavas (Parthians akin to the Scythians) now rule eastern Iran • Roman poet Publius Vergilius (Virgil) completes the Aeneid, c. 20 BC • King Herod of Judaea starts rebuilding temple at Jerusalem, c. 20 BC • Revolts in China, c. 20 BC, reflect financial crisis, including heavy tax burdens on the poor • German barbarian tribes defeat Roman army under Marcus Lollius; as a result, Emperor Augustus and his general Tiberius Claudius Nero carry out punitive campaigns in Gaul and Germany respectively, 16–15 BC; Rome absorbs Noricum, Thaetica and Vindelicia, moving frontiers of Roman Empire to upper Danube River • Roman general Claudius Drusus leads Roman troops to Elbe River, 9 BC • Titus Livius (Livy) finishes his history of Rome, c. 9 BC • Astronomy develops rapidly in China under Han Dynasty • Moche culture is evolving in Peru • About this time, Roman palaces feature voice-pipes for oral messages • Birth of Jesus at Bethlehem, probably 6 BC • Herod the Great of Judaea dies, 4 BC • Herod's sons Archelaus, Antipas and Philip inherit Samaria, Galilee and Batanaea respectively, 4 BC • Rome annexes Judaea, 4 BC

Roman theater at Leptis Magna in North Africa is begun, AD 1 • Wang Mang becomes regent in China, AD 1 • Romans recognize Cunobelinus (Cymbeline) as king of Britain, AD 5 • Roman poet Ovid writes Metamorphoses, c. AD 5 • Roman Emperor Augustus arranges bonus payments for retiring soldiers, AD 6 • In China, civil service candidates are made to take examinations, AD 6 • Roman general Tiberius suppresses revolts in Dalmatia and Pannonia by AD 9; Rome's frontier now runs to middle and lower Danube River • Germanic tribe the Cherusci, under Arminius, destroy Roman army under Varus in the Teutoberg Forest, AD 9; Roman expansion east of Rhine River ends • Roman poet Ovid starts writing Tristia, books of poetic complaints, AD 9 • Wang Mang becomes emperor of China, AD 9–23, founding the short-lived Hsia Dynasty; he introduces sweeping reforms • Augustus dies, AD 14 and is succeeded by Tiberius as emperor (to AD 37) • Tiberius's nephew and heir Germanicus Caesar puts down revolt by the Pannonian legions, AD 14 • Germanicus campaigns in Germany, defeating Arminius, AD 14–16 • Germanicus Caesar dies, AD 19, allegedly poisoned by Piso, governor of Syria • Tiberius comes under the influence of Lucius Aelius Sejanus, prefect of the Praetorian Guard, AD 23–31 • Sejanus reputedly poisons Tiberius' son Drusus, hoping to become emperor, AD 23 • Chinese Emperor Wang Mang dies in a revolt, AD 23 • Liu Hsiu founds China's Later Han Dynasty, AD 25–220

Pontius Pilate becomes procurator of Judaea, AD 26 • Sejanus persuades Tiberius to leave Rome for Capri, AD 26 • Jesus is baptized, c. AD 27 • Jewish prophet John the Baptist executed, AD 28 • Jesus is hailed by his followers as the Messiah (Christos in Greek) and is crucified for alleged sedition, c. AD 30 • Roman medical writer Aulus Cornelius Celus's De Re Medica appears, c. AD 30 • Buddhism reaches China • Roman Emperor Tiberius executes the prefect Lucius Sejanus, AD 31 • Saul (in Latin, Paul) of Tarsus becomes a Christian, AD 32 • Tiberius dies, AD 37, and is succeeded by Tiberius Gemellus and Gaius Caesar ("Caligula," or "Little Boot") • Caligula kills Gemellus and rules with megalomaniac folly • Rome annexes Mauretania, AD 41 • Praetorian Guard assassinates Caligula, AD 41; Caligula's uncle Claudius becomes emperor • Julius Agrippa ("Herod Agrippa") enlarges Jerusalem, AD 41–44 • Roman troops under Aulus Plautius invade Britain, where Claudius accepts the surrender of Camulodunum (Colchester), AD 43 • Romans begin fortification of London, AD 43 • China conquers Annam and Tonkin, AD 43 • Christian leader Paul starts his missionary journeys, AD 45 • Claudius marries his niece, Agrippina, AD 48 • Claudius adopts Nero, Agrippina's son by a previous marriage, as his successor, AD 50 • Greek physician Pedanius Dioscorides' Materia Medica describes medicinal plants, c. AD 50

Roman troops capture Caractacus, British defender of southwest England, 51 • Claudius dies, 54, allegedly poisoned by his wife Agrippina; her son Nero becomes emperor, at first ruling wisely under the tutelage of the philosopher Lucius Annaeus Seneca • Rome sends general Gnaeus Domitius Corbulo to subdue Parthia • Rockcut Buddhist temples at Ajanta, India, date from this period • Roman general Corbulo invades Armenia, 58 • Nero murders his mother Agrippina, 59 • Scientist Hero of Alexandria invents a steam engine, c. 60 • Boudicca, queen of the Iceni tribe in Britain, revolts against Rome in 61, but is defeated and killed by Seutonius Paulinus • Romans are defeated by the Parthians at Rhandeia in Armenia, 62 • Tiridates founds an Arsacid dynasty in Armenia, 63 • Rome is burned, 64; Nero is blamed and kills Christians as scapegoats • The apostles Peter and Paul become martyrs at Rome, 64 • Philosopher Seneca commits suicide, 65 • Judaea revolts, 66 • Roman general Vespasian begins subduing Judaea, 67 • Nero kills himself, and Galba, commander in Spain, becomes Roman emperor in 68 • Rhine legions in Germany acclaim their general, Vitellius, as emperor in opposition to Galba, 69 • Otho, former friend of Nero, murders Galba and the Senate declares Otho emperor, but he kills himself after defeat by Vitellius, 69 • Eastern governors proclaim Vespasian, general in Judaea, emperor, and Vitellius dies in the ensuing struggle, 69 • Vespasian rules as emperor, 69–79, founding the Flavian Dynasty and strengthening the Roman empire's eastern boundaries • Titus, son of Vespasian, completes subjection of Judaea and destroys Jerusalem in 70

Agricola continues Rome's conquest of Britain, 77–84 • Roman emperor Vespasian dies, 79, and his son Titus succeeds him • Volcano Vesuvius erupts, burying Pompeii and Herculaneum, 79 • Titus dies and is succeeded by his younger brother Domitian, 81 • Targums—Aramaic versions of parts of the Old Testament—appear about now • Roman metallurgists are extracting gold, silver and other rare metals from their ores • Buddhism gains ground in China • Domitian campaigns across the Rhine, 83, and founds a line of forts, the *limes*, which eventually guards the empire's Rhine and Danube boundaries • Romans defeat Caledonians at Mt Graupius, perhaps near Aberdeen, 83, in Rome's deepest northward penetration of Britain • Domitian throws back a barbarian invasion across the Danube, 85 • Agricola builds forts between Clyde and Forth rivers in Scotland, 85 • Marcomanni and Quadi of Bohemia defeat Domitian, 89 • The Gospel according to John written, c. 94 • Romans found city of Lindum (Lincoln) in England, 94 • Roman Emperor Domitian persecutes Christians, 96 • Domitian is assassinated and Rome's Flavian Dynasty ends, 96 • Nerva, an elderly senator, is Roman emperor, 96–98 • Nerva adopts the general Trajan as his successor, 97 • Roman orator Quintilian dies, c. 96 • Indian ruler Kanishka dies, c. 96, after founding a powerful Kushan dynasty in northern India • Chinese influence in Turkestan helps East-West silk trade expand by 97 • Trajan rules Rome as emperor, 98–117 • Roman historian Cornelius Tacitus writes his *Life of Agricola*, c. 98

Roman Emperor Trajan fights the Dacian Wars, c. 101–117, and Rome takes Dacia (now part of Romania) • Chinese begin making paper • Chinese drive the Hsiung-nu (Huns) towards western Asia • Trajan's Column in Rome is built early on in this period • Massive Roman aqueduct at Segovia, Spain, is built, 110 • Proconsul Pliny the Younger reorganizes Bithynia, 112, after top-heavy administration has raised problems • Chosroes of Parthia installs a puppet king in Armenia in defiance of Rome, and Roman Emperor Trajan launches a Parthian war, 113–117 • Trajan annexes Armenia, 114 • Roman author Cornelius Tacitus writes his *Historiae*, c. 115 • Trajan creates the Roman province of Mesopotamia, 115 • Trajan makes Assyria a Roman province, 116 • Trajan represses Jewish and other revolts, 116 • Trajan dies, 117, and is succeeded by his cousin Hadrian • Hadrian abandons lands east of the Euphrates River • Alexandrian astronomer-geographer Claudius Ptolemaeus (Ptolemy) experiments with refraction, c. 120 • Hadrian builds a defensive wall across northern England, 122–127 • Chinese writers first refer to lodestones, 122 • Pantheon at Rome in its present form is built on the site of an older structure by 124

126-150

Andhra (Satakani) ruler Gotamiputra Siri Satakani claims the Deccan in India, *c.* 126 • Greek physician Galen is born, *c.* 130 • Under changed rules of succession, empresses rule China during this period • Kingdom of Axum (founded after 100 BC) flourishes in northeastern Ethiopia • Ironworking spreads across Africa south of the Sahara, and trans-Saharan trade begins to expand • Roman lawyer Salvius Julianus formulates the *Praetor's Edict*, by which Imperial decree becomes the sole source of Roman law, 131 • Romanization of Jerusalem provokes Jewish revolt led by Simon Bar-Kokhba, 132 • Rome suppresses the Jewish revolt by 135, killing Simon Bar-Kokhba, ending the Jewish nation, depopulating Judaea, and forcing Jews abroad in the *Diaspora* (dispersion) • Emperor Hadrian adopts Antoninus Pius as his successor, 138, and dies; Antoninus Pius becomes emperor • Stoic philosopher Epictetus, a freed Greek slave, dies, 140 • Roman general Quintus Lollius Urbicus crushes a revolt in northern Britain, 143, and builds . temporary Antonine Wall between Forth and Clyde rivers • Greek surgeon Antyllus operates on arteries • Claudius Ptolemaeus's major astronomical work, the *Almagest*, locates the Earth in the heart of the universe; this erroneous notion is to dominate astronomical thinking until 16th century • Goths settle in Black Sea region • Christian heresy of Montanism appears • Latin translation of the Bible is made from a Greek version, *c.* 150

151-175

Polycarp of Smyrna, an early Christian martyr, dies, *c.* 155 • Rome fights inconclusive war with Vologesus of Parthia, 155 • Basketmaker culture develops in what is now the southwestern USA • Eskimo culture (originating *c.* 500 BC) continues to develop in American Arctic • Chang Ling, founder of Religious Taoism in China, dies, 156 • Buddhism in India splits into two schools: Hinayana (Lesser Vehicle) and Mahayana (Great Vehicle) • Greek physician Galen uses pulse rate as indicator of health and sickness, *c.* 160 • Roman lawyer Gaius writes his *Institutes*, expounding elements of Roman law, *c.* 160 • Emperor Antoninus Pius dies, 161, and is succeeded by his nephew Marcus Aurelius, who shares power with Lucius Aurelius Verus • Stoicism is now a dominant force in Rome • Verus's troops make Mesopotamia a Roman province and gain control of Armenia, 162–165 • Early Maya monuments date from 164 • Plague from the Middle East hits Roman Empire • Marcomanni tribesmen from Bohemia invade the Empire, 166 • Lucius Aurelius Verus dies, 169 • Marcus Aurelius makes peace with Marcomanni tribes, *c.* 172, and lets many of them settle plague-ravaged Roman lands • Avidius Cassius, governor of Syria, revolts and is crushed, 175

176-200

Greek geographer Pausanias completes his 10-volume *Description of Greece*, *c.* 176 • Roman emperor Marcus Aurelius makes his son Commodus coemperor, 177 • Roman persecution of Christians is intensified, *c.* 177 • Marcomanni renew war with Rome, 178 • Marcus Aurelius dies at Vindobona (Vienna), 180, and Commodus becomes sole Roman emperor • In Roman Britain, the Antonine Wall is breached, 180; Romans fall back on Hadrian's Wall • Revived Carthage in north Africa (destroyed 146 BC) flourishes as major Roman city • Commodus abandons war against the Marcomanni tribes by 181 • Revolt of the, Yellow Turbans against corrupt rule by eunuchs shakes China, 184 • Greek physician Galen uses plant juices as medicines, *c.* 190 • Hsien, last of China's Later Han emperors, comes to the throne, 190 • Roman writer Quintus Tertullianus embraces Christianity, *c.* 190 • Commodus' murder in 192 ends Antonine rule and begins an age of political and economic collapse • Praetorian Guard murders Pertinax, briefly emperor in 193 • Provincial Roman armies back rival claimants to imperial power; Septimius Severus, governor of Upper Pannonia (now mostly Hungary), seizes Rome and reigns from 193 • Septimius Severus defeats his rival, Pescendinius Niger, at Issus (now in Turkey) killing him, 194 • In Britain, barbarian tribes overrun and damage Hadrian's Wall, 196 • Septimius Severus defeats and kills another rival, Septimius Albinus, at Lugdunum (Lyon), 197 • Septimius Severus wins a Parthian war, 198, reaching Ctesiphon and reorganizing Mesopotamia • Preeminence of the bishop of Rome in Christian Church emerges by 200 under Pope Victor I (189–199)

201–225

Arch of Septimius Severus is raised in Rome, 203 • Roman lawyer Aemilius Papinianus is one of two Praetorian prefects created by Emperor Septimius Severus, 205 • Most of Japan is split into small states at this time • Septimius Severus campaigns in Britain, 208–211, and repairs Hadrian's Wall, 208 • Septimius Severus dies at Eboracum (York), 211, and is succeeded by his eldest son, Caracalla • Caracalla builds the immense Baths of Caracalla in Rome, 212 • Caracalla gives Roman citizenship to most free inhabitants of the Roman Empire, 212 • Caracalla fends off the Alamanni in southern Germany and Goths farther east, 214 • Clement of Alexandria, a Greek Father of the Church, dies, c. 215 AD • Caracalla annexes Armenia, 216 • Caracalla is murdered, 217 • The prefect Macrinus becomes emperor, 217–218, and is followed by the priest Elagabulus, 218–222 • China's Later Han Dynasty ends with death of Emperor Hsien, 220 • Goths invade Asia Minor and the Balkans, c. 220 • China fragments under three competing dynasties (Wei, Shu and Wu) by 222 • Praetorian guards assassinate Roman emperor Elagabalus, who is succeeded by his adopted son Severus Alexander, 222 • Southern India's Satakani Empire collapses, c. 225

226–250

Artabanus V, last Arsacid king of Parthia, is killed by the Persian rebel Ardashir I, who founds Persia's Sassanid Empire, 227 • Ardashir I wars with Rome and seizes Armenia after death of its king, Chosroes, 229–232 • Christian artists produce catacomb paintings • Roman emperor Severus Alexander purchases peace from the Alamanni tribes on Rome's Rhine River boundary and his own troops kill him, 235, starting a period of military anarchy • Rome's Rhine legions nominate Maximinus emperor, 235 • Rival claimants (Gordian I, Gordian II, Pupienus, Balbinus) contest Rome's leadership, but by mid-238 all are dead, and Maximinus is killed by his troops • Gordian III becomes Roman emperor, 238 • China's Wei Dynasty seizes part of northern Korea, c. 238 • Shapur I rules Persia, 240–271 • Shapur I starts a war with Rome by invading Mesopotamia, 241 • Persian sage Manes, founder of Manichaeism religion, starts to preach in Persia, c. 242 • Roman prefect Furius Timesitheus drives Persian forces from Antioch, 243 • Romans defeat Persians in Mesopotamia, 244 • Praetorian prefect Philippus the Arabian kills Gordian III, 244 and becomes emperor; he makes peace with Persia • Goths raid across Danube River, 247 • Philippus is killed in battle by Roman general Decius, who becomes emperor, 249 • Decius launches indiscriminate persecution of Christians • State of Paekche emerges in southwest Korea, c. 250

251–275

Roman emperor Decius is killed in Dacia, 251; Gallus becomes Roman emperor, and kills his coemperor Hostilian, son of Decius • Gallus is killed by his troops, 253 • Valerian, commander in Germany, becomes emperor, 253, with his son Gallienus as coemperor • Greek mathematician Diophantus of Alexandria invents algebra, c. 251 • Classic Maya period emerges in Central America • Valerian fails to stop Franks, Goths and Alamanni advancing into the Empire from 256 • Persian ruler Shapur I invades Mesopotamia, 258 • Cyprian, bishop of Carthage, is martyred, 258 • Shapur captures Valerian, who dies in captivity; Gallienus becomes sole Roman emperor, 259 • Goths based near the Black Sea raid Asia Minor and the Aegean region • Odenathus of Palmyra defeats Syria and takes Mesopotamia for Rome by 263 • The Western Chin nominally reunite China, 265 • Queen Zenobia of Palmyra declares independence from Rome, 267 • Gallienus is killed by his troops, 268, and Claudius II becomes Roman emperor • Claudius II repulses a Gothic attack on the Balkans, 269 • Claudius II dies of plague, 270 • Quintillius is briefly Roman emperor, and is followed by Aurelian, 270 • Aurelian renounces Dacia north of the Danube River • Aurelian drives the Alamanni from Italy, 271 • Aurelian seizes the rebel Queen Zenobia and destroys Palmyra, 273 • Aurelian recaptures Gaul in a struggle at Châlons, c. 274 • Aurelian is murdered, 275, and is succeeded by an elderly senator, Tacitus • Tacitus crushes the Alans and Goths in Asia Minor

276–300

Roman emperor Tacitus is killed by his troops, 276 • Florian is briefly Roman emperor before being murdered, 276 • Probus becomes Roman emperor, from 276 to 282; he drives Alamanni and Franks from Gaul and pacifies Asia Minor • Probus is killed by his troops, 282 • Marcus Aurelius Carus becomes Roman emperor, 282, making his son Numerian coemperor • Carus subdues Mesopotamia, takes Ctesiphon from the Persians under Varahran II, and dies, 283 • Numerian becomes Roman emperor with his brother Carinus as coemperor • Numerian is murdered, 284 • Rome's eastern army proclaims Gaius Aurelius Valerius Diocletianus (Diocletian) emperor, 284 • Carinus is killed by his troops while fighting in Moravia, 285 • Marcus Aurelius Carausius, commanding Rome's British fleet, proclaims himself emperor of Britain, 285 • Diocletian establishes the empire's administrative division under two coemperors: Diocletian reigns in the east, the general Marcus Aurelius Valerius Maximianus (Maximian) in the west, 285 • Carausius is defeated by a rival general, Allectus, who claims Britain, 293 • Diocletian crushes revolt in Egypt, 294 • Narses of Persia routs Galerius (Diocletian's Caesar, or deputy) in Mesopotamia, 296 • Galerius crushes Narses and recaptures Roman Mesopotamia, 297; Armenia returns to Roman influence and its king, Tiridates III, is converted to Christianity • Maximian's Caesar, Constantius, ends Allectus' revolt in Britain, 297 • Constantius crushes the Alamanni in Gaul, 298

301–325

Roman emperor Diocletian launches major persecution of Christians, 303 • Turkish, Mongol and Tibetan kingdoms emerge on China's northern borders, 304–439 • The immense Baths of Diocletian are built in Rome, c. 303 • Diocletian and Maximian abdicate, 305, to be succeeded by their deputies Galerius and Constantius • St. Anthony pioneers monasticism in Egypt by 300 • Constantius dies, 306, and his troops declare his son Constantinus I (Constantine the Great) Roman emperor, but he agrees to be Caesar (deputy) to Flavius Valerius Severus, who has been Constantius's Caesar • Maximian again rules in Rome, 306–308; his son Maxentius kills Severus, 306 • Maxentius rules in Rome, 308–312 • Valerius Licinianus Licinius is formally emperor in the west, 311 • Galerius dies, 311, and his nephew Maximin Daia grabs Asia Minor • Constantine defeats Maxentius at the Milvian Bridge, 312, and becomes a Christian • Edict of Milan restores Christians' property, 313 • Licinius defeats Maximin, 313 • Council of Arles recognizes Rome's primacy in Christian Church, 314 • China's Eastern Chin Dynasty comes to power, 317 • Chandragupta I founds the Gupta Dynasty (320–c. 535) which reunites northern India and produces a rich culture • Constantine defeats his rival Licinius at Adrianople, 323 • Constantine reigns as sole emperor from 324, and reunites east and west parts of Roman empire • Ethiopian Kingdom of Axum invades the old Egyptianized kingdom of Kush, c. 325 • Constantine calls the Council of Nicaea to settle doctrinal disputes in Christian Church, 325

326–350

Constantine the Great, Roman emperor, founds Constantinople on site of Byzantium as the new Roman capital, 330 • Chandragupta I of India dies, 330, and is succeeded by his son Samudragupta • Great cult center of Teotihuacan is developing in Mexico • Persia's ruler Shapur II (309–379) defeats Roman forces, 337 • Constantine the Great dies, 337; Constantine's son Constantine II, Constantius II and Constans become coemperors • Constantine II attacks Constans and is killed, 340 • Athanasius, Bishop of Alexandria, introduces monasticism to western Christendom, 340 • Ulfilas becomes bishop of the Goths, 341, converts many of them to Arian Christianity, and invents a Gothic alphabet for use in Biblical translations • As imperial power wanes in the west, papal power based on Rome is gaining strength • Settlement of Micronesia and Polynesia is now well under way • German-born Roman general Flavius Magnus Magnentius tries to usurp Roman throne and kills coemperor Constans, 350 • Tea drinking is recorded in China, c. 350 • Scots and Picts raid Roman Britain, c. 350 • Persia campaigns against Huns in the east

351–375	376–400	401–425

Armenia aligns itself with Rome against Persia, 351 • Samudragupta enlarges India's Gupta Empire • Roman coemperor Constantius II defeats Magnentius at Mursa, near the Danube-Drave confluence, 351 • Magnentius commits suicide, leaving Constantius in complete command of Roman Empire, 353 • Constantius II makes Julian his Caesar (deputy), 355, and sends him to make war against Franks and Almanni • Roman general Julian defeats the Alamanni, 357 • Julian rebels against Constantius II, 360 • Japanese win footholds in Korea, c. 360–390 • Constantius II dies, 361 • Julian "the Apostate" becomes Roman emperor, 361, and starts substituting a pagan religion for Christianity • Julian campaigns against Persians and is killed near Samarra, 363 • Soldiers elect Jovian Roman emperor, 363 • Jovian makes peace with Persia, relinquishing provinces beyond the Tigris River, but dies, 364 • Soldiers elect Valentinian Roman emperor, 364, with his brother Valens as coemperor in the east • Valentinian copes with barbarian onslaughts in Gaul, Illyricum and Africa, 365–370 • Valentinian's son Gratian becomes western coemperor, 367 • Roman general Theodosius drives Picts and Scots from Britain by 369 • Huns moving west overrun the Ostrogoths, settled north of the Black Sea, c. 370 • Third war between Rome and Persia starts, 371 • Huns crush the Heruls and Alans, 372 • Valentinian I dies, 375 • Gratian becomes Roman emperor, 375, with his half-brother Valentinian II as western coemperor • Samudragupta dies, c. 375, and is succeeded by his son Chandragupta II, ruler until 415

Visigoths (West Goths), retreating from Huns, advance across the Danube River, 376, and settle in lower Moesia, in northern Balkans • Valens, Roman emperor in the east, dies fighting Visigoths near Adrianople, 378 • Theodosius becomes coemperor in the east, 379 • Persian power reaches its peak by the time Shapur II dies, 379 • Barbarians finally overrun Hadrian's Wall in Britain, 383 • Roman general Magnus Maximus seizes Gaul, and his troops kill Emperor Gratian at Lugdunum (Lyon), 383 • Rome and Persia partition Armenia, 384 • Tatars establish Northern Wei Dynasty in China, 386 • Magnus forces coemperor Valentinian II from Italy, 387 • Theodosius kills Magnus, 388 • Theodosius massacres Thessalonicans after a revolt, 390, but Ambrose, Archbishop of Milan, makes him perform penance for this act • Japanese armies range through Korea, c. 391 • Arbogast, a Frankish count, kills Valentinian II and declares Eugenius, a pagan, emperor, 392 • Frankish Salian and Ripuarian tribes occupy lands between the Meuse and Rhine rivers, as allies of Rome • Theodosius bans Greek Olympic Games, c. 393 • Theodosius defeats and kills Eugenius, 394 • Theodosius dies, 395, and his sons Arcadius and Honorius divide the empire • Augustine becomes bishop of Hippo, North Africa. 395 • Alaric becomes king of the Visigoths, 395, invades Greece 396, but is expelled by the Vandal leader Stilicho, 397 • Yamato becomes the leading kingdom in Japan and adopts Chinese writing • Chinese Buddhist pilgrim Fahsien visits India • Major Indian dramatist Kalidasa is born, c. 400

Pope Innocent I (401–417) strengthens papal power • Alaric, King of the Visigoths, invades northwestern Italy, 401, fights the Vandal leader Stilicho, 402, and withdraws, 403 • St. Jerome completes his Latin translation of the Bible (the Vulgate), 405 • White Huns dominate Central Asia, 407–554 • Sanskrit literature reaches its peak in Gupta India • Jutes, Angles and Saxons invade Britain • Alchemy first recorded • Alans, Burgundians, Sueves and Vandals invade Gaul, c. 406 • Roman troops abandon Britain, 407 • Avars establish the first Mongolian empire, 407 • Roman Emperor Honorius has Stilicho killed, 408 • Theodosius II becomes Roman emperor of the east, 408 • Persia permits Christians freedom of worship, 409 • Alans, Sueves and Vandals enter Spain, 409 • Alaric invades Italy again, 409, sacks Rome, 410, and dies • Ataulf succeeds Alaric and takes Visigoths into Gaul, 412 • Japan establishes direct contact with China, 413 • Visigoths begin wresting Spain from the Vandals, 415 • British monk Pelagius proclaims freedom of will, 415 • Visigoth king Wallia forms the Kingdom of Toulouse, and builds Visigothic power in Spain, 419 • Eastern Chin Dynasty ends in China, and the Sung Dynasty begins, 420 • Persian persecution of Christians leads to war with Rome, 420–422; Rome wins • Pope Celestine I (422–432) asserts theory of papal supremacy • Honorius dies at his new capital, Ravenna (It), 423 • Johannes makes himself Roman emperor in the west, 423 • Troops of Theodosius II kill Johannes, 425 • Valentinian III, nephew of Honorius, becomes Roman emperor of the west, 425

City of Pyongyang becomes capital of Korea's Koguryo kingdom, 427 • Vandals under Gaiseric invade North Africa, 429, and set up a kingdom • St. Augustine dies in Vandal siege of Hippo, North Africa, 430 • First Christian mission to Ireland is launched, c. 431 • Romano-British missionary St. Patrick arrives in Ireland, probably from Gaul, c. 432, to become bishop • Attila becomes king of the Huns, c. 433, and advances west through Europe • Roman general Aëtius rids Gaul of barbarians, defeating the Visigoths, 436 • Aëtius smashes a peasant uprising, 437 • Theodosian Code, a collection of Roman imperial laws, is published in Eastern Empire, 438 • Vandals in Africa take Carthage, and their North African kingdom becomes formally independent of Rome, 439 • Pope Leo I (Leo the Great; 440–461) immensely strengthens papal spiritual and temporal authority, and attacks the Manichaean heresy, a religion founded by Persian mystic Mani • Saxons establish settlements by the Thames estuary in England, c. 441 • Merovech, second king of the Salian Franks (448–458), establishes the Merovingian Dynasty (432–c. 751) • Jutish leaders Hengist and Horsa invade Kent (Eng), c. 449 • Theodosius II, Roman Emperor of the East, dies, 450: his brother-in-law Marcian succeeds him

Huns under Attila, invade Gaul, 451, but lose the Battle of Châlons to Aëtius • Attila briefly invades Italy, 452 • Refugees from Attila found Venice • Attila dies, 453, and his army breaks up • Ostrogoths settle Pannonia (western Hungary), c. 454 • Valentinian III, Roman Emperor in the West, is murdered, 455; he is succeeded by puppet emperor • Vandals invade Italy from Africa, and sack Rome, 455 • Indian Gupta Emperor Skandagupta stems a White Hun invasion, 455 • Jutes, Angles and Saxons settle in Britain • Peru's Mochica culture flourishes • Ricimer, a Suevian general in Roman service, deposes Avitus (Emperor from 455) and puts his nominees on the Western throne, 456–472 • Majorian becomes West Roman Emperor, 456 • Childeric becomes king of the Salian Franks, 456 • Leo I succeeds Marcian as East Roman Emperor, 457 • Franks take Cologne 460 • Severus becomes West Roman Emperor, 461 • Pope Leo I dies, 461 • Anthemius becomes West Roman Emperor, 467 • East Romans under Basiliscus attack the Vandals in Africa, but Vandal leader Gaiseric defeats them off Cape Bon (Tunisia), 468 • Euric the Visigoth murders his brother Theodoric II and becomes King of Toulouse, 466–484; under Euric, Visigoth kingdom extends from Loire River to southern Spain • Burgundians, a Germanic tribe, make Lyon their capital, 470 • Theodoric becomes Ostrogoth king, 471, soon invading the Balkans • Olybrius becomes West Roman emperor, 472, then dies; he is followed by Glycerius, 473, and Julius Nepos, 473–475 • Romulus Augustus, son of Julius Nepos, becomes West Roman emperor, 475

Germanic barbarian leader Odoacer (Odovacer) deposes Roman emperor Romulus Augustus, ending the West Roman Empire, 476; traditionally regarding as starting date for the Middle Ages • In the East, Emperor Leo I dies, 474, and is succeeded by his colleague, Leo II; Leo II dies soon after and is succeeded by his father, Zeno • Basiliscus, a pretender, usurps East Roman throne, 476, but Zeno recovers it aided by Theodoric the Great, the Ostrogoth ruler • Shinto shrines appear in Japan, c. 478 • China's Sung Dynasty ends and Southern Ch'i Dynasty begins, 479 • Amerindians build animal-shaped earth mounds in Mississippi Valley • Clovis becomes king of the Salian Franks, 481, and founds the Frankish Kingdom • Bulgarians (related to the Huns) settle northeast of Danube River by 482 • Clovis crushes a Gallo-Roman force at Soissons, 486, and seizes lands as far as Loire River • Theodoric the Great threatens Constantinople, 487 • Anastasius becomes Byzantine (East Roman) Emperor, 491 • Pope Gelasius I (492–496) proclaims the papacy independent in matters of faith • Theodoric the Great makes Italy an Ostrogothic kingdom, 494, but rules largely in Roman tradition • China's Northern Wei Dynasty shifts its capital to Loyang, 495 • Clovis, King of the Salian Franks, defeats the Alamanni, 496, and becomes king of the Ripuarian Franks, thus uniting all Franks • Clovis becomes a Christian, 496 • Byzantine emperor Anastasius I quells revolt in Isauria (now part of Turkey), 497 • Indian mathematician Aryabhata works out the ratio of a circle's circumference to its diameter (3.14159), and declares that the Earth rotates, c. 400 • Saxons establish kingdom of Wessex in southern Britain, c. 500

501–525

China's Southern Ch'i Dynasty ends and the Southern Liang Dynasty begins, 502 • Persia at war with Byzantium, 503–505 • Lombards, a Germanic tribe, expand southward from Austria in this period • Picts and others hold kingdoms in various parts of Scotland at this time • Anglo-Saxons continue to set up kingdoms in England • Bulgars, Huns and Slavs invade the Byzantine (East Roman) Empire, 507–512 • Franks crush the Visigoths, 507, and take their French possessions • Spain's Visigothic kingdom is in decline, 507–711 • Germanic tribe the Lombards smash the Heruli from Scandinavia, 508 • Clovis, King of the Franks, dies, 511, and his four sons divide his kingdom • Byzantine Emperor Anastasius I builds the Anastasian Wall from the Black Sea to the Sea of Marmara to keep out the barbarians, 512 • Persians crush the White Huns, 513 • Anastasius I dies, 518, and is succeeded by Justinus I, an Illyrian • Clonard monastery —source of missions to much of Europe—is founded in Ireland, c. 520 • Ancius Boethius, last classical philosopher, writes *Consolation of Philosophy*, 524 • Persia again at war with Byzantine Empire, 524–531

526–550

Theodoric the Great, Ostrogothic ruler of Italy, dies, 526 • Justinian succeeds his uncle Justinus as Byzantine Emperor, 527; influenced by his wife Theodora, he proceeds to strengthen imperial power and to rebuild a united Christian Roman Empire • Byzantines under their general Belisarius defeat Persians at Daras, 528 • Rise of the Korean state of Silla and a revolt in Kyushu weaken Japan's hold on Korea by 528 • St. Benedict of Nursia founds a monastery at Monte Cassino, Italy, 529 • Justinian attacks heresy and shuts the Academy at Athens, 529 • Anushirwan the Just (Chosroes I), becomes Persian Emperor, 531 • Franks conquer the Burgundians, 532 • Belisarius crushes the Nika Rebellion—named for the rebels' cry "Nika!" (victory)—532 • Belisarius conquers Vandal North Africa, 533–534 • Justinian publishes *Digest* and *Institutes*, legal works, 533 • Persia makes peace with the Byzantine Empire, 533 • St. Columba develops monasticism in Ireland, c. 533 • China's Eastern Wei Dynasty rules at Ye (Anyang), 534–550 • Belisarius reconquers Sicily and Italy, 535–540 • China's Western Wei Dynasty rules from Ch'angan, 535–556 • Bulgars and Huns raid the Balkans, 540 • Persians invade Syria and take Lazica (ancient Colchis), 540 • Totila's Ostrogoths retake much of Italy, 541–543 • Bubonic plague is rampant in Europe, 542–546 • Justinian lets Lombards settle in Noricum and Pannonia (modern Austria and Hungary), 546 • Northern Ch'i Dynasty flourishes in China, 550–557

551–575

Buddhism is officially brought to Japan, 552 • Byzantine general Narses defeats the Ostrogoths at Tagina, 552, and Byzantines retake Italy • Revolt ends the first Mongol Empire, 553 • Persians defeat the White Huns, 554 • Byzantine general Belisarius invades Spain, but secures only the southeast, 554 • State of Silla expands in Korea during this period • England is split among seven Anglo-Saxon kingdoms (the Heptarchy): Saxon Essex, Sussex and Wessex; Anglian East Anglia, Mercia and Northumbria; and Jutish Kent • Mayas build ceremonial centers in Central America in their "classical" period, c. 300–900 • China's Western Wei Dynasty ends, 556; Southern Liang and Northern Ch'i dynasties end, 557, and Southern Ch'en and Northern Chou begin • Lothair (Clotaire) I, sole survivor of Clovis's warring sons, reunites Frankish kingdom, 558–561 • Ethelbert of Kent is chief Anglo-Saxon king, 560–616 • Lothair I dies, 561, and his four sons divide the Frankish kingdom • Silla ends Japan's power in Korea, 562 • Avar tribesmen from Volga River area reach Thuringia, 562 • Christian missionary St. Columba founds monastery on Scottish island of Iona, 563 • Columba converts Scotland's Pictish king Brude, c. 565 • Byzantine Emperor Justinian publishes new laws (*Novellae*) and dies, 565; succeeded by nephew Justin II • Power struggles, 567–613, split Frankish kingdom into Austrasia, Neustria, Burgundy • Lombards under Alboin invade Italy, 568 • The prophet Muhammad is born at Mecca, in Arabia, 570 • Lombards win most of north and central Italy by 571 • Short-lived Turkish empire in Central Asia splits in two, 572 • New war begins between Persia and Byzantine Empire, 572

Persians drive Axumite invaders from southern Arabia, 576 • Turks and Byzantines combine in unsuccessful invasion of Persia, 576–578 • Tiberius becomes Byzantine Emperor, 578, but fails to stop a huge influx of Slavs into the Balkans • Persian ruler Anushirwan dies, 579; succeeded by Hormisdas IV • War between Persia and Byzantine Empire continues to 589 • China's Sui Dynasty emerges at Ch'ang-an, 581 • Maurikios (Maurice) reigns as Byzantine Emperor, 582–602 • Avars seize Danube forts, 583 • Kurt becomes first known Bulgarian ruler, 584 • Japan's Emperor Yomei becomes a Buddhist, c. 587 • Persian general Varahran defeats Turkish invaders, 589 • China reunited in 589 under the Sui Dynasty, the first time since 220 • Khusru Parviz (in Greek, Chosroes II) becomes Persia's last important Sassanid king, 590 • Persian general Varahran rebels against Khusru and rules as Varahran (Bahram) VI, 590–591 • Agilulf, Duke of Turin, builds Lombard state in Italy, 590–615 • Pope Gregory I, the Great, (590–604) increases papal influence in political matters • Maurice restores Khusru Parviz to Persian throne, 591, in return for most of Armenia • Avars threaten Constantinople, 591 • Byzantine general Priscus attacks Avars, 593 • After 593, Empress Suiko and Crown Prince Shotoku firmly establish Buddhism and Chinese culture in Japan • Pope Gregory I sends the Roman monk Augustine to Britain to become its first archbishop, 596; Augustine converts Kent to Roman orthodoxy • Spanish scholar Isidore becomes Bishop of Seville, 600; his *Etymologies* becomes a basic general reference work for five centuries • Indian mathematicians invent a symbol (a dot) for zero

West African state of Ghana exists by now • Coptic art is established in Egypt • Byzantine forces under their general Priscus crush the Avars at Viminacium, 601 • The incompetent soldier Phocas deposes Maurice and becomes Byzantine Emperor, 602 • Persians and Byzantines start a fresh war, 603 • Lombards adopt Christianity, c. 603 • Indian mathematicians use decimal position by 604 • Shotoku's Chinese-inspired "Constitution" proclaims need for centralized power in Japan, 604 • Harsha (606–647) wins a short-lived empire in northern India • Arabs defeat Persians at Dhu-Qar, 610 • China builds Grand Canal by 610 • Mob kills Phocas, who is succeeded by Heraclius 1, 610 • The Arab trader Muhammad feels call to be a prophet, 610 • Persians sack Antioch, 611 • Muhammad begins preaching Islam ("submission" to the will of God), 612 • Persians invade Cappadocia, 612 • Lothair II reunites the Frankish kingdom, 613 • Persians take Damascus, 614 • Persians sack Jerusalem, 615 • Visigoths win Byzantine lands in Spain, 616 • Persian troops threaten Constantinople, 617 • T'ang Dynasty replaces Sui in China, 618, establishing a centralized form of administration that lasts to 1912 • Avars and Persians threaten Constantinople, 619 • Bulgar king Kurt adopts Christianity, 619 • Persians take Rhodes and Ancyra, 620 • Edwin of Northumbria enlarges his kingdom in the north of England • Windmills are in use in Persia by the end of this period

Persecution forces Muhammad to flee from Mecca to Yathrib (later called Medina, "City of the Messenger of God") 622: this event, the *Hegira*, marks the start of the Muslim era • Byzantine emperor Heraclius I begins driving Persians from the Byzantine Empire, 622 • Byzantines invade Armenia, 623 • Persians and Avars unsuccessfully beseige Constantinople, 626 • Under T'ai Tsung (622–649), Chinese conquests in Central Asia forge cultural links with India and Persia • In Britain, Edwin becomes first Christian king of Northumbria, 627 • Heraclius invades Assyria and Mesopotamia, 627 • Persian troops mutiny and kill their ruler, Khusru Parviz, 628 • Byzantines regain all possessions lost to Persia, 628–630 • Persia lapses into anarchy, 629–634 • Dagobert, last strong Merovingian King of the Franks, reigns 629–639 • Muhammad captures Mecca, 630 • Muhammad subdues many Arab tribes, then dies, 632 • Abu Bakr, first Muslim caliph ("successor") ends Arab revolts, 632–634 • Arabs under Khalid ibn al-Walid invade Iraq, 633 • Mercians kill Edwin and end Northumbrian dominance among Anglo-Saxon kingdoms • Irish monk Aidan spreads Celtic Christianity through Northumbria, 633 • Yezdigird III becomes Persia's last Sassanid ruler, 634 • Caliph Abu Bakr dies, 634; succeeded by Omar • Arabs win Syria, 636 • Arabs take Jerusalem and Ctesiphon, 637 • Arabs seize Mesopotamia and enter Fars and Susiana, 639 • Frankish King Dagobert dies, 639, and Carolingian "mayors of the palace" (viceroys) emerge as powers behind the throne • Arabs invade Egypt, 640 • Chinese traveler and philosopher Hsüan-tsang visits India, 630–643

641–660

Byzantine Emperor Heraclius I dies, 641; his grandson Constans II (641–668) forms *themes* (provinces under military governors) to resist Arabs • Tibet's first king, Srong-tsan-sgam-po, marries a Chinese princess, 641 • Arabs conquer Persian Empire, 642 • Arabs complete occupation of Egypt, 643 • Caliph Omar murdered, 644; succeeded by Othman, an Omayyad • Nakatomi Kamatari, founder of the Fujiwara clan, helps depose Japan's ruling Soga clan, 645 • Chinese philosopher Hsüan-tsang returns from India, 645, with account of Indian culture • Indian ruler Harsha dies, 647 • Arabs thrust west across North Africa, 647 • Arab fleet takes Cyprus, 648–649 • Arabs take Armenia, 653 • Mercian king Penda dies, 654, after making Mercia a powerful kingdom in Britain • Arabs destroy Byzantine fleet off Lycia, Anatolia, 655 • Arab ruler Caliph Othman murdered, 656; succeeded by Muhammad's cousin Ali, against opposition from Omayyad family • Muawiya, Omayyad governor of Syria, revolts and seizes Egypt, 658 • Grimoald, mayor of palace (viceroy) in Austrasia, part of the Frankish kingdom, dies trying to usurp Frankish throne, 656 • Lothair III succeeds to Frankish throne, 656 • Caedmon, first known English poet, enters monastery at Whitby, c. 660 • Chalukyas and Pallavas vie for dominance in southern India • Japanese culture is now closely modeled on that of China • Peru's Moche culture is drawing to an end

661–680

Caliph (Arab ruler) Ali murdered, 661; Muawiya becomes caliph, founds Omayyad Dynasty (661–750) and makes Damascus capital of Arab Empire • Japanese abandon Korea, 663 • Emperor Constans II transfers Byzantine court to Italy, 663–668, while Arabs ravage Asia Minor • Synod of Whitby establishes Roman orthodoxy in Britain, in place of Celtic Church, 664 • Constans II killed, 668; succeeded by his son Constantine IV • Theodore of Tarsus, a Greek monk, is appointed Archbishop of Canterbury (Eng), 669–690 • Sutton Hoo ship burial (discovered 1939) takes place in Suffolk (Eng), c. 670 • Bulgars, under pressure from Avars and Khazars, cross Danube River by 670 • Arabs hold North Africa westward to what is now Algeria by 670 • Silla is dominant state in Korea by 670 • The Venerable Bede, English monk, so-called "Father of English literature," born 673 • Arabs unsuccessfully besiege Constantinople, 673–678 • Slavs unsuccessfully assault Thessalonica, 675–681 • English monk St. Cuthbert temporarily retires to Farne Island, 676 • Arab armies advance east to Samarkand in Central Asia by 676 • Byzantines using "Greek fire" smash besieging Arab fleet and save Constantinople, 677 • Bulgars under Isperikh defeat Byzantine force, 680, and settle between Balkan Mountains and Danube • Sixth Ecumenical Council at Constantinople, 680–681, condemns doctrine of Monothelitism • Patriarch of Constantinople, not the pope, is now effective leader of Byzantine Christians • Caliph (Arab ruler) Muawiya dies, 680, and rival claimants fight for the caliphate

681–700

Marwan I becomes caliph (Arab ruler), 684, after civil war in Arab Empire • *Ravenna Cosmography,* anonymous Italian MS, c. 685, lists world's known rivers, nations and towns • Marwan I dies, 685; succeeded by Abdalmalik who sets up new administration for Arab Empire • Byzantine Emperor Constantine IV dies, 685; succeeded by son Justinian II • Picts halt Northumbrian expansion northward into Scotland at Battle of Nechtanesmere, 685; Scotland develops independently of England • In Britain, Northumbrian power wanes after death of its king, Egfrith, 685 • Victory at Tertry, 686, gives Pepin II, "mayor of the palace," control over Austrasia and Neustria, hence over most of the Frankish kingdom • First doge (chief official) of Venice is elected, 687 • Byzantines defeat Slavs in Thrace, 689 • Council of Constantinople reaffirms that the pope and the patriarch of Constantinople are equal, 692 • Arabs crush Byzantine troops at Sevastopol, 692 • Byzantine Emperor Justinian II deposed, 695 • succeeded by his rival Leontius, but Byzantine Empire enters two decades of anarchy • Arabs seize Carthage and and all Byzantine North Africa by 698 • Leontius deposed by revolt, 698; succeeded by Tiberius II • Kharijites and Shi'ites revolt against Omayyad rule of Arab Empire, but crushed by 699 • Anglo-Saxon priest Willibrord is first Christian missionary to Denmark, c. 700 • *Lindisfarne Gospels,* produced in Northumbria (Eng), date from c. 700 • Amerindians build temple mounds in what is now southeast USA, c. 700 • By 700 the city of Teotihuacan (Mex) covers c. 1750 acres

Pueblo culture succeeds Basket-maker culture in what is now southwestern USA • Arabs and Berbers make peace in North Africa; Berbers align themselves with Muslim Arabs, 703 • Srivishaya in Sumatra develops as a powerful trading state • Indian-influenced states evolve in what is now Thailand • Byzantine emperor Justinian II regains throne from Tiberius II, 705 • Arab ruler Caliph Abdalmalik dies, 705; succeeded by Walid I • Arabs extend Asian conquests north to Aral Sea and northeast of Samarkand, 705–715 • In the Indian subcontinent, Arabs invade the Punjab, 708–715 • City of Nara, designed on lines of T'ang Chinese capital Ch'ang-an, becomes Japan's first permanent capital, 710, and the Nara period (710–784) starts • Arab-Berber army commanded by Tariq invades Spain from Africa, defeating Visigothic king Roderick at Rio Barbate, 711 • Bulgars threaten Constantinople, 712 • China enjoys cultural renaissance under Hsüan-tsung, 712–756 • Lombard kingdom in Italy reaches its peak under Liutprand, 712–744 • Muslims master most of Spain by 715 • Byzantine Emperor Leo III (717–741) restores order in empire after period of incompetent rulers • Arabs besiege Constantinople, 717–718 • Caliph Omar (717–720) makes non-Arab subjects equal with Arabs for taxation • Muslims invade France from Spain, 720 • Charles Martel becomes mayor of the palace (chief minister) in Austrasia, Neustria, Burgundy, 717, reuniting Frankish kingdom

Charles Martel, mayor of the palace (chief minister), strengthens his hold on the Frankish kingdom • Anglo-Saxon missionary Boniface, the "Apostle of Germany," begins his missionary work, c. 719 • Arab attacks devastate Gujarat in India, 724–743 • Japan's Nara period reaches its cultural peak after 724 • Civil wars trouble the Arab Empire; descendants of Muhammad's uncle, Abbas, begin to press claims to the caliphate • First known clock escapement invented in China, c. 725 • Pala Buddhist kings rule Bengal and Magadha from c. 725 • Byzantine Emperor Leo III, first of the so-called Iconoclasts, forbids image-worship in bid to end supersition • Arabs conquer Georgia, on the Black Sea, 727–733 • Pope Gregory III excommunicates iconoclasts, 731 • Most English kings acknowledge Ethelbald of Mercia as their overlord, 731 • Charles Martel, Frankish mayor of the palace (chief minister) defeats a Muslim force at Tours (Fr), 732, halting the Muslims' northward thrust in the West • Byzantine emperor Leo III removes southern Italy from papal jurisdiction, 733 • English monk and scholar Bede dies, 735 • York (Eng) becomes an archbishopric, 735 • Pope Gregory III seeks Frankish aid against Lombards, 739 • Byzantines crush Arabs at Akroinon in Anatolia, 739 • Shi'ite and Kharijite revolts continue in the Arab Empire • Gurjara-Prathihara Dynasty (c. 740–1036) unites much of northern India against Muslim attacks • Some Ajanta (India) cave frescoes date from this time

Byzantine Emperor Leo III dies, 741; succeeded by Constantine V • Charles Martel, Frankish ruler, dies 741, dividing the kingdom between his sons: Carloman takes Austrasia, Pepin the Short takes Neustria and Burgundy • Byzantine forces invade Arab-held Syria, 745 • Uighur Turks defeat eastern Turks and found an empire in Central Asia, 745 • Byzantines retake Cyprus, 746 • Chinese troops campaign beyond the Pamirs, 747 • Pepin the Short becomes sole ruler of the Franks, 747 • Abbasids revolt against Omayyad rule of the Arab Empire, 747 • Lombard expansion continues in Italy under Aistulf after 749 • Abu-al-Abbas becomes first Abbasid caliph of Arabia, 750 • Heavy government-spending causes financial crisis in China • Byzantines fight Arabs in Armenia, 751–752 • Pepin the Short ousts Chilperic III, last Merovingian king of the Franks, 751; as Pepin III, he founds Carolingian Dynasty (752–987) • Arab caliph Al-Mansur (754–775) consolidates Abbas-id rule • Pepin III invades Italy (754–756), forcing Lombards to yield lands formerly held by the Byzantines • Byzantines campaign against Bulgars, 755–764 • Revolt disrupts China, 755 • Pepin hands over former Byzantine lands in Italy to the papacy—the "Donation of Pepin," 756—forming nucleus of Papal States • Abd ar-Rahman I founds Omayyad Dynasty of Córdoba (Sp) • English kingdom of Mercia reaches its peak under Offa II, 757–796 • Byzantines defeat Slavs in Thrace, 758 • Pepin III extends Frankish rule to the Pyrenees, 759

HOLY ROMAN EMPIRE

Irish *Book of Kells* (illuminated Latin gospels) is produced • Khazars, a group of Turkish tribes, hold an empire north of Black and Caspian seas • Barmecide family gains power as vizirs (ministers) to Arab caliphs • Caliph Al-Mansur founds Baghdad as new Abbasid capital of Arab Empire, 762 • Uighur Turks sack Chinese city of Loyang, and Tibetans sack China's capital Ch'ang-an, 763 • A monk, Dokyo, defeats a statesman, Nakamaro, in Japanese power struggle, 764 • Tu Yu starts writing China's first historical encyclopedia, 766 • York (Eng) becomes a major center of Western learning, *c.* 766 • Pepin III, king of the Franks, dies, 768; succeeded by sons Charles and Carloman

Charlemagne (Charles the Great, son of Pepin III) is sole king of Franks from 771, following death of his brother Carloman • Bulgars and Byzantines renew hostilities, 772 • Charlemagne invades Italy, 773–774, absorbing Lombard kingdom in his Frankish Empire; Corsica, Dalmatia, Istria, Venetia also come under him • Arab caliph Al-Mahdi (775–785) fosters education and communications in Arab Empire • Byzantine emperor Leo IV (775–780) continues iconoclast policy • Charlemagne builds splendid palace at Aachen, 777–786 • Charlemagne invades Spain but is halted at Saragossa, 777 • Retreating Franks are ambushed in Pyrenees, 778 • Leo IV dies 780, succeeded by Constantine VI, a child controlled by his mother, Irene

Pope Adrian I crowns Pepin, son of Frankish ruler Charlemagne, as king of Italy, 781 • Japanese under Emperor Kammu (781–806) subdue Ainu territory • Monk Alcuin of York helps found Charlemagne's Palace School at Aachen, *c.* 781 • Arabs again threaten Constantinople, 782–783 • Byzantines defeat Slavs in the Balkans, 783 • Charlemagne subdues Saxony by 785, establishing Christianity there • Charlemagne wins Catalonia, 785–811 • Harun al-Rashid becomes caliph of Arab Empire, 786 • Danes begin raiding England, 787 • Arabs win Kabul, Afghanistan, 787 • Charlemagne's empire absorbs Bavaria, 787–788 • Religious Council of Nicaea rejects iconoclasm (destruction of idols), 787 • Irish monks discover Iceland, *c.* 790

ENGLAND
HOLY ROMAN EMPIRE — **Louis I**

Egbert

Japanese culture develops independently of China • Bulgars establish Great Preslav as their capital, 821 • During the caliphate of Abdar-Rahman II (822–852) in Spain, Alfonso of León's invasion of Aragon fails, and Muslims repulse Franks in Catalonia • Byzantine emperor Michael II ends a revolt by 824 • Arab mathematician Al-Khwarizmi establishes Hindu use of decimals in the Arab world; from his *Al-jebr v'al muqâbalah* comes our term algebra ("reduction") • In England, Egbert of Wessex defeats Beornwulf of Mercia at Ellendun (modern Wroughton, Wiltshire) destroying Mercian power, 825 • Law school is established at Pavia (It) by 825

Muslims expelled from Omayyad-ruled Spain capture Crete, which becomes a pirate base, 826 • Aghlabid Muslims based in Tunis invade Sicily, 827 • Bulgars raid Croatia and Pannonia, 827–829 • Scholars translate work on astronomy by Greek scientist Claudius Ptolemaeus (Ptolemy) into Arabic as the *Almagest*, *c.* 828 • Church of St. Mark's, Venice, is founded, *c.* 828 • In England, Egbert of Wessex conquers Mercia, 829, and becomes first ruler to unite the English • Byzantine emperor Michael II dies, 829; succeeded by son Theophilus

Oldest order of chivalry, Venetian Order of St. Marc, is founded, *c.* 831 • Lateen sails are now in use in ships in the Mediterranean Sea • Trans-Saharan trade in ivory, salt and gold enriches the ancient empire of Ghana in West Africa • Aghlabid Muslims take Palermo, Sicily, 831 • Archbishop of Hamburg (founded *c.* 831) becomes a springboard for northern missions • Kenneth MacAlpin, King of the Scots, conquers the Picts and unites most of Scotland, *c.* 832 • Illustrated *Utrecht Psalter* is produced at Rheims, *c.* 832 • Arab caliph Al-Mamun dies, 833; succeeded by Al-Mu'tasim, who forms a corps of Turkish troops • Mojmir (833–836) founds Slav state of Moravia

□ **Charlemagne** ——————————————————— □ **Louis I** →

Heian (Kyoto) becomes Japan's capital, 794, and Japan enters its so-called Heian period (794–1185) • Vikings begin pillaging Scotland, 794 • Danes attack Ireland, 795 • Frankish ruler Charlemagne subdues the Avars on Danube River by 796 • Charlemagne organizes his border lands as defensive *marks* or *marches* • Irene, window of Byzantine emperor Leo IV, deposes and blinds her son Constantine VI, and becomes first ruling empress, 797–802 • Oseberg Ship, an early Viking vessel, is built, *c.* 800 • Pope Leo III crowns Charlemagne as emperor, 800, reviving West Roman (later to be called Holy Roman) Empire • Amerindian cultures thriving in what is now the USA include Woodland (northeast), Mississippian (southeast), and Southwestern farming cultures

Aghlabid Dynasty (801–909) takes Tunis out of Arab Empire • Egbert becomes king of the West Saxons in southern England, 802 • Finance minister Nicephorus deposes Byzantine empress Irene, 802, and becomes emperor • Nicephorus and Frankish emperor Charlemagne settle a territorial dispute: Byzantine empire keeps Dalmatia, southern Italy, and Venice, 803 • Arab caliph Harun al-Rashid topples powerful Barmecide family from power, 803 • Arabs attack Asia Minor and Cyprus, 804–806 • Minuscule (small letter) handwriting is developing • Charlemagne completes Palatine Chapel, Aachen, 805 • Harun al-Rashid dies, 809; succeeded by his son Al-Amin • Krum, Khan of the Bulgars (802–814) wars with Byzantium from 809

Arab caliph Al-Mamun (813–833) founds center for classical and oriental studies at Baghdad; Arab culture at its zenith • Byzantine emperor Nicephorus dies fighting Bulgars, 811 • Bulgars threaten Constantinople, 813 • Frankish emperor Charlemagne dies, 814; succeeded by son, Louis the Pious • Leo V, a successful general, is Byzantine emperor from 813 • Council of St. Sophia revives iconoclasm (destruction of images); Byzantine monks persecuted, 815 • Louis the Pious divides Carolingian Empire among his sons and himself, 817 • Byzantines crush Bulgars at Mesembria and make peace, 817 • County of Barcelona becomes independent in the Carolingian Empire, 817 • Emperor Leo V is killed, 820; succeeded by another general, Michael II

———————————— □ **Ethelwulf** —————————————————————— ▷
——————————————— □ **Lothair I** ———————————————————— ▷

Muslims invade southern Italy, 837–840 • They crush revolt at Toledo (Sp) by Jews and Christians, 837 • Byzantine troops invade Arab-held lands, but are forced back, 837–842 • Charles the Bald, son of Frankish emperor Louis the Pious, receives Neustria and Aquitaine—roughly the area of medieval France—838 • Bulgars take Serbia, 839 • Egbert of Wessex dies, 839; succeeded by son Ethelwulf • Uighur Empire in Central Asia declines, 840 • Louis the Pious dies, 840; succeeded by son Lothair I, but rivals fight over waning Carolingian Empire • Tiahuanaco culture, named for a ceremonial center in Bolivia, thrives, *c.* 700–1100 • Danes establish towns of Dublin and Limerick (Ire), 840

Norsemen invade northern France and establish Normandy, 841 • Arab caliphate is in decline under rule of Al-Wathiq, 842–847 • Christians persecuted in China under Taoist emperor Wu Tsung, 841–846 • Byzantine emperor Theophilus dies; succeeded by son, Michael III, "the Drunkard," 842 • Image-worship allowed again in Byzantine Empire, 843 • Treaty of Verdun, 843, splits Carolingian Empire: Lothair I gets Burgundy, Italy, Lotharingia, Provence; Louis the German rules the nucleus of Germany; Charles the Bald gets lands roughly tallying with modern France

Muslims attack Rome, 846 • Tamil invasions force rulers of Sri Lanka (Ceylon) to abandon Anuradhapura and build a capital at Polonnaruwa in the south, 846 • Pope Leo IV builds Rome's Leonine Wall, to protect Vatican from attack, 847–848 • Irish-born philosopher Johannes Scotus (Erigena) becomes head of Frankish king Charles the Bald's court school, 847 • Bremen replaces Hamburg as a center for evangelization in Germany, 848 • Swedish tribe the Rus (Varangians) move down Russian rivers toward Black Sea • University of Constantinople founded, *c.* 850 • Hinduism is replacing Buddhism in northern India • Jews begin settling in Germany

ENGLAND—**Ethelwulf**————————☐ **Ethelbald-**☐ **Ethelbert**————————
HOLY ROMAN EMPIRE—**Lothair I**—☐ **Louis II**————————————————

Aragon in Spain becomes independent of Carolingian rule • Feudalism emerges in France • Danes sack Canterbury Cathedral (Eng) but Ethelwulf of Essex crushes a Danish invasion force, 851 • Orthodox Muslims persecute Shi'ites, Christians and Jews in the Arab Empire during this period • Moors under Muhammad I (852–886) attack Galicia, León and Navarre in Christian Spain • Germans defeat the Bulgarians led by Boris I, 853 • Western polyphonic music is evolving • Emperor Lothair I divides his lands among his sons, 855: Italy goes to Louis II; Provence to Charles; Lotharingia (Lorraine) to Lothair II

Wessex leads English resistance to full-scale Viking attacks, 856–875 • Fujiwara regents dominate Japanese emperor, 858–1160, starting when Yoshifusa becomes regent for Emperor Seiwa • Pope Nicholas I, powerful arbiter of Roman Christendom, takes office, 858 • Ethelwulf dies, 858; succeeded by brothers Ethelbald (858) and Ethelbert (860) • Viking ships winter on Rhône River delta, 859 • Serbs check a Bulgarian force led by Boris I, 860 • Danes sack Winchester (Eng), 860 • Russians (Varangians) raid south to Constantinople, 860 • Khmers (Cambodians) begin building great temple complexes at Siemreap in Cambodia • Borobudur, magnificent Buddhist structure, completed in Java

Muslims advance against Christians in Spain, 861 • Arab caliph Al-Mutawakkil murdered by his Turkish guards, 861 • Russians under Rurik found Novgorod, c. 862 • Greek preacher Cyril and his brother Methodius evangelize Bohemian and Moravian Slavs, linking them with the Eastern Church, 863–885 • Pope Nicholas I disciplines Lothair II of Lorraine over divorce, and affirms the need for papal approval in election or deposition of bishops, 863 • Louis II of France, in dispute with the pope, invades Rome, 864 • Tsar Boris of Bulgaria becomes a Christian, 865 • Major Danish invasions of eastern England start, 865

ENGLAND—**Alfred the Great** ————————————————————————
HOLY ROMAN EMPIRE—**Charles III**————————————☐ **Guido**————☐ **Lambert**——

First German historical ballad appears, c. 881 • Pope John VIII is murdered, 882, and papacy becomes a pawn of Roman aristocracy • Arabs crush Zanj revolt of Negro slaves in Mesopotamia, 883 • Byzantines take Calabria (It), 885 • West Frankish crown passes to East Frankish king and Carolingian emperor, Charles III, the Fat, 885 • Count Odo (Eudes) of Paris repulses Viking attack on the city, 885 • First known French poem (*Vie de Sainte Eulalie*) appears, c. 885 • Bantu-speaking chiefdoms are evolving in what is now Zaïre • Muslim merchants build up trade on East African coast • Chinese porcelain exported to western Asia

Great fiefs are established in France as bastions against anarchy by 886 • Alfred the Great of Wessex (Eng) captures London, 886 • Leo VI succeeds father, Michael III, as Byzantine emperor, 886 • Charles the Fat is deposed as Carolingian emperor and West Frankish king, 887 • His distant relative Charles III, the Simple, becomes West Frankish king, opposed by Odo of Paris, 888 • In southern India, the Chola Dynasty of Tamil kings defeats Pallavas, 888 • Muslims raid Lombardy, 889 • Harold I unifies Norway after 890 • *Anglo-Saxon Chronicle*, a source of early English history, is begun on orders of Alfred the Great, 890

Guido of Spoleto becomes German emperor, 891 • Japan's Fujiwara dictatorship is briefly halted by emperor Uda (891–897) • Centralized T'ang rule is collapsing in China • Charles III the Simple rules France from Laon, 893–923, as the last Carolingian with real power in the country • Lambert of Spoleto becomes German emperor, 893 • Arnulf, as East Frankish (German) king, repulses Moravians with Magyar help, 893 • Byzantine emperor Leo VI publishes the *Basilica*, a list of post-Justinian laws, 887–893 • Bulgarians under Symeon I war with the Byzantine empire, 894–897 • Alfred the Great of Wessex (Eng) defeats Danish invasion fleet, 895

866–870	871–875	876–880

□ Ethelred I————————□ Alfred the Great————————————▷
————————————————————□ Charles II———————————□ Vacancy

Ethelbert dies; succeeded by brother Ethelred I, 866 • Danes capture York (Eng), 866 • Photius, Patriarch of Constantinople, denies Rome's primacy, 867, creating East-West schism • Papacy declines after Nicholas I dies, 867 • Byzantine emperor Michael III deposed, and Basil I (first Macedonian emperor) gains throne, 867; Byzantine empire enters a golden age • Under the Tulunid Dynasty (868–905), Egypt leaves Arab empire • Danes kill St. Edmund, last English king of East Anglia, 869 • First known printed book appears in China, 868 • Lothair II of Lorraine dies, 869; Treaty of Mersen, 870, divides Lorraine between France and Germany • Danes attack Wessex (Eng), 870

Alfred the Great becomes king of Wessex (Eng), 871, at a time when Danes are destroying East Anglian, Mercian and Northumbrian kingdoms and founding Danish colonies • Arab empire's eastern provinces hive off under the Saffarid Dynasty, 870–903 • West African state of Kanem-Bornu is emerging • Hausa and Yoruba states evolve in northern and western Nigeria • Harold I (872–930) begins unification of Norway • Alkindi (Arab pioneer in optics) dies, c. 873 • Vikings from Norway colonize Iceland, 874 • Byzantines begin recapturing southern Italy from the Arabs, 875 • Louis II of Germany dies, 875; succeeded by Charles II

Charles II of Germany dies, 877; throne vacant • Danes under their leader Guthrun overrun Wessex (Eng), but Alfred the Great of Wessex wins victory at Edington, 878, forcing Peace of Wedmore: England divided between Alfred (south) and Danelaw (northeast) • France is partitioned by Louis II's sons, 879: Louis III takes the north, Carloman the south • Boso of Provence founds the Kingdom of Burgundy, 879 • In Russia, Prince Oleg (c. 880–912) unites Novgorod and Kiev • Revolts disrupt the Korean state of Silla, 880 • Fujiwara Mototsune becomes Japan's first civil dictator, 880 • Classic period of Maya culture draws to an end (800–950) as cities and ceremonial centers are abandoned

896–900	901–905	906–910

————————————————□ Edward the Elder————————————▷
————————————□ Arnulf———□ Louis III————————————————▷

Arnulf claims German crown, 896 • Nomadic Hungarians, displaced from southern Russia and led by the Magyar tribe, settle middle Danube River valley by 896 • Magyars raid Lombardy, 898 • Louis the Child becomes last Carolingian king of Germany, 899; Germany is divided into duchies which grow in power • Alfred the Great of Wessex dies, 899; succeeded by son Edward the Elder • Santiago de Compostela (Sp) becomes a pilgrimage center after 899 • Byzantium renews union with the papacy, 900 • Salerno (It) has a medical school by 900 • Persian physician Rhazes differentiates smallpox from measles, c. 900 • Toltecs enter Valley of Mexico, c. 900 • Fujiwara rule again in Japan, 897

Louis III becomes German emperor, 901 • Ancient West African Empire of Ghana is at its peak during this period • Arab and Persian traders visit Chinese ports • Iron-Age cultures evolve in south-central Africa's grasslands • Toltec Indians extend empire over central Mexico • Egypt's Tulunid Dynasty is crushed by 905; Egypt once more under Abbasid Dynasty, rulers of Arab empire • Pope Sergius III (904–911) has two rivals strangled; his mistress bears the future Pope John XI • Leo of Tripoli storms Thessalonica, 904 • Kokinshu, anthology of Japanese verse, reflects diminishing Chinese influence in Japan, 905

Hungarians crush newly-formed kingdom of Moravia, 906, and start onslaught on Germany • Russian prince Oleg wins trading rights at Constantinople, 907 • Arpad, founder of Hungarian monarchy, dies, 907 • T'ang Dynasty in China ends, 907; followed by five minor dynasties (to 960) • Khitan Mongols conquer Inner Mongolia and much of northern China, 907–926 • Fatimids destroy Aghlabid Dynasty in Tunis and eastern Algeria, 909 • Welsh bishop Asser dies 909, having helped Alfred the Great revive learning in England • Edward the Elder, King of Wessex (Eng) defeats Northumbrian Danish army in Staffordshire, 910 • Abbey of Cluny (Fr) founded 910

| **911-915** | **916-920** | **921-925** |

ENGLAND—**Edward the Elder**—————————————————————————————————— ☐ **Athelstan**————
HOLY ROMAN EMPIRE—**Konrad I**——————— ☐ **Heinrich I**—————————————————————————————

Edward the Elder, King of Wessex (Eng), founds boroughs (fortified enclosures) • Charles III (Fr) grants lands in Normandy to Viking invader Rollo (Hrolf the Ganger), 911 • Louis the Child's death, 911, ends Carolingian rule in Germany • German magnates elect Konrad I (911–918); he faces revolts and barbarian raids • Rollo of Normandy baptized, as Robert, 912 • Muslim rule in Spain at its peak under Abd ar-Rahman III (912–961); Córdoba is the West's leading cultural center • Constantine VII becomes Byzantine emperor, 912 • Bulgarians threaten Constantinople, 913 • Kingdom of León expands in Spain, 910–914 • Byzantines defeat Muslims at Garigliano (It), 915

Saxon leader Edward the Elder, King of Wessex, recaptures much of central and eastern England from Danes, 917 • Bulgarians defeat Byzantines at Anchialus, 917 • Bulgarians defeat Serbs, 918 • Koryo, a new state, appears in west-central Korea, 918 • Danes defeat Irish at Dublin, 919 • Election of Heinrich I, "the Fowler" (919–936), founds Germany's Saxon or Ottonian Dynasty • By 920 all rulers in Britain and Scotland acknowledge Edward the Elder as overlord • Romanus Lecapenus (Byz) makes himself coemperor with Constantine VII • Byzantine forces campaign in east • Most of Polynesia, except New Zealand, is now peopled

Arab Idrisid Kingdom in North. Africa is crushed by rival Fatimids, 922 • Robert of Normandy expands his territories, 924 • Symeon I of Bulgaria makes peace with Byzantines, 924 • Robert, Count of Paris, expels Charles III, the Simple, 922, seizes West Frankish crown, but is killed, 923 • In two campaigns (923–925) Heinrich I (Ger) wins Lorraine from the West Franks • Edward the Elder (Eng) dies 924, and is succeeded by his son Athelstan, first Saxon king with effective rule over all England • Heinrich I's tribute payments buy 9 years' peace with the Magyars, 924–933 • Byzantines defeat pirate fleets of Leo of Tripoli, 924

| **941-945** | **946-950** | **951-955** |

ENGLAND—**Edmund I**——— ☐ **Edred**—————————————————————————————————— ☐ **Edwy**
HOLY ROMAN EMPIRE—**Otto I**——

Byzantines smash a Russian fleet under Prince Igor, 941 • English king Edmund I recovers Mercian lands conquered by Viking raiders, 942 • St. Dunstan becomes Bishop of Glastonbury, c. 943, and proceeds to revive monasticism in England on Benedictine lines • Magyars attack Bulgarians, 943 • Bulgarians suffer a major raid by Patzinaks, 944 • Bavarians defeat army led by Otto I (Ger) at Wels, 944 • Sayf al-Dawla establishes Hamdanid rule in Aleppo, Syria, 944 • Romanus Lecapenus (Byzantine coemperor deposed, 944; Constantine VII sole emperor, helped by general Bardas Phocas • Most of North Africa comes under Fatimid rule of Al-Mansur, 945–952

Edmund I (Eng) dies, 946; succeeded by his brother Edred, whose chief adviser is St. Dunstan • Edred ravages Northumbria, which has declared Eric Bloodax of Norway king, 948 • Otto I (Ger) crushes Boleslav of Bohemia, which Otto puts under Bavarian control, 950 • The priest Bogomil (Bulgarian form of Theophilus) founds the Bulgarian-based Bogomil heresy, c. 950 • Danish power extends to Norway, Schleswig and the Oder estuary under King Harold II, c. 950–985 • Boleslav I of Bohemia is forced to concede German supremacy • By 950, Toltecs led by Nahua Indians make central Mexico nucleus of a Central American Toltec empire

Otto I (Ger) enters Italy, and weds Adelheid (widow of Lothair II, claimant to Italian throne), 951 • Louis IV of West Franks dies, 954; succeeded by his son Lothair who is under thumb of Hugh the Great, Count of Paris • Eric Bloodax (Norw) dies, 954; Edred (Eng) regains control of Northumbria • Otto I crushes revolts by dukes of Lorraine and Swabia, 955 • Otto I ends Magyar threat at the Battle of the Lechfeld, 955, and crushes Wends (Slav people) on the Recknitz River; Otto reorganizes the Caroligian East Mark (Austria) • Muslim Spain recognizes independence of León and Navarre, 955 • Edred dies, 955; succeeded by his nephew Edwy, who expels St. Dunstan

926-930	931-935	936-940

☐ Edmund I ⟶
☐ Otto I ⟶

Bulgarians devastate Serbia, 926 • Byzantine Empire in the grip of famine, 927 • Byzantines campaigning in the east take Erzerum (Turk), 928 • Heinrich I of Germany attacks the Wends, a Slav people, takes Brandibor (Brandenburg), and forms *marks* (border territories) of Brandibor and Meissen • Charles III, the Simple, (Fr) dies, 929; Rudolf, Duke of Burgundy, rules West Franks, 929–936 • Bohemia expands under Duke Boleslav I (929–967) • Muslim Spain's Omayyad ruler Abd ar-Rahman III claims title of caliph, in opposition to Abbasid caliph based in Baghdad, 929 • Iceland's *Allthing* (general assembly) established, 930 • Four Arab houses (families) and one Kurdish dynasty rule Mesopotamia and Syria, 929–1096

Arab Buwayhid dynasty subdues and divides Persia and Iraq, 932–1055, and dictates to Baghdad's Abbasid caliph • Fernán González becomes first Count of Castile (Sp), 932 • German king Heinrich I withholds tribute payments to Magyars, who resume attacks on Germany, 932 • Robert gains western Normandy, 933, completing the Duchy of Normandy • Heinrich I crushes Magyars at Riade on Thuringian–Saxon border, 933 • Heinrich I dominates Denmark, 934 • English King Athelstan raids Scotland by land and sea, 934 • Magyars start series of raids on Bulgaria, 934 • King Haakon I (935–961) tries to convert Norway to Christianity

Koryo state of central Korea controls whole of Korea by 936 • Carolingian rule of West Franks restored under Louis IV, 936, but power rests largely with Hugh the Great, Count of Paris and Duke of the French • German King Heinrich I dies, 936; succeeded by son Otto I, the Great • Otto I dominates Arles (Burgundy and Provence) as protector of its young king, Conrad, 937 • By 939, Otto I crushes rebellions by Franconia, Bavaria, Lorraine, Saxony • English king Athelstan defeats Scots and Scandinavians at Brunanburh, 937 • Byzantines take Melitene, near the Euphrates River, 934 • Athelstan dies, 939; succeeded by brother, Edmund I

956-960	961-965	966-970

☐ Edgar ⟶

Hugh the Great, Count of Paris, secures control of Burgundy but dies, 956; succeeded as powerful Duke of the French by his son, Hugh Capet • In England, Mercians and Northumbrians revolt against Edwy and make his brother Edgar king, 957; Edgar recalls St. Dunstan from exile • Constantine VII (Byz) dies, 959; succeeded by Romanus II • Edwy dies, 959, and Edgar is sole king of England, receiving vague allegiance from Welsh and Scots • St. Dunstan becomes Archbishop of Canterbury, 959 • Sung Dynasty is founded in China, 960; great cultural advances follow, largely based on printing

Otto I crowns son Otto II king of Germany to assure succession, 961 • Byzantines win Crete from Muslim pirates, 961 • Pope John XII crowns Otto I emperor, 962, in formal revival of Charlemagne's West Roman Empire • Subaktagin, a Turk, founds Ghaznavid Dynasty (962–1186) in Ghazni, Afghanistan • Otto I claims control over Lombards in southern Italy, 962 • Otto I replaces Pope John XII with Pope Leo VIII, establishing imperial power over papal elections, 963 • Infant Basil II becomes Byzantine emperor, 963; a general, Nicephoras II Phocas, really rules • Pope Leo VIII expelled by Romans, 964 • Russian ruler Sviatoslar crushes Khazar empire on Volga, 965

Otto I (Ger) makes a third expedition to Italy (966–972), to restore his new pope, John XIII, deposed by Romans • Boleslav II becomes Duke of Bohemia, 967 • By 968, Byzantines retake Cyprus and invade Egypt • Arab Fatimids win Egypt, 968 • Fujiwara clan dominates Japan, 967–1068 • Russian pressure forces Byzantines to end war with Bulgars (966–969) • Russian ruler Sviatoslav invades Bulgaria, 967 • John I (Tzimisces) (Byz) ousts Nicephoras II (Phocas), 969 • Cairo (Egypt) founded, 969 • Fatimads crush Ikhshidids, 969 • Christian kingdoms of León and Navarre forced to make peace with Muslim Spain, 970 • Cairo's Al-Azhar University founded, 970

971–975	976–980	981–985

ENGLAND—**Edgar**—□ **Edward the Martyr**—□ **Ethelred II** ——————————————

HOLY ROMAN EMPIRE—**Otto I**—□ **Otto II** ——————————————————————— □ **Otto III** ——

Byzantines extend conquests in the Levant, 972 • Otto, son of German Emperor Otto I, marries Byzantine princess Theophano, 972, theoretically adding Byzantine Italy to Holy Roman Empire • Book *De Legatione Constantinopolitana* (c. 972) by Bishop Liutprand (It) describes Byzantine court • Spain's Omayyad Muslims crush Fatimids in Morocco, 973 • Otto I dies, 975, having largely unified Germany and begun the "Ottonian Renaissance"; succeeded by son Otto II • Otto II crushes Danish invasion, 975 • Edgar (Eng) dies, 975; succeeded by his son, Edward the Martyr

Spain's Muslim Omayyad Dynasty declines under Hisham II (976–1009) • Byzantines capture Beirut and Damascus, 976 • John I Tzimisces, the acting Byzantine emperor, dies, 976; coemperor Basil II becomes sole emperor • Otto II (Ger) ends Bavarian-centered revolt, 978 • Edward the Martyr (Eng) assassinated, 978; succeeded by his half-brother Ethelred II, the Redeless (badly advised) • West Frankish king Lothair tries to take Lorraine from Otto II, 978 • Otto II beseiges Paris, 979, and Lothair renounces claim to Lorraine • New Bulgarian empire grows under Tsar Samuel, 976–1014 • Ce Atl Topiltzin founds Toltec capital Tula (Mex) before 980

Viking Eric the Red discovers Greenland, 981, and colonizes it from Iceland • Tsar Samuel of Bulgaria defeats army of Byzantine emperor Basil II near Sofia (Bulg), 981 • German emperor Otto II's campaign to crush Muslims in southern Italy ends in defeat, 982 • Otto II dies, 983; his young son Otto III reigns under regency of his mother, Theophano, guided by the scholar-monk Gerbert of Aurillac (Fr) • Under Rajaraja (985–1014) the Chola Dynasty of Tamil kings dominates the Deccan and unites southern India • Sven I (Forked-beard) becomes king of Denmark, 985, and strengthens power of Danish crown

1001–1005	1006–1010	1011–1015

ENGLAND—**Ethelred II** ————————————————————————————————

HOLY ROMAN EMPIRE—**Otto III**—□ **Heinrich II** ————————————————————

Mahmud of Ghazni (now in Afghanistan) starts invasions of India, 1001 • Romans rebel against emperor Otto III (Ger), 1001 • Byzantines win Macedonia, 1002 • Viking Leif Ericsson, son of Eric the Red, discovers North America, c. 1002 • Brian Boru of Munster is chief ruler in Ireland, 1002–1014 • Ethelred II (Eng) marries Emma of Normandy, 1002 • Otto III dies, 1002; succeeded by his cousin, Heinrich II • Poland seizes Bohemia, 1003 • Bulgaria retakes Macedonia from Byzantium, 1003 • Thorfinn Karlsefni founds Norse settlement in North America, 1003 • Scottish crown gains power under Malcolm II (1005–1034) • Heinrich II drives Poles out of Bohemia, 1005

Thorfinn Karlsefni's Norse settlement in "Wineland" (New England ?) ends, 1006, perhaps destroyed by American Indians • Basil II (Byz) retakes Macedonia from Bulgarians, 1007 • Heinrich II (Ger) suppresses revolt by Baldwin of Flanders, 1006–1007, and puts down rebellion in Burgundy • Persian poet Firdausi completes the epic *Book of Kings*, 1010 • By 1010, civil war is breaking up Spain's Omayyad kingdom into many small Muslim states • In Central America, Teotihuacan, Monte Alban, and the "classic" Maya cities are now abandoned

Mesa Verde of Pueblo cliff dwellings are built in what is now southwest Colorado • Counts of Tusculum (It) dominate the papacy, 1012–1046 • Sven I (Den) invades England, 1013, forcing Ethelred II to flee to his wife's home, Normandy • Sven I dies, 1014; succeeded as king of Denmark by Canute (Cnut) • Ethelred II recaptures England, 1014, forcing Canute back to Denmark • Brian Boru of Ireland is killed defeating Viking invaders at Clontarf, 1014 • Basil II (Byz) defeats Bulgarians at Balathista, 1014, and has 15,000 prisoners blinded • Canute invades England, 1015 • Muslims overrun Sardinia, 1015

Lothair, king of West Franks, dies, 986; succeeded by his son Louis V, last Carolingian ruler in France • Louis V dies, 987, and Hugh Capet is elected king of France, founding France's Capetian Dynasty (direct line rule to 1328) • Hugh personally rules only the Île de France • Byzantine barons Bardas Phocas and Bardas Skleros revolt against emperor Basil II and seize much of Anatolia, 987 • Basil II defeats Bardas Phocas, 989, and the Byzantine revolt collapses • Vladimir the Saint (Russ) is converted to Eastern Orthodox Christianity, c. 989, and his people follow suit • By 990, Bulgarian rule extends from the Black Sea to the Adriatic

Ethelred II (Eng) raises a tax, Danegeld, to pay off Danish raiders under Sven I, 991 • Venice wins Byzantine trading concessions, 992 • Olaf Skutkonung (993–1024) is Sweden's first Christian king • Boleslav I Chrobry of Poland (992–1025) extends his kingdom to the Baltic Sea by 994 • Byzantines recapture Syria, 995 • Otto III (Ger) campaigns against Slavs, 995 • Olaf I Trygvesson (995–1000) converts Norway, Iceland and Greenland to Christianity • Japan's Fujiwara period is at its cultural peak under the shogun (generalissimo) Fujiwara Michinaga, 995–1028

Hugh Capet (Fr) dies, 996; succeeded by son Robert II, the Pious • Pope John XV dies, 996, and German emperor Otto III nominates Gregory V (first German pope) • Basil II (Byz) retakes Greece, 996 • China reunited, 997 • Mahmud of Ghazni (now in Afghanistan) becomes Sultan of Ghazni, 997 • Otto III deposes antipope (pope illegally elected) John XVI, 998 • St. Stephen I (997–1038) builds up Hungary, establishing Latin Christianity • Pope Gregory V dies, 999; succeeded by Gerbert of Aurillac, former tutor of Otto III, as Sylvester II (first French pope) • Poland gains Cracow, Moravia, Silesia, 999 • Polynesians colonize New Zealand, c. 1000

□ Edmund II—□ Canute

□ Konrad II

Italians from Pisa drive Muslims out of Sardinia, 1016 • Ethelred II (Eng) dies, 1016; he is succeeded by his son, Edmund Ironside but England's Witan (council) elects Canute as king • Edmund dies, 1016; Canute becomes sole ruler of England • Olaf II (St. Olaf) reunites divided Norway, 1016–1028 • Scotland is firmly united under Malcolm II, 1018 • Byzantines defeat Lombards and Normans at Cannae (It), 1018 • Byzantine empire defeats and absorbs Bulgaria, 1018 • Yaroslav becomes forceful Grand Prince of Kiev (Russ), 1019 • Murasaki Shikibu, a Japanese court lady, completes novel *The Tale of Genji*, 1020

Avicenna, Persian physician-philosopher, becomes vizir at Hamadan (Persia), c. 1021 • Under Caliph Az-Zahir (1021–1036) Egypt's Fatimid Dynasty loses most of Syria • Heinrich II (Ger) dies, 1024; his distant cousin Konrad II, first of the Salian or Franconian Dynasty (1024–1125) is elected to succeed him • Basil II (Byz) dies, 1025; succeeded by brother Constantine VIII • Boleslav I (Pol) dies, 1025; succeeded by weak king Mieszko II, who proceeds to lose Boleslav's conquests • Tamil king Rajendra Choladeva invades Bengal, 1024

Hisham III becomes last Omayyad caliph of Córdoba (Sp), 1027 • St. Stephen I (Hung) wins Slovakia from Poland, 1027 • Constantine VIII (Byz) dies, 1028; succeeded by his daughter, Empress Zoë, and her first husband, Romanus III • Norman settlement in southern Italy begins at Aversa, c. 1029 • Muslims defeat Byzantines in Syria, 1030 • Mahmud of Ghazni (now in Afghanistan) dies, 1030; Ghazni is a center of Islamic culture and capital of a Muslim empire stretching from the Tigris to the Ganges • King Rajendra Choladeva of southern India exacts tribute from states in East Indies, c. 1030 • Monk Guido of Arezzo (It) devises modern musical notation, c. 1030

1031–1035	**1036–1040**	**1041–1045**

ENGLAND—**Canute** ——☐ **Harold I** ————☐ **Hardicanute** ————☐ **Edward the Confesso**
HOLY ROMAN EMPIRE— **Konrad II** ————————☐ **Heinrich III**——

Robert II (Fr) dies, 1031; succeeded by son Henri I • Death of Hisham III ends Omayyad Dynasty of Córdoba (Sp), 1031 • Konrad II (Ger) inherits Burgundy, 1033 • Sancho the Great of Navarre (conqueror of Castile and León) dies, 1035; succeeded by Fernando I of Castile; Aragon regains lost independence • Canute dies, 1035; succeeded in England by son Harold I (Harefoot), and in Denmark by nephew Sven • Guillaume (William) I, illegitimate son of Robert the Devil, succeeds his father as Duke of Normandy, 1035 • Michael IV (Byz) becomes Empress Zoë's second husband, 1034 • Scandinavian mercenaries help Byzantine fleets crush Muslim pirates, 1034–1035

Egypt's Fatimid period at its peak under Al-Mustansir, 1036–1094 • Yaroslav, Grand Prince of Kiev, controls all Russia by 1036 • Seljuk Turks invade Khorasan, crushing Ghaznavids, 1037 • Fernando I of Castile subdues León, 1037 • Muslim Spain ruled as petty kingdoms, 1037–1086 • Bohemia annexes Silesia, 1038 • Casmir I restores lost Polish unity, 1038–1058 • Konrad II (Ger) dies, 1039; succeeded by son Heinrich III (the Black), strongest of all German emperors • Harold I (Eng) dies, 1040; succeeded by half-brother Hardicanute • Duncan I (Scot) is killed by Macbeth, chief of Moray, who makes himself king, 1040

Bohemia's king, Bratislav I is forced to do homage to emperor Heinrich III (Ger) and relinquish Polish lands, 1041 • Hardicanute (Eng) dies, 1042, ending Canute's line; Earl Godwin of Wessex secures election of Edward the Confessor, a younger son of Ethelred II and Emma of Normandy • Byzantine defenses neglected after 1042 under rule of Empress Zoë and her third husband, Constantine • Northern Korea walled off against Manchurians, 1044 • Edward the Confessor marries Edith, daughter of Godwin of Wessex, 1045 • Gregory VI elected pope, 1045, having paid his licentious predecessor, Benedict IX, to resign

1061–1063	**1064–1066**	**1067–1069**

ENGLAND—**Edward the Confessor** —☐ **Harold II** —☐ **William I** ————————
HOLY ROMAN EMPIRE—**Heinrich IV**————————————

Pope Nicholas II dies, 1061; succeeded by Alexander II without formal approval of Emperor Heinrich IV (then aged 11); Synod of Basel declares Alexander's election void • Poland regains upper Slovakia, 1061–1063 • Archbishop Anno of Köln (Ger) abducts Heinrich IV, 1062, rules in his name, and shares German monasteries between himself and Archbishop Adalbert of Hamburg-Bremen • Minamoto clan is gaining power in Japanese imperial service by 1062 • Under Duke William I, Normandy gains Maine (Fr), 1063 • Alp Arslan succeeds Tughril Beg as Seljuk sultan, 1063, and proceeds to conquer Armenia and Georgia; Seljuks are a major force in Middle East

Harold of Wessex (Eng), shipwrecked off Normandy, *c.* 1064, is forced to swear to help William of Normandy become king of England • Alp Arslan's Seljuk Turks overrun Armenia, 1064 • Northumbrians expel their earl, Tostig, brother of Harold of Wessex, 1065 • Diet of Tribur restores Heinrich IV (Ger) to power, 1066 • Edward the Confessor (Eng) dies, 1066; the Witan (council) elects Harold of Wessex king • Tostig and King Harold III Haardrade (Norw) invade northern England, but Harold defeats them at Stamford Bridge • William of Normandy invades southeastern England, defeats and kills Harold near Hastings, and becomes England's first Norman king, all in 1066

William I, the Norman Conqueror, subjugates all England, 1067–1070, and begins building garrison forts • Bayeux Tapestry (*c.* 1067) commemorates William's successful invasion of England • Emperor Constantine X (Byz) dies, 1067; succeeded 1068 by Romanus IV Diogenes • Normans wrest Otranto (It) from Byzantines, 1068 • Byzantines repel Seljuk Turks' advance in Armenia, 1068–1069 • William I crushes a revolt in northern England, 1069 • Chinese prime minister Wang An-shih implements sweeping economic reforms to reduce tax burdens and control prices, 1069–1074 • Fujiwara clan loses power in Japan under Emperor Sanjo II (1068–1073)

1046–1050

1051–1055

1056–1060

□ Heinrich IV

German emperor Heinrich III replaces rival popes Gregory VI, Sylvester III and Benedict IX with Clement II, first of several German reforming popes, 1046 • By 1047 William I of Normandy smashes revolts by his subjects • Baldwin of Flanders and Godfrey of Upper Lorraine rebel against Heinrich III, 1047 • Mecca and Medina reject Fatimid rule, 1047 • Pope Clement II dies, 1047; succeeded by Damasus II, who also dies • Byzantines defeat invading Seljuk Turks at Sragna, 1048 • Leo IX becomes pope, 1049 • Byzantine empress Zoë dies, 1050; her third husband, Constantine, rules alone • Pagan becomes the capital of Burma • Polyphonic (many-voiced) music develops in Europe

Edward the Confessor (Eng) names his cousin William of Normandy heir, 1051 • Westminster Abbey founded, 1052 • Romanesque architecture emerging in Europe • Stigand (a Saxon) becomes Archbishop of Canterbury, 1052 • Byzantine emperor Constantine II dies, 1054; succeeded by sister-in-law Theodora • Poland regains Silesia, 1054 • Kiev's power fails after Grand Prince Yaroslav dies, 1054 • Pope Leo IX backs Normans against Greeks in south Italy, provoking east-west Church schism, 1054 • Leo IX dies, 1054; succeeded by Victor II • Almoravids overrun West Africa, 1054 • Fernando I of Castile starts Christian reconquest of Portugal, 1055 • Seljuk Turks capture Baghdad and invade Anatolia, 1055

Almoravids conquer Morocco, 1056 • German emperor Heinrich III dies, 1056; succeeded by son Heinrich IV • Byzantine Empress Theodora dies, 1056; succeeded by Michael VI • Malcolm III, son of Duncan I, kills Macbeth and becomes king of Scotland, 1057 • Michael VI (Byz) is deposed by Isaac Comnenus, a soldier, 1057 • Poland under Boleslav II, the Bold, 1058–1079 • Henri I of France overruns Normandy, 1058 • Synod of the Lateran (1059) establishes papal election by a college of cardinals • Emperor Isaac I Comnenus (Byz) abdicates in favor of Constantine X, 1059 • Henri I of France dies, 1060; succeeded by son Philippe I

1070–1072

1073–1075

1076–1078

Knights of St. John founded, c. 1070 • Norman feudal system established in England by 1070, but Anglo-Saxon laws and shires (local government units) persist • Benedictine abbot Lanfranc (It) is made Archbishop of Canterbury (Eng), 1070, and reforms English Church • Norman ruler Robert Guiscard ends Byzantine power in Italy, 1071 • Seljuk Turks crush Byzantine power in Anatolia at Battle of Manzikert, 1071 • Romanus IV (Byz) dies, 1071; succeeded by Michael VII • William I (Eng) smashes resistance led by Saxon Hereward the Wake, 1071 • Robert Guiscard takes Palermo, 1072; Normans absorb Sicily • William I raids Scotland, 1072

Saxony rebels against German emperor Heinrich IV, 1073 • Hildebrand (It) becomes Pope Gregory VII, 1073 • Seljuk Turks are overrunning Anatolia, Syria and Palestine by 1075 • Gregory VII insists on extensive papal powers (including exclusive right to make and depose bishops) and triggers off 47-year investiture struggle between popes and emperors, 1075 • Heinrich IV exploits disagreements among Saxon rebels and regains control over Saxony, 1075 • Synod of Rome severely condemns simony (buying promotion in the Church), and lay investiture (people outside the Church giving bishops their symbols of office), 1075

In Spain, Aragon annexes Navarre, 1076 • Almoravids ravage Kumbi, capital of ancient Empire of Ghana, 1076 • Synod of Worms, 1076: bishops backed by German emperor Heinrich IV declare Pope Gregory VII deposed; Gregory declares Heinrich and the bishops deposed and excommunicated • Robbed of papal support, Heinrich IV faces fresh German revolts, and humbles himself before Gregory at Canossa (It), 1077 • Revolt by Rudolf of Swabia against Heinrich IV starts civil war in Germany, 1077 • Hungarian prosperity increases under St. Ladislas I (1077–1095) • Nicephorus III becomes Byzantine emperor, 1078 • The Seljuk Turkish sultan Nizam al Mulk stimulates Muslim scholarship

| 1079-1081 | 1082-1084 | 1085-1087 |

ENGLAND—**William I** ────────────────────────────────── □ **William II** ──────

HOLY ROMAN EMPIRE—**Heinrich IV** ─────────────────────────────────────

French towns gain some independence from the king, by 1080 • Emperor Heinrich IV (Ger) ends civil war by killing Rudolf of Swabia, 1080 • Pope Gregory VII again deposes and excommunicates Heinrich IV, but German and pro-German bishops declare Gregory deposed and elect antipope (rival pope) Clement III, 1080 • Heinrich IV begins attacks on Italy, 1081 • After fighting in the service of Castile, El Rodrigo Diáz de Bivar, known as El Cid (The Lord), is banished, 1081, and becomes a soldier of fortune • Byzantine general Alexius Comnenus overthrows Nicephorus III, 1081, and rules forcefully as Emperor Alexius I Comnenus

Cuzco (Peru), future capital of Inca empire, is founded • Byzantines grant Venetians important trading concessions (1082) for help against attacks launched by the Norman Robert Guiscard, who takes Durazzo (now in Albania) • The Norman Bohemund takes much of Macedonia, 1083 • Emperor Heinrich IV (Ger) beseiges Rome, 1083, and Pope Gregory VII asks Robert Guiscard for help • Robert Guiscard drives Heinrich IV from Rome and sacks the city, 1084 • Seljuk Turks seize Antioch, 1084 • Chinese historian Ssu-ma Kuang completes *The Mirror of History* (1084), a major account of Chinese history, 403 BC–AD 959

Peru's Tiahuanaco culture is in its final phase • Pope Gregory VII dies in exile, 1085 • Byzantines and Venetians crush Normans off Corfu, 1085 • Norman invasion of Balkans abandoned after death of Robert Guiscard, 1085 • Alfonso VI of Castile wrests Toledo from Muslims, 1085 • *Domesday Book* records land ownership as a basis for taxation in England, 1086 • Almoravids defeat Alfonso VI of Castile at Zallaka, 1086, and rule most of Muslim Spain • "El Cid" helps Alfonso VI against Almoravids, 1087 • William the Conqueror (Eng) dies, 1087; succeeded as Duke of Normandy by eldest son, Robert II, Curthose, and as King of England by second son, William II, Rufus

| 1097-1099 | 1100-1102 | 1103-1105 |

ENGLAND—**William II** ──·── □ **Henry I** ──────────────────────────────

HOLY ROMAN EMPIRE—**Heinrich IV** ─────────────────────────────────────

Anselm, Archbishop of Canterbury, leaves England after William II rejects his claim that Church law overrides civil law, 1097 • Kalman I (Hung) invades Dalmatia, 1097 • Greeks and Crusaders seize Nicaea, chief Seljuk center in Asia Minor, 1097 • Crusader Baldwin of Flanders captures Edessa, 1097 • Bohemund of Otranto captures Antioch after a siege, 1098; Byzantines and Normans at war in Asia Minor • "El Cid" dies, 1099, having fought off two Almoravid assaults on Valencia (Sp) • Crusaders seize and sack Jerusalem, 1099; Godfrey of Bouillon is elected king of Jerusalem • Mississippian culture now fully developed in North America

Provencal troubadours develop courtly love lyrics at this time; French epic poem *Chanson de Roland* is written down • William II (Eng) murdered in the New Forest; succeeded by younger brother, Henry I, 1100 • Godfrey of Bouillon dies, 1100, and Baldwin of Flanders becomes King Baldwin I of Jerusalem • After 1100, Seljuk army leaders, *atabegs*, seize most of Seljuk Empire • Count Roger I of Sicily dies, 1101; succeeded by son, Simon • Venice gains trading rights in Sidon 1102 • Kalman I (Hung) wrests Dalmatia from Venice by 1102

Chinese statesman Wang An-shih's reforms of the 1070s are mostly undone by bureaucrats • Chinese landscape painting at its peak with artists like Li Kung-lin and Mi Fei; Emperor Hui Tsung founds Imperial Academy of Painting • Anselm, Archbishop of Canterbury, opposes Henry I (Eng) in investiture struggle, 1103–1107 • Baldwin I of Jerusalem seizes port of Acre, 1104, takes Beirut and Sidon, and repulses Saracen (Muslim) counter-attacks • Future Heinrich V (Ger) rebels against his father Heinrich IV, 1104 • Crusader Raymond of Toulouse beseiges Tripoli (now in Lebanon), 1104; siege continues after Raymond dies, 1105 • Count Simon of Sicily dies, 1105; succeeded by brother Roger II, aged 9

1088-1090

1091-1093

1094-1096

Urban II (Fr) becomes Pope, 1088 • William II (Eng) crushes a revolt by Norman nobles, 1088 • Archbishop Lanfranc of Canterbury (Eng) dies, 1089; William II seizes his revenues but appoints no successor • "El Cid" masters Valencia (Sp) for himself, 1089–1094 • Collapse of ancient Empire of Ghana is followed in West Africa by rise of so-called succession states, Diara, Manding, Mossi, Soso • Toltec temple pyramids are established at Chichén Itzá (Mex) • Hasan Sabbah founds the Assassins, 1090, a terrorist Ismaili groups based in Persia • The Norman Roger I of Sicily captures Malta from Muslims, 1090

St. Ladislas I (Hung) seizes Bosnia and Croatia, 1091 • Indian Muslim prince Nizam al-Mulk murdered by the Assassins, 1091 • Pope Urban II excommunicates Philippe I (Fr) for adulterous marriage, 1092 • Seljuk Turkish rule over Anatolia weakens with death of Malik Shah, 1092 • Walcher of Malvern (Eng) uses timed observations of lunar eclipse to compute longitudes in England and Italy, 1092 • Anselm (It) becomes Archbishop of Canterbury (Eng), 1093 • German prince Konrad, supported by Pope Urban II, rebels against his father, Emperor Heinrich IV, 1093 • King Alfonso VI of Castile grants county of Portugal to Henri of Burgundy, 1093

Barkyaruk becomes Seljuk Turkish sultan, 1094, but civil war breaks up the Seljuk empire • At Synod of Piacenza (It), Byzantines ask papacy for help against Seljuks, 1095 • At Synod of Clermont (Fr), 1095, Pope Urban II preaches the first Crusade, publicized by Peter the Hermit (Fr) • First Crusade starts 1096, with Normans under Bohemund of Otranto, Provençals under Raymond of Toulouse, Lorrainers under Godfrey of Bouillon and Baldwin of Flanders • Anglo-Norman penetration of Scotland is now under way • Compasses are used in China

1106-1108

1109-1111

1112-1114

☐ Heinrich V

Henry I (Eng) defeats his brother Robert II, Duke of Normandy, at Tinchebrai and gains Normandy, 1106; Robert stays prisoner for rest of his life • German emperor Heinrich IV dies, 1106; succeeded by son, Heinrich V • Alfonso VI of Castile dies, 1106; succeeded by daughter, Urraca • Hsi Hsia kingdom of the Tibetan-speaking Tanguts (founded 1038) flourishes in north-west China (to 1227) • Compromise of 1107 between Henry I and Pope Paschal II: Church and state invest bishops with spiritual and temporal powers respectively • Philippe I of France dies, 1108; succeeded by Louis VI, the Fat • Heinrich V attacks Hungary, 1108 • Normans in Asia Minor make peace with Byzantines, 1108

Forceful Polish king Boleslav III crushes Pomeranians at Naklo, and halts German Emperor Heinrich V's advance at Hundsfeld, 1109 • Tripoli, besieged since 1104, falls to Crusaders, 1109 • Louis VI (Fr) at war with Henry I (Eng) over Normandy; Louis supports William Clito, son of Duke Robert II, 1109–1112 • Heinrich V reestablishes supremacy over Bohemia, 1110 • Heinrich V invades Italy, 1110 • Pope Paschal II renounces Church lands in return for right to invest bishops, 1111; but prelates in Rome reject this settlement, forced on Paschal II by Heinrich V • Byzantines grant Pisa important trade concessions, 1111

Afonso Henriques (founder of Portuguese independence) succeeds Henri of Burgundy in Portugal, 1112 • Cambodian (Khmer) ruler Suryavarman II (1113–1150) builds colossal funerary temple, Angkor Wat • Kiev's hold on Russia is in its last phase of importance, under Vladimir II Monomakh (1113–1125), who campaigns against Cumans (Turkish nomads) in the steppes • Emperor Heinrich V (Ger) marries Matilda, daughter of Henry I (Eng), 1114 • Revolts in Rhineland and other parts of Germany against Heinrich V, 1114 • Tungus-speaking Juchen tribes, ancestors of the Manchus, oust Khitan overlords in Manchuria, 1114–1116

1115-1117 | 1118-1120 | 1121-1123

ENGLAND—**Henry I**
HOLY ROMAN EMPIRE—**Heinrich V**

Emperor Heinrich V (Ger), helped by south German towns, puts down revolts, 1115 • St. Bernard founds the Abbey of Clairvaux (Fr), 1115 • Peter Abélard (Fr theologian-philosopher) teaches at Paris after 1115, arguing that Scripture should be subject to scrutiny of reason • Florence (It) develops on independent lines after death of its overlord, Countess Matilda of Tuscany, 1115 • Alexius I Comnenus (Byz) defeats Seljuks at Philomelion, 1116, and recovers much of Anatolia • Henry I (Eng) again at war with Louis VI (Fr) over Normandy, 1116–1120 • Heinrich V enters Italy, 1116; in 1117 he claims lands left to him by Matilda of Tuscany

Great Mosque of Córdoba (Sp) is completed, 1118 • Alfonso I of Aragon captures Muslim state of Saragossa, 1118 • Emperor Heinrich V (Ger) forces Pope Gelasius II to leave Rome, 1118; Gelasius excommunicates Heinrich • Emperor Alexius I Comnenus (Byz) dies, 1118; succeeded by son, John II Comnenus • Calixtus II becomes Pope, 1119 • Henry I assures England's hold on Normandy by defeating Louis IV of France at Brémule, 1119 • Crusading order of Knights Templars founded in Jerusalem, c. 1119 • Henry I makes his daughter Matilda heir to English throne after his son William is drowned, 1120 • William Clito, son of captive Duke Robert of Normandy, makes a last unsuccessful bid for Normandy, 1120

Emperor John II Comnenus (Byz) recovers much of south-western Asia Minor from Seljuk Turks, 1121 • Venice starts war with Byzantium over lost trading concessions, 1122 • Byzantine victory ends a threat of invasion by the Patzinaks (nomadic Turkish people), 1122 • Emperor Heinrich V (Ger) and Pope Calixtus II end investiture controversy, 1122, by the Concordat of Worms (Ger), broadly based on the English settlement of 1107 • Juchen tribes of northern China rebel against the Sung Dynasty, 1122 • Venice wins trading rights in Tyre, 1123 • Boleslav III (Pol) absorbs Pomerania by 1123

1133-1135 | 1136-1138 | 1139-1141

ENGLAND—**Henry I**——☐**Stephen**
HOLY ROMAN EMPIRE—**Lothair II**——☐**Konrad III**

Alfonso I of Aragon dies, 1134, and Navarre regains independence • King Sverker of Sweden (1134–1150) unites Goths and Swedes and strengthens Swedish unity • Council of Pisa excommunicates antipope Anacletus II, 1134 • Germany's Welf-Waiblinger struggle ends in so-called Year of Pacification, 1135 • Henry I (Eng) dies, 1135; his nephew Stephen of Blois seizes the throne, ignoring the claim of Henry's daughter Matilda • Chimu culture emerging in northern coastal Peru; based on urban centers in irrigated valleys, separated by desert • China's Southern Sung Dynasty establishes its capital at Lin-an (Hangchow), 1135

Suger, Abbot of St. Denis (Fr), begins first Gothic church, 1136 • Geoffrey of Monmouth (Eng) completes *Historia Regum Britanniae*, c. 1136 • Louis VI (Fr) dies, 1137; succeeded by son Louis VII, the Young • John II Comnenus (Byz) subordinates Latin kingdom of Antioch by 1137 • Emperor Lothair II (Ger) dies, 1138; clergy elect Konrad III, founder of Hohenstaufen Dynasty (1138–1268) • Welf leader Heinrich the Proud of Saxony and Bavaria refuses allegiance to Konrad III, who hands Bavaria to Leopold of Austria, Saxony to Albert the Bear; Welf-Waiblinger civil war renewed • Stephen (Eng) defeats David I (Scot) at Northallerton, 1138

Matilda—heiress of Henry I, dispossessed by her nephew Stephen—invades England, 1139; civil war follows to 1153 • Pope Innocent II excommunicates Roger II of Sicily, 1139 • Second Lateran Council, 1139, ends a papal schism: Innocent II now reigns unchallenged • Afonso Henriques (Port) defeats Muslims at Ourique (Port), 1139 • *Cantar de Mio Cid*, early Spanish epic poem, written c. 1140 • Roger II of Sicily captures Pope Innocent II, forcing recognition of Roger's territorial claims, 1140 • Stephen (Eng) is captured by Matilda's forces, but freed • Hohokam culture of what is now the southwestern USA is in its classical period (1100–1400)

1124-1126

1127-1129

1130-1132

□ Lothair II

David I rules Scotland, 1124–1153, with an Anglo-Norman aristocracy • In Russia, Volynia and Suzdal gain power at expense of Kiev after 1125 • Emperor Heinrich V (Ger) dies, 1125; support from the Church brings about election of the Welf family emperor, Lothair II • Civil war follows between Welfs and their rivals the Waiblingers (Hohenstaufens), known in Italy as Guelphs and Ghibellines • Scientist Adelard of Bath (Eng) translates Arabic astronomical tables into Latin, 1126 • Queen Urraca of Castile dies, 1126; succeeded by her son, Alfonso VII • Juchen tribes overrun northern China, and put an effective end to the Northern Sung Dynasty, 1126 • First artesian well produces water in Artois (Fr), 1126

Sung rule persists in form of Southern Sung Dynasty, founded in southern China (1127) by a Sung prince escaping the north's Juchen invaders • Roger II of Sicily becomes Duke of Apulia, 1127 • Matilda, heiress of Henry I (Eng) and widow of German emperor Heinrich V, marries Geoffrey Plantagenet, 1128 • Land reclamation and road-making are developed by monks in England from 1128 • David I (Scot) founds Holyrood Abbey, 1128 • Afonso Henriques rejects Castile's dominion over Portugal and defeats Spanish forces, 1128 • Geoffrey Plantagenet becomes Count of Anjou, Maine and Touraine, 1129 • Heraldry is developing by 1129

Innocent II, supported by influential reformer, Bernard of Clairvaux, becomes Pope, 1130; Cardinal Pierleone is illegally elected as antipope (rival pope) Anacletus II • Roger II becomes King of Sicily, Calabria, and Apulia, 1130 • By 1130, France's Capetian monarchy is replacing feudal lords with loyal career-men as administrators • Berber Muslim prophet Muhammad ibn Tumart founds dynasty of the Almohades in north-western Africa, 1130 • Rievaulx Abbey is founded in Yorkshire (Eng), 1131 • Baldwin I of Jerusalem dies, 1131; succeeded by Fulk of Anjou • Fountains Abbey founded in Yorkshire (Eng), 1132

1142-1144

1145-1147

1148-1150

Emperor Konrad III (Ger) acknowledges Welf leader's claim to Saxony by Heinrich the Lion (son of Heinrich the Proud), 1142 • Revolt against papal rule establishes a Roman republic, 1143 • Afonso Henriques proclaimed King of Portugal, 1143 • John II Comnenus (Byz) dies, 1143; succeeded by Manuel I Comnenus, chief of the Comnenus line of Byzantine emperors • Alfonso VII of Castile steps up Christian reconquest of Muslim Spain, 1144 • Almohades Arabs destroy Almoravid force in North Africa, 1144 • Muslims recapture Edessa (now in Turkey) from Crusaders, 1144 • Pueblo culture is influencing the Great Basin area of what is now the south-western USA, continuing a process begun by Basketmakers

Stephen (Eng) splits his rival Matilda's forces, 1145 • Medical school emerging at Montpellier (Fr) • Arnold of Brescia (It) joins new Roman republic, 1145, denouncing Church corruption • Pope Eugenius III preaches the second Crusade, 1145 • Almohades invade Spain, 1145, and master Morocco • Alfonso VII of Castille wins Almería (Sp) from Muslims, 1147 • Portuguese- capture Lisbon from Muslims, 1147 • Second Crusade starts, 1147, under Emperor Konrad III (Ger) and Louis VII (Fr) • Saxon king Heinrich the Lion crusades against Wends and Slavs, 1147: Poles driven from Baltic • First recorded mention of Moscow, 1147 • Roger II of Sicily's Norman fleets ravage parts of Greece, 1147

Matilda leaves England, 1148; but anarchy continues under feeble rule of Stephen • Arnold of Brescia excommunicated, 1148 • Venetians, promised trading rights, help Byzantines retake Corfu from Roger II of Sicily, 1149 • Second Crusade ends in failure, 1149 • Almohades continue conquest of Muslim Spain, 1150 • Albert the Bear, made Margrave (count ruling a *mark* or military district) of Brandenburg, 1150, helps lead German eastward expansion in Europe • German immigrants settle in southern Hungary, 1150 • Henry, son of Matilda, inherits Duchy of Normandy, 1150 • Ramón Berenguer IV, Count of Barcelona, becomes king of Aragon by marriage, 1150, uniting Catalonia and Aragon

1151-1153	1154-1156	1157-1159

ENGLAND—**Stephen** ————□**Henry II** ————

HOLY ROMAN EMPIRE—**Konrad III**—□**Friedrich I** ————

City of Ghazni (now in Afghanistan) sacked by Sultan of Ghur, 1151 • Byzantines take Ancona (It) from Normans, 1151 • Henry of Normandy, son of Matilda of England, inherits Anjou, Maine and Touraine from his father, 1151 • Henry marries Eleanor of Aquitaine, ex-wife of Louis VII of France, 1152; her lands of Gascony, Guyenne and Poitou go from French king's control to Henry, now master of more than half France • Emperor Konrad III (Ger) dies, 1152; succeeded by nephew Friedrich I Barbarossa • Almohades win Algeria, 1152 • Empire-building Roger II of Sicily holds extensive lands in North Africa by 1153 • Stephen (Eng) makes his cousin Henry of Normandy his heir, 1153

Stephen (Eng) dies, 1154; succeeded by his cousin Henry II, first of the Plantagenet Dynasty (1154–1399) • Nicholas Breakspear becomes Adrian IV, the only English Pope, 1154 • Adrian IV "gives" (without any right to do so) Ireland to Henry II, 1154 • By 1154, Welsh prince Owaiṇ Gwynedd dominates north Wales • Roger II of Sicily dies, 1154 • Nur al-Din sets up strong Seljuk state in Syria, 1154 • Emperor Friedrich I (Ger) helps Adrian IV regain Rome; Arnold of Brescia executed, 1155 • Henry II makes Thomas Becket chancellor, 1155 • Heinrich the Lion of Saxony regains Bavaria, 1156 • Prince electors emerge as powerful body at Diet of Regensburg (Ger), 1156

German merchants settle in London (Eng) by 1157 • Henry II (Eng) forces Malcolm IV (Scot) to quit northern England, 1157, and begins subduing Welsh princes • Denmark expands eastward under Waldemar I (1157–1182) • Alfonso VII of León and Castile dies, 1157; his lands are split between his two sons, Sancho III (Castile), and Fernando II (León) • Sancho dies, 1158; succeeded by infant son Alfonso VIII • Henry II takes *scutage* (cash payments) in lieu of military service, 1159 • In 1159, Henry II seeks to enforce his wife's claim to Toulouse, but Louis VII (Fr) forces withdrawal • Milan revolts against Holy Roman Emperor Friedrich I, and Lombard towns backed by Pope Adrian IV unite against him, 1159

1169-1171	1172-1174	1175-1177

ENGLAND—**Henry II** ————

HOLY ROMAN EMPIRE—**Friedrich I** ————

Andrei Bogoliubski, Prince of Suzdal (Russ), conquers Kiev, 1169 • Spanish Arab philosopher Ibn-Rushd (Averroës) active in Seville, 1169; from him the West rediscovers works of Greek philosopher Aristotle • Norman baron Richard de Clare ("Strongbow") invades Ireland from Wales, 1170 • Archbishop Becket returns to England from exile and is murdered at Canterbury (Eng), 1170 • Palermo Cathedral, Sicily, founded, 1170 • University of Paris effectively dates from *c.* 1170 • Byzantines at war with Venice, 1170–1177 • Leipzig trade fairs start, *c.* 1170 • Henry II (Eng) lands in Ireland, 1171; Irish leaders submit • Salah al-Din ("Saladin"), Kurdish vizir in Egypt, ends Fatimid rule, 1171, founding Ayyubid Dynasty

Henry II (Eng) is reconciled with Church, 1172 • Synod of Cashel (Ire) reforms Irish Church along English lines, 1172 • Muslim Spain is a province of the Almohades' North African-based empire by 1172 • Catalonia (Sp) acquires Roussillon (Fr), 1172 • Minnesingers (German troubadours) active by 1170s • –Henry II crushes revolt by his sons in his French lands, 1173 • Béla III, married to daughter of Louis VII of France, becomes King of Hungary, 1173 • Henry II ends a Scottish invasion of England, 1174 • Canterbury Cathedral (Eng) burned down, 1174 • Emperor Friedrich I (Ger) launches fifth futile expedition to Italy, 1174 • *Fabliaux* (French burlesque verse tales) developing by 1174

William the Lion (Scot) does homage to Henry II (Eng), 1175 • Rebuilding of Canterbury Cathedral (Eng) begins, 1175 • Buddhist priest Honen (Genku) founds Pure Land Sect in Japan, 1175 • Religious mystery plays begin to appear in France • Venetian-Norman alliance forces Byzantines to agree humiliating peace with Venice, 1176 • Lombard League defeats German emperor Friedrich I at Legnano (It), 1176 • Byzantines and Seljuks at war, 1176–1177 • Henry II's youngest son John Lackland is made Lord of Ireland, 1177 • Chrétien de Troyes (Fr) writes *Lancelot* (1177), among best early Arthurian romances to survive • In India, girls are forbidden by law to marry below their own caste

Benjamin of Tudela (Sp Jew) travels overland to China, 1160–1173 • *Nibelungenlied* (German epic) dates from *c.* 1160 • Soissons Abbey Church and Laon Cathedral (Fr) begun, 1160 • Greek scientist Claudius Ptolomaeus's *Almagest* translated from Greek into Latin, *c.* 1160 • Civil war in Japan, 1160 • Normans are driven out of northern Africa, 1160 • Chinese troops use explosives to help crush a revolt near Nanking, 1161 • Emperor Friedrich I (Ger) destroys Milan, 1162 • Henry II (Eng), seeking to reduce clerical privilege, makes his friend Thomas Becket archbishop of Canterbury, 1162, but Becket sides with the Church

Bishopric of Uppsala (Swe) founded, 1163 • Building of Nôtre Dame Cathedral, Paris, begun, 1163 • Henry II (Eng) again campaigns against the Welsh, 1163 • Henry II issues the *Constitutions of Clarendon*, 1164, extending royal power over English clerics, and provoking quarrel with Thomas Becket, Archbishop of Canterbury; Becket flees to France • Henry II secures nominal homage of the Welsh, 1165 • Pope Alexander III excommunicates Emperor Friedrich I (Ger), 1165, for supporting a series of antipopes • Toltec capital of Tula (Tollan) in Mexico destroyed by Chichimec invaders, and its population is scattered

Henry II (Eng) introduces legal reforms: in 1166 he sets up system of traveling judges, dispensing the king's justice rather than local justice • Oxford University (Eng) founded, 1167 • Emperor Friedrich I's fourth expedition to Italy, 1167, forces Pope Alexander III to flee, but disease decimates Friedrich's army • Lombard League formed, 1168, to defy Friedrich • Yoruba and Wolof states emerging respectively in what are now western Nigeria and Senegal; kingship of ancient Benin is becoming established in western Africa • According to tradition, Aztecs start their wanderings in Mexico, 1168

Henry II (Eng) creates a permanent central court, 1178 • Third Lateran Council makes rules for papal election, 1179 • Pope Alexander III recognizes Portugal's independence, 1179 • Jewish philosopher Maimonides publishes *Mishne Torah*, 1180; greatest ever exposition of Jewish Law • Saxon king Heinrich the Lion dispossessed and exiled, 1180 • Louis VII (Fr) dies, 1180; succeeded by son Philippe II "Augustus," who consolidates French royal authority, crushing dissident barons • Stevan Nemanya makes Serbia independent of Byzantium after 1180 • Manuel I Comnenus (Byz) dies, 1180, succeeded by son Alexius II Comnenus • Srivishaya, in Sumatra, is supreme in East Indies by 1180

Alcazar palace, Seville (Sp), begun, *c.* 1181 • Canute VI of Denmark (1182–1202) invades Pomerania and Mecklenburg • Jews expelled from France, 1182 • Andronicus I Comnenus becomes Byzantine co-emperor, 1183, kills nephew Alexius II Comnenus, and proceeds to end government corruption • Egyptian ruler Saladin seizes Aleppo (Syria), 1183 • German emperor Friedrich I, Pope Martin IV and Lombard cities agree Peace of Constance, 1183; Lombard cities virtually freed from imperial rule • Rebuilt after destruction of 1162, Milan (It) is growing rapidly • German river trade developing at Dortmund, Köln, Münster; and German Baltic Sea trade expands

German emperor Friedrich I's sixth expedition to Italy rebuilds imperial influence, 1184 • Canterbury Cathedral (Eng) completed, 1184 • Lincoln Cathedral (Eng) built, 1185–1200 • Afonso Henriques (Port) dies, 1185; succeeded by son Sancho I • Ivan and Petr Asen (Bulg) revolt against Byzantines, 1185 • Military dictator Yoritomo establishes Japan's Kamakura period (1185–1333) • Andronicus I Comnenus (Byz) deposed and killed, 1185; succeeded by insurgent leader Isaac Angelus • Heinrich, heir to German emperor Friedrich I, marries Constance, daughter of Roger II of Sicily, 1186 • Saladin of Egypt secures Mesopotamia, 1186 • English rule in Ireland limited to area around Dublin, "The Pale," 1186

ENGLAND—**Henry I** —□ **Richard I**
HOLY ROMAN EMPIRE—**Friedrich I**——□ **Heinrich VI**

Muhammad of Ghur in north-western Afghanistan overruns Punjab, India, 1187 • Saladin (Egypt) takes Jerusalem, 1187, and Latin states shrink • Ranulf de Glanvil writes first major work on English common law, c. 1188 • Papal charter recognizes commune of Rome, 1188 • Bulgarian leaders, Ivan and Petr Asen, create independent Bulgaria north of the Balkan Mountains by 1188 • Philippe II (Fr) and Richard of Normandy defeat Henry II (Eng) at Angers (Fr), 1189 • Henry II dies, 1189; succeeded by son Richard I, "Coeur de Lion" • Third Crusade begins, 1189, led by German emperor Friedrich I with Richard I and Philippe II • Fujiwara family crushed by Japan's Minamoto rulers, 1189

Jews persecuted in England, 1190 • Jewish teacher Maimonides' *Guide of the Perplexed* (1190) influences Jewish and Christian philosophy • German emperor Friedrich I dies, 1190; succeeded by son Heinrich VI • Heinrich VI at war with Heinrich the Lion of Saxony, 1190–1195 • Byzantines drive Normans from Balkans by 1191 • Richard I takes Cyprus, but sells it to Guy de Lusignan, King of Jerusalem, 1191 • Crusaders capture Acre (now Akko, Israel), 1191 • By treaty with Saladin of Egypt, Richard I secures Palestinian ports and access to Jerusalem, 1192 • Minamoto Yoritomo (Jap) becomes *shogun* (generalissimo or military dictator), 1192 • Richard I captured, 1192, and handed over to Heinrich VI

Muhammad of Ghur in north-western Afghanistan occupies Delhi, India, 1193 • German emperor Heinrich VI and Heinrich the Lion of Saxony at war to 1195 • Richard I (Eng) ransomed from Heinrich VI, 1194 • Richard I begins war against Philippe II of France, 1194 • China's Yellow River alters course dramatically, 1194 • Chartres Cathedral (Fr) under construction, 1194 • Heinrich VI establishes claim to Sicily after death of its Norman king, Tancred, 1194 • Almohades defeat Alfonso VIII of Castile at Alarcos (Sp), 1195 • Emperor Isaac Angelus (Byz) deposed and blinded by his brother, who succeeds him as Alexius III (1195)

ENGLAND—**John**
HOLY ROMAN EMPIRE—**Otto IV**

Bulgarians capture Byzantine emperor Baldwin I, who dies, 1205 • St. Dominic (Sp) goes on mission to heretic Albigensians (Fr), 1206 • Sultanate of Delhi established by slave dynasty of Muhammad of Ghur (Afghanistan), 1206 • Mongol leader Temujin proclaimed *Genghis Khan* ("Very Mighty King"), 1206 • Waldemar II (Den) crusades in eastern Baltic, 1206 • Philippe II (Fr) wins Anjou, Maine, Touraine and most of Poitou from John (Eng) by 1206 • Llewellyn the Great wins power in South Wales, 1207 • Pope Innocent III appoints Stephen Langton Archbishop of Canterbury (Eng), 1207 • Geoffroy de Villehardouin's *Conquête de Constantinople* (to 1207) is first French vernacular history

Pope Innocent III lays interdict on England, 1208, after its king, John, rejects Stephen Langton as Archbishop of Canterbury • Innocent III preaches crusade against Albigensians and Waldensians, 1208 • King John's confiscation of Church property leads to his excommunication, 1209 • John invades Scotland, 1209 • Cambridge University (Eng) founded, 1209 • Gottfried von Strassburg (Ger), author of *Tristan* epic, active c. 1210 • Mongols attack Chin in northern China, 1210 • German emperor Otto IV excommunicated, 1210 • Innocent III authorizes St. Francis of Assisi and 11 companions to be roving preachers, 1210 • Aztecs active in Valley of Mexico; influence of Toltec Indians wanes

Friedrich II, "Stupor Mundi" (Wonder of the World), elected German emperor, 1211; but Otto IV also continues to reign • Friedrich's Golden Bull (proclamation) allows nobles of Bohemia to elect their own king, 1212 • Children's Crusade: thousands of European children set out for Holy Land, but most of them perish, 1212 • Byzantine Nicaea expanding in Anatolia, 1212 • King John (Eng) exploits feudal rights, provoking plot against him, 1212 • Spain's Christian kings crush Moorish Almohades at Las Navas de Tolosa, 1212, ending major Muslim resistance to Christian reconquest of Spain • Pope Innocent III declares King John deposed, forcing his submission, 1213 • Council of St. Albans (Eng) foreshadows Parliament, 1213

| 1196-1198 | 1199-1201 | 1202-1204 |

□ John ⟶▷

□ Otto IV ⟶▷

Richard I (Eng) builds Château Gaillard as a Seine outpost against the French, 1196 • Stevan Nemanya, ruler of Serbia, abdicates, 1196; succeeded by son, Stevan Nemanya II (1196–1223) • German emperor Heinrich VI dies, 1197; Otto of Brunswick (Welf son of Heinrich the Lion) and Heinrich's brother Philip of Swabia (Waiblinger) fight for succession • Medieval papacy at its peak under Innocent III (1198–1216); he becomes guardian of Heinrich's young son Friedrich, 1198 • Innocent III forces Philippe II (Fr) to acknowledge his rejected wife Ingeborg • Teutonic Knights, formerly a charitable organization, become military order open only to German nobles, 1198 • Ottokar I becomes King of Bohemia, 1198

North India is under Muslim rule by 1199 • Richard I (Eng) killed in battle, 1199; succeeded by brother John Lackland • Port of Liverpool (Eng) founded, 1199 • Siena Cathedral (It) begun, c. 1199 • First Inca emperor rules, c. 1200, according to tradition • Llewellyn the Great of Gwynedd (Wales) takes Anglesey, 1200 • Denmark conquers Holstein, 1200–1201 • Culture featuring corn and temple mounds thrives in Middle Mississippi region • John (Eng) weds Isabella of Angoulême (Fr), who is already betrothed to Hugh of Lusignan, 1200 • Otto of Brunswick is supported as Emperor Otto IV (Ger) by Pope Innocent III, 1201 • Bulgarians and Byzantines make peace, 1201

Fourth Crusade begins, 1202 • Controversial marriage of King John (Eng) provokes Anglo-French war, 1202 • German Order of Livonian (Latvian) Brothers of the Sword founded, 1202 • Leonardo Fibonacci of Pisa (It) writes mathematical treatise *Liber Abaci*, 1202 • King John murders his nephew, Arthur, 1203 • Crusaders enter Constantinople, 1203 • In West Africa, Sumanguru of Soso ravages Kumbi, 1203 • Wolfram von Eschenbach (Ger poet) writes epic *Parzival*, c. 1203 • Philippe II (Fr) captures Normandy, 1204 • Instead of campaigning in the Holy Land, Crusaders storm and sack Constantinople, 1204, and crown Baldwin of Flanders as Byzantine emperor

| 1214-1216 | 1217-1219 | 1220-1222 |

□ Henry III ⟶▷

□ Friedrich II ⟶▷

William the Lion (Scot) dies, 1214; succeeded by son, Alexander II • Phillipe II (Fr) and Friedrich II (Ger) crush anti-French alliance led by John (Eng), Otto IV (Ger) and the Count of Flanders at Bouvines (Fr), 1214; Friedrich becomes supreme in Germany • Fourth Lateran Council expounds doctrine of transubstantiation—belief that Christ's body is present in the bread and wine of communion—1215 • Pope Innocent III formally approves Dominican Order, 1215 • Discontent among English barons leading to civil war forces King John to accept *Magna Carta*, 1215 • Innocent III annuls *Magna Carta*, 1216 • John dies, 1216; succeeded by infant Henry III • Pope Innocent III dies, 1216; succeeded by Honorius III

Louis, son of Philippe II (Fr) claims English throne; defeated by barons • Fifth Crusade (against Egypt) starts, 1218 • Second Bulgarian empire reaches its peak under Ivan Asen II (1218–1241) • Crusaders capture Damietta (Egypt), 1219 • William Marshal, chief minister of Henry III (Eng), dies, 1219; succeeded by the *justiciar* (chief judge), Hubert de Burgh • Waldemar II (Den) subdues Estonia, 1219 • Latin emperor of Byzantium, Robert of Courtenay (1219–1228), loses all his lands except Constantinople • Genghis Khan's Mongols seize Bokhara (now in Uzbekistan), 1219 • Hojo family ends Minamoto power and rules Japan as regents for the shoguns (dictators), 1219–1333

Mongols invade Persia, 1220 • Dominican monks reach England, 1220 • Salisbury Cathedral (Eng) begun, 1220 • Leonardo Fibonacci (It) completes *Practica Geometriae*, 1220 • Friedrich II (Ger) tightens hold on Sicily, 1221–1225 • Mongols penetrate Sultanate of Delhi, India, 1221 • Crusaders lose city of Damietta (Egypt) and abandon Fifth Crusade, 1221 • Hungarian nobles force charter of feudal privileges on their king, Andras II, 1222 • University of Padua (It) established, 1222 • Snorri Sturluson (Iceland) writes *Edda* (poetic myths) by 1222 • Eastern Byzantine empire strong under John III Vatatzes (1222–1254), ruling from Nicaea (Iznik, Turkey)

1223-1225   1226-1228   1229-1231

ENGLAND—**Henry III** —————————————————————

HOLY ROMAN EMPIRE—**Friedrich II** —————————————

Philippe II (Fr) dies, 1223; succeeded by son, Louis VIII • Waldemar II (Den) loses most of his Baltic empire, 1223 • Mongol invaders under Subutai defeat Russians and Cumans (Turkish nomads) at Kalka River, near Sea of Azov, 1223 • French seize English lands between Garonne and Loire rivers, 1224 • Franciscan friars arrive in England, 1224 • Naples becomes first European university granted royal charter (by Friedrich II), 1224 • In West Africa, Soso absorbs Manding, 1224 • True Pure Land Sect emerges in Japan, 1224 • *Sumer is icumen in* (Eng round), *c.* 1225 • English win Gascony, 1225, regaining much land lost in 1224

Louis VIII (Fr) dies, 1226; succeeded by son, Louis IX (St. Louis, most chivalrous medieval king) • Lombard League reestablished, 1226, to resist Friedrich II (Ger) • Teutonic Knights begin conquest of Prussia, 1226 • Henry III (Eng), now 20, begins to reign without a guardian, 1227; but Hubert de Burgh is real ruler • Mongols crush Hsi Hsia Kingdom in China, 1227 • Genghis Khan dies, 1227, leaving Mongol empire to sons Ogadai, Chagatai, Tului and grandson Batu • North Germans crush Danes, 1227, and again Holstein, Mecklenburg, Lübeck, Pomerania • Pope Honorius III dies, 1227; succeeded by Gregory IX • Friedrich II leads Sixth Crusade, to Palestine, 1228

Mongol leader Ogadai elected Great Khan, 1229 • Raymond of Toulouse, semi-independent French province, submits to Louis IX (Fr), 1229 • In Sixth Crusade, Friedrich II (Ger) recaptures Jerusalem, 1229 • Henry III (Eng) fails to regain Aquitaine (Fr), 1229 • Friedrich II expels papal forces invading Apulia (It), 1229 • Fernando III of Castile succeeds to León, 1230 • Friedrich II grants Privilege of Worms to German princes, 1231 • Friedrich II issues Constitutions of Melfi, 1231 • Swiss canton of Uri recognized as virtually independent, 1231 • Mongols invade Korea, 1231

1241-1243   1244-1246   1247-1249

ENGLAND—**Henry III** —————————————————————

HOLY ROMAN EMPIRE—**Friedrich II** —————————————

Mongols overrun Hungary, Poland and Bulgaria; but withdraw on death of the Great Khan, Ogadai, 1241 • Siena University (It) founded, 1241 • Friedrich II (Ger) ravages papal Italy, 1241 • Aleksandr Nevski (Russ) crushes Teutonic Knights on icebound Lake Peipus, 1242 • Salamanca University (Sp) founded, 1242 • Henry III (Eng) foments revolt against Louis IX in southwestern France, 1242, but Parliament refuses him cash to pay for French wars, 1242 • Mongol kingdom of the Golden Horde established on lower Volga River, 1242 • Innocent IV becomes pope, 1243 • Mongols defeat Seljuk Turks, 1243 • Castile subdues the Muslim state of Murcia, 1243

Muslims recapture Jerusalem from Christians, 1244 • Mongols invade Anatolia, 1244 • Friedrich II (Ger) invades Campagna (It), 1244 • Synod of Lyon (Fr) declares Friedrich II deposed, 1245 • Jaime I of Aragon wins Valencia, 1245 • Franciscan friar Giovanni da Pian del Carpine (It) visits Karakorum, Mongolia, 1245–1247 • Mongols ravage Armenia, Azerbaijan, Georgia and Mesopotamia, 1245–1253 • Present structure of Westminster Abbey (Eng) begun, 1245 • Heinrich Raspe (Ger) becomes antiking, 1246, in opposition to Friedrich II • Nicaean emperor John Vatatzes III wins northern Macedonia and Thessalonica from Bulgarians, 1246

Heinrich Raspe, nominated as German king by Pope Innocent IV, dies, 1247; succeeded by Wilhelm of Holland • Friar Roger Bacon (Eng) starts experimental research in optics, alchemy, astronomy, 1247 • Birger Magnusson runs Swedish government, 1248–1266 • Albertus Magnus (Ger), Dominican philosopher, teaching at Köln, 1248–1252; Thomas Aquinas his chief pupil • German emperor Friedrich II is defeated by Lombard League after besieging Parma (It), 1248 • Louis IX (Fr) launches Seventh Crusade, 1248 • Louis IX captures Damietta (Egypt), 1249, and marches on Cairo • Founding of University College, 1249, initiates collegiate system in Oxford (Eng) • Explosives are mentioned by Roger Bacon, 1249

1232-1234

1235-1237

1238-1240

The Nasrids of Granada are last Muslims to withstand Christian reconquest of Spain (1232–1492) • Henry III (Eng) dismisses chief minister, Hubert de Burgh, 1232; Peter des Roches and Peter of Rivaux become his chief advisers • Pope Gregory IX entrusts the investigation of heresy to the Dominican and Franciscan orders, 1233 • Welsh join Earl of Pembroke in revolt against Henry III, 1233 • Toulouse university (Fr) founded, 1233 • Under pressure from English barons, Henry III expels his foreign advisers, 1234 • Friedrich II (Ger) faces revolt by son Heinrich, 1234 • Dominic, founder of Dominican order, canonized, 1234 • France conquers Navarre, 1234 • Mongols capture Chin Empire, 1234

Manding in West Africa, under its leader Sun Diata, frees itself from Soso, 1235 • Aragon captures the Balearic Islands, 1235 • Almohades lose Algeria, 1235 • Friedrich II (Ger) issues reforms at Diet of Mainz, 1235 • Henry III (Eng) weds Eleanor of Provence, 1236 • The monk Matthew Paris becomes chronicler at St. Albans (Eng), 1236 • Fernando III of Castile takes Córdoba (Sp) from Muslims, 1236 • Friedrich II crushes Second Lombard League at Cortenuova (It), 1237 • Teutonic Knights absorb Livonian order, Brothers of the Sword, 1237 • Mongol ruler Batu renews conquest of Russia, 1237 • Guillaume de Lorris (Fr) completes first part of *Roman de la Rose*, major poem with a theme of courtly love, 1237

Sung Chinese attack on Mongols leads to Mongols' capture of Szechwan, 1238 • Simon de Montfort, Earl of Leicester (Eng), marries sister of King Henry III, 1238 • Mongols seize Moscow, 1238 • Pope Gregory IX excommunicates Friedrich II (Ger), who is threatening papal power in Italy, 1239 • Mongols capture Kiev and begin to exact tribute from Russians, 1240 • Aleksandr Nevski, Prince of Novgorod (Russ) halts Swedish advance at the Neva River, 1240 • Richard of Cornwall and Simon de Montfort start Crusade to Jaffa, 1240 • England's Great Council is called "Parliament" from *c.* 1240

1250-1252

1253-1255

1256-1258

☐ Konrad IV —————————— ☐ Great Interregnum —————————

Stockholm (Swe) founded, *c.* 1250 • Statesman Birger Magnusson's son Waldemar founds Sweden's Folkung Dynasty, 1250 • Friedrich II (Ger) dies, 1250; succeeded by son Konrad IV • Mamluks, powerful descendants of Turkish slave troops, dominate Ayyubid sultans from 1250 • Louis IX (Fr) defeated, captured and ransomed while crusading in Egypt, 1250 • Konrad IV campaigns in Italy, 1251–1254, to secure Hohenstaufen right to succession • Mangu, grandson of Genghis Khan, elected Great Khan of Mongols, 1251 • Aleksandr Nevski (Russ) becomes Prince of Vladimir, 1252 • Florence mints first gold florin, 1252 • Fernando III of Castile dies, 1252; succeeded by son, Alfonso X

Venice and Genoa at war, 1253 • Castile ends war with Portugal, 1253 • Teutonic Knights crush Prussian revolt, 1253 • Bohemian power at its peak under Ottokar II (1253–1278) • Franciscan friar Willem of Rubruck (Flem) visits Great Khan, Mangu, 1253–1255 • Hungary masters Bosnia and Herzegovina, 1254 • Papal invasion of Naples collapses, 1254 • Konrad IV, last Hohenstaufen German emperor dies, 1254; Great Interregnum (struggle for power) ensues (to 1273) • Manfred, half-brother of Konrad IV, wins southern Italy, 1255 • First journey to China by the Polo brothers, Niccolò and Maffeo, Venetian merchants (1255–1266)

Manfred, bastard son of German emperor Friedrich II, gains control of Sicily, 1256 • Mongol Hulagu, a grandson of Genghis Khan, founds Il-Khan dynasty in Persia, 1256–1349 • Mongols destroy the Assassins, 1256 • Last Ayyubid sultan of Egypt murdered, 1257 • Richard of Cornwall and Alfonso X of Castile claim Holy Roman Empire (1257–1272) • Robert de Sorbonne endows University of Paris, 1257 • Provisions of Oxford, 1258: Henry III (Eng) to rule on advice of a 15-member privy council chosen by barons • Genoa loses war with Venice, 1258 • France and Aragon agree Treaty of Corbeil, 1258, to France's territorial advantage • Asen Dynasty (Bulg) ends, 1258 • Mongols sack Baghdad, 1258

ENGLAND—**Henry III** ———————————————————————————————
HOLY ROMAN EMPIRE—**Great Interregnum** —————————————————

Mangu, Great Khan of the Mòngols, dies, 1259 • Provisions of Westminster (Eng) introduce reforms, 1259 • England and France make peace, 1259 • Bohemia absorbs Styria, 1260 • Mali ruler Sun Diata dies, *c.* 1260, after founding nucleus of Mali Empire in West Africa • King Manfred of Sicily becomes master of most of Italy • Kublai Khan founds China's Yüan (Mongol) Dynasty, 1260 • Mamluks crush Mongols at Ain Jalut, Palestine, 1260 • Haakon IV (Norw) secures submission of Greenland, 1261 • Michael VIII Paleologus of Nicaea ousts Baldwin II, 1261, reestablishing the Byzantine Empire • Papal Bull (proclamation) frees Henry III (Eng) from Provisions of Oxford, 1261

Haakon IV (Norw) secures submission of Iceland, 1262 • In England, Simon de Montfort's revolt, 1263–1265, forces Henry III to restore Provisions of Oxford; England once more ruled by a council of 15 barons • Last Norse invasion of Scotland fails, 1263 • Kublai Khan becomes supreme ruler of Mongol Empire, 1264 • Louis IX (Fr) supports Henry III against Provisions of Oxford, 1264; Simon de Montfort defeats and captures Henry at Lewes, 1264, then rules as military dictator • Venetians destroy Genoese fleet off Trapani, Sicily, 1264

Knights and burgesses (town representatives) included for first time in English parliament, 1265 • Henry III's son Edward defeats and kills rebel Simon de Montfort at Evesham, restoring Henry III, 1265 • Bohemia and Hungary at war 1265–1270 • English friar Roger Bacon writes scientific treatise *Opus Majus*, 1266 • Balban, chamberlain to King Malmud of Delhi, India, founds a new dynasty of slave kings at Delhi, 1266 • Charles of Anjou, brother of Louis IX of France, kills Sicilian ruler Manfred at Benevento (It), 1266 • Scotland receives Isle of Man from Norway, 1266 • Kublai Khan (China) founds Peking, 1267 • England recognizes Llewellyn ap Gruffyd as Prince of Wales, 1267

ENGLAND—**Edward I** ———————————————————————————————
HOLY ROMAN EMPIRE—**Rudolf I** —————————————————————————

Scientist-friar Roger Bacon (Eng) imprisoned for heresy, 1277 • Edward I (Eng) defeats Welsh prince Llewellyn ap Gruffyd, 1277 • Milan (It) is under rule of Visconti family, 1277–1447 • Alexander III (Scot) performs homage (a ritual act of submission) to Edward I for lands he holds in England, 1278 • Statute of Gloucester (Eng) curbs barons' rights to hold public courts, 1278 • Rudolf I (Ger) defeats and kills Ottokar II of Bohemia in Battle of Marchfeld, 1278 • Kublai Khan takes over southern China and ends Sung rule by 1279 • By England's Statute of Mortmain, 1279, royal consent is needed for gifts of land to clergy • Portugal thrives under rule of Diniz the Worker (1279–1325)

French poet Jean de Meung completes *Roman de la Rose*, *c.* 1280 • Japan crushes huge Mongol invasion, 1281 • Serbia expands under its ruler Milyutin (1281–1321) • Rudolf I's Habsburg sons receive Austria, Carniola, Styria, 1282 • Erik V (Den) forced to sign Danish version of *Magna Carta*, 1282 • German traders in London (Eng) form own corporation, 1282 • Welsh prince Llewellyn ap Gruffyd is killed fighting Edward I (Eng), 1282 • Revolt in Sicily against French rule, 1282, begins with massacre of French people there, ironically called "The Sicilian Vespers" • Pedro III of Aragon invades Sicily, 1282, ousting Charles of Anjou • East-West Church schism reopened, 1282

Mongol army briefly invades Champa (now part of Vietnam), 1283 • Edward I (Eng) begins building of Harlech and Caernarvon castles in Wales, 1283 • Philippe, heir to French throne, marries 12-year-old Jeanne, heiress of Champagne and Navarre, which becomes part of France, 1284 • First ducat is coined in Vienna, 1284 • Wales is split into counties, 1284 • Power of Pisa wanes after naval defeat by Genoa, 1284 • Teutonic Knights complete subjection of Prussia, 1285 • England's Second Statute of Westminster (1285) tightens landholding laws and deals with defense and roads • France invades Catalonia, 1285 • Philippe III (Fr) dies, 1285; succeeded by son Philippe IV, the Fair

1268-1270	1271-1273	1274-1276

□ Edward I ————————————————————————▷
□ Rudolf I ————————————————————————▷

Defeat and death of Hohenstaufen leader Conradin in Italy, 1268, leaves Charles of Anjou undisputed king of Naples and Sicily (as Charles I) • Mamluks, Muslim rulers of Egypt and Syria, win Antioch from Christians, 1268 • Ottokar II of Bohemia absorbs Carinthia, Carniola, Istria, 1269 • Louis IX (Fr) dies, 1270, on Eighth Crusade against Tunis; succeeded by son Philippe III, the Bold • Portuguese begin to explore Africa's west coast, 1270 • Amharic culture thrives under Ethiopia's Solomonid Dynasty, founded c. 1270

Edward, heir to English throne, crusades at Acre, 1271 • Charles I of Naples and Sicily invades Greece and Albania, 1271 • Alfonso X of Castile (Sp) weakens crown by concessions to nobles, 1271 • Philippe III (Fr) inherits Languedoc, 1271 • Venetian merchants Niccolò and Maffeo Polo start second journey to China, taking with them Niccolò's son, Marco (1271–1295) • Ramón Lull (Catalan) writes first philosophical treatise in a Romance language, 1272 • Henry III (Eng) dies, 1272; succeeded by son Edward I, an outstanding legislator • Dominican monk Thomas Aquinas (It) completes *Summa Theologica*, work on religion, 1273 • Rudolf I is elected first Habsburg King of Germany, 1273, ending Great Interregnum

Mongols invade Japan but withdraw, 1274 • Council of Lyon (Fr) secures seclusion of conclaves for papal elections and purports to end schism (break) between Roman and Eastern Churches, 1274 • English parliament of 1275 grants Edward I an increase in export duty on leather and wool • Marco Polo (It) travels in Asia in service of Kublai Khan, 1275–1292 • Portolan charts (coastal maps for sailors) first appear, c. 1275 • Ottokar II of Bohemia's refusal to acknowledge Rudolf I as German emperor leads to war, 1276 • Welsh prince Llewellyn ap Gruffyd refuses homage to Edward I, 1276 • Mongols capture Sung capital Hangchow, 1276 • Pope Gregory X dies, 1276; his Ninth Crusade is abandoned

1286-1288	1289-1291	1292-1294

————————————————————————————————▷
□ Adolf I————————————————————————▷

Alexander III (Scot) dies, 1286; succeeded by infant niece, Margaret of Norway • Philippe IV (Fr) receives homage (a ritual act of submission) from Edward I (Eng) for Guyenne in southwestern France, 1286 • Alfonso III of Aragon forced to agree so-called *Magna Carta* of Aragon, 1287 • Il-Khans of Persia send first of several missions to England, 1287; free travel and trade between Mongol Empire and Europe flourish • Mongols destroy Burmese capital, Pagan, 1287 • Annam and Champa (Vietnam) repulse Mongol invasions, 1287–1288, but acknowledge Mongol overlordship • Florence (It) involved in continuing struggles between Guelphs and Ghibellines • Peru's north-coastal Chimu culture continues

Wood-block printing is carried on at Ravenna (It), 1289 • Mamluks of Syria capture Tripoli, Lebanon, 1289 • Osman founds Osmanli (Ottoman) Turkish principality in Bithynia (northern Turkey), c. 1290 • In India, Firuz founds Delhi's Khalji Dynasty, 1290 • Edward I (Eng) expels Jews, 1290 • University of Lisbon (Port) founded, 1290 • Spectacles in use, c. 1290 • Scottish queen Margaret of Norway dies, aged 8, 1290; Scottish throne claimed by John Balliol, Robert Bruce, John Hastings and others • Uri, Schwyz, Unterwalden form League of Three Forest Cantons (in what is now Switzerland), 1291 • Turks capture Acre (now Akko, Israel), 1291 • Rudolf I (Ger) dies, 1291; succeeded by Adolf of Nassau

Most of southern India comes under rule of Viraballala III, 1292 • Edward I (Eng), as arbitrator, chooses John Balliol as King of Scotland, 1292 • Dante Alighieri (It) writes *Vita Nuova*, lyric poems, c. 1292 • Mongols send naval expedition to Java, 1292; repulsed 1293 by King Madjapahit • Lithuanian state is formed, 1293 • Anglo-Gascon fleet defeats French, 1293; Philippe IV (Fr) seizes Gascony • Edward I (Eng) and Philippe IV (Fr) war over Guyenne, 1294 • Siamese states acknowledge Mongol supremacy, 1294 • Portugal makes trade treaty with England, 1294 • Starting with Pope Boniface VIII, the papacy becomes chiefly concerned with politics, 1294–1534

1295-1297 | 1298-1300 | 1301-1303

ENGLAND—**Edward I**

HOLY ROMAN EMPIRE—**Adolf I** ———□ **Albrecht I**

Franco–Scottish alliance formed, 1295 • Edward I (Eng) summons "Model Parliament," 1295 • Papal bull (proclamation) *Clericis laicos* forbids kings to tax clergy without papal approval, 1296 • Because of French alliance, Edward I invades Scotland, crushing Balliol at Dunbar, 1296, and claims Scottish throne; Balliol dies in exile • Edward I takes Stone of Scone (Scottish coronation stone) to Westminster • Florence Cathedral (It) is begun, 1296 • Edward I invades northern France, 1297 • Edward I outlaws English clergy, 1297, for refusing tax payments; Pope Boniface VIII virtually cancels bull of 1296 • Scottish knight William Wallace leads revolt against English rule, 1297

Edward I (Eng) defeats Scottish patriot William Wallace at Falkirk (Scot), 1298 • Barcelona Cathedral (Sp) building begun, 1298 • Giotto (It) creates Navicella mosaic, *c.* 1298 • Electors depose Adolf (Ger) in favor of Albrecht I (Habsburg), 1298 • Mongols invade Sultanate of Delhi, India, 1299 • Pope Boniface VIII secures truce between Edward I and Philippe IV (Fr), 1299 • War between Venice and Genoa ends, 1299 • So-called "Regressive" Pueblo Period of Amerindian culture (1300–1700) begins in southwestern North America • Philippe IV (Fr) gains Flanders, 1300 • Wenceslas II of Bohemia is made King of Poland, 1300 • Mali empire in West Africa expands under Sakuru

Edward, son of Edward I (Eng), becomes first English Prince of Wales, 1301 • Hungary's Arpad Dynasty ends with death of Andras III, 1301 • Peace of Caltabelotta, 1302: Frederick II of Sicily marries daughter of Charles of Anjou • Estates General (parliament) first meets in France, 1302 • French massacred by Flemings in "Matins of Bruges," 1302 • Flemings defeat French at Courtrai, 1302 • Pope Boniface VIII issues bull (proclamation) *Unam sanctam* (1302), claiming papal supremacy over temporal rulers • Supporters of Philippe IV (Fr) threaten Boniface VIII at Anagni (It), 1303 • Boniface VIII dies, 1303; succeeded by Benedict XI

1313-1315 | 1316-1318 | 1319-1321

ENGLAND

HOLY ROMAN EMPIRE—**Heinrich VII** —□ **Ludwig IV**

Scots capture Perth from English, 1313 • In India, Delhi sultanate absorbs central Deccan, 1313 • Heinrich VII (Ger) dies, 1313; succeeded (1314) by Ludwig IV, of the Wittelsbach family • Giotto (It) paints frescoes in church of St. Croce, Florence, *c.* 1314 • Philippe IV (Fr) dies, 1314, succeeded by son Louis X, the Quarrelsome • Ex-Grand Master of Knights Templars, Jacques de Molay, burned at the stake in France for heresy, 1314 • England is governed by Thomas, Duke of Lancaster, nephew of Edward II, by 1314 • Edward II invades Scotland, and is defeated by Robert Bruce at Bannockburn, 1314 • Robert's daughter Marjory weds Walter "the Steward," 1315; ancestor of royal house of Stuart

Rumors of Prester John, legendary Christian king in East Africa, lead Pope John XXII to send eight Dominican friars to Ethiopia, 1316 • Edward Bruce, brother of Robert I (Scot), is crowned king of Ireland, 1316 • Louis X (Fr) dies, 1316; succeeded by brother Philippe V, the Tall • Gedymin, founder of Lithuanian Empire, becomes Prince of Lithuania, 1316, and extends rule south and east • Ottoman Turks besiege Brusa in northwestern Asia Minor, 1317 • Swiss and Habsburgs agree truce, 1318 • Edward Bruce is killed in battle, 1318 • Scots capture Berwick from English, 1318

Sweden and Norway unite under Magnus II of Sweden (Magnus VII of Norway), 1319 • Scots defeat English at Myton-upon-Swale, 1319 • Tughluk (a Turk) founds Delhi Sultanate's Tughluk Dynasty in India, 1320 • Lithuania conquers Kiev, 1320 • Coronation of Vladislav IV, 1320, underlines Poland's revived independence after a struggle against Bohemian rule • Hansa towns (cities with close trade links) dominate Danish politics by reign of Christopher II (1320–1332) • English Parliament banishes Edward II's new favorite, Hugh le Despenser, 1321 • Civil war in Byzantine empire between Andronicus II and his grandson Andronicus, 1321–1328

1304–1306 | 1307–1309 | 1310–1312

□ Edward II ──────────────────────────────▷
□ Heinrich VII ────────────────────────────▷

Pope Benedict XI dies, 1304, reputedly poisoned . • French defeat Flemings at Mons-en-Pévèle, 1304 • Sultanate of Delhi, India, smashes Mongol army, 1304 • Edward I (Eng) captures and executes Scottish patriot William Wallace, and subjugates Scotland, 1305 • A French archbishop becomes Pope Clement V, crowned at Lyon (Fr), 1305 • Wenceslas II of Bohemia dies, 1305, after relinquishing Polish throne • France expels Jews, 1306 • Bohemia's Premyslid dynasty (founded 1198) ends, 1306 • Robert Bruce (Scot) revolts against English rule, 1306; crowned Robert I of Scotland • Giotto (It) completes Arena Chapel frescoes, Padua, c. 1306

Philippe IV (Fr) starts seizing property of crusading order, the Knights Templars, 1307 • Mali empire of West Africa is at its peak under Gongo Musa, 1307–1332 • Edward I (Eng) dies, 1307; succeeded by son Edward II • Piers Gaveston, a Gascon of dubious morals, becomes Edward II's chief minister • John of Montecorvino becomes Archbishop of Peking, 1307 • Barons force Edward II to banish Gaveston, 1308 • Albrecht I (Ger) dies, 1308; succeeded by Heinrich VII (Count of Luxemburg) • At the invitation of Philippe IV (Fr), Pope Clement V moves headquarters of papacy from Rome to Avignon, 1309: the so-called "Babylonian Captivity" • Edward II recalls Gaveston, 1309

Hungary becomes westernized under its king Charles I (Charles Robert of Anjou), 1310–1342 • Edward II (Eng) is forced to accept barons' reform committee, the Lords Ordainers, 1310 • Robert Bruce (Scot) invades England, 1311 • Heinrich VII (Ger) subdues north Italian towns, 1311 • Duccio di Buoninsegna (It) paints *Maestà*, 1311 • English Parliament confirms baronial reforms, 1311; Piers Gaveston is again banished from England • Synod of Vienne (in south-eastern France): order of Knights Templars abolished • Norway cedes Western Isles to Scotland, 1312 • English barons seize and kill Gaveston, 1312 • Visconti family (Ghibelline) crush Della Torre (Guelph) rivals in Milan, 1312

1322–1324 | 1325–1327 | 1328–1330

□ Edward III ──────────────────────────────▷

Emperor Daigo II (Jap) ends court domination by retired emperors, 1322 • Edward II (Eng) defeats his rebellious nephew Thomas of Lancaster at Boroughbridge, executes him, and issues Statute of York revoking baronial ordinances, 1322 • Philippe V (Fr) dies, 1322; succeeded by brother Charles IV, the Fair • Ludwig IV (Ger) defeats Habsburg rival Friedrich the Handsome • Vilna established as Lithuanian capital by 1323 • Pro-French Pope John XXII declares Ludwig IV deposed and excommunicated, 1324, but to no effect • Friar Oderic of Pordenone's travels in Asia (1324–1328) form basis for a detailed account of China •

Aztecs found Tenochtitlán (Mexico City), c. 1325 • Mali empire in West Africa absorbs Songhoy (based on city state of Gao), 1325 • In England, Edward II's favorites Hugh Despenser and his son Hugh antagonize Queen Isabella, who leaves for her native France, 1325 • *Luttrel Psalter* (Eng illustrated manuscript) c. 1325 • Teutonic Knights raid Poland in first Polish War, 1326–1333 • Army under Edward II's wife Isabella and her lover Roger Mortimer invades England, 1326; Despensers are executed; Edward II is imprisoned, deposed by parliament, and murdered in 1327; succeeded by son, Edward III, with Mortimer as regent to 1330

France takes over Flanders, 1328 • Robert Bruce (Scot) invades England, 1328, forcing recognition of Scotland's independence • Charles IV (Fr) dies, 1328; succeeded by his cousin Philippe VI (founding the Valois line which lasts to 1498) • Emperor Andronicus III (Byz) forces abdication of his grandfather Andronicus II, 1328 • Ivan I Kalita becomes Grand Prince of Moscow, 1328 • Robert Bruce (Scot) dies, 1329; succeeded as king by son, David II • Edward III (Eng) performs homage (a ritual act of subservience) for French holdings, 1329 • Serbs defeat Greeks and Bulgarians, 1330, ending Bulgar power • Edward III imprisons and executes his mother's lover Roger Mortimer, 1330

| 1331-1333 | 1334-1336 | 1337-1339 |

ENGLAND—**Edward III**
HOLY ROMAN EMPIRE—**Ludwig IV**

Emperor Daigo II restores imperial power in Japan, 1331–1333 • Perpendicular Gothic style appears in England when building of Gloucester Cathedral choir is begun, 1331 • Stevan Dušan, medieval Serbia's greatest ruler, deposes his father, Stevan Dechanski, 1331 • Lucerne joins Switzerland's three Forest Cantons, 1332 • Christopher II (Den) is deposed, 1332; German merchants now largely control Denmark • First Polish War ends, 1333 • Vladislav IV (Pol) dies, 1333; succeeded by Casimir III the Great, who strengthens the nation • Edward III (Eng) defeats Scots at Halidon Hill, 1333, deposes Scots king David II and replaces him with puppet king, Edward Balliol

Giotto (It) appointed architect to Florence, 1334 • Arab traveler Ibn Batuta visits India, 1334–1342 • Poland grants Jews generous privileges, 1334 • Edward III (Eng) invades Scotland, 1335 • Artillery is used in Europe by 1335 • France buys province of Dauphiné from its rulers, 1336; from it, heirs to French crown later took title *dauphin* • Count Louis II of Flanders stops trade with England; Edward III blocks English wool exports to Flanders, 1336 • Japanese general Ashikaga Takauji expels Emperor Daigo II from Kyoto and sets up a new emperor with himself in control, starting Japan's Ashikaga period (1336–1568) • Hohokam culture of American southwest is at height of its classical period

Edward III (Eng) claims French crown, 1337, and Philippe VI (Fr) demands Gascony • Ottoman Turks capture Nicomedia (modern Izmit), 1337 • In India, Delhi Sultanate loses Bengal, 1338 • Ashikaga Takauji (Jap) appointed shogun (military dictator), 1338 • Diet of Frankfurt, 1338, declares popes should not interfere in imperial elections • Flemish weavers led by Jan van Arteveldt make trade treaty with England, 1338 • Edward III forms alliance with Ludwig IV (Ger), 1338 • England and France start Hundred Years' War, 1338: Philippe VI attacks Guyenne, southwestern France • Edward III invades France via Flanders, 1339

| 1349-1351 | 1352-1354 | 1355-1357 |

ENGLAND—**Edward III**
HOLY ROMAN EMPIRE—**Karl IV**

Germans persecute Jews, 1349 • Giovanni Boccaccio (It) writes *Decameron*, 1349–1351 • In England, the Commons and Lords emerge as separate houses of Parliament • Royal ordinance of 1349 (Eng) regulates wages and prices, dislocated by Black Death (bubonic plague) and war • Philippe VI (Fr) dies, 1350; succeeded by son, Jean II • Siamese invade Cambodia, 1350 • Karl IV (Ger) grants states of Brandenburg and Tyrol to Wittelsbach family, 1350 • England's Statute of Laborers, 1351, seeks to relieve labor shortage • Milan at war with Venice, 1351 • Zurich joins Forest Cantons in what is now Switzerland, 1351 • Black Death kills one-third of Europe's people by 1351

Arab traveler Ibn Batuta visits Mali empire, in Africa, 1352–1353 • Glarus joins Forest Cantons in what is now Switzerland, 1352 • King Stevan Dušan (Serbia) defeats a Hungarian invasion and captures Belgrade, 1353 • England's Statute of Praemunire forbids appeals to courts abroad, particularly papal courts, 1353 • Bern joins Forest Cantons (Switz), 1353 • John VI Cantacuzene (Byz) employs Ottoman Turks to defeat Serbs, 1353 • German towns form a new Rhine League, 1354 • Roman lawyer and former rebel Cola di Rienzo is appointed a Roman senator, 1354, but is murdered • Ottoman Turks are established in Europe at Gallipoli by 1354 • John V regains Byzantine throne, deposing father-in-law John VI

Hundred Years' War between England and France is renewed, 1355: Edward the Black Prince, eldest son of Edward III (Eng) lays waste western France • Habsburgs regain Glarus and Zug, 1355 • English forces enter Brittany and Artois, 1355 • English under Black Prince defeat French near Poitiers and capture King Jean II, 1356 • Rebel Chu Yüan-chang wins Nanking from Mongols, 1356 • Edward Balliol hands over Scottish crown to Edward III, 1356 • Korean state of Koryo revolts against Mongol rulers of China, 1356 • Karl IV (Ger) issues Golden Bull (proclamation), 1357, nominating 7 electors to choose future emperors • Edward III frees captive Scottish king David II, 1357

1340–1342	1343–1345	1346–1348

▷
☐ Karl IV ——▷

Waldemar IV of Denmark (1340–1375) attacks Hansa (German traders) power in Denmark • Battle of Sluys near Bruges, between English and French fleets, gives England control of English Channel, 1340 • English Parliament appoints auditors of royal expenditure, 1340 • Castile and Portugal defeat Muslims at Río Salado, greatest battle in Christian reconquest of Spain, 1340 • Civil war in the Byzantine Empire, 1341–1347 • Ludwig IV (Gèr) sides with Philippe VI (Fr), 1341 • David II recovers Scots throne, 1341 • Charles I (Hung) dies, 1342; succeeded by Lajos I the Great (Louis of Anjou)

Peace of Kalisch deprives Poland of access to Baltic Sea, 1343 • Bardi bank (It), creditor of Edward III (Eng), fails, 1344 • Edward III begins rebuilding of Windsor Castle, 1344 • First record of the term "Hanseatic League" for the Hansa towns, a north German trading federation, 1344 • Order of the Garter (Eng) established, c. 1344 • England's Parliament demands that money grants to the Crown be spent as stipulated, 1344 • King Stevan Dušan (Serbia) wins Albania, Macedonia, Thessaly and Epirus by 1344 • Flemish leader Jan van Arteveldt is murdered, 1345 • Ottoman Turks first enter Europe, 1345 • Ludwig IV (Ger) acquires Frisia, Hainault, Holland, Zeeland

Teutonic Knights take Estonia from Denmark, 1346 • Edward III (Eng) invades Normandy, 1346, crushes French at Crécy and besieges Calais • Jan of Luxemburg, King of Bohemia, dies, 1346; succeeded by son Karl I • English crush Scottish invasion at Battle of Neville's Cross, near Durham, capturing David II, 1346 • Lugwig IV (Ger) dies 1347; succeeded by Luxenburgian Karl IV (Karl I of Bohemia) • England takes Calais in 1347, but makes truce with France • John Cantacuzene deposes his son-in-law John V and becomes John VI of Byzantium, 1347 • Roman lawyer Cola di Rienzo revolts against patrician rule of Rome, 1347 • Black Death (bubonic plague) sweeps Europe, 1348–1350 • Cola di Rienzo driven from Rome, 1348

1358–1360	1361–1363	1364–1366

▷
▷

Edward III (Eng) and captive Jean II (Fr) agree Treaty of London, 1358, restoring French territories to England • French nobles crush *Jacquerie* peasant rising, 1358 • Hungary gains most of Dalmatia from Venice, 1358 • Muhammad I (1358–1375) consolidates Bahmani kingdom in Deccan, India • Edward III again invades France, 1359, when French Estates General (parliament) reject Treaty of London • Ottoman Turks take Ankara, 1359 • Under Dmitri Donskoi (1359–1389), Moscow wars with Tver, Lithuania and Tatars • Treaty of Bretigny, 1360, ends first part of Hundred Years' War: French promise land and cash to ransom their king, Jean II

Duchy of Burgundy reverts to French crown, 1361 • Ottoman Turks under Murad I (c. 1361–1389) dominate Asia Minor and Balkans • Waldemar IV (Den) defeats Hansa (Ger) fleets at Helsingborg, 1362 • William Langland (Eng) writes poetic allegory *Piers Plowman, c.* 1362 • Edward III (Eng) gives principality of Aquitaine to his heir, Edward, the Black Prince, 1362 • Ottoman Turks take Adrianople, 1362, and make it their capital • Haakon VI (Norw) marries Margaret of Denmark, 1363 • Jean II (Fr) gives Burgundy to his son Philippe, 1363

Jean II (Fr) returns voluntarily to captivity in England following a breach of ransom terms, and dies there, 1364; succeeded by son, Charles V • Scottish parliament rejects King David II's plan for union with England, 1364 • Swiss Confederation regains Zug from the Habsburgs, 1364 • Vienna university is founded, 1365 • Hansa (German trading) towns lose privileges in Denmark, 1365 • Italian poet Petrarch writes *Canzoniere*, 1366 • In 1366, the English parliament rejects Pope Urban V's request for renewal of tribute payments, stopped since 1333 • Statute of Kilkenny, 1366, forbids English colonists to marry Irish citizens; designed to keep English colony in Ireland loyal to Crown

| 1367-1368 | 1369-1370 | 1371-1372 |

ENGLAND—**Edward III**

HOLY ROMAN EMPIRE—**Karl IV**

Pedro II, the Cruel, of Castile, supported by Edward the Black Prince (Eng) defeats Enrique of Trastamare and French forces led by Bertrand du Guèsclin at Navarrete, in northern Spain, 1367 • 77 German towns form Confederation of Köln, to sist Waldemar IV (Den), 1367 • In India, Bahmanis use artillery to crush Vijayanagar forces, 1367 • Nobles of English-ruled Aquitaine, provoked by heavy taxes, appeal to Charles V (Fr) for help, 1368 • Second war begins between Denmark and Hansa (German trading) towns, 1368 • Habsburgs and Swiss agree new truce, 1368 • Yüan (Mongol) Dynasty ends in anarchy; replaced by Ming Dynasty, founded by monk Chu Yüan-chang, 1368

Edward III (Eng) is dominated by his mistress Alice Perrers, 1369–1376 • The Hundred Years' War resumes, 1369; John of Gaunt, Duke of Lancaster, 4th son of Edward III, leads a cavalry raid into France from Calais • *The Book of the Duchesse*, earliest datable poem by Geoffrey Chaucer (Eng) appears, 1369 • Mongol leader Timur the Lame builds power in central Asia, 1369 • Philippe the Bold of Burgundy weds Margaret, daughter of last Count of Flanders, 1369 • Hansa (German trading) towns force Danes to submit, 1370 • Edward the Black Prince (Eng) sacks Limoges in France, 1370 • Louis of Anjou (Lajos I of Hungary) is elected King of Poland, 1370

Jean Froissart (Fr) completes Book 1 of his *Chronicles* • Revolt in France forces Edward the Black Prince to return to England, 1371 • In England, parliament dismisses the chancellor, William of Wykeham (who is also Bishop of Winchester), and declares that a layman should hold the post, 1371 • David II (Scot) dies, 1371; succeeded by Robert II, grandson of Robert Bruce and first Stuart king • Zeta (Montenegro) becomes independent principality, 1371 • In China, the Ming drive Mongols from Szechwan, 1371 • Edward III's last effort to invade France fails; contrary winds prevent landing • French and Castilian fleets defeat English fleet off La Rochelle (Fr), 1372

| 1379-1380 | 1381-1382 | 1383-1384 |

ENGLAND—**Richard I**

HOLY ROMAN EMPIRE—**Wenzel**

Church leader John Wycliffe (Eng) urges reformation of Church by temporal rulers, rejects transubstantiation (idea that the body of Christ is present in the communion bread and wine) and denies Biblical basis for the Pope's authority, 1379 • Ottoman Turks help John V recover Byzantine throne from his son Andronicus IV, 1379 • Dmitri Donskoi, Grand Prince of Moscow, defeats Tatars at Kulikovo, 1380 • Charles V (Fr) dies, 1380; succeeded by 11-year-old son Charles VI; France is disrupted by rivalry of young king's uncles, the dukes of Anjou, Berri, Burgundy • Olaf IV (Den) succeeds to Norwegian throne, 1380 • English defeat Franco-Castilian fleet off Ireland, 1380

Peasants' Revolt (Eng) in 1381: forces led by Jack Straw, Wat Tyler, John Ball march on London, forcing concessions from Richard II; Richard goes back on his word, and ringleaders are executed • Venice defeats Genoa, 1381 • First English translation of the Bible appears, c. 1382 • Richard II (Eng) weds Anne of Bohemia, 1382 • Term Lollard ("mutterer") first used in 1382 for Church reformer John Wycliffe's followers • Wycliffe is expelled from Oxford University, 1382; Lollards are persecuted • All China comes under Ming rule by 1382 • French crush Flemish revolt, 1382 • Poet Geoffrey Chaucer (Eng) completes *The House of Fame* and probably *The Parliament of Fowls* by 1382

Timur the Lame, self-styled restorer of the Mongol Empire, conquers eastern Persia and Khorasan, 1383–1385 • Geoffrey Chaucer (Eng) writes *The Consolation of Philosophy* (translation of Boethius's Latin work) about this time • Juan I of Castile nominally gains Portuguese crown by marriage, 1383, but Portuguese nationalists rally under João, Mestre de Avis • Quarantine is established at Marseille (Fr) to guard against bubonic plague, 1383 • Successions in Poland and Hungary disputed after death of Lajos I: Jadwiga, daughter of Lajos I, is elected Queen of Poland, 1384 • Flanders passes to Philippe the Bold of Burgundy, 1384

1373-1374	1375-1376	1377-1378

In the Hundred Years' War, John of Gaunt, son of Edward III (Eng), leads a cavalry raid through France from Calais to Bordeaux, 1373 • Bohemia acquires Brandenburg, 1373 • Dutch develop canal locks by 1373 • Charles V (Fr) sets up an organized staff and chain of command in his army, 1374 • Lajos I of Hungary and Poland exempts his nobles from taxation, 1374 • John of Gaunt, allied with his father's mistress, Alice Perrers, effectively gains power in England, 1374 • By 1374, France regains lands lost to England • Under Suleiman-Mar, Gao in West Africa wins independence from Mali empire, c. 1374 • Stone buildings of Great Zimbabwe (Rhodesia) constructed by peoples of uncertain origin

England and France agree a truce at Bruges (Flanders), 1375: English lose all French possessions except some coast towns • Juan, son of Enrique II of Castile, weds daughter of Pedro IV of Aragon, 1375 • Edward the Black Prince, son and heir of Edward III (Eng) supports work of the reforming "Good Parliament," 1376, but dies soon after • Church reformer John Wycliffe (Eng) asserts in treatise *Civil Dominion* (1376) that the Church should not own property • Swabian League of German towns is formed, 1376 • Tvrtko I, powerful Lord of Bosnia, styles himself King of Serbia and Bosnia, 1376 • Emperor Andronicus IV (Byz) dethrones his father, John V, 1376

Parliamentary treasurers and collectors are appointed in England, 1377 • Parliament reverses reforms of 1376, and introduces a poll tax, 1377 • Alhambra's Court of Lions (Granada) is built, 1377 • Edward III (Eng) dies, 1377; succeeded by 10-year-old grandson Richard II, under a council led by his uncle, John of Gaunt • Karl IV (Ger) dies, 1378; succeeded by Wenzel (Wenceslas IV of Bohemia) • Pope Urban VI, elected 1378, moves the papal headquarters back to Rome from Avignon, (Fr), ending so-called "Babylonian captivity"; but 13 cardinals dislike him and elect rival antipope, Clement VII, based at Avignon: start of the Great Schism (split) in the western Church

1385-1386	1387-1388	1389-1390

Richard II (Eng) leads futile expedition to Scotland, 1385 • Turks take Sofia, (Bulg), 1385 • João I establishes Portugal's Avis Dynasty, 1385 • Portuguese crush Castilians, and affirm independence, at Aljubarrota, 1385 • Grand Duke Jagiello of Lithuania weds Queen Jadwiga (Pol) 1386, becoming King Vladislav V of Poland • Swiss Confederation and Swabian League win Battle of Sempach against Leopold III of Habsburg, 1386 • Building of Milan Cathedral (It) is begun, 1386 • Geoffrey Chaucer (Eng) completes poems *Troilus and Criseyde* and *The Legend of Good Women* by 1386 • Alliance between England and Portugal, 1386

Geoffrey Chaucer (Eng) begins writing *The Canterbury Tales,* 1387 • Afghanistan, Azerbaijan, Kurdistan fall to Mongol leader Timur by 1387 • Richard II (Eng) and his supporters are defeated in battle by opposing barons, 1387 • Denmark, Norway and Sweden come under the rule of Margaret of Denmark, 1387 • Swiss defeat Habsburgs at Nafels, 1388 • Gian Galeazzo, ruler of Milan, wins Padua, Verona, Vicenza by 1388 • England's so-called "Merciless Parliament" of 1388 appoints five Lords Appellant, who find Richard II's supporters guilty of treason • Scots defeat English at Battle of Otterburn, Northumberland (also called "Chevy Chase"), 1388 • Chinese drive Mongols from Karakorum, 1388

Richard II (Eng) begins a period of direct rule, 1389 • England and France agree truce in Hundred Years' War, 1389 • Struggle for power in Germany between citizens of the towns and the knights and nobles ends with towns' defeat in the Town War of 1387–1389 • Ottoman Turks crush a Balkan alliance in the Battle of Kossovo, 1389, and make Serbia a vassal state • Ottoman sultan Murad I is killed in battle, 1389; succeeded by son, Bayazid I • Indonesian kingdom of Madjapahit collapses after death of King Hayam Wuruk, 1389 • Swiss Confederations' conquests over Habsburgs confirmed by Truce of Zürich, 1389 • Scottish king Robert II dies, 1390 • Succeeded by son Robert III

1391–1392

1393–1394

1395–1396

ENGLAND—**Richard II**
HOLY ROMAN EMPIRE—**Wenzel**

Geoffrey Chaucer (Eng) writes *The Astolabe,* a treatise on astronomy, 1391 • Mongol leader Timur crushes Tartars under Toqtamish, Khan of the Golden Horde, 1391 • Ottoman Turks expand their territories in northern Asia Minor, 1391 • John V (Byz) dies, 1391; succeeded by younger son Manuel II • Korean leader Songgye declares himself king, founds Korea's Li Dynasty (1392–1910), with Secul as its capital • Japan reunited by submission of its southern emperor to its northern emperor, 1392 • Charles VI (Fr) suffers first spell of insanity, 1392 • Philippe the Bold of Burgundy becomes regent of France, ousting Louis of Orléans from leadership

William of Wykeham, Bishop of Winchester, founds Winchester College (Eng), 1393 • Mongol leader Timur captures Baghdad and overruns Mesopotamia, 1393 • Bayazid I (Turk) strengthens Ottoman imperial hold on Asia Minor and Bulgaria, 1393 • Wenceslas IV of Bohemia has John of Npomuk, a leading churchman, tortured and killed, 1393 • Ottomans, Tatars and Mamluks form an alliance against Timur, 1394 • Dutch sculptor Claus Sluter is active at Dijon (Fr) • Richard II (Eng) takes an army to Ireland and secures the apparent submission of the Irish, 1394 • Swiss Confederation extends its truce with the Duke of Austria, 1394 • Antipope Clement VII dies at Avignon, 1394; succeeded by Benedict XIII

Gian Galeazzo, ruler of Milan, is made hereditary Duke of Milan, 1395 • Ottoman Turks invade Hungary and blockade Constantinople, 1395 • Mongol kingdom of the Golden Horde breaks up into khanates of Astrakhan, Crimea, Kazan • French, German, English and Balkan crusaders are crushed by Ottomans near Nicopolis (Bulg), 1396 • Manuel Chryseloràs becomes first lecturer on Greek language and culture in Western Europe (at Florence, 1396–1400) • England's Richard II weds Isabella, daughter of the French king Charles VI, 1396; France and England extend truce by 20 years • By 1396, Bessarabia, Moldavia and Wallachia acknowledge Lithuanian suzereinty • Bulgaria is under Ottoman rule from 1396

1403–1404

1405–1406

1407–1408

ENGLAND—**Henry IV**
HOLY ROMAN EMPIRE—**Ruprecht**

English king Henry IV defeats revolt by the Percies, leading barons of northern England, at Shrewsbury, 1403 • Bayazid I (Turk) dies a prisoner of Mongol leader Timur, 1403; civil war racks Ottoman Empire to 1413 • Henry IV sends army against rebellious Welsh prince Owen Glendower, 1403 • China starts major naval expeditions into southern seas, 1403 • English Parliament enforces reforms in royal administration, 1404 • Henry IV rejects House of Commons' demand to seize Church property, 1404 • Philippe the Bold of Burgundy dies, 1404; succeeded by Jean, the Fearless • Owen Glendower captures Harlech Castle, 1404

Mongol leader Timur dies, 1405, on way to invade China; Timurid rule continues in Persia to 1469 • French-aided Welsh are defeated by English at Usk, Gwent, 1405 • Henry IV (Eng) crushes baronial revolt, executes Thomas Mowbray and Richard Scrope, the Archbishop of York, and imprisons Edward, Duke of York, 1405 • Florence (It) buys Pisa, 1405 • Venice wins Bassano, Padua, Verona, Vicenza from enfeebled Milan, 1405 • English capture and imprison James, heir of Scotland's king Robert III, 1406 • English Parliament, aggrieved at royal mismanagement, forces Henry IV to nominate a new council, 1406 • Scotland's Robert III dies 1406; is succeeded by the captive James I

Thomas Arundel, Archbishop of Canterbury, becomes England's Chancellor, with wide powers, 1407 • Louis, Duke of Orléans, is murdered by order of his rival, Jean, Duke of Burgundy, 1407; civil war ensues in France • Genoa controls Corsica, 1407 • Chinese admiral Cheng Ho's naval expedition to East Indies (1405–1407) returns with captive Prince of Palembang, and also secures submission of many Malay states • Armies of Henry IV quell rebellion in northern England, 1408 • Bohemian religious reformer Jan Hus is accused of heresy, 1408 • Moscow (Russ) resists attack by Tatars under Yedigei, 1408

1397-1398	1399-1400	1401-1402

──────────────────── □ Henry IV ────────────────────▷

──────────────────────── □ Ruprecht ────────────────▷

Richard II (Eng) forces Parliament to convict three of his political opponents—the Earls of Arundel and Warwick, and the Duke of Gloucester—for treason, 1397 • Ottoman Turks attack Constantinople 1397 • Union of Kalmar unites the kingdoms of Norway, Sweden and Denmark under Erik of Pomerania, 1397 • Richard II banishes his cousin Henry Bolingbroke and Thomas Mowbray, Duke of Norfolk, 1398 • French clergy vote to refuse payment of papal taxes, 1398 • Wicklow Irish kill Richard II's viceroy, 1398 • Ottomans conquer lands west of Euphrates River, 1398–1390 • Mongol leader Timur invades India and sacks Delhi, 1398

John of Gaunt, uncle of King Richard II (Eng) dies, 1399; the king confiscates his estates • Richard II makes fruitless expedition to pacify Ireland, 1399 • Gaunt's exiled son, Henry Bolingbroke, now Duke of Lancaster, invades England, 1399, captures and deposes Richard and, as King Henry IV, founds the ruling House of Lancaster (1399–1461) • Milan acquires Pisa and Siena, 1399 • Henry IV crushes a revolt in favor of Richard II, 1400 • Milan acquires Assisi and Perugia, 1400 • Richard II dies in prison, 1400, perhaps murdered • Wolof empire is established in Senegal, West Africa, by 1400 • German emperor Wenzel is deposed for drunkenness, 1400; succeeded by Ruprecht, the Elector Palatine

England introduces a law *De Heretico Comburendo,* giving the Church power to put to death Lollards (religious dissenters), 1401 • Bohemian religious reformer Jan Hus becomes dean of philosophy at Prague University, 1401 • Mongol leader Timur devastates Baghdad and occupies Damascus, 1401 • Sculptor Lorenzo Ghiberti (It) wins competition to design bronze doors of Florentine Baptistery, 1402 • A Scottish invasion of England is defeated at Homildon Hill, Northumberland, 1402 • Welsh prince Owen Glendower revolts, 1402 • Building of Seville Cathedral is begun, 1402 • Timur defeats Ottoman Turks and captures Bayazid I in Battle of Angora (Ankara), 1402

1409-1410	1411-1412	1413-1414

── □ Henry V ──────▷

──────────────────── □ Sigismund ──────────────────────────▷

English recapture Harlech Castle from Welsh rebels, 1409 • Sicily is reunited with Aragon, 1409 • Thomas Beaufort (Eng) replaces Thomas Arundel as Chancellor, 1409 • Trying to end Great Schism in the church, the Council of Pisa (It) declares Roman and Avignonese popes deposed and elects Alexander V, 1409; result is three rival popes instead of two • Donatello (It) completes his first known sculpture, *David,* 1409 • Bohemian religious leader Jan Hus becomes rector of a reformed Prague University, 1409 • German emperor Ruprecht (Ger) dies, 1410; succeeded by Sigismund, King of Bohemia, who is challenged by Jobst, Margrave of Moravia and Brandenburg • Antipope Alexander V dies; succeeded by John XXIII, 1410

England's Prince Henry, heir of Henry IV, joins plot against his father, 1411 • St. Andrews University, Scotland, is founded, 1411 • Teutonic Knights agree First Peace of Thorn with Poles, 1411 • Castile and Portugal finally make peace, 1411 • Cheng Ho's Chinese naval mission visits Sri Lanka, 1408–1411 • City of Ahmadabad, (northwest India) is founded 1411 by Ahmad Shah of Gujarat's Muslim Rajput Dynasty (1390–1572) • English army defeats Orléanist French force at St. Cloud (Fr), 1411 • Fernando I of Castile inherits Aragon, 1412 • In northern coastal Peru, the vast royal Chimu necropolis-capital, Chan Chan, is expanding

Revolt led by a skinner, Simon Caboche, shakes Paris (Fr), 1413 • Henry IV (Eng) dies 1413; is succeeded by his son Henry V, the first king of England to read and write English easily • Ottoman Empire is reunited by Mehmed I, 1413 • Medici family of Florence become bankers to the papacy, 1414 • Henry V puts down Lollard (heretical) rebellion, 1414 • German monk Thomas à Kempis (Ger) writes devotional book *Imitation of Christ* • Council of Constance is held to reform Church, restore unity and remove heresy (1414–1417) • Mehmed I masters Anatolia, 1414 • Under Sayyid rule (1414–1451) the Sultanate of Delhi (India) is reduced to Jumna Valley • Chinese fleet visits Persian Gulf, 1414–1415

1415	1416	1417

ENGLAND—**Henry V** ————————————————————————————
HOLY ROMAN EMPIRE—**Sigismund** ————————————————————

Bohemian religious reformer Jan Hus is burned for heresy • Henry V (Eng) revives English claim to the French throne, invades France and wins the Battle of Agincourt • Antipope John XXIII is deposed and Pope Gregory XII resigns, removing 2 of the 3 rival popes; Benedict XIII (Avignon) refuses to resign

English forces win the Battle of the Seine against the French, assuring England's control of the English Channel • Henry V (Eng) makes a treaty with the Emperor Sigismund (Ger) • Venice fights its first war with the Ottoman Turks • Donatello (It) completes his statues of *St. Mark* and *St. George*

Sir John Oldcastle (Eng), the last Lollard aristocrat, is executed for heresy • The English begin reconquering Normandy • The Council of Constance deposes Antipope Benedict XIII (Avignon); election of Martin V ends the papal schism • Ottoman Turks under Mehmed I invade Wallachia

1421	1422	1423

ENGLAND—**Henry V** ————————————□ **Henry VI** ———————————
HOLY ROMAN EMPIRE—**Sigismund** ————————————————————

Henry V (Eng) invades France again • Florence (It) buys Livorno (Leghorn) • Floods in the Netherlands drown 10,000 people • Hussites in Bohemia repel an attack from Germany • Mehmed I is succeeded by Murad II as Ottoman sultan • Building of the Church of St. Lorenzo, Florence, designed by Filippo Brunelleschi, is begun

Ottoman Turks attack Constantinople • England's king Henry V dies; he is succeeded by his infant son Henry VI under the regency of Humphrey, Duke of Gloucester and John, Duke of Bedford • Charles VI (Fr) dies; is succeeded by his son Charles VII, who is not crowned king because of lack of power

Pope Martin V calls the Council of Pavia, which achieves nothing • The House of Wettin is established in Saxony • English free the captive Scottish king James I • Block-printed playing cards appear in Europe • Venetians take over Thessalonica (Greece) • An English army led by the Earl of Salisbury defeats French and Scottish forces at Cravant (Fr)

1427	1428	1429

ENGLAND—**Henry VI** ————————————————————————————
HOLY ROMAN EMPIRE—**Sigismund** ————————————————————

French troops led by Jean Dunois defeat English forces under the Duke of Bedford at Montargis (Fr) • Florence (It) introduces income tax • George Brankovich becomes Despot of Serbia and seeks to withstand Turkish attacks • Portuguese explorer Diogos de Silves discovers the Azores • Masaccio (It) paints church frescoes in Florence

English troops besiege French forces in Orléans • Country lairds are represented in the Scottish parliament • Venice wins Bergamo from Milan • Jeanne d'Arc, 16-year-old French peasant girl guided by "voices," resolves to help the Dauphin Charles gain his throne

French peasant girl Jeanne d'Arc convinces the Dauphin Charles that she has a divine mission to defeat the English; under her leadership French forces raise the siege of Orléans and defeat an English army at Patay • Urged on by Jeanne, the Dauphin is crowned as Charles VII at Rheims

1418

English victories in northern France force the Dauphin, regent for his insane father, Charles VI, to flee to the south • Burgundian forces drive those of their rivals, the Armagnacs, out of Paris • Collective decisions of the Hanseatic League (German trading towns) are made binding on all members • Cheng Ho's Chinese fleet visits Aden • Portuguese explorers visit Madeira

1419

English forces conquer Normandy and reach Paris • Filippo Brunelleschi (It) designs the Foundling Hospital in Florence • An Anglo-Burgundian alliance is formed against France • Vaclav IV of Bohemia dies; the Bohemians reject the Emperor Sigismund (Ger) as his successor

1420

Pope Martin V preaches a crusade against followers of reformer Jan Hus • Venice controls the Dalmatian and Albanian coasts • By the Treaty of Troyes Henry V (Eng) is declared heir to Charles VI (Fr); he marries Charles' daughter Catherine of Valois • Masaccio (It), paints *Virgin and Child with St. Anne* • Filippo Brunelleschi (It) begins designing the dome of Florence Cathedral

1424

James I is crowned as King of Scots • English forces under the Duke of Bedford crush the French and Scots at Verneuil (Fr); another army led by the Duke of Gloucester invades Hainault • The Hussite Church reform movement in Bohemia splits into two sects: Utraquists and the more extreme Taborites • Muslim trade spreads throughout the East Indies, where many people are converted to Islam

1425

English troops capture Le Mans (Fr) • Venice starts a second war against the Ottoman Turks • Byzantine emperor John VIII succeeds his father, Manuel II • Giovanni de' Medici becomes probably the richest man in Italy • Donatello (It) sculpts *Zuccone*

1426

Bohemian priest Prokop the Great repels an anti-Hussite crusade • Germans led by their emperor Sigismund fight the Ottoman Turks (to 1427) • The leaders of England's government, Humphrey, Duke of Gloucester, and Henry Beaufort, Bishop of Winchester, fall out: England is close to civil war • Masaccio (It) paints the altarpiece at Pisa

1430

French heroine Jeanne d'Arc is captured by the Burgundians, allies of England • English parliament gives the vote to all freeholders of property worth 40 shillings (the law continues in force until 1832) • In southern Africa, Shona king Mutota extends his rule between the Limpopo and Zambezi rivers • The Aztecs' power increases in Mexico under the rule of Itzcoatl (1427–1440)

1431

The English burn French peasant leader Jeanne d'Arc for heresy • Henry VI (Eng) is crowned king of France in Paris • Pope Martin V dies; is succeeded by Eugenuis IV • The Religious Council of Basel meets (to 1449) • Bohemian Hussite reformers defeat crusading forces led by Cardinal Beaufort (Eng) at Domazlice

1432

The Duke of Holstein (Ger), helped by the Hansa (trading) towns, seizes Schleswig from Denmark • Chinese admiral Cheng Ho on an expedition (1431–1433) secures tribute from Mecca (Arabia) • Jan van Eyck (Flem) paints *The Adoration of the Lamb* • Donatello (It) completes the bronze *David*

1433	1434	1435

ENGLAND—**Henry VI** ————————————————————
HOLY ROMAN EMPIRE—**Sigismund** ——————————————

Portugal is ravaged by bubonic plague • In Italy, Florence's ruler Cosimo de' Medici is imprisoned and exiled as a scapegoat for Florence's disastrous war with Lucca • Tuaregs (Saharan tribesmen) seize and sack Timbuktu • Portuguese mariners sail south of Cape Majador, Western Sahara, for the first time

Peasants' leader Engelbrecht Engelbrechtson seizes castles in Sweden • Exiled ruler Cosimo de' Medici is recalled to Florence (It) and dominates its government • Civil war splits the Bohemian Hussites (Church reformers): the Utraquists defeat the Taborites at Lipany, killing the warrior-priest Prokop the Great

The alliance between Burgundy and England ends; the Burgundians join forces with France, where civil war ends • Alfonso V of Aragon secures Naples, reuniting it with Sicily

1439	1440	1441

ENGLAND—**Henry VI** ————————————————————
HOLY ROMAN EMPIRE—**Albrecht II** —□ **Friedrich III** ——————

Cardinal Beaufort, great-uncle of Henry VI, takes control of the English government • Denmark and Sweden depose their king, Erik • The Council of Basel elects the antipope Felix V • Schism between Eastern and Western Christian Churches is ended • By the Pragmatic Sanction of Mainz, the German Church stops payments to the pope • German emperor Albrecht II dies

Friedrich III is elected as Holy Roman Emperor • Vladislav VI (Pol) becomes king of Hungary as Ladislas I • Charles VII (Fr) crushes the Praguerie, a coalition of nobles • Richard of York again becomes English regent in France • The Aztec king Itzcoatl dies and is succeeded by Montezuma I

Philippe the Good of Burgundy keeps a fleet operating in the Mediterranean and Black seas, 1441–1445 • János Hunyadi (Hung) wins victories in Transylvania against the Ottoman Turks • Henry VI (Eng) founds King's College, Cambridge

1445	1446	1447

ENGLAND—**Henry VI** ————————————————————
HOLY ROMAN EMPIRE—**Friedrich III** ——————————————

Henry VI (Eng) marries Margaret of Anjou • Charles VII creates France's first permanent royal army • Portuguese navigator Dinis Dias rounds Cape Verde, West Africa • Jean Fouquet (Fr) paints portrait of Charles VII • Guillaume Dufay (Fr-Flem composer) is active at the Burgundian court

The Dauphin Louis, heir to Charles VII (Fr), is exiled to Dauphiné for his part in a plot • Aztecs under Montezuma I extend their conquests in Mexico • Architect Leon Alberti (It) designs the Palazzo Rucellai façade, Florence • Japanese No drama is perfected

French merchant and royal counsellor Jacques Coeur builds up French trade with the Levant • William de la Pole, Duke of Suffolk, controls England's government (to 1449) • Pope Eugenius IV dies; he is succeeded by Nicholas V, restores the lost papal sovereignty at the Concordat of Vienna • A republic replaces the rule of the Visconti family in Milan

1436	1437	1438

☐ Albrecht II ──────▷

Zurich wars with rival Swiss cantons over who should possess the lands of the extinct Counts of Toggenburg in northeastern Switzerland • French regain Paris from the English • Hussites (religious reformers) in Bohemia accept the *Compactata* compromise of the Council of Basel, offering them recognition within the Church • All Bohemians finally accept German emperor Sigismund as king

Richard Beauchamp, Earl of Warwick, becomes English regent in France, replacing Richard, Duke of York • Moors defeat the Portuguese at Tangier • Henry VI (Eng) becomes legally of age at 16 • Emperor Sigismund (Ger) dies • James I (Scot) is murdered; is succeeded by son James II • Albrecht of Austria, Sigismund's son-in-law, is elected king of Bohemia

The Pragmatic Sanction of Bourges (Fr) declares the French Church independent of the pope • Albrecht II of Habsburg is elected as German emperor; Habsburg imperial rule lasts to 1806 • The Inca empire in Peru expands under Pachacutec, 1438–1471 • Laurens Koster (Neth) experiments with movable type for printing

1442	1443	1444

Zurich joins the German emperor Friedrich III against its rival Swiss cantons • Pope Eugenius recognizes Alfonso V of Aragon as king of Naples • French forces capture most of Gascony, except Bordeaux, from the English • Benin is now a powerful state in West Africa • Norway expels its king, Erik

Philippe the Good of Burgundy occupies Luxembourg • Forces of Zurich are defeated by armies of rival Swiss cantons at Battle of Schwyz • Christian armies capture Sofia from the Ottoman Turks • Cosimo de' Medici (It) founds the Laurentine Library in Florence

Ottoman Turkish army crushes Christian crusaders at Varna (Bulg), killing Ladislas I of Hungary • Armagnacs defeat Zurich's Swiss enemies near Basel • William de la Pole, Earl of Suffolk, negotiates an Anglo-French truce at Tours • János Hunyadi becomes regent of Hungary • Portuguese explorer Nuno Tristam reaches the Senegal River

1448	1449	1450

French armies capture Maine from the English • Bohemian Hussite (religious reform) leader Georg Podiebrad seizes Prague • Constantine XI becomes the last Byzantine emperor • Lancastrians and Yorkists, branches of the royal family, are rivals for power in England • Fra Angelico paints frescoes in the Vatican

A French army led by King Charles VII captures Rouen from the English • Richard of York (Eng) is sent to Ireland as Lord Lieutenant • Felix V, the last antipope, abdicates • Rogier van der Weyden (Flem) paints *The Entombment* • In Japan, Ashikaga art is at a new peak under Yoshimasa

French armies recapture Normandy from the English • In Jack Cade's Rebellion, a mob of 30,000 marches on London (Eng) • Francesco Sforza becomes Duke of Milan • Zurich makes peace with its rivals in the Swiss Confederation • Shona ruler Matope dominates most of what is now Rhodesia and Mozambique

1451	1452	1453

ENGLAND—**Henry VI**
HOLY ROMAN EMPIRE—**Friedrich III**

Charles VII (Fr) recaptures Bordeaux and Bayonne from English • Vasili II, Grand Duke of Moscow, repels Tatar invasion • Muhammed II (creator of centralized Ottoman rule) succeeds Murad II • Buhlul Lodi, an Afghan, founds Delhi's Lodi Dynasty in India • Glasgow University (Scot) founded • Flanders and Burgundy in trade war with Hansa towns

English recapture Bordeaux from French • Richard of York fails to win power by force in England • James II (Scot) crushes Earl of Douglas • Dauphin Louis (heir to Charles VII) makes anti-Burgundian alliance • Friedrich III (Ger) is crowned at Rome by the Pope—last emperor to be crowned in this way • Leon Alberti (It) publishes first Renaissance work on architecture

French retake Bordeaux, and Hundred Years' War ends; England keeps only Calais • Richárd of York is regent of England while Henry VI is insane • Philippe the Good of Burgundy subdues Ghent (Flanders) • Ottoman Turks besiege and take Constantinople, killing Emperor Constantine XI; end of Byzantine Empire; this date marks the end of the Middle Ages

1457	1458	1459

ENGLAND—**Henry VI**
HOLY ROMAN EMPIRE—**Friedrich III**

Revolt drives Karl VIII from Sweden; he is replaced by Christian I of Denmark and Norway; real power in Sweden is held by the Sture Family • Sculptor Donatello (It) makes bronze *St. John* for Siena and *Judith and Holofernes* for Florence • Poles capture Marienburg, forcing Teutonic Knights to move capital to Königsburg • *Mainz Psalter,* first book printed in more than one color, is published

Alfonso V of Aragon dies; of his possessions Aragon passes to his brother Juan II, Naples to his son Ferrante (Ferdinand I), in dispute with King René of Anjou • Pope Calixtus III dies; is succeeded by Pius II • Janós Hunyadi's son Matthias Corvinus is elected King of Hungary • Georg Podiebrad is elected King of Bohemia • Ottoman Turks build Old Serai Palace in Constantinople

Wars of the Roses continue in England: Yorkists defeat Queen Margaret at Bloreheath, but are routed at Ludford Bridge • After several reverses, Ottoman Turks finally crush and absorb Serbia • Pitti Palace, Florence (It), is under construction • Andrea Mantegna (It) is appointed court painter at Mantua • Mantegna paints altarpiece *Madonna Enthroned* for St. Zeno, Verona

1463	1464	1465

ENGLAND—**Edward IV**
HOLY ROMAN EMPIRE—**Friedrich III**

Edward IV (Eng) puts down Lancastrian rebellions • France and England agree Truce of St. Omer: France regains Somme towns • Portuguese campaign in Africa gains kingdom of Fez • Venice starts major war with Ottoman Turks • Ottoman Turks overrun Bosnia • Fra Filippo Lippi (It) paints *The Annunciation* • Cambridge University introduces England's first degrees in music

Yorkist forces led by Earl of Warwick (Eng) rout Lancastrians at Hedgeley Moor • Anglo-Scottish peace is made permanent • Edward IV (Eng) weds Elizabeth Woodville, a commoner, and angers nobles by favors shown to her relatives • Philippe the Good of Burgundy launches abortive anti-Ottoman expedition • Pope Pius II dies; is succeeded by Paul II

Edward IV, Yorkist King of England, imprisons his defeated Lancastrian rival Henry VI • Defeated by League of Public Weal, Louis XI (Fr) restores Normandy to the Duc de Berri, and Somme towns to Burgundy • Philippe the Good hands government of Burgundy to his son, Charles the Bold • Pope Paul II ineffectually declares Georg Podiebrad of Bohemia deposed

1454	1455	1456

Henry VI (Eng) regains sanity • Support of the towns for the monarchy saves Castile (Sp) from feudal anarchy under Enrique IV (1454–1474) • Johannes Gutenberg (Ger) invents printing from movable metal type • Prussian nobles and towns revolt against oppression by Teutonic Knights • Casimir IV (Pol) launches war against Teutonic Knights

Edmund, Duke of Somerset, ousts Richard of York as regent of England • The Wars of the Roses (1455–1485) begin between Yorkists (badge a white rose) and Lancastrians (badge a red rose) • King Henry VI's Lancastrian army is defeated at Battle of St. Albans; Duke of Somerset is killed • Richard of York is in power as Lord Protector • Pope Nicholas dies; is succeeded by Calixtus III

Margaret of Anjou, queen-consort of Henry VI (Eng) has Richard of York removed as Henry's chief adviser • Janós Hunyadi (Hung) repels Ottoman Turks from Belgrade, but dies of plague • Navigator Alvise Cadamosto (a Venetian in Portuguese service) discovers Cape Verde Islands • Paolo Uccello (It) paints *Rout of San Romano* • French poet Francois Villon writes *Le Petit Testament*

1460	1461	1462

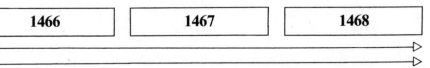

□ Edward IV

In English Wars of the Roses, Yorkists capture Henry VI at Battle of Northampton; Henry recognizes Richard of York as his heir • Queen Margaret's army defeats Yorkists at Wakefield, killing Richard of York • James II (Scot), killed in battle against the English, is succeeded by his son, James III, aged 8 • Swiss Confederation wins Thurgau from Austria • Schleswig and Holstein are united under Danish crown

Edward of York (Richard's son) defeats Lancastrians at Mortimer's Cross • London proclaims Edward of York king as Edward IV (House of York rules to 1485) • Second Battle of St. Albans: Lancastrians recapture Henry VI • Edward of York wins Battle of Towton • Charles VII (Fr) dies; is succeeded by his son Louis XI, the Spider • Andrea Mantegna (It) paints *Agony in the Garden*

Richard Neville, Earl of Warwick ("Warwick the Kingmaker") crushes Lancastrian resistance in northern England, 1462–1464 • Vasili II, Grand Prince of Moscow dies; is succeeded by his son, Ivan III, the Great • Castile (Sp) captures Gibraltar • Pope Pius II rejects Basel compact with Hussites • Friedrich III (Ger) abandons his claims to Hungarian throne

1466	1467	1468

Earl of Warwick loses influence with Edward IV (Eng) • Lord Boyd kidnaps boy-king James III (Scot) and rules Scotland as governor, with parliamentary backing • Louis XI (Fr) reoccupies Normandy • Georg Podiebrad's Bohemian Hussites war with Catholics, claiming Matthias Corvinus (Hung) as king • Second Peace of Thorn: Poland wins West Prussia; Teutonic Knights keep East Prussia

Philippe the Good dies; is succeeded as Duke of Burgundy by Charles the Bold • Warlords Yamana Mochitoyo and Hosokawa Katsumoto embroil Japanese feudal nobility in the Onin War • Dieric Bouts (Neth) paints *Five Mystic Meals* • Maya-Toltec civilization is in decline in Central America • So-called Regressive Pueblo (Pueblo IV) period continues in North America

Charles the Bold of Burgundy weds Margaret of York, cementing Anglo-Burgundian alliance • Louis XI (Fr) invades Brittany • Charles briefly imprisons Louis for supposed role in a Flemish revolt • Estates General (French parliament) holds its only meeting of Louis' reign • Pope Paul II declares King Georg Podiebrad of Bohemia deposed and supports claim by King Matthias Corvinus (Hung)

1469	1470	1471

ENGLAND—**Edward IV** ———————————□ **Henry VI** ———————————□ **Edward IV** ———

HOLY ROMAN EMPIRE—**Friedrich III** ————————————————————————————

In England, Earl of Warwick and George, Duke of Clarence (brother of Edward IV), foment risings against Edward, who defeats them; Warwick and Clarence flee to France • In Spain, Isabel, heiress to Castile, weds Fernando, heir to Aragon • Andrea del Verrocchio (It) produces his bronze *David* • Lorenzo de' Medici succeeds his father, Piero, as ruler of Florence (It)

Lancastrians led by Earl of Warwick invade England; Edward IV flees to Flanders and Warwick restores Henry VI to the throne • Louis XI (Fr) forms an alliance with the Swiss cantons • Leon Alberti (It) designs the Church of St. Andrea, Mantua • Turks win Euboea from Venice • Explorer João de Santarem (Port) reaches Mina, on West Africa's Gold Coast

Earl of Warwick (Eng) defeated and killed by army led by Edward IV at Battle of Barnet; Edward finally crushes Lancastrians at Tewkesbury • Henry VI is deposed and murdered • Burgundians invade Normandy • Portuguese win Tangier from the Moors • Pope Paul II dies; succeeded by Sixtus IV • King Georg Podiebrad of Bohemia dies; is succeeded by Ladislas II, son of the king of Poland

1475	1476	1477

ENGLAND—**Edward IV** ————————————————————————————————————

HOLY ROMAN EMPIRE—**Friedrich III** ————————————————————————————

English army under Edward IV invades France; but Edward is bought off by Louis XI (Treaty of Picquigny) and a trade agreement follows • France makes peace with Burgundy and Brittany • Charles the Bold (Burgundy) gains Nancy (Fr) • Pazzi family handle papal revenues after the Medicis break with Pope Sixtus IV • University of Buda (Hung) is founded

William Caxton (Eng) starts printing in London • Charles the Bold (Burgundy) overruns Lorraine, but is defeated by Swiss at Grandson and at Mornt, and loses Nancy • Fernando of Aragon defeats Portuguese in Battle of Toro • Sandro Botticelli (It) paints *Adoration of the Magi* • Galeazzo Maria Sforza, ruler of Milan (It) is assassinated; succeeded by son Gian Galeazzo II

Charles the Bold (Burgundy) is killed by Swiss at Nancy (end of Burgundian rule) • Charles the Bold's heiress Mary marries Austrian archduke Maximilian (later Emperor Maximilian I) • Hans Memlinc (Flem) paints *Donne Triptych* • Turks reach edge of Venetian territory • Japan's Onin War ends • Sandro Botticelli (It) paints *Primavera* • William Caxton (Eng) prints Chaucer's *Canterbury Tales*

1481	1482	1483

ENGLAND—**Edward IV** ———————————————————————□ **Edward V**—□ **Richard III** —

HOLY ROMAN EMPIRE—**Friedrich III** ————————————————————————————

Louis XI (Fr) annexes Maine and Provence • Afonso V (Port) dies; is succeeded by son Joao II, who promotes exploration • Sandro Botticelli, Domenico Ghirlandaio and Pietro Perugino (It) contract to paint frescoes for the Sistine Chapel, Rome • Leonardo da Vinci (It) is commissioned to paint *Adoration of the Magi* • Swiss Confederation admits Solothurn and Fribourg

Concordat limits papal power over the Spanish Church • Forces of Pope Sixtus IV and Venice attack Ferrara (It) • Through the peace of Arras, Louis XI (Fr) gets Burgundy, Picardy, Boulonnais, Franche-Comté and Artois; Austrians keep Netherlands • Filippino Lippi (It) paints *Madonna Kneeling Before the Child* • Sandro Botticelli (It), paints *Madonna of the Pomegranate*

Louis XI (Fr) repudiates Treaty of Picquigny with England (signed 1475) . • Edward IV (Eng) dies; is succeeded by his son Edward V, aged 12, under guardianship of his uncle Richard, Duke of Gloucester; in mysterious circumstances Edward is deposed and Richard III becomes king • Edward V and his younger brother are murdered • Louis XI (Fr) dies; is succeeded by son Charles VIII

| 1472 | 1473 | 1474 |

Scotland gains Orkney and Shetland islands from Norway in compensation for non-payment of dowry of Margaret of Denmark, who had married James III • Hans Memlinc (Flem) paints *Last Judgment* altarpiece • Leonardo da Vinci (It) joins painters' guild in Florence • Ivan III (Russ) weds Zoë, niece of last Byzantine emperor • Explorer Ruy de Sequeira (Port) crosses the Equator off West Africa

Charles the Bold (Burgundy) acquires Gelderland and occupies Alsace and Lorraine • Building of Sistine Chapel, Rome, is begun • Sandro Botticelli (It) paints *St. Sebastian* • Leonardo da Vinci (It) paints *The Annunciation* • Armenia, Azerbaijan, Iran and Kurdistan under Turkoman rule of Uzun Hasan • Yamana Mochitoyo and Hosokawa Katsumoto die but Japan's Onin War continues

English king Edward IV, in league with Burgundy, prepares to invade France • England makes trade treaty with Hanseatic League • Swiss, south German cities, Louis XI of France, and German emperor Friedrich III combine forces against Burgundy • Isabel becomes queen of Castile on death of her stepbrother, Enriques IV • Andrea Mantegna (It) finishes painting his frescoes of *Camera degli Sposi,* Mantua

| 1478 | 1479 | 1480 |

Edward IV (Eng) executes his rebellious brother Edmund, Duke of Clarence • The Inquisition is established in Spain • Pazzi Conspiracy (It) against the Medici family leads to war between Florence and Naples • Swiss defeat Milanese • Ivan III (Russ) conquers city of Novgorod • Peace of Olomouc: King Mathias Corvinus (Hung) recognizes Ladislas II as King of Bohemia

Fernando II, husband of Isabel of Castile, inherits Aragon; Christian Spain is united under their joint rule as the "Catholic Kings" • Hans Memlinc (Flem) paints *Mystic Marriage of St. Catherine* • Lorenzo de' Medici visits Naples to seek peace • Venice loses war with Turkey, ceding Scutari • Copenhagen University is founded

René of Anjou, titular king of Naples, dies; Louis XI (Fr) annexes Anjou and part of Bar • Lorenzo de' Medici secures peace in Italy • Domenico Ghirlandaio (It) paints fresco *St. Jerome* • Hans Memlinc (Flem) paints *Madonna and Child with Angels* • Giovanni Bellini (It) paints *St. Francis in Ecstasy* • Ivan III (Russ) ends Tatar overlordship of Muscovy • Turks take Otranto (It), and besiege Rhodes

| 1484 | 1485 | 1486 |

□ Henry VII

Richard III (Eng) loses his only son, Edward • Sir Thomas Malory's *Morte d'Arthur* is printed by William Caxton • Pope Sixtus IV dies; is succeeded by Innocent VIII • Venetian war with Ferrara ends • Diogo Cão (Port) reaches Cape Cross in southwestern Africa • Christopher Columbus (It) unsuccessfully asks João II (Port) to back a westward voyage to the Indies

Henry Tudor, Earl of Richmond, Lancastrian claimant to the English throne, defeats and kills Richard III at Bosworth; end of Wars of Roses • Richmond becomes Henry VII, founding House of Tudor (1485–1603) • King Matthias Corvinus (Hung) invades Austria and drives Emperor Friedrich III from Vienna • Ivan III (Russ) takes Tver (modern Kalinin)

English King Henry VII marries Elizabeth of York, eldest daughter of Edward IV, ending succession dispute • Cardinal Morton becomes Archbishop of Canterbury (Eng) • Sandro Botticelli (It) paints *Birth of Venus* and *Madonna with the Two St. Johns* • Maximilian, son of German emperor Friedrick III, is elected King of the Romans—i.e. heir to the Empire • Fernando and Isabel (Sp) refuse cash for Christopher Columbus's proposed voyage

1487 | 1488 | 1489

ENGLAND—**Henry VII**

HOLY ROMAN EMPIRE—**Friedrich III**

Politics and Wars

Henry VII (Eng) establishes Star Chamber administrative court; power of the throne increases • Lambert Simnel, pretended Earl of Warwick, backed by John de la Pole, Earl of Lincoln, invades England from Ireland supported by Irish chiefs and German mercenaries • Henry VII defeats Simnel at Stoke and makes him a kitchenhand • Aztec expansion in Mexico is boosted under rule of Ahuitzotl (1486–1502)

Science and Discovery

João II (Port) sends explorer Pedro de Covilha to Ethiopia and India via Egypt and Aden, and Bartolomeu Dias to seek the same places via southern Africa

Politics and Wars

Members of Japan's Ikko (True Pure Land) Sect kill a feudal lord in the first of many rebellions • Duke of Brittany dies; France's bid to obtain Brittany antagonises England, Spain and the Holy Roman Empire • James III (Scot) is defeated in battle at Sauchieburn by rebellious nobles, and murdered • England and Scotland agree a truce

Arts and Letters

PAINTING: Hieronymus Bosch (Neth) is active

Science and Discovery

Bartholomeu Dias (Port) rounds Cape of Good Hope and reaches Great Fish River, South Africa

Politics and Wars

Henry VII (Eng) agrees the Treaty of Dordrecht with Friedrich III (Ger) • England makes an alliance with Brittany • Venice acquires Cyprus from the widow of James of Lusignan • Jem, the captured brother of Ottoman sultan Bayazid II, falls into the hands of Pope Innocent VIII • Ottoman Turks war with Egypt Cilicia, southeastern Turkey (1485–1491) • Ivan III (Russ) seizes Novgorod's last colony, Khylnov (modern Kirov)

Arts and Letters

LITERATURE: Philippe de Commines (Fr), *Mémoires*, best critical history since classical times

1493 | 1494 | 1495

ENGLAND—**Henry VII**

HOLY ROMAN EMPIRE—**Maximilian I**

Politics and Wars

England and Flanders engaged in a trade war • German emperor Friedrich III dies; is succeeded by his son Maximilian I • Under Askia Muhammad (1493–1529) the Songhoy Empire in Western Africa absorbs most of Manding Empire and expands east of Niger River • Pope Alexander VI fixes boundary between Portuguese and Spanish spheres of interest at 100 leagues west of Cape Verde Islands • France and the Holy Roman Empire agree Treaty of Senlis

Science and Discovery

On second voyage of discovery, Christopher Columbus (It) discovers Guadeloupe and Puerto Rico, and founds city of Isabela, on Hispaniola

Politics and Wars

Ferrante (Ferdinand I) of Naples dies; Charles VIII (Fr) invades Italy to claim Naples • Reformer Girolamo Savonarola starts democratic government in Florence (It) • Ivan III (Russ) crushes the Hanseatic League's center in Novgorod • Treaty of Tordesillas moves boundary between spheres of Spanish and Portuguese colonial interest further west, enabling Portugal to claim Brazil • Statute of Drogheda states terms of Ireland's political subordination to England

Science and Discovery

Christopher Columbus (It) discovers Jamaica during his second voyage of exploration

Politics and Wars

Perkin Warbeck, Flemish imposter claiming the English throne, lands in Scotland • Holy League (the Emperor, the Pope, Milan, Spain and Venice) is formed to protect Italy from French ambition • Army of French king Charles VIII enters Naples • Holy League defeats French forces at Fornovo (It), forcing Charles VIII back to France

Arts and Letters

PAINTINGS: Perugino (It), *Pietà;* Bernardino Pintorrichio (It), Borgia apartments frescoes in the Vatican; MUSIC: sackbuts (early trombones) are in use; OTHER: contact with Italy stimulates Renaissance (revival of learning) in France

1490

Politics and Wars
Anglo-Dutch treaty is agreed • Matthias Corvinus (Hung), most powerful ruler in central Europe, dies; the ineffectual Ladislas II of Bohemia is elected to succeed him • Chief Changamir founds an independent Shona state in the region of present-day Bulawayo

Arts and Letters
PAINTING: Domenico Ghirlandaio (It), fresco *Zaccharias and the Angel*; Andrea Mantegna (It), *Triumphs of Caesar*

Science and Discovery
Portuguese explorers travel 200 miles (320 km) up the Congo (Zaïre) River through the so-called kingdom of Kongo, and establish relations with its king in his capital, Mbanza

1491

Politics and Wars
England and Scotland agree a 5-year truce • Charles VIII (Fr) weds Anne, heiress of Brittany, thereby uniting Brittany with France and provoking war with England • Ladislas II of Bohemia (Laszlo VI of Hungary) agrees Treaty of Pressburg, acknowledging the Habsburg family's right to succeed him

Arts and Letters
PAINTING: Domenico Ghirlandaio (It), fresco *Birth of the Virgin*, Church of St. Maria Novella, Florence

Religion and Philosophy
Girolama Savonarola (It), reforming preacher, becomes prior of St. Mark's Florence

1492

Politics and Wars
Perkin Warbeck, a Flemish lad, impersonates Edward V's murdered brother Richard, Duke of York • Capture of Granada from the Moors completes the Christian conquest of Spain • Spain expels Jews • Lorenzo de' Medici dies; is succeeded in Florence by his son Piero the Unfortunate • Christopher Columbus (It) wins the support of Isabel of Spain for a westward voyage to the Indies; he finds Bahamas, Cuba and Hispaniola, believing them to be near Japan • France and England sign the Peace of Etaples

Religion and Philosophy
Pope Innocent VIII dies; is succeeded by the worldly Rodrigo Borgia as Alexander VI

1496

Politics and Wars
England joins the Holy League • Bartholomew Columbus (It) transfers Isabela settlement from original location to Santo Domingo in southern Hispaniola • James IV of Scotland invades England • Intercursus Magnus treaty is signed between England and Burgundy • Philipp the Handsome, son of Emperor Maximilian I (Ger), weds Juana, heiress to Castile

Arts and Letters
PAINTING: Perugino (It), *Crucifixion with Saints*

Science and Discovery
Christopher Columbus (It) completes his second voyage to the west

1497

Politics and Wars
Flemish imposter Perkin Warbeck lands in Cornwall to claim throne of England; the rising is crushed and Warbeck is captured • England makes peace with Scotland • Turkoman ruler Rustam Shah dies, leaving Persia in turmoil • Denmark defeats Sweden in Battle of Brunkenberg

Arts and Letters
PAINTING: Leonardo da Vinci (It), *The Last Supper*

Science and Discovery
Vasco da Gama (Port) rounds Cape of Good Hope, bound for India • John Cabot (It), sailing from England, discovers Newfoundland • Amerigo Vespucci (It) claims to have discovered the Gulf of Mexico

1498

Politics and Wars
Charles VIII (Fr) dies; is succeeded by his distant cousin Louis XII

Arts and Letters
PAINTING: Sandro Botticelli (It), *Calumny of Apelles*; WOODCUT: Albrecht Dürer (Ger), *Apocalypse*; SCULPTURE: Michelangelo Buonarroti (It), *Pietà*

Science and Discovery
Explorer Vasco da Gama (Port) reaches East Africa and India • Christopher Columbus (It) on a third voyage of discovery reaches Trinidad

Religion and Philosophy
Reformer Domenico Savonarola (It) is burned in Florence for heresy

1499 · 1500 · 1501

ENGLAND—**Henry VII**

HOLY ROMAN EMPIRE—**Maximilian I**

1499

Politics and Wars
Treaty allows English cloth duty-free into all Burgundian lands except Flanders • Imposter Perkin Warbeck, claimant to English throne, tries to escape from prison and is executed • Swiss defeat Emperor Maximilian I (Ger) at Dornach and force Treaty of Basel by which Swiss Confederation is effectively independent

Arts and Letters
DRAWING: Albrecht Dürer (Ger), 7 *Great Passion* woodcuts

Science and Discovery
Explorers Alonso de Ojeda (Sp) and Amerigo Vespucci (It) discover the Guianas and Venezuela

1500

Politics and Wars
Hungary and Turkey are at war • Sweden rebels against Danish rule • Christopher Columbus (It) is relieved of governorship of Hispaniola, for incompetence, on orders from Fernando and Isabel of Spain • Columbus is sent back to Spain in chains, but is freed and pardoned

Arts and Letters
PAINTING: Sandro Botticelli (It), *Mystic Nativity* • Giovanni Bellini (It), *Madonna and Child in a Landscape*

Science and Discovery
Portuguese navigator Pedro Cabral reaches Brazil • Vicente Pinzón (Sp) explores Brazilian coast • Diego Diaz (Port) discovers Madagascar

1501

Politics and Wars
Arthur, heir of Henry VII (Eng) weds Spanish princess Catherine of Aragon • Swiss Confederation absorbs Basel and Schaffhausen • French forces enter Rome and conquer Naples

Arts and Letters
PAINTING: Giovanni Bellini (It), *Doge Loredano;* ARCHITECTURE: Palace of Holyroodhouse, Edinburgh, built

Science and Discovery
Vasco da Gama (Port) sets out to cut Arabs' Red Sea trade route • Gaspar de Corte Real (Port) explores Labrador

Social and Economic
First African slaves are transported to the West Indies

1505 · 1506 · 1507

ENGLAND—**Henry VII**

HOLY ROMAN EMPIRE—**Maximilian I**

1505

Politics and Wars
Francisco de Almeida (Port) is made first governor of the Portuguese Indies • Portuguese take Mombasa and burn Kilwa, Arab trading centers on East African coast

Arts and Letters
PAINTING: Gentile Bellini (It), commission for *St. Mark Preaching at Alexandria;* Raphael (It), *St. George and the Dragon;* Mathias Grünewald (Ger), *Crucifixion;* ARCHITECTURE: Building of Archangel Cathedral, Moscow, begins

Science and Discovery
Portuguese explorers discover Mauritius

1506

Politics and Wars
English merchants gain control of Flemish cloth trade • Juana, daughter of Fernando and Isabel of Spain, and her husband Philippe of Burgundy, Archduke of Austria, enter Spain to claim Juana's inheritance, Castile • Philippe of Burgundy (Felipe I of Spain) dies, and Juana becomes insane; Fernando continues ruling Castile • Christian son of King Hans (Den), becomes regent of Norway

Arts and Letters
PAINTING: Raphael (It) *Ansidei Madonna;* LITERATURE: William Dunbar (Scot), poem *Dance of the Sevin Deidly Synnis*

1507

Politics and Wars
Empire of Kanem-Bornu expands in Western Africa • Portuguese set up trading posts in Mozambique • Portuguese traders are established at Hormuz Island, Persian Gulf

Arts and Letters
PAINTING: Giorgione (It) *The Three Philosophers;* Raphael (It) *Entombment*

Science and Discovery
Geographer Martin Waldseemüller (Ger) produces map of the known world showing South America, which he names for explorer Amerigo Vespucci (It)

Religion and Philosophy
Pope Julius II authorizes sale of indulgences to help pay for St. Peter's Basilica, Rome

1502

1503

1504

Politics and Wars
Castile expels Moors • Scottish king James IV marries Margaret, daughter of Henry VII (Eng) • France and Spain are at war over Naples • Shah Ismail founds Persia's Safavid Dynasty and establishes Shi'ism faith in Persia

Arts and Letters
WOODCUT: Albrecht Dürer (Ger), *Great Fortune*

Science and Discovery
Christopher Columbus (It) starts his fourth voyage to the West, and explores coast of Honduras • Amerigo Vespucci (It) explores coast of Brazil

Social and Economic
Last year chronicled in *Mendoza Codex* (pictorial Aztec history)

Politics and Wars
Casa de Contratación (colonial office) is founded at Seville (Sp) to help control colonial trade • Spaniards retake Naples and defeat French at Garigliano (It) • Portugese build first European fort in India, at Cochin

Arts and Letters
PAINTING: Leonardo da Vinci (It), *Battle of Anghiari;* SCULPTURE: Michelangelo Buonarroti (It), *David*

Religion and Philosophy
Pope Alexander VI dies; succeeded by Pius III, who dies within a few weeks; succeeded by Julius II, creator of the Papal States • Dutch humanist Desiderius Erasmus writes a guide to Christian faith

Politics and Wars
France and the Empire make peace by the Treaty of Blois • Treaty of Lyon: France hands Naples to Spain • Isabel of Castile dies: Fernando of Aragon rules Castile on behalf of his daughter, Juana, who shows signs of insanity

Arts and Letters
PAINTING: Leonardo da Vinci (It), *Mona Lisa*; Raphael (It), *Marriage of the Virgin;* WOODCUT: Albrecht Dürer (Ger), *Adam and Eve*

Science and Discovery
Christopher Columbus (It) returns to Spain from his last voyage, having reached Panama

Social and Economic
England mints first shilling

1508

1509

1510

—□ Henry VIII —————————————▷

Politics and Wars
France and the Holy Roman Empire found League of Cambrai against Venice • Persia seizes Iraq

Arts and Letters
PAINTING: Michelangelo Buonarroti (It) begins Sistine Chapel ceiling: Giorgione (It) *The Tempest* (first landscape of mood); Raphael (It), 'Cowper' *Madonna*

Science and Discovery
Vicente Pinzon (Sp) explores coast from Honduras to easternmost tip of Brazil

Religion and Philosophy
Martin Luther (Ger) becomes professor of divinity at Wittenberg

Politics and Wars
Portuguese defeat Muslims at Diu, Western India, and dominate Indian seas • Afonso de Albuquerque, founder of Portugal's Asian empire, becomes governor of the Portuguese Indies • Henry VII (Eng) dies; succeeded by son, Henry VIII • Henry VIII marries Catherine of Aragon, widow of his brother Arthur

Arts and Letters
LITERATURE: Dutch humanist Desiderius Erasmus, satire *Encomium Moriae*

Science and Discovery
Diego Lopez de Sequira (Port) circumnavigates Sumatra • Alonso de Ojen (Sp) establishes city of San Sebastián in Colombia

Politics and Wars
Henry VIII (Eng) is granted tunnage and poundage taxes by parliament • Pope Julius II abandons League of Cambrai and joins Venice • Aragon becomes neutral • Portuguese capture Goa (India), making it their capital in Asia

Arts and Letters
PAINTING: Giorgione (It) *The Adoration of The Shepherds*; Hieronymous Bosch (Neth), *Hell*

Science and Discovery
Vasco Nuñez de Balboa (Sp) founds Darién on Isthmus of Darién (now Panama)

1511 | 1512 | 1513

ENGLAND—**Henry VIII**
HOLY ROMAN EMPIRE—**Maximilian I**

1511

Politics and Wars
Portuguese capture Malacca, in Malaya • Spanish conquest of Puerto Rico is completed • Adventurer Diego Velázquez (Sp) conquers Cuba • Holy League, renewed to protect Italy from French, involves Papacy, Spain, Venice and Swiss cantons

Arts and Letters
PAINTING: Titian (It), frescoes in Padua; Piero di Cosimo (It), *Triumph of Death*; Raphael (It) completes frescoes for the Stanza della Segnatura; Albrecht Dürer (Ger), *Reunion of the Saints*

Science and Discovery
Francisco Serrano (Port) visits Java and other islands

1512

Politics and Wars
Government in Holy Roman Empire is partly reorganized by Diet of Köln (Ger) • England joins the Holy League against France • Spanish forces conquer Navarre, which is added to Castile • Medicis are restored to power in Florence (It)

Arts and Letters
PAINTING: Michelangelo Buonarroti (It) completes Sistine Chapel ceiling frescoes; Albrecht Dürer (Ger), *Madonna and Child*

Science and Discovery
Juan Ponce de León (Sp) discovers Florida

Religion and Philosophy
Pope Julius II calls Fifth Lateran Council

1513

Politics and Wars
Armies of Henry VIII (Eng) and Emperor Maximilian (Ger) defeat French at Battle of the Spurs in Artois • James IV (Scot) is killed at Flodden Field in defeat of his army invading England; he is succeeded by his son James V, aged 2

Arts and Letters
PAINTING: Raphael (It), *Sistine Madonna*; LITERATURE: Niccoló Machiavelli (It), *Il Principe*

Science and Discovery
Jorge Alvarez (Port) reaches Canton (China) • Vasco Núñez de Balboa (Sp) crosses Darién (Panama) and sights Pacific Ocean

Religion and Philosophy
Pope Julius II dies; is succeeded by Leo X, a Medici

1517 | 1518 | 1519

ENGLAND—**Henry VIII**
HOLY ROMAN EMPIRE—**Maximilian I** ☐ **Karl V**

1517

Politics and Wars
Ottoman Turks conquer Egypt and end independent Mameluke rule

Arts and Letters
PAINTING: Andrea del Sarto (It), *Madonna del Arpie*; Hans Holbein the Elder (Ger), *St. Sebastian Altar*

Science and Discovery
Francisco Hernandez de Córdoba (Sp) discovers Yucatán (Mex) • Vasco Núñez de Balboa (Spanish explorer) is beheaded for treason ,

Religion and Philosophy
Priest Martin Luther (Ger) launches the Reformation by protesting against sale of indulgences • Cardinal Wolsey is made Papal Legate to England

1518

Politics and Wars
France buys city of Tournai (now in Belgium) from England for 600,000 crowns • Hernán Cortés (Spanish conquistador) leads expedition of 600 men against Aztecs in Mexico

Arts and Letters
PAINTING: Titian (It), *The Assumption,* for Frari Church, Venice; Antonio Correggio (It), first frescoes for Camera di St. Paolo, Parma; Raphael (It), *The Holy Family*

Religion and Philosophy
Ulrich Zwingli establishes Reformation of the Church in Switzerland • Reformer Martin Luther (Ger), questioned by Cardinal Cajetan at Augsburg, refuses to recant • Reformation is established in Poland

1519

Politics and Wars
Conquistador Hernan Cortés (Sp) penetrates Mexico, enters Aztec capital Tenochtitlán, and takes Aztec emperor Montezuma II prisoner • Maximilian I (Ger) dies; is succeeded as Holy Roman Emperor by his grandson Karl V (Carlos I of Spain), uniting Austrian and Spanish Habsburg territories

Science and Discovery
Alvárez Pineda (Sp) completes exploration of Gulf of Mexico • Ferdinand Magellan (Port) in Spanish service, begins first attempt to sail around the world

Social and Economic
Panama City founded • Havana (Cuba) founded

1514

Politics and Wars
England makes peace with France and Scotland; England gets Tournai from France • Louis XII (Fr) marries Henry VIII's sister Mary (Mary of France) • Pedro Arias de Avila (Sp) becomes governor of Darien, (Panama) Central America

Arts and Letters
PAINTING: Andrea del Sarto (It), fresco *Birth of the Virgin;* Raphael (It), frescoes for the Stanza d'Elidoro • Lucas Cranach (Ger), *Henry the Pious of Saxony* and *Duchess;* Titian (It), *The Tribute Money*

1515

Politics and Wars
Thomas Wolsey (Eng) becomes Cardinal, Archbishop of York and Chancellor of England • Louis XII (Fr) dies; is succeeded by his distant cousin François I • French defeat Swiss at Marignano (It) and retake Milan • French and Swiss sign Treaty of Geneva

Arts and Letters
PAINTING: Leonardo da Vinci (It), *St John;* Mathias Grünewald (Ger) *Isenheim Altar;* ARCHITECTURE: Michelangelo Buonarroti (It), façade of St. Lorenzo, Florence

1516

Politics and Wars
Ottoman Turks conquer Syria • France and Papacy agree Concordat of Bologna • Fernando of Aragon dies; is succeeded by grandson Carlos I, ruling Spain, Burgundy, Netherlands, Spanish America and Sicily

Arts and Letters
PAINTING: Hans Holbein the Younger (Ger), *Burgomaster Meyer and His Wife;* SCULPTURE: Michelangelo Buonarroti (It), *Moses;* LITERATURE: Thomas More (Eng), *Utopia;* Ludovico Ariosto (It), epic poem *Orlando Furioso*

Religion and Philosophy
Scholar Desiderius Erasmus (Neth) publishes new edition of the New Testament

1520

Politics and Wars
Henry VIII (Eng) meets François I (Fr) at the Field of the Cloth of Gold (Fr) • Henry VIII and Karl V (Ger) make anti-French Treaty of Calais • Gustavus Vasa (Swe) leads a revolt against Christian II (Den) • Suleiman I becomes sultan of Ottoman Empire • Aztects oust Spaniards from Tenochtitlán (Mex), but their emperor Montezuma II is killed

Arts and Letters
PAINTING: Titian (It), *Bacchanalia;* ARCHITECTURE: Michelangelo Buonarroti (It), Medici tombs, Florence; ENGRAVING: Lucas Cranach (Ger), portrait *Martin Luther*

1521

Politics and Wars
Turks capture Belgrade • François I (Fr) and Karl V (Ger) are at war, 1521–1529

Science and Discovery
Francisco de Gordillo (Sp) explores coast of North America northward to South Carolina • Ferdinand Magellan (Port) discovers Philippines, where he is killed • Hernán Cortés (Sp) destroys Tenochtitlán (refounded as Mexico City)

Religion and Philosophy
Anabaptists founded in Germany • Diet of Worms (Ger) condemns reformer Martin Luther • Luther translates the Bible into German • Pope Leo X grants Henry VIII (Eng) title "Defender of the Faith" • Leo excommunicates Luther, then dies

1522

Politics and Wars
Habsburg empire is partitioned: Karl V entrusts Germany to his brother Ferdinand • France loses Milan and Genoa

Arts and Letters
PAINTING: Hans Holbein the Younger (Ger), *Solothurn Madonna;* Antonio Correggio (It), nativity scene *Night;* Titian (It) *Bacchus and Ariadne*

Science and Discovery
Circumnavigation of the globe, begun under Ferdinand Magellan's leadership, is completed by crew under Sebastian del Cano (Sp) • Spanish explorers reach Peru

Religion and Philosophy
Adrian Boeyens (Neth) becomes Pope Adrian VI—last non-Italian Pope

1523	1524	1525

ENGLAND—**Henry VIII**
HOLY ROMAN EMPIRE—**Karl V**

Politics and Wars
England and Holy Roman Empire are at war with France • Charles, Duke of Bourbon, in service of the Empire, invades France • Gustavus Vasa becomes King of Sweden, founding House of Vasa

Arts and Letters
PAINTING: Hans Holbein the Younger (Ger), *Erasmus*; Albrecht Altdorfer (Ger), *Nativity*, on wood; Titian (It) *Entombment of Christ*; Perugino (It), *Adoration of the Shepherds*; LITERATURE: Hans Sachs (Ger), poem *The Wittenberg Nightingale* about Luther

Religion and Philosophy
Pope Adrian VI dies; is succeeded by Clement VII, a Medici

Politics and Wars
France recaptures Milan • Peasants' War, rebellion by peasants against their overlords' injustices, begins in Germany • Spaniards subdue Mexico, Salvador and Honduras

Arts and Letters
DRAWING: Hans Holbein the Younger (Ger), *Dance of Death* and *Alphabet of Death*

Science and Discovery
In French service, Giovanni de Verrazzano (It) discovers New York Bay and Hudson River

Religion and Philosophy
First Lutheran hymnbook appears

Politics and Wars
Peasants' War in Germany ends in peasants' defeat • England and France make peace • Karl V defeats French forces at Pavia (It) and captures François I (Fr).

Arts and Letters
PAINTING: Andrea del Sarto (It), fresco *Madonna del Sacco*; Albrecht Altdorfer (Ger), *Virgin and Child in Glory*

Religion and Philosophy
Matteo di Bassi (It) founds Capuchin Order • Lutheranism grows in Denmark

Science and Discovery
Santa Maria, oldest city in Columbia, and Trojillo, Honduras, are founded

1529	1530	1531

ENGLAND—**Henry VIII**
HOLY ROMAN EMPIRE—**Karl V**

Politics and Wars
Sir Thomas More is appointed Chancellor of England by Henry VIII; Thomas Wolsey loses all his offices except Archbishopric of York • Treaty of Barcelona formally restores Papal States • Peace of Cambrai between France and Holy Roman Empire: the Empire renounces claims to Burgundy, while France renounces claim to Naples and Flanders; Venice loses conquests

Arts and Letters
PAINTING: Albrecht Altdorfer (Ger), *The Battle of Arbela*; Andrea del Sarto (It), *The Holy Family*

Politics and Wars
Karl V is crowned Holy Roman Emperor at Bologna (It) by Pope Clement VII—last such coronation • Thomas Wolsey (Eng) dies in disgrace • François I (Fr) weds Eleanor of Austria, sister of Karl V • Medicis regain power in Florence • Karl V gives Malta to Knights of St. John

Arts and Letters
PAINTING: Michelangelo Buonarroti (It), *Leda and the Swan* (now lost); SCULPTURE, Michelangelo, *The Virgin and the Child Jesus*

Religion and Philosophy
Philip Melanchthon (Ger) states Protestant standpoint in "Confession of Augsburg"

Politics and Wars
Schmalkaldic League—a defensive alliance—is formed at Schmalkalden (now in East Germany) by Protestant princes and cities of the Holy Roman Empire • Karl V's brother Ferdinand is elected king of Rome • Swiss Confederation is split by War of the Catholic Cantons; Zürich is defeated and reformer Huldrich Zwingli is killed in Battle of Kappel

Arts and Letters
PAINTING: Lucas van Leyden (Neth), triptych *Blind Man of Jericho Healed by Jesus Christ*

Science and Discovery
Francisco Pizarro (Sp) with 180 men sets out for Peru

1526

Politics and Wars
François I (Fr) is released by Karl V (Ger) after signing Treaty of Madrid under duress • Holy Roman Empire is at war with Ottoman Turks (to 1532) • Turks kill Lajos II of Hungary (Ludwig of Bohemia) at Mohács • Ferdinand (Ger) is elected king of Bohemia • Ferdinand and John Zápolya, king of Hungary, fight over Hungary • Mongol leader Babar wins Battle of Panipat and founds Mogul empire in India

Religion and Philosophy
William Tyndale's English translation of the New Testament is printed • Lutheranism becomes established in Sweden

1527

Politics and Wars
Florence drives out the Medicis and forms a republic • Henry VIII (Eng) asks the Pope to annul his marriage to Catherine of Aragon • Treaty of Amiens creates Anglo-French alliance • Troops of the Holy Roman Empire sack Rome, ending its Renaissance greatness • England ends Anglo-Spanish alliance

Arts and Letters
PAINTING: Antonio Correggio (It), *Day,* depicting St. Jerome; Hans Holbein the Younger (Ger), *Thomas More*; Titian (It), *Venus of Urbino*

Science and Discovery
Jorge de Menezes (Port) lands on New Guinea

1528

Politics and Wars
England is at war with Holy Roman Empire • 5 Swiss cantons including Basel and Bern embrace the Reformation; 7 stay Catholic • Welsers (Ger bankers) colonize northwest Venezuela • Spanish colony in Carolinas is abandoned • Navigator Pánfilo de Nárvaez (Sp) lands colonists in Florida

Arts and Letters
PAINTING: Hans Holbein the Younger (Ger), *The Artist's Family*; LITERATURE, Baldassare Castiglione (It), *Il Libro del Cortegiano*, a courtier's handbook; ARCHITECTURE: Michelangelo Buonarrotti (It), designs fortifications for Florence; building of Granada Cathedral (Sp) is begun

1532

Politics and Wars
Henry VIII (Eng) curbs bishops' cash payments to the papacy • Sir Thomas More resigns as English Chancellor • Henry VIII sends theologian Thomas Cranmer to Rome and to German Emperor Karl V, to argue for the annulment of Henry's marriage to Catherine of Aragon • Ottoman invasion of Hungary is halted

Arts and Letters
PAINTING: Hans Holbein the Younger (Ger), *Noli Me Tangere*; Antonio Correggio (It), *Leda and the Swan*; LITERATURE: François Rabelais (Fr), *Pantagruel*

Science and Discovery
Francisco Pizarro (Sp) penetrates Peru and captures Inca emperor Atahualpa

1533

Politics and Wars
Henry VIII (Eng) secretly marries Anne Boleyn and is excommunicated by Pope Clement VII • Ivan IV, the Terrible, accedes to Russian throne at age of 3 • Peace settlement between Ferdinand I (Hung) and Suleiman (Turk) • Death of Frederick I of Denmark precipitates civil war

Arts and Letters
PAINTING: Hans Holbein the Younger (Ger), *The Ambassadors*; Titian (It), *Karl V*

Science and Discovery
Regiomontanus (Ger) publishes a treatise on trigonometry

Religion and Philosophy
Thomas Cranmer becomes Archbishop of Canterbury (Eng)

1534

Politics and Wars
Suleiman (Turk) conquers Iraq • Revolutionary Anabaptists gain short-lived control of Münster (Ger)

Arts and Letters
LITERATURE: François Rabelais (Fr) *Gargantua*; Martin Luther (Ger) completes translation of the Bible into German

Science and Discovery
Jacques Cartier (Fr) explores Gulf of St. Lawrence

Religion and Philosophy
Act of Supremacy makes English monarch head of English Church, independent of Rome • Ignatius Loyola (Sp) founds fraternity, (later Jesuits) • Pope Clement VII dies; is succeeded by Paul III

1535

1536

1537

ENGLAND—**Henry VIII** ————————————————————————————
HOLY ROMAN EMPIRE—**Karl V** ————————————————————————

Politics and Wars
German city of Lübeck's failure to regain commercial control of Scandinavian ports puts an end to Hanseatic League • Milan comes under direct Spanish rule following death of last member of ruling Sforza family

Science and Discovery
Niccoló Tartaglia (It) produces a solution of the quadratic equation

Religion and Philosophy
Thomas Cromwell becomes Henry VIII's viceregent for English Church affairs: Thomas More, refusing to take oath of supremacy, is beheaded • Miles Coverdale (Eng), first complete English-language version of the Bible

Politics and Wars
Act of Union unites Wales with England • Dissolution of monasteries and economic grievances provoke insurrection in northern England (Pilgrimage of Grace) • Henry VIII (Eng) has Anne Boleyn executed for treason, and marries Jane Seymour

Arts and Letters
SCULPTURE: Michelangelo Buonarroti (It), figures *Day* and *Night* for Medici Chapel, Florence

Science and Discovery
Jacques Cartier (Fr) sails up St. Lawrence River to region of Montreal, founding French claim to Canada

Politics and Wars
Cosimo de' Medici becomes Duke of Florence • War breaks out between Ottoman Empire and Venice, following Turkish threat to close Strait of Otranto • France joins Turks in abortive siege of Corfu • Robert Aske (Eng) leader of Pilgrimage of Grace rebellion, is executed

Arts and Letters
PAINTING: Hans Holbein the Younger (Ger), *Jane Seymour*

Science and Discovery
Niccoló Tartaglia (It) founds modern science of ballistics in *Nuova Scienzia* • First dictionary of science published in Bohemia

1541

1542

1543

ENGLAND—**Henry VIII** ————————————————————————————
HOLY ROMAN EMPIRE—**Karl V** ————————————————————————

Politics and Wars
Ottoman Turks complete conquest of Hungary • Karl V (Ger) launches unsuccessful attack on Algiers • Henry VIII (Eng) adopts title 'King of Ireland

Arts and Letters
PAINTING: Michelangelo Buonarroti (It), *The Last Judgment*

Science and Discovery
Pedro de Valdivia (Sp) follows Inca coast road from Cuzco southward to Coquimbo and founds Santiago

Religion and Philosophy
Reformer Jean Calvin (Fr), recalled to Geneva, begins process of eliminating ungodliness and establishing "City of God"

Politics and Wars
Henry VIII (Eng) executes his fifth wife, Catherine Howard, and marries Catherine Parr • Scots, at war with England, are defeated at Solway Moss • Karl V (Ger) makes his son Philipp ruler of Milan, provoking France to renewal of war • Spain institutes viceroyalties of Peru and New Spain • James V (Scot) dies; is succeeded by his baby daughter Mary

Science and Discovery
In first English-language arithmetic book, Robert Recorde (Eng) introduces the mathematical symbols " = " and " × "

Religion and Philosophy
Pope Paul III founds Roman Inquisition to combat Protestantism

Politics and Wars
Henry VIII (Eng) proposes to marry his son Edward to Mary, Queen of Scots; Scots refuse • Henry retaliates by making alliance with Holy Roman Empire in war against France

Arts and Letters
METALWORK: Benvenuto Cellini (It), gold salt-cellars for François I of France

Science and Discovery
Nicolaus Copernicus (Pol) suggests that Earth rotates around the Sun in *De Revolutionibus Orbium Coelestium,* published just before he dies • Andreas Vesalius (Flem) publishes *De Humani Corporis Fabrica,* the first well-illustrated printed book on human anatomy

Politics and Wars
Truce of Nice ends 3-year war between France and Spanish-Imperial forces of Karl V • Karl V joins Venice and Pope Paul III in Holy League against Turks • Gonzalo de Quesada (Sp) founds Bogota (Colombia) after subduing Chibcha Indians

Arts and Letters
MUSIC: First five-part madrigals are published

Science and Discovery
Francisco de Ulloa (Sp) sails to head of Gulf of California, proving Lower California to be part of American mainland

Religion and Philosophy
Reformer Jean Calvin is banished from Geneva

Politics and Wars
Truce is made between Karl V (Ger) and German Protestant princes • Year-old Truce of Nice between France and Karl V is converted into peace agreement at Toledo

Science and Discovery
Hernando de Soto (Sp) lands in Florida and begins exploring southeastern North America

Religion and Philosophy
Statute of Six Articles gives English Church's definition of heresy, punishable by death • Henry VIII decrees that a Bible be placed in every parish church in England

Other Events
First New World printing press operates in Mexico

Politics and Wars
England's chief minister, Thomas Cromwell, negotiates Henry VIII's marriage to Anne of Cleves; Henry, dissatisfied, divorces Anne, marries Catherine Howard and has Cromwell executed for treason

Arts and Letters
SCULPTURE: Michelangelo Buonarroti (It) *Brutus*

Science and Discovery
Francisco de Coronada (Sp) begins exploration that takes him across what are now Texas, Oklahoma and part of Kansas • Hernando de Soto (Sp) discovers Mississippi River

Religion and Philosophy
Pope Paul III officially institutes the Society of Jesus (Jesuits)

Politics and Wars
English army invades Scotland and takes Edinburgh • Karl V (Ger), in alliance with Henry VIII (Eng), invades France, penetrating east to Soissons • Allied French and Turkish fleets bombard Nice • France settles differences with Karl V by Treaty of Crespy

Science and Discovery
Pedro de Valdivia (Sp) sends ships to Magellan's Strait and founds Chilean city bearing his name

Religion and Philosophy
First English-language, Litany is issued

Politics and Wars
Scots defeat English at Ancram Moor • English invade Scotland again • Spain institutes annual sailings of convoyed fleets from Peru and New Spain to safeguard New World treasure

Arts and Letters
PAINTING: Jacopo Tintoretto (It), *Ascension of Mary*; LITERATURE: the first book fair is held at Leipzig (Ger)

Science and Discovery
Europe's oldest botanical garden is established in Padua

Religion and Philosophy
Council of Trent begins reforming Roman Catholic Church, under guidance of Jesuits

Politics and Wars
England and France make peace treaty; England to hold Boulogne for 8 years • Karl V (Ger) and Pope Paul III make joint war on the Schmalkaldic League of Protestant German states; Karl V defeats several south German states • Maya revolt is put down in New Spain

Arts and Letters
PAINTING: Lucas Cranach the Younger (Ger), *Martin Luther*; ARCHITECTURE: Rebuilding of the Louvre, Paris; LITERATURE: Roger Ascham (Eng), *Toxophilus*, a work on archery

Religion and Philosophy
Scots begin revolt against Church of Rome

1547   1548   1549

ENGLAND—**Henry VIII** ☐ **Edward VI** ──────────────
HOLY ROMAN EMPIRE—**Karl V** ──────────────

Politics and Wars
Henry VIII (Eng) dies; is succeeded by son Edward VI, aged 10 • François I (Fr) dies; is succeeded by his son Henri II • English again invade Scotland • Ivan IV, the Terrible, assumes full power in Russia, taking the title Tsar • Karl V (Ger) defeats Saxony, winning Schmalkadic War • Brittany is finally united with France

Arts and Letters
PAINTING: Tintoretto (It), *Last Supper*

Religion and Philosophy
England repeals Statute of Six Articles (1530) • First Protestant doctrines are introduced into English Church • Calvinist reformer John Knox (Scot) is exiled to France

Politics and Wars
Emperor Karl V (Ger) separates government of the 17 Netherlands provinces from that of the Holy Roman Empire • Turks launch campaign against Persia

Arts and Letters
PAINTING: Tintoretto (It), *Miracle of St. Mark* and *Miracle of the Slave*; ARCHITECTURE: building of Pitti Palace, Florence, begins

Religion and Philosophy
By Interim of Augsburg, Karl V makes limited liturgical concessions to German Protestants • Reformation begins gaining ground in Poland • Heresy laws temporarily abolished in England

Politics and Wars
War erupts between France and England • Robert and William Kett, brothers of Norfolk, England, lead a rebellion and seize Norwich; both are hanged • Thomé de Souza (Port), first Governor-General of Brazil, founds São Salvador (Bahia)

Arts and Letters
LITERATURE: Poet Joachim du Bellay says French authors should write in French

Religion and Philosophy
Francis Xavier (Sp) leads the first Christian (Jesuit) mission to Japan • First Jesuit missions are founded in Brazil • English replaces Latin for English Church services: Book of Common Prayer is published • Pope Paul III dies

1553   1554   1555

ENGLAND—**Edward VI** ☐ **Mary I** ──────────────
HOLY ROMAN EMPIRE—**Karl V** ──────────────

Politics and Wars
Edward VI (Eng) ignoring claims of his half-sisters Mary and Elizabeth, nominates Lady Jane Grey as his successor, and dies • Duke of Northumberland proclaims Lady Jane Grey (his daughter-in-law) queen; she rules for nine days before Mary I succeeds to throne.

Arts and Letters
LITERATURE: Hans Sachs (Ger), cobbler-poet, *Tristan und Isalde*; Nicholas Udall (Eng), *Ralph Roister Doister*

Science and Discovery
Explorer Richard Chancellor (Eng), sails to Novaya Zemlya in the Arctic Ocean

Religion and Philosophy
Mary I reconciles English Church with Rome

Politics and Wars
In England, Sir Thomas Wyatt leads an abortive rebellion against Mary I • Lady Jane Grey, rival to English throne, is executed • Mary I marries Philipp, son and heir of Holy Roman Emperor Karl V (Ger) • French, at war with Karl V, invade the Netherlands

Arts and Letters
PAINTING: Titian (It), *Venus and Adonis*; LITERATURE: Matteo Bandello (It), short stories; MUSIC: Giovanni da Palestrina (It), *Missa Ecce Sacerdos*

Religion and Philosophy
England repeals Act of Supremacy, and admits a Papal legate, Cardinal Pole; Roman Catholicism is restored

Politics and Wars
Holy Roman Emperor Karl V abdicates: his brother Ferdinand I of Austria, Hungary and Bohemia becomes emperor (from January 1556); Spain, the Netherlands and the Spanish Empire go to his son Philipp as Felipe II of Spain

Religion and Philosophy
Persecution of English Protestants begins: Bishops Ridley and Latimer are burned at Oxford • Preacher John Knox returns home from Geneva to unite Scottish Protestants • Religious Peace of Augsburg allows religious freedom in German states • Pope Julius III dies; is succeeded first by Marcellus II, who dies 22 days later, then by Paul IV

Politics and Wars

England makes peace with France, giving up Boulogne • Peace between England and Scotland • Duke of Somerset, Lord Protector of England for the young Edward VI, falls from power; is replaced by Duke of Northumberland • Gustavus Vasa (Gustavus I of Sweden), furthering Swedish expansion around the Baltic, founds Helsinki

Arts and Letters

PAINTING: Michelangelo Buonarroti (It), frescoes *Conversion of St. Paul* and *Crucifixion of St. Peter*

Religion and Philosophy

John Marbeck (Eng) produces first English-language concordance (index) to the Bible • Election of Pope Julius III

Politics and Wars

Karl V (Ger) names his son Philipp as sole heir • Turks renew war with Hungary

Arts and Letters

LITERATURE: English translation of Thomas More's *Utopia* (originally in Latin)

Religion and Philosophy

Archbishop Thomas Cranmer (Eng) publishes 42 Articles of Religion, making English Church basically Protestant • Russia limits the right of Church to acquire land • Pope Julius III concedes Portugal the right to spiritual jurisdiction within her overseas empire

Politics and Wars

Duke of Somerset, former Lord Protector of England, is executed • Ivan IV the Terrible (Russ) captures Kazan from Tatars • France, having made treaty with Saxony, goes to war with Holy Roman Emperor Karl V and seizes Toul, Metz and Verdun • Persians capture Erzerum from Turks

Arts and Letters

LITERATURE: Pierre de Ronsard (Fr) *Les Amours de Cassandre*; MUSIC: Thomas Tallis (Eng), *Service in the Dorian Mode*

Science and Discovery

Physician Bartolommeo Eustachio (It) discovers (eustachian) tube connecting throat and middle ear

□ Elizabeth I ▷

□ Ferdinand I

Politics and Wars

Akbar the Great becomes Mogul emperor of India • Akbar crushes the Afghans at Panipat as first step toward consolidating Mogul power throughout northern India

Arts and Letters

LITERATURE: Pierre de Ronsard (Fr), poems *Les Amours de Marie*

Science and Discovery

German mineralogist Georg Agricola's *De re Metallica*, foundation work on minerals, published posthumously

Religion and Philosophy

Thomas Cranmer, Archbishop of Canterbury, is burned at Oxford • Cardinal Pole takes see of Canterbury

Politics and Wars

Permanent Portuguese settlement is established at Macao, China • England supports Spain in war against France • French are defeated at St. Quentin • João III (Port) dies; is succeeded by 3-year-old grandson Sebastian I • Emperor Karl V's daughter, Joanna of Austria, becomes Portuguese regent for five years

Arts and Letters

LITERATURE: George Cavendish (Eng) completes biography of Thomas Wolsey (published in 1641); ARCHITECTURE: Mosque of Suleiman I completed in Istanbul

Religion and Philosophy

Disputation at Worms fails to reconcile Lutheran and Catholic theology

Politics and Wars

French capture Calais, Britain's last possession in Continental Europe • Mary I (Eng) dies; half-sister Elizabeth I succeeds her • William Cecil becomes English Secretary of State • Mary, Queen of Scots, daughter of James V, marries French Dauphin François

Arts and Letters

PAINTING: Pieter Brueghel the Elder (Flem), *Wedding Feast*

Science and Discovery

Sailor Anthony Jenkinson (Eng), on mission for Ivan IV of Russia, sails down Volga River to Caspian Sea

Religion and Philosophy

John Knox (Scot), *First Blast of the Trumpet against the Monstrous Regiment of Women*

1559

1560

1561

ENGLAND—**Elizabeth I**
HOLY ROMAN EMPIRE—**Ferdinand I**

Politics and Wars
Henri II of France, killed in tournament, is succeeded by his son François II • François's wife, Mary Queen of Scots, styles herself Queen of England and Scotland • War between Spain and France ends

Arts and Letters
PAINTING: Titian (It), *Diana and Actaeon*

Religion and Philosophy
Acts of Supremacy and Uniformity are re-enacted in England, establishing the Church of England and breaking with Rome • Vatican issues its first *Index Expurgatorius*, listing banned books • Pope Paul IV dies; is succeeded by Pius IV

Politics and Wars
François II of France dies, aged 16; is succeeded by his 10-year-old brother, Charles IX; the Queen Mother, Catherine de Médicis, rules as regent

Arts and Letters
PAINTING: Jacopo Tintoretto (It), *Christ Before Pilate* and *Last Supper*; Pieter Brueghel the Elder (Flem) *Children at Play*; ARCHITECTURE: Building of Uffizi Palace, Florence, begins

Religion and Philosophy
Scottish Parliament establishes Reformed Church and breaks with Rome

Other Events
Madrid becomes Spanish capital

Politics and Wars
Mary Queen of Scots returns from France to Scotland • In Livonian War, Poles take Livonia, Swedes take Reval and much of Estonia

Arts and Letters
LITERATURE: Thomas Norton and Thomas Sackville (Eng), *Tragedy of Gorboduc* first performance of an English tragedy on London stage

Science and Discovery
Gabriel Fallopius (It) discovers fallopian tubes

Religion and Philosophy
Mary Queen of Scots clashes with Calvinists • Colloquy of Poissy attempts to reconcile French Roman Catholics and Protestants

1565

1566

1567

ENGLAND—**Elizabeth I**
HOLY ROMAN EMPIRE—**Maximilian II**

Politics and Wars
Turks make an abortive attempt to take Malta, haunt of Spanish corsairs • Mary Queen of Scots marries her cousin Henry Stuart, Lord Darnley • Willem of Orange (the Silent), earlier appointed governor of the Netherlands by Felipe II of Spain, champions a Protestant move to throw off Spanish rule

Arts and Letters
PAINTING: Pieter Breughel the Elder (Flem), *Autumn* and *Winter*; Titian (It), *Toilet of Venus*; LITERATURE: Pierre de Ronsard (Fr), *Abrégé de l'art poetique français*

Religion and Philosophy
Pope Pius IV dies

Politics and Wars
Darnley, husband of Mary, Queen of Scots, instigates murder of musician David Rizzio, his wife's favorite • Suleiman I dies, leaving Ottoman Empire strong in Europe; is succeeded by his son Selim II

Arts and Letters
LITERATURE: George Gascoigne (Eng), *Supposes,* earliest surviving English comedy

Religion and Philosophy
Election of Pius V, last Pope to be canonized • Decisions of Council of Trent are further clarified in *Catechismus Romanus*

Other Events
Royal Exchange is founded in London

Politics and Wars
Earl of Bothwell, a Scottish nobleman, murders Darnley, husband of Mary Queen of Scots, who then marries Bothwell • Scottish nobles force Mary to abdicate; her infant son (by Darnley) succeeds as James VI • Felipe II (Sp) sends 20,000 men to crush revolt in Netherlands • Second Religious War in France

Arts and Letters
MUSIC: Giovanni Palestrina (It), *Missa Papae Marcelli,* dedicated to Pope Marcellus II

Other Events
Rugby School, England, is founded • Portuguese found the city of Rio de Janeiro, Brazil

1562

1563

1564

⟶

────────────────────────────── □ **Maximilian II** ⟶

Politics and Wars
Huguenots (Protestants) take up arms in First French Religious War: Huguenots are defeated at Dreux • Huguenots begin emigrating to England and German Protestant states • Netherlanders launch revolt against Spanish rule

Arts and Letters
LITERATURE: Benvenuto Cellini (It), *Autobiography*

Religion and Philosophy
Akbar the Great furthers policy of religious toleration by abolishing tax on Indian Muslims

Other Events
Seaman John Hawkins (Eng) begins selling African slaves to New World colonists

Politics and Wars
Ivan IV (Russ) seizes part of Livonia from Poland • Brief truce in First Religious War in France

Arts and Letters
LITERATURE: John Foxe (Eng) English version of *Actes and Monuments,* (first written in Latin) better known as *Foxe's Book of Martyrs;* ARCHITECTURE: Work begins on Escorial Palace, near Madrid

Religion and Philosophy
Council of Trent ends: resulting Tridentine Decrees, reforming Roman Catholic Church, begin winning back ground lost to Protestants

Other Events
Bubonic plague sweeps Europe

Politics and Wars
Peace of Troyes ends Anglo-French War • England at war with Spain • Holy Roman Emperor Ferdinand I (Ger) dies; is succeeded by his son Maximilian II • Spain occupies Philippine Islands

Arts and Letters
PAINTING: Pieter Breughel the Elder (Flem), *Two Chained Monkeys*; Jacopo Tintoretto (It), *Christ at the Sea of Galilee*; Paolo Veronese (It), *The Marriage at Cana*

Religion and Philosophy
Final establishment of the Church of England: Thirty-Nine Articles are adopted, Elizabeth I tries to enforce uniformity • Counter-Reformation begins in Poland

1568

1569

1570

⟶

⟶

Politics and Wars
Mary Queen of Scots flees to England; is held prisoner by Elizabeth I • Truce between French Roman Catholics and Huguenots is followed by further war • Elizabeth I orders seizure of vessels carrying supplies to the army of Felipe II (Sp) in Netherlands • Oda Nobunga seizes power in central Japan, inaugurating a 20-year period of national unification

Science and Discovery
Jacques Besson (Fr) publishes illustrated book on iron machinery, which is replacing wooden machines

Religion and Philosophy
School for training English Jesuits set up in Netherlands

Politics and Wars
Rebellion of Roman Catholic earls in northern England is crushed by forces led by Earl of Sussex • Rebellion breaks out in Ireland (not ended until 1574) • Union of Lublin merges Lithuania and Poland • In France, Roman Catholics defeat Huguenots (Protestants) at Moncontour • Revolt of Spanish Moriscos—Moors who profess Christianity but are suspected of remaining Muslims

Arts and Letters
PAINTING: El Greco (Domeniko Theotokopoulos; Gk): *Coronation of a Saint*

Science and Discovery
Gerhardus Mercator (Flem) invents his projection for maps

Politics and Wars
Third French Religious War ends: Huguenots (Protestants) give up La Rochelle and other strongholds in return for 2 years' freedom of worship • Ivan IV, the Terrible, (Russ) destroys city of Novgorod, suspected of pro-Polish sympathies

Arts and Letters
LITERATURE: Roger Ascham (Eng), one-time teacher to Elizabeth I *The Schoolmaster*; Andrea Palladio (It), treatise on architecture, *I quattro libri dell' architettura*

Religion and Philosophy
Pope Pius V excommunicates Elizabeth I (Eng)

1571 | 1572 | 1573

ENGLAND—**Elizabeth I**
HOLY ROMAN EMPIRE—**Maximilian II**

1571

Politics and Wars
Turks seize Famagusta (Cyprus) from Venice, Tunis from Spain • Combined fleets of Spain, Venice and Genoa, under Don Juan of Austria, overwhelm a Turkish fleet at Battle of Lepanto • Empire of Kanem, or Bornu, around Lake Chad, Africa, reaches its height

Science and Discovery
First known theodolite is constructed

Religion and Philosophy
Importation of Papal Bulls (proclamations) into England is prohibited

Other Events
Laurenziana Library is founded in Florence (It)

1572

Politics and Wars
Massacre of St. Bartholomew: mass slaughter of Huguenots (Protestants) in France • Fourth French Religious War begins with siege of Huguenot stronghold La Rochelle • In northern Netherlands, Willem of Orange leads revolt

Arts and Letters
LITERATURE: Luis de Camöens (Port), *Os Lusíados,* epic poem

Science and Discovery
Adventurer Francis Drake (Eng) climbs mountain in Panama to see the Pacific Ocean

Religion and Philosophy
Pope Pius V dies; is succeeded by Gregory XIII

1573

Politics and Wars
Huguenots (Protestants) gain marginal advantages as Fourth French Religious War ends with Edict of Boulogne • Henri, duc d'Anjou (Fr) becomes the first elected king of Poland • Venice makes peace with Turks by abandoning Cyprus, one of its few remaining possessions • Don Juan of Austria seizes Tunis from Turks • Akbar (India) completes conquest of Gujarat, gaining sea access for Mogul empire

Arts and Letters
LITERATURE: Torquato Tasso (It), *Aminta,* pastoral poem

Other Events
Construction of Mexico City's cathedral begins

1577 | 1578 | 1579

ENGLAND—**Elizabeth I**
HOLY ROMAN EMPIRE—**Rudolf II**

1577

Politics and Wars
Huguenots (Protestants) are defeated in Sixth French Religious War • Don Juan of Austria, Spain's Governor in Netherlands, fails in an effort to pacify the Dutch • English make treaty with Dutch

Arts and Letters
PAINTING: El Greco (Gk), *Assumption of the Virgin;* LITERATURE: Raphael Holinshed (Eng), *Chronicles of England, Scotland and Ireland*

Science and Discovery
Francis Drake (Eng) begins voyage around the world in the *Pelican* (later renamed *Golden Hind*)

1578

Politics and Wars
Don Juan of Austria dies; is succeeded as Spanish governor of the Netherlands by Alessandro Farnese, Duke of Parma, who begins subduing southern provinces • Sebastian I of Portugal, leading crusade against Moors, is defeated and killed at Al Kasr Al-Kabir

Arts and Letters
LITERATURE: Pierre de Ronsard (Fr), *Les Amours d'Hélène*

Science and Discovery
Martin Frobisher (Eng) reaches Baffin Island and Hudson Strait

Other Events
Foundation of Levant Trading Company, London, to promote trade with Ottoman Empire

1579

Politics and Wars
By Union of Utrecht, seven Protestant northern provinces of Netherlands unite to make a concerted drive against Spanish domination • Southern provinces acknowledge Felipe II of Spain

Arts and Letters
PAINTING: El Greco (Gk), *The Espolio;* SCULPTURE: Giambologna (It), *Rape of the Sabines;* LITERATURE: Thomas North (Eng), English translation of Plutarch's *Lives;* Edmund Spenser (Eng), *Shepheardes Calendar*

Science and Discovery
Francis Drake (Eng) spends winter in San Francisco Bay

1574	1575	1576

□ Rudolf II ⟶

Politics and Wars
Charles IX of France dies; is succeeded by his brother Henri d'Anjou, king of Poland, who returns to France as Henri III • In the Netherlands, Guezen guerrillas relieve a year-long Spanish siege of Leiden • Spain again loses Tunis to Turks • Fifth Religious War begins in France • Rebellion in Ireland ends

Arts and Letters
DRAMA: James Burbage (Eng) obtains a licence to build England's first permanent theater

Religion and Philosophy
Undercover Roman Catholic mission is organized to bring England back to the "Old Faith"

Politics and Wars
English Parliament establishes freedom of arrest for its members • Henri III of France refuses to return to his Polish kingdom; Poles depose him • Maximilian II (Ger) bids for Polish crown, but Poles elect István Báthory, prince of Transylvania, their king

Arts and Letters
PAINTING: Paolo Veronese (It), *Moses Saved from the Waters*; MUSIC: William Byrd and Thomas Tallis (Eng composers) are granted a virtual monopoly of music printing in England; LITERATURE: Torquato Tasso (It), *Jerusalem Delivered*, epic poem on Crusades; English comedy *Gammer Gurton's Needle*

Politics and Wars
Spaniards sack Antwerp (Neth) • By Pacification of Ghent, all Netherlands provinces, whatever their religion, unite against Spanish rule • Fifth French Religious War ends: Huguenots (Protestants) are granted freedom of worship outside Paris • German emperor Maximilian II dies; is succeeded by his son Rudolf II

Arts and Letters
DRAMA: John Burbage (Eng) opens the first English theater at Shoreditch, London

Science and Discovery
Tycho Brahe (Den) begins his epoch-making astronomical observations at Danish royal observatory, Uraniborg

1580	1581	1582

Politics and Wars
Seventh French Religious War ends with Treaty of Felix • Seven claimants vie for Portuguese throne following death of King Enrico • Spaniards invade Portugal and win decisive Battle of Alcantara; Portugal comes under Spanish rule (until 1640) • Spanish occupy Ceuta, Portugal's oldest African possession

Arts and Letters
LITERATURE: Philosopher Michel de Montaigne (Fr), *Essais*, Books I and II

Science and Discovery
Francis Drake (Eng) completes circumnavigation of the world • Cossack leader Yermak Timofeyevich (Russ) pioneers conquest of Siberia

Politics and Wars
United Provinces of the Netherlands proclaim independence from Spain • Poles invade Russia and take Polotsk • Ivan IV, the Terrible (Russ) murders his heir, Ivan, in a fit of fury

Arts and Letters
DANCE: Production of *Le Ballet comique de la reyne* at Versailles marks the beginning of modern ballet; LITERATURE: Sir Philip Sidney (Eng), *The Defense of Poesie*

Science and Discovery
Galileo Galilei (It) discovers law of the pendulum

Religion and Philosophy
Conversion to Roman Catholicism is made treasonable in England

Politics and Wars
Livonian War ends: Poland takes Livonia and excludes Russia from access to Baltic Sea • Assassination of dictator Oda Nobunga precipitates power-struggle in Japan

Science and Discovery
Richard Hakluyt (Eng) publishes *Divers Voyages Touching the Discovery of America*

Religion and Philosophy
Akbar the Great (India) decrees new *Divine Faith*, not exclusively Muslim, but wins little support

Other Events
Reformed Gregorian Calendar is adopted by most Roman Catholic countries in Europe

ENGLAND—**Elizabeth I**
HOLY ROMAN EMPIRE—**Rudolf II**

Politics and Wars
Francis Throgmorton (Eng) and the Spanish ambassador to England plot against Elizabeth I • Portuguese-French fleet, attempting to seize Azores, is defeated by Spanish fleet • Sir Humphrey Gilbert (Eng) takes possession of Newfoundland for England

Arts and Letters
LITERATURE: Joseph Justus Scaliger (Fr), "father of historical criticism," *De Emendatione Temporum,* advocating recognition of Middle East historical records

Science and Discovery
Galileo Galilei (It), studies acceleration under gravity and learns that missiles follow parabolic trajectories

Politics and Wars
Death of François, younger brother of Henri III (Fr), leaves Henri of Navarre, Huguenot (Protestant) leader, as apparent heir to French throne • Spain backs Roman Catholic leader Henri, Duc de Guise, in a bid to ensure Catholic succession • Ivan IV, the Terrible (Russ) dies; is succeeded by his feeble son Feodor I; power is in hands of Boris Godunov, Feodor's brother-in-law • Dutch leader, Willem Prince of Orange, is murdered, and succeeded by his son Maurice of Nassau, aged 17

Science and Discovery
Sir Walter Raleigh (Eng), discovers and names Virginia; founds first short-lived colony there

Politics and Wars
Spain captures Antwerp from Dutch • Elizabeth I (Eng) sends troops to aid Netherlands, making war on Felipe II (Sp) • Eighth French Religious War (War of the Three Henris—Henri III of Valois, Henri of Navarre, and Henri of Guise)

Arts and Letters
ARCHITECTURE: Domenico Fontana (It), Quirinal Palace, Rome; LITERATURE: Miguel de Cervantes (Sp), *Galatea*

Science and Discovery
Explorer John Davis (Eng) rounds South Greenland into the strait now bearing his name

Religion and Philosophy
Pope Gregory XIII dies; is succeeded by Sixtus V

ENGLAND—**Elizabeth I**
HOLY ROMAN EMPIRE—**Rudolf II**

Politics and Wars
Catherine de Médicis, Queen Mother of France, dies • Henri III (Fr), assassinated by a monk, is succeeded by Huguenot (Protestant) leader Henri of Navarre, first Bourbon king of France as Henri IV; Roman Catholics contest the throne, some backing the Duc de Mayenne, others Felipe II of Spain • Portuguese expatriates march on Lisbon, but are defeated by Spanish troops

Arts and Letters
LITERATURE: Richard Hakluyt (Eng), *Principall Navigations, Voiages, and Discoveries of the English Nation*; Thomas Nashe (Eng), *Anatomie of Absurdities,* criticism of current English literature

Politics and Wars
Army of Henri IV (Fr) defeats his rival, Duc de Mayenne, at Battle of Ivry • Japanese dictator Toyotomi Hideyoshi completes unification of Japan

Arts and Letters
PAINTING: Jacopo Tintoretto (It), *Paradise* for Doge's Palace, Venice; LITERATURE: Edmund Spenser (Eng), first three books of *The Faerie Queene*

Science and Discovery
Galileo Galilei (It) publishes results of experiments with falling bodies

Religion and Philosophy
Pope Sixtus V dies; is succeeded first by Urban VII, who dies after 14 days, then by Gregory XIV

Politics and Wars
German Protestants form League of Torgau • Spanish and Portuguese mercenaries take Timbuktu for Morocco, wiping out Negro culture there • Sir Richard Grenville (Eng) killed when his lone ship *Revenge* battles with a large Spanish fleet

Arts and Letters
LITERATURE: Sir Philip Sidney (Eng), sonnets *Astrophel and Stella* (published posthumously)

Science and Discovery
François Vieta (Fr) introduces letter symbols into algebra, and simplifies cubic equations

Religion and Philosophy
Pope Gregory XIV dies; is succeeded by Innocent IX, who dies after two months

1586

Politics and Wars
Politician Anthony Babington (Eng) leads a plot against Elizabeth I and is executed; Mary Queen of Scots, implicated in the plot, is tried at Fotheringay Castle and convicted of treason • English troops in Netherlands win Battle of Zutphen • Francis Drake (Eng) plunders Spanish West Indies, sacking Cartagena and Domingo

Science and Discovery
Thomas Cavendish (Eng) begins 2-year voyage destined to be the third circumnavigation of the globe

1587

Politics and Wars
Mary Queen of Scots is executed for treason • Felipe II of Spain fits out an Armada to invade England • Francis Drake (Eng) destroys a Spanish fleet at Cadiz • Swiss Roman Catholic cantons make alliance with Spain • Sigismund III (Vasa), son of Sweden's king, is elected king of Poland

Arts and Letters
MUSIC: Claudio Monteverdi (It), first book of madrigals; LITERATURE: Christopher Marlowe (Eng), *Tamburlaine the Great*

Religion and Philosophy
Sigismund III of Poland backs Counter-Reformation • Japanese dictator Toyotomi Hideyoshi banishes Christian missionaries

1588

Politics and Wars
Spanish Armada is defeated by English fleet under Lord Howard of Effingham • Henri III (Fr) instigates assassination of Henri of Guise and his brother, Louis, Cardinal de Lorraine; a third brother, Charles, Duc de Mayenne, becomes leader of the Holy League • Frederick II of Denmark dies; is succeeded by his son, Christian IV

Arts and Letters
MUSIC: Thoinot Arbeau (Fr), *Orchésographie,* earliest treatise on dancing and valuable source of dance tunes; LITERATURE: Michel de Montaigne (Fr), *Essais,* Book III; Bishop William Morgan, *Welsh Bible,* crystallizing modern Welsh language

1592

Politics and Wars
Dictator Toyotomi Hideyoshi (Jap) sends 200,000 men to invade Korea; the country is laid waste, but Chinese army drives invaders back to coast • Jan III (Swe) dies; is succeeded by son Sigismund, King of Poland

Arts and Letters
LITERATURE: William Shakespeare (Eng), *Henry VI* (parts I, II, III), *Richard III*; Christopher Marlowe (Eng), *The Tragical Historie of Dr. Faustus*

Science and Discovery
John Davis (Eng) discovers Falkland Islands • Galileo Galilei (It) publishes *Della Scienza Meccanica*

Religion and Philosophy
Clement VIII is elected pope

1593

Politics and Wars
Henri IV (Fr) renounces Protestant faith to win Roman Catholic support • 13-year war breaks out between Austria and Ottoman Empire • Wallachia gains independence from Turks

Arts and Letters
LITERATURE: Christopher Marlowe (Eng), *Edward II*; he is murdered soon afterwards

Religion and Philosophy
Sigismund of Sweden tries to restore Roman Catholicism; his people react against him and hold Convention of Uppsala, which accepts Lutheran catechism • In England absence from church on Sundays is made punishable

1594

Politics and Wars
Henri IV of France is crowned at Chartres; Paris at once surrenders to him • Felipe II of Spain closes the Lisbon spice market to Dutch and English ships

Arts and Letters
PAINTING: Jacopo Tintoretto (It), *The Last Supper*; LITERATURE: William Shakespeare (Eng), *Titus Andronicus* and *The Taming of the Shrew*; Thomas Nashe (Eng), *The Unfortunate Traveller*; Thomas Kyd (Eng), *The Spanish Tragedie*

Science and Discovery
Jan Huygen van Linschoten (Neth) reaches Kara Sea, in search of Northeast Passage

ENGLAND—**Elizabeth I** ——————————————

HOLY ROMAN EMPIRE—**Rudolf II** ——————————

Politics and Wars
Karl of Södermanland (a Protestant) becomes Lieutenant-Governor (regent) of Sweden despite opposition from Sigismund, king of Poland and Sweden • Russia and Sweden end Livonian War by Treaty of Teusina; Russia recognizes Sweden's right to Narva and Estonia • First Dutch settlements on the coast of Guinea and in the East Indies are founded

Arts and Letters
PAINTING: Caravaggio (It), *Narcissus*; LITERATURE: William Shakespeare (Eng), *A Midsummer Night's Dream*; Robert Southwell (Eng), *St. Peter's Complaint,* outlining closing events of Jesus's life

Science and Discovery
Inspired guess that a liquid expands by equal amounts in response to equal increases of heat leads to invention of thermometer, possibly by Galileo Galilei (It) • Alvaro de Mendaña (Sp) sails from Peru and discovers Marquesas Islands

Religion and Philosophy
Jesuits thwart efforts to reunite Greek Orthodox Church in Poland with Roman Catholic Church • Robert Southwell (Eng), Roman Catholic priest and poet, is executed after three years' imprisonment for celebrating Mass

Social and Economic
Europeans begin to make walking shoes with heels

Other Events
Warsaw becomes Poland's capital

Politics and Wars
Turks defeat Austrians at Battle of Keresztes, northern Hungary • England, France and Netherlands form alliance against Spain • English sack Cadiz • Spaniards briefly capture Calais from France • Peasants rebel in Oxfordshire, England, protesting against bad conditions for farm laborers

Arts and Letters
PAINTING: Caravaggio (It), still life, *Fruit Basket*; LITERATURE: William Shakespeare (Eng) *Sonnets*; Edmund Spenser (Eng) *Prothalamium* and Books IV to VI of *The Faerie Queene*

Science and Discovery
Willem Barents (Neth) discovers Bear Island and Spitsbergen, and becomes first explorer to survive an entire winter in the high Arctic; his discoveries pave way for valuable Dutch sealing and whaling industries • First trigonometric tables for all six ratios, compiled by astronomer Rhaticus (Aus), are published

Religion and Philosophy
Pope Clement VIII ends excommunication of Henri IV of France after French ambassadors in Rome do penance • French League against Protestants ends

Social and Economic
Tomatoes, from the New World, are introduced into England • Sir John Harington (Eng) equips Elizabeth I's palace at Richmond with early water closet

Politics and Wars
Second Spanish Armada sent against England is destroyed by storm • Hugh O'Neill, Earl of Tyrone, leads Spanish-supported Irish rebellion against English rule • English raid Azores, Portuguese possession under Spanish control • Dutch found Batavia (now Djakarta), Java • Japanese dictator Hideyoshi launches a second invasion of Korea • Persia defeats Uzbeks, ending their sporadic raids on Khorasan

Arts and Letters
PAINTING: El Greco (Gk), *St. Martin and the Beggar*; MUSIC: John Dowland (Eng) *First Book of Songs*; Jacopo Peri (It), *Dafne*, world's first opera; LITERATURE: Francis Bacon (Eng), first version of *Essays*; William Shakespeare (Eng) *The Merchant of Venice*

Science and Discovery
Astronomer Tycho Brahe (Den) leaves Uraniborg observatory, following quarrels with Christian IV of Denmark

Religion and Philosophy
Toyotomi Hideyoshi (Jap) renews ban on Christian missionaries, executing 7 and also 17 Japanese Christians • Much of Upper Austria is forcibly re-converted to Roman Catholicism • Clergyman Richard Hooker (Eng) publishes final volume of *Laws of Ecclesiastical Politie,* a spirited defense of the Church of England

Social and Economic
England makes statutory provision for relief of the poor and makes begging illegal • England begins transporting convicts to its colonies

Politics and Wars

Religious wars end in France; Henri IV issues Edict of Nantes, giving Huguenots (Protestants) limited freedom of worship and equal political rights with Roman Catholics • Franco-Spanish war ends with Peace of Vervins, thanks to mediation by Pope Clement VIII • Felipe II of Spain dies; is succeeded by his son, Felipe III • Dutch occupy Mauritius • Fedor I of Russia dies without issue; statesman Boris Godunov is elected tsar • Japanese abandon invasion of Korea • Japanese dictator Toyotomi Hideyoshi dies, precipitating a power struggle in Japan • Karl of Södermanland leads rebellion against Sigismund, king of Poland and Sweden

Arts and Letters

PAINTING: Jan Breughel (Flem), second son of Breughel the Elder, *Adoration of the Kings*; LITERATURE: Ben Jonson (Eng) *Every Man in His Humour*; Lope de Vega (Span) *La Dragontea,* on exploits of Francis Drake

Science and Discovery

Admiral Vicunin (Korea) designs the first ironclad ships, used against Japanese invaders • Carlo Riani (It) publishes pioneer work on veterinary science

Other Events

Sir Thomas Bodley begins rebuilding a library at Oxford, England, now known as Bodleian Library

Politics and Wars

Earl of Essex, appointed English governor of Ireland, fails to end rebellion led by Earl of Tyrone; he returns unbidden to England and is arrested • Swedish Diet (parliament) deposes Sigismund III; the crown goes to Karl of Södermanland (Vasa) as Karl IX; Sigismund remains king of Poland • Army of Michael of Wallachia conquers Transylvania

Arts and Letters

LITERATURE: Ben Jonson (Eng), *Every Man out of His Humour*; Wiliam Shakespeare (Eng), *Much Ado about Nothing, As You Like It, Twelfth Night, Henry V* and *Julius Caesar*; James VI (Scot), *Basilikon Doron,* on art of kingly rule

Science and Discovery

Publication of first 3 volumes of *Natural History*, by naturalist Ulisse Aldrovandi (It), marks first serious approach to zoology

Social and Economic

Duc de Sully (Fr) institutes vigorous measures to restore crippled French finances and trade

Other Events

Globe Theatre, Southwark, London, is opened

Politics and Wars

Maurice of Nassau (Neth) defeats Spanish force at Nieuport • Elizabeth I (Eng) dismisses Earl of Essex as governor of Ireland • Lord Mountjoy becomes governor of Ireland and begins starving rebels into submission • Tokugawa Ieyasu (Jap) defeats coalition of rivals at Battle of Sekigahar; he becomes supreme ruler of Japan • Spanish force lands at Kinsale, Ireland

Arts and Letters

PAINTING: Caravaggio (It), *Doubting Thomas*; MUSIC Jacopo Peri (It), opera *Euridice*; LITERATURE: Thomas Dekker (Eng playwright), *Old Fortunatus* and ·*The Shoemaker's Holiday*

Science and Discovery

Astronomer Tycho Brahe (Den), working at Prague observatory by invitation of Rudolf II, chooses brilliant young Johann Kepler (Ger) as assistant • Physician William Gilbert (Eng) publishes *De Magnete,* coining name "electricity" and describing the magnetic poles

Religion and Philosophy

Philosopher Giordano Bruno (It) is burned for heresy • Karl IX of Sweden persecutes Roman Catholics, and executes nobles who opposed his accession

Social and Economic

English East India Trading Company founded • Ieyasu transfers Japan's capital city from Kyoto to Edo (now Tokyo), starting its phenomenal growth

ENGLAND—**Elizabeth I** ——————————————————— □ **James I** ———————
HOLY ROMAN EMPIRE—**Rudolf II** ——————————————————————————————

Politics and Wars

Earl of Essex (Eng) raises abortive rebellion against Elizabeth I, and is executed for treason • Spanish force, having landed at Kinsale, Ireland in 1600, fortifies the town • French make an unsuccessful attempt to found a colony on lower St. Lawrence River • Dutch oust Portuguese from Malacca

Arts and Letters

PAINTING: Caravaggio (It), *The Conversion of St. Paul*; MUSIC: Thomas Morley (Eng), *The Triumphes of Oriana*, a collection including several of his own madrigals and canzonets; Carlo Gesualdo (It), lyrics by Torquato Tasso (It)

Science and Discovery

Astronomer Tycho Brahe dies, leaving a wealth of unpublished astronomical observations to Johann Kepler, who now takes charge at Prague observatory • Olivier van Noort (Neth) completes the fourth circumnavigation of the world (first for Dutch Republic)

Social and Economic

New Poor Law in England makes parishes responsible for providing for the needy • England abolishes grants of monopolies • English East India Company despatches its first trading fleet to Sumatra

Religion and Philosophy

Jesuit missionary Matteo Ricci is received in Peking

Politics and Wars

Victory by English governor Lord Mountjoy over Spanish-Irish force around Kinsale virtually ends Irish rebellion • Persia and the Ottoman Empire begin a war destined to last 25 years • Dutch establish a trading post at Patani, Thailand • Sri Lanka welcomes Dutch ships as potential allies against Portugal • Spaniards from the Philippines begin short-lived trade with Japan

Arts and Letters

MUSIC: Hans Hassler (Ger), *Lustgarten*, collection of songs; LITERATURE: Thomas Dekker (Eng), play *Satiromastix*; William Shakespeare (Eng), *All's Well that Ends Well, Troilus and Cressida,* and *Hamlet*

Science and Discovery

Astronomer Johann Kepler (Ger) edits and publishes Tycho Brahe's *Astronomiae Instaurate Progymnastata,* putting forward theory that planets other than Earth circle Sun, while Sun circles Earth • Sebastian Vizcaino (Sp) surveys Californian coast with view to Spanish settlement

Social and Economic

Foundation of Amsterdam (Neth) Stock Exchange underlines growing commercial and maritime importance of Netherlands at the expense of Portugal's decline in the Far East

Other Events

Bodleian Library, Oxford, opens • Ambrosian Library, Milan, is founded

Politics and Wars

Elizabeth I (Eng) dies; is succeeded by her distant cousin James VI of Scotland as James I of England • Two plots against James discovered—Main Plot to dethrone him in favor of Arabella Stuart, Bye-Plot to wring religious concessions from him; explorer Sir Walter Raleigh, implicated in Main Plot, is imprisoned in Tower of London • James grants amnesty to Irish rebels against English rule; Earl of Tyrone is allowed to retain his title and lands • Persians retake Tabriz from Turks

Arts and Letters

PAINTING: Caravaggio (It) *Madonna of the Serpent* and *Death of the Virgin*; ARCHITECTURE: Carlo Maderna (It) begins work on façade of St. Peter's Rome; LITERATURE: Ben Jonson (Eng) tragedy *Sejanus*; Thomas Heywood (Eng), *A Woman Killed with Kindnesse,* romantic comedy

Science and Discovery

Explorer Samuel de Champlain (Fr) sails through Belle Isle Strait, up St. Lawrence River, and begins exploration of Saguenay River • Surgeon Geronimo Fabrizio (It) publishes first accurate description of valves in the veins

Social and Economic

English East India Company sends trade mission to Agra, India

Other Events

Severe plague epidemic in London

Politics and Wars

James I (Eng) proposes full union of England and Scotland • Edict banishing Roman Catholic priests from England provokes Roman Catholic leader Robert Catesby to instigate "Gunpowder Plot" to blow up Houses of Parliament in London • Peace is restored between England and Spain • Maurice of Nassau (Neth) captures Sluys from Spain • "False Dmitri," Russian nobleman claiming to be a son of Ivan IV, the Terrible, claims Russian throne

Arts and Letters

PAINTING: Caravaggio (It), *The Deposition*; LITERATURE: William Shakespeare (Eng), *Measure for Measure* and *Othello*; Lope de Vega (Sp), first volumes of *Comedias*

Science and Discovery

Astronomer Johann Kepler (Ger), in *Astronomiae Pars Optica*, defines light rays and nature of vision, laying foundations of optics

Religion and Philosophy

Convocation convened by James I (Eng) strengthens Church of England's stand against Puritans; strong measures are taken against people who attend Roman Catholic Mass or refuse to attend Anglican services • 300 English clergy resign livings in protest against anti-Puritan measures

Social and Economic

Silk manufacture begins in England • French East India Company is founded

Politics and Wars

"Gunpowder plot" to blow up English Houses of Parliament is discovered: conspirator Guy Fawkes is arrested in vaults of Houses of Parliament • Mogul emperor Akbar the Great (India) dies; is succeeded by his son Jahangir • Tsar Boris Godunov (Russ) dies; is succeeded by his son, Fedor II, who is assassinated ; "False Dmitri" (nobleman claiming to be son of Ivan IV) becomes Tsar • Ieyasu (Jap) retires as shogun (generalissimo); succeeded by his son, Hidetada • English colonists land in Barbados • Karl IX is confirmed as king of Sweden

Arts and Letters

THEATRE: Inigo Jones, founder of English classical school of architecture, is employed at James I's court to design scenes for a masque; MUSIC: Claudio Monteverdi (It), fifth book of madrigals; LITERATURE: William Shakespeare (Eng), *Macbeth*; Miguel de Cervantes (Sp), first half of *Don Quixote*; François de Malherbe (Fr), proponent of simplicity in poetry, *Poésies*

Science and Discovery

Explorer Samuel de Champlain (Fr) explores coastal areas of Cape Breton Island and Nova Scotia

Religion and Philosophy

Philosopher Francis Bacon (Eng), *The Advancement of Learning,* a critique of current educational methods with suggestions for reform • Pope Clement VIII dies; is succeeded by Leo XI, who dies after 25 days, then succeeded by Paul V

Politics and Wars

In England, Guy Fawkes and other "Gunpowder Plotters" are executed • James I (Eng) imposes additional customs duties without parliamentary sanction; English courts uphold his right to do so • Dutch fleet routs Portuguese-Spanish fleet in East Indies • Boyar (rich landowner) leader Basil Shuisky (Russ) dethrones and assassinates "False Dmitri" (claiming to be a son of Ivan IV) and becomes tsar in his place

Arts and Letters

LITERATURE: Joseph Justus Scaliger (Fr), *Thesaurus Temporum,* a chronology of ancient times; Ben Jonson (Eng), *Volpone,* comedy; William Shakespeare (Eng), *King Lear*

Science and Discovery

Navigator Lois Vaez de Torres (Sp) discovers Torres Strait between Australia and New Guinea

Religion and Philosophy

James I (VI of Scotland) confirms episcopacy—government of the Church by bishops—in Scotland, defying a move to introduce presbyterian form of church administration

Other Events

First open-air opera is produced in Rome • Two English companies are given charters to colonize the Atlantic seaboard of North America—one around Virginia; one from Delaware Bay almost to Cape Cod

ENGLAND—**James I** —————————————————————————

HOLY ROMAN EMPIRE—**Rudolf II** ————————————————————

Politics and Wars
A second pretender—the "New Dmitri" — claims Russian throne • Peasants and Cossacks rebel against Tsar Basil Shuisky • Jamestown Colony (Va), first permanent English settlement on the American mainland, is founded • "Flight of the Earls": leading Ulster nobles flee to Spain, leaving the way clear for colonization of northern Ireland by settlers from Scotland

Arts and Letters
MUSIC: Claudio Monteverdi (It), opera *La Favola d'Orfeo*; William Byrd (Eng) Volume I of *Gradualia*; LITERATURE: William Shakespeare (Eng), *Timon of Athens*; Honoré d'Urfé (Fr), pastoral romance *L'Astrée*

Science and Discovery
Topographer John Norden (Eng) publishes a manual for surveyors • Navigator Pedro Fernandez de Quirós (Sp) reaches islands to the east of Tahiti, goes on to New Hebrides and crosses Pacific Ocean to America • Explorer Henry Hudson (Eng), seeking Northeast Passage between Spitsbergen and Novaya Zemlya, sights Jan Mayen Island

Social and Economic
Table forks come into use in France and England, having originated in Italy

Politics and Wars
Religious dissension in Germany leads to the formation of Protestant Union by German states, led by Elector Frederick IV of the Palatinate; Emperor Rudolf II, weak and mentally ill, loses control of the Holy Roman Empire • In Russia, a rebel army led by claimant the "New Dmitri" advances almost to Moscow; Tsar Basil Shuisky cedes Karelia (now in northwestern Russia) to Sweden in exchange for military aid

Arts and Letters
PAINTING: El Greco (Gk), portrait *Cardinal Taverna*; LITERATURE: Thomas Middleton (Eng), plays *The Familie of Love, A Trick to Catch the Old One,* and *A Mad World, My Masters*

Science and Discovery
Invention of the microscope, attributed to Hans Lippershey (Neth) • First primitive telescope is made, also in Netherlands • Explorer Samuel de Champlain (Fr), on second voyage to North America, founds Quebec settlement

Religion and Philosophy
Confucian scholar Hayashi Razon (Jap) is made adviser to the shogun (military dictator) with object of stabilizing society • St. Francis de Sales (Fr), Bishop of Geneva, writes *Introduction to a Devout Life*

Social and Economic
Dutch East India Company begins import of China tea to Europe

Politics and Wars
12-year truce agreed between Spain and Netherlands marks virtual end of Dutch struggle for independence, although Spain delays official recognition • Spain expels Moriscos (Moors nominally converted to Christianity) • Catholic League is formed in Germany, headed by Maximilian, Duke of Bavaria • Sigismund of Poland makes war on Russia and claims the Russian throne

Arts and Letters
MUSIC: Orlando Gibbons (Eng), *Fantazies in Three Parts*; LITERATURE: Francis Beaumont and John Fletcher (Eng), play *Knight of the Burning Pestle*; William Shakespeare (Eng), *Coriolanus*; philosopher Francis Bacon (Eng), *De Sapienta Veterum* (The Wisdom of the Ancients), a collection of myths

Science and Discovery
Astronomer Johann Kepler (Ger) publishes *Astronomia Nova,* stating that planets move in elliptical orbits around Sun • Galileo Galilei (It) makes an improved telescope

Religion and Philosophy
Emperor Rudolf II (Ger) grants religious freedom to Bohemia

Social and Economic
Lawyer Hugo Grotius (Neth) writes *Mare Librum,* on freedom of the seas

Other Events
Work begins on the Blue Mosque, Constantinople

□ Matthias

Politics and Wars
Civil war continues in Russia; Swedish troops fighting for Tsar Basil Shuisky relieve a siege of Moscow; Poles advance into Russia; Russian nobles depose Basil and offer the throne to Vladislav, son of King Sigismund of Poland; the Poles decline the offer • English Parliament rejects plan for James I to give up his feudal dues in return for a fixed income • Henry IV (Fr) assassinated; is succeeded by his infant son Louis XIII; his widow, Marie de Médicis, is appointed regent • Lord Delaware is appointed governor of the English colony of Virginia

Arts and Letters
PAINTING: Peter Paul Rubens (Flem), *Raising of the Cross*; LITERATURE: Ben Jonson (Eng), comedy *The Alchemist*; Perez de Hita (Sp), novel *The Civil Wars of Granada*

Science and Discovery
Galileo Galilei (It) publishes *Siderius Nuncius,* announcing first observations of Moon mountains and craters, the four moons of Jupiter, and apparent movement of sunspots across face of Sun • Astronomer Nicolas Pieresc (Fr) observes Orion Nebula

Religion and Philosophy
St. Francis de Sales (Fr), Bishop of Geneva, founds Order of Visitation nuns • Dounai Old Testament is published, for use of English Roman Catholics • Explorer Henry Hudson (Eng) sails through Hudson Bay to James Bay

Politics and Wars
James I (Eng) grants lands in northern Ireland, forfeited after Irish rebellion, to Scottish and English Protestants ("Plantation of Ulster") • James I raises funds by sale of baronetcies (minor titles) • Kolmar War begins between Denmark and Sweden • Rudolf II abdicates throne of Bohemia in favor of his brother, Matthias • Karl IX of Sweden dies; is succeeded by his son Gustavus II Adolphus

Arts and Letters
MUSIC: John Bull, William Byrd and Orlando Gibbons (Eng), *Parthenia,* collection of virginal music; LITERATURE: scholar George Chapman (Eng), translation of Homer's *Iliad*; William Shakespeare (Eng), *The Winter's Tale* and *The Tempest*; lawyer Etienne Pasquier (Fr), *Les Recherches de la France,* history

Science and Discovery
Astronomer Johann Kepler (Ger) publishes *Dioptrice,* dealing with properties of convex lenses • Explorer Henry Hudson (Eng) loses his life in St. James Bay, Canada, when his crew mutiny and cast him adrift

Social and Economic
Traveler, William Hawkins (Eng) on a mission to India, fails to gain trading concessions • Dutch East Indies Company begins limited trade with Japan

Religion and Philosophy
"Authorized" Version of the Bible is published in England

Politics and Wars
Holy Roman Emperor Rudolf II dies; is succeeded by his old, ill and childless brother, Matthias • Archduke Ferdinand of Styria, the emperor's cousin and a Roman Catholic, is nominated as Matthias's heir • Last recorded executions for heresy in England • Russian national militia drives Poles away from besieging Moscow • Persia makes peace with Ottoman Empire

Arts and Letters
PAINTING: Peter Paul Rubens (Flem), *Descent from the Cross*; El Greco (Gk), *Baptism of Christ*; LITERATURE: John Webster (Eng), play *The White Devil*; William Shakespeare (Eng) *Henry VIII*, probably in collaboration with John Fletcher

Science and Discovery
Increasing use of telescope in astronomy results in rediscovery of the Andromeda Nebula, first described by an Arab astronomer in 963 • Trigonometrical tables published in Germany employ decimal point

Social and Economic
First tobacco plantations in Virginia • English East India Company spreads joint stock holdings over series of voyages for first time • Dutch make trade treaty with Ceylon

Other Events
Group of English settlers from Virginia begin colonizing Bermuda

ENGLAND—**James I** ———————————

HOLY ROMAN EMPIRE—**Matthias** ———————————

Politics and Wars
Russian national assembly elects as tsar Mikhail Romanov, first of Romanov dynasty which lasts till 1917 • Denmark and Sweden end War of Kolmar with Peace of Knarod • German Protestant Union forms alliance with Netherlands • Hungarian nobleman Bethlen Gabor becomes Prince of Transylvania and begins making it the hub of Hungarian culture • Elizabeth, daughter of James I (Eng), marries Elector Frederick V of the Palatinate (Ger)

Arts and Letters
LITERATURE: Thomas Middleton (Eng), masque *The Triumphs of Truth*

Science and Discovery
Explorer Samuel de Champlain (Fr) explores Ottawa River upstream of present-day Ottawa • Explorer Etienne Brulé (Fr) nears Lake Huron, stays with Huron Indians • Galileo Galilei (It) publishes his acceptance of the Copernican theory that the Earth goes round the Sun, contrary to the Church's teachings

Religion and Philosophy
Theologian Francisco Suaréz (Sp) publishes *A Defense of the Catholic Faith*

Other Events
English trading stations are established at Hirado, Japan, and Surat, India • Fire destroys Globe Theatre, London

Politics and Wars
Gustavus II Adolphus of Sweden captures Novgorod (Russ), marking start of phenomenal rise in prestige of Swedish army • James I (Eng) summons so-called "Addled Parliament"; the members quarrel with king about finances but make no decisions • French Estates General (parliament), summoned to curb power of nobility, fails; last meeting until 1789 • Dutch found Fort Nassau, near modern Albany, NY

Arts and Letters
PAINTING: Zampieri Domenichino (It), *Last Communion of St. Jerome*; LITERATURE: George Chapman (Eng), translation of Homer's *Odyssey*; John Webster (Eng), tragedy *The Duchess of Malfi*; Ben Jonson (Eng), comedy *Bartholomew Fayre*; explorer Sir Walter Raleigh (Eng), imprisoned in the Tower of London for treason, *History of the World* (to 130 BC)

Science and Discovery
Captain John Smith (Eng) begins exploring and charting New England coast • Mathematician John Napier (Scot) announces his development of natural logarithms

Social and Economic
Growth of glassmaking in England begins to bring about bigger windows and lighter homes

Other Events
Pocahontas, daughter of an American Indian chief, becomes a Christian and marries John Rolfe, an English settler

Politics and Wars
Duke of Somerset (Eng), James I's Lord Treasurer since 1613, falls from power; George Villiers, later Duke of Buckingham, becomes the king's favorite • Shogun (dictator) Tokugawa Ieyasu (Jap) captures Osaka castle and kills Hideyori, son of Hideyoshi, establishing his heirs as effective rulers of Japan until 1868 • Spaniards take the Moluccas from Portugal, which is still united with Spain

Arts and Letters
PAINTING: Peter Paul Rubens (Flem), *The Battle of the Amazons;* Domenichino (It), *Scenes from the Life of St. Cecilia*; LITERATURE: Miguel de Cervantes (Sp), Part II of *Don Quixote*; Francis Beaumont and John Fletcher (Eng), tragedy *Cupid's Revenge*

Science and Discovery
Explorers Samuel de Champlain and Etienne Brulé (Fr) travel up Ottawa River to Georgian Bay, then overland to Lake Ontario and Lake Oneida • Navigator William Baffin (Eng) discovers Baffin Island and Baffin's Bay, Canada

Religion and Philosophy
First French missionaries (Recollet friars) reach Quebec

Other Events
White settlers in Latin America begin learning use of rubber from American Indians

Politics and Wars

Armand-Jean du Plessis de Richelieu, Bishop of Luçon, becomes Secretary of State to Louis XIII (Fr) • England returns to Netherlands towns of Flushing and Brill, held as security for money lent by Elizabeth I to aid Dutch war of independence • James I (Eng) dismisses Chief Justice Sir Edward Coke for repeated failures to give judgments favorable to the king

Arts and Letters

PAINTING: Peter Paul Rubens (Flem), *The Last Judgment*; Frans Hals (Flem), *The Banquet of the Civic Guard of the Archers of St. George*

Science and Discovery

Gaspar Boccaro (Port), pioneer explorer of African interior, journeys from upper Zambesi River to Mozambique coast • Navigator Willem Schouten (Neth) ventures south of Magellan Strait, discovers and rounds Cape Horn • Explorer Sir Walter Raleigh (Eng) is released from imprisonment to go in search of El Dorado • Roman Catholic Church forbids scientist Galileo Galilei (It) to defend theory that Earth revolves around Sun, but permits him to discuss it as a mathematical supposition • Physician Sir William Harvey (Eng) first speaks of his discovery of the circulation of blood

Religion and Philosophy

Roman Catholics intensify oppressive measures against Protestants in Bohemia • St. Francis de Sales (Fr), Bishop of Geneva, writes *On the Love of God*

Politics and Wars

Archduke Ferdinand of Styria, a Roman Catholic, is proclaimed king of Bohemia, which is largely Protestant; he promises religious freedom • Treaty of Stolbovo ends war between Sweden and Russia: Sweden returns Russian city of Novgorod, but gets Russian territory on Baltic Sea coast • War breaks out between Sweden and Poland • James I (Eng; VI of Scot) meets Scots parliament

Arts and Letters

PAINTING: Peter Paul Rubens (Flem), *The Lion Hunt*; Domenichino (It), *Diana's Hunt*; Anton van Dyck (Flem), *Study of Four Negro Heads*; LITERATURE: James I (Eng) grants pension to poet and playwright Ben Jonson; lawyer John Selden (Eng), *De diis Syris Syntagmata*, work on Near Eastern religions

Mathematician John Napier (Scot) publishes *Rabdologia*, describing "Napier's bones," devices to simplify multiplication and division • Explorer Sir Walter Raleigh (Eng) fails to find El Dorado

Shogun (dictator) Hidetada (Jap) makes determined effort to stamp out Christianity; begins executing missionaries and Japanese converts

Politics and Wars

Louis XIII (Fr) dismisses Armand-Jean de Richelieu as Secretary of State for intriguing with the Queen Mother, Marie de Médicis • Thirty Years' War begins with "Defenestration of Prague"—Bohemian Protestant rebels throw two Roman Catholic governors, appointed by Holy Roman Emperor Matthias, out of a window in Prague • Philosopher and lawyer Francis Bacon is appointed Lord Chancellor of England and made Baron Verulam

Arts and Letters

SCULPTURE: Giovanni Bernini (It), *Anaeas, Anchises and Ascanius*; LITERATURE: John Fletcher (Eng): drama *The Loyal Subject*; James I (Eng): *Book of Sports*

Science and Discovery

Astronomer Johann Kepler (Ger) outlines third law of planetary motion

Social and Economic

Colony of Virginia offers substantial land grants to settlers who induce others from England to join them

Other Events

Explorer Sir Walter Raleigh (Eng) is beheaded following his failure to find El Dorado • Teatro Farnese opens at Parma, Italy • Epsom, England, begins exploiting mineral spring to become a spa

ENGLAND—**James I** ————————————————
HOLY ROMAN EMPIRE—**Matthias -□ Ferdinand II** ————————

Politics and Wars
Death of Holy Roman Emperor Matthias; King Ferdinand of Bohemia is elected to succeed him as Emperor Ferdinand II • Protestant rebels depose Ferdinand from Bohemian throne and choose Elector Frederick of the Palatinate, son-in-law of James I (Eng), as king; James refuses to help him • Quarrel between Louis XIII (Fr) and his mother, Marie de Médicis, ends; Armand-Jean de Richelieu is recalled as secretary of State • America's first elected assembly meets in Virginia

Arts and Letters
PAINTING: Diego Velázquez (Sp), *Adoration of the Kings*; MUSIC: Marco da Gagliano (It), opera *Medoro*; compilation of *Fitzwilliam Virginal Book*, important collection of English keyboard music; LITERATURE: Francis Beaumont and John Fletcher (Eng), plays *The Maid's Tragedy* and *A King and No King*; Thomas Kyd (Eng), play *The Spanish Tragedie*

Science and Discovery
Astronomer Johann Kepler (Ger), based in Prague, writes *De Harmonice Mundi*, further outlining his support for the theory that Earth revolves around the Sun

Social and Economic
First Negro slaves in Virginia

Politics and Wars
Troops of Holy Roman Emperor under command of Count Tilly rout Protestant forces of Frederick of Bohemia at Battle of White Mountain; Frederick, his lands confiscated, flees to Netherlands • Relentless drive against Bohemian Protestantism begins • Imperial and Spanish forces conquer Palatinate • Protestant Union is dissolved • Spain seizes Valtelline Pass, Switzerland, vital communications link between Austrian and Spanish Habsburg lands

Arts and Letters
PAINTING: Anton Van Dyck (Flem), *St. Sebastian* and *The Three Graces*; Diego Velázquez (Sp), *The Water Seller of Seville* and *St. John in The Wilderness*; SCULPTURE: Gian Lorenzo Bernini (It), *Neptune and Triton*; LITERATURE: John Fletcher (Eng), comedy *The Chances*

Science and Discovery
Terms *cosine* and *cotangent* are first introduced into trigonometrical terminology

Religion and Philosophy
Philosopher and lawyer Francis Bacon (Eng) publishes *Novum Organum Scientiarum*, advocating the application of inductive reasoning to fruits of experience in search for scientific truth

Social and Economic
English merchants begin trading with Gambia

Other Events
Voyage of the *Mayflower*: Pilgrim Fathers, group of English settlers, arrive at Cape Cod, and form Plymouth settlement

Politics and Wars
In England, third Parliament of James I meets: it impeaches Lord Chancellor Francis Bacon for accepting gifts from parties to lawsuits coming before him as a judge • James I rebukes Parliament for daring to criticize his plan to marry his heir, Prince Charles, to a Spanish princess; Parliament replies with the "Great Protestation," setting out Parliament's rights • Spain and Netherlands renew hostilities after 12-years truce • Sweden goes to war with Poland

Arts and Letters
SCULPTURE: Gian Lorenzo Bernini (It), *The Rape of Proserpine*; LITERATURE: Robert Burton (Eng), *Anatomy of Melancholy*, "the inbred malady in every one of us;" Edmwnd Prys (Wales) publishes metrical Welsh version of psalms; Thomas Middleton (Eng), play *The Triumphs of Honor and Virtue*

Science and Discovery
Astronomer Johann Kepler (Ger) completes publication of *Epitome Astronomiae Copernicanae*, on theory that Earth revolves around the Sun; Roman Catholic Church bans the work

Religion and Philosophy
Pope Paul V dies; is succeeded by Gregory XV

Social and Economic
Potato-growing becomes popular in Germany • Dutch West Indies Company is founded

Politics and Wars

Thirty Years' War continues: troops of Holy Roman Empire under Count Tilly are defeated by Protestants at Battle of Wiesloch, but defeat Protestant forces at Battles of Bad Wimpfen and Höchst; Tilly takes Heidelberg • James I (Eng) dissolves Parliament and imprisons three members who opposed him—John Pym, Edward Coke and John Selden • Negotiations for Anglo-Spanish royal marriage are resumed • Failure of Huguenot (Protestant) rising in France starts wane of Huguenot power • French statesman Armand-Jean de Richelieu increases his power, and is made a cardinal • English merchants, with Persian military help, seize Hormuz (Persia) from Portugal

Arts and Letters

PAINTING: Guido Reni (It), *Job*; LITERATURE: Charles Sorel (Fr), humorous novel *Françion* • Francis Bacon (Eng), *History of Henry the Seventh*; Michael Drayton (Eng), *Polyobion,* great topological poem on England

Science and Discovery

Mathematician William Oughtred (Eng) invents slide-rule

Religion and Philosophy

Pope Gregory XV organizes *Congregatio de Propaganda Fide* to coordinate all Roman Catholic missionary activity

Social and Economic

London Weekly Newes begins publication in England

Politics and Wars

Charles, heir to James I (Eng), visits Spain to negotiate marriage treaty; negotiations are broken off when Spain refuses concessions to the Elector Palatine, Charles' brother-in-law • Thirty Years' War continues: Protestant forces are defeated at Stadtlohn by armies of the Holy Roman Emperor under Count Tilly, who advances to Westphalia • Dutch massacre English and Japanese merchants at Amboina (now Ambon, Indonesia) • In North America, English colonists establish settlements at Casco Bay, Me, and at Portsmouth and Dover, NH; George Calvert (Eng) secures a charter to found a colony in Newfoundland, to be called Avalon

Arts and Letters

PAINTING: Anton Van Dyck (Flem), portrait *Cardinal Bentivoglio*; Peter Paul Rubens (Flem), *The Landing of the Medicis*; Guido Reni (It), *The Baptism of Christ*; SCULPTURE: Gian Lorenzo Bernini (It), *David*; LITERATURE: "First Folio" edition of works of William Shakespeare (Eng), published

Science and Discovery

Scientist Galileo Galilei (It), urges new pope, Urban VIII, to persuade Church to accept Copernican theory of Earth revolving around Sun; Urban replies that theory is not heretical, merely unproven

Religion and Philosophy

Pope Gregory XV dies; is succeeded by Urban VIII • Rulers of Bohemia forbid Protestant worship

Politics and Wars

France and England sign treaty for marriage of Charles, heir to James I (Eng) to Henrietta Maria, sister of Louis XIII (Fr) • English parliament votes money for defense against Spain • Thirty Years' War continues: German soldier Ernst von Mansfeld raises small English army to aid Netherlands against Spain, provoking real breach with Spain • Virginia becomes a Crown colony • Cardinal Richelieu becomes chief minister of Louis XIII, and the real master of France • Dutch capture Bahia, Brazil, from the Portuguese • Japan expels Spanish traders and bans all contact with the Philippines

Arts and Letters

PAINTING: Franz Hals (Neth), *The Laughing Cavalier*; Nicolas Poussin (Fr), *Rape of the Sabine Women*; SCULPTURE: Gian Lorenzo Bernini (It), *Apollo and Daphne*; LITERATURE: Thomas Middleton (Eng), *A Game of Chesse*, political drama which brings him a summons before the Privy Council

Science and Discovery

Chemist Jan Baptist van Helmont (Flem) recognizes that "vapours" may be alike in appearance, different in other properties, and coins word "gas" (corruption of "chaos") for them

Religion and Philosophy

John Donne, English poet and clergyman, publishes *Devotions Upon Emergent Occasions*

ENGLAND—**James I**—□ **Charles I** —————————————
HOLY ROMAN EMPIRE—**Ferdinand II** —————————————

Politics and Wars

James I (Eng; VI of Scot) dies; is succeeded by his son Charles I • Charles I marries Princess Henrietta Maria of France, and secretly sends ships for Louis XIII (Fr) to use against Huguenot (Protestant) revolt; English parliament retaliates by cutting supplies and Charles dissolves it • English expedition against Cadiz (Sp) fails • Holy Roman Emperor Ferdinand II appoints Albrecht von Wallenstein to command his armies • Maurice of Nassau, stadtholder (chief executive) of Dutch Republic dies; is succeeded by his brother Frederick Henricus • Spaniards seize Breda from the Dutch • Spanish fleet captures Bahia, Brazil from the Dutch

Arts and Letters

PAINTING: Peter Paul Rubens (Flem), portrait of his sons, *Albert and Nicolas*; LITERATURE: Ben Jonson (Eng), last play, *The Staple of News*; Francis Bacon (Eng) *Essays* (in their final form)

Science and Discovery

Chemist Johann Glauber (Ger) discovers Glauber's salt (sodium sulphate): hailed as salis mirabilis, "marvelous salt"

Religion and Philosophy

French priest St. Vincent de Paul founds Order of Sisters of Mercy in Paris

Other Events

Plague in London (Eng) causes parliament to move to Oxford

Politics and Wars

Second parliament of Charles I (Eng) impeaches Charles's friend and adviser the Duke of Buckingham for failure of an expedition against Spain; Charles saves Buckingham by dissolving parliament • Thirty Years' War continues; Holy Roman Emperor Ferdinand II's general Albrecht von Wallenstein defeats Protestant army under Ernst von Mansfeld at Bridge of Dessau; Mansfeld retreats to Hungary, counting on support of Hungarian Protestants, but Bethlen Gabor, their leader, makes peace with the Emperor; Count Tilly (for the Emperor) inflicts heavy defeat on Protestant army of King Christian IV of Denmark • Sweden gains upper hand in war with Poland • French establish settlements in Senegal and Madagascar • Dutch "buy" Manhattan Island from Amerindians for 60 guilders' worth of goods and establish New Amsterdam (later New York)

Arts and Letters

LITERATURE: Francis Bacon (Eng) *The New Atlantis*, treatise on political philosophy disguised as a fable, published in year of his death; George Sandys (Eng), translation of Ovid's *Metamorphoses*

Science and Discovery

Galileo Galilei (It) makes improved microscopes

Religion and Philosophy

Christian missionary efforts in Japan virtually cease as a result of persecution ordered by shogun (military dictator) Tokugawa Hidetada

Politics and Wars

Huguenots (French Protestants) are besieged at La Rochelle (Fr Atlantic port) by armies of King Louis XIII supervised by chief minister Cardinal Richelieu • England goes to war with France; Duke of Buckingham leads unsuccessful attempt to relieve La Rochelle • Holy Roman Emperor Ferdinand II's armies score great successes in Thirty Years' War: Albrecht van Wallenstein conquers Schleswig, subdues Jutland and Silesia, Count Tilly and Wallenstein together conquer Holstein • Bohemia gets a new constitution confirming and strengthening hereditary Habsburg rule there • Indian Mogul emperor Jahangir dies; is succeeded by his son Shah Jahan • Manchus occupy Korea

Arts and Letters

PAINTING: Peter Paul Rubens (Flem), *Mystic Marriage of St. Catherine;* Franz Hals (Neth), *The Merry Drinker;* MUSIC: Heinrich Schutz (Ger), *Dafne,* first German opera; LITERATURE: Gabriel Naude (Fr), treatise on librarianship

Science and Discovery

Astronomer Johann Kepler (Ger) publishes *Rudolphine Tables* (named for late Holy Roman Emperor Rudolf II, Kepler's patron), giving positions of more than 1000 stars; based on observations of Danish astronomer Tycho Brahe (1564–1601)

Social and Economic

France's chief minister Cardinal Richelieu organizes company to colonize "New France" (then implying entire Atlantic seaboard of North America)

1628 | 1629 | 1630

Politics and Wars

Third parliament of Charles I (Eng) passes Petition of Right, demanding that no taxes should be levied without parliamentary approval; Charles agrees, but continues to levy "tonnage and poundage" taxes; parliament protests and is dissolved • Huguenots (French Protestants) surrender La Rochelle to Roman Catholic royal armies after 14-month siege; end of Huguenots as an important political force • Thirty Years' War continues: armies of Holy Roman Emperor Ferdinand II capture much of the Pomeranian coast on the Baltic Sea • English troops capture Quebec City from France

Arts and Letters

PAINTING: Nicolas Poussin (Fr), *Martyrdom of St. Erasmus*; Peter Paul Rubens (Flem), portrait of *Felipe IV* of Spain; MUSIC: Marco da Gagliano (It), opera *Flora*; LITERATURE: Juan Ruiz de Alarcón (Sp), comedy *La Verdad Sospechosa*

Science and Discovery

William Harvey (Eng) publishes his treaty on the circulation of the blood—*Exercitatio Anatomica de Motu Cordis et Sanguinis in Animalibus*

Religion and Philosophy

Highchurchman William Laud (Eng), largely responsible for King Charles I's provocative ecclesiastical policy, becomes Bishop of London

Other Events

Duke of Buckingham (Eng) is assassinated

Politics and Wars

Third parliament of Charles I (Eng) passes resolutions against the King's action in levying tonnage and poundage taxes without parliamentary consent, and against his introducing religious innovations; Charles has nine members arrested and dissolves parliament • Last Huguenot (French Protestant) rebels in Languedoc defeated • Peace of Alais gives Huguenots freedom of worship • Holy Roman Emperor Ferdinand II and King Christian IV of Denmark sign Treaty of Lubeck: lands Christian has lost in Thirty Years' War are restored in return for promise to abandon his allies • Poland ends war with Sweden; Sweden's title to Livonia is confirmed

Arts and Letters

PAINTING: Anton Van Dyck (Flem), *Rinaldo and Armida*; LITERATURE: John Milton (Eng), *On the Morning of Christ's Nativity*

Science and Discovery

Architect Giovanni Branca (It) designs a primitive turbine—boiler with spout to direct steam against wooden blades of wheel • Mathematician Albert Gerard (Neth) makes advance toward modern algebraic notation by use of brackets

Social and Economic

Russia and France agree trade treaty

Other Events

Charles I (Eng) knights Flemish artist Peter Paul Rubens • Company of Massachusetts Bay is founded

Politics and Wars

England makes peace with France and Spain • Charles I (Eng) beginning 11-year rule without parliament, resorts to *ad hoc* and unpopular means of raising money • Electoral Assembly at Ragensburg (Ger) forces Holy Roman Emperor Ferdinand II (Ger) to dismiss Albrecht von Wallenstein from army command for cruelty and financial malpractice • King Gustavus Adolphus of Sweden declares war on Ferdinand, invades Pomerania and captures Frankfurt-an-der-Oder • Turks capture Hamadan from Persia • Dutch seize Recife and Olinda, Brazil, from Portugal

Arts and Letters

PAINTING: Diego Velázquez (Sp), *The Forge of Vulcan*; Jusepe de Ribera (Sp), *Archimedes*, a "naturalist" painting; LITERATURE: Pierre Corneille (Fr), Clitandre, a tragicomedy; Thomas Dekker (Eng), Part 2 of drama *The Honest Whore*

Science and Discovery

Galileo Galilei (It) completes his *Dialogue on The Two Chief Systems of the World* (Ptolemaic and Copernican) but delays publication pending permission from the Church

Other Events

About 1000 English settlers arrive in Massachusetts; Boston is founded • Colony's first general court sits • Buccaneers seize and fortify Tortuga, a small island off Hispaniola

ENGLAND—**Charles I** —————————————————————————

HOLY ROMAN EMPIRE—**Ferdinand II** ——————————————————

Politics and Wars

Thirty Years' War continues: Gustavus Adolphus of Sweden gains powerful allies against Holy Roman Emperor Ferdinand II—France, the Netherlands, Saxony, Brandenburg and Hesse • Imperial general Count Tilly's troops massacre Swedish garrison at Neu Brandenburg: Gustavus retaliates by massacring Frankfurt garrison • Tilly sacks cities of Magdeburg, Halle and Merseberg, and occupies Leipzig • Gustavus with a Swedish-Saxon army defeats Imperial army at Battle of Breitenfeld, near Leipzig • Bohemian Protestants with Saxon aid seize cities of Prague and Magdeburg • Ferdinand II recalls Albrecht von Wallenstein to supreme army command: Wallenstein recaptures Prague and drives the Saxons out of Bohemia

Arts and Letters

PAINTING: Rembrandt van Rijn (Neth), portrait of his mother; Diego Velázquez (Sp), *Infanta Maria, Queen of Hungary*; LITERATURE: Thomas Dekker (Eng), tragicomedy *Match Mee in London*; William D'Avenant (Eng), tragedy *The Cruel Brother*

Science and Discovery

Scientist Pierre Vernier (Fr) invents the secondary scale (vernier)

Social and Economic

First French newspaper is published in Paris—*La Gazette*

Other Events

Earthquake at Naples (It) and first serious eruption of volcano Vesuvius since 1068: 3,000 killed

Politics and Wars

England returns Quebec City to France • France's chief minister, Cardinal Richelieu, foils a conspiracy by the Duc de Montmorency and Gaston d'Orleans to overthrow him; Montmorency is executed for treason • Thirty Years' War continues: Gustavus Adolphus of Sweden advances to Danube River • Holy Roman Emperor Ferdinand II's general Count Tilly is killed in battle • Albrecht von Wallenstein, supreme Imperial commander, overruns Saxony; Gustavus attacks him at Battle of Lutzen: Swedes win the battle, but Gustavus is killed; his infant daughter Christina succeeds him

Arts and Letters

PAINTING: Rembrandt van Rijn (Neth), *The Anatomy Lesson of Dr. Nicolaes Tulp*; ARCHITECTURE: Building of *Taj Mahal*, Agra, India, begins

Science and Discovery

Galileo Galilei (It) publishes *Dialogue On the Two Chief Systems of the World*, having received the Church's permission to do so provided it would treat Copernican theory that Earth revolves around Sun as a hypothesis, not as fact; tone of work suggests that only a fool could accept the alternative (Ptolemaic) theory

Other Events

Lord Baltimore (Eng) is granted charter to found American colony named Maryland • Large influx of English settlers arrives in Massachusetts Bay colony

Politics and Wars

Thomas Wentworth, adviser to Charles I (Eng), becomes Lord Leiutenant of Ireland • Thirty Years' War continues: Protestant Duke Bernhard of Saxe-Weimar invades Franconia, seizes Bamberg and Höchstädt from the Bavarians, and occupies much of the Palatinate; Holy Roman Emperor Ferdinand II's supreme commander Albrecht von Wallenstein fights Swedish and Saxon armies in Silesia, but also conducts secret negotiations with Sweden and Saxony; later he winters in Bohemia instead of going to aid Bavaria as Ferdinand demands: Ferdinand suspects him of plotting to gain crown of Bohemia

Arts and Letters

PAINTING: Anton Van Dyck (Neth), portrait *Charles I*: Rembrandt van Rijn (Neth), *The Shipbuilder*; LITERATURE: John Milton (Eng), poems *L'Allegro* and *Il Penseroso*; John Donne (Eng), *Poems* (published posthumously) John Ford (Eng), tragedy *'Tis Pity She's a Whore*

Religion and Philosophy

Scientist Galileo Galilei (It) is brought before a special commission of Roman Catholic Church charged with disobeying Church's ruling of 1616 that theory Earth revolves around the Sun is just a hypothesis; admits "error" and is put under house arrest for life • Highchurchman William Laud, adviser to Charles I (Eng), becomes Archbishop of Canterbury

Other Events

Dutch build fort near site of present-day Hartford, Conn

1634	1635	1636

Politics and Wars

Charles I (Eng) provokes resentment by levying ship-money tax on all parts of England, not just coastal towns; Puritan leader John Hampden refuses payment, loses his case in the courts, and becomes a popular hero • Thirty Years' War continues: Holy Roman Emperor Ferdinand II dismisses Albrecht von Wallenstein from supreme army command; Wallenstein is murdered at the emperor's instigation • Ferdinand's son, Ferdinand of Hungary, becomes Imperial commander-in-chief: he defeats the Swedes at Nordingen and regains territory lost to Protestants • Poland and Russia sign Treaty of Ploianov: King Ladislaus of Poland gets city of Smolensk in return for renouncing claim to Russian throne

Arts and Letters

LITERATURE: Jean Mairet (Fr), tragedy *Sophonisbe*; Pierre Corneille (Fr), comedy *La Suivante*; John Milton (Eng), masque *Comus*

Science and Discovery

Explorer Jean Nicolet (Fr) travels west from St. Lawrence River to Lake Huron and northern end of Lake Michigan, and explores Wisconsin to upper Mississippi River • Scientist Thomas Mouffet (Eng), father of "Little Miss Muffet" of nursery-rhyme fame, compiles *Theatrum Insectorum*, work on entòmology

Religion and Philosophy

Citizens of Oberammergau, Bavaria, perform first of their 10-yearly Passion Plays in thankfulness for being saved from bubonic plague

Politics and Wars

Thirty Years' War continues: Holy Roman Emperor Ferdinand II makes peace with Saxony by Treaty of Prague; France and Sweden agree treaty of alliance against the emperor; France subsidizes the Protestant army of Duke Bernhard of Saxe-Weimar; Ferdinand's armies invade the Palatinate • France declares war on Spain: the Netherlands form alliance with France against Spain and the emperor • Turks retake Tabriz from Persia • Council of New England gives up its charter • French occupy island of Martinique • Dutch seize Portuguese trading posts in Taiwan (Formosa)

Arts and Letters

PAINTING: Diego Velázquez (Sp), *Prince Baltasar Carlos*; Francisco de Zurbarán (Sp) *St. Veronica's Kerchief*; MUSIC: Girolamo Frescobaldi (It), *Fiori Musicali de' Toccate*, organ music which influences later composers; LITERATURE: Pierre Corneille (Fr), tragedy *Médée*; Thomas Heywood (Eng), poem *Hierarchy of the Blessed Angels*

Social and Economic

London's hackney coaches are limited to speed of 4.8 kph (3 mph) • Postal service between London and Edinburgh begins

Other Events

Académie Française is empowered to rule on all questions of French language • University of Budapest is founded

Politics and Wars

Thirty Years' War continues: Holy Roman Emperor Ferdinand II's general Prince Ottavio Piccolomini (It) invades northern France from the Spanish Netherlands but is driven back; Swedes defeat imperial forces at Wittstock and dominate north and central Germany • Austrian troops invade Burgundy but are forced out • Manchus found an imperial dynasty ruling from Mukden, Manchuria

Arts and Letters

PAINTING: Peter Paul Rubens (Flem), *The Judgment of Paris*; Anton Van Dyck (Neth), *Charles I on Horseback*; Nicolas Poussin (Fr), *The Worship of the Golden. Calf*; MUSIC: Heinrich Schütz (Ger), *Kleine Geistliche Concerten,* motets; LITERATURE: Pierre Corneille (Fr), tragedy *Le Cid*; Pedro Calderón de la Barca (Sp), romantic play *La Vida es Sueño*

Social and Economic

Japanese citizens are forbidden to leave the country • Plague recurs in London (Eng)

Other Events

Harvard College is founded at Cambridge, Mass, and becomes North America's first university • Anton van Diemen is made Governor of the Dutch East Indies • Expelled from Massachusetts, Welsh Puritan Roger Williams establishes settlement of Providence, RI, on democratic principles • Colonists from Cambridge, Mass, establish Hartford; others from Watertown establish Wethersfield

ENGLAND—**Charles I** ——————————————

HOLY ROMAN EMPIRE—**Ferdinand II**–☐ **Ferdinand III** ——————

Politics and Wars

In Thirty Years' War, French forces penetrate the Netherlands; Dutch troops capture Breda, southwestern Netherlands; France repulses a Spanish invasion from the south • Holy Roman Emperor Ferdinand II dies; is succeeded by his son Ferdinand III • Russian Cossacks take Azov from Crimean Tatars, but hand it back when Tsar Mikhail Romanov of Russia declines it for fear of Turkey • Manchus forcibly turn Korea into a vassal state

Arts and Letters

PAINTING: Rembrandt van Rijn (Neth), *Angel Raphael Leaving Tobias*; José de Ribera (Sp), *Pietà*; Peter Paul Rubens (Flem), *Allegory of War*; LITERATURE: John Milton (Eng), elegaic poem *Lycidas*

Science and Discovery

Pierre Fermat (Fr founder of modern number theory) and René Descartes (Fr) independently develop analytic geometry

Religion and Philosophy

Scottish Presbyterians sign the Solemn League and Covenant against Episcopacy (bishops) —hence term "Covenanters" • Scots riot against the introduction by the Scottish bishops of a new liturgy • Descartes publishes *Discours de la Méthode,* introducing his philosophy

Other Events

Peter Minuit (Neth) helps start the New Sweden Company to colonize the Delaware River

Politics and Wars

Thirty Years' War continues: Protestant armies under Duke Bernhard of Saxe-Weimar and Vicomte de Turenne (Fr) defeat armies of Holy Roman Emperor Ferdinand III and Bavaria; the fall of Breisach, southwestern Germany, cuts Spain's Rhine River route from Milan to the Spanish Netherlands • France and Sweden renew their alliance

Arts and Letters

PAINTING: Anton Van Dyck (Neth), *The Three Graces*; Rembrandt van Rijn (Neth), *Marriage of Samson*; Diego Velázquez (Sp), *Christ on the Cross*; MUSIC: Claudio Monteverdi (It), eighth book of madrigals

Science and Discovery

Galileo Galilei (It) publishes *Dialogues Concerning Two New Sciences,* describing laws of motion for falling bodies and projectiles

Religion and Philosophy

General assembly in Scotland abolishes episcopacy (rule by bishops) in Scottish Church • Covenanters (Scottish Presbyterians) prepare for war • 37,000 Christians on the Shimabara Peninsula (Jap) die in rebellion against repression by Japan's Tokugawa rulers

Other Events

Dutch occupy Mauritius • Swedish ships reach Delaware River and Swedes establish Fort Christina • Anne Hutchinson, banished from Massachusetts Bay Colony, settles on Aquidneck, RI, and establishes Portsmouth • John Davenport and Theophilus Eaton establish New Haven, Conn

Politics and Wars

Scottish Covenanters (Presbyterians) protesting against episcopalianism capture Edinburgh Castle in the First Bishops' War, outmaneuvering King Charles I (Eng and Scot), who agrees a truce at Berwick-on-Tweed (Eng) • Admiral Maarten Tromp (Neth) defeats a Spanish fleet off Dover (Eng), cutting Spain's sea route to Flanders and preventing Spain retaking the Dutch Netherlands • Dutch oust Portuguese from Trincomalee (Sri Lanka) • Settlements of Hartford, Wethersfield and Windsor (now collectively called Connecticut) produce "Fundamental Orders," first written constitution in North America

Arts and Letters

PAINTING: Diego Velázquez (Sp), *The Surrender of Breda*; Nicolas Poussin (Fr), *The Israelites Collecting Manna*; LITERATURE: Philip Massinger (Eng), *The Unnatural Combat*; John Milton (Eng), poem *Epitaphium Damonis*

Science and Discovery

Astronomer Jeremiah Horrocks (Eng) makes first observation of transit of Venus (passage between Earth and Sun)

Social and Economic

Portuguese are expelled from Japan

Other Events

Rhode Island settlers establish town of Newport • Francis Day (Eng) founds Indian city of Madras as a fort for the English East India Company • Stephen Daye (Eng) at Cambridge, Mass, establishes North America's first printing press

Politics and Wars

Charles I (Eng) summons the so-called Short Parliament, which refuses to vote him money without concessions; he dissolves it • Scots wage the Second Bishops' War against Charles; to raise money for the war, Charles summons the so-called Long Parliament (1640–1660); Charles tries to conciliate parliament but it opposes and moves to impeach his advisers, Archbishop Laud and Thomas Wentworth (now Earl of Strafford) • Friedrich Wilhelm (the Great Elector) becomes elector of Brandenburg • Portuguese revolt and overthrow their Spanish rulers: Duke João of Bragança becomes King João IV

Arts and Letters

PAINTING: Rembrandt van Rijn (Neth), *Self Portrait*; LITERATURE: Pierre Corneille (Fr), tragedy *Horace*; John Donne (Eng) 80 sermons (posthumous publication); *The Bay Psalm Book*, first book printed in the North American colonies

Religion and Philosophy

Augustinus, a posthumous publication of theologian Cornelius Jansen (Neth), antagonizes Jesuits by stressing inner regeneration of the Church rather than its external reorganization

Social and Economic

English East India Company sets up trading station in Bengal, India • Japanese execute most Portuguese envoys who try to renew trade links

Politics and Wars

English parliament passes Triennial Act, declaring that recall of parliament is no longer dependent on the king; Presbyterians introduce the Root and Branch Bill to abolish bishops; parliament abolishes the Star Chamber and High Commission courts • 30,000 Protestants are massacred in an Ulster Roman Catholic rebellion • English parliament's "Grand Remonstrance" lists grievances against King Charles I; parliament has Charles's adviser, Earl of Strafford, executed • French occupy Alsace • Sweden and German state of Brandenburg sign a truce • Dutch take Malacca from Portuguese and become masters of the East Indies

Arts and Letters

PAINTING: Claude Lorrain (Fr), *Seaport: Embarkation of St. Ursula;* MUSIC: Claudio Monteverdi (It), opera *Il Ritorno d'Ulisse in Patria*; LITERATURE: Pierre Corneille (Fr), tragedy *Cinna*

Religion and Philosophy

Priest-diplomat Jules Mazarin (It) becomes a cardinal • René Descartes (Fr) publishes major work on metaphysics, *Meditationes de Prima Philosophia* • England's House of Commons authorizes the destruction of altars and images

Other Events

Jesuits establish mission at Sault Ste. Marie, first settlement in Michigan

Politics and Wars

English House of Commons refuses to let King Charles I arrest five of its members • Charles leaves London for York; parliament and king raise armies • Charles raises his standard at Nottingham and English Civil War between royalists (Cavaliers) and parliamentarians (Roundheads) begins: parliamentary army repulses Charles's advance on London • In Thirty Years' War, Swedish forces beat army of Holy Roman Emperor Ferninand III of Leipzig (Ger) • Cardinal Richelieu dies; is succeeded as France's chief minister by Cardinal Mazarin (It) • Sir William Berkeley becomes governor of Virginia

Arts and Letters

PAINTING: Rembrandt van Rijn (Neth), *The Night Watch*; MUSIC: Claudio Monteverdi (It), last opera *L'Incoronazione di Poppea*

Science and Discovery

Mathematician Blaise Pascal (Fr) designs an adding machine • Navigator Abel Tasman (Neth) discovers Tasmania (which he names Van Diemen's Land) and New Zealand

Religion and Philosophy

Philosopher Sir Thomas Browne (Eng) writes *Religio Medici*

Social and Economic

England's Puritan parliament abolishes theaters • Bubonic plague sweeps England

Other Events

Paul de Chomedey, Sieur de Maisonneuve (Fr), founds Montreal city

ENGLAND—**Charles I**

HOLY ROMAN EMPIRE—**Ferdinand III**

1643

Politics and Wars
In English Civil War, parliament's agreement to make sweeping religious reforms wins it Scottish aid; parliamentary cavalry leader Oliver Cromwell's "Ironsides" win several battles, but royalist cavalry leader Prince Rupert sacks Bristol; by December, King Charles I holds most of England except the southeast • In Thirty Years' War, French troops under Duc d'Enghien defeat Spanish forces at Rocroi, northeastern France; Austro-Bavarian forces defeat a French army at Tuttlingen (Ger) • Denmark and Sweden are at war: Sweden invades Jutland • Louis XIII (Fr) dies; is succeeded by his son Louis XIV, aged 5 • England's North American colonies form the New England Confederation for defense

Arts and Letters
LITERATURE: Molière (Jean-Baptiste Poquelin, Fr) joins L'Illustre Théatre players in Paris

Science and Discovery
Physicist Evangelista Torricelli (It) makes the first barometer • Navigator Abel Tasman (Neth) discovers Fiji after circumnavigating Australia without seeing it

Religion and Philosophy
Theologian Antoine Arnauld (Fr) becomes leader of Jansenists, heretical sect emphasizing free will • Pope Urban VIII condemns certain Jansenist doctrines • French crown confirms remaining rights of Huguenots (Fr Protestants)

1644

Politics and Wars
In English Civil War, Scots invade England; parliamentary general Thomas Fairfax crushes Irish royalists at Nantwich, Cheshire, and takes York; parliamentary cavalry general Oliver Cromwell defeats royalists under Prince Rupert at Marston Moor, Yorkshire, a major battle; King Charles I wins battles in Cornwall • In Thirty Years' War, French army under Vicomte de Turenne and Duc d'Enghien invades the Rhineland • In China, Manchu Ch'ing Dynasty replaces Ming Dynasty • At 18, Queen Christina (Swe) comes of age and is crowned • Providence and Rhode Island towns unite

Arts and Letters
PAINTING: Jan van Goyen (Neth), *Village Church in the Sand*; LITERATURE: John Milton (Eng), *Areopagitica*, tract to defend press freedom; Pierre Corneille (Fr), tragedy *Pompée*

Science and Discovery
Ars Magna Lucis et Umbrae by Jesuit scientist Athanasius Kircher (Ger) describes his invention of the magic lantern

Religion and Philosophy
Philosopher René Descartes (Fr) explains many phenomena mechanistically in *Principia Philosophiae* • Pope Urban VIII dies; is succeeded by Innocent X

Social and Economic
China's new Manchu rulers order the Chinese to have shaven heads with queues ("pigtails")

1645

Politics and Wars
In English Civil War, Marquis of Montrose arouses Scottish clans to fight for Charles I, but is defeated by a parliamentary army under David Leslie and flees; Archbishop Laud, former adviser to Charles, is executed; Generals Thomas Fairfax and Oliver Cromwell lead parliament's reformed "New Model" Army which defeats Charles conclusively at Naseby, Northamptonshire • In Thirty Years' War, Swedes invade Saxony, forcing its elector to agree a truce; Swedish troops beat forces of Holy Roman Emperor Ferdinand III in Bohemia and take Moravia; Sweden and Denmark make peace • Turks start a long war with Venice • Tsar Mikhail Romanov (Russ) dies; is succeeded by his son Alexis, aged 16

Arts and Letters
PAINTING: Nicolas Poussin (Fr), *St. John on Patmos*; SCULPTURE: Giovanni Bernini (It), *Ecstasy of St. Theresa* for Cornaro Chapel, Rome; ARCHITECTURE: François Mansart (Fr) establishes Baroque art in France with the Val-de-Grace convent and church, Paris; LITERATURE: Pierre Corneille (Fr), tragedy *Rodogune*; Edmund Waller (Eng), *Poems*

Science and Discovery
English scientists start regular meetings, creating the so-called Invisible College, precursor of the Royal Society

Religion and Philosophy
Presbyterianism becomes the official religion in England

Politics and Wars

English Civil War ends with the royalist surrender of Oxford; King Charles I escapes to the Scots at Newcastle; negotiations between king and parliament collapse when Charles refuses to accept Presbyterianism as England's national religion, and parliamentary control of the militia for a period of 20 years • In Thirty Years' War, Swedes and French invade Bavaria; Swedish forces enter Prague • João IV of Portugal survives a Spanish plot

Arts and Letters

PAINTING: Rembrandt van Rijn (Neth), *Winter Landscape*; Bartolomé Murillo (Sp), *Ecstasy of St. Diego of Alcalá*; LITERATURE: Pierre Corneille (Fr), tragedy *Théodore*; Henry Vaughan (Eng), *Poems*; exiled Earl of Clarendon (Eng) begins his *History of the Great Rebellion*; Richard Crashaw (Eng), devotional poems *Steps to the Temple*; Sir John Suckling (Eng), poems *Fragmenta Aurea* (published posthumously)

Religion and Philosophy

American clergyman John Eliot starts missionary travels among Massachusetts Indians • English clergyman Jeremy Taylor urges religious tolerance in his book *Liberty of Prophesying*

Other Events

Laying-out of Berlin's Unter den Linden avenue begins

Politics and Wars

Scottish army hands over King Charles I to English parliament in exchange for back pay • Cornet Joyce kidnaps Charles for the English army, now at odds with parliament • Charles I is recaptured by parliament, but Scots secretly offer to reinstate him if he abolishes episcopacy (rule of Church by bishops) • In Thirty Years' War, Swedish and French armies invade Bavaria and force its elector, Maximilian, to concede the Truce of Ulm—which he soon breaks • Frederick Henricus of Orange, Stadtholder (chief executive) of Dutch Republic, dies; is succeeded by his son Willem II, who is married to Mary, daughter of Charles I (Eng)

Arts and Letters

PAINTING: Pietro da Cortona (It), *The Age of Gold*; Rembrandt van Rijn (Neth), *Susannah and the Elders*; LITERATURE: Pierre Corneille (Fr), tragedy *Héraclius*; Abraham Cowley (Eng), poetic love cycle *The Mistress*

Religion and Philosophy

Lutherans recognize Calvinists as coreligionists • Church of England professors lose their posts at Oxford University (Eng)

Social and Economic

England's parliament passes further ordinances against the theater: performers to be whipped and audiences fined

Other Events

The Eleutherian Adventurers' Company (Eng) sends settlers to the Bahamas

Politics and Wars

Second English Civil War: Scots invade England on behalf of Charles I, but are defeated at Preston, Lancashire by parliamentary army under Oliver Cromwell • Colonel Thomas Pride expels Presbyterian members from England's parliament; remainder of parliament becomes known as "The Rump" • The Rump calls for Charles I's trial • In Thirty Years' War, French and Swedes again overrun Bavaria; Treaty of Westphalia ends the war (begun 1618) and recognizes independence of the Dutch Republic • Fronde (literally "sling") rebellions: parlement (judicial body) of Paris opposes government moves to limit its powers • King Wladyslaw IV (Pol) dies; is succeeded by his half-brother Jan II Casimir

Arts and Letters

PAINTING: Claude Lorrain (Fr), *Embarkation of the Queen of Sheba*; Rembrandt van Rijn (Neth) *The Pilgrims at Emmaus*; ARCHITECTURE: Jacob van Kampen (Neth) designs Amsterdam Town Hall; LITERATURE: Robert Herrick (Eng), book of poems *Hesperides*

Science and Discovery

Scientist Blaise Pascal (Fr) shows atmospheric pressure diminishes as altitude increases

Religion and Philosophy

Preacher George Fox (Eng) establishes the Society of Friends ("Quakers") • Treaty of Westphalia puts Catholic and Protestant states of the Holy Roman Empire on equal basis

ENGLAND—**Charles I**—□ **The Commonwealth** ————————
HOLY ROMAN EMPIRE—**Ferdinand III** ————————————

Politics and Wars

England's High Court condemns defeated king Charles I to death as tyrant, traitor, public enemy and murderer; he is executed • A republican Commonwealth replaces England's monarchy, under the "Rump" parliament; actual power rests with the army and its general, Oliver Cromwell • Charles's son is proclaimed as King Charles II in Scotland; royalist revolts flare up there and in Ireland; Cromwell brutally crushes the Irish revolt, storming towns of Drogheda and Wexford and massacring their garrisons • First Fronde revolt ends in France in the Treaty of Rueil

Arts and Letters

PAINTING: Diego Velázquez (Sp), *Pope Innocent X*; Gerard Terborch (Neth), *Felipe IV of Spain*; MUSIC: Pietro Francesco Cavalli (It), opera *Giasone*

Religion and Philosophy

Society for Propagating the Gospel in New England is incorporated in England • Maryland's Toleration Act makes the colony America's first civil authority to acknowledge freedom of conscience

Social and Economic

New Russian law code, intended to reform, actually helps entrench serfdom • Portuguese traders set up the Commercial Company of Brazil to monopolize trade with Brazil • In England, English language replaces Latin in legal documents • Merchant Gerrard Winstanley (Eng) establishes the Diggers, an agrarian communist society in Surrey

Politics and Wars

Royalist leader, Marquis of Montrose, leads rebellion in Scotland; is defeated and executed • Exiled Prince Charles (eldest son of Charles I) lands in Scotland and is again proclaimed king; parliamentary general Oliver Cromwell defeats Scots at Battle of Dunbar • Willem II of Orange, Stadtholder (chief minister of Dutch Republic) dies; his son Willem is born posthumously and the States-General (parliament) assumes power • Iroquois Indians almost wipe out Hurons

Arts and Letters

PAINTING: Rembrandt van Rijn (Neth), *Jewish Merchant*; Nicolas Poussin (Fr), *The Arcadian Shepherds*; MUSIC: John Playford (Eng), *The English Dancing Master*, a treasury of traditional dances; LITERATURE: Anne Bradstreet of Mass, poems *The Tenth Muse*; Pierre Corneille (Fr), drama *Andromède*

Science and Discovery

Physicist Otto von Guericke (Ger) invents an air pump

Religion and Philosophy

Preacher Jeremy Taylor (Eng) writes *The Rule and Exercises of Holy Living* • Anglican clergyman James Ussher (Ire) uses Biblical "proofs" to put the date of creation at 4004 BC

Social and Economic

World population reaches *c.* 500 million • Wallpaper becomes popular in England • England's Puritan rulers make adultery punishable by death

Politics and Wars

Prince Charles, son of Charles I (Eng), is crowned king of the Scots at Scone • His Scottish army invades England but parliamentary army under Oliver Cromwell routs it at Worcester; Charles escapes to France • Tokugawa Iemitsu, shogun (military dictator) of Japan, dies; is succeeded by his son Ietsuna • Ietsuna quells last revolts against Tokugawa rule before the 1800s • In France, Fronde (rebel) disturbances force chief minister Cardinal Mazarin to flee from Paris

Arts and Letters

PAINTING: Rembrandt van Rijn (Neth) paints *Girl With a Broom*; SCULPTURE: Gian Lorenzo Bernini (It), *Four Rivers Fountain*, Rome; LITERATURE: Pierre Corneille (Fr), dramas *Nicomède* and *Perathrite*

Science and Discovery

Astronomer Giovanni Riccioli (It) makes a Moon map giving names still used for many lunar features

Religion and Philosophy

Book *Leviathan* by philosopher Thomas Hobbes (Eng) acknowledges the sovereign's absolute power, provided he makes proper use of it • Preacher Jeremy Taylor (Eng) writes *The Rule and Exercises of Holy Dying*

Social and Economic

England's first Navigation Act, aimed against Dutch commercial competition, declares that only English-owned and English-manned ships may carry goods to England or its colonies

Politics and Wars

First Anglo-Dutch War (provoked by England's first Navigation Act) begins with an English naval victory off Dover; naval commanders are Robert Blake and George Monk (Eng), Michel de Ruyter and Maarten van Tromp (Neth) • England's "Rump" parliament passes "Acts of Indemnity and Oblivion", to conciliate royalists, and an Act of Settlement for Ireland • Fronde (rebel) government appears in Paris, but King Louis XIV restores royal authority with aid of chief minister Cardinal Mazarin • Commissioners sent from England by Puritan general Oliver Cromwell clash with Governor William Stone of Maryland and oust Governor Sir William Berkeley (a royalist) from Virginia • King Felipe IV (Sp) crushes a Catalan revolt after besieging Barcelona for more than a year

Arts and Letters

PAINTING: Rembrandt van Rijn (Neth), *Hendrickje*; Carel Fabritius (Neth), *View of Delft*; Adriaen van Ostade (Neth), *Cottage Dancers*; LITERATURE: Andrew Marvell (Eng), poem *The Garden*

Science and Discovery

Scientists found the Imperial German Academy of Naturalists at Schweinfurth (Ger)

Religion and Philosophy

Pamphleteer Gerrard Winstanley (Eng) outlines a communist society in his book, *The Law of Freedom in a Platform*

Other Events

Dutch settlers found Cape Town in South Africa

Politics and Wars

In England, army leader Oliver Cromwell ejects the "Rump" parliament; new parliament consists of members nominated by army council • Cromwell becomes Lord Protector of the Commonwealth of England, Scotland and Ireland • English fleet led by Robert Blake and George Monk defeats Dutch fleet under Maarten van Tromp in English Channel; Tromp dies in battle off Texel (Neth) • Massachusetts gains jurisdiction over southern Maine • Fronde rebellions in France continue; Fronde leader Prince de Condé (formerly Duc d'Enghien) invades France with Spanish troops, but is repulsed • Dutch statesman Jan de Witt becomes Grand Pensionary (chief minister) of Dutch republic

Arts and Letters

PAINTING: Nicolas Poussin (Fr), *The Holy Family*; Peter Lely (Neth), *Oliver Cromwell*; LITERATURE: Isaak Walton (Eng) *The Compleat Angler*

Science and Discovery

Armamentarium Chirurgicam, a surgeon's handbook by Johann Schultes (Ger) appears posthumously

Religion and Philosophy

Controversy over the heretical teachings of theologian Cornelius Jansen (1585–1638) develops when Pope Innocent X condemns five propositions in Jansen's book *Augustinus*

Other Events

Louis XIV (Fr) plays role of the Sun in a court ballet, earning his nickname *Le Roi Soleil*, "The Sun King"

Politics and Wars

Treaty of Westminster ends first Anglo-Dutch War: Dutch acknowledge England's Navigation Act which rules that certain goods carried to England and its colonies can travel only in English ships • Lord Protector Oliver Cromwell (Eng) clashes with parliament, and excludes republicans protesting against his dictatorial powers • Portuguese drive Dutch from Brazil • Queen Christina (Swe) becomes a Roman Catholic and abdicates; is succeeded by her cousin Karl Gustavus • Poland and Russia fight for the Ukraine • French troops end the Fronde leader Prince de Condé's siege of Arras

Arts and Letters

PAINTING: Carel Fabritius (Neth), *The Goldfinch*, he is killed soon after by an exploding powder magazine; Pieter de Hooch (Neth), *Delft After the Explosion*; Rembrandt van Rijn (Neth), Portrait of *Jan Six*; LITERATURE: Johann Amos Comenius (Moravia), *Orbis Sensualium Pictus*, first textbook with illustrations as important as text

Science and Discovery

Scientist-philosopher Blaise Pascal and Pierre de Fermat (Fr) begin developing probability theory • Robert Boyle (Ire) uses a pneumatic pump to prove that air supports respiration • Otto van Guericke (Ger) demonstrates that atmospheric pressure can prevent horse teams pulling apart two hollow copper hemispheres emptied of air by pumping

ENGLAND—**The Commonwealth**
HOLY ROMAN EMPIRE—**Ferdinand III**

Politics and Wars

Dissension in England persuades Lord Protector Oliver Cromwell to dissolve parliament; Cromwell organizes England into 12 military districts, each commanded by a major-general • Force led by Admiral William Penn and Robert Venables (Eng) captures Jamaica from Spain • Sweden begins the first Northern War against Poland to win Baltic lands • In North America, the Dutch West India Company occupies New Sweden (founded 1638 in what is now Delaware)

Arts and Letters

PAINTING: Rembrandt van Rijn (Neth), *Woman Bathing in a Stream*; ARCHITECTURE: work begins on Church of St. Sulpice, Paris (Fr); LITERATURE: Molière (Fr), *L'Etourdi*; GENERAL: Puritanism curbs artistic expression in England

Science and Discovery

Book *Arithmetica Infinitorum* by John Wallis (Eng) introduces the sign ∞ representing infinity

Religion and Philosophy

England's Anglican clergy are forbidden to preach, and Roman Catholic priests are expelled • Pope Innocent X dies; is succeeded by Alexander VII • Waldenses (a Protestant minority) are massacred in Savoy • Clergyman Thomas Fuller (Eng) publishes *A Church History of Britain*

Social and Economic

England's republican government introduces Press censorship

Politics and Wars

War breaks out between England and Spain; English seize Spanish treasure ships off Cadiz • Lord Protector Oliver Cromwell (Eng) calls second parliament; he again excludes hostile members • João IV of Portugal dies; is succeeded by son Afonso VI, a dissolute young man • Roman Catholic Swiss cantons defeat Protestant cantons in the First Villmergen War • Armies of Sweden and Brandenburg invade Poland • Muhammad Kiuprili becomes Grand Vizir (chief minister) of Turkey and bolsters the sagging Ottoman Empire

Arts and Letters

ARCHITECTURE: Giovanni Bernini (It), colonnade flanking the square of St. Peter's, Rome; Pietro da Cortona (It), Baroque church of St. Maria della Pace, Rome; THEATRE: Sir William D'Avenant (Eng), produces *The Siege of Rhodes,* first English opera; LITERATURE: Abraham Cowley (Eng), verse *Miscellanies*

Science and Discovery

Physician Thomas Wharton (Eng) publishes an account of glands • Physicist Christiaan Huygens (Neth) develops the pendulum as a time-controller for clocks

Religion and Philosophy

Sorbonne College (Paris) expels Jansenist leader Antoine Arnauld for heresy • Scientist-philosopher Blaise Pascal (Fr) begins his *Lettres Provinciales,* supporting Jansenists against Jesuits • Jewish authorities denounce Jewish philosopher Baruch Spinoza (Neth) for heresy

Politics and Wars

Lord Protector Oliver Cromwell (Eng) rejects parliament's offer of the crown but accepts its Humble Petition and Advice, a new constitution reintroducing a second house • France's chief minister Cardinal Mazarin agrees with Cromwell on Anglo-French treaty against Spain • War begins between Dutch and Portuguese • Denmark and Sweden's former ally Brandenburg (a German state) side with Russia, Austria and Poland against Sweden; Swedes are driven from Poland • Holy Roman Emperor Ferdinand III dies

Arts and Letters

PAINTING: Nicolas Poussin (Fr), *Birth of Bacchus*; Rembrandt van Rijn (Neth), portrait of son *Titus*; ARCHITECTURE: Gian Lorenzo Bernini (It), Throne of St. Peter for St. Peter's, Rome; Louis Le Vau (Fr) Chateau of Vaux-le-Vicomte; LITERATURE: Thomas Middleton (Eng) tragedy *Women Beware Women* (posthumously); Cyrano de Bergerac (Fr) *Etats et empires de la lune,* a novel of imaginary travel (posthumously); Japanese shogun (military dictator) Tokugawa Mitsutuni employs scholars to compile a History of Japan

Science and Discovery

Accademia del Cimento in Florence (It) becomes the first organized scientific academy • Scientist Olaf Rudbeck (Swe) discovers the lymph vessels of the body

Social and Economic

English East India Company sets up permanent fund to finance ventures, hitherto subscribed individually

☐ Charles II ⟶ ▷

☐ Leopold I ⟶ ▷

Politics and Wars

Spanish troops try to relieve Dunkirk (then in Spanish Netherlands) from siege by English and French troops; Spaniards are defeated in Battle of the Dunes; England takes Dunkirk • English parliament reconvenes but wrangles over the new constitution and is dissolved • Lord Protector Oliver Cromwell (Eng) dies; is succeeded by his son, Richard • Swedes invade Denmark, which agrees to cede to Sweden lands in Norway and south Sweden; King Karl X of Sweden wants more territory and reopens the war • Leopold I, son of Ferdinand III, is elected Holy Roman Emperor • In India, Aurangzib deposes his father Shah Jehan to become Mogul emperor • Lord Baltimore regains control of Maryland, lost when Puritans deposed his appointed governor in 1654

Arts and Letters

LITERATURE: Philip Massinger (Eng), comedy *The City Madam* (posthumously); Edward Phillips (Eng), philological dictionary *A New World of Words*

Science and Discovery

Naturalist Jan Swammerdam (Neth) is the first person to see red blood corpuscles, using a microscope • Explorers Médart Chouart, Sieur de Groseilliers, and Pierre Esprit Radisson (Fr) probe west of Lake Superior

Religion and Philosophy

Physician Sir Thomas Browne (Eng) publishes *Urn Burial,* a mystical historical study of the disposal of the dead

Politics and Wars

Lord Protector Richard Cromwell (Eng) recalls parliament, but dissolves it after it disagrees with the army; the army then reconvenes the "Rump Parliament" and Richard Cromwell is forced to resign • General John Lambert stages a coup to replace the "Rump" with military rule; another general, George Monk, supports civil government and prepares to march on London from Scotland • Treaty of the Pyrenees ends the Franco-Spanish War • King Louis XIV (Fr) marries Maria Teresa, daughter of King Felipe IV of Spain at Elvas (Port) • Danes repel Swedish assault on Copenhagen (Den) • American colony of Virginia declares its allegiance to Charles II • Tribal leader Sivaji, a Maratha from peninsular India, gains power at Mogul expense in India

Arts and Letters

PAINTING: Diego Velazquez (Sp), *Infanta Maria Theresa*; LITERATURE: Pierre Corneille (Fr), *Oedipe*; Molière (Fr), *Les Précieuses ridicules*; John Dryden (Eng), *Heroic Stanzas* to mark Oliver Cromwell's death

Science and Discovery

Systema Saturnium by physicist Christiaan Huygens (Neth) correctly describes Saturn's rings

Religion and Philosophy

Quebec (Can) gets its first bishop, François Xavier de Laval Montmorency (Fr) • Philosopher Henry More (Eng), one of the Cambridge Platonists, writes *The Immortality of the Soul* to combat skepticism • Massachusetts' Puritan government persecutes Quakers; the Puritans do not acknowledge religious freedom

Politics and Wars

In English constitutional crisis, General John Lambert agrees not to use the army against General George Monk; Monk's forces enter London and he reestablishes the Long Parliament, which soon dissolves itself • Prince Charles, exiled son of Charles I, issues Declaration of Breda, promising amnesty and tolerance upon his succession; a Convention Parliament proclaims Charles II king, and the English monarchy is restored • King Karl X (Swe) dies; is succeeded by his son Karl XI • Treaties of Oliva and Copenhagen hand Polish and Danish lands to Sweden, and confirm German state of Brandenburg's claim to East Prussia • Virginia's former royal governor Sir William Berkeley is reappointed by Charles II • Bambara kingdoms grow strong along the Niger River in West Africa

Arts and Letters

LITERATURE: John Dryden (Eng), poem *Astraea Redux* celebrating Charles II's return; civil servant Samuel Pepys (Eng) begins his coded diary; Molière (Fr), *Sganarelle*

Science and Discovery

Royal Society is created in London • Scientist Otto von Guericke (Ger) makes the first machine to produce (static) electricity

Social and Economic

Dancing and theater revive in England's anti-Puritan Restoration period • English parliament passes new Navigation Act stipulating that only English-built ships may carry goods for England and its colonies, and forbidding North American colonies to sell sugar or tobacco to foreign countries

1661   1662   1663

ENGLAND—**Charles II**

HOLY ROMAN EMPIRE—**Leopold I**

Politics and Wars
Pro-royalist "Cavalier" parliament meets in England • General John Lambert (Eng) is executed for treason • France's chief minister Cardinal Mazarin (Fr) dies, and King Louis XIV rules as absolute monarch • Sweden and Russia agree the Peace of Kardis • Dutch and Portuguese settle colonial disputes • Arabs raid Portuguese settlement in Mombasa (now in Kenya)

Arts and Letters
PAINTING: Claude Lorrain (Fr), *Landscape with the Rest on the Flight to Egypt*; BALLET: King Louis XIV (Fr) establishes the Académie Royale de Danse, which develops a system of correct ballet steps; LITERATURE: Molière (Fr), comedy *L'Ecole des maris*

Science and Discovery
Anatomist Marcello Malpighi (It) describes lung structure • *The Sceptical Chymist* by Robert Boyle (Ire) attacks old notions of the nature of the chemical elements

Religion and Philosophy
Repressive laws (so-called Clarendon Code) reëstablish Anglicanism in England, starting with the Corporation Act to ensure all magistrates are loyal Anglicans • Episcopacy (Church rule by bishops) is resumed in Scotland • Preacher John Eliot (Eng) begins translating the Bible into Massachusetts Indian dialect

Social and Economic
Stockholm's Banco (Swe) issues world's first banknote

Politics and Wars
England sells city of Dunkirk to France • King Charles II (Eng) marries Catherine of Braganza (Port) • Spaniards attempt to invade Portugal • Chinese pirate Cheng Ch'engkung ("Koxinga") captures Taiwan (Formosa) from Dutch

Arts and Letters
PAINTING: Charles le Brun (Fr) appointed first painter to King Louis XIV (Fr); MUSIC: Giovanni Battista Lulli (It) becomes master of music to Louis XIV; LITERATURE: Pierre Corneille (Fr), drama *Sertorius*; Molière (Fr), comedy *L'Ecole des femmes*; GENERAL: Chinese culture attains new heights under emperor Sheng-tsu (1662–1722)

Science and Discovery
Robert Boyle (Ire) describes pressure-volume relationship for gases, called Boyle's law • Royal Society of London receives its charter • Statistician John Graunt (Eng) writes a pioneer work on vital statistics

Religion and Philosophy
England's Act of Uniformity bans teaching or preaching by Nonconformists (those priests who do not accept the entire, Book of Common Prayer) • Massachusetts' General Court grants civil liberties to citizens outside the Congregational Church

Social and Economic
Statesman Jean Baptiste Colbert (Fr) becomes Louis XIV's controller-general of finances

Other Events
Charles II (Eng) grants the Charter of Connecticut

Politics and Wars
Portugal defeats Spain at Ameixal, south-central Portugal • Swiss confederation practically collapses; the Federal Diet does not meet 1663–1776 • Austria and the Ottoman Empire start a war • Dutch help China's emperor Sheng-tsu to drive Cheng Chin (pirate successor to Koxinga) away from mainland China

Arts and Letters
LITERATURE: Pierre Corneille (Fr), *Sophonisbe*; Samuel Butler (Eng) first part of verse satire *Hudibras*

Science and Discovery
Philosopher-scientist Blaise Pascal (Fr) outlines his principles of hydrostatics and pneumatics

Religion and Philosophy
Société des Missions Etrangères founded in France

Social and Economic
England's Turnpike Act allows levy of road tolls • Slave-trading is first specified as an objective of an English chartered company • England's Staple Act insists that products made in Continental Europe must reach English colonies via England

Other Events
King Charles II (Eng) grants the American colony of Carolina (31°–36°N) to 8 proprietors and grants the Charter of Rhode Island and Providence Plantations • Charles II founds Sheerness Dockyard, but English sea power is weak

Politics and Wars

England seizes New Netherlands (modern New York), which is handed to James, Duke of York; also Dutch coastal posts in Africa • Duke of York grants Lord Berkeley and Sir George Carteret the Delaware-Hudson region • Portugal wins further victories against Spain • Austrians and French defeat Turks southeast of Vienna, and Turks sue for peace • American colonies of Connecticut and New Haven unite

Arts and Letters

MUSIC: Heinrich Schütz (Ger), *Christmas Oratorio*; LITERATURE: Jean Baptiste Racine (Fr), first tragedy, *La Thébaïde*; Pierre Corneille (Fr), *Othon*; Molière (Fr), *Tartuffe*; John Evelyn (Eng), *Sylva,* book on tree cultivation

Science and Discovery

L'Homme, a posthumous work by philosopher René Descartes (Fr), explains the animal body in mechanistic terms

Religion and Philosophy

England's Conventicle Act allows only small private meetings of Nonconformists

Social and Economic

France starts a state coach service • French gain right to trade in Persia • Siam (Thailand) grants Dutch monopoly in foreign trade (invalidated by actions of the French) • French statesman Jean Baptiste Colbert founds French East India and West India companies

Other Events

City of New Amsterdam, now in English hands, is renamed New York

Politics and Wars

In the Second Anglo-Dutch War, English fleet defeats Dutch off Lowestoft (Eng) • Felipe IV of Spain dies; is succeeded by his 4-year-old son Carlos II • American colony of Maine goes to the heirs of its former proprietor, Sir Ferdinando Gorges • An English Royal Commission visiting New England finds fault only with autocratic Massachusetts

Arts and Letters

PAINTING: Meindert Hobbema (Neth), The *Water Mill*; LITERATURE: Jean Baptiste Racine (Fr), *Alexandre le Grand*; Molière (Fr), *Don Juan*; John Dryden (Eng), heroic drama *The Indian Emperor*; GENERAL: Louis XIV (Fr) begins to make Versailles Europe's most splendid palace: designed by architects Louis Le Vau and Jules Hardouin-Mansart, landscape gardener André Le Nôtre, and painter Charles Le Brun

Science and Discovery

Philosophical Transactions of the Royal Society (Eng) becomes the world's first scientific journal in English • Scientist Robert Hooke (Eng) publishes *Micrographia,* featuring first biological use of the term "cell" • Mathematician Isaac Newton (Eng) develops differential calculus, and begins research into light and gravitation

Religion and Philosophy

England's Five-Mile Act forbids Nonconformist ministers to live within 5 miles (8 km) of corporate towns, or to teach

Social and Economic

Serious outbreak of bubonic plague in London (Eng); 68,596 people die, thousands flee

Politics and Wars

French join Dutch in war against England • Dutch fleet under Michel de Ruyter and Grand Pensionary Jan de Witt defeats English fleet under George Monk (now Duke of Albemarle) off North Foreland (Eng); Albemarle defeats Dutch in another encounter off the Dutch coast • Scottish Covenanters rebelling against episcopalianism (rule of Church by bishops) lose Battle of the Pentland Hills, Lothian • Dutch tighten their hold on East Indies by taking Celebes from Portugal • French capture West Indies islands of Antigua and Montserrat from English • English privateers seize island of Tobago

Arts and Letters

LITERATURE: Pierre Corneille (Fr), *Agésilas*; Molière (Fr), *Le Misanthrope*

Science and Discovery

King Louis XIV (Fr) establishes the Académie Royale des Sciences • Physician Thomas Sydenham (Eng), founder of modern clinical medicine, publishes *Methodus Curandi Febres* • Astronomer Giovanni Cassini (It) sees polar caps on Mars • Scientist Isaac Newton (Eng) develops integral calculus, and continues research into light and gravitation

Religion and Philosophy

Preacher John Bunyan (Eng) publishes *Grace Abounding,* a major work of religious experience • Philosopher Baron Gottfried von Leibniz (Ger) publishes his first major philosophical work, *Dissertatio de Arte Combinatoria*

Social and Economic

Five-day fire destroys much of London (Eng), including Old St. Paul's Cathedral

ENGLAND—**Charles II**
HOLY ROMAN EMPIRE—**Leopold I**

Politics and Wars

Dutch ships enter Medway River (Eng), revealing the weakness of English sea power • Dutch, French, English and Danes conclude the Treaty of Breda: England keeps the North American territory which now forms New York, New Jersey and Pennsylvania; Dutch keep Surinam • English statesman Earl of Clarendon (wrongly blamed for the Clarendon Code, repressive laws re-establishing Anglicanism) is impeached and exiled • England's Cabal ministers (named for its members' initials) foreshadow cabinet government • King Louis XIV (Fr) launches War of Devolution to seize Flanders from Spain • Portugal's profligate king Afonso VI is exiled • Russia gets eastern Ukraine from Poland in the Treaty of Andrussovo

Arts and Letters

ARCHITECTURE: Giovanni Bernini (It) completes colonnaded square of St. Peter's, Rome; LITERATURE: Jean Baptiste Racine (Fr), tragedy *Andromaque*; Pierre Corneille (Fr), *Attila*; John Milton (Eng), *Paradise Lost*

Science and Discovery

Scientist Robert Hooke (Eng) proves that respiration requires fresh air

Religion and Philosophy

Pope Alexander VII dies; is succeeded by Clement IX, who unavailingly tries to reconcile Jansenists and Jesuits • Patriarch Nikon revises Russian Church ritual on Greek lines, provoking secession by so-called Old Believers

Other Events

King Charles II (Eng) grants Bahamas islands to the Carolina proprietors

Politics and Wars

England, Netherlands and Sweden form Triple Alliance to counter encroachment by France into the Spanish Netherlands • Holy Roman Emperor Leopold I joins War of Devolution against France • France seizes Burgundy, but by Treaty of Aix-la-Chapelle, Spain regains it: France keeps Spanish Netherlands border towns • Spain recognizes Portugal's independence • Polish king Jan II Casimir of Poland abdicates: a power struggle follows

Arts and Letters

MUSIC: Dietrich Buxtehude (Den) becomes organist at Lübeck (Ger); LITERATURE: Jean Baptiste Racine (Fr), satirical comedy *Les Plaideurs*; Molière (Fr), *L'Avare*; Jean de la Fontaine (Fr), first six books of *Fables*; Sir George Etherege (Eng), comedy *She Would If She Could*

Science and Discovery

Naturalist Anton van Leeuwenhoek (Neth) makes improved observations of capillaries in the human body • Physiologist John Mayow (Eng) shows that a certain part of the air is needed for respiration

Religion and Philosophy

Quaker lawyer William Penn (Eng) is imprisoned in the Tower of London for questioning the doctrine of the Trinity in his book *Sandy Foundation Shaken*

Social and Economic

French begin founding trading posts in India • King Charles II (Eng) leases city of Bombay to the English East India Company

Other Events

Dutch pioneers settle at Mossel Bay in South Africa

Politics and Wars

James, Duke of York, brother and heir of King Charles II (Eng), is suspected to have rejected Anglicanism for Roman Catholicism • Venice loses Mediterranean island of Crete to Ottoman Empire • Michael Wisinowiecki is elected king of Poland • Carolina receives an outmoded Fundamental Constitution • Statesman Jean Baptiste Colbert (Fr) becomes Louis XIV's Minister of Marine

Arts and Letters

MUSIC: Louis XIV (Fr) founds Académie Royale de Musique; LITERATURE: Jean Baptiste Racine (Fr), tragedy *Britannicus*; Molière (Fr), comedy ballet *Monsieur de Pourceaugnac*; Samuel Pepys (Eng) ends his diary because of failing eyesight

Science and Discovery

Giovanni Cassini (It) becomes first director of Paris Observatory • Isaac Newton (Eng) first describes his calculus • Naturalist Jan Swammerdam (Neth) publishes a work describing insect metamorphosis • Johann Joachim Becher (Ger) pioneers theory of *phlogiston,* a substance supposed to be lost in burning • Nicolaus Steno (Den) explains the true nature of fossils • Phosphorus is first prepared, by Hennig Brand (Ger)

Religion and Philosophy

India's Muslim Mogul rulers ban Hinduism and smash Hindu temples • Peace of Pope Clement IX briefly ends the Jansenist controversy • Quaker leader William Penn (Eng) writes *No Cross No Crown* (stressing Christian self-sacrifice) • Pope Clement IX dies

Politics and Wars

King Charles II (Eng) signs secret Treaty of Dover with King Louis XIV (Fr) promising to help France against Spain and the Dutch Republic • James, Duke of York, heir to Charles II, openly declares his Roman Catholicism • Cossack leader Stenka Razin starts a peasant revolt in southeastern Russia • Africa's Mandingo Empire is defeated by the Bambara kingdoms

Arts and Letters

PAINTING: Jan Vermeer (Neth), *Allegory of the Art of Painting*; Jacob van Ruisdael (Neth), *Haarlem*; ARCHITECTURE Christopher Wren (Eng) begins designing London churches to replace those destroyed by Great Fire of 1666; LITERATURE: Pierre Corneille (Fr) *Tite et Bérénice*; Molière (Fr), ballet comedy *Le Bourgeois gentilhomme*; Jean Baptiste Racine (Fr), tragedy *Bérénice*

Science and Discovery

Astronomer Jean Picard (Fr) makes the first exact measurement of an arc of the meridian • William Clement (Eng) invents the anchor escapement to regulate clocks

Religion and Philosophy

Clement X is elected Pope • Jewish philosopher Baruch Spinoza (Neth) publishes *Tractatus Theologico Politicus* • In his book *Pensées,* French philosopher Blaise Pascal defends Christianity against skeptics

Social and Economic

In England, the Hudson's Bay Company is chartered to trade and colonize

Other Events

Town of Charleston (now S.C.) is founded

Politics and Wars

English buccaneer Henry Morgan destroys Panama City • Russian government puts down Stenka Razin's peasant revolt with difficulty • Cossack disturbances affect Polish Ukraine • King Louis XIV (Fr) acts to isolate his Dutch opponents, signing treaties with German states of Brunswick, Hanover, Lüneburg and Osnabruck; he wins a promise of neutrality from Holy Roman Emperor Leopold I (Ger)

Arts and Letters

PAINTING: Adriaen van Ostade (Neth), *Travelers Resting*; LITERATURE: John Milton (Eng), *Paradise Regained* and *Samson Agonistes*; Pierre Corneille, Molière, Philippe Quinault (Fr), *Psyché*; Molière, *Les Fourberies de Scapin*; William Wycherley (Eng), comedy *Love in a Wood*

Science and Discovery

Astronomer Giovanni Cassini (It) discovers satellites of the planet Saturn

Religion and Philosophy

Philosopher John Locke (Eng) begins *Essay Concerning Human Understanding* • Preacher John Bunyan (Eng) publishes *A Confession of My Faith*

Social and Economic

England's parliament forbids all freeholders of property worth less than £100 a year to kill game, even on their own land

Other Events

Jean Baptiste Colbert, French Minister of Marine, raises strength of French navy to nearly 200 ships

Politics and Wars

King Charles II (Eng) issues second Declaration of Indulgence, granting freedom to nonconformist Protestants and Roman Catholics • England and France are at war with Dutch Republic • France forms secret alliance with Sweden • French invade southern Holland • As a result of war, Dutch mob murders Grand Pensionary Jan de Witt and his brother Cornelius; Willem III of Orange, now aged 22, elected Stadtholder • Dutch defeat an Anglo-French fleet in Sole Bay, off Suffolk coast (Eng) • Turks invade Poland

Arts and Letters

LITERATURE: Molière (Fr), comedy *Les Femmes savantes*; Thomas Shadwell (Eng) *Epsom Wells,* play of contemporary manners

Science and Discovery

Physicist N. Cassegrain (Fr) designs a reflecting telescope utilizing a secondary mirror opposite a pierced main mirror • Giovanni Cassini (It) estimates Sun's distance from Earth to within 7 percent of accuracy

Social and Economic

England opens Baltic trade to all English merchants

Other Events

African Trading Company (Eng) relinquishes its charter • Royal African Company is founded • English architect Christopher Wren is knighted

ENGLAND—**Charles II**

HOLY ROMAN EMPIRE—**Leopold I**

Politics and Wars
English parliament compels King Charles II to withdraw second Declaration of Indulgence, and passes Test Act making it virtually impossible for Roman Catholics and Nonconformists to hold offices in England; Charles II's brother and heir, James Duke of York, a Roman Catholic, resigns all his offices • German state of Brandenburg joins Netherlands in alliance against France • Dutch fleet under Michel De Ruyter defeats English and French fleets at Schooneveld Banks, in mouth of Scheldt River • English seize St. Helena from Dutch • Dutch capture New York City from English • Brandenburg makes separate peace with France

Arts and Letters
PAINTING: Willem Van de Velde the Elder (Neth) *Three Ships in a Gale*; Adriaen van Ostade (Neth), *The Violin Player*; LITERATURE: Jean Baptiste Racine (Fr), tragedy *Mithridate*; Molière (Fr), last play of importance, *Le Malade imaginaire*; John Dryden (Eng) comedy *Marriage à la Mode*; Mrs. Aphra Behn (Eng), onetime spy for Charles II in Antwerp, comedy *The Dutch Lover*

Science and Discovery
Jesuit explorer Jacques Marquette (Fr) follows Wisconsin River to Mississippi River, and travels down Mississippi to confluence with Arkansas River

Politics and Wars
Treaty of. Westminster ends Third Anglo-Dutch War; Dutch return New York City to English • Holy Roman Empire and Spain declare war on France; French army under Vicomte de Turenne invades the German state of the Palatinate • France's Swedish allies invade Brandenburg; Brandenburg joins the alliance against France • King Michael Wisniowiecki of Poland dies; Jan III Sobieski is elected to the throne • Poland forms an alliance with France

Arts and Letters
PAINTING: Bartolomé Murillo (Sp), *St. Francis*; LITERATURE: Jean Baptiste Racine (Fr), tragedy *Iphigénie*; Andrew Marvell (Eng), *Last Instructions to a Painter,* satirizing England's conduct of Dutch Wars; Nicolas Boileau (Fr), *L'Art Poétique,* aimed at improving literary taste; John Evelyn (Eng), *Navigation and Commerce*; Giovanni Battista Basile (It), short stories *Il Pentamerone*; Thomas Shadwell (Eng), *The Enchanted Island,* based on William Shakespeare's *The Tempest*

Science and Discovery
Physicist Robert Boyle (Ire) confirms that oxidation increases weights of metals • Anatomist Thomas Willis (Eng) publishes *Pharmaceutie Rationalis*

Religion and. Philosophy
Philosopher Nicolas Malebranche (Fr) publishes the important *De la recherche de la vérité*

Politics and Wars
In the Dutch War against France, army of German state of Brandenburg defeats the Swedes, France's allies, at Battle of Fehrbellin (Ger); sharp decline in prestige of Swedish army; German troops defeat French at Sasbach, Baden, on Rhine River; French commander, Vicomte de Turenne, is killed; French retreat across Rhine but stand firm in Alsace • King Christian V (Den) makes war on Sweden and regains Scania (Skåne province, southern Sweden, ceded to Denmark 1658) • Army of King Jan III Sobieski (Pol) defeats Turks at Lemberg (modern Lvov, Ukraine) • "King Philip's War" begins between Wampanoag Indians and English settlers in New England; named for Wampanoag chief Metacom, also called "King Philip"

Arts and Letters
PAINTING: Bartolome Murillo (Sp), *Girl and Her Duenna*; MUSIC: Jean-Baptiste Lully (Fr; formerly Giovanni Battista Lulli, It) opera *Thesée*; LITERATURE: William Wycherley (Eng), comedy *The Country Wife*

Science and Discovery
Greenwich Royal Observatory is founded in England, and John Flamsteed becomes the first Astronomer Royal • Pioneer Dutch microscopist Anton van Leeuwenhoek first observes protozoa, which he calls "animalcules" • Dutch scientist Christiaan Huygens invents balance-wheels for watches

Religion and Philosophy
Book *Christian Ethics* by poet-clergyman Thomas Traherne (Eng) is published posthumously • Benedictus de Spinoza (Neth) finishes *Ethics*

Politics and Wars

In Dutch War against France, French fleet routs Dutch fleet off Sicily; Dutch Admiral Michel de Ruyter is killed • Denmark, at war with Sweden since 1675, joins Dutch in successful attack on Götland; Swedes defeat Danes at Lund, Sweden • In Spain, Don Juan, bastard elder brother of 15-year-old King Carlos II, leads revolt against incompetent rule of the regent, Carlos's mother, Mariana de Austria, and takes over the government • War between Poles and Turks ends with Treaty of Zuravna; Turks gain Polish Ukraine • "King Philip's War" in New England ends with death of Metacom ("King Philip"), chief of the Wampanoag Indians • New Jersey colony is divided into East Jersey and West Jersey

Arts and Letters

PAINTING: Bartolomé Murillo (Sp), *Madonna Purissima,* and two self-portraits; Godfrey Kneller (Gottfried Kniller, Ger, settled in Eng), portrait *Mr. Banks*; MUSIC: Jean-Baptiste Lully (Fr) opera *Atys*; LITERATURE: John Dryden (Eng), rhymed tragedy *Aurangzebe*; Sir George Etheredge (Eng), comedy *The Man of Mode*

Science and Discovery

English astronomer Edmund Halley catalogues the southern stars • Microscopist Anton van Leewenhoek (Neth) examines and compares spermatazoa of various mammals

Religion and Philosophy

Pope Clement X dies; is succeeded by Innocent XI, who begins campaign to reorganize Roman Catholic Church finances, improve morality of the clergy and eliminate nepotism (favors shown to relatives)

Politics and Wars

Mary, daughter of James, Duke of York, brother and heir of Charles II (Eng) marries Willem III of Orange, Stadtholder (head of state) of the Netherlands; Dutch merchants are hostile to the marriage • In Dutch War against France, French troops defeat those of Willem III at Kassel (Ger); troops of German state of Brandenburg capture Stettin (now Szczecin, Poland); Swedes defeat Danes in naval battles in Baltic Sea off Rostock (Ger), and off Landskrona (Swe) • French capture Dutch posts on Senegal River, West Africa • War breaks out between Turkey and Russia following Cossack (Russ) raids on Turkish territory

Arts and Letters

PAINTING: Pieter de Hooch (Neth), *Musical Party in a Courtyard*; MUSIC: Jean-Baptiste Lully (Fr), opera *Isis*; LITERATURE: Jean Baptiste Racine (Fr): tragedy *Phèdre*; Mrs Aphra Behn (Eng), Part I of play *The Rover*; Thomas Wycherley (Eng), comedy *The Plain Dealer*

Science and Discovery

English astronomer Edmund Halley observes transit of Venus across the face of the Sun

Religion and Philosophy

Posthumous publication of *Ethics,* by Benedict de Spinoza (Neth) in the year of his death, defines government of God as "the unalterable order of nature and the interconnection of natural things"

Politics and Wars

Renegade Anglican priest Titus Oates (Eng) "discloses" largely invented "Popish plot" to murder King Charles II and put his Roman Catholic brother James, Duke of York, on the throne; panic trials of leading Roman Catholics follow and 35 are executed after false evidence • Papists' Disabling Act is passed barring Roman Catholics from English parliament • English Lord High Treasurer Thomas Osborne, Earl of Danby, is impeached for treasonable negotiations with France • Two Treaties of Nijmegen ends wars between Netherlands and France, and Spain and France: Netherlands keeps its territories intact, France gains lands in Flanders from Spain

Arts and Letters

PAINTING: Bartolomé Murillo (Sp), *The Immaculate Conception*; LITERATURE: Comtesse de La Fayette (Fr), novel *La Princesse de Clèves*; Jean de La Fontaine (Fr), *Fables, choisies, mises en vers*; John Dryden (Eng), *All for Love*

Science and Discovery

Scientist Robert Hooke (Eng) discovers that the extension of a coil spring is proportional to its tension • Astronomer Olaus Roemer (Den) builds a planetarium

Religion and Philosophy

Preacher John Bunyan (Eng) publishes *The Pilgrim's Progress,* an allegory of the Christian journey through life, written while in jail for unlicensed preaching

Other Events

Netherlands gets its first chrysanthemums from Japan

113

ENGLAND—**Charles II**

HOLY ROMAN EMPIRE—**Leopold I**

Politics and Wars

King Charles II (Eng) dissolves parliament • James, Duke of York, Charles's Roman Catholic brother and heir, leaves England for exile abroad • Charles calls his third parliament, which tries to pass a Bill excluding James from the succession: Charles thwarts it • Habeas Corpus Act is passed by English parliament, restating checks on illegal imprisonment • Rebellion of Scottish Covenanters (Presbyterians) is ruthlessly put down by troops led by Charles II's illegitimate son the Duke of Monmouth • War between Sweden and the German state of Brandenburg continues

Arts and Letters

MUSIC: Alessandro Scarlatti (It), first opera *Gli Equivoci nell' Amore*; Jean Baptiste Lully (Fr), opera *Bellérophon*; LITERATURE: John Dryden and Nathanial Lee (Eng), tragedy *Oedipus*

Science and Discovery

English astronomer Edmund Halley publishes catalog of stars in the southern hemisphere • French explorers Louis de Hennepin and René Cavalier, Sieur de la Salle discover the Niagara Falls, then sail through the Great Lakes to the southern end of Lake Michigan • French scientist Denis Papin invents "steam digester" (pressure cooker)

Social and Economic

Political economist Sir William Petty (Eng) publishes *A Treatise on Taxes and Contributions* • Germany gets its first coffee-house (in Hamburg)

Politics and Wars

King Charles II (Eng) calls his fourth parliament; the House of Commons passes an Exclusion Bill, aimed at excluding Charles's Roman Catholic brother James, Duke of York, from succession to the crown, but the House of Lords rejects it; parliament is dissolved • King Louis XIV (Fr) establishes Chambers of Reunion (special courts) to decide what lands France should possess; as a result of its decisions, he annexes Luxembourg and Saarbrucken to France • Swedish parliament passes a law by which earldoms and all large territorial holdings revert to the crown • New Hampshire separates from Massachusetts

Arts and Letters

LITERATURE: Thomas Otway (Eng) blank-verse tragedy *The Orphan, or the Unhappy Marriage*; John Bunyan (Eng), novel *The Life and Death of Mr. Badman*; Andrew Marvell (Eng), *Poems* (published posthumously)

Science and Discovery

Scientist Giovanni Borelli (It) publishes work *On the Motion of Animals*, applying mathematics and mechanics to the study of muscular movements

Social and Economic

Diplomat Sir William Temple (Eng) publishes his essay *Upon the Origin and Nature of Government*

Other Events

Last dodo is hunted to death in Mauritius • Ballet is introduced into Germany

Politics and Wars

King Charles II calls his fifth parliament, sitting at Oxford; it reintroduces the Exclusion Bill to bar his brother James, Duke of York from succession to the crown; Charles at once dissolves parliament • France annexes German city of Strasbourg, and seizes town of Casale from Savoy • Turks sign Treaty of Radzin with Russia: Russia gains greater part of Ukraine and trading rights on Black Sea • Portuguese establish settlement of Colonia on left bank of Rio de la Plata, South America • Charles II grants Charter of Pennsylvania to Quaker leader William Penn • In India, Akbar leads abortive revolt against the misrule of his father, Mogul emperor Aurangzeb; Akbar flees to the Deccan, giving Aurangzeb a pretext for invading it

Arts and Letters

MUSIC: Jean Baptiste Lully formally acquires French citizenship; LITERATURE: John Dryden (Eng), satirical poem *Absalom and Achitophel* and play *Spanish Fryar* (attacking papists); GENERAL: Comédie Francaise is founded

Science and Discovery

Trader René Cavalier, Sieur de La Salle, (Fr) explores Mississippi River to its mouth and claims river valley for France (as Louisiana) • Architect Christopher Wren becomes president of the Royal Society (Eng)

Social and Economic

Spain passes laws to ameliorate lot of Indian workers in Spanish America • Oil lamps are used to light streets in London (Eng)

Politics and Wars

Charles II's illegitimate son, the Duke of Monmouth, at the height of his popularity, is greeted royally on progress through England • Spain and Holy Roman Empire make pact against French aggression • King Louis XIV (Fr) calls Church assembly at St. Germain: it decides that popes have no temporal rights over kings and are inferior to French church councils • Pope Innocent XI refuses to invest any participants in St. Germain council as bishops • Austria and Poland begin a war with the Turks to liberate ʻHungary • Fedor III of Russia dies; is succeeded by his brother Ivan V and his half-brother Petra I as joint tsars, and his sister Sophia as regent • Quaker leader William Penn (Eng), new owner of Pennsylvania, calls a general assembly in the colony which adopts the "Great Law," guaranteeing religious freedom there • James, Duke of York, gives Delaware to William Penn

Arts and Letters

MUSIC: Jean Baptiste Lully (Fr), opera Persée; LITERATURE: Thomas Otway (Eng), last blank-verse tragedy, Venice Preserved

Science and Discovery

Scientist Isaac Newton (Eng) gives mathematical explanation for astronomer Johann Kepler's laws of planetary motion • Astronomer Edmund Halley (Eng) observes what is called Halley's Comet, and sets himself the task of calculating its highly elliptical orbit

Religion and Philosophy

Preacher John Bunyan (Eng) publishes The Holy War

Politics and Wars

So-called "Rye House" plot to murder King Charles II (Eng) roughly coincides with lawful attempt to curb his powers, made by many leading statesmen; the statesmen concerned suffer severe treatment as a result: Lord William Russell and Algernon Sidney are executed, Earl of Essex is driven to suicide, Duke of Monmouth (Charles's bastard son) is exiled • Renegade preacher Titus Oates (Eng), whose evidence had led to many executions for treason, is proved to be a liar • James, Duke of York, brother of Charles II, is reinstated in office • Spain and France are at war; France invades Spanish Netherlands • Turks lay siege to Vienna; a German-Polish army relieves the city • René Cavalier, Sieur de La Salle (Fr), establishes colony near mouth of Mississippi River • Quaker leader William Penn makes peace treaty with Indians in Pennsylvania

Arts and Letters

PAINTING: Godfrey Kneller (Eng), Sir Charles Cotterell; LITERATURE: William Penn (Eng), General Description of Pennsylvania

Science and Discovery

French ecclesiastic Edmé Mariotte completes his investigation of the rise of sap in plants, and foreshadows concept of osmosis (the passage of one fluid into another through a membrane)

Social and Economic

A former Lord Chief Justice of England, Sir Matthew Hale, publishes A Discourse Touching Provision for the Poor

Politics and Wars

In Franco-Spanish War, French seize city of Trier and duchy of Luxembourg from Holy Roman Empire (Spain's ally), and invade the Spanish Netherlands • By the Truce of Regensburg between Louis XIV (Fr) and Holy Roman Emperor Leopold I, France keeps all its gains since 1680 • Louis XIV secretly marries his mistress, Mme. de Maintenon, a devout Roman Catholic, and begins campaign against heretics: Huguenots (Protestants) in the Cavennes of southern France revolt • Venice joins Austria and Poland in Holy League against the Turks, backed by Pope Innocent XII • Holy Roman Empire makes minor gains against Turks in Hungary

Arts and Letters

PAINTING: Godfrey Kneller (Eng), portrait The Duchess of Portsmouth; MUSIC: Jean Baptiste Lully (Fr), opera Amadis de Gaule; Alessandro Scarlatti (It) becomes maestro di capella at Naples, Italy's leading center of music; LITERATURE: Physician Alexander Esquemeling (Neth), History of the Buccaneers of America

Science and Discovery

Philosopher-statesman Gottfried Leibnitz (Ger) publishes his method of calculus, using different nomenclature from that of Isaac Newton (Eng) • Scientist Robert Hooke (Eng) invents the heliograph

Religion and Philosophy

In Massachusetts, Presbyterian preacher Cotton Mather begins his voluminous puritanical writings

ENGLAND—**Charles II**–□ **James II**
HOLY ROMAN EMPIRE—**Leopold I**

Politics and Wars

Charles II (Eng) dies; is succeeded peacefully by his Roman Catholic brother, James II • Renegade preacher Titus Oates (Eng) is flogged for fabricating the "Popish Plot" of 1678: five Roman Catholic peers alleged to have been in the plot are freed from jail • Double rebellion by Protestant leaders against King James II: the Duke of Argyle lands with an army in Scotland, but fails to win support and is captured and executed; Duke of Monmouth, exiled bastard son of Charles II, lands from the Netherlands with 82 followers in west of England and proclaims himself king; he raises an army but is defeated at Battle of Sedgemoor and executed • Lord Chief Justice Jeffreys holds "Bloody Assize"—harsh and biased trials of English rebels, many of whom are executed or transported • Louis XIV (Fr) revokes Edict of Nantes, which gave religious freedom to Huguenots (Protestants)

Arts and Letters

MUSIC: Jean-Baptiste Lully (Fr), opera *Roland*; ARCHITECTURE: building of Pont Royal begins in Paris

Science and Discovery

Mathematician John Wallis (Eng), publishes an important treatise on algebra • Scientist Isaac Newton (Eng), formulates the law of gravitation

Social and Economic

French Huguenots (Protestants), fleeing from persecution, pour into England, Netherlands and Brandenburg (Ger), taking with them many arts and crafts • French settlers arrive in Texas

Politics and Wars

King James II defies England's religious laws by making Sir Edward Hales, a Roman Catholic, an army officer; judges nominated by James uphold his action in court • Louis XIV (Fr) lays claim to lands of the Palatinate (Ger) following the death of its last Elector, Charles, without heir (1885): as a result, the League of Augsburg is formed against France by the Holy Roman Empire, the Palatinate, the Netherlands, Saxony, Spain and Sweden • England's New England colonies are formed into the Dominion of New England, with Sir Edmund Andros as governor • France formally annexes the island of Madagascar • German armies capture city of Buda (Hung) from the Turks • French seize North American trading posts from Hudson's Bay Company

Arts and Letters

THEATER: Kabuki theaters gain popularity in Japan; Sweden's first theater opens in Stockholm; MUSIC: Jean-Baptiste Lully (Fr), last opera, *Armide et Renaud*; LITERATURE: John Dryden (Eng), *Ode to the Memory of Mrs. Anne Killigrew*

Science and Discovery

Scientist Isaac Newton (Eng) exhibits first book of his *Philosophiae Naturalis Principia Mathematica* to Royal Society (Eng)

Religion and Philosophy

Fellows of Magdalen College, Oxford (Eng) are expelled for refusing to accept as their president a Roman Catholic appointed by James II

Other Events

Henri de Tonty (Fr) establishes settlement on Lower Arkansas River

Politics and Wars

King James II issues general first Declaration of Liberty of Conscience, granting freedom of worship in England and Scotland • Venice completes its conquest of Morea (Greece) from Turks, and captures Athens • German army liberating Hungary defeats Turks at Battle of Mohacs; as a result, Turkish army leaders depose sultan Muhammad IV and install his brother Suleiman III

Arts and Letters

ARCHITECTURE: work begins on Grand Trianon palace, Versailles (Fr); LITERATURE: John Dryden (Eng), poem *The Hind and the Panther,* contrasting eternal meek Hind (Church of Rome) with fierce Panther (Church of England); Francois Fénelon (Fr), *Traité de l'éducation des filles*

Social and Economic

Under pressure from Aurangzeb, Mogul emperor of India, the English East India Company shifts its headquarters from Surat to Bombay

Other Events

Parthenon in Athens is badly damaged by explosion when Venetians capture the city • Huguenot (French Protestant) settlement is founded at Cape of Good Hope, South Africa

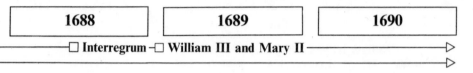

Politics and Wars
King James II (Eng) issues his second Declaration of Liberty of Conscience, ordering it to be read in all churches: seven bishops who refuse are arrested, tried for seditious libel, and acquitted • Birth of James II's first son (the king is aged 57) raises fears of a continuing Roman Catholic monarchy: leading members of the nobility petition Willem III of Orange, Stadtholder (chief of state) of the Netherlands, to save England from "Catholic tyranny" • Willem lands at Torbay, Devon, with 14,000 Dutch troops, and many English nobles and army leaders support him, including John Churchill, a general; James flees to France • France invades Palatinate • Austrians capture Belgrade from Turks • In War of the League of Augsburg, French troops invade the Palatinate (Ger)

Arts and Letters
LITERATURE: Mrs. Aphra Behn (Eng), novel *Oroonoko*; Thomas Shadwell (Eng), comedy *The Squire of Alsatia*

Science and Discovery
Navigator William Dampier (Eng) sails from Cochin China to northwestern coast of Australia before going on to Batavia (Djakarta, Indonesia), and thence via Cape of Good Hope back to England

Social and Economic
Underwriters in London form habit of meeting regularly at Lloyd's coffee-house

Other Events
Earthquake shatters Smyrna (Turk)

Politics and Wars
English peers summon a Convention Parliament, which offers the throne jointly to Willem III of Orange and his wife Mary Stuart (daughter of runaway king James II); they accede as William III and Mary II; Declaration of Rights assures parliamentary supremacy; James II lands in Ireland and besieges Londonderry; Scottish Highlanders on James's side win Battle of Killicrankie, but their rebellion then dies out • Scottish bishops are abolished • The League of Augsburg makes war on France, and is joined by England to form a Grand Alliance • Colonists in North America joyfully proclaim William and Mary as sovereigns; New Englanders overthrow the Dominion of New England and its governor, Sir Edmund Andros, and restore charter government in Massachusetts, Rhode Island and Connecticut • Petr I (Russ) overthrows his sister Sophia as regent, and takes command of the government; his co-tsar Ivan V lives on in retirement

Arts and Letters
PAINTING: Meindert Hobbema (Neth), *The Avenue, Middelharnis*; MUSIC: Henry Purcell (Eng), opera *Dido and Aeneas*; LITERATURE: Jean Baptiste Racine (Fr), tragedy *Esther*; Thomas Shadwell (Eng), *Bury Fair*

Science and Discovery
Baron Louis de Lahontan, French officer and traveler, reaches Great Salt Lake, Utah

Religion and Philosophy
English dissenters win the right not to attend Church of England services • John Locke (Eng), book *On Civil Government*

Politics and Wars
English parliament passes Act of Grace, giving indemnity to supporters of ex-king James II; in Ireland, an army led by William III defeats that of James at Battle of the Boyne: James returns to exile in France • War of the League of Augsburg continues: a French fleet defeats an English fleet at Battle of Beachy Head; French armies defeat German forces at Fleurus (now Belg) and Italian forces in Piedmont (It) • Schenectady Massacre: village of Schenectady, NY, is virtually wiped out by French and Indians • English capture Port Royal, S.C. from French

Arts and Letters
PAINTING: Meindert Hobbema (Neth), *The Mill*; LITERATURE: John Dryden (Eng), tragi-comedy *Amphitryon*

Science and Discovery
Scientist Christiaan Huygens (Neth) publishes his theory that light travels by wave motion • Physicist Denis Papin (Fr) invents a crude piston-and-cylinder steam engine

Religion and Philosophy
Philosopher John Locke (Eng) publishes *An Essay Concerning Human Understanding*

Social and Economic
English economist Sir William Petty publishes Political Arithmetic, foundation stone of social statistics

Other Events
Radical Benjamin Harris issues newspaper *Publick Occurrences Both Forreign and Domestick* in Boston, Mass; it is suppressed

ENGLAND—**William III and Mary II** ────────────────────

HOLY ROMAN EMPIRE—**Leopold I** ──────────────────────

1691

Politics and Wars
Irish rebellion against William and Mary (Eng) continues; English force defeats French-supported Irish rebels at Battle of Aughrim; Limerick surrenders after second siege in 2 years; revolt ends with Pacification of Limerick, guaranteeing full civil and religious freedom to Irish Roman Catholics • In War of the League of Augsburg, French seize town of Nice from Savoy • In war to liberate Hungary, Germans defeat Turks at Battle of Salem Kemen; Turkish Grand Vizier Mustafa Kiuprili is killed • Massachusetts (now including Maine, Plymouth Colony and Nova Scotia) receives a new charter, broadening its franchise and granting freedom of worship to all except Roman Catholics • English general John Churchill, Earl of Marlborough, is imprisoned, suspected of plotting with the exiled James II

Arts and Letters
MUSIC: Henry Purcell (Eng), opera King Arthur (words by John Dryden); LITERATURE: Jean Baptiste Racine (Fr), scriptural tragedy Athalie; Anthony à Wood (Eng) Athenae Oxonienses, brief and sometimes scathing biographies of Oxford notabilities

Religion and Philosophy
Witch-hunt begins in Salem, Mass

Social and Economic
English parishes are compelled to levy taxes for upkeep of roads, and face fines if roads fall into disrepair

1692

Politics and Wars
Massacre of Glencoe (Scot): government soldiers of Clan Campbell treacherously slaughter 40 members of Clan MacDonald because their chief fails to take an oath of allegiance to William and Mary within prescribed time • War of the League of Augsburg continues: French troops defeat army of William III (Eng) at Steenkerke (Neth); an English-Dutch fleet defeats a French fleet at Cap La Hogue, ending French threat to invade England • Hanover (Ger) becomes an electorate—that is, its ruler has the right to help elect Holy Roman emperors

Arts and Letters
MUSIC: Henry Purcell (Eng), opera The Fairy Queen; LITERATURE: Florent Dancourt (Fr), witty comedy Les Bourgeoises à la mode; William Congreve (Eng), novel Incognito; OTHER: German painter Godfrey Kneller receives an English knighthood

Religion and Philosophy
Witch trials at Salem, Mass, result in 19 people being hanged for witchcraft, as a result of voodoo tales told by Tituba, a West Indian slave • Pope Innocent XII restricts the sale of Church offices, and limits the number of posts which can be held by a pope's relations

Social and Economic
Lloyd's Coffee House in London becomes the official headquarters of English marine insurance

1693

Politics and Wars
War of the League of Augsburg continues: French defeat the forces of William III (Eng) at Battle of Neerwinden (Neth), and the army of Savoy at Marsaglia (It); a French fleet heavily defeats an English fleet at Battle of Lagos • The Protestant Swiss cantons agree to supply England and the Netherlands with mercenary soldiers, while the Roman Catholic cantons make similar terms with Spain, also a member of the Grand Alliance • Carolina colony is divided into North Carolina and South Carolina

Arts and Letters
PAINTING: Sir Godfrey Kneller (Eng), portrait of Dr. Burnet; MUSIC: Alessandro Scarlatti (It), opera Teodora; LITERATURE: William Penn (Eng), An Essay on the Present and Future Peace of Europe

Religion and Philosophy
New England Puritan preacher Increase Mather publishes book Case of Conscience Concerning Evil Spirits Personating Men, vindicating his family's part in the Salem witchcraft trials of 1692

Social and Economic
English government borrows £1,000,000 in loans from the public at 10 percent., starting England's National Debt • Increasingly effective Jesuit protection of Indians in Brazil makes slave-dealing unprofitable, so colonists begin intensive and successful new search for gold; more white settlers flock to Brazil

Other Events
William and Mary College is founded in Virginia • City of Kingston, Jamaica, is founded

Politics and Wars

War of the League of Augsburg continues: English naval attack on Brest fails • English parliament passes Triennial Act, providing that a new parliament must be elected every 3 years • Queen Mary II (Eng) dies, leaving her husband, William III, as sole ruler, and without a direct heir • Elector Johann Georg IV of Saxony dies; is succeeded by his brother, Frederick Augustus I

Arts and Letters

PAINTING: Sir Godfrey Kneller (Eng), *Hampton Court Beauties*; MUSIC: Henry Purcell (Eng), *Te Deum*; LITERATURE: William Congreve (Eng), comedy of manners *The Double Dealer*; John Dryden (Eng), last tragicomedy *Love Triumphant* (incidental music by Purcell); Académie Française publishes its first official French dictionary

Science and Discovery

Physician Antonio Vallisnieri (It), unwilling to accept the theory of spontaneous generation of insects, begins work to prove that larvae in galls originate from eggs

Social and Economic

At the suggestion of Scottish economist William Paterson, the English parliament establishes the Bank of England, with initial capital of £1,200,000 and empowers it to issue notes • England gets freedom from press censorship when the Licensing Act expires and is not renewed

Other Events

Royal Hospital for disabled soldiers Chelsea (Eng) opens • University of Halle (Ger) is founded

Politics and Wars

In War of the League of Augsburg, the army of William III (Eng) recaptures city of Namur (now Belg) from French • Russia and Turkey are at war: army led by Russia's Tsar Petr I, the Great, fails in a bid to capture Azov, gateway to the Black Sea • Protestant Irish parliament refuses to ratify terms of the Pacification of Limerick, agreed with England in 1691

Arts and Letters

MUSIC: Henry Purcell (Eng), operas *The Indian Queen, The Tempest*; LITERATURE: William Congreve (Eng), comedy *Love for Love*

Science and Discovery

Botanist Nehemiah Grew (Eng) isolates magnesium sulphate (Epsom salt) from natural spring water

Religion and Philosophy

English philosopher John Locke publishes *Essay on the Reasonableness of Christianity,* arguing that reason cannot grasp the whole of reality without the aid of religious faith • Thomas Ken (Eng), earlier deprived of the bishopric of Bath and Wells as a *non-juror*—one who would not take the oath of allegiance to William III and Mary II— writes the hymn *Awake My Soul*

Social and Economic

Scientist Isaac Newton (Eng) becomes Master of the Mint, supervising England's coinage • Royal Bank of Scotland is established

Politics and Wars

Quaker leader William Penn (Eng) issues third "Frame of Government" for his colony of Pennsylvania • English parliament passes Trials for Treason Act, requiring minimum of 2 witnesses to prove an act of treason • A plot to assassinate William III (Eng) is uncovered; the plotters are executed • France and Savoy (It) sign Peace Treaty of Turin, marking beginning of end of the War of the League of Augsburg; they persuade League powers to cease all fighting in Italy • In combined land and sea operation, Tsar Petr I, the Great, (Russ) seizes Azov from Turks • Petr the Great sends young Russians to study shipbuilding in England, Venice and Netherlands as a step in the westernization of Russia • Polish king Jan III Sobieski dies without an heir

Arts and Letters

LITERATURE: John Dryden (Eng), *Ode on the Death of Mr. Henry Purcell*; William Congreve (Eng), tragedy *The Mourning Bride*; Sir John Vanbrugh (Eng), play *The Relapse*

Science and Discovery

Swiss mathematician Jacques B. Bernouilli publishes first systematic treatise on probability, *Artis Conjectandi*

Religion and Philosophy

General Court (legislature) of Massachusetts adopts a resolution of repentance for the Salem witchcraft trials of 1692

Social and Economic

A Board of Commissioners is formed to control all trade between England and its American colonies • English parliament imposes a tax on windows

1697   1698   1699

ENGLAND—**William III**

HOLY ROMAN EMPIRE—**Leopold I**

1697

Politics and Wars
Treaty of Ryswick ends war between France and the Grand Alliance; little territory changes hands but Rhine River is declared free to navigation, and Louis XIV (Fr) recognizes William III as king of England • King Karl XI of Sweden dies; is succeeded by his son Karl XII, aged 15. • Austrian general Prince Eugene of Savoy defeats Turkish armies at Battle of Zenta • 18 claimants to vacant throne of Poland; Poles choose Elector Frederick Augustus I of Saxony, who becomes Augustus II "The Strong" of Poland • Russian tsar Petr I visits England and Netherlands incognito and works in shipyards there

Arts and Letters
MUSIC: John Blow (Eng), anthem *I Was Glad When They Said*; LITERATURE: John Dryden (Eng), *Alexander's Feast* (his favorite poem); philosopher Pierre Bayle (Fr), *Dictionnaire historique et critique,* analyzing and criticizing legendary beliefs; Charles Perrault (Fr), *Histoires ou contes du temps passé* ("Mother Goose's Tales")

Social and Economic
Peace between England and France results in cession of Hudson's Bay Company's forts to French-Canada

Religion and Philosophy
Judge Samuel Sewall admits that the witchcraft trials of 1692 at Salem, Mass, over which he presided, were unjust

Other Events
Fire destroys greater part of London's Palace of Whitehall

1698

Politics and Wars
Childlessness of aging King Carlos II (Sp) raises question of Spanish succession; to maintain balance of power, France, England, Holy Roman Empire and Netherlands agree on how Spanish inheritance shall be divided when Carlos II dies (First Treaty of Partition); Carlos, not having been consulted, makes Josef Ferdinand, Prince Elector of Bavaria, his sole heir • Tsar Petr I, the Great (Russ) breaks off visit to western Europe to crush Revolt of the Streltsy (soldier-nobility of Moscow garrison) • Arabs expel Portuguese from their East African trading posts

Arts and Letters
PAINTING: Rachel Ruysch (Neth), paintings of fruit and flowers; ARCHITECTURE: Jules Hardouin Mansart (Fr) designs Place Vendôme, Paris

Science and Discovery
Engineer Thomas Savery (Eng) invents "engine to raise water by fire"—an atmospheric steam engine designed to pump water from mines

Social and Economic
England's Woolens Act prohibits American colonists from shipping locally-manufactured woolen goods from one colony to another • English companies introduce their own fire-brigades

Other Events
Explorer Pierre Lmoyne, Sieur d'Iberville, founds French settlement in Louisiana • Engineer Henry Winstanley (Eng) completes building of the Eddystone Lighthouse, on rocks off Plymouth, England

1699

Politics and Wars
Death of Josef Ferdinand, Prince Elector of Bavaria, and heir to throne of Spain reopens Spanish succession question; France and Holy Roman Empire maneuver for advantage while negotiating new treaty of partition with England and Netherlands • Austria, Poland and Venice end war with Turks by Treaty of Karlowitz: Turks lose large territories to all three opponents • French establish military posts in lower Mississippi River region, to prevent English expansion there

Arts and Letters
BALLET: Raoul Feuillet (Fr), *Choréographie,* containing first ballet notation; LITERATURE: Bishop François Fénelon (Fr), *Télémaque,* criticizing Louis XIV (Fr) and postulating that kings are subject to law; George Farquhar (Ire), comedy *Love and a Bottle*; John Dryden (Eng), *Fables, Ancient and Modern*

Science and Discovery
Explorer Dr. C. Poncet (Fr), follows Nile River from Cairo (Egypt) to area of Singa (Sudan), then travels east to Gondar (Ethiopia) • Navigator William Dampier (Eng) begins 2-year voyage to East Indies, northwest Australia, New Guinea and Ascension Island

Religion and Philosophy
English parliament decrees life imprisonment for Roman Catholic priests and teachers

Other Events
Billingsgate fish market opens in London (Eng)

1700

Politics and Wars

Second Treaty of Partition fails to settle Spanish succession: King Carlos II names Philippe of Anjou, grandson of Louis XIV (Fr), his sole heir, and dies six weeks later; Spain accepts Philippe as Felipe V • Holy Roman Emperor Leopold I and Elector Frederick III of Brandenburg (Ger) agree to act against France; France gains support of Savoy and Bavaria • Russia ends war with Turkey, retaining Azov • Start of Great Northern War: Russia, Poland and Denmark attack Sweden, in effort to break Swedish Baltic supremacy; Danes invade Schleswig; Poland's Saxon allies invade Livonia.

Arts and Letters

PAINTING: Sir Godfrey Kneller (Eng), portrait *Matthew Prior*; LITERATURE: William Congreve (Eng), comedy *The Way of the World*; George Farquhar (Ire), comedy *The Constant Couple*

Science and Discovery

Prussian Academy of Science founded, with mathematician Baron Gottfried von Leibnitz as first president

Social and Economic

American diarist and judge Samuel Sewall publishes *The Selling of Joseph*, first strong American protest against slavery

Religion and Philosophy

Pope Innocent XII dies; is succeeded by Clement XI

1701

Politics and Wars

English parliament passes Act of Settlement, providing that future sovereigns must be Protestants • Exiled ex-king James II dies; his son James Edward is hailed by Louis XIV (Fr) as "king of England" • War of the Spanish Succession begins: France, Savoy and Bavaria support King Felipe V (grandson of Louis XIV); Holy Roman Emperor Leopold I, England, Netherlands and many German states form the Grand Alliance to support claim of Leopold's son, Archduke Karl, to the Spanish throne; French troops seize fortresses in the Spanish Netherlands, while Austrian general Prince Eugene of Savoy invades Italy • Elector Frederick III of Brandenburg adopts title of King Frederick I of Prussia • In Great Northern War, a Swedish army led by King Karl XII invades Poland

Arts and Letters

PAINTING: Hyacinthe Rigaud (Fr), portrait of *Louis XIV*; Ogata Korin (Jap), *Irises* (screen); LITERATURE: Daniel Defoe (Eng), satirical poem *The True-born Englishman*; Sir Richard Steele (Ire), moral comedy *The Funeral*

Science and Discovery

Scottish physician and mathematician John Arbuthnot publishes *The Usefulness of Mathematics*

Social and Economic

English agricultural reformer Jethro Tull devises a horse-drawn seed drill

Other Events

Pioneer Antoine Cadillac (Fr) founds Detroit settlement • Yale College established at New Haven, Conn

1702

Politics and Wars

William III (Eng and Neth) dies; is succeeded in Britain and Ireland by his sister-in-law Anne, younger daughter of James II; in Netherlands the States-General assumes control • In War of Spanish Succession, England declares war on France; John Churchill, now Earl of Marlborough, is captain-general of its land forces; English naval attack on Cadiz (Sp) fails, but an assault on Spanish treasure fleet in Vigo Bay (Sp) succeeds; Austrians under Prince Eugene and French under Duc de Vendome clash in indecisive Battle of Luzzara • War spreads to North American colonies (Queen Anne's War) • In Great Northern War, Swedes seize Warsaw and Cracow (Pol) • East Jersey and West Jersey are reunited as New Jersey

Arts and Letters

LITERATURE: Cotton Mather (Amer) *Magnalia Christi Americana*; George Farquhar (Ire), comedy *The Twin Rivals*; Edward Hyde, Earl of Clarendon (Eng), *The True Historical Narrative of the Rebellion and Civil Wars in England* (published posthumously)

Religion and Philosophy

Journalist Daniel Defoe (Eng) publishes pamphlet *The Shortest Way with the Dissenters,* lampooning the absurdity of religious intolerance; it results in his imprisonment • American Puritan preacher Cotton Mather publishes a history of church affairs in New England

Other Events

A French settlement is established in Alabama

ENGLAND—**Anne**

HOLY ROMAN EMPIRE—**Leopold I** ———————————————— ☐ **Josef I**

Politics and Wars

War of Spanish Succession continues: John Churchill, now Duke of Marlborough (Eng), captures Bonn and Limburg (Ger); Archduke Karl, German claimant to Spanish throne, invades Catalonia and proclaims himself Carlos III of Spain; Savoy, France's ally, changes sides and joins the Grand Alliance headed by the Holy Roman Empire • Hungarians begin revolt against Austrian rule • In Great Northern War, Swedes defeat Saxons at Pultusk, Saxony • Methuen Treaty improves trade relations between England and Portugal

Arts and Letters

MUSIC: Cleric and musician Sebastien de Brossard (Fr), *Dictionnaire de Musique,* first work of its kind in France; LITERATURE: Daniel Defoe (Eng), begins publishing periodical *The Review*; Sir Richard Steele (Ire), comedy *The Lying Lover*

Science and Discovery

Scientist Isaac Newton (Eng) becomes President of the Royal Society

Other Events

Storm destroys first Eddystone lighthouse off Plymouth (Eng) • A strong earthquake rocks Tokyo, killing 100,000 people • Tsar Petr I, the Great, (Russ) founds the city of St. Petersburg (now Leningrad)

Politics and Wars

War of the Spanish Succession continues: Austrians under Prince Eugene and English under Duke of Marlborough inflict a heavy defeat on French-Bavarian force at Blenheim (modern Blindheim, Ger), knocking Bavaria out of the war; English fleet captures Gibraltar from Spain; Spaniards invade Portugal, England's ally; French overrun Savoy • In Queen Anne's War, French and Indians attack English colonists in the Connecticut Valley • In Great Northern War, Poles depose Augustus II and elect nobleman Stanislaw Leszczynski as their king

Arts and Letters

MUSIC: Johann Sebastian Bach (Ger), first cantata; Georg Friedrich Händel (Ger), *St. John Passion*; LITERATURE: Jean-François Regnard (Fr), comedy *Les Folies amoureuses*; George Farquhar (Ire) and Peter Motteux (Eng), comedy *The Stage Coach*; Colley Cibber (Eng), play *The Careless Husband*; Jonathan Swift (Ire), *The Battle of the Books* and *A Tale of a Tub*

Science and Discovery

Scientist Isaac Newton (Eng) publishes *Opticks,* propounding the corpuscular theory of light and explaining his "Method of Fluxions" (calculus)

Religion and Philosophy

Mathematician Baron Gottfried von Leibnitz (Ger) publishes philosophical work *New Essays Concerning Human Understanding*

Other Events

Weekly *Boston News-letter* is issued in Boston, Mass

Politics and Wars

War of Spanish Succession continues; on behalf of Archduke Karl, a British force under Lord Peterborough captures Barcelona; much of eastern Spain accepts Karl as King Carlos III; Austrians under Prince Eugene begin pushing French out of Savoy • Holy Roman Emperor Leopold I dies; is succeeded by his son, Josef I • An Ottoman officer, Hussein ibn Ali, frees city of Tunis from Turkish rule and founds the Husseinite dynasty • Chinese compel Tibetans to enthrone their candidate as Dalai Lama—spiritual and temporal ruler of Tibet—arousing strong Tibetan hostility

Arts and Letters

ARCHITECTURE: Sir John Vanbrugh (Eng) begins Blenheim Palace; MUSIC: Georg Friedrich Händel (Ger), opera *Almira*; LITERATURE: Sir Richard Steele (Ire), comedy *The Tender Husband*; London-based Dutch physician Bernard de Mandeville, *The Grumbling Hive, or Knaves Turned Honest*

Science and Discovery

Astronomer Edmund Halley (Eng) predicts date of return of Halley's Comet • Engineer Thomas Newcomen (Eng) patents his first steam engine

Religion and Philosophy

English metaphysician and moralist Samuel Clarke publishes *A Demonstration of the Being and Attributes of God*

Other Events

Ship's wheel begins to replace tiller for steering larger vessels

Politics and Wars

Queen Anne's War continues, with French and Indian raids on Charleston, SC • In War of Spanish Succession, Portuguese invade Spain, capturing Madrid and holding it for four months before being driven out; Duke of Marlborough (Eng) defeats Duc de Villeroi's French force at Battle of Ramillies; Austrians under Prince Eugene defeat French at Turin, virtually ending French war effort in Italy • In Great Northern War, Swedes invade and defeat Saxony • Augustus II of Poland is forced to renounce his crown and to recognize Stanislaw Leszczynski as Poland's king

Arts and Letters

LITERATURE: Daniel Defoe (Eng), ghost story *True Relation of the Apparition of one Mrs. Veal*; George Farquhar (Ire), comedy *The Recruiting Officer*; John Evelyn (Eng), ends his *Diary* (not published until 1818)

Science and Discovery

Astronomer Olaus Roemer (Den) issues a new star catalog

Religion and Philosophy

English deist Matthew Tindal publishes *Rights of the Christian Church Asserted*; it provokes a storm of protest

Other Events

Work begins on a second Eddystone lighthouse, off Plymouth (Eng) • Earthquake disaster in Abruzzi, Italy

Politics and Wars

England and Scotland are united under the name of Great Britain, with a single parliament and flag; but Scots retain their own legal system; the Act of Union also provides that Sophia, Princess of Hanover, a Protestant, granddaughter of James I and VI, should be heir to the British throne • War of Spanish Succession continues: Spaniards defeat Portuguese at Almanza; Austrians occupy Naples • In Queen Anne's War, British forces attack French colony of Acadia (Nova Scotia), but fail to capture Port Royal • Mogul emperor Aurangzeb dies in India after 58 years' reign; his empire begins rapidly to disintegrate

Arts and Letters

LITERATURE: Alain-René Lesage (Fr), comedy *Crispin rival de son maître* and novel *Le Diable boiteux*; George Farquhar (Ire), *The Beaux' Stratagem* (Farquhar dies soon after)

Science and Discovery

German alchemist Johann Freidrich Böttger discovers how to make hard white porcelain, formerly a Chinese monopoly

Religion and Philosophy

Theologian Isaac Watts (Eng) publishes *Hymns and Spiritual Songs,* including "When I Survey the Wondrous Cross"

Other Events

Serious eruption of Fujiyama (Jap) • Physicist Denis Papin (Fr) builds a paddlewheel boat, intending to fit it with a steam engine, but the boat is destroyed by watermen

Politics and Wars

Statesman Robert Walpole becomes British Secretary for War • James Edward Stuart, the "Old Pretender," lands with an army in Scotland, but returns to France after defeat of a supporting French fleet by a British fleet under Admiral Byng (GB) • War of Spanish Succession continues: Duke of Marlborough (GB) defeats French at Oudenarde; armies of Holy Roman Emperor capture Lille (Fr) and drive French from West Flanders; French win battles in Spain • In Great Northern War, Karl XII (Swe), allied with Cossack leader Ivan Mazepa, advances in Russia

Arts and Letters

MUSIC: Johann Sebastian Bach (Ger) becomes court organist at Weimar; Georg Friedrich Händel (Ger), oratorio *Il Trionfo del Tempo*

Science and Discovery

Dutch physician Hermann Boerhaave writes *Institutiones Medicae,* a pioneer physiology textbook • Jean Baptiste Régis (Fr) begins making first accurate maps of China

Religion and Philosophy

Religious leader Govind Singh molds the Sikhs of India into a militant order • Alexander Mack (Ger) founds first congregation of German Baptist Brethren (Dunkards) at Schwarzenau

Other Events

A gas explosion kills 100 miners at Chester-le-Street (Eng)

GREAT BRITAIN—**Anne** ————————————————————————

HOLY ROMAN EMPIRE—**Josef I** ———————————————— □ **Karl VI** ————

Politics and Wars

War of Spanish Succession continues: forces led by the Duke of Marlborough (GB) and Prince Eugene (Ger) defeat a French army at Malplaquet, near Mons; British capture the island of Minorca; Austrians defeat the forces of Spain's king Felipe V at Almenara and Saragossa • In Great Northern War, Russians crush Swedes at Poltava (Russ) and become the chief northern power • Russia, Saxony and Denmark form an anti-Swedish coalition • Afghan state wins independence from Persia

Arts and Letters

MUSIC: Bartolomeo Cristofori (It) builds first fortepiano; LITERATURE: Richard Steele (GB) founds influential periodical *The Tatler,* with Joseph Addison as a regular contributor

Science and Discovery

British ironmaster Abraham Darby uses coked coal to smelt iron at Coalbrookdale, Shropshire, pioneering new technique

Religion and Philosophy

George Berkeley (Anglo-Irish bishop) publishes *Essay Towards a New Theory of Vision*

Social and Economic

Japan receives financial reforms under the shogun (military dictator) Tokugawa (1709–1713)

Other Events

Portuguese begin to colonize the Brazilian interior • Johann Maria Farina (It) makes eau-de-cologne in Köln (Ger)

Politics and Wars

Tory party oust Whig party in British parliamentary election: Robert Harley becomes Lord High Treasurer • In War of Spanish Succession, armies of Grand Alliance capture Mons and Douai; French forces crush the alliance in Spain, Archduke Karl is expelled from Madrid, and Felipe V is reëstablished as king of Spain • Tunis becomes virtually independent of the Ottoman Empire • In America, British troops capture Port Royal from the French: Acadia is renamed Nova Scotia and Port Royal becomes Annapolis Royal • Stanislaw Leszczynski is deposed and Augustus II is reinstated as king of Poland

Arts and Letters

ARCHITECTURE: Building of St. Paul's Cathedral, London (Eng), is completed; MUSIC: Georg Friedrich Händel (Ger) becomes Kapellmeister (chief court musician) to Elector Georg of Hanover

Religion and Philosophy

German engraver J. C. Le Blon invents a 3-color printing process

Social and Economic

George Berkeley (Anglo-Irish bishop) publishes Part I of *Treatise Concerning Principles of Human Knowledge,* launching empiricist movement in philosophy • Massachusetts Puritan preacher Cotton Mather publishes *Essays to Do Good*

Other Events

A gas explosion kills 80 miners at Bensham in North Durham (Eng) • First English copyright act becomes law • University of Lyon (Fr) is founded

Politics and Wars

Holy Roman Emperor Josef I dies; is succeeded by his brother, Karl VI • In Britain, the Duke of Marlborough's Tory enemies dismiss him, and appoint the Duke of Ormonde commander-in-chief of the British army • The Grand Alliance ends: negotiations begin to end the War of Spanish Succession • Peace of Szatmar ends the Hungarian war of independence: grievances to be redressed • Turks surround the army of Petr I, the Great, (Russ), forcing the Treaty of Pruth: the town of Azov is returned to Turkey • Governing senate replaces council of boyars in Russia • Tuscarora Indians kill 200 English settlers in North Carolina • British troops launch an abortive attack on French-controlled Montreal

Arts and Letters

MUSIC: Georg Friedrich Händel (Ger), establishes Italian opera in Britain with *Rinaldo*; LITERATURE: Jonathan Swift (GB), *Conduct of the Allies* (attack on war policy); Alexander Pope (GB) verse *Essay Criticism*; Richard Steele and Joseph Addison (GB) found periodical *The Spectator*; OTHER: Roman statues are excavated at Herculaneum (It)

Religion and Philosophy

British parliament passes Occasional Conformity Act, penalizing dissenters

Social and Economic

South Sea Company (GB) is incorporated, and assumes £9 million of Britain's national debt • Queen Anne (GB) founds Ascot races

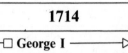

□ George I ⟶▷

Politics and Wars

Felipe V (Sp), grandson of French king Louis XIV, is persuaded to renounce his claims to succeed to the French throne • Peace moves between England and France continue • Protestant cantons secure supremacy in Switzerland's Second Villmergen War • Tuscarora Indians of North Carolina are crushed with help from the colonists of South Carolina and Virginia • Louis XIV grants the Louisiana territory to art-collector Joseph Antoine Crozat

Arts and Letters

MUSIC: Georg Friedrich Händel (Ger), opera *Il Pastor Fido*; Arcangelo Corelli (It), *Concerti grossi,* popularizing early concerto form in music; LITERATURE: Richard Steele and Joseph Addison (GB) cease publishing *The Spectator*; Alexander Pope (GB), poems *Windsor Forest* and *The Rape of the Lock*

Science and Discovery

Thomas Newcomen (GB) uses atmospheric pressure in a steam pump devised to clear flooded mines

Religion and Philosophy

British parliament passes a Religious Toleration Act for Scotland

Social and Economic

Newspaper Stamp Act is passed in Britain—advertisements are taxed

Other Events

Slaves revolt in New York colony • Britain's last execution for witchcraft is carried out • Madrid University is founded • St. Petersburg (modern Leningrad) becomes Russia's capital

Politics and Wars

Treaty of Utrecht ends War of Spanish Succession between most belligerents: Great Britain receives Acadia, Hudson Bay, Newfoundland and St. Kitts from France; Gibraltar and Minorca from Spain; Felipe V is acknowledged as king of Spain, provided French and Spanish crowns stay separate; Spanish Netherlands pass to Dutch Republic in trust for Austria, which receives Milan; Savoy takes Sicily • In Great Northern War, Swedes invade Denmark • King Friedrich I (Pr) dies; is succeeded by his son Friedrich Wilhelm I • Russo-Turkish Peace of Adrianople is signed • Having no son, Holy Roman Emperor Karl VI introduces Pragmatic Sanction, bequeathing his Austrian lands to his daughter, Maria Theresa

Arts and Letters

MUSIC: Georg Friedrich Händel (Ger), *Utrecht Deum*; Alessandro Scarlatti (It), oratorio *St. Francis Neri*; LITERATURE: Richard Steele (GB) starts a periodical, *The Guardian*

Science and Discovery

First proof of binomial theorem appears in *De Arte Conjectandi* by Jacques Bernoulli (Switz)

Religion and Philosophy

Anthony Collins (GB) writes *A Discourse of Free-Thinking* • Pope Clement XI condemns Jansenism in bull (proclamation) *Unigenitus*

Social and Economic

Treaty of Utrecht hands Britain the Asiento (concession for supplying slaves to Spanish America) for 30 years • South Sea Company (GB) wins a monopoly of British trade outside Europe

Politics and Wars

Following a British parliamentary election, the Earl of Shrewsbury succeeds the Earl of Oxford (Harley) as Lord High Treasurer • Princess Sophia of Hanover, heir to British throne, dies • Queen Anne (GB), dies; is succeeded by Sophia's son, the Elector Georg of Hanover, as George I • Treaties of Rastatt and Baden end remainder of war of Spanish Succession: Austria secures the Spanish Netherlands and keeps Milan, Naples and Sardinia • Venice and Turkey are at war • Russians defeat Swedes at Storkyrø and gain control of Finland

Arts and Letters

MUSIC: Johann Sebastian Bach (Ger) becomes Konzertmeister (chief musician) at Weimar • Giovanni Buononcini (It), opera *Astarte*; LITERATURE: Daniel Defoe (GB), *A General History of Trade*

Science and Discovery

Physicist Gabriel Fahrenheit (Ger) develops a mercury thermometer • English agricultural reformer Jethro Tull introduces a horse-drawn hoe

Religion and Philosophy

Schism Act affects dissenting schoolteachers in Britain

Social and Economic

Chartered Company of Spanish Honduras is formed in Spain • German, Swiss and Scots-Irish immigrants cross the fall line—the edge of the Appalachian plateau—to settle the New York-Pennsylvania Piedmont area • King Felipe V bans use of the Catalan language in Spain

125

GREAT BRITAIN—**George I**
HOLY ROMAN EMPIRE—**Karl VI**

Politics and Wars
Whigs win majority in first parliament of George I (GB): the Earl of Halifax becomes First Lord of the Treasury; the Duke of Marlborough is recalled as army commander-in-chief • Jacobite (Stuart) rising begins in Scotland; James Edward Stuart, the "Old Pretender," arrives from France • Louis XIV (Fr) dies; is succeeded by his 5-year-old great grandson Louis XV • French take the island of Mauritius • The Spanish Netherlands (Belgium) effectively pass to Austria • Sweden is opposed by a new coalition • Turks retake the Morea (Greece) from Venice • Colonists drive Yamassee Indians from Carolina into Florida • Maryland reverts to proprietory form of government under the Calvert family

Arts and Letters
MUSIC: Georg Friedrich Händel (Ger/GB) suite *Water Music*; LITERATURE: Nicholas Rowe (GB) *Tragedy of Lady Jane Grey*; Alain René Lesage (Fr), Vol. I of novel *Gil Blas*

Science and Discovery
Mathematician Brook Taylor (GB) publishes *Methodus Incrementorum Directa et Inversa*: earliest work on finite differences, and origin of *Taylor's series* • George Graham (GB) designs an improved anchor escapement for clocks

Religion and Philosophy
Theologian Isaac Watts (GB) writes the earliest English children's hymnal

Social and Economic
Japan sharply curbs copper exports by Dutch traders • British East India Company establishes a trading post in Canton (China)

Politics and Wars
Jacobite (pro-Stuart) rebellion in Scotland collapses; James Edward Stuart, the "Old Pretender," returns to France; leading rebels are executed • Septennial Act fixes 7-year term for British parliaments • Austrians under Prince Eugene of Savoy defeat Turks at Peterwardein • Japan comes under rule of shogun (military dictator) Tokugawa Yoshimune, the ablest Tokugawa ruler after Ieyasu

Arts and Letters
PAINTING: Giovanni Battista Tiepolo (It), *The Sacrifice of Isaac*; MUSIC: François Couperin (Fr) *Art de toucher le clavecin,* work on harpsichord technique; LITERATURE: Chinese scholars produce the *K'ang Hsi* dictionary

Science and Discovery
Governor Alexander Spotswood of Virginia penetrates the Shenandoah Valley and urges colonial control of the Blue Ridge mountain passes

Religion and Philosophy
Emperor K'ang Hsi forbids the teaching of Christianity in China

Social and Economic
France establishes a body of civil engineers, Corps des Ponts et Chaussées • Economic reforms are introduced in Japan, together with attempts to revive old military virtues • Scottish financier John Law founds a joint-stock bank in Paris (Fr)

Other Events
Carolinian settlers build a fort on the Savannah River • Petr I, the Great (Russ), visits Europe

Politics and Wars
Britain, France and Netherlands form a Triple Alliance • Troops of Felipe V (Sp) seize island of Sardinia • Austrians under Prince Eugene capture Belgrade from Turks • Spanish colonies of New Granada, Quito, Panama and Venezuela form Viceroyalty of New Granada • Louis XV (Fr) grants charter for Louisiana territory to Scottish financier John Law and his Company of the West • Mongols seize city of Lhasa (Tibet) • Treaty of Amsterdam allows for French mediation in the Great Northern War

Arts and Letters
PAINTING: Antoine Watteau (Fr), *Embarkation for Cythera*; MUSIC: Johann Sebastian Bach (Ger), *Orgelbüchlein* (organ chorales); LITERATURE: Alexander Pope (GB), poem *Eloisa to Abelard*

Science and Discovery
Tsar Petr I, the Great (Russ), sends envoys to Khiva in Central Asia • German physicist Gabriel Fahrenheit announces his Fahrenheit system for measuring temperatures • Mathematician Abraham de Moivre (GB) publishes *Doctrine of chances*

Social and Economic
East India Company (GB) gets trading concessions from India's Mogul emperor, Farrukh-Siar • Compulsory education is introduced in Prussia—the first country to do this

Other Events
British government grants Sir Robert Montgomery (GB) land in Georgia between the Altamaha and Savannah rivers

Politics and Wars

Troops sent by Spanish king Felipe V seize the island of Sicily • Austria joins the Triple Alliance, forming a Quadruple Alliance to stop Spain wrecking the Utrecht peace settlement; Allied invasions of Sicily and northern Spain follow • Austro-Turkish war ends in Treaty of Passarowitz • Sweden attacks Norway; King Karl XII (Swe) is killed and succeeded by his sister, Ulrika Eleanora

Arts and Letters

PAINTING: Antoine Watteau (Fr), *Fête in a Park*; ARCHITECTURE: Elysée Palace, Paris (Fr), built; MUSIC: Georg Friedrich Händel (Ger/GB) masque *Acis and Galatea*; LITERATURE: Voltaire (Fr) tragedy *Oedipe*

Science and Discovery

Lady Mary Wortley Montagu introduces into Britain the Turkish practice of inoculation against smallpox • British astronomer Edmund Halley discovers the true motion of fixed stars

Religion and Philosophy

British parliament repeals the Occasional Conformity and Schism acts

Social and Economic

French government backs Scots financier John Law's Company of the West, founded to monopolize trade with Louisiana

Other Events

French establish the port of New Orleans • Yale University is established at New Haven, Conn, and named for its benefactor, Elihu Yale (GB), who made a fortune in the service of the English East India Company

Politics and Wars

Spain sends an unsuccessful expedition to Scotland to help Jacobites (Stuart supporters) • George I (GB), as Elector Georg of Hanover, acquires the port of Bremen • Irish parliament passes Declaratory Act allowing British parliament to pass laws for Ireland • France is at war with Spain • Liechtenstein becomes an independent principality within the Holy Roman Empire • Muhammad Shah becomes Mogul emperor in India

Arts and Letters

MUSIC: Georg Friedrich Händel (Ger/GB) *Chandos Anthems*; Thomas D'Urfey (GB) songs and ballads *Wit and Mirth, or Pills to Purge Melancholy*; LITERATURE: Daniel Defoe (GB), first part of *Robinson Crusoe*

Science and Discovery

Explorer Bernard de la Harpe (Fr) starts expeditions along the Red, Arkansas and Canadian rivers

Religion and Philosophy

The first German Baptist Brethren (Dunkards) to reach America settle in Germantown, Penn, under Peter Becker

Other Events

Bubonic plague spreads from Russia to eastern-central Europe • Two American newspapers are founded: *The Boston Gazette* in Massachusetts and *The American Weekly Mercury* in Philadelphia, Penn

Politics and Wars

Quadruple Alliance (Britain, France, Netherlands, Austria) and Spain agree Treaty of the Hague: Felipe V (Sp) gives up claims in Italy; Holy Roman Emperor Karl VI (Aus) abandons claims to Spain; Sicily goes to Austria; Savoy gets Sardinia • Chinese set up garrisons in Tibet • Sweden's Queen Ulrika abdicates in favor of her husband, Frederik of Hesse-Kassel • Treaties of Stockholm largely end the Great Northern War

Arts and Letters

PAINTING: Giovanni Battista Tiepolo (It): *The Martyrdom of St. Bartholomew*; MUSIC: Johann Sebastian Bach (Ger) begins *Klavierbüchlein* (keyboard pieces) Georg Friedrich Händel (Ger/GB), first harpsichord suites; LITERATURE: Voltaire (Fr) tragedy *Artémise*; Alexander Pope (GB) translation of Homer's *Iliad*

Social and Economic

Collapse of Scottish financier John Law's Mississippi scheme triggers financial panic in France and England: bursting of "South Sea Bubble"—craze for company speculation in England—leaves many people ruined • Japanese shogun (military dictator) Tokugawa Yoshimune lifts ban on the study of European culture

Other Events

Colonial settlement starts in Vermont • William Burnet, appointed by British crown governor of New York and New Jersey provinces, bans trade between Iroquois Indians and the French

GREAT BRITAIN—**George I**
HOLY ROMAN EMPIRE—**Karl VI**

1721

Politics and Wars
Whig statesman Sir Robert Walpole becomes Britain's First Lord of the Treasury and effectively the first-ever prime minister; he establishes Cabinet (committee) system of government • Spain joins Franco-British defensive alliance • Sweden and Russia agree the Peace of Nystadt: Russia gains much of eastern Baltic; Sweden is left as a minor nation

Arts and Letters
MUSIC: Johann Sebastian Bach (Ger), *Brandenburg Concertos*; Georg Friedrich Händel (Ger/GB), opera *Floridante* and serenata *Acis and Galatea*; LITERATURE: Nathan Bailey (GB), *Universal Etymological Dictionary*; Charles de Montesquieu (Fr), *Lettres persanes* (fictional "Persian" view of French society)

Science and Discovery
George Graham (GB) invents a cylinder escapement for watches • Fourth *London Pharmacopoeia* omits remedies based on superstition

Religion and Philosophy
Pope Clement XI dies; is succeeded by Innocent XIII

Other Events
Carolinians man Fort George on the Altamaha River to guard against Indians • James Franklin founds newspaper *The New-England Courant* • Modern colonization of Greenland is begun by a Norwegian pastor Hans Egede (founder of Godthaab city) • Bubonic plague kills 9000 people in the French cities of Marseille and Toulon

1722

Politics and Wars
Prussia's government is centralized in a General Directory controlled by its king, Friedrich Wilhelm I • Mir Mahmud, ruler of Kandahar (India), leads an Afghan invasion of Persia and becomes Shah of Persia • Tsar Petr I, the Great (Russ) exploits Persian disunion to capture Persian city of Derbent

Arts and Letters
MUSIC: Johann Sebastian Bach (Ger), first book of *Well-Tempered Clavier* and Anna Magdalena suites; Georg Friedrich Händel (Ger/GB), trio sonatas; Jean Philippe Rameau (Fr), treatise on harmony; LITERATURE: Daniel Defoe (GB), novels *Moll Flanders* and *Colonel Jacque*, also *A Journal of the Plague Year* and *The History of Peter the Great*

Science and Discovery
Physicist René de Réaumur (Fr) publishes *L'Art de convertir le fer forgé en acier et l'art d'adoucir le fer fondu*, first sound handbook on iron technology • Dutch navigator Jacob Roggeveen discovers Easter Island and Samoa in the Pacific Ocean

Social and Economic
William Burnet, governor of New York, founds a trading post at Oswego and persuades Indians to help stop French encroachment from the west

Other Events
Guy's Hospital, London (Eng), is founded with cash given by bookseller Thomas Guy

1723

Politics and Wars
Duc de Bourbon-Condé becomes first minister of France following the death of Duc d'Orléans; at 13, King Louis XV is deemed to be "of age" • Abraham Davel (Switz) launches a doomed revolt in Vaud against rule by Bern • Hungarian Diet (parliament) accept's Holy Roman Emperor Karl VI's Pragmatic Sanction, settling Habsburg succession on his daughter Maria Theresa • Russian force take city of Tiflis (modern Tbilisi) in the Causasus, from disunited Persia • Ashanti tribes of what is now Ghana expand under their leader Opoku Ware

Arts and Letters
MUSIC: Johann Sebastian Bach (Ger), *Magnificat* and *St. John Passion*; he becomes cantor of St. Thomas's School, Leipzig; Georg Friedrich Händel (Ger/GB), opera *Ottone*; LITERATURE: Richard Steele (GB), drama *The Conscious Lovers*

Science and Discovery
German physician and chemist Georg Ernst Stahl coins the term *phlogiston* for the supposed inflammable substance emitted in air by burning objects

Religion and Philosophy
Preacher Peter Becker organizes the first Dunkard (German Baptist) church in North America, at Germantown, Penn

Other Events
British traders claim the Gambia area for the African Company

1724	1725	1726

Politics and Wars

Spanish king Felipe V abdicates, but resumes throne after the death of his son Luis I • Austria accepts the Pragmatic Sanction of Holy Roman Emperor Karl VI, settling succession on his daughter Maria Theresa • Russia and Turkey plot to carve up Persia, and Turks invade Kermanshah province and other parts of western Persia • In a fit of insanity, Mir Mahmud, ruler of Kandahar, massacres Persian nobles and others in Isfahan (Persia) • Nizam-ul-Mulk makes city and kingdom of Hyderabad virtually independent of Delhi; city state of Oudh (modern Ayodhya) wins independence from Delhi • Oyo tribe reestablishes supremacy over South Dahomey, Africa

Arts and Letters

MUSIC: Johann Sebastian Bach (Ger), 39 cantatas and *Sanctus* for *Mass in B Minor*; Georg Friedrich Händel (Ger/GB), opera *Giulio Cesare*; Three Choirs Festival is started at Gloucester (Eng); LITERATURE: Cotton Mather (Amer), *Curiosa Americana*; Daniel Defoe (GB), *Tour Through the Whole Island of Great Britain* (first part)

Science and Discovery

Mathematician Abraham de Moivre (GB) publishes *Annuities on Lives,* a contribution to actuarial mathematics

Religion and Philosophy

Pope Innocent XIII dies; is succeeded by Benedict VIII

Social and Economic

Bourse (stock exchange) is opened in Paris (Fr)

Politics and Wars

On advice of his First Minister the Duc de Bourbon-Condé, Louis XV (Fr) cancels his plans to marry a Spanish princess • Spain and Austria sign the Treaty of Vienna; Britain, France, Prussia and Netherlands retaliate with the Treaty of Hanover • Louis XV marries Maria, daughter of former king of Poland Stanislaw Leszczynski • Petr I, the Great (Russ) dies; is succeeded by his second wife, Ekaterina I • Ashraf Shah succeeds Mir Mahmud as Shah in Persia • The Imamate (Muslim country) of Futa Djallon (Guinea) is established.

Arts and Letters

PAINTING: Antonio Canaletto (It), *View of the Grand Canal, Venice*; MUSIC: Johann Sebastian Bach (Ger), 52 chorale cantatas; Georg Friedrich Händel (Ger/GB), opera *Rodelinda*; Prague Opera House is opened; LITERATURE: Marquise de Sévigné (Fr), *Letters* (published posthumously)

Science and Discovery

Academy of Sciences is founded at St. Petersburg (Russ) • *Historia Coelestis Britannica* by John Flamsteed (GB) becomes a standard star catalog • Navigator Vitus Bering (Den) starts exploring seas off northeastern Siberia

Religion and Philosophy

A "Great Awakening" movement in America is led in Pennsylvania by German immigrants; in New Jersey by Dutch Reformed and Presbyterian churches

Other Events

The New-York Gazette, New York City's first newspaper, is started by printer William Bradford

Politics and Wars

Britain is at war with Spain • France comes under the able administration of King Louis XV's tutor, Cardinal Fleury, who sends Duc de Bourbon-Condé, former First Minister, into exile • William Burnet, Governor of New York, places Cayuga, Seneca and Onondaga Indian lands under British protection • Persians defeat Turks marching on Isfahan, Persia's capital • An anti-Turkish alliance is formed by Russia and Austria • Prussia approves the Pragmatic Sanction by which Holy Roman Emperor Karl VI's daughter Maria Theresa is to inherit Habsburg lands

Arts and Letters

PAINTING: Giovanni Battista Tiepolo (It), ceiling frescoes in the archbishop's palace, Udine (It); MUSIC: Georg Friedrich Händel (Ger/GB), opera *Scipione*; he becomes a British subject as George Frideric Handel; BALLET: ballerina Marie Anne de Cupis de Carmargo (Aust. Neth) pioneers the short ballet skirt; LITERATURE: Alexander Pope (GB), translation of Homer's *Odyssey*; Jonathan Swift (Ire), *Gulliver's Travels*; Daniel Defoe (GB), *The Four Years' Voyages of Captain George Roberts*; Cotton Mather (Amer), *Manuductio and Ministerium*; Chinese scholars produce a 5,020-volume encyclopedia

Science and Discovery

Process of flint-grinding under water is patented in Britain to protects grinders' lungs from damage by silica dust

Other Events

Spanish colonists settle the site of Montevideo (Uru).

GREAT BRITAIN—**George I**-☐ **George II**
HOLY ROMAN EMPIRE—**Karl VI**

Politics and Wars
King George I (GB) dies; is succeeded as ruler of Britain and Hanover by his son George II, who is influenced by his wife Caroline • Spain, at war with Britain and France, blockades Gibraltar • Russia's ruler Ekaterina I dies; is succeeded by Petr II, a grandson of Petr I, the Great • Turks are entrenched in western Transcaucasia • Persia and Turkey make peace; Turkey keeps conquered lands • China and Russia modify their Amur River boundary in the Treaty of Kiachta

Arts and Letters
PAINTING: Antonio Canaletto (It), *The Mole and the Ducal Palace* (Venice); MUSIC: George Frideric Handel (GB) Coronation Anthem and operas *Admeto* and *Riccardo I*; LITERATURE: John Gay (GB), *Fables* (1st series)

Science and Discovery
Physiologist Stephen Hales (GB) publishes *Vegetable Staticks,* describing experiments on plant physiology • J. H. Schulze of Nuremberg (Ger) discovers that sunlight darkens silver salts; an important discovery for the subsequent development of photography • Benjamin Franklin (Amer) founds the Junto at Philadelphia, Penn—precursor of the American Philosophical Society

Religion and Philosophy
First Annual Act (GB) relieves Protestant dissenters who hold public office from penalties for not conforming to the law

Other Events
A hospital for foundlings is established by Thomas Coram in London (Eng) • Brazil's first coffee plantation is established

Politics and Wars
Whig Prime Minister Sir Robert Walpole (GB) stays in office in the first parliament of George II • Anglo-Spanish war formally ends with the Convention of Prado • William Burnet, Governor of Massachusetts, clashes with the colony's legislature over his salary

Arts and Letters
MUSIC: John Gay (GB), *The Beggar's Opera;* George Frideric Handel (GB), operas *Siroe* and *Tolomeo;* LITERATURE: Voltaire (Fr), epic poem *La Henriade* on Henri IV of France; Alexander Pope (GB), *The Dunciad*

Science and Discovery
James Bradley (GB) explains motion of fixed stars in terms of the aberration of light • Navigator Vitus Bering (Den) enters what is now known as the Bering Strait without sighting Alaska • Explorer Sieur de La Vérendrye (Fr) sails along Lake Superior • Pierre Fauchard (Fr) writes the first handbook for dentists

Religion and Philosophy
Clergyman William Law (GB) publishes *A Serious Call to a Devout and Holy Life,* precursor of Methodism • First Amish Mennonites, a European Christian sect, reach America • Johann Beissel, preaching celibacy, forms the first Dunkard (German Baptist) splinter group in North America

Social and Economic
Chartered Company of Guipuzcoa (Caracas) is formed in Spain to promote trade with South America

Politics and Wars
Treaty of Seville ends war involving Spain, Britain, France and Netherlands: Britain keeps Gibraltar, but Britain and France recognize right for Carlos, third son of Spain's king, Felipe V, to succession in Parma, Piacenza and Tuscany (It) • British government makes North and South Carolina Crown colonies because of the incompetence of their proprietors

Arts and Letters
MUSIC: Johann Sebastian Bach (Ger), *St. Matthew Passion;* George Frideric Handel (GB), opera *Lotario;* LITERATURE: Jonathan Swift (Ire) attacks Irish poverty in satire *A Modest Proposal* (he suggests feeding children of the poor to the wealthy!)

Science and Discovery
Scientist Stephen Gray (GB) differentiates between electrical conductors and non-conductors

Religion and Philosophy
Preacher John Wesley (GB) becomes head of the Oxford "Methodist" society founded by his brother Charles • Dunkard (German Baptist) leader Alexander Mack takes the Dunkard congregation to Germantown, Penn

Social and Economic
British parliament investigates the horrors of debtors' prisons • Pennsylvanian printer Benjamin Franklin (Amer) publishes *Modest Enquiry into the Nature and Necessity of a Paper Currency*

Other Events
Baltimore, Md, founded as a "tobacco port" • Benjamin Franklin starts publishing *The Pennsylvania Gazette*

1730

Politics and Wars
Mediterranean island of Corsica revolts against Genoese rule • Petr II (Russ) dies; is succeeded by Anna, daughter of Ivan V, who is dominated by her German lover, statesman Ernst Johann Biron • Persians under warrior Nadir Kuli drive Turks from Transcaucasia and end alien Afghan rule; Persian rule is restored under Shah Tahmasp II, with Nadir Kuli as the real power • Sir Alexander Cuming, on behalf of the British government, secures submission of the Cherokee Indians of eastern Tennessee and the western Carolinas

Arts and Letters
PAINTING: William Hogarth (GB): *A Musical Party*; LITERATURE: James Thomson (GB), pastoral poem *The Seasons*

Science and Discovery
Statesman Charles Townshend (GB), having resigned as Secretary of State after a disagreement with Prime Minister Robert Walpole, turns to agricultural innovation, exploiting crop rotation • Physicist René Antoine de Réaumur (Fr) devises a thermometer scale with 0° as the freezing point of water • Scientist Stephen Hales (GB) proves that the spinal cord controls reflex movement in a frog

Religion and Philosophy
Conrad Beissel (Ger) founds "Economy", a Dunker (Baptist) community at Ephrata, Pa • Pope Benedict XIII dies; is succeeded by Clement XII

Other Events
Diamonds are discovered in Brazil by the Portuguese

1731

Politics and Wars
Britain, Netherlands, Spain, Austria agree two treaties of Vienna • Felipe V (Sp) and maritime powers recognize Holy Roman Emperor Karl VI's Pragmatic Sanction, bequeathing Habsburg lands to his daughter Maria Theresa • Carlos, son of Felipe V, succeeds to Farnese family's Italian duchies • Shah Tahmasp II (Persia) dies; is succeeded by infant Abbas III, last Safavid ruler • Spanish troops kill rebel leader Jose de Antequera in Paraguay

Arts and Letters
PAINTING: William Hogarth (GB), *The Conquest of Mexico*; MUSIC: Johann Sebastian Bach (Ger), Part I of *Klavierübung,* and *St. Mark Passion*; LITERATURE: L'Abbé Prévost (Fr), novel *Manon Lescaut*; Voltaire (Fr), *Histoire de Charles XII* (of Sweden); George Lillo (GB), prose tragedy *George Barnwell*

Science and Discovery
Mathematician John Hadley (GB) demonstrates his octant, a navigation aid

Social and Economic
Holy Roman Empire dissolves the Ostend East India Company • Printer Benjamin Franklin founds first American subscription library

Other Events
A Spanish coastguard pillages a British ship and lops an ear from its captain, Robert Jenkins—an incident which later leads to war • Louisiana becomes a royal French province • French erect a fort at Crown Point on Lake Champlain, in North America

1732

Politics and Wars
Persia and Russia agree Treaty of Resht: Russia abandons claims to Astrabad, Gilan and Mazandaran • All the Holy Roman Empire except Bavaria, the Palatinate and Saxony now at least nominally supports Pragmatic sanction of Emperor Karl VI, leaving his Habsburg lands to his daughter Maria Theresa

Arts and Letters
MUSIC: Covent Garden Opera House opens in London; LITERATURE: Voltaire (Fr), tragedy *Zaïre*; Benjamin Franklin (Amer) publishes first issue of *Poor Richard's Almanack* in Philadelphia, Penn

Science and Discovery
Chemist Hermann Boerhaave (Neth) publishes *Elementa Chemiae,* long a standard chemistry text • Agriculturist Jethro Tull (GB) publishes *New Horse Hoeing Husbandry*

Social and Economic
British parliament bans imports of hats from colonies, to discourage colonists from competing with home manufacturers

Other Events
Philanthropist James Oglethorpe (GB) gets charter granting him land between the Altamaha and Savannah rivers, in Georgia • Western Japan suffers a severe famine • Explorer Sieur de La Vérendrye (Fr) establishes Fort St. Charles on the Lake of the Woods (now between Canada and USA)

GREAT BRITAIN—**George II**
HOLY ROMAN EMPIRE—**Karl VI**

Politics and Wars

Augustus II of Poland dies: succession contested by ex-king Stanislaw Leszczynski (backed by Poles, French and Spaniards) and Augustus's son Augustus of Saxony (backed by Russians and Austrians); France opens War of the Polish Succession against the Holy Roman Empire, occupying Lorraine and invading Lombardy; Russia invades Poland • Persians blockade Baghdad

Arts and Letters

MUSIC: Johann Sebastian Bach (Ger), *Mass in B Minor*; George Frideric Handel (GB), oratorios *Deborah* and *Athaliah*, and harpsichord suites; LITERATURE: Alexander Pope (GB), poem *Essay on Man,* and *Imitations of Horace*; William Byrd (Amer) *A Journey to the Land of Eden*

Science and Discovery

Scientist Stephen Hales (GB) publishes *Haemastaticks* on animal physiology • John Kay (GB) patents the flying shuttle, a landmark in textile mass-production • Vitus Bering (Den) leads 600 men to explore the Siberian coast for Russia • Charles Fay (Fr) discovers that charges of static electricity may be resinous (positive) or vitreous (negative)

Social and Economic

Molasses Act places heavy duties on molasses and sugar imported into British colonies • Prussia introduces military conscription

Other Events

British philanthropist James Oglethorpe founds Georgia, last of the 13 British colonies in North America; colonists begin building town of Savannah

Politics and Wars

In the War of the Polish Succession, Spanish troops defeat Austrians at Bitonto (It) and take Naples and Sicily; Russians take Danzig; Polish ex-king Stanislaw Leszczynski flees to Prussia, and Augustus of Saxony becomes king as Augustus III • Persians campaign in Transcaucasia

Arts and Letters

MUSIC: Johann Sebastian Bach (Ger), *Christmas Oratorio*; George Frideric Handel (GB), opera *Arianna* and *concerti grossi,* Opus 3; LITERATURE: Carlo Goldoni (It), tragedy *Amalasunta*

Science and Discovery

Physicist René Antoine de Réaumur (Fr) starts publication of his *Histoire des insectes* • John Atkins (GB) publishes first authentic description of sleeping sickness (trypanosomiasis)

Religion and Philosophy

Jonathan Edwards revives Puritan intensity in *New England's Great Awakening* (1734–1742) • Voltaire (Fr) writes *Lettres sur les Anglais,* championing representative rule as practiced in England • Philosopher Emanuel Swedenborg (Swe) publishes his mystical *Prodromus Philosophiae*

Social and Economic

Russia and Britain agree a trade treaty

Other Events

Explorer Sieur de La Vérendrye (Fr) establishes Fort Maurepas on Lake Winnipeg • *Lloyd's List,* precursor of *Lloyd's Register of Shipping,* first published in London (Eng)

Politics and Wars

Statesman Sir Robert Walpole (GB) continues as Prime Minister in 2nd parliament of George II • Preliminary Peace of Vienna settles War of the Polish Succession: Augustus III confirmed as king of Poland; Austria recognizes Carlos of Spain as Carlo IV of Naples and Sicily; Russia is now largely master of Polish affairs • Russia returns Baku and Derbent to Persia; Persians win Tiflis from Turks

Arts and Letters

PAINTING: William Hogarth (GB), picture sequence *A Rake's Progress*; MUSIC: Georg Frideric Handel (GB), opera *Alcina,* Johann Sebastian Bach (Ger), "*Italian Concerto*" and Part II of *Klavierübung*; LITERATURE: Alexander Pope (GB), *Moral Essays* and *Epistle to Dr. Arbuthnot*; James Thomson (GB), poem *Liberty*

Science and Discovery

Horologist John Harrison (GB) invents his first chronometer, accurate clock for navigation at sea • Charles La Condamine (Fr) travels to Peru to determine the length of a degree of meridian near the Equator • Naturalist Carolus Linnaeus (Swe) publishes *Systema Naturae,* a pioneer work in plant classification

Religion and Philosophy

Preacher John Wesley (GB) visits America • Moravian missionary Augustus Gottlieb Spangenberg visits America

Social and Economic

Publisher John Peter Zenger (Amer) wins libel case which secures freedom of press in New York • Sugar production established at Mauritius

Politics and Wars

Riots in Edinburgh (Scot): mob seizes Captain John Porteous, who ordered guard to fire on, crowd, and hangs him • Franz Stephen, Duke of Lorraine, marries Maria Theresa of Austria, heir to Holy Roman Emperor Karl VI • Ex-king Stanislaw Leszczynski formally renounces Polish crown • Russia and Austria start war with Turks; Russia retakes Azov • Abbas III (Persia), last Safavid shah, dies; is succeeded by Persian warrior Nadir Kuli

Arts and Letters

MUSIC: Giovanni Pergolesi (It), *Stabat Mater*; George Frideric Handel (GB), *Alexander's Feast*

Science and Discovery

Swiss mathematician Leonhard Euler publishes first systematic mechanics textbook • Spanish navigator Antonio d'Ulloa describes platinum • Dutch physicist Pieter van Musschenbroek invents a moving magic-lantern show

Religion and Philosophy

Preachers John and Charles Wesley (GB) form evangelical groups in England • Nadir Shah fails to convert Persia from Shi'ite to Sunni Islam • Joseph Butler, Bishop of Durham (Eng) defends Christianity against Deism in *Analogy of Religion*

Social and Economic

British parliament repeals law punishing witchcraft with death

Other Events

Colonists build a fort at Augusta, Ga

Politics and Wars

Death of George II's wife Queen Caroline (GB) robs Prime Minister Sir Robert Walpole of important political support • Medici family's rule in Tuscany ends with death of Gian Gastone: Duke Franz Stephen of Lorraine becomes Grand Duke of Tuscany • Russians invade Turkish-held Moldavia and ravage Crimea, but Turks win upper hand against Russians and Austrians • Forces of Nadir Shah (Persia) subdue cities of Balkh (now in Afghanistan) and Baluchistan (now in Pakistan)

Arts and Letters

MUSIC: George Frideric Handel (GB), operas *Arminio* and *Giustino*; Jean Philippe Rameau (Fr), opera *Castor et Pollux*; LITERATURE: Pierre Marivaux (Fr) comedy *Les Fausses confidences*

Science and Discovery

Atlas Général by B. D'Anville (Fr) removes mythical Southern Continent shown in earlier atlases • Joshua Ward (GB) produces sulfuric acid in England • *Biblia Naturae* by Jan Swammerdam (Neth) disproves old notion that nervous action presupposed a nervous fluid • Naturalist Carolus Linnaeus (Swe) publishes *Genera Plantorum*, a landmark in botany

Religion and Philosophy

Preacher John Wesley (GB), on a mission to Georgia, publishes there the first of his 23 collections of hymns • Bookseller Alexander Cruden (GB) compiles his *Concordance to the Bible*

Social and Economic

Theater censorship by the Lord Chamberlain is introduced in Britain

Politics and Wars

Treaty of Vienna: Austria formally abandons Naples, Sicily and Elba to Spain and gets Parma and Piacenza (It); ex-king Stanislaw Leszczynski of Poland receives duchy of Lorraine and Bar from Franz Stephen of Austria • European powers seemingly agree to Pragmatic Sanction, which secures Habsburg lands to Maria Theresa of Austria • "Hawkish" Count Gyllenborg overthrows Arvid Horn as chief Swedish minister • Armies of Nadir Shah (Persia) overruns Afghanistan and invade India • Austria loses Orsova and Semindria to Turks

Arts and Letters

PAINTING: Jean-Baptiste-Siméon Chardin (Fr), *Scouring Maid*; MUSIC: George Frideric Handel (GB), oratorio *Saul* and Opus 4 organ concertos: LITERATURE: Samuel Johnson (GB), poem *London* and articles for *The Gentleman's Magazine*; John Gay (GB), *Fables*, 2nd series (published posthumously)

Science and Discovery

Pierre de Maupertuis (Fr) publishes *Sur la figure de la terre*, confirming that Earth is flattened near the poles • Scientist Daniel Bernoulli (Switz) publishes *Hydrodynamica*, on fluid forces • Russian explorers reach the Arctic Sea estuaries of the Ob and Yenisei rivers, east of the Ural Mountains

Religion and Philosophy

Preacher George Whitefield (GB) visits America • Pope Clement XII attacks Freemasonry in bull (proclamation) *In Eminenti* • Moravian missionary Peter Boehler arrives in North America • John Wesley (GB), under Moravian influence, begins preaching in England

GREAT BRITAIN—**George II**
HOLY ROMAN EMPIRE—**Karl VI** ——□ **Interregnum**

1739

Politics and Wars
Britain starts War of Jenkins' Ear with Spain over mutilation of an English seaman in 1731: Admiral Edward Vernon (GB) storms Porto Bello, Darien • Russia and Turkey agree Treaty of Belgrade: Russia keeps Azov but is forbidden to build a Black Sea fleet • Forces of Nadir Shah (Persia) crush Mogul army and capture Delhi, India • Felipe, son of Felipe V (Sp), marries daughter of Louis XV (Fr)

Arts and Letters
PAINTING: Jean-Baptiste-Siméon Chardin (Fr), *Saying Grace*; MUSIC: Jean Philippe Rameau (Fr), opera *Dardanus*; Johann Sebastian Bach' (Ger) Part III of *Klavierübung*; George Frideric Handel 12 *Grand Concertos*, Opus 6, and oratorio *Israel in Egypt*

Science and Discovery
Russian explorers reach Cape Sterlegov in northern Siberia • Explorers Pierre and Paul Mallet (Fr) make an expedition from Missouri westward to the high plains and back via the Arkansas River

Religion and Philosophy
Preacher George Whitefield (GB) influences Great Awakening in North America • Clergyman Charles Wesley (GB) writes hymn "Hark the Herald Angels Sing" • Philosopher David Hume (GB) develops empiricist philosophy in *Treatise on Human Nature*

Other Events
Dick Turpin, notorious British highwayman, is executed • Nadir Shah takes the Peacock Throne of Delhi to Persia

1740

Politics and Wars
Tsarina Anna (Russ) dies; is succeeded by her great-nephew, Ivan VI • British colonists invade Spanish Florida • Bengal becomes independent of Delhi • Friedrich Wilhelm I of Prussia dies; is succeeded by his son Friedrich II, the Great • Holy Roman Emperor Karl VI (Aus) dies; Europe's Great Powers refuse recognition of his daughter, Maria Theresa, as heir to Austria, despite earlier agreement to do so: Karl Albrecht of Bavaria, Felipe' V of Spain and Augustus III of Saxony claim Austria, leading to War of the Austrian Succession • Prussians occupy Silesia in First Silesian War against Austria

Arts and Letters
PAINTING: François Boucher (Fr), *Triumph of Galatea*; Antonio Canaletto (It), *The Square of St. Mark's*; MUSIC: George Frideric Handel (GB), opera *Imeneo* and organ concertos; Thomas Arne (GB), song "Rule Britannia;" LITERATURE: Samuel Richardson (GB), novel *Pamela*

Science and Discovery
Swiss naturalist Charles Bonnet describes parthenogenesis (development without fertilization) in aphids

Religion and Philosophy
Clergyman George Whitefield (GB) preaches in New England • Preacher John Wesley (GB) ends his connection with the Moravian Church • Pope Clement XII dies; is succeeded by Benedict XIV

Social and Economic
Spanish chartered company of Havana formed • Land enclosure develops in England • Famine affects Paris (Fr)

1741

Politics and Wars
In First Silesian War, now part of the War of the Austrian Succession, Prussians defeat Austrians at Mollwitz • Bavaria, France and Spain (later with Saxony and Prussia) conclude a secret anti-Austrian alliance • Franco-Bavarian troops invade Austria and Bohemia • Concordat curbs papal wealth and power in Naples • Diet of Pressburg (modern Bratislava, Czech): Hungarian nobles are freed from taxation • Sweden, at war with Russia, loses battle at Vilmanstrand (modern Lappeenranta, Fin) • Military revolt overthrows Russian tsar Ivan VI and puts Elizaveta, youngest daughter of Petr I, the Great, on the throne

Arts and Letters
MUSIC: George Frideric Handel (GB), oratorios *Messiah* and *Samson*; Christoph Willibald Gluck (Ger), opera *Artaxerxes*; Jean Philippe Rameau (Fr), trio sonatas; LITERATURE: Voltaire (Fr), tragedy *Mahomet*

Science and Discovery
Explorers Vitus Bering (Den) and Alexei Chirikov (Russ) sight Alaska • Nicolas Andry (Fr) coins term "orthopedics"

Religion and Philosophy
David Hume (GB) writes *Essays Moral and Political*

Social and Economic
Burials outnumber baptisms by 2 to 1 in London (Eng) at height of gin-drinking craze; 75 percent of children die before age 5 in England at this time

□ Karl VII

Politics and Wars
British Prime Minister Sir Robert Walpole (Tory) falls from power; the Earl of Wilmington forms Whig government • Karl Albrecht of Bavaria is elected Holy Roman Emperor Karl VII • First Silesian War ends with Treaty of Breslau and Berlin: Austria cedes upper and lower Silesia to Prussia • In rest of the War of the Austrian Succession, Austrians overrun Bavaria and Bohemia • In War of Jenkins Ear, Spanish forces attack Georgia from Florida

Arts and Letters
PAINTING: François Boucher (Fr), *Diana Resting*; MUSIC: Johann Sebastian Bach (Ger), *Goldberg Variations*; LITERATURE: Henry Fielding (GB), novel *Joseph Andrews*; Thomas Gray (GB), poem *Elegy in a Country Churchyard*; Edward Young (GB) poem *Night Thoughts*

Science and Discovery
Mathematician Colin Maclaurin (GB) first uses calculus in dynamics • Chelyuskin (Russ) reaches Siberia's northernmost point • Engineer Thomas Bolsover (GB) develops Sheffield plate • Military engineer Benjamin Robins (GB) invents ballistic pendulum for finding velocity of projectiles • Chemist Georg Brandt (Swe) identifies cobalt • Astronomer Anders Celsius (Swe) devises centigrade temperature scale

Religion and Philosophy
Religious disturbances produce backlash against the Great Awakening movement in North America

Politics and Wars
British Prime Minister the Earl of Wilmington dies; Henry Pelham forms new Whig government • Russo-Swedish Treaty of Abö cedes Finnish territory to Russia • Turkey and Persia are at war • In War of Jenkins' Ear between Britain and Spain, British general James Oglethorpe invades Florida • King George's War (American aspect of War of the Austrian Succession) begins • In European part of the war, English, Hanoverian, and Hessian forces defeat French at Dettingen, Bavaria • France and Spain sign Treaty of Fontainebleau • Austria hands over Piacenza and Parma to Sardinia

Arts and Letters
PAINTING: William Hogarth (GB) *Marriage à la Mode*: ARCHITECTURE: Johann Balthasar Neumann (Ger), rococo church of Vierzehnheiligen; MUSIC: George Frideric Handel (GB), *Dettingen Te Deum*; LITERATURE: Henry Fielding (GB) novel *Jonathan Wilde*

Science and Discovery
American scientist Benjamin Franklin establishes American Philosophical Society • French naturalist Charles-Marie de La Condamine makes first scientific exploration of the Amazon River • French explorers François and Louis Joseph de La Vérendrye (Fr) explore part of South Dakota

Religion and Philosophy
British preacher George Whitefield's followers split from those of John Wesley as Calvinist Methodists • Congregational clergyman Jonathan Edwards (GB) preaches "New England" sermons

Politics and Wars
Armies of King Friedrich II, the Great, of Prussia invade Saxony and Bohemia, starting Second Silesian War (part of the War of the Austrian Succession) • France goes to war with Austria and Britain • French and Indians invade Nova Scotia, but have to withdraw

Arts and Letters
MUSIC: Johann Sebastian Bach (Ger), *Twenty-four New Preludes and Fugues* (second volume of *The Well Tempered Clavier*); LITERATURE: Samuel Johnson (GB), *Life of Mr. Richard Savage*; Publication of the *Harleian Miscellany* (extracts from manuscripts collected by Robert and Edward Harley, first and second Earls of Oxford)

Science and Discovery
French encyclopedist Jean d'Alembert publishes *Treatise on Dynamics*; British admiral Lord Anson completes a four-year circumnavigation of the Earth, having explored islands north of Strait of Magellan • French cartographer César François Cassini begins survey of France

Religion and Philosophy
Philosopher George Berkeley (Ire) publishes his last work, *Siris*

Other Events
First recorded cricket match: Kent v Rest of England

GREAT BRITAIN—**George II**
HOLY ROMAN EMPIRE—**Karl VII**–☐ **Franz I**

1745

Politics and Wars
Charles Edward Stuart ("the Young Pretender") lands in Scotland from France and starts Jacobite rebellion on behalf of his father, James ("the Old tender"); he wins battles of Prestonpans and Penrith • War of the Austrian Succession continues: Saxony and Netherlands join Britain and Austria against France and Bavaria: Bavaria makes separate peace with Austria; French defeat allied army under Duke of Cumberland (GB) at Battle of Fontenoy • Holy Roman Emperor Karl VII dies: Maria Theresa of Austria's husband Franz Stephen is elected emperor as Franz I • In American phase of the war, British volunteers from Massachusetts, New Hampshire and Connecticut capture French fortress of Louisburg, Cape Breton Island

Arts and Letters
PAINTING: William Hogarth (GB), Self Portrait; LITERATURE: Jonathan Swift (Ire), Direction to Servants

Science and Discovery
Naturalist Charles Bonnet (Switz) discovers instances of parthenogenesis (reproduction without mating) among insects

Religion and Philosophy
Physician Julien Offroy de La Mettrie (Fr) publishes Natural History of the Soul, regarded as so subversive of religious belief that he is compelled to flee from France • British nonconformist divine Philip Doddridge publishes The Rise and Progress of Religion in the Soul

1746

Politics and Wars
In Jacobite rebellion in Britain, army of Charles Edward Stuart ("the Young Pretender") wins battle at Falkirk Moor, but is decisively defeated at Culloden; Charles Edward escapes to France after many adventures • Harsh "pacification" of Highland Scotland begins • In War of the Austrian Succession, French army defeats army of Austria and its allies at Raucoux, and conquers the Austrian Netherlands; Russia makes an alliance with Austria • French capture Madras, India, from British • In American phase of the war, French fail to recapture Nova Scotia and Cape Breton, and attack frontiers of New York colony

Arts and Letters
PAINTINGS: Francois Boucher (Fr), portrait Madame Bergeret; MUSIC: Jean Jacques Rousseau (Fr), opera Les Muses galantes; George Frideric Handel (GB), oratorio Judas Maccabaeus; LITERATURE: William Collins (GB), Odes

Science and Discovery
Swiss mathematician Leonhard Euler supports wave theory of light and suggests possibility of correcting distortion in telescope lenses

Religion and Philosophy
French encyclopedist Denis Diderot writes Philosophical Thoughts

Social and Economic
Wearing of tartans made illegal in Scotland as retribution against Jacobite Highlanders' rebellion

1747

Politics and Wars
In the War of the Austrian Succession, British fleets defeat French fleets off Cape Finisterre, northwest Spain, and in the West Indies • The Dutch Republic appoints Willem IV of Orange as hereditary Stadtholder (chief of state) • In Persia, the assassination of Nadir Shah sparks off serious unrest, with three claimants to the throne; Ahmed Shah Durani becomes ruler of an independent Afghanistan

Arts and Letters
DRAWINGS: William Hogarth (GB), Industry and Idleness (issued as prints); MUSIC: Johann Sebastian Bach (Ger), The Musical Offering (dedicated to King Frederick the Great of Prussia); LITERATURE: Charles Collé (Fr), comedy Truth in Wine; David Garrick (GB), comedy Miss in Her Teens; Thomas Gray (GB), Ode on Eton College and Ode on the Death of a Favorite Cat

Science and Discovery
British astronomer James Bradley discovers the nutation of Earth's axis—nodding movement responsible for precession of equinoxes

Religion and Philosophy
Voltaire (Fr) publishes a fictional tale, Zadig, using it as a vehicle to show the difficulties of attempts to improve human institutions

Politics and Wars

The Treaty of Aix-la-Chapelle (Aachen) ends the War of Austrian Succession: Pragmatic sanction in Austria (the succession of Empress Maria Theresa) and right of Hanoverian succession in Britain is agreed by all parties; Spanish prince Don Felipe, gets Parma and Piacenza; Silesia goes to Prussia; all other conquests are reciprocally restored • In India, French forces repel a British naval attack on Pondichery, but return Madras to Britain

Arts and Letters

PAINTING: William Hogarth (GB), *Calais Gate*; MUSIC: Johann Sebastian Bach (Ger) begins writing *The Art of Fugue*, illustrating almost every possibility of fugal treatment of a single subject; LITERATURE: André-Joseph Panckoucke (Fr), dictionary of French proverbs; Samuel Richardson (GB), novel *Clarissa Harlowe*; Tobias Smollett (GB), novel *Roderick Random*

Science and Discovery

British physician John Fothergill describes diptheria

Religion and Philosophy

French political philosopher Charles de Montesquieu publishes *Spirit of Law*, an entirely new approach to the study of social and political institutions • British philosopher David Hume publishes his *Enquiry Concerning Human Understanding*

Other Events

Excavation begins on the site of Pompeii (It)

Politics and Wars

France and Britain, at peace in Europe, maneuver for position in North America • Prominent Virginian colonists found the Ohio Company, get land grant on the upper Ohio River and initiate exploration as far as Ohio Falls • The French send provincial governor Jean Baptiste de Bienville to take possession of the Ohio Valley, and meanwhile establish a fort on the site of modern Toronto • Spain and Britain sign a commercial treaty

Arts and Letters

PAINTING: Thomas Gainsborough (GB), *Cornard Wood*; SCULPTURE: Jean Baptiste Pigalle (Fr), *Madame de Pompadour*; MUSIC: George Frideric Handel (GB), *Music for the Royal Fireworks*; LITERATURE: Samuel Johnson (GB), poem *The Vanity of Human Wishes*; Henry Fielding (GB), novel *Tom Jones*

Science and Discovery

Naturalist Georges de Buffon (Fr) publishes the first three volumes of his 44-volume *Natural History*

Religion and Philosophy

British philosopher and physician David Hartley publishes *Observations on Man, his Fame, Duty, and Expectations*, arguing that Man's moral sense is not innate but is derived from the association of ideas

Other Events

A sign language for deaf mutes is devised in Portugal

Politics and Wars

King João V of Portugal dies; is succeeded by his son José; government passes into the hands of statesman Sebastião José Carvalho e Mello, a ruthless dictator who begins 27 years of absolute power by breaking the power of the Church and the nobility while promoting trade and agriculture • Britain joins Austria and Russia in a defensive alliance against Prussia • Britain gives up the Asiento, a monopoly of slave trade with the Spanish colonies

Arts and Letters

PAINTING: François Boucher (Fr), *The Sleeping Shepherdess*; MUSIC: George Frideric Handel (GB) oratorio *Theodora*; LITERATURE: Thomas Gray (GB), *Elegy in a Country Churchyard*; Samuel Johnson (GB) launches periodical *The Rambler*, mostly written by himself; Benedictine Monks of Congrégation de Saint-Maur publish a dictionary of dates

Science and Discovery

Dutch physicist Pieter van Musschenbroek invents a thermometer capable of registering higher temperatures than before; a step towards the true pyrometer • Printing of music from movable type begins in Germany

Social and Economic

Interest on Britain's national debt falls from 10 percent to 3 percent

Other Events

New York City gets its first playhouse • The construction of London's first Westminster Bridge is completed

GREAT BRITAIN—**George II**
HOLY ROMAN EMPIRE—**Franz I**

1751

Politics and Wars
Dutch Stadtholder (chief of state) Willem IV of Orange-Nassau dies; his queen, Anne, acts as regent for his infant son, Willem V • In India, a British force under Robert Clive seizes Arcot from the French, greatly diminishing French prestige • King Fredrik I of Sweden dies; the pro-French Adolf Fredrik, Bishop of Lübeck, is chosen to succeed him

Arts and Letters
PAINTING: François Boucher (Fr), *The Toilet of Venus*; William Hogarth (GB), *Gin Lane*; LITERATURE: Tobias Smollett (GB), novel *Peregrine Pickle*; Henry Fielding (GB), novel *Amelia*; French writers Denis Diderot, Voltaire, Jean-Jacques Rousseau, Charles de Montesquieu, Jean d'Alembert, first volume of the *Encyclopédie*

Science and Discovery
Swedish botanist Karl von Linné (Carolus Linnaeus) publishes his *Philosophia Botanica*, introducing a new system of describing and naming living things

Religion and Philosophy
British philosopher David Hume publishes *Enquiry Concerning the Principles of Morals* • Portuguese statesman Sebastião Carvalho curbs the powers of the Portuguese Inquisition

1752

Politics and Wars
Saxony sides with Austria against possible Prussian aggression • In India, British troops led by Robert Clive capture Trichinopoly from the French • Marquis Michel-Ange Duquesne is appointed governor of Quebec • In Anatolia (Turk), derebeys (valley barons) set themselves up as semi-autonomous rulers in defiance of the Turkish government

Arts and Letters
MUSIC: George Frideric Handel (GB), oratorio *Jephtha*; in Paris rival supporters of opera-composers Christoph Willibald Gluck (Ger) and Niccolò Piccini (It) come to blows; LITERATURE: Mrs. Charlotte Edwards (Amer), novel *The Female Quixote*; Viscount Bolingbroke (GB), *Letters on the Study and Use of History* (published posthumously)

Science and Discovery
American scientist Benjamin Franklin conducts his kite-and-key experiment, proving lightning flash and electric spark discharge to be the same

Religion and Philosophy
New England philosopher and revivialist preacher Jonathan Edwards publishes *Misrepresentations Corrected and Truth Vindicated* • William Law (GB) publishes mystical work *The Way to Divine Knowledge*

Other Events
Britain changes from the Julian to the Gregorian Calendar, omitting 11 days from September to get in step with countries already using it • In Moscow a great fire renders thousands homeless

1753

Politics and Wars
French troops are sent by Marquis Duquesne, governor of Quebec, to occupy the British-held Ohio Valley; the colonial government of Virginia sends surveyor George Washington to demand that the French withdraw; the French decline, and build two forts • Portuguese dictator Sebastião Carvalho takes vigorous measures to increase trade between Portugal and Brazil, where he urges racial equality and the appointment of native Brazilians to key government posts • Burma, broken into several petty states since 1600, is reunited with British aid, the French opposing the move

Arts and Letters
PAINTING: Sir Joshua Reynolds (GB), portrait *Commodore Keppel*; LITERATURE: Tobias Smollett (GB), novel *Ferdinand, Count Fathom*; Samuel Richardson (GB), novel *Sir Charles Grandison*; Carlo Goldoni (It), play *La Locandiera*

Science and Discovery
Swiss mathematician Leonhard Euler states the fundamental theorem: In any simple polyhedron $V+F-E=2$ (vertices plus faces minus edges equals two)

Other Events
British physician and naturalist Sir Hans Sloane dies, leaving a massive collection of books and manuscripts; the government buys it, together with the Harleian collection (see 1744), and founds the British Museum • The Vienna stock exchange is founded

Politics and Wars

Britain's Prime Minister Henry Pelham (Whig) dies; his brother, the Duke of Newcastle, takes office • A Concordat between the Vatican and Spain makes the Spanish Church largely independent of Rome but subject to greater control by the state • French forces build Fort Duquesne at a fork on the Ohio River; American troops led by George Washington build Fort Necessity at Great Meadows; the French attack Washington's force and compel its surrender • Representatives of the American colonies discuss a common defense plan at the Albany Convention; Benjamin Franklin's proposal of union is rejected • France recalls its governor-general, Marquis Dupleix, from India, leaving British influence unopposed there

Arts and Letters

PAINTING: François Boucher (Fr), *Judgment of Paris*; William Hogarth (GB), *The Election* (series); LITERATURE: David Hume (GB), first volume of *History of Great Britain*; Prosper Jolyot Crébillon (Crébillon père; (Fr), melodramatic tragedy *Le Triumvirat*; Thomas Gray (GB), ode on *The Progress of Poesy*

Religion and Philosophy

French encyclopedist Denis Diderot publishes a philosophical essay, *Thoughts on the Interpretation of Nature*

Other Events

George Hepplewhite (GB) is at the peak of his career as a furniture-maker: Hepplewhite chairs are famed for their grace, lightness and delicacy

Politics and Wars

The "French and Indian Wars" begin in North America: British colonial governors meet and plan a four-point attack on French forces; a British army led by General Edward Braddock is defeated near Fort Duquesne (modern Pittsburgh); British troops defeat a French army at the Battle of Lake George • Britain signs a treaty with Russia for the defense of Russia and Hanover against possible Prussian attack • Corsican patriot Pasquale Paoli leads a determined revolt against Genoese rule

Arts and Letters

PAINTING: Thomas Gainsborough (GB), *Milkmaid and Woodcutter*; LITERATURE: Voltaire (Fr), play *The Maid of Orleans*; Gotthold Lessing (Ger), domestic tragedy *Miss Sara Sampson*; Samuel Johnson (GB), *Dictionary of the English Language* and *An Account of the Attempt to Ascertain the Longitude at Sea*

Science and Discovery

British chemist Joseph Black publishes his *Experiments upon Magnesia alba, Quicklime, and some other Alcaline Substances* (the first work on quantitative chemistry)

Religion and Philosophy

Swiss-born philosopher-musician Jean-Jacques Rousseau vents his discontent with the existing social order in his *Discourse on the Origin of Inequality*

Other Events

A great earthquake devastates Lisbon (Port) and 30,000 people are killed • Moscow University is founded, the first in Russia

Politics and Wars

Britain, fearing a French attack on Hanover, makes treaty of neutrality with Prussia, nullifying effect of Britain's 1755 treaty with Russia • France forms a defensive alliance with Austria • Friedrich II, the Great, of Prussia starts Seven Years' War by attacking Saxony, weakest member of the anti-Prussian alliance, and compelling its surrender; Britain declares war on France; French seize Minorca; British admiral George Byng is court-martialed and shot for failing to relieve the island • In North America, French troops under the Marquis de Montcalm take Fort Oswego and Fort William Henry • In India, the Nawab of Bengal captures Calcutta and locks 156 British captives in a small room, the notorious "Black Hole": many die

Arts and Letters

MUSIC: George Frideric Handel (GB) oratorio *The Triumph of Time and Truth*; Karl Philipp Emmanual Bach (Ger), *Easter Cantata*; LITERATURE: Voltaire (Fr) *Poem on the Lisbon Disaster,* attacking the idea of a benign providence

Science and Discovery

French mathematician Joseph Louis Lagrange—first man to provide compelling evidence that neither Earth nor Moon is perfectly spherical—develops calculus of variations

Other Events

Sèvres porcelain factory is founded in France • Rebuilding of earthquake-shattered Lisbon begins

GREAT BRITAIN—**George II**
HOLY ROMAN EMPIRE—**Franz I**

1757

Politics and Wars
A coalition government headed by Duke of Newcastle and William Pitt (the Elder), with Pitt as dominant figure, takes over the direction of Britain's war against France (the Seven Years' War); a British force, defeated by the French at Hastenbeck, capitulates at Kloster-Zeven; French occupy Hanover; an army under Prussian king Friedrich II, the Great, defeats a French-Austrian force at Rossbach (Ger) and an Austrian force at Leuthen (Pol) • Russia and Sweden join the Austro-French alliance against Prussia and Britain • In India, Britain retakes Calcutta; troops led by Robert Clive defeat French decisively at Battle of Plassey • In North America, a French force

Arts and Letters
PAINTING: Thomas Gainsborough (GB) *The Artist's Daughter with a Cat*; Giovanni Battista Tiepolo (It), Venetian fresco *Cleopatra's Banquet*; LITERATURE: Johann Jakob Bodmer (Swiss) edits *Das Nibelungenlied*

Religion and Philosophy
Philosopher David Hume (GB) publishes *The Natural History of Religion*, tracing the origins of religion to human hopes and fears and its development through polytheism to monòtheism • Welsh-born divine Richard Price publishes *Review of the Principal Questions in Morals* • Economist François Quesnay (Fr) founds physiocrats, claiming that government according to natural order is inherent in society

Social and Economic
Britain's canal era begins with the completion of the Sankey Canal in Lancashire

1758

Politics and Wars
In Seven Years' War, an army led by Duke Ferdinand of Brunswick defeats a French force at the Battle of Créfeld; a Prussian army defeats Russian invaders at the Battle of Zorndorf; Austrians under Count von Daun defeat Prussians at Battle of Hochkirch • Britain captures French Senegalese possessions • In North America, British successes include the capture of Louisbourg, Nova Scotia, and Île St. Jean (now Prince Edward Island); also Fort Frontenac on Lake Ontario, and Fort Duquesne on the Ohio River; French defeat British at Ticonderoga, NY • In India, Robert Clive (GB) becomes Governor of Bengal

Arts and Letters
PAINTING: François Boucher (Fr), *The Mill at Charenton*; Jean Baptiste Greuze (Fr), *The Wool Winder;* LITERATURE: Denis Diderot (Fr), *The Father of the Family*; Samuel Johnson (GB) contributes the *Idler* papers to the *Universal Chronicle or Weekly Gazette*

Science and Discovery
John Dolland (GB), one of several opticians making achromatic lenses, markets the first achromatic refracting telescope

Social and Economic
Foreign trade with China is restricted to Canton

Religion and Philosophy
Claude-Adrien Helvétius (Fr) publishes *De l'Esprit*, arguing that enlightened self-interest is the mainspring of human conduct

1759

Politics and Wars
In the Seven Years' War, an army commanded by Duke Ferdinand of Brunswick defeats the French at the Battle of Minden (Ger); the Russians and Austrians inflict a major defeat on the Prussians at Kunersdorf (modern Kowice, Pol); a British fleet under Sir Edward Hawke defeats a French fleet at Quiberon Bay, western France • In North America, British forces under Major-General James Wolfe capture Quebec City from the French; Wolfe and the French commander, the Marquis de Montcalm, are killed • Fernando VI of Spain dies; is succeeded by his son Carlos III, formerly Carlo VII of Naples; Carlos's third son becomes Ferdinando IV of Naples

Arts and Letters
MUSIC: Josef Haydn (Aus), first symphony; William Boyce (GB), song "Heart of Oak"; LITERATURE: Samuel Johnson (GB), romance *Rasselas*; Oliver Goldsmith (Ire), *Enquiry into the Present State of Polite Learning*; Voltaire (Fr), satirical novel *Candide*; Edmund Burke (Ire) and Robert Dodsley (GB) start the *Annual Register*

Religion and Philosophy
Portuguese dictator Sebastião de Carvalho expels Jusuits from Portugal and its possessions • Philosopher-economist Adam Smith (GB) writes *Theory of Moral Sentiments*, arguing that moral sense derives from sympathy and is therefore essentially a social sense

Other Events
Engineer James Brindley (GB) begins work on the Bridgewater Canal, Manchester • Halley's Comet reappears

Politics and Wars

British king George II dies; is succeeded by his grandson, George III • In Seven Years' War, Prussians defeat Austrians at the Battle of Leignitz; Russians burn Berlin; a Prussian army defeats Austrians at the Battle of Torgau • In North America, British capture Montreal from the French, marking the virtual end of French power in Canada • In India, British troops under Sir Eyre Coote defeat a combined French and Indian force at Wandiwash • Robert Clive, former Governor of Bengal, returns to England and enters parliament

Arts and Letters

PAINTINGS: Thomas Gainsborough (GB), portrait *Mrs. Philip Thicknesse*; MUSIC: Josef Haydn (Aus), symphonies 2-5; LITERATURE: Laurence Sterne (Ire), first two volumes of novel *Tristam Shandy*; Scottish poet James Macpherson publishes *Fragments of Ancient Poetry Collected in the Highlands of Scotland* (later shown to have been partly his own writings)

Science and Discovery

Chemist Joseph Black (GB) begins quantitative measurement of heat, discovering "characteristic capacity for heat" (specific heat) • American scientist Benjamin Franklin's first effective lightning conductor is installed in Philadelphia, Penn

Other Events

Edmond Hoyle (GB) formulates the "laws" of whist, regarded as sacrosanct until 1864

Politics and Wars

Seven Years' War continues: Spain makes defensive pact with France against Britain • Portugal, refusing to close her ports to Britain, is invaded by Spanish and French troops • British secretary of state William Pitt (Whig), unable to persuade King George III to make war on Spain, resigns; Earl of Bute (Tory) succeeds him as the king's adviser • Prussia's fortunes are at low ebb as Austrians seize Schweidnitz (now Swidnica, Pol) and Russians occupy Kolberg (now Kolobrzeg, Pol)

Arts and Letters

PAINTING: François Boucher (Fr), *Girl and Birdcatcher*; MUSIC: Christoph Willibald Gluck (Ger), ballet *Don Juan*; Josef Haydn (Aus), becomes Kapellmeister to Prince Esterházy; LITERATURE: Thomas Gray (GB), lay *The Descent of Odin*; Charles Churchill (GB), *The Rosciad*, satirizing contemporary actors; Jean Jacques Rousseau (Fr), novel *The New Héloïse*, discussing return to nature in relation to sex and family life

Science and Discovery

Traveler Karsten Niebuhr (Den) begins two years of exploration in Arabia, traveling south along the coast from Jidda to the Yemen, and inland to San'a • Horologist John Harrison (GB) makes his fourth (and first supremely accurate) chronometer

Social and Economic

England's Bridgewater Canal opens

Politics and Wars

Seven Years' War continues: Britain declares war on Spain, and seizes Cuba and Manila; with British help, Portugal repels Spanish invaders; a British fleet hits hard at the French West Indies, forcing the surrender of Grenada, Martinique and St. Vincent • Prussians defeat Austrians at Battles of Burkersdorf and Freiburg • Earl of Bute (Tory) becomes Britain's prime minister • Tsarina Elizaveta of Russia dies; is succeeded by nephew Petr III, who makes peace with Prussia; Petr is assassinated and is succeeded by his widow, Ekaterina II (the Great)

Arts and Letters

PAINTING: George Stubbs (GB), *Mares and Foals*; ARCHITECTURE: work begins on Petit Trianon, Paris MUSIC: Thomas Arne (GB), ballad-opera *Love in a Village*; 6-year-old Wolfgang Amadeus Mozart (Aus), begins 4-year concert-tour of Europe; LITERATURE: Denis Diderot (Fr), novel *Rameau's Nephew*; Jean Jacques Rousseau (Fr), *Emile*; Edward Young (GB), poem *Resignation*; Tobias Smollett (GB), founds periodical *The Briton* to support Prime Minister Bute; John Wilkes (GB), founds more successful anti-Bute periodical *The North Briton*

Religion and Philosophy

France follows Portuguese example and expels Jesuits • Rousseau publishes *The Social Contract*, arguing that, by an implied contract, the state is bound to guarantee the rights and liberties of the subject

GREAT BRITAIN—**George III** ——————————————————————
HOLY ROMAN EMPIRE—**Franz I** ————————————————— □ **Josef II** ————

1763

Politics and Wars
Seven Years' War is ended by the Treaty of Paris (among Britain, France and Spain) and the Treaty of Hubertsburg (between Austria and Prussia); France loses Canada, Grenada and Senegal to Britain and cedes Louisiana to Spain; Spain cedes Florida to Britain in return for the restoration of Cuba and Manila; France is left with few possessions in India beyond Pondichery and Chandernagor; Prussia retains Silesia • George Grenville (Whig) succeeds the Earl of Bute (Tory) as British prime minister; he begins imposing direct taxes on the American colonies and enforcing the navigation laws regulating trade with the colonies • Pontiac, Ottawa Indian chief, organizes an uprising; tribes seize British posts formerly held by the French • King George III (GB) issues a proclamation creating four provinces (Quebec, East Florida, West Florida, Grenada) from British conquests in the Seven Years' War • Politician John Wilkes (GB) is arrested for denigrating King George III in a periodical, *The North Briton*

Arts and Letters
PAINTING: Francesco Guardi (It), *Election of the Doge of Venice*; LITERATURE: Voltaire (Fr) *Saul*, attacking sections of the Old Testament of the Bible, and *Treatise on Tolerance*; Gotthold Lessing (Ger), comedy *Minna von Barnhelm*

Social and Economic
Almanach de Gotha, guide to European royalty and aristocracy, is first published in Gotha (Ger) • New York City's chamber of commerce is founded

1764

Politics and Wars
British parliament passes a Sugar Act to raise revenue from the American colonies; it also hits colonists' earnings from their trade with the West Indies • Colonial Currency Act simultaneously prevents colonists from paying British debts in depreciated colonial currency • Russia and Prussia agree to cöoperate in Polish policy • Stanislaw Poniatowski, favorite of Tsarina Ekaterina II, the Great, succeeds Augustus III as king of Poland • British East India Company takes over full control of Bengal • British politician John Wilkes is expelled from the House of Commons

Arts and Letters
ARCHITECTURE: Robert Adam (GB), Kenwood House, London; LITERATURE: Oliver Goldsmith (Ire), poem *The Traveller*; Horace Walpole (GB), bloodcurdling romance *The Castle of Otranto*; "The Club" (later The Literary Club) is formed in London; its founder-members include the writers Samuel Johnson, Oliver Goldsmith and Edmund Burke; and the painter Joshua Reynolds

Science and Discovery
French naturalist Jacques-Christophe Valmont publishes *Universal Dictionary of Natural History*

Religion and Philosophy
French philosopher Voltaire publishes *Pocket Philosophical Dictionary,* attacking oppression, untruth and religious dogma

Social and Economic
King Carlos III of Spain authorizes intercolonial trade between New Spain and Peru, New Granada and Guatemala

1765

Politics and Wars
British prime minister George Grenville (Whig) persuades parliament to pass a Stamp Act, levying duty on documents and newspapers in North American colonies; also a Quartering Act, providing for the quartering of British troops in the colonies; riots follow in Boston, Mass; at New York Stamp Congress, delegates from 9 colonies adopt a Declaration of Rights and Liberties • Grenville quarrels with King George III and resigns; he is succeeded as prime minister by the Marquess of Rockingham (Whig) • Holy Roman Emperor Franz I dies; he is succeeded by his son Josef II, but real power lies with Josef's mother, Maria Theresa • Robert Clive (GB) takes over the administration of Bengal, India • Chinese begin an invasion of Burma

Arts and Letters
PAINTING: Jean Baptiste Greuze (Fr), *La Bonne mère*; François Boucher becomes director of the French Académie; LITERATURE: Thomas Chatterton (GB), aged 12, begins passing off his own poems as those of an imaginary 15th-century priest, Thomas Rowley; Thomas Percy (GB), publishes *Reliques of Ancient English Poetry*, an influential anthology of old songs and ballads.

Science and Discovery
Engineer James Watt (GB) invents the separate condenser, soon to make the steam engine the power source of the age

Social and Economic
Lawyer Sir William Blackstone (GB) publishes his *Commentaries on the Laws of England*

Politics and Wars

Britain appeases its American colonies by repealing the hated Stamp Act; then antagonizes them with the Declaratory Act, affirming the right of the British government to pass laws binding on all colonies • The Marquess of Rockingham (Whig) resigns as British prime minister; he is succeeded by the Earl of Chatham (formerly William Pitt), also a Whig • Willem V, Stadtholder (chief of state) of the Dutch Republic, assumes power on reaching the age of 18 • King Fredrik V of Denmark dies; he is succeeded by his mentally unstable son Christian VII

Arts and Letters

PAINTING: Jean Fragonard (Fr), *The Swing*; LITERATURE: Denis Diderot, (Fr), *Essay on Painting*; Oliver Goldsmith (Ire), novel *The Vicar of Wakefield*; Jonathan Swift (Ire), *Journal to Stella* (published posthumously); OTHER: Britain's oldest surviving theater, the Theatre Royal, Bristol, opens

Science and Discovery

French explorer Louis Antoine de Bougainville begins a three-year voyage that takes him to Tahiti, Samoa and New Hebrides • Chemist Henry Cavendish (GB) isolates hydrogen

Religion and Philosophy

Russia and Prussia rouse the hostility of Polish Roman Catholics by forcing Poland to grant equal rights to Protestant and Greek Orthodox Churches

Politics and Wars

British Government suspends New York's colonial assembly for refusing to enforce the Quartering Act • Townshend Acts: British Chancellor of the Exchequer Charles Townshend persuades Parliament to tax lead, paint, paper and tea imported into the colonies; Boston, Mass, begins boycott of imports • The Earl of Chatham (Whig) resigns as British Prime Minister; he is succeeded by the Duke of Grafton (Whig) • Burmese invade and conquer Siam (Thailand)

Arts and Letters

PAINTING: Allan Ramsay, Scottish portraitist, becomes court painter to King George III (GB); MUSIC: Christoph Willibald Gluck (Ger), opera *Alceste*

Science and Discovery

Chemist Tobern Olaf Bergman (Swe) improves tables of chemical "affinities" produced by Etienne Geoffroy (Fr) in 1718 • Clergyman-chemist Joseph Priestley (GB) publishes *History and Present State of Electricity*, suggesting that inverse square law applies to electrical as well as to gravitational attraction

Religion and Philosophy

Spain, Naples and Spanish colonies expel Jesuits • Paraguayan missions, formerly in Jesuit hands, are handed over to Franciscans • Methodism takes firm root in the American colonies

Other Events

The newly invented fortepiano reaches Britain

Politics and Wars

Massachusetts assembly petitions King George III (GB), and sends circular letter to legislatures of other colonies calling on them for support; royal governor at Boston dissolves Massachusetts assembly; Boston refuses to quarter British troops • In Britain, politician John Wilkes is three times elected Member of Parliament for Middlesex and three times excluded by vote of the House of Commons • Genoa cedes Corsica to France • Poles fleeing into Turkish territory are pursued by Russians; Turkey, urged on by France, declares war on Russia

Arts and Letters

PAINTING: Royal Academy in London (Eng) founded; MUSIC: Jean Jacques Rousseau (Fr), *Dictionary of Music*; LITERATURE: Laurence Sterne (Ire), *A Sentimental Journey*; Sterne dies soon after; Thomas Gray (GB), *Poems*

Science and Discovery

Chemist Joseph Black (GB) proves disappearance of heat in melting, reappearance in freezing (latent heat) • Navigator James Cook (GB) begins two-year voyage to Tahiti and New Zealand • Explorer James Bruce (GB) begins five-year journey of African exploration

Religion and Philosophy

Clergyman-chemist Joseph Priestley (GB) publishes *Essay on the First Principles of Government*, anticipating Jeremy Bentham's "greatest happiness for greatest number" ideal

Other Events

First weekly parts of the *Encyclopaedia Britannica* are issued in Scotland

GREAT BRITAIN—**George III**

HOLY ROMAN EMPIRE—**Josef II**

Politics and Wars

British parliament urges application of 16th-century act to bring American colonists charged with treason to Britain for trial; Virginia assembly passes resolution of protest; Russians overrun Turkish provinces of Moldavia and Wallachia • Austrians, alarmed by Russia's successes, are on verge of war • King Friedrich II, the Great, of Prussia, plans to partition Poland as a means of keeping the peace • Portugal's chief minister, Sebastião de Carvalho, is created Marquis de Pombal

Arts and Letters

PAINTING: Jean Fragonard (Fr), *The Study*; Joshua Reynolds (GB) is knighted, and succeeds Allan Ramsay as Painter-in-Ordinary to George III; ARCHITECTURE: The Adam brothers (GB), The Adelphi, London

Science and Discovery

French artillery officer Nicolas Cugnot road-tests his steam-driven gun carriage, regarded as the first mechanically-propelled vehicle

Religion and Philosophy

Statesman Edmund Burke (Ire) publishes *Observations on the Present State of the Nation*, denying that taxes on American colonies are justified by the cost of the Seven Years' War and urging that people must be governed "in a manner agreeable to their disposition" • Pope Clement XIII dies; is succeeded by Pius VI

Other Events

"Letters of Junius" attacking George III and several leading politicians begin appearing in London's *Public Advertiser* (to 1771) • Famine kills one-third of the people of Bengal (India)

Politics and Wars

Lord North (Tory) succeeds Duke of Grafton (Whig) as British prime minister • "Boston Massacre": several citizens of Boston (Mass) are killed in a protest riot against presence of British troops; as a placatory gesture, Britain lifts all colonial duties other than that on tea • Count Johann von Struensee forms administration in Denmark, and introduces sweeping reforms aimed at creating an enlightened despotism, with the crown independent of the nobility • Russian fleet defeats Turkish fleet off the Anatolian coast • Spain disputes British possession of the Falkland Islands

Arts and Letters

PAINTING: Thomas Gainsborough (GB), *The Blue Boy*; Jean Fragonard (Fr), *The Love Letter*; MUSIC: Wolfgang Amadeus Mozart (Aus), opera *Mithridate*; LITERATURE: Oliver Goldsmith (Ire), poem *The Deserted Village*; Johann Wolfgang Goethe (Ger) begins his greatest dramatic work, *Faust*; poet Thomas Chatterton (GB) commits suicide at age of 18

Science and Discovery

Weaver James Hargraves (GB) patents his "spinning jenny" • British explorer Samuel Heane begins two years of Canadian exploration, from Hudson Bay to mouth of Coppermine River and Great Slave Lake • Navigator James Cook (GB) discovers Botany Bay, Australia

Religion and Philosophy

German philosopher Immanuel Kant becomes professor of logic and metaphysics at Königsberg (Ger)

Politics and Wars

Publication of British parliamentary speeches is permitted for the first time • French *parlements* are abolished in favor of a simpler system of courts • King Adolf Fredrik of Sweden dies, is succeeded by his son, Gustaf III • Russians seize Crimea from Turks • Austria and Turkey make pact to force Russian withdrawal from Moldavia and Wallachia

Arts and Letters

PAINTING: Benjamin West (Amer), *The Death of Wolfe*; MUSIC: Josef Haydn (Aus), "Sun" string quartets, Nos 31–36; LITERATURE: Louis-Antoine de Bougainville (Fr), *Voyage Around the World*, an account of his journey of 1766–69; Henry Mackenzie (GB) novel *The Man of Feeling*; Tobias Smollett (GB), novel *The Expedition of Humphry Clinker*; he dies soon after; William Robertson (GB), *History of America*

Science and Discovery

John Hunter, surgeon-extraordinary to George III (GB), publishes an important treatise on dentistry • French geographer Jean Bourguignon d'Anville publishes *States Formed in Europe* • British traveler and naturalist Thomas Pennant publishes *British Zoology*

Social and Economic

New York City Hospital founded

Other Events

First bound edition of *Encyclopaedia Britannica* is published in Edinburgh (GB)

Politics and Wars

British government decides that salaries of Massachusetts judges and governors will be paid by the Crown, making them independent of the assembly • Rhode Island colonists burn a British revenue boat • American statesman Samuel Adams forms Committees of Correspondence in Massachusetts, for action against the British • Gustaf III of Sweden, fearing Austrian and Russian aggression, seizes absolute power by military *coup d'état*, and begins a programme of social reform and religious tolerance • Count Johann von Struensee's administration is overthrown in Denmark; a reactionary aristocrat, Ore Güldberg, takes control • First Partition of Poland: 30 percent of its territory is taken by Russia, Austria and Prussia • Warren Hastings (GB) becomes Governor of Bengal (India) and initiates reforms, including control of opium manufacture

Arts and Letters

MUSIC: Josef Haydn (Aus), symphony No 45 ("Farewell"); LITERATURE: David Garrick (GB) farce *The Irish Widow*; Gotthold Lessing (Ger), tragedy *Emilia Galotti*

Science and Discovery

Chemist Karl Wilhelm Scheele (Swe) isolates oxygen, but does not publish the fact • Navigator James Cook (GB) begins a second great voyage of discovery, to New Zealand, South Pacific and Antarctic waters

Other Events

Norwegian students in Copenhagen form the Norwegian Society, aimed at accentuating the nationhood of Norway, now under Danish rule

Politics and Wars

Virginia assembly appoints a Committee of Correspondence, to keep in touch with the other American colonies; its example is followed by ten other colonies • Tea duty is lifted in Britain but retained in the colonies; in protest, colonists dump a cargo of tea in the harbor at Boston, Mass ("Boston Tea Party") • King José I of Portugal becomes insane; his wife, Maria Anna, is made regent and begins undermining the power of chief minister Marquis de Pombal • Formidable peasant rising occurs in southeast Russia (Pugachev's revolt); Russia's war effort against Turkey slackens as result

Arts and Letters

SCULPTURE: Jean-Antoine Houdon (Fr), bust *Gluck*; LITERATURE: Gottlieb Klopstock (Ger), last five cantos of epic poem Der Messias; Oliver Goldsmith (Ire), comedy *She Stoops to Conquer*; Johann Wolfgang Goethe (Ger), drama *Goetz von Berlichingen*

Science and Discovery

James Cook (GB) becomes the first navigator intentionally to sail south of the Antarctic circle

Religion and Philosophy

Pope Clement XIV, under heavy Bourbon pressure, orders dissolution of the Jesuit Order

Other Events

The waltz becomes the rage in Vienna (Aus)

Politics and Wars

British parliament passes "Coercive Acts" against American colonies: Port of Boston is to be closed; Massachusetts is to be deprived of most of its self-government, and any of its citizens accused of murder in connection with law enforcement are to be tried elsewhere; troops are to be quartered in Massachusetts; the boundary of Quebec province is to be extended south to the Ohio River • First Continental Congress meets in Philadelphia to protest against the Acts; it draws up a Declaration of Rights and Grievances • King Louis XV of France dies; is succeeded by his grandson, Louis XVI • Treaty of Kuchuk Kainarji ends Russo-Turkish War; Russia makes only minor territorial gains, but is granted the right to protect Christians under Turkish rule • Regulating Act limits powers of British East India Company and provides for government of India by a governor-general and council; Warren Hastings becomes India's first governor-general

Arts and Letters

PAINTING: Thomas Gainsborough (GB), portrait *Lord Kilmorey*; MUSIC: Christoph Willibald Gluck (Ger), opera *Iphigénie en Aulide*; LITERATURE: Johann Wolfgang Goethe (Ger), romance *The Sorrows of Young Werther*; Earl of Chesterfield (GB) *Letters to His Son*

Science and Discovery

Clergyman-chemist Joseph Priestley (GB) publishes *Experiments and Observations on Different Kinds of Air*, in which he demonstrates that plants immersed in water give off oxygen • Scientist Antoine Lavoisier (Fr) proves that water and carbon dioxide are produced in breathing

GREAT BRITAIN—**George III**
HOLY ROMAN EMPIRE—**Josef II**

Politics and Wars

Belated British moves to conciliate American colonists fail; British troops sent from Boston destroy stores at Concord, Mass, clash with armed colonists at Lexington, and Revolutionary War breaks out; Americans repulse British forces and capture Fort Ticonderoga and Crown Point, NY • Second Continental Congress meets at Philadelphia, and appoints George Washington commander-in-chief of its forces • British defeat Americans at Bunker Hill, Mass; Boston is besieged • Americans besiege Quebec • Tsarina Ekaterina the Great (Russ) reforms local government

Arts and Letters

PAINTING: Ralph Earl (Amer), portrait *Roger Sherman*; Joshua Reynolds (GB), portrait *Miss Bowles*; MUSIC: Karl Philipp Emmanuel Bach (Ger), oratorio *The Israelites in the Wilderness*; LITERATURE: Pierre de Beaumarchais (Fr), comedy *The Barber of Seville*; Samuel Johnson (GB), *Journey to the Western Islands of Scotland*; Richard Brinsley Sheridan (Ire), comedy *The Rivals*; Augustus Toplady (GB), hymn *Rock of Ages*

Science and Discovery

Austrian physician Franz Mesmer uses his "animal magnetism" (mesmerism) to cure hysterical patients

Social and Economic

British manufacturer Matthew Boulton takes Scottish inventor James Watt into partnership and they begin production of steam engines

Politics and Wars

In America, the Revolutionary War continues; British evacuate Boston, Mass, but drive American colonists from Canada • Continental Congress adopts a Declaration of Independence (July 4), drafted by Thomas Jefferson, Benjamin Franklin and John Adams • British recruit 20,000 German mercenaries from Hesse ("Hessians") • British occupy New York City; American general George Washington defeats Hessians at Trenton, NJ • India's Governor-General, Warren Hastings, establishes central control of the country's finances • King Louis XVI appoints Jacques Necker as France's Finance Minister

Arts and Letters

PAINTING: Jean Fragonard (Fr), *The Washerwoman*; MUSIC: Wolfgang Amadeus Mozart (Aus), *Serenade in D* ("Haffner"); LITERATURE: Thomas Paine (GB), *Common Sense*, favoring independence for American colonies; Edward Gibbon (GB), Volume I of *Decline and Fall of the Roman Empire*

Science and Discovery

Navigator James Cook (GB) sets out on his last voyage of discovery, destined to take him to Kerguelen Island, New Zealand, Hawaii and northeast of the Bering Strait

Social and Economic

Scottish philosopher and economist Adam Smith publishes *Inquiry into the Nature and Causes of the Wealth of Nations*, holding labor, rather than land, to be the main source of wealth

Politics and Wars

American Revolutionary War continues: George Washington's troops defeat the British at Princeton, NJ; Americans defeat British at Bennington, Vt; a British force under John Burgoyne surrenders at Saratoga, NY; British defeat Americans and occupy Philadelphia, Pa; Washington's army goes into winter quarters at Valley Forge, Pa where it suffers great privations • José I of Portugal dies; is succeeded by his daughter, Maria I: Portugal's chief minister, the Marquis de Pombal, is exiled

Arts and Letters

PAINTING: Thomas Gainsborough (GB), *The Watering-Place*; MUSIC: Christoph Willibald Gluck (Ger), opera *Armide*; LITERATURE: Richard Brinsley Sheridan (Ire), comedies *A Trip to Scarborough* and *The School for Scandal*

Science and Discovery

Physicist Charles Augustin de Coulomb (Fr) invents torsion balance • Chemist Carl Wilhelm Scheele (Swe) publishes his *Treatise on Air and Fire*, in which he proves that air consists of two gases (now known as nitrogen and oxygen)

Social and Economic

British philanthropist and prison reformer John Howard publishes *The State of the Prisons in England and Wales*

Other Events

America's Continental Congress adopts Stars and Stripes flag (originally with 13 stars and 13 stripes)

Politics and Wars

France makes an alliance with the new United States of America, and war breaks out between France and Britain • The Marquis de Lafayette, already fighting in America, coördinates plans for a French expeditionary force to America; a former Prussian general, Baron von Steuben, becomes inspector-general of the American army, and issues the first US Army drill manual • Americans under George Washington win Battle of Monmouth, NJ • In India, British seize Pondicherry and Mahé from the French • Russia intervenes in the Turkish-held Crimea • War of the Bavarian Succession breaks out, following the death of its last ruler, Maximilian Josef, without heir: Prussian and Austrian forces confront each other

Arts and Letters

PAINTING: John Singleton Copley (Amer), *Brook Watson and the Shark*; LITERATURE: Fanny Burney (GB), novel *Evelina*

Science and Discovery

Navigator James Cook (Br) discovers Hawaiian islands • Austrian physician Franz Mesmer, accused of dabbling in magic, is forced to leave Vienna

Religion and Philosophy

In British parliament, statesman Edmund Burke (Ire) makes a memorable speech against employing American Indians in the Revolutionary War; and later he advocates emancipation of Roman Catholics, who are restricted by law from holding certain posts

Politics and Wars

Spain joins France and America in war against Britain and begins siege of Gibraltar • Americans under George Rogers Clark defeat a British force at Vincennes, near Mississippi River • American seaman John Paul Jones begins a series of successful attacks on British shipping • The war causes a sharp increase in France's financial deficit • Treaty of Teschen ends the War of Bavarian Succession; Austria gains some Bavarian territory

Arts and Letters

PAINTING: Charles Willson Peale (US), portrait *George Washington*; MUSIC: Christoph Willibald Gluck (Ger), opera *Iphigenia in Tauris*; LITERATURE: Gotthold Lessing (Ger), play *Nathan der Weise*; Richard Brinsley Sheridan (Ire), farce *The Critic*; Samuel Johnson (GB) first part of *Lives of the Poets*

Science and Discovery

Chemist Karl Wilhelm Scheele (Swe) discovers glycerine and a wide range of organic acids

Religion and Philosophy

A Protestant Association (leader Lord George Gordon) is formed in England to oppose the removal of Roman Catholic disabilities • Posthumous publication of David Hume's *Dialogues Concerning Natural Religion*

Other Events

Navigator James Cook (GB) is killed in skirmish at Hawaii • Pope Pius VI initiates draining of Pontine Marshes (It)

Politics and Wars

Dutch refusal to let the British navy search its ships during the war with France and Spain brings the Netherlands into the alliance against Britain • Russia, Sweden and Denmark adopt a policy of armed neutrality at sea • A British fleet led by Admiral George Rodney (GB) defeats a Spanish fleet off Cape St. Vincent, Portugal • In America, the British take Charleston and overrun South Carolina, but are defeated at King's Mountain, NC • A British agent, John André, taken prisoner, reveals a plot by American general Benedict Arnold to betray West Point to the British • Holy Roman Emperor Josef II becomes sole ruler of Austria on the death of his mother, Maria Theresa

Arts and Letters

PAINTING: Thomas Gainsborough (GB), portrait *Miss Haverfield* • John Singleton Copley (US), *The Death of Chatham*; MUSIC: Josef Haydn (Aus), "Toy" symphony for children

Science and Discovery

Scientist Luigi Galvani (It) notes that legs of newly-killed frogs twitch when in contact with two different metals, iron and copper—a pioneer discovery in electricity • American Academy of Science is founded

Religion and Philosophy

British politician Lord George Gordon heads 60,000 London marchers to protest against the granting of greater political freedom to Roman Catholics; resultant Gordon Riots, culminating in an attack on the Bank of England and the forcing of prisons, are suppressed by troops

GREAT BRITAIN—**George III**
HOLY ROMAN EMPIRE—**Josef II**

1781

Politics and Wars
In the Revolutionary War, colonists defeat British at battles of Cowpens and Eutaw, NC • British commander Lord Cornwallis, besieged in Yorktown, Va, surrenders to George Washington; United States begins peace negotiations with Britain, to the chagrin of its allies, France and Spain • Britain loses several of its West Indian possessions to France • French finance minister Jacques Necker, dismissed from office, publishes his *Comte rendu*, revealing the deplorable state of French finances • Holy Roman Emperor Josef II demands that the Dutch should reopen the Scheldt River to the Spanish Netherlands • Austria and Russia conclude a treaty designed to end Turkish power and divide the Balkans between them

Arts and Letters
PAINTING: Jacques-Louis David (Fr), *Belisarius*; MUSIC: Wolfgang Amadeus Mozart (Aus), opera *Idomeneo*; LITERATURE: Friedrich Schiller (Ger), play *The Robbers*; Philosopher Jean Jacques Rousseau (Fr), *Confessions* (published posthumously)

Science and Discovery
Musician and astronomer William Herschel (GB) discovers the planet Uranus

Religion and Philosophy
Emperor Josef II issues the Edict of Tolerance, weakening Roman Catholic power in Austria, and leading to the closure of half the country's monasteries within 10 years • Philosopher Immanuel Kant (Ger) publishes his *Critique of Pure Reason*

1782

Politics and Wars
Britain and the United States sign a preliminary peace treaty in Paris: British lose Minorca to Spain, and Spain acquires all Florida • British raise the siege of Gibraltar • Lord North's government falls in Britain; is succeeded by a Whig coalition under Marquess of Rockingham • A British fleet under Admiral George Rodney defeats a French fleet commanded by Admiral François de Grasse at Battle of the Saints in West Indies; British sea power is restored • Britain abandons its judicial and legislative supremacy over the Irish parliament

Arts and Letters
PAINTING: Henry Fuseli (GB), *The Nightmare*; MUSIC: Wolfgang Amadeus Mozart (Aus), opera *Il Seraglio* and symphony K385 ("Haffner"); LITERATURE: Fanny Burney (later Madame d'Arblay, GB) *Cecilia*; William Cowper (GB), poem *John Gilpin*

Science and Discovery
Karl Wilhelm Scheele (Swe) makes hydrocyanic acid • Montgolfier Brothers (Fr) build the first hot-air balloon

Religion and Philosophy
Theologian Joseph Priestley (GB) writes *A History of the Corruptions of Christianity*

Social and Economic
Economic reforms in Britain give parliament greater control over royal expenditure • Bank of North America is established in Philadelphia

Other Events
About 800 men die when British warship *Royal George* capsizes at Spithead

1783

Politics and Wars
Britain, USA, France and Spain sign the Peace of Versailles, recognizing independence of the United States of America; British and French possessions in the West Indies are confirmed; navigation of Mississippi River is opened to both Britain and the USA • William Pitt becomes British prime minister • Russia seizes Baku and assumes sovereignty over Georgia • British forces in India surrender to Tippoo Sahib, Sultan of Mysore • Holy Roman Emperor Josef II imposes the German language on Czech-speaking Bohemia

Arts and Letters
MUSIC: Wolfgang Amadeus Mozart (Aus), Mass in C Minor and symphony K425 ("Linz"), John Broadwood (GB) patents piano pedal; LITERATURE: William Blake (GB), *Poetical Sketches*

Science and Discovery
Pilâtre de Rozier (Fr) makes the first manned hot-air balloon ascent in Paris, using a Montgolfier balloon • The first paddlewheel steamboat sails on the Saône River, France

Religion and Philosophy
Charles Simeon (GB), later founder of the Church Missionary Society, starts an evangelical movement • Philosopher Moses Mendelssohn (Ger) writes book *Jerusalem*

Other Events
In Japan, there is famine in the north, and Mount Asama erupts • Iceland's Skaptarjökul volcano erupts • America's first daily newspaper, *The Pennsylvania Evening Post and Daily Advertiser*, is published

Politics and Wars

Russia annexes Crimea and Kuban • British parliament curbs the authority of the East India Company, which is put under a Board of Control • Holy Roman Emperor Josef II removes the Hungarian crown to Vienna and causes outcry; emperor is forced to restore the crown to Hungary • Naval clash on River Scheldt ruptures relations between the Netherlands and Austria • USA suffers economic depression

Arts and Letters

PAINTING: Joshua Reynolds (GB), *Mrs. Siddons as the Tragic Muse*; LITERATURE: Beamarchais (Pierre Augustin Caron; Fr), play *The Marriage of Figaro*; Friedrich von Schiller (Ger), *Kabale und Liebe*

Science and Discovery

Ironmaster Henry Cort (GB) patents a revolutionary "puddling" process in smelting • Henry Cavendish (GB) discovers the composition of water • Joseph Bramah (GB) invents a specially secure lock • Andrew Meikle (GB) invents a threshing machine

Religion and Philosophy

Evangelist John Wesley (GB) formalizes the foundation of Methodism

Other Events

Serfdom is abolished in Denmark

Politics and Wars

USA and Prussia sign a commercial treaty • US Land Ordinance establishes a survey system • India's Governor-General, Warren Hastings, returns to England to face trial on corruption charges • Holy Roman Emperor Josef II tries to exchange the Austrian Netherlands for Bavaria • Friedrich II, the Great, of Prussia creates a League of German Princes to combat Austrian expansion • The Treaty of Fontainebleau between Austria and Netherlands recognizes Austrian rights over part of the Scheldt River • Russians colonize Aleutian Islands

Arts and Letters

PAINTING: Jacques-Louis David (Fr), *The Oath of the Horatii*; SCULPTURE: Jean Antoine Houdon (Fr), statue of George Washington and busts of Benjamin Franklin and Thomas Jefferson; LITERATURE: William Cowper (GB), poem *The Task*; James Boswell (GB), *Journal of a Tour to the Hebrides*

Science and Discovery

Henry Cavendish (GB) discovers the composition of nitric acid • Edmund Cartwright (GB) patents a power loom

Religion and Philosophy

Virginia passes a Statute of Religious Freedom on separative Church and State • Philosopher Immanuel Kant (Ger) writes *Groundwork of the Metaphysics of Ethics* • Anglican priest William Paley (GB) writes *Principles of Moral and Political Philosophy*

Other Events

Coal-dealer and printer John Walter (GB) founds *The Daily Universal Register* (later *The Times*) newspaper

Politics and Wars

Friedrich II, the Great, of Prussia dies; is succeeded by his nephew, Friedrich Wilhelm II • China suppresses a revolt in Formosa • Massachusetts farmers rebel against high taxes (Shays' Rebellion) and are suppressed by state militia • British prime minister William Pitt starts sinking fund in Britain to reduce national debt by annual allocations; he negotiates with France a trade treaty reducing duties • Britain acquires the Malayan island of Penang • Willem V of Orange, Stadtholder (chief of state) of the Netherlands, loses command of the Dutch army in conflict with the French-supported Patriot party

Arts and Letters

MUSIC: Wolfgang Amadeus Mozart (Aus), opera *Marriage of Figaro*; LITERATURE: William Beckford (GB), *Vathek*; John Burgoyne (GB), play *The Heiress*; Robert Burns (GB), *Poems chiefly in the Scottish dialect*

Science and Discovery

Count Alessandro Volta (It) invents a primitive electric battery • Chemist Martin Heinrich Klaproth (Ger) discovers uranium and zirconium

Religion and Philosophy

Mennonite religious sect from Europe settles in Canada

Social and Economic

Philanthropist Thomas Clarkson (GB) publishes *Essay on Slavery*

Other Events

Famine in Japan • Jacques Balmat (Fr) and Michel Paccard (Fr) make the first ascent of Mont Blanc

UNITED STATES OF AMERICA
GREAT BRITAIN—**George III**
HOLY ROMAN EMPIRE—**Josef II**

George Washington

Politics and Wars

US Constitution is signed in Philadelphia; first states to ratify it are Delaware (1), Pennsylvania (2) New Jersey (3) and Georgia (4) • The Northwest Ordinance is enacted, providing for government of US northwest territories • Tsarina Ekaterina II of Russia forms a defensive alliance with Holy Roman Emperor Josef II • Josef makes the Netherlands an Austrian province • France moves towards revolution because of financial crisis • Stadtholder (chief of state) Willem V of Orange regains authority in Netherlands with Prussian help • Turkey declares war on Russia • Warren Hastings, former Governor-General of India, is impeached by British parliament for corruption and cruelty

Arts and Letters

MUSIC: Wolfgang Amadeus Mozart (Aus), *Eine kleine Nachtmusik* and opera *Don Giovanni*; LITERATURE: Friedrich Schiller (Ger), *Iphigenie auf Tauris*

Science and Discovery

John Fitch (US) sails steam-propelled boat on the Delaware River

Religion and Philosophy

Methodist leader John Wesley (GB) publishes *Sermons* • Essays in *The Federalist* by James Madison, Alexander Hamilton and John Jay explain the US Constitution

Social and Economic

New York state assembly imposes tariffs on imported goods

Politics and Wars

More states ratify the US Constitution — Connecticut (5) Massachusetts (6), Maryland (7), and South Carolina (8); ratification by New Hampshire (9) automatically brings the Constitution into force; Virginia (10) and New York (11) follow • Seven-year trial of Warren Hastings (former Governor-General of India, accused of corruption) begins in Britain • Louis XVI summons French Estates-General (national assembly) for 1789 after demands by Paris parlement (local court); former Finance Minister Jacques Necker is recalled from exile to handle French financial crisis • British, Dutch and Prussians form Triple Alliance to preserve peace • Swedes invade Finland • Danes invade Sweden • Austria is at war with Turkey

Arts and Letters

MUSIC: Wolfgang Amadeus Mozart (Aus), symphonies 39, 40 and 41; Josef Haydn (Aus), symphony 92

Science and Discovery

Navigator Comte de la Pérouse (Fr) completes his exploration of the Pacific coasts of Asia and North America • Port Jackson settlement for British convicts is founded in Australia

Religion and Philosophy

Philosopher Immanuel Kant (Ger) publishes *Critique of Practical Reason*

Social and Economic

New York City becomes US federal capital • Britain founds Sierra Leone as a haven for former slaves

Politics and Wars

First US Congress meets in New York • George Washington becomes first US President • North Carolina ratifies the US Constitution and becomes 12th State • Judiciary Act establishes federal court system in USA • French Estates-General (assembly) meets for the first time since 1614; Third Estate (the commons) insists on new constitution; French Revolution begins when Paris mob storms fortress-prison of the Bastille; French National Assembly adopts Declaration of the Rights of Man and prohibits its members from working for the king; for safety from the mob, Louis XVI is forced to move from Versailles to Paris • Belgium, encouraged by France, declares independence from Austria

Arts and Letters

MUSIC: Wolfgang Amadeus Mozart (Aus), opera *Cosi fan tutte*; LITERATURE: William Blake (GB), *Songs of Innocence*; Johann Wolfgang von Goethe (Ger), *Tasso*

Science and Discovery

Sir Alexander Mackenzie (Can) begins exploration of northern Canada • Scientist Antoine Laurent Lavoisier (Fr) publishes the first modern chemistry textbook, *Elements of Chemistry*

Religion and Philosophy

US Episcopal Church separates from Church of England

Social and Economic

Political philosopher Jeremy Bentham (GB) publishes *Introduction to the Principles of Morals and Legislation*

───▷
───▷

□ Leopold II ──────────────────────────── □ Franz II ──▷

Politics and Wars

Rhode Island ratifies the US Constitution and becomes 13th State • Spain gives up claim to Vancouver Island, Canada, in favor of Britain • French Revolution continues; finance minister Jacques Necker resigns; political clubs, led by Maximilien Robespierre and others, increase their authority; moderate leader Comte de Mirabeau tries to prevent overthrow of monarchy; Louis XVI accepts new constitution • Holy Roman Emperor Josef II dies; is succeeded by his brother Leopold II • Poland cedes Thorn and Danzig to Prussia • Russia gains part of Finland from Sweden, and Russian-Swedish war ends • Austrians suppress independence movement in Belgium

Arts and Letters

LITERATURE: Robert Burns (GB), *Tam O'Shanter*

Science and Discovery

Explorer James Bruce (GB) publishes *Travels to Discover the Source of the Nile*

Religion and Philosophy

Philosopher Immanuel Kant (Ger) writes *Critique of Judgment* • Politician Edmund Burke (Ire) opposes revolutionaries in France in his *Reflections on the Revolution in France* • John Carroll is appointed first Roman Catholic bishop in USA (Baltimore)

Social and Economic

In France, Jews are given civil liberties, clergy are placed under civil organization, titles are abolished and sweeping administrative reforms are introduced

Politics and Wars

Vermont becomes 14th state of the USA • President Washington selects site on Potomac River for new US capital • Upper and Lower Canada, with separate legislative assemblies, are created by Britain's Canada Constitution Act • In French Revolution, King Louis XVI and royal family are stopped trying to escape from France (the Flight to Varennes); French National Assembly adopts constitutional monarchy, then dissolves • Britain declares neutrality over French revolution, following declaration by Austria and Prussia that they will intervene only with agreement of other powers • In India, Tippoo Sahib's army is defeated by the British at Seringapatam

Arts and Letters

PAINTING: George Morland (GB), *The Stable*; MUSIC: Wolfgang Amadeus Mozart (Aus), opera *The Magic Flute*; he dies soon after; Joseph Haydn (Aus), symphony 94 ("Surprise"); LITERATURE: James Boswell (GB) *Life of Samuel Johnson*; Marquis de Sade (Fr), novel *Justine*

Science and Discovery

Samuel Slater and Moses Brown (US) introduce power-driven cotton spinning • An ordnance survey mapping all Britain is begun • Claude Chappé (Fr) invents a visual signaling system by semaphore

Social and Economic

British-born journalist Thomas Paine (US) writes Part 1 of *The Rights of Man* • Economist Jeremy Bentham (GB) proposes his "panopticon"— a scheme for prison administration

Politics and Wars

Kentucky becomes the 15th state of the USA • Republican and Federalist parties are formed in the USA • French Revolution continues: Swiss guards are massacred in Paris; royal family is imprisoned; France is proclaimed a republic; trial of Louis XVI on treason charge begins before the National Convention • Austria and Prussia form an alliance against France, which declares war on them and Sardinia; Austrian and Prussian troops invade France and are defeated at Valmy; French take Mayence, capture Brussels and gain Austrian Netherlands; France annexes Savoy and Nice • Franz II (Aus) becomes last Holy Roman Emperor • King Gustavus III (Swe) is assassinated; is succeeded by his son, Gustavus IV

Arts and Letters

MUSIC: Claude Rouget de Lisle (Fr), *La Marseillaise*

Science and Discovery

Navigator George Vancouver (GB) explores the island now named after him • Gas lighting is introduced in England

Religion and Philosophy

Thomas Paine publishes Part 2 of *The Rights of Man* in Britain and is accused of treason; he leaves for France and is declared a French citizen

Social and Economic

Denmark abolishes the slave trade • The dollar becomes US currency unit • Mary Wollstonecraft (GB), publishes *Vindication of the Rights of Women*

USA—**George Washington**
GREAT BRITAIN—**George III**
HOLY ROMAN EMPIRE—**Franz II**

Politics and Wars

French Revolution continues: King Louis XVI and Queen Marie Antoinette are executed; unsuccessful royalist revolt in the Vendée, western France; Committee of Public Safety with dictatorial powers is appointed in Paris; revolutionary leader Jean Paul Marat is murdered by Charlotte Corday; Maximilien Robespierre rises to power: Reign of Terror • USA declares its neutrality • Russia and Britain agree to close Baltic trade to France • France declares war on Britain and Netherlands, which join coalition with Austria, Prussia, Spain and Sardinia • British capture Toulon, but lose it again • Britain seizes French possessions in India • Coalition forces are driven back across the Rhine by French • Second partition of Poland by Prussia and Russia

Arts and Letters

PAINTING: Jacques Louis David (Fr), *The Death of Marat*; Gilbert Charles Stuart (US), portrait, *George Washington*; SCULPTURE: Antonio Canove (It), *Cupid and Psyche*

Science and Discovery

Eli Whitney (US) invents the cotton gin

Religion and Philosophy

Christianity is abolished in France under the Cult of Reason • William Godwin (GB) writes *An Enquiry concerning the Principles of Political Justice*

Social and Economic

Compulsory education is introduced in France • French government fixes wages and maximum prices

Politics and Wars

John Jay Treaty between USA and Britain stabilizes trade relations and provides for evacuation by Britain of Great Lakes frontier posts • Eleventh amendment to US Constitution is passed • "Whiskey Rebellion" in Pennsylvania over excise duty on whiskey is put down by state militia • French Revolution continues: many revolutionary leaders are executed including Georges Danton and Maximilien Robespierre; Reign of Terror ends; Paris Commune is abolished • In war between France and coalition, French win victories at Tourcoing, Charleroi, Fleurus and reach the Rhine; Prussia withdraws from war; Britain, Russia and Austria form an anti-French alliance; Spain and Prussia begin peace negotiations with France; French invade Netherlands; a French fleet is defeated by British in the English Channel

Arts and Letters

PAINTING: John Trumbull (US), *The Declaration of Independence*; MUSIC: Josef Haydn (Aus), symphony 101 ("Clock"); LITERATURE: William Blake (GB), *Songs of Experience*

Science and Discovery

Chemist John Dalton (GB) discovers color blindness

Religion and Philosophy

William Paley (GB) writes *A View of the Evidences of Christianity* • In France, Robespierre organizes the Feast of the Supreme Being, replacing the Cult of Reason • Thomas Paine (now a US citizen) writes *The Age of Reason*

Politics and Wars

French troops occupy the Netherlands and create Batavian Republic there • France and Prussia conclude Peace Treaty of Basel • Britain acquires Ceylon (Sri Lanka) from the Dutch • Bread riots in Paris • Third French Constitution creates a five-director executive (the Directory) • Britain occupies the Cape of Good Hope on behalf of Willem V of Orange • Troops under General Napoleon Bonaparte put down royalist insurrection in Paris • Belgium is absorbed by France • Russia and Austria partition Poland for the third time • Stanislaus II of Poland abdicates • Spain and the USA establish boundaries between Florida and USA and navigational rights on the Mississippi River • Warren Hastings, former Governor-General of India, is found not guilty of high treason by British parliament

Arts and Letters

PAINTING: Francisco Goya (Sp), *The Duchess of Alba*

Science and Discovery

Inventor Joseph Bramah (GB) patents his hydraulic press • Mungo Park (GB) explores the Niger River • Metric system is adopted in France

Religion and Philosophy

Freedom of worship is restored in France

Politics and Wars

Tennessee becomes the 16th state of the USA • French general Napoleon Bonaparte marries Josephine Beauharnais • Napoleon's Italy campaign: his forces defeat the Austrians at Millesimo and Lodi; the Republic of Lombardy is established • Savoy and Nice are ceded to France • Britain captures the island of Elba • France and Spain form an alliance against Britain • Austrians defeat the French at Amberg, but are beaten at Arcole • Britain captures West Indian islands, including Grenada and St. Lucia • Britain opens negotiations for peace with France • Ekaterina II, the Great, of Russia dies, and is succeeded by her son, Paul I • George Washington declines to stand again as US president; John Adams is elected, with Thomas Jefferson as his vice-president

Arts and Letters

ARCHITECTURE: Thomas Jefferson (US), Monticello; LITERATURE: Fanny Burney (Madame d'Arblay; GB), novel *Camilla*

Science and Discovery

Physician Edward Jenner (GB) introduces vaccination against smallpox • Astronomer Pierre Simon de Laplace (Fr) publishes *Exposition du système du monde* – a nebular theory of cosmogony

Social and Economic

The newspaper press becomes free in France

Politics and Wars

John Adams assumes office as second President of the USA • Adams sends three special ambassadors to France to try to settle US-French differences; French negotiators seek bribes and Adams recalls his envoys (so-called "XYZ Affair") • Napoleon's army defeats the Austrians at Rivoli • A British fleet defeats a French fleet at Battle of Cape St. Vincent • Britain seizes Trinidad from Spain • Napoleon's troops advance on Rome, and Pope Pius VI is forced to cede territories through the Treaty of Tolentino • French forces cross the Alps into Austria • The Peace of Campo Formio between France and Austria gives Belgium and Lombardy to France in exchange for Venice, Istria and Dalmatia • France proclaims the Cisalpine Republic, comprising most of northern Italy • Charles Maurice de Talleyrand becomes French foreign minister • Napoleon is appointed to command a French invasion of Britain

Arts and Letters

PAINTING: J. M. W. Turner (GB), *Millbank by Moonlight*; MUSIC: Josef Haydn (Aus), "Emperor" quartet; Ludwig van Beethoven (Ger), 1st piano concerto; LITERATURE: Samuel Taylor Coleridge (GB), poem *The Ancient Mariner*

Science and Discovery

Charles Newbold (US) patents a cast-iron plow • Louis Vauquelin (Fr) discovers chromium

Social and Economic

British government settles sailors' grievances after mutiny at Spithead, then later suppresses a second mutiny at the Nore, in the Thames River

Politics and Wars

Strained relations between USA and France lead to the creation of a US Navy Department to control operations in the West Indies • US Congress passes Naturalization Act, Aliens Act, Enemies Act and Seditions Act against its opponents • French troops annex Geneva and the French government proclaims a Helvetian Republic in Switzerland • French forces occupy Rome and proclaim a Roman Republic • Pope Pius VI moves to Valence, France • Napoleon begins an Egyptian campaign, occupies Alexandria and wins Egypt in the Battle of the Pyramids • A British fleet led by Horatio Nelson defeats a French fleet in Battle of the Nile; Napoleon's communications with France are cut • French forces take Malta, British take Minorca

Arts and Letters

MUSIC: Ludwig van Beethoven (Ger), 2nd piano concerto; Josef Haydn (Aus), oratorio *The Creation*; LITERATURE: William Wordsworth (GB) and Samuel Coleridge Taylor (GB), *Lyrical Ballads* (joint work)

Science and Discovery

Henry Cavendish (GB) calculates the density of the Earth • Iron-frame printing press is invented by the Earl of Stanhope (GB) • Count von Rumford (Benjamin Thompson, American-born) determines that heat is a form of motion

Social and Economic

British government introduces income tax to meet the cost of the Napoleonic wars • Thomas Robert Malthus (GB) writes *Essay on the Principle of Population*

USA—**John Adams** ———————————————————————— □ **Thomas Jefferson** ———
GREAT BRITAIN—**George III** ——————————————————————————————————————
HOLY ROMAN EMPIRE—**Franz II** ———————————————————————————————————

Politics and Wars

Napoleon enters Syria and besieges Acre • France establishes the Parthenopean Republic in northern Italy • Austrians defeat the French at Stockach and Magnano • Russians and Austrians enter Milan after victory at Cassano; the Cisalpine Republic is dissolved; Russians recapture Naples; the Parthenopean and Roman Republics are ended • In the Netherlands, the Allies have to capitulate, and British forces withdraw; British ships blockade the Dutch coast • A Russian army is defeated at Zurich and Russia leaves the coalition against France • Napoleon abandons the siege of Acre, but defeats the Turks at Aboukir • In a *coup d'etat*, Napoleon returns suddenly to Paris, ends the Directory and establishes the Consulate with himself as first consul and virtual dictator of France

Arts and Letters

MUSIC: Ludwig van Beethoven (Ger), piano sonata in C minor ("Pathétique") • LITERATURE: Friedrich Schiller (Ger), trilogy *Wallenstein*

Science and Discovery

Mungo Park (GB) publishes *Travels in the Interior of Africa* • The Royal Institution is founded in Britain

Social and Economic

Trade monopoly in Alaska is granted to a Russo-American company • Teacher Johann Pestalozzi opens a school for destitute children at Burgdorf, Switzerland

Politics and Wars

US government departments move to the new capital, Washington, DC • British parliament passes an Act of Union creating the United Kingdom of Great Britain and Ireland • Spain sells its Louisiana territory in America to France • Napoleon leads an army through the Great St. Bernard Pass over the Alps and defeats the Austrians at Marengo; Napoleon reconquers Italy; an Austrian army is defeated at Hohenlinden; French troops advance on Vienna • Northern European powers form the Armed Neutrality group as a counter to the British naval blockage • In US presidential elections, John Adams is defeated; Thomas Jefferson (Republican) is selected as new President after a tied vote with Aaron Burr

Arts and Letters

PAINTING: Jacques-Louis David (Fr), *Portrait of Madame Recamier*; MUSIC: Ludwig van Beethoven (Ger), 1st symphony and 3rd piano concerto • LITERATURE: Madame de Staël (Fr), *Literature in relation to Social Institutions*

Science and Discovery

Engineer Eli Whitney (US) designs muskets with interchangeable parts • William Herschel (UK) discovers infra red solar rays

Social and Economic

British Royal College of Surgeons is founded

Other Events

Philemon Wright (US) founds first settlement on site of Ottawa • Library of Congress in Washington, D.C, is established

Politics and Wars

Thomas Jefferson is inaugurated as 3rd President of the USA • Under the terms of a concordat between France and the Pope, French archbishops and bishops are to be appointed by the government and confirmed by the Pope, who is to retain some but not all the Papal States • Austria and France sign the Peace of Luneville, by which France gains large territories; The Armed Neutrality powers are joined by Prussia • Danish actions against British ships lead to the Battle of Copenhagen • A British fleet defeats a Danish fleet and forces a truce • The Armed Neutrality group breaks up and its members recognize the British right to search neutral ships • Russia and Britain are reconciled • Britain and France agree to peace preliminaries • Tsar Paul I of Russia is assassinated, and succeeded by his son Aleksandr I

Arts and Letters

PAINTING: J. M. W. Turner (UK), Calais Pier; MUSIC: Josef Hadyn (Aus) oratorio *The Seasons*; LITERATURE: Friedrich Schiller (Ger), play *The Maid of Orleans*

Science and Discovery

Chemist John Dalton (UK) formulates his law of gas pressures • Astronomer Guiseppe Piazzi (It) discovers Ceres, the first known asteroid (minor planet)

Religion and Philosophy

The clergy become ineligible to sit as members of the British parliament

Social and Economic

Napoleon founds the Bank of France

Politics and Wars

The Treaty of Amiens between Britain and France brings temporary peace to Europe: Britain returns her maritime conquests – Cape of Good Hope, Guadeloupe, Haiti, Malacca, Pondicherry, St. Lucia, Trincomalee – but retains Trinidad and Ceylon (Sri Lanka); British and French troops evacuate Egypt; the French quit Naples; Portugal's independence is recognized; Malta is returned to the Knights of St. John • France and Turkey conclude a separate treaty • Napoleon makes himself First Consul of France for life, with the right to appoint his successor • A new French constitution reduces the powers of legislative bodies • Napoleon annexes Piedmont, Parma and Piacenza • French crush a rebellion in Haiti by Negro leader Toussaint L'Ouverture

Arts and Letters

PAINTING: François Gérard (Fr), *Madame Récamier*; MUSIC: Ludwig van Beethoven (Ger), 2nd symphony and piano sonata op. 27 No. 2 ("Moonlight"); LITERATURE: Madame de Staël (Fr), novel *Delphine*

Religion and Philosophy

William Paley (UK) writes his last book, *Natural Theology*

Social and Economic

Napoleon creates the Legion of Honor • Philosopher Jeremy Bentham (UK) writes *Civil and Penal Legislation* • Health and Morals of Apprentices Act in Britain aims at improving standards for young factory workers • Political journalist William Cobbett (UK) founds a weekly paper, *The Political Register*

Politics and Wars

Ohio becomes the 17th state of the USA. • The Louisiana Purchase: USA buys Louisiana Territory, including New Orleans, from France for 80 million francs • The US Supreme Court (Marbury v. Madison) rules that Acts of Congress may not be enforceable if they violate the Constitution • Napoleon gives Switzerland a new constitution and establishes a federal republic of 19 cantons • Britain embargoes French and Dutch ships in British ports • War is renewed between Britain and France over French interference in Switzerland and Italy • Britain captures the West Indian islands of St. Lucia and Tobago, and Dutch Guiana • Irish nationalist Robert Emmet leads an abortive rebellion against British rule in Ireland; is captured and hanged

Arts and Letters

PAINTING: Benjamin West (US) *Christ Healing the Sick*; MUSIC: Ludwig van Beethoven (Ger), sonata for violin and piano op. 47 ("Kreutzer")

Science and Discovery

Construction is begun of the Caledonian Canal across Scotland, linking the North Sea with the Atlantic Ocean • William Hyde Wollaston (UK) discovers the metals rhodium and palladium • US inventor Robert Fulton's steamboat makes a successful debut on the Seine River in France

Social and Economic

Economist Jean Baptiste Say (Fr) writes his *Treatise on Political Economy* • Educationist Joseph Lancaster (UK) writes *Improvements in Education as it Respects the Industrious Classes*

Politics and Wars

A Twelfth Amendment to the US Constitution is passed, requiring separate ballots for Presidency and Vice-Presidency • US statesman Alexander Hamilton is killed in a duel with Vice-President Aaron Burr • Holy Roman Emperor Franz II assumes the title of Austrian Emperor • Spain declares war on Britain • Austria and Russia announce support for the Ottoman Empire against France • The French Empire is proclaimed; later Napoleon crowns himself emperor at a ceremony conducted by Pope Pius VII

Arts and Letters

MUSIC: Ludwig van Beethoven (Ger), piano sonatas op. 53, 54, 57, concerto for piano, violin and cello, op 56, and 3rd symphony ("Eroica"); LITERATURE: William Blake (UK), poem *Jerusalem*; Friedrich Schiller (Ger), play *William Tell*

Science and Discovery

US soldiers Meriwether Lewis and William Clark begin an exploration of the western United States • John Leslie (UK) writes *Experimental Enquiry into the Nature and Properties of Heat*

Religion and Philosophy

The British and Foreign Bible Society is founded

Social and Economic

The Napoleonic Code, a system of laws, is introduced in France

USA—**Thomas Jefferson** ————————————
UK—**George III** ————————————————
HOLY ROMAN EMPIRE—**Franz II** ——————————☐

Politics and Wars

Thomas Jefferson starts a second term as US President • US war with Tripoli ends • The Third Coalition of Britain and Russia against France is formed; Austria joins later • Napoleon abandons his plan to invade England • Napoleon is crowned King of Italy • Genoa (It) becomes French • At the Battle of Trafalgar, a British fleet under Horatio Nelson destroys combined French and Spanish fleets; Nelson is killed in the action • Napoleon's troops defeat the Austrians at Ulm, and the Russians and Austrians at Austerlitz • By the Peace of Pressburg, Austria loses Bavaria, Württemberg, Baden and all its Italian possessions • The Bourbon dynasty in Naples is ended

Arts and Letters

PAINTING: Francesco Goya (Sp), portrait *Doña Isabel Cobos de Porcal*; J. M. W. Turner (UK), *Shipwreck*; MUSIC: Ludwig van Beethoven (Ger), opera *Fidelio*; LITERATURE: William Wordsworth (UK), poem *Ode to Duty*; Walter Scott (UK), poem *Lay of the Last Minstrel*

Science and Discovery

Mungo Park (UK) explores the Niger River in West Africa • Thomas Telford (UK) builds the Ellesmere Canal aqueduct • Chemist F. W. A. Sertürner (Ger) discovers morphine

Politics and Wars

British prime minister William Pitt dies; "Ministry of All the Talents" begins • Naples is occupied by French forces • Napoleon makes his brothers kings: Louis rules Naples and Joseph rules Holland • Britain declares war on Prussia • With the Confederation of the Rhine, Napoleon dominates most of Germany • Prussia declares war on France • Emperor Franz II formally ends the Holy Roman Empire • Napoleon's troops defeat the Prussians at Jena and Auerstadt, and occupy Berlin • Napoleon launches the Continental System, blocking all continental European ports to British shipping • Former US Vice-President Aaron Burr raises a force to threaten Mexico and the southwestern USA

Arts and Letters

PAINTING: David Wilkie (UK), *Village Politicians*; MUSIC: Ludwig van Beethoven (Ger), 4th symphony and violin concerto, op. 61; LITERATURE: Ernst Moritz Arndt (Ger), poem *Spirit of the Age*

Science and Discovery

US soldiers Meriwether Lewis and William Clark complete their exploration of the western USA • Scientist Humphry Davy (UK) demonstrates the existence of potassium, sodium and chlorine

Social and Economic

James Madison (US) writes *An Examination of the British Doctrine which Subjects to Capture a Neutral Trade Not Open in Time of Peace*

Politics and Wars

Former Vice-President Aaron Burr (US) is tried for treason and acquitted • A British ship, *Leopard*, fires on the US ship *Chesapeake* carrying Royal Navy deserters; President Thomas Jefferson orders all British ships out of American waters: Embargo Act is passed which prohibits any ships sailing from the USA to foreign ports • Napoleon's troops defeat the Russians and Prussians at Friedland • Napoleon, Tsar Aleksandr I and Friedrich Wilhelm III of Prussia meet on a raft on the Neman River at Tilsit (now Sovetsk, Soviet Union) • By the Treaty of Tilsit, Russia recognizes French conquests and agrees to back France against Britain if the British do not make peace; the size of Prussia is reduced by nearly one-half • The kingdom of Westphalia is created, ruled by Napoleon's brother Jerome • French forces invade Portugal; Portugal's royal family flees to Brazil

Arts and Letters

PAINTING: Jacques-Louis David (Fr), *The Coronation of Napoleon*; MUSIC: Ludwig van Beethoven (Ger), overtures *Leonora No. 3* and *Coriolanus*; LITERATURE: Charles and Mary Lamb (UK), *Tales from Shakespeare*; Lord Byron (UK), *Hours of Idleness*; William Wordsworth (UK), *Ode on Intimations of Immortality*; Washington Irving (US), *The Salmagundi Papers*

Science and Discovery

US inventor Robert Fulton's steamboat *Clermont* sails on the Hudson River

Social and Economic

Britain abolishes the slave trade in Jamaica and in British ships

─────────────── □ **James Madison** ───────────────▷
▷

Politics and Wars

Pope Pius VII refuses to recognize the kingdom of Naples • French troops occupy Rome and Madrid: Carlos VI of Spain abdicates • Joseph Bonaparte is made king of Spain • The Spaniards begin a general resistance against Napoleon; British troops under Arthur Wellesley land in Portugal; the Peninsular War begins • The French, defeated at Vimiero, withdraw troops from Portugal • Russia conquers Finland • Spanish insurgents are beaten at Burgos, in the north • Emperor Napoleon I (Fr) annexes Tuscany • Sierra Leone becomes a British Crown colony • Secretary of state James Madison is elected president of the USA

Arts and Letters

PAINTING: Jean Auguste Ingres (Fr), *La Grande baigneuse*; MUSIC: Ludwig van Beethoven (Ger), 5th symphony and 6th symphony ("Pastoral"); LITERATURE: Walter Scott (UK), poem *Marmion*; Johann Wolfgang Goethe (Ger), drama *Faust*, part I

Science and Discovery

Chemist John Dalton (UK) publishes *A New System of Chemical Philosophy* • The element boron is isolated by Humphry Davy (UK) and independently by J. L. Gay-Lussac (Fr)

Religion and Philosophy

The Inquisition is abolished in Spain

Social and Economic

USA bans the import of slaves from Africa

Politics and Wars

James Madison becomes 4th president of the USA • US Embargo Act is repealed • Non-Intercourse Act in USA bans commerce with France and Britain • British troops land in northwest Spain but retreat to Corunna: the British general Sir John Moore dies of wounds • British forces commanded by Arthur Wellesley defeat the French at Oporto and Talavera: Wellesley is made Viscount Wellington • French forces overrun Andalusia, Spain • Austria declares war on France the French take Vienna and defeat the Austrians at Wagram • By the Peace of Schönbrunn, Austria loses territories and joins Napoleon's Continental System • Emperor Napoleon I (Fr) is excommunicated for annexing Papal States and seizing Pope Pius VII • Gustavus IV of Sweden abdicates after defeat by Russia: is succeeded by his uncle, Karl XIII, who adopts French marshal Jean Bernadotte as his heir • Napoleon I divorces Empress Josephine.

Arts and Letters

PAINTING: John Constable (UK), *Malvern Hall*; MUSIC: Ludwig van Beethoven (Ger), piano concerto op. 73 ("Emperor"); LITERATURE: Washington Irving (US), *Knickerbocker's History of New York*; Lord Byron (UK), poem *English Bards and Scotch Reviewers* (satire replying to his critics)

Science and Discovery

John Heathcoat (UK) invents a lace-making bobbin machine • Humphry Davy (UK), invents an arc lamp • William Maclure, "Father of American geology," makes a geological chart of the USA

Politics and Wars

Emperor Napoleon I (Fr), marries Princess Marie-Louise of Austria • Movement begins toward independence in Spain's South American colonies: Simón Bolívar emerges as leader in Venezuelan uprising; revolts follow in Mexico, New Granada and Chile • In Portugal, the French take Ciudad Rodrigo, but British troops hold the Line of Torres Vedras, forcing the French army to withdraw • British forces occupy the French colonies of Mauritius, Seychelles and Guadaloupe • Napoleon I orders the sale of all seized US vessels • Napoleon annexes the Netherlands

Arts and Letters

PAINTING: Francisco Goya (Sp), *Majas on a Balcony*; MUSIC: Ludwig van Beethoven (Ger), incidental music to play *Egmont*; LITERATURE: Walter Scott (UK), poem *The Lady of the Lake*

Science and Discovery

Statesman-scientist Johann Wolfgang Goethe (Ger) writes his *Theory of Color* • Samuel Friedrich Hahnemann (Ger), founder of homeopathy, writes *Principles of Rational Medicine* • Scientist Nicolas Appert (Fr) develops a method of food preservation in heat-sealed bottles

Social and Economic

The French government assumes a monopoly of the sale of tobacco • Educational reforms are introduced in Prussia

USA—**James Madison**
UK—**George III**

Politics and Wars

In Britain, King George III's insanity results in the passing of a Regency Act: the Prince of Wales is made Prince Regent • In Portugal, British troops led by Lord Wellington defeat the French at Fuentes d'Onoro and Albuhera • Russian forces take Belgrade and defeat the Turks • Egyptian Viceroy Mehemet Ali has Mamelukes —the ruling dynasty—massacred • A son is born to the French emperor Napoleon I; he is named King of Rome • Venezuela and Paraguay declare their independence from Spain • In the USA, Indians opposing the white man's drive to the northwest are defeated at the Battle of Tippecanoe • President James Madison (US) threatens war over Britain's maritime trade policy

Arts and Letters

PAINTING: Thomas Lawrence (UK), portrait *Benjamin West*; MUSIC: Carl Maria von Weber (Ger), opera *Abu Hassan*; LITERATURE: Jane Austen (UK), *Sense and Sensibility*; Johann Wolfgang Goethe (Ger), *My Life, Poetry and Truth*; Friedrich de la Motte Fouqué (Ger), romance *Undine*

Science and Discovery

Anatomist Charles Bell (UK) writes *New Idea of the Anatomy of the Brain* • Physicist Amedeo Avogadro (It) publishes a hypothesis that equal volumes of all gases contain the same number of molecules (Avogadro's Law)

Social and Economic

Krupp's steelworks is founded in Essen (Ger) • Mechanization of industry leads to destruction of machinery in British factories by "Luddites," named after a mythical Ned Ludd

Politics and Wars

Louisiana becomes the 18th US state • USA declares war on Britain: US plans to invade Canada are frustrated by defeats at Detroit and Queenston Heights • In Spain, British general Viscount Wellington's forces take Ciudad Rodrigo and Badajoz, defeat French at Salamanca, and enter Madrid; Wellington is made a marquess • Emperor Napoleon I (Fr) leads an invasion of Russia: wins victory at Borodino, and enters Moscow, which is burned by Russians; French army meets disaster crossing Beresina River and begins a punishing retreat in bitter conditions • A conspiracy to overthrow Napoleon fails: he returns hurriedly to Paris • British prime minister Spencer Perceval is assassinated in the House of Commons

Arts and Letters

PAINTING: Francisco Goya (Sp), portrait *Lord Wellington*; MUSIC: Ludwig van Beethoven (Ger), 7th and 8th symphonies; LITERATURE: Lord Byron (UK), *Childe Harold's Pilgrimage*; the Grimm Brothers (Ger), *Fairy Tales*

Science and Discovery

Scientist Humphry Davy (UK) writes *Elements of Chemical Philosophy* • John Blenkinsop (UK) constructs first cog railway • First steamboat to appear in Europe is Henry Bell's *Comet*, launched on the Clyde River, Scotland

Religion and Philosophy

Restrictions on Nonconformists in England are relaxed by repeal of the Conventicle Acts

Politics and Wars

In War of 1812 between Britain and USA, US forces occupy Fort St. George; a British fleet is defeated on Lake Erie; US forces reoccupy Detroit and win Battle of Thames River; British capture Fort Niagara and burn Buffalo • Prussia declares war on France • Russians occupy Hamburg and Dresden • British forces under Marquess of Wellington (UK) defeat French at Vittoria (Sp), and drive King Joseph (brother of French emperor Napoleon I) from Spain; British troops enter France and besiege Bayonne • Napoleon is defeated by allied armies at Leipzig (Ger) • Confederation of the Rhine is dissolved • Popular risings drive French from Netherlands • Prussians cross the Rhine • Austrians invade France by way of Switzerland • Simón Bolívar becomes virtual dictator of independent Venezuela

Arts and Letters

PAINTING: J. M. W. Turner (UK), *Frosty Morning*; MUSIC: Giacchino Rossini (It), opera *The Italian Girl in Algiers*; LITERATURE: Jane Austen (UK), novel *Pride and Prejudice*; Lord Byron (UK), poems *The Giaour* and *The Bride of Abydos*; Percy Bysshe Shelley (UK), poem *Queen Mab*

Social and Economic

Industrialist reformer Robert Owen (UK) writes *A New View of Society* • New charter for British East India Company ends its trade monopoly in India, and recognizes British Crown's sovereignty there

Politics and Wars

In War of 1812 between Britain and USA, Britain reinforces troops in Canada; US forces beat British at Chippewa, Ont., but withdraw from Canada; a British fleet is destroyed on Lake Champlain; British land at Chesapeake Bay, defeat Americans at Bladensburg, occupy Washington and burn the Capitol; a British force is repulsed at Baltimore; Treaty of Ghent (December 24) ends the war • In Europe, peace negotiations between Napoleon I (Fr) and his opponents break down; French forces are defeated at Bar-sur-Aube and Laon; British general Wellington, now a duke, takes Bordeaux; Allies enter Paris; Napoleon I abdicates and is exiled to Elba • Louis XVIII, brother of Louis XVI, becomes king of France • Congress of Vienna meets to settle future of reconquered territories • Cape of Good Hope becomes a British colony

Arts and Letters

PAINTING: Francisco Goya (Sp), *3 May 1808*; LITERATURE: Walter Scott (UK), novel *Waverley*; William Wordsworth (UK), poem *The Excursion*; Jane Austen (UK), novel *Mansfield Park*; Lord Byron (UK), poem *The Corsair* • Francis Scott Key (US), poem *The Star Spangled Banner*

Science and Discovery

Engineer George Stephenson (UK) builds the first successful steam locomotive • J. J. Berzelius (Switz) writes *Theory of Chemical Proportions and the Chemical Action of Electricity*

Religion and Philosophy

Pope Pius VII revives the Inquisition and the Index

Politics and Wars

The Hundred Days: Napoleon I returns from Elba to France; Louis XVIII flees to Ghent; Britain, Austria, Russia and Prussia form a new alliance • The Waterloo Campaign: Napoleon's troops beat the Prussians at Ligny, but are decisively defeated by Wellington's army at Waterloo; Napoleon abdicates again and is exiled to St. Helena • Louis XVIII returns to throne of France • In War of 1812, US forces beat British at New Orleans before news of the Peace of Ghent arrives • Congress of Vienna decides on future map of Europe; Britain to retain most of the overseas territory acquired • British occupy Ascension Island • Britain, Austria, Russia and Prussia renew the Quadruple Alliance • US Navy captain Stephen Decatur frees American ships and prisoners held by pirates of the Barbary Coast—Morocco, Algeria and Tunisia

Arts and Letters

PAINTING: J. M. W. Turner (UK), *Dido building Carthage*; SCULPTURE: Antonio Canova (It), *The Three Graces*; LITERATURE: Walter Scott (UK), novel *Guy Mannering*

Science and Discovery

Scientist Humphry Davy (UK) invents miner's safety lamp • John Macadam (UK) introduces roads made of broken stone • USA builds the first steam warship, *Fulton*

Social and Economic

British Corn Law prohibits import of wheat below fixed price • Income tax ends in Britain

Other Events

Tambora Volcano in Sumbawa (Indon) erupts: 50,000 dead

Politics and Wars

Indiana becomes 19th state of the USA • US administration introduces tariffs as a protection against dumping of British goods • Maria I of Portugal dies; is succeeded by her son, João VI, who prefers to remain in Brazil, which becomes an empire • United Provinces of Rio de la Plata (Arg) declare independence • Demands for parliamentary reform are made in Britain: violent demonstrations in London • James Monroe is elected President of the USA • Britain restores Java to the Netherlands

Arts and Letters

MUSIC: Franz Schubert (Aus), song "Erl King"; Giacchino Rossini (It), opera *The Barber of Seville*; LITERATURE: Jane Austen (UK), novel *Emma* • Samuel Taylor Coleridge (UK), poem *Kubla Khan*; Walter Scott (UK), novels *The Antiquary* and *Old Mortality*; Thomas Love Peacock (UK), novel *Headlong Hall*; Lord Byron (UK), poem *The Prisoner of Chillon*

Science and Discovery

The kaleidoscope is invented by David Brewster (UK) • Réné Laennec (Fr) invents the stethoscope • Johann Maelzel (Ger) patents the metronome

Religion and Philosophy

American Bible Society is founded

Social and Economic

Friedrich Froebel (Ger) establishes an educational community at Keilau, Thuringia • William Cobbett (UK) begins issuing *Political Register* (founded 1802) as a twopenny paper to avoid tax

USA—**James Madison**—☐ **James Monroe**
UK—**George III**

Politics and Wars

Mississippi becomes 20th state of the USA • James Monroe is inaugurated as 5th President of the USA • Rush-Bagot Agreement between USA and Britain prohibits fortifications on the Great Lakes • High food prices in Britain cause industrial unrest: Habeas Corpus Act is suspended • British Parliament passes acts protecting the king and prince regent and banning seditious meetings and publications • Quadruple Alliance powers (Austria, Britain, Prussia, Russia) begin reducing their army of occupation in France • War against Seminole Indians in Florida begins (to 1818)

Arts and Letters

PAINTING: John Constable (UK), Flatford Mill; ARCHITECTURE: Thomas Jefferson (US), University of Virginia; LITERATURE: Lord Byron (UK), poem Manfred • Percy Bysshe Shelley (UK), poem The Revolt of Islam • Samuel Taylor Coleridge (UK), Biographia Literaria • Thomas Moore (Ire), Lalla Rookh

Religion and Philosophy

Georg Wilhelm Friedrich Hegel (Ger) writes Encyclopaedia of Philosophical Sciences

Social and Economic

Economist David Ricardo (UK) writes Principles of Political Economy and Taxation • Spain agrees to end slave trade • Quaker philanthropist Elizabeth Fry (UK) forms association for improved treatment of women in prison

Other Events

Construction of Erie Canal begins

Politics and Wars

Illinois becomes 21st state of the USA • Britain and USA agree to 49th Parallel boundary between USA and Canada; Oregon is left to joint occupation • Former French Marshal Jean Bernadotte becomes King Karl XIV of Sweden on death of Karl XIII • In Britain, suspension of the Habeas Corpus Act is ended; attempts at parliamentary reform are defeated • Conference of the Quadruple Alliance (Austria, Britain, Prussia, Russia) at Aix-la-Chapelle (Aachen): Allies agree to remove occupation troops from France • France is invited to join the Concert of Europe, an informal alliance of European powers • Chile and Venezuela become independent

Arts and Letters

MUSIC: Franz Schubert (Aus), 6th symphony; Giacchino Rossini (It), opera Moses in Egypt; LITERATURE: Jane Austen (UK), Northanger Abbey and Persuasion (both published posthumously); Thomas Love Peacock (UK), Nightmare Abbey; John Keats (UK), poem Endymion; Walter Scott (UK), Heart of Midlothian and Rob Roy • Mary Wollstonecraft Shelley (UK), novel Frankenstein • Lord Byron (UK), poem Don Juan

Science and Discovery

Polar explorers John Ross and Edward Parry (UK) explore Baffin Bay, Northwest Territories • Astronomer Friedrich Wilhelm Bessel (Ger) lists over 3,000 stars in Fundamente Astronima

Politics and Wars

Alabama becomes 22nd state of the USA • Spain cedes Florida to the USA • US Supreme Court decision (McCulloch v. Maryland) strengthens power of federal authority over states • Britain establishes a settlement in Singapore • "Peterloo" massacre in Manchester, England: 11 people are killed when troops disperse demonstrators seeking parliamentary reform and repeal of Corn Laws • Repressive Carlsbad Decrees are passed by Diet of the German Confederation • Simón Bolívar becomes president of independent Colombia

Arts and Letters

PAINTING: Théodore Géricault (Fr), The Raft of the Medusa; MUSIC: Franz Schubert (Aus), The "Trout" quintet; LITERATURE: Lord Byron (UK), Mazeppa; John Keats (UK), Hyperion; Johann Wolfgang Goethe (Ger), The West-Eastern Divan

Science and Discovery

Hans Christian Oersted (Den) discovers electromagnetism • Engineer Thomas Telford (UK) begins building Menai suspension bridge

Religion and Philosophy

Philosopher Arthur Schopenhauer (Ger) writes The World as Will and Idea

Other Events

Mehemet Ali, ruler of Egypt, gives Cleopatra's Needles to USA and Britain

□ George IV

Politics and Wars

Maine becomes 23rd state of the USA • Under the Missouri Compromise, Missouri is to be admitted without restriction on slavery • US Land Law abolishes credit system and fixes minimum price for land • Revolution in Spain: Fernando VII gives way, restores liberal Constitution of 1812 and abolishes the Inquisition • Cato Street conspiracy in Britain: attempt to murder cabinet ministers fails • Britain's King George III dies, and is succeeded by the prince regent as George IV • George IV's attempt to divorce his wife Caroline fails • Conference of Troppau meets to consider revolutionary threats in Spain and Italy • US President James Monroe is unopposed for a second term

Arts and Letters

PAINTING: John Constable (UK), *Dedham Mill*; William Blake (UK), illustrations for *The Book of Job*; MUSIC: Franz Schubert (Aus), *The Wanderer*; LITERATURE: Walter Scott (UK), *Ivanhoe*; Percy Bysshe Shelley (UK), *Prometheus Unbound*; Washington Irving (US), *Sketchbook of Geoffrey Crayon, Gent*; John Keats (UK), *The Eve of St. Agnes and other Poems*

Science and Discovery

André Ampère (Fr) develops his law of electromagnetism

Religion and Philosophy

Metaphysician Thomas Brown (UK) publishes *Lectures on the Philosophy of the Human Mind*

Social and Economic

Thomas Robert Malthus (UK) writes *Principles of Poltical Economy*

Politics and Wars

James Monroe begins 2nd term as President of the USA • Missouri becomes the 24th state of the USA • Greek war of independence against Turkey begins: the Greeks successful in the Morea, where Turks are massacred, but Turks defeat Greeks at Dragashan • Revolt in Piedmont: Austria intervenes • Force led by South American patriot Simón Bolívar defeats Spanish army at Carabobo, Venezuela • Peru, Mexico, Guatemala, Panama, and San Domingo declare independence from Spain • Britain's Queen Caroline dies • British Africa Company is ended • British West Africa—comprising Gambia, Gold Coast and Sierra Leone—is formed • Portuguese king João VI agrees to leave Brazil and return to Portugal

Arts and Letters

PAINTING: John Constable (UK), *The Hay Wain*; MUSIC: Karl Maria von Weber (Ger), opera *Der Freischutz*; LITERATURE: Walter Scott (UK), *Kenilworth*; James Fenimore Cooper (US), *The Spy*; Thomas de Quincey (UK), *Confessions of an English Opium Eater*; Percy Bysshe Shelley (UK), poem *Adonais*

Science and Discovery

Michael Faraday (UK) develops the electric motor • Thomas Johann Seebeck (Ger) invents the thermocouple, used in measuring temperatures • Egyptian hieroglyphics are deciphered by Jean-François Champollion (Fr)

Social and Economic

Hudson's Bay Company combines with North-West Trading Company in Canada • James Mill (UK) writes *Elements of Political Economy*

Politics and Wars

Greeks declare independence from Turkey: Turks massacre inhabitants of the island of Chios • Mexican nationalist Agustín de Iturbide is proclaimed emperor of newly-independent Mexico • Brazil is formally declared independent of Portugal; Dom Pedro, eldest son of King João of Portugal, is proclaimed emperor • American Colonization Society founds Liberia as a colony for freed American slaves • Viscount Castlereagh, Britain's foreign secretary, commits suicide • Bottle Riots: Orangemen attack the viceroy of Ireland in Dublin • New Corn Laws reduce price at which wheat may be imported into Britain

Arts and Letters

PAINTING: Eugène Delacroix (Fr), *The Bark of Dante*; MUSIC: Ludwig van Beethoven (Ger), Mass in D; Franz Schubert (Aus), symphony in B minor ("Unfinished"); LITERATURE: Washington Irving (US), *Bracebridge Hall*; Walter Scott (UK), *The Fortunes of Nigel*

Science and Discovery

Louis Jacques Mandé Daguerre (Fr) opens the Diorama theater in Paris • Alexander Laing (UK) explores the Niger River basin in West Africa

Social and Economic

In France, the sale of newspapers which are not government-approved is banned • Gas street-lighting is introduced in Boston, Mass

Other Events

The Sunday Times newspaper is founded in London

USA—**James Monroe** ——————————————————— □ **John Quincy Adams** ———
UK—**George IV** ——————————————————————————————

Politics and Wars

The Monroe Doctrine, barring further European colonization of America, is promulgated by US President James Monroe • Mexican emperor Agustín Iturbide abdicates under pressure; Mexico becomes a republic • French forces invade Spain to help crush rebellion and restore Fernando VII to the throne • British move towards free trade with Warehousing of Goods Act • Rising in Portugal, partly over loss of Brazil: João VI dismisses the Cortés (parliament) • Costa Rica, Guatemala, Honduras, Nicaragua and San Salvador form the Confederation of United Provinces of Central America • Argentine soldier-patriot José de San Martín quits Pèru; Simón Bolívar arrives to take over

Arts and Letters

PAINTINGS: Jean Ingres (Fr), *La Source*; LITERATURE: James Fenimore Cooper (US), *The Pioneers*; Stendhal (Marie Henri Beyle, Fr), *Racine and Shakespeare*; Walter Scott (UK), *Quentin Durward*; Charles Lamb (UK) *Essays of Elia*, in book form

Science and Discovery

Michael Faraday (UK) analyzes hydrate of chlorine, leading to chlorine's discovery • Charles MacIntosh (UK) patents a waterproof fabric • Explorers Hugh Clapperton and Walter Oudney (UK) discover Lake Chad in Central Africa • Navigator James Weddell (UK) discovers the Weddell Sea in Antarctica

Religion and Philosophy

Pope Pius VII dies; is succeeded by Leo XII

Politics and Wars

Greek War of Independence continues: Turks abandon the siege of Missolonghi; Egyptians capture Crete; Turks are defeated at Mitylene • War between Britain and Burma: British capture Rangoon • King Louis XVIII of France dies; is succeeded by his brother, Charles X • South American patriot Simón Bolívar defeats Spanish armies in Peru and is proclaimed President • Agreement is reached between USA and Russia on rights in northwest America and the Pacific Ocean • US presidential election ends with no-one having a clear majority; House of Representatives chooses John Quincy Adams as President

Arts and Letters

PAINTING: Thomas Lawrence (UK), *Portrait of Master Lambton*; MUSIC: Ludwig van Beethoven (Ger), symphony No. 9 ("Choral") and *Missa Solemnis*; LITERATURE: Walter Scott (UK), *Redgauntlet*; Walter Savage Landor (UK), first two volumes of *Imaginary Conversations*

Science and Discovery

Joseph Aspdin (UK) produces Portland cement • Alexander Hamilton Hume (Austral) discovers Murray River, Australia

Religion and Philosophy

American Sunday School Union is founded • Johann Friedrich Herbert (Ger) writes *Psychology as a Science*

Social and Economic

Repeal of the Combination Act in Britain legalizes trade unions • Robert Owen (UK) founds the New Harmony settlement in Indiana • French Press laws are relaxed

Politics and Wars

John Quincy Adams is inaugurated as 6th President of the USA • British and Russians sign treaty on their rights in northwest America and the Pacific Ocean • French aristocrats are compensated for their losses during the Revolution • Britain relaxes controls over European shipping under Navigation Acts • Javanese revolt against the Dutch • Portugal recognizes the independence of Brazil • Bolivia declares independence from Peru • Uruguay declares independence from Brazil • Tsar Aleksandr I of Russia dies, is succeeded by his brother, Nikolai I

Arts and Letters

PAINTING: Samuel F. B. Morse (US), *Lafayette*; Thomas Cole founds Hudson River School of painting in USA; MUSIC: Franz Schubert (Aus), string quartet D810 ("Death and the Maiden"); ARCHITECTURE: John Nash (UK), new design for Buckingham Palace, London; LITERATURE: William Hazlitt (UK), *The Spirit of the Age*; Samuel Pepys (UK, 1633–1703), *Diary* (deciphered for first time); Walter Scott (UK), *The Talisman*

Science and Discovery

In England, the world's first passenger railroad—from Stockton to Darlington—begins to operate • In North America, the Erie Canal is opened to shipping • Michael Faraday (UK) distills benzine • Chemist Hans Christian Oersted (Den) produces aluminum

Social and Economic

Violence in trade union action is prohibited by law in Britain

1826

Politics and Wars
King João VI of Portugal dies, and is succeeded by his son Pedro, emperor of Brazil; Pedro refuses to leave Brazil and cedes the Portuguese throne to his 7-year-old daughter Maria, with his brother Dom Miguel as regent • Greek War of Independence continues: Egypt takes Missolonghi • Janizaries, crack Turkish troops, mutiny and are ruthlessly suppressed • Britain's war with Burma ends • Russia declares war on Persia • The Panama Congress, planned by patriot leader Simón Bolívar to produce unity among American republics, is ineffective

Arts and Letters
MUSIC: Karl von Weber (Ger), opera *Oberon*; he dies soon after; Felix Mendelssohn (Ger), music for *A Midsummer Night's Dream*; LITERATURE: James Fenimore Cooper (US), *The Last of the Mohicans*; Benjamin Disraeli (UK), *Vivian Grey*; Walter Scott (UK), *Woodstock*; Giovanni Casanova (1725–1798; It), *Memoirs* (published posthumously); Alfred de Vigny (Fr), *Cinq Mars*

Science and Discovery
André Marie Ampère (Fr) publishes his *Theory of Electric Phenomena* • The chemical aniline is discovered

Religion and Philosophy
Jesuits are permitted to return to France

Other Events
London Zoological Society is founded • Menai Bridge, connecting mainland Wales with the Isle of Anglesey, is opened

1827

Politics and Wars
Britain sends troops to Portugal to support Queen Maria, but withdraws them after Regent Miguel undertakes to support the constitution • Turks capture Athens and occupy the Acropolis; by the Treaty of London, Russia, France and Britain recognize Greek autonomy; but Turkey rejects their proposal for truce with Greece; in the naval Battle of Navarino, Turkish and Egyptian fleets are destroyed by the Allies; Count Capo d'Istria is elected President of Greece

Arts and Letters
PAINTING: J. M. W. Turner (UK), *Ulysses Deriding Polyphemus*; LITERATURE: Victor Hugo (Fr), *Cromwell*; Alessandro Manzoni (It), *I Promessi Sposi* • Heinrich Heine (Ger), *Book of Songs*; Edgar Allan Poe (US), *Tamerlane and Other Poems*; John James Audubon (US), first part of *Birds of North America* (published in Britain); John Clare (UK), *The Shepherd's Calendar*

Science and Discovery
Striking matches, called "Congreves" or "Lucifers," are invented • Joseph N, Niepce (Fr) makes a crude photograph on sensitized metal plate • Georg Simon Ohm (Ger) formulates his mathematical law of electric currents

Religion and Philosophy
The Plymouth Brethren sect is founded in Britain • Concordat is established between Pope Leo XII and the Netherlands

Social and Economic
Britain reforms its criminal law, reducing the number of capital offenses

1828

Politics and Wars
US Congress passes the "Tariff of Abominations" controlling the import of foreign goods • The Duke of Wellington (Tory) becomes Britain's prime minister • Pedro IV abdicates the throne of Portugal: a *coup d'état* makes his brother Miguel king • Russia declares war on Turkey and occupies Varna • Britain, France and Russia guarantee Greece independence after the withdrawal of Turkish and Egyptian forces • Uruguay becomes independent from Brazil • Andrew Jackson is elected President of the USA

Arts and Letters
PAINTING: John Constable (UK), *Salisbury Cathedral from the Meadows*; MUSIC: Franz Schubert (Aus), 7th symphony; he dies soon after; LITERATURE: James Fenimore Cooper (US), *The Red Rover*; Aleksandr Pushkin (Russ), poem *Poltava*; Noah Webster (US), *American Dictionary of the English Language*; OTHER: National Academy of Design incorporated in USA

Science and Discovery
Chemist Friedrich Wohler (Ger) founds the science of organic chemistry • Biologist Karl Ernst von Baer (Ger) writes *The Embryology of Animals*

Religion and Philosophy
Dugald Stewart (UK) writes *The Philosophy of the Active and Moral Powers of Man* • By the repeal of the Test and Corporation Acts, Nonconformists and Roman Catholics are permitted to hold public office in Britain

USA—**J. Q. Adams**—☐ **Andrew Jackson** ————————————
UK—**George IV** ————☐ **William IV** ————————————————

Politics and Wars
Andrew Jackson is inaugurated as 7th President of the USA • The Treaty of Adrianople ends Russo-Turkish War: Russia gains navigation rights in Dardanelles and Bosphorus • Britain, France and Russia extend their guarantees of independence to the whole of Greece; Turkey acknowledges Greek independence • Western Australia is colonized by British settlers

Arts and Letters
PAINTING: Eugène Delacroix (Fr), *The Assassination of the Bishop of Liège*; Katsushika Hokusai (Jap), *36 Views of Mount Fuji*; MUSIC: Giacchiano Rossini (It), opera *William Tell*; LITERATURE: Honoré de Balzac (Fr), *The Human Comedy*; Alfred de Musset (Fr), *Stories of Spain and Italy*

Science and Discovery
Joseph Henry (US) devises an electro-magnetic motor • James Neilson (UK) invents a high-temperature blast furnace • Wealthy chemist James Smithson (UK) dies, bequeathing his fortune to found the Smithsonian Institution in Washington, DC

Religion and Philosophy
In Britain, the Catholic Emancipation Act is passed; the first Roman Catholic Member of Parliament (Daniel O'Connell) is elected • James Mill (UK) writes *Analysis of the Human Mind* • Pope Leo XII dies; is succeeded by Pius VIII

Social and Economic
London's Metropolitan police force is founded by statesman Robert Peel • Louis Braille (Fr) publishes a raised alphabet for the blind • The Working Men's Party founded in New York City

Politics and Wars
George IV of Britain dies; is succeeded by his brother, William IV • Citizens of Paris revolt: King Charles X abdicates; his distant relative Louis Philippe is appointed lieutenant-general, then king • New French Constitution provides for an elected monarchy • French forces invade Algeria and capture Algiers • Belgians revolt against Dutch rule and are supported by a conference of Britain, France, Austria and Russia; a provisional Belgian government declares independence • Venezuela becomes independent from Colombia • Ecuador becomes independent

Arts and Letters
MUSIC: Hector Berlioz (Fr), *Symphonie Fantastique*; LITERATURE: Victor Hugo (Fr), *Hernani*; Stendhal (Fr), *Scarlet and Black*; William Cobbett (UK), *Rural Rides*; Alfred Tennyson (UK), *Poems, Chiefly Lyrical*

Science and Discovery
First railroad in USA—Baltimore and Ohio—is opened • Charles Lyell (UK) publishes the first volume of *Principles of Geology* • John and Richard Lander (UK) explore the Niger River • Charles Sturt (UK) explores the Murray River region of Australia

Religion and Philosophy
Evangelist Joseph Smith (US) writes *Book of Mormon* • Roman Catholicism ceases to be the state religion of France • Auguste Comte (Fr) writes *Course of Positive Philosophy*

Other Events
The Liverpool-to-Manchester railroad is opened in England

Politics and Wars
Poland declares independence from Russia, but Russian troops take Warsaw and the Polish revolt ends • Leopold of Saxe-Coburg is declared first king of the Belgians; Dutch troops invade Belgium but withdraw when French forces go to the Belgians' aid • Austrian forces enter Italy after revolutionary outbreaks • President Capo d'Istria of Greece is assassinated • Two Reform Bills fail to pass through the British parliament • Emperor Pedro I of Brazil abdicates and returns to Portugal to aid his daughter Maria against the regent, his brother Miguel

Arts and Letters
PAINTING: Barbizon School of artists exhibit in Paris; MUSIC: Vincenzo Bellini (It), opera *La Sonnambula* and *Norma*; Louis Hérold (Fr), opera *Zampa*; LITERATURE: Victor Hugo (Fr), *Notre Dame de Paris*; Aleksandr Pushkin (Russ), *Boris Godunov*

Science and Discovery
Naturalist Charles Darwin (UK) begins his scientific voyage on HMS *Beagle* • Michael Faraday (UK) discovers electromagnetic induction • Explorer James Clark Ross (UK) reaches the magnetic North Pole

Religion and Philosophy
Farmer William Miller (US), founder of Second Adventists, begins preaching • Pope Pius VIII dies; is succeeded by Gregory XVI

Social and Economic
Abolitionist William Lloyd Garrison (US) publishes newspaper *The Liberator* in Boston, Mass

Politics and Wars

South Carolina challenges the US Tariff Act, and declares it void in the state; Vice-President John C. Calhoun resigns in support of South Carolina • President Jackson vetoes renewal of the charter of Second Bank of the United States • British parliament passes a Reform Bill, extending franchise to many new voters and including many reforms of electoral system • Tsar Nikolai I (Russ) abolishes the Polish Constitution • Turkey declares war on Egypt: Turks are defeated at Konieh • In Portugal, ex-king Pedro defeats Regent Miguel's forces and takes Oporto • Prince Otto of Bavaria is elected Greek king • Andrew Jackson is reëlected President of the USA

Arts and Letters

MUSIC: Gaetano Donizetti (It), opera *L'Elisir d'amore*; LITERATURE: Washington Irving (US), *A Town of the Prairie*; Honoré de Balzac (Fr), *Contes drôlatiques*; Alfred Tennyson (UK), poem *The Lady of Shallot* • Johann Wolfgang Goethe (Ger), drama *Faust*, part II; Victor Hugo (Fr), play *Le Roi s'amuse*

Religion and Philosophy

Pope Gregory XVI issues an encyclical condemning unrestrained liberty of conscience and the Press

Other Events

The Gotha Canal in Sweden is completed

Politics and Wars

Andrew Jackson is inaugurated for his 2nd term as President of the USA • US Congress passes the Force Act, authorizing the collection of revenues from South Carolina by force if necessary • Britain acquires the Falkland Islands as a Crown Colony • An armistice is declared between the Netherlands and Belgium • In the Portuguese civil war, King Pedro's forces occupy Lisbon; Queen Maria returns • King Fernnando VII of Spain dies, and is succeeded by his 3-year-old daughter Isabel II • British Tory party takes the name "Conservative" • A Customs Union (Zollverein), excluding Austria, is established in Germany

Arts and Letters

MUSIC: Gaetano Donizetti (It), opera *Lucrezia Borgia*; Felix Mendelssohn (Ger), 4th symphony ("Italian"); LITERATURE: Robert Browning (UK), *Pauline*; Thomas Carlyle (UK), *Sartor Resartus*; Nikolai Gogol (Russ) *The Government Inspector*

Religion and Philosophy

The Oxford movement begins in England

Social and Economic

Journalist William Lloyd Garrison (US) forms the American Anti-slavery Society • A General Trades' Union is formed in New York • The British East India Company loses its China trade monopoly • The Education Grant Act provides state aid for education in Britain • The Factory Act regulates British children's working hours • Slavery is declared abolished in the British Empire

Politics and Wars

Ex-king Pedro IV of Portugal dies; his 15-year-old daughter Maria II, queen since 1826, is declared of age to rule • Civil war starts in Spain with a claim to the throne by Don Carlos, uncle of 4-year-old Isabel II; Carlos is opposed by an alliance of England, France and Portugal with the established Spanish government • Civil war erupts in Ecuador • The South Australia Association receives a charter to found a British colony

Arts and Letters

PAINTING: Eugène Delacroix (Fr), *Arabic Fantasy*; MUSIC: Hector Berlioz (Fr), *Harold in Italy*, for viola and orchestra; Robert Schumann (Ger), *Carnaval*; LITERATURE: Honoré de Balzac (Fr), *Le Père Goriot* • Edward Bulwer-Lytton (UK), *The Last Days of Pompeii*; Frederick Marryat (UK); *Peter Simple*; William Dunlap (US), *History of the Rise and Progress of the Arts of Design in the United States*

Science and Discovery

Cyrus McCormick (US) patents a harvesting machine

Social and Economic

Robert Owen (UK) forms the Grand National Consolidated Trade Union; six Dorset laborers (the Tolpuddle Martyrs) are sentenced to transportation for joining it

Other Events

The hansom cab is patented in London by an architect, Joseph Aloysius Hansom • Robin Carver (US) writes the first description of "base, or goal ball" in *Book of Sports* • Britain's Houses of Parliament are gutted by fire

USA—**Andrew Jackson** ———————————————— ☐ **Martin Van Buren** ———
UK—**George IV** —————————————————————— ☐ **Victoria** ———————

1835

Politics and Wars
Emperor Franz I of Austria dies and is succeeded by his son, Ferdinand I • Civil war continues in Spain: British and French foreign legions are formed to support Queen Isabel II • French republicans try to shoot King Louis Philippe of France; the king escapes, but 18 people die; strict laws are introduced in France to curb the Press and expedite the trial of insurgents • The city of Melbourne, Australia, is founded • In Argentina, politician Juan de Rosas imposes a dictatorship • The Second Seminole War begins in Florida

Arts and Letters
PAINTING: Caspar David Friedrich (Ger), *Rest During the Harvest*; MUSIC: Gaetano Donizetti (It), opera *Lucia di Lammermoor*; LITERATURE: Hans Christian Andersen (Den), *Fairy Tales*; Nikolai Gogol (Russ), *Dead Souls*; Edward Bulwer-Lytton (UK), *Rienzi*; William Wordsworth (UK), poem *Yarrow Revisited*; J. P. Kennedy (US), *Horse Shoe Robinson*; Robert Browning (UK), poem *Paracelsus*

Science and Discovery
Samuel Colt (US) patents his revolver

Social and Economic
The Municipal Reform Act provides for locally elected councils in Britain

Other Events
The New York Herald newspaper is founded • Madame Tussaud's waxworks are opened in London, Eng

1836

Politics and Wars
Arkansas becomes the 25th state of the USA • Texas declares independence from Mexico; Davy Crockett and James Bowie are among 150 Americans killed at the Siege of the Alamo: defeat of the Mexicans at San Jacinto wins Texas freedom as a republic • In South Africa, many Boers move northwards from Cape Colony in the "Great Trek" and found the Orange Free State • Adelaide is founded as the capital of South Australia • Martin van Buren (Dem) is elected President of the USA • Peru and Bolivia form a federation

Arts and Letters
MUSIC: Mikhail Glinka (Russ), opera *A Life for the Tsar*; Giacomo Meyerbeer (Ger), opera *Les Huguenots*; LITERATURE: Charles Dickens (UK), *The Pickwick Papers* and *Sketches by Boz*; Frederick Marryat (UK), *Mr. Midshipman Easy*; Nikolai Gogol (Russ), *The Inspector-General*

Science and Discovery
Edmund Davy (UK) discovers acetylene gas • John Ericsson (Swed) patents a screw propeller for ships

Religion and Philosophy
Philosopher Ralph Waldo Emerson (US) writes *Nature*, outlining principles of Transcendentalism

Social and Economic
The Chartist Movement begins in Britain

Other Events
Canada's first railroad, the Champlain and St. Lawrence line, is opened

1837

Politics and Wars
Martin van Buren is inaugurated as 8th President of the USA • Michigan becomes the 26th state of the Union • Financial panic in USA is caused by a wave of speculation • William IV of England dies; is succeeded by his niece Queen Victoria as ruler of England, and by his brother, the Duke of Cumberland, as King Ernst August of Hanover • A rebellion in Lower Canada led by Joseph Papineau is defeated after initial success • Rebellion in Upper Canada is led by William Lyon Mackenzie; relations between USA and Canada are strained when Canadians seize the US ship *Carolina*, which is helping the rebels • Boers (Dutch farmers) begin occupying Zululand and Natal in South Africa

Arts and Letters
MUSIC: Hector Berlioz (Fr), opera *Benvenuto Cellini* and *Requiem*; Robert Schumann (Ger), *Studies in the form of Variations*; LITERATURE: Nathanial Hawthorne (US), *Twice-Told Tales*; Thomas Carlyle (UK), *The French Revolution*; Charles Dickens (UK), *Oliver Twist*

Science and Discovery
Artist Samuel Morse (US) demonstrates his telegraph • H. W. Craufurd (UK) patents galvanized iron

Social and Economic
Educationist Horace Mann (US) becomes secretary of the Massachussets State Board of Education

Other Events
Isaac Pitman (UK) publishes *Stenographic Soundhand,* developing shorthand

Politics and Wars

Rebellion in Upper Canada is suppressed; rebels' leader William Lyon Mackenzie is arrested • A People's Charter, demanding parliamentary reforms, is published in Britain • British economist Richard Cobden forms an Anti-Corn-Law League • Boers (Dutch farmers) defeat forces of Zulu chief Dingaan at Blood River • French troops occupy Vera Cruz, Mexico • The British military mission at Herat, Persia, is besieged • The First Afghan War begins

Arts and Letters

LITERATURE: Edgar Allan Poe (US), *Arthur Gordon Pym*; Karl Immermann (Ger), *Münchhausen*; William Makepeace Thackeray (UK), *The Yellowplush Papers*; Charles Dickens (UK), *Nicholas Nickleby*; Victor Hugo (Fr); *Ruy Blas*; R. S. Surtees (UK), *Jorrocks' Jaunts and Jollities*; Charlotte Guest (UK) translates the Welsh *Mabinogion*

Science and Discovery

Louis Jacques Daguerre (Fr) makes a daguerrotype photograph • Astronomer Friedrich Wilhelm Bessel (Ger) measures the parallax of a star

Religion and Philosophy

The Dominican Order is revived in France

Social and Economic

An "underground railroad" is organized for escaping slaves in USA

Other Events

A regular transatlantic steamship service starts • The National Gallery is opened in London, England

Politics and Wars

The Chartists' petition is rejected by Britain's parliament, and riots follow • The First Opium War between Britain and China begins; Chinese burn British opium; British sink Chinese junks and take Hong Kong • The Peru-Bolivian Federation is dissolved after Chilean victory at Yungay • Uruguay is at war with Argentina • French forces withdraw from Mexico • Belgium's independence is recognized by the Netherlands • Luxemburg becomes an independent Grand Duchy • The Treaty of London guarantees Belgium's independence and perpetual neutrality

Arts and Letters

PAINTING: J. M. W. Turner (UK), *The Fighting Téméraire*; MUSIC: Frédéric Chopin (Pol), *Préludes*; LITERATURE: Henry Wadsworth Longfellow (US), poem *Voices of the Night*; Stendhal (Fr), *The Charterhouse of Parma*

Science and Discovery

Charles Goodyear (US) discovers vulcanization of rubber • James Nasmyth (UK) develops the steam hammer • William Fox Talbot (UK) reveals his invention of photographic paper

Social and Economic

Horace Mann founds the USA's first teacher-training school at Lexington, Mass • Britain's P & O Line starts a regular steamship service to Egypt, connecting with the Red Sea

Other Events

Baseball is first played—at Cooperstown, N.Y. • Britain's Grand National horserace is run for the first time

Politics and Wars

Britain's Queen Victoria marries Prince Albert of Saxe-Coburg-Gotha • Upper and Lower Canada are united by the Canadian Act of Union • An uprising in France led by Louis Napoleon, nephew of Napoleon I, fails • The First Afghan War ends • Russia, Britain, Austria and Prussia unite in a war against Egypt; British forces capture Acre; the Egyptians evacuate Syria • The Treaty of Waitangi between Britain and the Maoris makes New Zealand a British colony • The city of Auckland, New Zealand, is founded • William Henry Harrison (Whig) is elected President of the USA

Arts and Letters

PAINTING: Eugène Delacroix (Fr), *The Justice of Trajan*; MUSIC: Gaetano Donizetti (It), opera *The Daughter of the Regiment*; Richard Wagner (Ger), overture to *Faust*; Adolphe Sax (Bel) invents the saxophone; LITERATURE: Charles Dickens (UK), *The Old Curiosity Shop*; Edgar Allan Poe (US), *Tales of the Grotesque and Arabesque*; James Fenimore Cooper (US), *The Pathfinder*; Richard Harris Barham (UK), *The Ingoldsby Legends*

Science and Discovery

Chemist Justus Liebig (Ger) writes *The Chemistry of Diet* • Jean Louis Agassiz (Swiss) writes *Study of Glaciers* • Charles Wilkes (US) explores the Antarctic coast • Charles Darwin (UK) publishes *Zoology of the Voyage of the Beagle*

Social and Economic

The penny post is introduced in Britain, together with the first adhesive postage stamps

USA—**M. Van Buren** –□ **William H. Harrison** –□ **John Tyler** ——————
UK—**Victoria** ——————————————————

Politics and Wars

William Henry Harrison, in-augurated as 9th President of the USA, dies a month later: Vice-President John Tyler becomes 10th President • The Dorr Rebellion against inadequate government in Rhode Island collapses • The Pre-Emption Distribution Act controls land settlement in USA • The Second Afghan War breaks out when British officers are massacred at Kabul • The Straits Convention closes Dardanelles and Bosphorus to all but Turkey's warships • Trade dispute leads to war between Britain and China

Arts and Letters

MUSIC: Robert Schumann (Ger), 1st symphony and piano concerto No 1 in A minor; Giacchino Rossini (It), oratorio *Stabat Mater*; LITERATURE: James Fenimore Cooper (US), *The Deerslayer*; James Russell Lowell (US), first volume of poems; Charles Dickens (UK), *Barnaby Rudge*; Thomas Carlyle (UK), *On Heroes and Hero-Worship*

Science and Discovery

Polar explorer James Ross (UK) discovers and names the Ross Sea in Antarctica

Religion and Philosophy

David Livingstone (UK) starts his missionary work in South Africa

Other Events

In London, Eng, *Punch* magazine makes its first appearance • The newspapers *New York Tribune, Jewish Chronicle* (London) and *Pesti Hirlap* (Hung) are founded • Thomas Cook (UK) starts his travel agency

Politics and Wars

A boundary dispute between USA and Britain over the frontier between Canada and Maine is settled by the Ashburton Treaty • Rhode Island receives a new constitution following the Dorr Rebellion • USA recognizes Hawaii's independence • British forces are defeated at Kabul, Afghanistan, and are massacred as they withdraw; soon after, Kabul is reoccupied, and the Second Afghan War ends • Industrial unrest in Britain is marked by Chartist risings • Britain's war with China ends: Chinese ports are opened to foreign trade • Hong Kong becomes British • The Second Seminole war ends

Arts and Letters

MUSIC: Richard Wagner (Ger), opera *Rienzi*; Mikhail Glinka (Russ), opera Russlan and Ludmilla; Felix Mendelssohn (Ger), 3rd symphony ("Scottish"); Giuseppe Verdi (It), opera *Nabucco*; New York Philharmonic Society is founded; LITERATURE: Lord Macaulay (UK), *Lays of Ancient Rome*; Alfred Tennyson (UK), *Morte d'Arthur and Other Idylls*; Edgar Allan Poe (US), *The Masque of the Red Death*; Henry Wadsworth Longfellow (US), *Poems of Slavery*; Nicolai Gogol (Russ), *Dead Souls*

Science and Discovery

Physician Crawford Long (US) uses ether as an anesthetic for an operation • Christian Döppler (Aus) describes the effect of velocity on sound and light waves

Social and Economic

Income tax is reintroduced into Britain • The Coal Mines Act prohibits British collieries from giving underground work to women and children

Politics and Wars

British troops led by General Charles Napier conquer the Sind region of India • Gambia in West Africa becomes a separate British Crown Colony • Greeks rise against King Otto I • Natal in South Africa is declared a British Crown Colony • Basutoland (modern Botswana) is put under British protection • A treaty with China gives Britain most-favored-nation status • In New Zealand, the First Maori War begins • Andrew Johnson (US) is first elected to Congress

Arts and Letters

MUSIC: Richard Wagner (Ger), opera *The Flying Dutchman*; Gaetano Donizetti (It), opera *Don Pasquale*; LITERATURE: John Ruskin (UK), *Modern Painters*; George Borrow (UK), *The Bible in Spain*; Charles Dickens (UK), *A Christmas Carol*; William H. Prescott (US), *The Conquest of Mexico*; William Wordsworth is appointed Britain's Poet Laureate

Science and Discovery

James Prescott Joule (UK) establishes the relation of heat to energy • Samuel Heinrich Schwabe (Ger) measures intensity of sunspots • Surveyor John Fremont (US) and frontiersman Kit Carson (US) cross the Sierra Nevada range into California

Religion and Philosophy

The Mormon Church recognizes polygamy • The United Free Church of Scotland is formed

□ James K. Polk ────────────────────────────▷

Politics and Wars

US Senate rejects a Texan proposal that the USA should annex the Republic of Texas • Karl XIV of Sweden dies; is succeeded by his son, Oskar I • Daniel O'Connell, Irishman who advocates repealing the Act of Union with Britain, is sentenced for sedition, but the verdict is not upheld by the House of Lords • The Treaty of Wanghsia between USA and China protects US citizens • James K. Polk is elected President of the USA

Arts and Letters

PAINTING: J. M. W. Turner (UK), *Rain, Steam and Speed*; MUSIC: Felix Mendelssohn (Ger), violin concerto, op. 64; Giuseppe Verdi (It), opera *Ernani*; LITERATURE: Alexandre Dumas (Fr), *The Three Musketeers*; Eugène Sue (Fr), *The Wandering Jew* • Charles Dickens (UK), *Martin Chuzzlewit* • James Russell Lowell (US), *Poems*

Science and Discovery

Samuel Morse's telegraph is first used to transmit a message (from Baltimore to Washington, DC) • Horace Wells (US) uses nitrous oxide ("laughing gas") in dentistry

Religion and Philosophy

The Young Men's Christian Association is founded in Britain by George Williams

Social and Economic

The Cooperative movement is founded in Rochdale, England • Economist John Stuart Mill (UK) writes *Unsettled Questions of Political Economy*

Politics and Wars

James K. Polk is inaugurated as 11th President of the USA • Florida becomes the 27th state of the USA • Texas is annexed and becomes the 28th state of the USA • Britain abolishes or modifies export and import duties • Seven Swiss Roman Catholic cantons unite to form the Sonderbund • The USA and Mexico disagree over frontiers • British are victorious in war with Sikhs in India

Arts and Letters

MUSIC: Franz Liszt (Hung), *Preludes for piano*; Richard Wagner (Ger), opera *Tannhäuser*; LITERATURE: Alexandre Dumas (Fr), *The Count of Monte Cristo*; Benjamin Disraeli (UK), *Sybil*; Honoré de Balzac (Fr), *Les Paysons* • Thomas Carlyle (UK), *Cromwell's Letters and Speeches*; Edgar Allan Poe (US), *Tales of Mystery and Imagination*

Science and Discovery

British archaeologist Austen Henry Layard begins excavation at Nineveh, Iraq

Religion and Philosophy

John Henry Newman, UK Anglican priest (later Cardinal Newman), becomes a Roman Catholic

Social and Economic

Friedrich Engels (Ger) writes *Condition of the Working Classes in England* • The potato crop fails in Ireland

Other Events

The US Naval Academy at Annapolis, Md, is established

Politics and Wars

Iowa becomes the 29th state of the USA • War breaks out between USA and Mexico: Americans capture Sante Fe; New Mexico is annexed • Oregon Treaty with Britain extends 49th Parallel as boundary between USA and Canada to Pacific coast • In India, British war against Sikhs ends and British possessions are expanded

Arts and Letters

MUSIC: Hector Berlioz (Fr), cantata *The Damnation of Faust*; Felix Mendelssohn (Ger), oratorio *Elijah*; Franz Liszt (Hung), 1st *Hungarian Rhapsody*; LITERATURE: William Hickling Prescott (US), *The Conquest of Peru*; Nathaniel Hawthorne (US), *Mosses from an Old Manse*; Ralph Waldo Emerson (US), *Poems*; Feodor Dostoievski (Russ), first novel, *Poor Folk*; Edward Lear (UK), *Book of Nonsense*; Henry Wadsworth Longfellow (US), *The Belfry of Bruges*; Hermann Melville (US), first book, *Typee*

Science and Discovery

Elias Howe (US) patents a sewing machine • Astronomer Johann G. Galle (Ger) discovers the planet Neptune • Chemist Ascanio Sobrero (It) makes nitroglycerine • John Deere (US) invents a plow with a steel mold-board

Religion and Philosophy

Mormons begin the migration which ends at the Great Salt Lake • Pope Gregory XVI dies; is succeeded by Pius IX

Social and Economic

In Britain, parliament repeals the Corn Laws • The Irish potato crop again fails and famine spreads

USA—**James K. Polk** ———————————————————— □ **Zachary Taylor** ———
UK—**Victoria** ————————————————————————————————

Politics and Wars

The Mexican–US war continues: American forces led by General Winfield Scott capture Mexico City • Liberia becomes an independent republic • Civil war begins in Switzerland when the Diet tries to dissolve the Sonderbund union of Roman Catholic cantons; Sonderbund forces are defeated and Lucerne is captured; the Sonderbund is dissolved

Arts and Letters

PAINTING: Eugène Delacroix (Fr), *St. George and the Dragon*; MUSIC: Friedrich von Flotow (Ger), opera *Martha*; LITERATURE: Charlotte Brontë (UK), *Jane Eyre*; Emily Brontë (UK), *Wuthering Heights*; William Makepeace Thackeray (UK), *Vanity Fair*; Prosper Merimée (Fr), play *Carmen*; Frederick Marryat (UK), *Children of the New Forest*; Benjamin Disraeli (UK), *Tancred*; Alfred Tennyson (UK), poem *The Princess*

Science and Discovery

Physician James Simpson (UK) pioneers the use of chloroform as an anesthetic • Gold is discovered in California • Hermann Helmholtz (Ger) writes *On the Conservation of Energy*

Religion and Philosophy

Karl Marx (Ger) writes *The Poverty of Philosophy* • The Mormons establish their headquarters at Salt Lake City • The United Presbyterian Church of Scotland is founded

Social and Economic

In Britain, the Factory Act reduces the working hours of women and children to 10 a day

Politics and Wars

The Treaty of Guadalupe Hidalgo ends war between the USA and Mexico; Mexico abandons its claim to Texas, and cedes California and New Mexico to USA • Wisconsin becomes the 30th state of the Union • It is a year of revolutions in Europe: there are uprisings in Berlin, Budapest, Milan, Naples, Rome, Prague, Venice, Vienna and Warsaw • Pope Pius IX flees from Rome • In France, King Louis Philippe abdicates and Louis Napoleon Bonaparte is elected president of the Second Republic • New constitutions are adopted in Austria, Switzerland and Germany • Emperor Ferdinand I of Austria abdicates and is succeeded by his nephew, Franz Josef • In South Africa, British forces drive the Boers across the Vaal River, and annex Orange Free State • Zachary Taylor is elected as President of the USA

Arts and Letters

PAINTING: Pre-Raphaelite Brotherhood of painters is founded in Britain; MUSIC: Carl Nicolai (It), opera *The Merry Wives of Windsor*; LITERATURE: James Russell Lowell (US), *The Biglow Papers*; Alexandre Dumas the Younger (Fr), *La Dame aux Camélias* • William Thakeray (UK), *Pendennis*; Lord Macaulay (UK), *History of England*

Science and Discovery

The American Association for the Advancement of Science is founded in Philadelphia, Pa

Social and Economic

Karl Marx (Ger) and Freidrich Engels (Ger) publish their *Communist Manifesto* • John Stuart Mill (UK) writes *Principles of Political Economy*

Politics and Wars

Zachary Taylor is inaugurated as 12th President of the USA • German National Assembly approves a new constitution and offers the crown of Emperor of the Germans to Friedrich Wilhelm IV of Prussia, who demurs • In Italy, the patriot Giuseppe Garibaldi fails in an attempt to prevent French troops entering Rome • The French restore Pope Pius IX to Rome • In the Battle of Novara, Austrian forces defeat the Piedmontese • King Carlo Alberto of Sardinia and Piedmont abdicates in favor of his son, Vittorio Emmanuele II • The siege of Venice ends uprisings in Italy • Denmark adopts a democratic constitution • Britain annexes the Punjab in India

Arts and Letters

PAINTING: Eugène Delacroix (Fr), *The Odalisk*; LITERATURE: Charles Dickens (UK), *David Copperfield*; Charles Kingsley (UK), *Alton Locke*; John Ruskin (UK), *The Seven Lamps of Architecture*; Charlotte Brontë (UK), *Shirley*

Science and Discovery

Walter Hunt (US) patents the safety pin • Joseph Monier (Fr) produces reinforced concrete • Armand Fizeau (Fr) measures the speed of light

Religion and Philosophy

Pope Pius IX condems socialism and communism

Social and Economic

The California Gold Rush is at its height • Amelia Bloomer (US) introduces "bloomers"—trousers for women

□ Millard Fillmore

Politics and Wars

US President Zachary Taylor dies and Vice-President Millard Fillmore becomes 13th President • California becomes the 31st state of the USA • Creation of the future States of New Mexico and Utah is agreed under the Compromise of 1850 • The Clayton–Bulwer agreement between USA and Britain curbs British involvement in Central America • South Australia, Victoria and Tasmania (Van Diemen's Land) obtain representative government

Arts and Letters

PAINTING: John Everett Mjllais (UK), *Christ in the House of His Parents*; MUSIC: Robert Schumann (Ger), 3rd symphony ("Rhenish"); LITERATURE: Nathaniel Hawthorne (US), *The Scarlet Letter*; Elizabeth Barrett Browning (UK), *Sonnets from the Portuguese*; Ralph Waldo Emerson (US), *Representative Man*; Ivan S. Turgeniev (Russ), play *A Month in the Country*; William Wordsworth (UK), poem *The Prelude*; Alfred Tennyson, poem *In Memoriam*; he becomes Poet Laureate in succession to Wordsworth

Science and Discovery

Physicist Rudolf Clausius (Ger) states the second law of thermodynamics • Chemist Robert Bunsen (Ger) invents his burner • John Brett (UK) establishes telegraphic communication with continental Europe by submarine cable

Social and Economic

Old-age insurance is introduced in France • Britain gets its first public libraries

Other Events

Architect Joseph Paxton (UK) designs the Crystal Palace for the Great Exhibition in London

Politics and Wars

Louis Napoleon, President of the French Republic, organizes a *coup d'etat* against the republican constitution; a popular rising is suppressed by troops and a plebiscite leads to a new constitution • British Foreign Secretary Lord Palmerston is forced to resign for supporting Louis Napoleon's actions • Victoria, Australia, becomes a separate British colony

Arts and Letters

MUSIC: Giuseppe Verdi (It), opera *Rigoletto*; LITERATURE: John Ruskin (UK), *The Stones of Venice*; Nathaniel Hawthorne (US), *The House of the Seven Gables*; Herman Melville (US), *Moby Dick*; George Borrow (UK), *Lavengro*; Harriet Beecher Stowe (US), *Uncle Tom's Cabin* (as a magazine serial)

Science and Discovery

Isaac Singer (US) makes a practical sewing machine • William Kelly (US) devises a converter for blast furnaces • Discovery of gold in Australia • Physicist Hermann Helmholtz (Ger), invents the ophthalmoscope • Unsuccessful search for missing explorer John Franklin (UK) adds to knowledge of the Arctic

Social and Economic

Maine and Illinois introduce prohibition • Britain's window tax (introduced in 1695) is repealed

Other Events

The Great Exhibition is held in Hyde Park, London (UK) • The *New York Times* is founded

Politics and Wars

The Second French Empire is proclaimed after a plebiscite: Louis Napoleon becomes emperor as Napoleon III • A new constitution for New Zealand gives the colony representative government • Britain recognizes the independence of Transvaal, South Africa, in the Sand River Convention • The Second Burmese War begins: Britain annexes Lower Burma • William Ewart Gladstone becomes Britain's Chancellor of the Exchequer • The Taiping revolution breaks out in China • Franklin Pierce is elected President of the USA

Arts and Letters

PAINTING: Ford Madox Brown (UK), *The Last of England*; Holman Hunt (UK), *The Light of the World*; LITERATURE: Charles Dickens (UK), *Bleak House*; William Makepeace Thackeray (UK), *The History of Henry Esmond*; Théophile Gautier (Fr), *Enamels and Cameos*; Book publication of *Uncle Tom's Cabin* by Harriet Beecher Stowe (US) causes storm over slavery

Science and Discovery

Missionary David Livingstone (UK) begins exploration of the Zambesi River • Heinrich Barth (Ger), explores Lake Chad in Central Africa • Chemist Robert Bunsen (Ger) develops a method of producing magnesium

Other Events

Victoria and Albert Museum is opened in London • Henry Wells and William G. Fargo found the Wells, Fargo Company in the USA

USA—**Millard Fillmore**—□ **Franklin Pierce** ─────────────
UK—**Victoria** ──────────────────────────────────

Politics and Wars

Franklin Pierce is inaugurated as 14th President of the USA • The Gadsden Purchase confirms southern New Mexico and southern Arizona as parts of USA • Turkey rejects Russia's claim to protect Christians in the Ottoman Empire; Russian troops invade Moldavia and Wallachia and destroy a Turkish fleet at Sinope • British and French fleets gather near the Dardanelles • Britain embarks on a Free Trade policy; duties are abolished or modified • Britain annexes Nagpur in India • France annexes New Caledonia

Arts and Letters

MUSIC: Giuseppe Verdi (It), operas *La Traviata* and *Il Trovatore*; LITERATURE: Nathaniel Hawthorne (US), *Tanglewood Tales*; Elizabeth Gaskell (UK), *Cranford*; Charlotte M. Yonge (UK), *The Heir of Redclyffe*; Charlotte Brontë (UK), *Villette*; Matthew Arnold (UK), poems *The Scholar Gipsy* and *Sohrab and Rustum*

Science and Discovery

Queen Victoria (UK) is given chloroform as an anesthetic during the birth of Prince Leopold • Alexander Wood (UK) introduces the hypodermic syringe

Social and Economic

In Britain, the tax on newspaper advertisements is abolished, and compulsory vaccination is introduced

Other Events

The first railroad between New York and Chicago is opened

Politics and Wars

The Crimean War begins: Britain and France join Turkey against Russia and land troops in the Crimea; they win victories at Alma, Balaclava (Charge of the Light Brigade) and Inkerman • USA makes a trade treaty with Japan • The Kansas–Nebraska Act repeals The Missouri Compromise of 1820 and creates the territories of Kansas and Nebraska; fierce controversy rages over whether slavery shall be allowed in these territories • The Republican Party is formed in the USA • By the Ostend Manifesto, the USA proposes taking Cuba by force if Spain refuses to sell the island • In South Africa, the Orange Free State declares its independence

Arts and Letters

MUSIC: Hector Berlioz (Fr), oratorio *The Childhood of Christ*; LITERATURE: Charles Dickens (UK); *Hard Times*; Alfred Tennyson (UK), poem *The Charge of the Light Brigade*; Henry D. Thoreau (US), *Walden, or Life in the Woods*; Charles Kingsley (UK), *Westward Ho!*

Science and Discovery

Heinrich Geissler (Ger) invents the tube named after him (resembling the neon tube) • Abraham Gesner (Can) refines kerosene • Elisha Graves Otis (US) demonstrates a safety lift at the New York Fair

Religion and Philosophy

The Immaculate Conception is proclaimed as dogma by Pope Pius IX

Social and Economic

Florence Nightingale (UK) pioneers modern nursing in the Crimea

Politics and Wars

Tsar Nikolai I of Russia dies; is succeeded by his son Aleksandr II • The Crimean War continues: Russians capitulate at Sevastapol • In Britain, the ministry of Lord Aberdeen falls: Lord Palmerston becomes prime minister • Sweden enters an anti-Russian alliance with Britain, France and Turkey • There are uprisings in Yunnan and Kweichow, China • The Taiping rebellion virtually ends • Austria threatens war against Russia

Arts and Letters

PAINTING: Gustave Courbet (Fr), *The Artist's Studio*; MUSIC: Hector Berlioz (Fr), opera *The Sicilian Vespers*; LITERATURE: Alfred Tennyson (UK), *Maud and Other Poems*; Anthony Trollope (UK), *The Warden*; Henry Wadsworth Longfellow (US), *The Song of Hiawatha*; Walt Whitman (US), *Leaves of Grass*; John L. Motley (US), *The Rise of the Dutch Republic,* George Meredith (UK), *The Shaving of Shagpat*

Science and Discovery

David Livingstone (UK) discovers the Victoria Falls on the Zambesi River • Physician Thomas Addison (UK) identifies an adrenal malfunction now known as Addison's disease • Alexander Parkes (UK) invents celluloid

Social and Economic

Stamp duty on newspapers in Britain is abolished

Other Events

The Daily Telegraph newspaper is founded in London (UK) • An international exhibition is held in Paris

James Buchanan ⟶

Politics and Wars

Abolitionists led by John Brown murder five pro-slavers at Pottawatomie Creek, Kan, in "Bleeding Kansas" war over slavery • Treaty of Paris ends Crimean War; the Black Sea is neutralized; the Danube River is reopened to international shipping; Russia gives up Bessarabia • Britain declares war on China after Chinese sailors board a British ship; the city of Canton is shelled • Natal in South Africa becomes a separate British Crown Colony • James Buchanan is elected President of the USA

Arts and Letters

PAINTING: William Holman Hunt (UK), *The Scapegoat*; J. D. Ingres (Fr), *The Source*; LITERATURE: Gustave Flaubert (Fr), *Madame Bovary*; Charles Reade (UK), *It's Never Too Late to Mend*; Charles Kingsley (UK), *The Heroes*; Ralph Waldo Emerson (US), *English Traits*; Elizabeth Barrett Browning (UK), poem *Aurora Leigh*

Science and Discovery

The steel industry is revolutionized by a converter designed by Henry Bessemer (UK) • Skull of early man (Neanderthal) is discovered in Neander Gorge, Germany • Explorers Richard Burton (UK) and John Speke (UK) set out to find the source of the Nile River

Social and Economic

Turkish edict *Hatt-I-Hamayu* guarantees reforms affecting lives of Christians

Other Events

The Victoria Cross for valor is instituted in Britain • *Harper's Weekly* magazine is founded in New York City • "Big Ben," largest bell of London's Houses of Parliament clock, is cast

Politics and Wars

James Buchanan becomes 15th President of the USA • Financial panic in USA follows over-expansion and speculation • The US Supreme Court rules that the Missouri Compromise of 1820 was unconstitutional • The Indian Mutiny (Sepoy Rebellion) breaks out when sepoys (Indian soldiers) revolt against their British officers at Meerut; British retake Delhi, Lucknow and Cawnpore after sieges • British destroy the Chinese fleet and take Canton • Giuseppe Garibaldi (It) forms the Italian National Association • The new Transvaal state is formally proclaimed as the South African Republic

Arts and Letters

PAINTING: Jean François Millet (Fr), *The Gleaners*; MUSIC: Franz Liszt (Hung), 1st piano concerto; LITERATURE: Charles Dickens (UK), *Little Dorrit*; George Borrow (UK), *The Romany Rye*; Thomas Hughes (UK), *Tom Brown's Schooldays*; Anthony Trollope (UK), *Barchester Towers*; Charles Baudelaire (Fr), *Les Fleurs du mal*; George Eliot (UK), *Scenes from Clerical Life*

Science and Discovery

The Science Museum in London is founded • Work begins on the Mont Cenis Tunnel connecting France and Italy

Social and Economic

Many countries in Europe suffer a financial crisis over railroad shares • Divorce courts are set up in Britain

Politics and Wars

Minnesota becomes the 32nd State of the USA • British Columbia is made a colony • Ottawa is named as the capital city of Canada • The Indian Mutiny is suppressed: the East India Company's powers are removed and the British Crown rules India • Britain's war with China ends with the Treaty of Tientsin: the opium trade is legalized and Chinese ports are opened to British and French trade • Under the Compact of Plombières, Emperor Napoleon III of France and Italian statesman Camillo Cavour (It) plan the unification of Italy

Arts and Letters

PAINTING: W. P. Frith (UK), *Derby Day*; MUSIC: Jacques Offenbach (Fr), operetta *Orpheus in the Underworld*; César Franck (Fr), *Messe Solonelle* • Johannes Brahms (Ger), 1st piano concerto; LITERATURE: Oliver Wendell Holmes (US), *The Autocrat of the Breakfast Table*

Science and Discovery

The world's largest steamship, *Great Eastern,* built by Isambard Kingdom Brunel (UK), is launched • British explorers Richard Burton and John Speke discover Lake Tanganyika • Speke discovers Lake Victoria

Religion and Philosophy

A vision of the Virgin Mary is claimed by Bernadette Subirous at Lourdes, France • The Society of Paulist Fathers is founded in New York City

Social and Economic

The Suez Canal Company is formed • Lionel de Rothschild becomes the first Jewish member of parliament elected in Britain

USA—**James Buchanan** ———————————————— ☐ **Abraham Lincoln** ——
UK—**Victoria** ——————————————————————————

1859

Politics and Wars
Anti-slaver John Brown leads an abortive attack on a US arsenal at Harper's Ferry, now in West Virginia; Brown is executed • Oregon becomes the 33rd State of the USA • Austria wages war on Sardinia and France and begins a move towards the unification of Italy: Austrian forces are defeated at Magenta and Solferino; Parma and Lombardy are ceded to Sardinia • Queensland becomes a separate Australian colony

Arts and Letters
PAINTING: Jean-Auguste Ingres (Fr), *The Turkish Bath*; Jean François Millet (Fr), *The Angelus*; Edouard Manet (Fr), *The Absinthe Drinker*; MUSIC: Charles Gounod (Fr), opera *Faust*; LITERATURE: Charles Dickens (UK), *A Tale of Two Cities*; George Meredith (UK), *The Ordeal of Richard Peverel*; George Eliot (UK), *Adam Bede*; Samuel Smiles (UK), *Self-Help*; Edward FitzGerald (UK) translates *The Rubáiyát of Omar Khayyám*; Alfred Tennyson (UK), poem *Idylls of the King*

Science and Discovery
British naturalist Charles Darwin publishes *The Origin of the Species by Natural Selection* • America's first oil well is drilled at Titusville, Pa • The steamroller is invented in France

Religion and Philosophy
Karl Marx (Ger) writes *Criticism of Poltical Economy*

Other Events
Charles Blondin (Fr) walks a tightrope across Niagara Falls • George Pullman (US) designs the Pullman railroad cars • Work begins on the Suez Canal

1860

Politics and Wars
Sardinia cedes Nice and Savoy to France • Giuseppe Garibaldi (It) forms the Redshirts, and takes Naples; Sardinian king Vittorio Emmanuele invades the Papal States and is proclaimed King of Italy by Garibaldi • The Russian port of Vladivostok is founded • Britain and France are at war with China: their troops occupy Peking and burn the Summer Palace; war ends with the Treaty of Peking • Republican antislavery candidate Abraham Lincoln is elected President of the USA, and South Carolina secedes from the Union in protest

Arts and Letters
PAINTING: Edgar Degas (Fr), *Spartan Boys and Girls Exercising*; Edouard Manet (Fr), *The Guitarist* (sometimes known as *The Spanish Singer*); LITERATURE: Charles Dickens (UK), *Great Expectations*; George Eliot (UK), *The Mill on the Floss*; Wilkie Collins (UK), *The Woman in White*; Ivan Turgeniev (Russ), *On the Eve*

Science and Discovery
Johann P. Reis (Ger) invents a type of telephone • Christopher Latham Sholes (US) invents a form of typewriter • Etienne Lenoir (Fr) invents an internal-combustion engine

Social and Economic
The Florence Nightingale School for Nurses is established in London

Other Events
The *Catholic Times* (UK) is published • Bronze coinage is introduced in Britain

1861

Politics and Wars
Abraham Lincoln becomes 16th President of the USA • Kansas becomes the 34th State of the USA • Ten Southern States—Mississippi, Florida, Alabama, Georgia, Louisiana, Texas, Virginia, Arkansas, North Carolina and Tennessee —join South Carolina in seceding from the Union, and form the Confederate States of America; Jefferson Davis becomes Confederate President • Confederate capture of Fort Sumter, SC, starts Civil War • Confederate forces win a victory at Bull Run, Va • Gold is discovered in New Zealand • Russian troops occupy Tsushima in Japan • The Kingdom of Italy is proclaimed by the Italian Parliament • Lagos, West Africa, is annexed by Britain to check the slave trade • Moldavia and Wallachia unite as Romania

Arts and Letters
LITERATURE: Charles Reade (UK), *The Cloister and the Hearth*; George Eliot (UK), *Silas Marner*; Mrs. Henry Wood (UK), *East Lynne*; Oliver Wendell Holmes (US), *Elsie Venner*; Feodor Dostoievsky (Russ), *House of the Dead*; Francis T. Palgrave (UK), compiles *The Golden Treasury*

Science and Discovery
Scientist William Crookes (UK) discovers the element thallium • Chemist Robert Bunsen (Ger) discovers elements caesium and rubidium • Chemist Ernest Solvay (Belg) invents a process for making soda from common salt • Open-hearth process is introduced into steelmaking in Britain and France

Social and Economic
Tsar Aleksandr II abolishes serfdom in Russia

Politics and Wars

The American Civil War continues: Confederate forces win battles at Bull Run (second battle), Va; Fredericksburg, Va; Chancellorsville, Va; and Shiloh, Tenn; Union forces are victorious at Antietam, Md; Fort Henry and Fort Donelson, Tenn; New Orleans, La; *Merrimack* (Confederate) and *Monitor* (Union) fight the first battle between ironclad ships; President Abraham Lincoln declares all slaves free • France annexes Cochin China • In Italy, the patriot Giuseppe Garibaldi is captured at Aspromonte by Italian government troops • Otto von Bismark becomes prime minister of Prussia

Arts and Letters

PAINTING: William P. Frith (UK), *The Railway Station*; MUSIC: Giuseppe Verdi (It), opera *The Force of Destiny*; LITERATURE: Julia Ward Howe (US), *The Battle Hymn of the Republic*; Elizabeth Barrett Browning (UK), *Last Poems* (published posthumously); Victor Hugo (Fr), *Les Misérables*; George Borrow (UK), *Wild Wales*; John Ruskin (UK), *Unto This Last*; Christina Rossetti (UK), *Goblin Market*; Ivan Turgeniev (Russ), *Fathers and Sons*; Henrik Ibsen (Nor), *Love's Comedy*

Science and Discovery

Richard Gatling (US) patents a machine-gun • Chemist Friedrich Wöhler (Ger) discovers the gas acetylene • Astronomer Friedrich W. Argelander (Ger) catalogs stars in the northern hemisphere

Religion and Philosophy

Philosopher Herbert Spencer (UK) writes *First Principles*

Social and Economic

The first legal paper money is issued in the USA

Politics and Wars

The American Civil War continues: in the East, Confederate troops win a victory at Chancellorsville (where their General Thomas "Stonewall" Jackson, dies), but lose at Gettysburg, Penn, the decisive battle of the war; in the west, Union forces win battles of Vicksburg and Chattanooga • President Abraham Lincoln, in his Gettysburg Address, promises government "of the people, by the people, for the people" • West Virginia breaks away from Virginia and forms the 35th State of the USA • Arizona and Idaho are created US Territories • Denmark annexes the Duchy of Schleswig, while German forces enter neighboring Holstein • French troops occupy Mexico City • Japan attempts to expel foreigners; British ships bombard the Japanese port of Kagoshima

Arts and Letters

PAINTING: Edouard Manet (Fr), *Luncheon on the Grass*; James Whistler (US), *Symphony in White*; Eugène Boudin (Fr), *The Beach at Trouville*; MUSIC: Georges Bizet (Fr), opera *The Pearl Fishers*; LITERATURE: Charles Kingsley (UK), *The Water Babies*; Edward Everett Hale (US), *The Man Without a Country*; Henry Wadsworth Longfellow (US), *Tales of a Wayside Inn*

Science and Discovery

Chemist Hippolyte Mège Mourries (Fr) develops margarine • Thomas H. Huxley (UK) writes *Man's Place in Nature* • Geologist Charles Lyell (UK) publishes *The Antiquity of Man*

Politics and Wars

The American Civil War continues: Union forces advance into Virginia, raid Washington, DC, fight battles at The Wilderness, Spotsylvania Court House, Cold Harbor, and besiege Petersburg, defended by Confederate troops led by General Robert E. Lee; Union soldiers commanded by General William T. Sherman advance through Georgia, laying the countryside waste • Nevada becomes the 36th State of the USA • Montana is created a US Territory • Prussia and Austria attack Denmark over its possession of Schleswig Holstein; Denmark is forced to cede both duchies • Cheyenne and Arapahoe Indians are massacred at Sand Creek, Colorado • Archduke Maximilian of Austria, backed by France, becomes Emperor of Mexico • Abraham Lincoln is reelected President of the USA

Arts and Letters

PAINTING: Arnold Böcklin (Switz), *Villa at the Sea*; MUSIC: Petr Tchaikovsky (Russ), opera *Romeo and Juliet*; Jacques Offenbach (Fr), operetta *La Belle Hélène*; Anton Bruckner (Aust), symphony in D minor; LITERATURE: Charles Dickens (UK), *Our Mutual Friend*; Alfred Tennyson (UK), *Enoch Arden*; Henrik Ibsen (Nor), play *The Pretenders*; Anthony Trollope (UK), *The Small House at Allington*; Lev Tolstoy (Russ), *War and Peace*

Science and Discovery

Louis Pasteur (Fr) invents pasteurization and saves France's wine industry

Social and Economic

The International Red Cross is founded in Geneva, Switzerland

175

USA—**Abraham Lincoln**–☐ **Andrew Johnson** ————————————
UK—**Victoria** ——————————————————————————————

Politics and Wars

General Robert E. Lee surrenders the Confederate armies to the Union General Ulysses S. Grant at Appomattox Court House, Va; the American Civil War ends • President Abraham Lincoln is assassinated; is succeeded by Vice-President Andrew Johnson • The Convention of Gastein gives Holstein to Austria and Schleswig to Prussia • Wellington becomes the capital city of New Zealand in succession to Auckland • USA presses France to withdraw its troops from Mexico

Arts and Letters

PAINTING: Edouard Manet (Fr), *Olympia*; Winslow Homer (US), *Prisoners at the Front*; James Whistler (US), *Old Battersea Bridge*; MUSIC: Richard Wagner (Ger), opera *Tristan and Isolde*; Nikolai Rimsky-Korsakov (Russ), 1st symphony; LITERATURE: Charles Dodgson (Lewis Carroll), *Alice's Adventures in Wonderland*; John Ruskin (UK), *Sesame and Lilies*; Mary Mapes Dodge (US), *Hans Brinker*; Walt Whitman (US), *Drum Taps*; Mark Twain (US), *The Celebrated Jumping Frog of Calaveras County*

Science and Discovery

Louis Pasteur (Fr) discovers a cure for silkworm disease • Pierre Lallement (Fr) patents a "boneshaker" pedal bicycle • A transatlantic cable is successfully laid • Explorer David Livingstone (UK) publishes *The Zambesi and its Tributaries*

Religion and Philosophy

Evangelist William Booth starts the Christian Mission (later the Salvation Army) in London

Social and Economic

Slavery is ended in the USA by the 13th Amendment to the Constitution

Politics and Wars

The 14th Amendment to the US Constitution ensures that no person is deprived "of life, liberty or property without due process of law" • Chile obtains territory between the Andes and the Pacific • Prussia and Austria war over Schleswig-Holstein; Germany annexes Holstein; Austrians are defeated at Sadowa; many German principalities and Schleswig-Holstein are incorporated with Prussia • There are riots in London after a new Reform Bill fails in parliament

Arts and Letters

PAINTING: Claude Monet (Fr), *Camille*; MUSIC: Ambroise Thomas (Fr), opera *Mignon* • Bedrich Smetana (Czech), opera *The Bartered Bride*; LITERATURE: Alphonse Daudet (Fr), *Letters from My Mill*; Fyodor Dostoievsky (Russ), *Crime and Punishment*; Victor Hugo (Fr), *Toilers of the Sea*; Charles Kingsley (UK), *Hereward the Wake*; Algernon C. Swinburne (UK), *Poems and Ballads*; Henrik Ibsen (Nor), *Brand*

Science and Discovery

Botanist Gregor Mendel (Aus) states principles of heredity • Robert Whitehead (US) develops the torpedo

Social and Economic

Dr. Thomas Barnardo opens his first home for orphans in London's East End • "Black Friday": financial panic in London follows failure of a bank

Other Events

The Queensberry Rules for boxing are introduced in England

Politics and Wars

USA buys Alaska from Russia for $7,200,000 • Nebraska becomes the 37th State of the USA • The Tenure of Office Act, designed to limit the US President's powers, is passed • The Dominion of Canada, consisting of New Brunswick, Nova Scotia, Quebec and Ontario, is created by the British North America Act • French troops leave Mexico; Emperor Maximilian is executed • The Italian revolutionary Giuseppe Garibaldi again marches on Rome, but is captured by French and Papal troops at Mentana • The Irish Fenian Brotherhood organizes terrorist activities in. Britain and Australia

Arts and Letters

PAINTING: Pierre Renoir (Fr), *The Skaters*; MUSIC: Giuseppe Verdi (It), opera *Don Carlos*; Charles Gounod (Fr), opera *Romeo and Juliet*; Johann Strauss (Aus), *Blue Danube* waltz; LITERATURE: George Meredith (UK), *Vittoria*; Algernon C. Swinburne (UK), *Song of Italy*; Henrik Ibsen (Nor), *Peer Gynt*; Ouida (UK), *Under Two Flags*

Science and Discovery

Joseph Lister (UK) introduces antiseptic surgery • Alfred Nobel (Swe) invents dynamite • David Livingstone (UK) explores the Congo

Religion and Philosophy

Karl Marx (Ger) writes the first volume of *Das Kapital*

Social and Economic

The Reform Act in Britain extends franchise and redistributes parliamentary seats

Other Events

Philip D. Armour starts a meat-packing company in Chicago, Ill.

□ Ulysses S. Grant

Politics and Wars
US President Andrew Johnson is impeached for alleged violation of the Tenure of Office Act, but is acquitted • British troops invade Ethiopia to rescue an imprisoned consul, capture Magdala, release other prisoners, and withdraw • Benjamin Disraeli (Conservative) becomes Britain's Prime Minister, but resigns after electoral defeat; William Ewart Gladstone (Liberal) succeeds him • After a Liberal revolution in Spain, Queen Isabel II is deposed • In Japan, Emperor Mutsuhito takes control of the government, replacing the Shogun (military dictator): the Meiji (Enlightened Rule) Period begins • Ulysses S. Grant is elected President of the USA

Arts and Letters
PAINTING: Edgar Degas (Fr), The Orchestra; Pierre Renoir (Fr), The Skaters; MUSIC: Edvard Grieg (Nor), piano concerto, op. 16; Richard Wagner (Ger), opera The Mastersingers of Nuremberg; LITERATURE: Louisa M. Alcott (US), Little Women; Fyodor Dostoievsky (Russ), The Idiot; Wilkie Collins (UK), The Moonstone; William Morris (UK), The Earthly Paradise; Robert Browning (UK), The Ring and the Book

Science and Discovery
Engineer George Westinghouse (US) perfects an air brake for railroad trains

Social and Economic
The first Trades Union Congress meets in Manchester, England

Other Events
The first professional baseball team is formed—the Cincinnati Red Stockings

Politics and Wars
General Ulysses S. Grant becomes 18th President of the USA • In Wyoming, women are given the vote • The National Prohibition Party is established in Chicago • Canada purchases North-West Territory from Hudson's Bay Company • European-Indian halfbreeds led by Louis Riel rebel against Canada's Dominion government at Red River, Manitoba • Emperor Napoleon III introduces a parliamentary system of government in France • Britain, France and Italy assume control of Tunis in North Africa

Arts and Letters
PAINTING: Claude Monet (Fr), The Balcony; MUSIC: Richard Wagner (Ger), opera The Rhinegold; Johann Brahms (Ger), Hungarian Dances 1 and 2; LITERATURE: Mark Twain (US), The Innocents Abroad; Francis Brett Harte (US), The Outcasts of Poker Flat; Richard Dodridge Blackmore (UK), 20,000 Leagues under the Sea

Science and Discovery
Francis Galton (UK) founds the science of genetics with his book Hereditary Genius, its Laws and Consequences • John Wesley Hyatt (US) invents celluloid • Dmitri Ivanovich Mendeleev (Russ) devises a periodic table classifying the chemical elements

Religion and Philosophy
Pope Pius IX summons the Vatican Council

Other Events
The Union Pacific and Central Pacific lines are linked in Utah, forming the first railroad to cross North America • The Suez Canal is opened to shipping

Politics and Wars
Prussia and France quarrel over the succession to the Spanish throne; France declares war in July and Prussian troops invade France, winning a series of victories; on September 2, Emperor Napoleon III surrenders with an army at Sedan • A new French government declares France a republic; Paris is besieged • French forces withdraw from Rome, which becomes Italy's capital • The 15th Amendment to the US Constitution ensures voting rights for former slaves • Manitoba becomes a province of Canada

Arts and Letters
PAINTING: Jean Corot (Fr), The Pearl; Henri Fantin-Latour (Fr), Homage to Manet; MUSIC: Richard Wagner (Ger), opera The Valkyrie; Léo Delibes (Fr), ballet Coppélia; LITERATURE: Francis Brett Harte (US), The Luck of Roaring Camp; Benjamin Disraeli (UK), Lothair; Charles Dickens (UK), The Mystery of Edwin Drood (unfinished at his death)

Science and Discovery
James Young Simpson (UK) develops chloroform as an anesthetic

Religion and Philosophy
Papal infallibility is proclaimed by the Vatican Council • Austria revokes its Concordat with the Papacy

Social and Economic
The Standard Oil Company is founded by John D. Rockefeller (US) • Compulsory education for all begins in Britain

USA—**Ulysses S. Grant**
UK—**Victoria**

Politics and Wars

King Wilhelm I of Prussia is proclaimed Kaiser (Emperor) of a united Germany at Versailles • Otto von Bismarck becomes German Chancellor • Paris capitulates to the Prussians: France cedes Alsace-Lorraine to Germany, and undertakes to pay heavy reparations • A radical group, the Commune, is set up in Paris, but is suppressed by troops in "Bloody Week" • Louis A. Thiers is elected President of France's Third Republic • The colony of British Columbia becomes a province of Canada

Arts and Letters

PAINTING: James Whistler (US), *Arrangement in Grey and Black*, No 1 ("Whistler's Mother"); Paul Cézanne (Fr), *Man with a Straw Hat*; MUSIC: Giuseppe Verdi (It), opera *Aïda*; LITERATURE: George Eliot (UK), *Middlemarch*; Lewis Carroll (UK), *Through the Looking Glass, and What Alice Found There*; Algernon C. Swinburne (UK), *Songs Before Sunrise*; Walt Whitman (US), *Democratic Vistas*

Science and Discovery

Journalist Henry Morton Stanley (US) sent to find explorer David Livingstone (UK), meets him at Ujiji, by Lake Tanganyika

Religion and Philosophy

Charles Taze Russell (US) founds the Jehovah's Witnesses

Social and Economic

Much of Chicago is destroyed by fire • The Mont Cenis Tunnel through the Swiss Alps is opened • Bank (public) holidays are introduced in Britain • British Trade Unions are legalized by Act of Parliament

Politics and Wars

Alabama dispute: an international tribunal awards to the USA heavy damages against Britain for losses inflicted by a British-built Confederate ship, *Alabama*, during the American Civil War • Carlist War in Spain: Don Carlos claims throne by succession through the female line • The emperors of Germany, Austria and Russia form an alliance • The Reuter Concession in Persia provides for economic development by Baron de Reuter (UK) in return for customs revenues • Rebellion against Spanish rule breaks out in the Philippines • Ulysses S. Grant is reelected President of the USA

Arts and Letters

PAINTING: Edgar Degas (Fr), *The Foyer of the Opera*; Camille Pissaro (Fr), *The Wash House*; MUSIC: Georges Bizet (Fr), incidental music to play *The Maid of Arles*; LITERATURE: Alphonse Daudet (Fr), *Tartarin of Tarascon*; Thomas Hardy (UK), *Under the Greenwood Tree*; Jules Verne (Fr), *Around the World in Eighty Days*; Samuel Butler (UK), *Erewhon*

Science and Discovery

A British naval vessel, *Challenger*, begins a world oceanographic survey • Eadweard Muybridge (UK) photographs a horse in motion (early movie picture)

Social and Economic

Britain introduces the secret ballot • France and Japan adopt conscription

Other Events

Work on the St. Gotthard Tunnel under the Alps starts • New York's Brooklyn Bridge is opened

Politics and Wars

Ulysses S. Grant begins his second term as US President • Prince Edward Island becomes a province of Canada • Marshal Patrice MacMahon is elected President of France on the resignation of Louis Thiers • France completes paying reparations for the Franco-Prussian War, and the German occupation ends • Carlist (rival monarchist) risings in Spain are followed by the declaration of a republic • Ashanti tribesmen fight British troops in West Africa • Japan embarks on a policy of religious toleration

Arts and Letters

PAINTING: Edouard Manet (Fr), *The Croquet Party*; Claude Monet (Fr), *Pleasure Boats*; MUSIC: Nikolai Rimsky-Korsakov (Russ), opera *Ivan the Terrible*; LITERATURE: John Stuart Mill (UK), *Autobiography*; Arthur Rimbaud (Fr), *A Season in Hell*

Science and Discovery

Physicist James Clerk Maxwell (UK) writes *Treatise on Electricity and Magnetism* • Farmer Joseph F. Glidden (US) invents barbed wire • Silver is discovered in Nevada

Social and Economic

Russia sinks its first oilwell at Baku • Germany adopts the mark as currency • Business panic in Europe spreads to the USA, causing withdrawal of foreign capital

Other Events

The cities of Buda and Pesth are united to form Budapest, capital of Hungary • Walter Wingfield (UK) introduces the game of lawn tennis

Politics and Wars

Conservative Benjamin Disraeli becomes Britain's prime minister when the Liberals are defeated in British elections • The Ashanti War in Africa ends in British victory • Iceland obtains self-government from Denmark • The Spanish Republic ends; Queen Isabel's son is proclaimed King Alfonso XII • Britain annexes Fiji • Annam in Indo-China becomes a French protectorate • Japanese occupy Formosa but withdraw

Arts and Letters

PAINTING: Pierre Renoir (Fr), *The Box at the Opera*; Claude Monet (Fr), paints *Impression: Sunrise* (giving name to Impressionists); first Impressionist exhibition in Paris; MUSIC: Modeste Mussorgsky (Russ), opera *Boris Godunov* and *Pictures at an Exhibition*; Johann Strauss (Aus), operetta *Die Fledermaus*; Giuseppe Verdi (It), *Requiem Mass*; LITERATURE: Thomas Hardy (UK), *Far from the Madding Crowd*; John Richard Green (UK), *Short History of the English People*; Victor Hugo (Fr), *Ninety-three*; Paul Verlaine (Fr), *Romances sans Paroles*

Science and Discovery

G. Annauer Hansen (Nor) discovers the bacillus of leprosy

Religion and Philosophy

Statesman William Ewart Gladstone (UK) criticizes the dogma of papal infallibility

Social and Economic

Civil marriage is made obligatory in Germany • The Society for the Prevention of Cruelty to Children is founded in New York

Politics and Wars

Britain buys 176,602 Suez Canal shares from the Khedive (ruler) of Egypt, gaining virtual control of the shortest route to India and Far East • France has a new Constitution and endorses the Third Republic • French fears of war with Germany are 'dispelled by British and Russian intervention • The Carlist (rival monarchist) war continues in Spain: Carlists are forced out of Valencia and Catalonia • Centralized government in New Zealand is strengthened • Rebellion breaks out in Cuba • Japan secures a treaty with Korea, establishing Korean independence from China

Arts and Letters

PAINTING: Claude Monet (Fr), *Boating at Argenteuil*; MUSIC: Georges Bizet (Fr), opera *Carmen*; first W. S. Gilbert and Arthur Sullivan light opera, *Trial by Jury*; Anton Dvorak (Czech), 5th symphony; Petr Tchaikovsky (Russ), 1st piano concerto

Science and Discovery

Richard M. Hoe of New York City invents a rotary printing press • Henry Morton Stanley (UK) begins exploration of the Congo (now Zaïre) River in Africa

Religion and Philosophy

Elena Petrovna Blavatsky founds the Theosophical Society in New York City • Mary Baker Eddy (US) writes *Science and Health with Key to the Scriptures*, leading to the Christian Science movement

Other Events

Matthew Webb (UK) becomes the first man to swim the English Channel • The Universal Postal Union is founded in Berne, Switzerland

Politics and Wars

Colorado becomes the 38th State of the USA • At Little Big Horn, Mont, Lieutenant-Colonel George Custer and his men are massacred by Sioux Indians • Bulgarians rebel against Turkish misrule; massacre by Turkish troops arouses widespread anger; Serbia and Montenegro declare war on Turkey; Russia, too, threatens war • Samuel Jones Tilden (Dem) obtains majority vote over Rutherford B. Hayes (Rep) in election for presidency of USA, but vote is challenged

Arts and Letters

PAINTING: Edgar Degas (Fr), *The Dancing Class*; MUSIC: Richard Wagner (Ger), opera *Siegfried*; first complete performance of Wagner's *Ring* cycle at Bayreuth; Léo Delibes (Fr), ballet *Sylvia*; LITERATURE: Mark Twain (US), *The Adventures of Tom Sawyer*; Lewis Carroll (UK), poem *The Hunting of the Snark*; Stéphane Mallarmé (Fr), poem *L'Après-midi d'un faune*

Science and Discovery

Scots-born speech teacher Alexander Graham Bell patents the telephone in the USA • Robert Koch (Ger) discovers the bacillus of anthrax • Nikolaus Otto (Ger) invents a form of internal-combustion engine • Cesare Lombroso (It) founds the science of criminal psychology

Social and Economic

In Britain, the Merchant Shipping Act imposes the Plimsoll line on merchant vessels, preventing overloading

Other Events

The US National Baseball League is formed

USA—**Ulysses S. Grant**—☐ **Rutherford B. Hayes** ——————————
UK—**Victoria** ————————————

Politics and Wars

Rutherford B. Hayes (Rep) becomes the 19th President of the USA • Queen Victoria (UK) is proclaimed Empress of India • Turkey rejects demands for reforms made by leading European powers: Russia, Romania and Serbia declare war on Turkey; Russians take Plevna, Bulgaria • British annex Transvaal, South Africa, and Walvis Bay in South-West Africa • In Japan, the Satsuma Rebellion led by General Saigo Takamori is suppressed

Arts and Letters

PAINTING: John Singer Sargent (US), portrait *Fanny Watts*; Winslow Homer (US), *The Cotton-Pickers*; SCULPTURE: Auguste Rodin (Fr), *The Bronze Age*; MUSIC: Camille Saint-Saëns (Fr), opera *Samson and Delilah*; Petr Tchaikovsky (Russ), 4th symphony; LITERATURE: Lev Tolstoi (Russ), *Anna Karenina*; Henry James (US), *The American*; Henrik Ibsen (Nor), *The Pillars of Society*; Anna Sewell (UK), *Black Beauty*; Sarah Orne Jewett (US), *Deephaven*

Science and Discovery

Thomas Alva Edison (US) invents the phonograph • The first shipments of refrigerated meat are made from Argentina to Europe • Carl Gustave de Laval (Swe) invents a machine to separate cream from milk • Henry Morton Stanley (UK) completes his exploration of the Congo (now Zaïre) River

Social and Economic

Compulsory education for young children is introduced in Italy

Other Events

The first All-England tennis championships are played at Wimbledon (UK)

Politics and Wars

Russians defeat Turks at Shipka Pass, Bulgaria, and take Adrianople (Edirne) in European Turkey • Britain sends a fleet to Constantinople • The treaties of San Stefano and Berlin (after a Berlin Congress of the Great Powers) reshape the Balkans; Romania, Montenegro and Serbia gain independence; Russia acquires Bessarabia, southwest of Ukraine; Cyprus goes to Britain • Britain warns the Zulu chief Cetawayo not to threaten the Boer republic of Transvaal, South Africa

Arts and Letters

PAINTING: Albert Bierstadt (US), *Sierra Nevada*; Pierre Renoir (Fr), *Madame Charpentier and her Children*; MUSIC: W. S. Gilbert and Arthur Sullivan (UK), opera *H.M.S. Pinafore*; LITERATURE: Henry James (US), *Daisy Miller*; Algernon C. Swinburne (UK), *Poems and Ballads*; Thomas Hardy (UK), *The Return of the Native*

Science and Discovery

Explorer Henry Morton Stanley (UK) writes *Through the Dark Continent* • David Hughes (US) invents the microphone • Explorer Nils Nordenskjöld (Swe) begins to navigate a northeast passage through the Arctic Ocean from Sweden to Japan

Religion and Philosophy

Evangelist William Booth (UK) names his Christian Mission "the Salvation Army" • Pope Pius IX dies; is succeeded by Leo XIII

Other Events

French vineyards are devastated by the disease phylloxera, accidentally imported from America

Politics and Wars

In South Africa the Zulu War begins: a British force is wiped out at Isandhlwana, but the Zulus are defeated at Rorke's Drift and Ulundi; the Zulu leader Cetawayo is captured, and the war ends • By agreement, Britain occupies the Khyber Pass between India and Afghanistan • Britain invades Afghanistan after the British legation at Kabul is massacred; Emir Ya'qub abdicates • Britain and France resume joint control of Egypt

Arts and Letters

SCULPTURE: Auguste Rodin (Fr), *St. John the Baptist Preaching*; MUSIC: Anton Bruckner (Aus), 6th symphony; Petr Tchaikovsky (Russ), opera *Eugène Onegin*; LITERATURE: Henrik Ibsen (Nor), *A Doll's House*; Robert Louis Stevenson (UK), *Travels with a Donkey in the Cevennes*; George Meredith (UK), *The Egoist*; Fyodor Dostoievsky (Russ), *The Brothers Karamazov*

Science and Discovery

Chemists Constantin Fahlberg (Ger) and Ira Remsen (US) discover saccharin • William Crookes (UK) develops the cathode ray tube • The Siemens brothers (Ger) demonstrate an electric tramway in Berlin • Thomas Alva Edison (US) invents an incandescent electric lamp

Religion and Philosophy

Mary Baker Eddy (US) organizes the Church of Christ, Scientist, in Boston, Mass

Other Events

The Tay Bridge in Scotland collapses in a storm while a train is passing over it

Politics and Wars

Britain's Conservative government is defeated over the question of Irish Home Rule; Liberal leader William Gladstone becomes Prime Minister • In Ireland, Charles Stewart Parnell, allied with the land league, leads a drive for Home Rule • The Irish decide to isolate uncooperative landlords and land agents: their first victim is Captain Charles Boycott • Transvaal (South Africa) declares independence from Britain and proclaims itself a republic under Boer leader Paul Kruger • Chile defeats Bolivia and Peru in the War of the Pacific; Chile gains valuable nitrate territory while Bolivia loses access to the sea • James Garfield (Rep) is elected President of the USA

Arts and Letters

PAINTING: Camille Pissaro (Fr), *The Outer Boulevards*; MUSIC: Petr Tchaikovsky (Russ), overture "1812"; W. S. Gilbert and Arthur Sullivan (UK), opera *The Pirates of Penzance*; LITERATURE: Guy de Maupassant (Fr), *Boule de Suif*; Lewis Wallace (US), *Ben Hur*; Emile Zola (Fr), *Nana*; Henry Wadsworth Longfellow (US), *Ultima Thule*; Joel Chandler Harris (US), *Uncle Remus, His Songs and His Sayings*; Guy de Maupassant (Fr), *Stories*

Religion and Philosophy

In Britain, an atheist Member of Parliament, Charles Bradlaugh, is unseated for refusing to take the oath of office

Other Events

The first cricket Test match between England and Australia is played at Melbourne • Scotland's Forth Bridge is opened • New York City gets its first electric street lights ·

Politics and Wars

James A. Garfield, 20th President of the USA, is assassinated four months after taking office; Vice-President Chester A. Arthur becomes the 21st President • In South Africa, the Boers defeat British forces at Laing's Neck and Majuba Hill; in the Treaty of Pretoria, Transvaal's independence is recognized by Britain • France invades Tunis and captures Bizerta; Tunis becomes a French protectorate • Tsar Aleksandr II of Russia is assassinated; his son, Aleksandr III, succeeds him

Arts and Letters

PAINTING: Claude Monet (Fr), *Sunshine and Snow*; MUSIC: Jacques Offenbach (Fr), opera *Tales of Hoffmann* (produced posthumously); Johannes Brahms (Ger), *Academic Festival Overture*; W. S. Gilbert and Arthur Sullivan (UK), opera *Patience*; LITERATURE: Henrik Ibsen (Nor), play *Ghosts*; Anatole France (Fr), *The Crime of Sylvestre Bonnard*; Henry James (US), *Portrait of a Lady*

Science and Discovery

Astronomer Samuel P. Langley (US) invents the bolometer— an ultra-sensitive thermometer • Louis Pasteur (Fr) develops an anthrax vaccine

Social and Economic

The American Federation of Trades and Labor Unions is founded

Other Events

Construction of Canadian Pacific Railway is started • The first US Lawn Tennis championships are played • St. Gotthard Tunnel under the Alps is completed • 300,000 people are reported killed when a tidal wave hits Indo-China

Politics and Wars

The Chinese Exclusion Act bans immigration of Chinese into the USA for 10 years • Korea signs trade treaties with the USA • Troubles continue in Ireland with the Phoenix Park murders in Dublin: Chief Secretary Lord Frederick Cavendish and Under-Secretary Thomas Burke are killed by Fenians • British and French naval squadrons sail to Alexandria to support the Khedive of Egypt against rebellions; Alexandria is bombarded • British forces occupy Cairo and Sudan after defeating rebel forces at Tel-el-Kebir; Anglo–French control of Egypt is restored • Italy makes Eritrea a colony

Arts and Letters

PAINTING: Edouard Manet (Fr), *The Bar at the Folies-Bergères*; Edgar Degas (Fr), *The Laundresses*; MUSIC: Richard Wagner (Ger), opera *Parsifal*; Nikolai Rimsky-Korsakov (Russ), opera *The Snow Maiden*; Charles Francois Gounod (Fr), oratorio *The Redemption*; Johannes Brahms (Ger), 2nd piano concerto; W. S. Gilbert and Arthur Sullivan (UK), opera *Iolanthe*; Berlin Philharmonic Orchestra formed; LITERATURE: Henrik Ibsen (Nor), *An Enemy of the People*; George Bernard Shaw (UK), *Cashel Byron's Profession*

Science and Discovery

Robert Koch (Ger) discovers the bacillus of tuberculosis • The Society for Psychical Research founded in Britain • US Army officer Adolphus Greely explores Greenland and the Arctic

Religion and Philosophy

Prebendary Wilson Carlile (UK) founds the Church Army • Repressive measures are taken against Jews in Russia

USA—**Chester A. Arthur** —————————————— ☐ **Grover Cleveland** —————
UK—**Victoria** —————————————————————————————————

Politics and Wars

Germany founds settlements in South-West Africa • Paul Kruger becomes President of the Boer South African Republic • France begins to colonize West Africa and gains control of Tunisia in North Africa • In Egypt, a Muslim agitator, Muhammad Ahmad — the Mahdi—declares himself a prophet, organizes the defeat of Egyptian troops at El Obeid and obtains control of most of Sudan • Annam and Tonkin in Indo-China become French protectorates • The Pendleton Act calls for reforms in the US civil service

Arts and Letters

PAINTING: Pierre Renoir (Fr), *Umbrellas*; MUSIC: Léo Delibes (Fr), opera *Lakmé*; Johannes Brahms (Ger), 3rd symphony; LITERATURE: Robert Louis Stevenson (UK), *Treasure Island*; Björnstjern Björnson (Nor), *Beyond Our Strength*; Olive Schreiner (S. Afr), *The Story of an African Farm*

Science and Discovery

John Carbutt (US) introduces a coated celluloid film for photography • Edwin Klebs (Ger) identifies the diptheria germ • Francis Galton (UK), founder of eugenics, writes *Human Faculty*

Religion and Philosophy

Philosopher Friedrich Nietzsche (Ger) writes *Thus Spake Zarathustra*

Social and Economic

Chancellor Otto von Bismarck introduces sickness insurance in Germany

Other Events

Around 36,000 people die in the Dutch East Indies when the Krakatoa volcano erupts

Politics and Wars

European colonization in Africa continues: the Berlin Conference establishes an independent State of the Congo, and ensures freedom of navigation on the Niger and Congo (Zaïre) rivers • Germany establishes protectorates over Togoland and Cameroons • Britain sets up protectorate over part of Somaliland • General Charles Gordon (UK) is sent to Khartoum in Sudan to negotiate with rebel leader, the Mahdi, who refuses to talk • Grover Cleveland (Dem) is elected President of the USA

Arts and Letters

PAINTING: John Singer Sargent (US), portrait *Madam X*; Edgar Degas (Fr), *The Ironers*; Georges Seurat (Fr), *Bathers at Asnières*; SCULPTURE: Auguste Rodin (Fr), *The Burghers of Calais*; MUSIC: Anton Bruckner (Aus), 7th symphony; Jules Massenet (Fr), opera *Manon*; LITERATURE: Henrik Ibsen (Nor), *The Wild Duck*; Mark Twain (US), *The Adventures of Huckleberry Finn*; Alphonse Doudet (Fr), *Sappho*; poet Alfred Tennyson (UK) becomes a baron

Science and Discovery

Charles Parsons (UK) devises a practical steam-turbine engine • Boston and New York City are connected by telephone • Hiram S. Maxim (US) develops a machine-gun • Ottmar Mergenthaler (US) patents the Linotype typesetting machine

Social and Economic

The Fabian Society, a Socialist group, is founded in Britain

Other Events

France presents the Statue of Liberty to the USA • In Chicago, the first skyscraper is built

Politics and Wars

Grover Cleveland (Dem) becomes 22nd President of the USA • In Sudan, rebel forces led by the Mahdi capture Khartoum from British: General Charles Gordon is killed; Khartoum relieved two days later; British leave Sudan; Mahdi dies; Dervishes control Sudan • Congo colony is established, with Leopold II of Belgium its ruler • Germany makes a protectorate of north New Guinea, and annexes Tanganyika and Zanzibar in East Africa • British establish protectorates in Nigeria, north Bechuanaland and south New Guinea • British at war with Burmese • Serbs invade Bulgaria and are defeated

Arts and Letters

PAINTING: Edgar Degas (Fr), *Jockeys at Training*; MUSIC: Anton Dvořak (Czech), 2nd symphony; W. S. Gilbert and Arthur Sullivan (UK), opera *The Mikado*; César Franck (Belg), *Symphonic Variations*; LITERATURE: Richard Burton (UK), *The Arabian Nights*; Guy de Maupassant (Fr), *Bel Ami*; George Meredith (UK), *Diana of the Crossways*; Emile Zola (Fr), *Germinal*

Science and Discovery

Louis Pasteur (Fr) successfully vaccinates a child against rabies • Karl Benz (Ger) produces a three-wheel automobile • Gottlieb Daimler (Ger) develops an internal-combustion gasoline engine • William Burroughs (US) invents an adding machine

Social and Economic

The Indian National Congress meets for the first time

Other Events

The Canadian Pacific Railway is extended from Montreal to British Columbia

Politics and Wars

The Presidential Succession Law is passed in USA, providing for succession in case both President and Vice-President die • Anarchists riot in Haymarket Square, Chicago: 10 are killed • In Britain, the Irish Home Rule Bill is defeated in the House of Commons • Britain annexes Upper Burma • Britain and Germany agree on the borders of Togoland and Gold Coast

Arts and Letters

PAINTING: Georges Seurat (Fr), *Sunday Afternoon on the Island of Grande Jatte*; John Everett Millais (UK), *Bubbles*; John Singer Sargent (US), *Carnation, Lily, Lily, Rose*; MUSIC: Camille Saint-Saëns (Fr), *Carnival of the Animals*; LITERATURE: Henry James (US), *The Bostonians*; Louisa May Alcott (US), *Jo's Boys*; Frances Hodgson Burnett (UK), *Little Lord Fauntleroy*; Robert Louis Stevenson (UK), *Doctor Jekyll and Mr. Hyde*; H. Rider Haggard (UK), *King Solomon's Mines*

Science and Discovery

Neurologist Richard von Krafft-Ebbing writes *Psychopathia Sexualis* • An inexpensive method of making aluminum is invented independently by Charles M. Hall (US) and Paul L. Hérault (Fr) • Carl Auer von Welsbach (Aus) invents an incandescent gas mantle

Social and Economic

Spain abolishes slavery in Cuba • The American Federation of Labor is formed

Other Events

The statue of Liberty is dedicated in New York • 60 people die in an earthquake at Charleston, SC

Politics and Wars

The Dawes Act authorizes the end of Indian tribal government and division of Indian land in the USA • The Interstate Commerce Act imposes controls on US railroads and sets up an Interstate Commerce Commission • German Chancellor Otto von Bismarck calls for a larger German army • Germany, Austria and Italy renew their Triple Alliance • France creates a Union of Indo-China, consisting of Annam, Cambodia, Cochin-China and Tonkin

Arts and Letters

PAINTING: Vincent van Gogh (Neth), *The Mill of la Galette*; MUSIC: Aleksandr Borodin (Russ), opera *Prince Igor* (he dies soon after); Giuseppe Verdi (It), opera *Otello*; John Stainer (UK), oratorio *The Crucifixion*; W. S. Gilbert and Arthur Sullivan (UK), opera *Ruddigore*; LITERATURE: Victorien Sardou (Fr), *La Tosca*; Arthur Conan Doyle (UK), first Sherlock Holmes story, *A Study in Scarlet*; Thomas Hardy (UK), *The Woodlanders*; Auguste Strindberg (Swed), play *The Father*

Science and Discovery

Physicist Heinrich Hertz (Ger) produces electromagnetic waves • Physicist Ernst Mach (Aus) creates a system of Mach numbers, related to the speed of sound • Gottlieb Daimler (Ger) produces the first successful automobile

Other Events

Ludovic Lagarno Zamenhof (Pol) devises an international language—Esperanto • Britain celebrates Queen Victoria's Golden Jubilee (50 years on the throne) • Central China suffers disastrous floods

Politics and Wars

Kaiser Wilhelm I of Germany dies; is succeeded by his son, Friedrich III, who also dies 100 days later; Wilhelm II, son of Friedrich, becomes Kaiser • Germany and Italy form a military alliance • A revolt in Ethiopia led by Menelik, Negus of Shewa and heir to the Ethiopian throne, is supported by Italy • Britain establishes protectorates in Sarawak, Brunei and North Borneo • Benjamin Harrison (Rep) is elected President of the USA

Arts and Letters

PAINTING: James Ensor (Belg), *Entry of Christ into Brussels*; Vincent van Gogh (Neth), *Sunflowers*; MUSIC: Petr Tchaikovsky (Russ), 5th symphony; Nikolai Rimsky-Korsakov (Russ), *Scheherazade*; LITERATURE: Rudyard Kipling (UK), *Plain Tales from the Hills*; Thomas Hardy (UK), *Wessex Tales*; Arthur Quiller-Couch (UK), *The Astonishing History of Troy Town*; Edward Bellamy (US), *Looking Backward*

Science and Discovery

Nikola Tesla (US) invents an alternating-current induction motor • John Boyd Dunlop (UK) invents pneumatic bicycle tyres • George Eastman (US) produces the Kodak box camera • Fritz Nansen (Nor) explores the icefields of Greenland • Charles Montagu Doughty (UK) writes *Travels in Arabia Deserta*

Social and Economic

Serfdom is ended in Brazil

Other Events

The Suez Canal is declared open to all ships at all times by the Convention of Constantinople • "Jack the Ripper" murders occur in London

USA—**Grover Cleveland**—☐ **Benjamin Harrison**
UK—**Victoria**

Politics and Wars

Benjamin Harrison becomes 23rd President of the USA • North Dakota, South Dakota, Montana and Washington become the 39th, 40th, 41st and 42nd States of the USA • Oklahoma is opened to settlement • The first Pan-American Conference, held in Washington, establishes a Pan-American Union • Italy claims Ethiopia as an Italian protectorate; Menelik becomes King of Ethiopia • Ivory Coast becomes a French protectorate • Japan receives a new constitution: a Diet (parliament) with upper and lower houses is created, but Emperor Mutsuhito retains wide powers • Pedro II of Brazil abdicates, and Brazil becomes a republic

Arts and Letters

PAINTING: Vincent van Gogh (Belg), *Landscape with Cypress Tree*; MUSIC: César Franck (Belg), symphony in D minor; Anton Dvořák (Czech), 4th symphony; W. S. Gilbert and Arthur Sullivan (UK), opera *The Gondoliers*; LITERATURE: Jerome K. Jerome (UK), *Three Men in a Boat*; James Barrie (UK), *A Window in Thrums*; Anatole France (Fr), *Thaïs*

Science and Discovery

George Eastman (US) produces roll film for cameras

Religion and Philosophy

Thomas H. Huxley (UK) writes *Agnosticism* • George Bernard Shaw (UK) writes *Fabian Essays*

Social and Economic

Old-age insurance is introduced in Germany

Other Events

The Eiffel Tower in Paris is completed • Construction of the Panama Canal is halted by lack of funds

Politics and Wars

Idaho and Wyoming become the 43rd and 44th States of the USA • The Force Bill, protecting Negro voters' rights, is rejected by the US Senate • Otto von Bismarck is dismissed as German Chancellor by Kaiser Wilhelm II • Britain gives Heligoland to Germany in return for Zanzibar and Pemba • German East Africa (Tanganyika) becomes a German colony • Japan's first elections are followed by the first meeting of the Diet (parliament) • Luxembourg becomes independent of the Netherlands • Britain annexes Uganda • Cecil Rhodes (UK) becomes Premier of Cape Colony

Arts and Letters

PAINTING: Paul Cézanne (Fr), *The Cardplayers*; Frederick Leighton (UK), *The Bath of Psyche*; MUSIC: Pietro Mascagni (It), opera *Cavalleria Rusticana*; Petr Tchaikovsky (Russ), opera *Queen of Spades*; LITERATURE: John Greenleaf Whittier (US), *At Sundown*; James Barrie (UK), *My Lady Nicotine*; Henrik Ibsen (Nor), play *Hedda Gabler*

Science and Discovery

Alphonse Bertillon (Fr) writes *Legal Photography* on criminal identification

Religion and Philosophy

James Frazer (UK) writes *The Golden Bough: A Study in Magic and Religion*

Social and Economic

The Sherman anti-Trust Law is enacted in the USA to restrict monopolistic business practices

Other Events

The Daughters of the American Revolution movement is formed in the USA

Politics and Wars

Germany, Austria and Italy renew their Triple Alliance; Kaiser Wilhelm II of Germany fails to persuade Britain to join • Nyasaland (now Malawi) becomes a British protectorate • Britain acquires Barotseland (now part of Zambia) from Portugal • Civil war breaks out in Chile • Revolt in Brazil • Franco-Russian agreement is reached after a French fleet visits Kronstadt • Britain and Italy agree spheres of influence in East Africa • Emperor Menelik of Ethiopia rejects Italy's claims that his country is an Italian protectorate

Arts and Letters

PAINTING: Paul Gauguin (Fr), *Women on the Beach*; Henri de Toulouse-Lautrec (Fr) produces his first music hall posters; MUSIC: Petr Tchaikovsky (Russ), *Nutcracker* ballet music; LITERATURE: Thomas Hardy (UK), *Tess of the D'Urbervilles*; Francis Thompson (UK), *The Hound of Heaven*; Rudyard Kipling (UK), *The Light that Failed*; Oscar Wilde (UK), *The Picture of Dorian Gray*; James Barrie (UK), *The Little Minister*

Science and Discovery

Physicist Johnstone Stoney (UK) first uses the word "electron" • Anthropologist Eugène Dubois (Neth) discovers bones of *Pithecanthropus erectus* (Java Man) • Samuel P. Langley (US) writes *Experiments in Aerodynamics*

Social and Economic

The first Labour Member is elected to Britain's Parliament

Other Events

Building of the Trans-Siberian railroad is begun

☐ **Grover Cleveland** ▷

Politics and Wars

The People's Party, founded in St. Louis, Mo, urges financial reforms • Workers strike at the Carnegie Steel Company in Pennsylvania: State troops are used to restore order • Corruption in Panama Canal dealings causes scandal in France • William Ewart Gladstone (Lib) becomes British prime minister for the 4th and last time • In Egypt, Abbas Hilmi II (pro-French, anti-British) succeeds Tewfik as Khedive (ruler) • Grover Cleveland (Dem) is elected President of the USA

Arts and Letters

PAINTING: Henri de Toulouse-Lautrec (Fr), *At the Moulin Rouge*; MUSIC: Ruggiero Leoncavallo (It), opera *I Pagliacci*; LITERATURE: Oscar Wilde (UK), play *Lady Windermere's Fan*; Henrik Ibsen (Nor), play *The Master Builder*; Rudyard Kipling (UK), *Barrack Room Ballads*; Israel Zangwill (UK), *Children of the Ghetto*; Emile Zola (Fr), *The Debacle*

Science and Discovery

C. F. Cross (UK) discovers viscose, leading to the manufacture of rayon • Oliver Heaviside (UK) discovers the ionosphere • Rudolf Diesel (Ger), patents a diesel internal-combustion engine • Whitcombe L. Judson (US) invents a slide-fastener

Social and Economic

The marriage age for girls in Italy is raised to 12 years

Other Events

Russia suffers famine • James ("Gentleman Jim") Corbett (US) defeats John L. Sullivan (US) to become world heavyweight boxing champion

Politics and Wars

Grover Cleveland becomes the 24th President of the USA • The US organizes overthrow of Hawaii's monarchy: the Hawaiian islands are annexed by a treaty, which Cleveland cancels • Financial panic in USA follows British investors' sales of US stock • Ivory Coast and Guinea become French colonies, and Dahomey becomes a French protectorate • Uganda becomes a British colony • In southern Africa, British troops suppress a rising by Matabele tribesmen • Anarchist outrages in France include a bomb explosion in the Chamber of Deputies • Laos becomes a French protectorate

Arts and Letters

PAINTING: Paul Gauguin (Fr), *Tahitian Landscape*; MUSIC: Petr Tchaikovsky (Russ), 6th symphony ("Pathetique")—he dies soon after; Antonin Dvořak (Czech) symphony "From the New World"; Giacomo Puccini (It), opera *Manon Lescaut*; Engelbert Humperdinck (Ger), opera *Hansel and Gretel*; LITERATURE: Victorien Sardou (Fr), *Madame Sans-Gêne*; Oscar Wilde (UK), play *A Woman of No Importance*; Arthur Pinero (UK), play *The Second Mrs. Tanqueray*

Science and Discovery

Fridtjof Nansen (Nor) sails on an expedition to the North Pole in the *Fram* • Wilhelm Maybach (Ger) introduces a float-feed carburetor for automobile engines

Social and Economic

Women are given the vote in New Zealand • The prohibitionist Anti-Saloon League is founded in the USA • The Independent Labour Party is founded in Britain

Politics and Wars

French president Sadi Carnot is assassinated by an anarchist • Alfred Dreyfus, a French army officer, is wrongly convicted of treason • Japan declares war on China; the Japanese capture Port Arthur • In the US, the Carey Act grants land to several states for irrigation; the Wilson-Gorman Tariff Act introduces income tax of 2 per cent on annual incomes over $4000 • Tsar Aleksandr III of Russia dies; is succeeded by his son, Nikolai II • Riots in Italy lead to the suppression of Italian Socialist societies • Italian forces invade Ethiopia

Arts and Letters

PAINTING: Edgar Degas (Fr), *Woman at Her Toilet*; MUSIC: Jules Massenet (Fr), opera *Thaïs*; Claude Debussy (Fr), *Prélude a l'apres-midi d'une faune*; LITERATURE: George Moore (UK), *Esther Waters*; George du Maurier (UK), *Trilby*; Anthony Hope (UK), *The Prisoner of Zenda*; Rudyard Kipling (UK), *The Jungle Book*; George Bernard Shaw (UK), play *Arms and the Man*; publication of *The Yellow Book*, with illustrations by Aubrey Beardsley (UK); George and Weedon Grossmith (UK), *Dairy of a Nobody*

Science and Discovery

British scientists William Ramsay and Lord Rayleigh discover the element argon • Inventor Hiram Maxim (US) experiments with a heavier-than-air flying machine • Bacteriologist Shibasaburo Kitasoto (Jap) isolates the bubonic plague germ

Social and Economic

An inheritance tax ("Death duty") is introduced in Britain

USA—**Grover Cleveland** ———————————————— □ **William McKinley** ————
UK—**Victoria** ————————————————————————————————————

Politics and Wars
Japanese troops defeat a Chinese army at Wei-hai-wei; China cedes Formosa and Port Arthur to Japan • Japan later returns Port Arthur after European powers protest • Korea's indepencence is recognized • Armenians in Turkey form revolutionary movement; Turks massacre many Armenians • Italian invaders are defeated by Ethiopians at Amba Alagi • Leander Starr Jameson (UK) leads an unsuccessful raid into Transvaal from South Africa • USA protests against brutal Spanish suppression of a Cuban uprising • US Supreme Court declares income tax—imposed by the Wilson-Gorman Tariff Act—unconstitutional

Arts and Letters
PAINTING: Edgar Degas (Fr), *Dancers at the Practice Bar*; MUSIC: Richard Strauss (Ger), *Till Eulenspiegel's Merry Pranks*; Gustav Mahler (Aus), 2nd symphony; LITERATURE: Joseph Conrad (UK), *Almayer's Folly*; H. G. Wells (UK), *The Time Machine*; Thomas Hardy (UK), *Jude the Obscure*; Henry Sienkiewicz (Pol), *Quo Vadis?*; Oscar Wilde (UK), play *The Importance of Being Earnest*; William Butler Yeats (UK), *Poems*

Science and Discovery
Wilhelm Konrad Röntgen (Ger) detects X-rays • Guglielmo Marconi (It) develops wireless telegraphy • Sigmund Freud (Aus) founds the science of psychoanalysis with *Studien über Hysterie* • King Gillette (US) invents a safety-razor

Other Events
Germany's Kiel Canal is completed

Politics and Wars
Utah becomes the 45th State of the USA • Ethiopians decisively defeat Italians at Adowa; Italy renounces its protectorate over Ethiopia • Turks accept self-government for Crete • British forces led by General Herbert Kitchener begin the reconquest of Sudan • France annexes the island of Madagascar • A telegram sent by Kaiser Wilhelm II to President Kruger of Transvaal causes a rift in Anglo-German relations • William McKinley (Rep) is elected President of the USA

Arts and Letters
PAINTING: Paul Gauguin (Fr), *Holiday*; MUSIC: Giacomo Puccini (It), opera *La Bohème*; LITERATURE: A. E. Housman (UK), *A Shropshire Lad*; Henrik Ibsen (Nor), *John Gabriel Borkman*; Anton Chekhov (Russ), *The Seagull*

Science and Discovery
Henry Ford (US) makes his first automobile • Samuel P. Langley (US) flies the first power-driven model aircraft • Robert Whitehead (UK) invents a gyroscopically-controlled torpedo • Antoine Henri Becquerel (Fr) detects radiation from uranium

Religion and Philosophy
Theodor Herzl (Aus) writes *The Jewish State*, advocating the founding of a Jewish state in Palestine

Social and Economic
In Canada, the Klondike gold rush begins • Scientist Alfred Nobel (Swed) dies: Nobel prizes instituted

Other Events
A tidal wave kills 22,000 people in Japan • The Olympic Games are revived in Athens

Politics and Wars
William McKinley becomes 25th President of the USA • Crete unites with Greece • Turkey declares war on Greece and defeats Greek forces in Thessaly; Russia and Austria intervene to end the war • Revelation of suppressed evidence in the Dreyfus case causes a scandal in France • Cecil Rhodes, Premier of Cape Colony, South Africa, is censured for his part in the Jameson raid and forced to resign • In China, German troops occupy Tsingtao, and Russian forces take Port Arthur

Arts and Letters
PAINTING: Paul Gauguin (Fr), *Girls Bathing in Tahiti* • Henri de Toulouse-Lautrec (Fr), *Marcelle*; MUSIC: Paul Dukas (Fr), *The Sorcerer's Apprentice*; LITERATURE: H. G. Wells (UK), *The Invisible Man*; Joseph Conrad (UK), *The Nigger of the Narcissus*; Edmond Rostand (Fr), *Cyrano de Bergerac*; George Bernard Shaw (UK), *Candida*; Henry James (US), *The Spoils of Poynton*

Science and Discovery
Physician Ronald Ross (UK) identifies the cause of malaria • Scientist James J. Thomson (UK) discovers the electron

Religion and Philosophy
A Zionist conference is held in Basel, Switzerland

Social and Economic
The Workmen's Compensation Act is passed in Britain

Other Events
Britain celebrates Queen Victoria's Diamond Jubilee (60 years on the throne)

Politics and Wars
The US warship *Maine* is blown up in Havana harbor, Cuba; USA declares war on Spain over the Cuban rebellion; a Spanish fleet is destroyed in the Philippines; Americans invade Puerto Rico and capture the Philippine capital Manila; by the Treaty of Paris, Spain withdraws from Cuba, and cedes Puerto Rico, Guam and Philippines to the USA ● The US annexes Hawaii ● Anglo-French rivalry flares in Sudan; French troops occupy Fashoda, but soon withdraw ● British forces defeat Dervishes at Omdurman, Sudan ● China leases Port Arthur to Russia, Wei-hai-wei and Kowloon to Britain ● Emile Zola writes an open letter, "J'Accuse," to the French president about the Dreyfus trial, and is jailed

Arts and Letters
SCULPTURE: Auguste Rodin (Fr), *The Kiss*; MUSIC: Samuel Coleridge-Taylor (UK), *Hiawatha's Wedding Feast*; LITERATURE: Henry James (US), *The Turn of the Screw*; Oscar Wilde (UK), *The Ballad of Reading Gaol*; H. G. Wells (UK), *The War of the Worlds*

Science and Discovery
Scientists Marie and Pierre Curie (Fr) discover radium ● Konstantin E. Tsiolkovsky (Russ) develops a theory of rocket propulsion ● William Ramsay (UK) discovers neon, krypton and xenon gases ● Ferdinand von Zeppelin (Ger) invents a rigid airship

Religion and Philosophy
The sale of Church of England livings is ended

Social and Economic
New Zealand introduces old-age pensions

Politics and Wars
In South Africa, war begins between British and Boers; the Boers win victories at Laing's Nek, Stromberg, Magersfontein and Colenso; they besiege Ladysmith and Mafeking ● In France, the trial of Alfred Dreyfus is reopened; he is reconvicted of treason, but immediately pardoned ● The USA faces insurrection of the Philippines ● US Secretary of State John Hay sends "Open Door" note to Britain, Germany, France and Russia urging those countries to keep to their own spheres of influence in China ● Britain acquires Tonga and Savage islands ● A Geneva conference establishes a permanent international Court of Arbitration at The Hague, Netherlands

Arts and Letters
PAINTING: Henri de Toulouse-Lautrec (Fr), *At the Circus*; MUSIC: Edward Elgar (UK) *Enigma Variations*; Jean Sibelius (Fin), *Finlandia*; LITERATURE: Henrik Ibsen (Nor), *When We Dead Awaken*; Lev Tolstoy (Russ), *The Resurrection*; Rudyard Kipling (UK), *Stalky and Co*; Ernest W. Hornung (Austral) introduces "Raffles" in *The Amateur Cracksman*

Science and Discovery
Zoologist Ernst Heinrich Haeckel (Ger) writes *The Riddle of the Universe* ● The metal actinium is discovered by André Debierne (Fr)

Social and Economic
The first "garden city" (Letchworth) is developed in Britain

Other Events
Motor omnibuses are introduced in London, England

Politics and Wars
Hawaii becomes a Territory of the USA ● The Boer War continues; Britain reinforces its troops in South Africa, defeats the Boers at Paardeberg, Bloemfontein, Pretoria and Bergendal, and relieves the besieged townships of Mafeking and Ladysmith ● Britain annexes Orange Free State and Transvaal; guerrilla warfare follows ● In the Boxer Rising, European legations in Peking are besieged by Chinese terrorists; an international expedition relieves them ● The Commonwealth of Australia becomes an independent British Dominion ● William McKinley (Rep) is reëlected president of the USA

Arts and Letters
PAINTING: Henri Rousseau (Fr), *The Customs House*; MUSIC: Edward Elgar (UK), oratorio *The Dream of Gerontius*; Giacomo Puccini (It), opera *Tosca*; LITERATURE: Joseph Conrad (UK), *Lord Jim*; Anton Chekhov (Russ), *Uncle Vanya*; Theodore Dreiser (US), *Sister Carrie*; H. G. Wells (UK), *Love and Mr. Lewisham*; Colette (Sidonie Gabrielle Colette; Fr), *Claudine at School*

Science and Discovery
Jacques Edwin Brandenburger (Swiss) invents Cellophane ● Physicist Max Planck (Ger) develops the quantum theory of light ● Walter Reed (US) discovers the transmission of yellow fever by mosquitos ● Sigmund Freud (Aus) writes *The Interpretation of Dreams* ● Archeologist Arthur Evans (UK) discovers relics of Minoan culture in Crete

Social and Economic
The Labour Party is founded in Britain

USA—**William McKinley** ⊣☐ **Theodore Roosevelt** ——————
UK—**Victoria** ⊣☐ **Edward VII** ——————————

Politics and Wars

William McKinley is assassinated six months after starting his second term as president of the USA; he is succeeded by vice-president Theodore Roosevelt as 26th President • The USA decides to proceed with building the Panama Canal • Panama becomes independent from Colombia • Queen Victoria of Britain dies; is succeeded by her son, Edward VII • In South Africa, the Boers continue guerrilla action • The Boxer Rising is suppressed and China agrees to pay reparations to European countries • Britain annexes the kingdom of Ashanti to the Gold Coast

Arts and Letters

PAINTING: Paul Gauguin (Fr), *Golden Bodies*; Pablo Picasso (Sp), *Bal Tabarin*; · MUSIC: Edward Elgar (UK), *Cockaigne Overture*; Sergei Rachmaninoff (Russ), 2nd piano concerto; LITERATURE: Rudyard Kipling (UK), *Kim*; Frank Norris (US), *The Octopus*; Thomas Mann (Ger), *Buddenbrooks*; Anton Chekhov (Russ), play *Three Sisters*; Auguste Strindberg (Swed), play *Dance of Death*; George Bernard Shaw (UK), play *Caesar and Cleopatra*

Science and Discovery

Guglielmo Marconi (It) transmits messages across the Atlantic by wireless telegraphy • Jokichi Takamine (Jap) isolates adrenalin • Otto Nordenskjöld (Swed) explores the Antarctic seas • Sigmund Freud (Aus) writes *The Psychotherapy of Everyday Life*

Other Events

The Trans-Siberian railroad begins operating

Politics and Wars

Britain and Japan form an alliance; Britain recognizes the independence of China and Korea, and acknowledges Japan's special interest in Korea • The Boer War in South Africa ends with the Treaty of Vereeniging; the Boers recognize British sovereignty • Germany, Italy and Austria renew their Triple Alliance • President Theodore Roosevelt is empowered to purchase French shares in the Panama Canal and so gain control of the Canal Zone for the USA • Russia agrees with China to evacuate Manchuria • Australia introduces immigration restrictions

Arts and Letters

PAINTING: Paul Gauguin (Fr), *Horsemen on the Beach*; Claude Monet (Fr), *Waterloo Bridge*; LITERATURE: Arthur Conan Doyle (UK), *The Hound of the Baskervilles*; Rudyard Kipling (UK), *Just So Stories*; Beatrix Potter (UK), *Peter Rabbit*; Henry James (US), *Wings of the Dove*; James Barrie (UK), plays *The Admirable Crichton* and *Quality Street*

Science and Discovery

British explorer Robert Falcon Scott sails to the Antarctic in the *Discovery* • William Maddock Bayliss (UK) and Ernest Henry Starling (UK) discovers the hormone secretin • Brain surgeon Harvey Cushing (US) investigates the pituitary gland

Other Events

In Martinique, the volcano Mont Pelée erupts and destroys the town of St. Pierre; 38,000 people are believed killed • Egypt's Aswan Dam is completed • The Pilgrim Association is founded in the USA

Politics and Wars

Japan protests at Russia's failure to evacuate Manchuria, but the Russians refuse to go • King Edward VII visits Paris and a period of Anglo-French friendship begins • Serbia's Alexander I and Queen Draga are assassinated • A treaty between the USA and Panama provides for perpetual US control of the Panama Canal Zone • Canada and the USA agree Alaska's frontier • The Russian Social Democratic Party divides into Mensheviks (Moderates) and Bolsheviks (extremists)

Arts and Letters

MUSIC: Edward Elgar (UK), oratorio *The Apostles*; LITERATURE: Henry James (US), *The Ambassadors*; Samuel Butler (UK), *The Way of All Flesh* (published posthumously); Erskine Childers (UK), *The Riddle of the Sands*; Joseph Conrad (UK), *Typhoon*; Jack London (US), *The Call of the Wild* • George Bernard Shaw (UK), *Man and Superman*

Science and Discovery

First flights in powered heavier-than-air machine by Orville and Wilbur Wright (US) • Betrand Russell (UK) writes *The Principles of Mathematics* • Willem Einthoven (Neth) invents string galvanometer (electrocardiograph)

Religion and Philosophy

Pope Leo XIII dies; is succeeded by Pope Pius X

Social and Economic

Emmeline Pankhurst (UK) founds the Women's Social and Political Union, beginning the suffragette movement in Britain

Other Events

The first "Teddy Bears," named for President Theodore Roosevelt, are made in the USA

Politics and Wars

Russia and Japan war over rival interests in China; Japanese forces besiege Port Arthur, Manchuria, partly destroy a Russian fleet and defeat a Russian army at Liaoyang • Russian warships on the way to Japan fire on British trawlers in the North Sea • An *Entente Cordiale* between Britain and France settles their differences over Egypt; Britain recognizes the Suez Canal Convention • Tibet's independence is established by a treaty with Britain • France's possessions in West Africa are reorganized as French West Africa, with Dakar as the capital • Herero tribesmen revolt against German rule in South-West Africa • Theodore Roosevelt (Rep) is elected to second term as president of the USA

Arts and Letters

PAINTING: Henri Rousseau (Fr), *The Wedding*; SCULPTURE: Auguste Rodin (Fr), *The Thinker*; MUSIC: Frederick Delius (UK), *Appalachia*; Giacomo Puccini (It), opera *Madame Butterfly*; LITERATURE: James Barrie (UK), *Peter Pan*; J. M. Synge (UK), *Riders to the Sea*; Anton Chekhov (Russ), *The Cherry Orchard;* G. K. Chesterton (UK), *The Napoleon of Notting Hill*; O. Henry (US), *Cabbages and Kings*; Romain Rolland (Fr), *Jean-Christophe;* Jack London (US), *Sea Wolf*; H. G. Wells (UK), *Food of the Gods*

Science and Discovery

Frederick Stanley Kipping (UK) discovers silicones • John Ambrose Fleming (UK) invents the thermionic valve • Ernest Rutherford (UK) publishes *Radio Activity*

Social and Economic

The Workers' Educational Association is founded in Britain

Politics and Wars

Russo-Japanese War continues: Japanese troops in Manchuria capture Port Arthur and defeat Russian forces at Mukden; a Russian fleet is destroyed in the Tsushima Strait between Japan and Korea; through the Treaty of Portsmouth, organized by US President Theodore Roosevelt, Russia cedes the Manchurian towns of Port Arthur and Talien • Revolution in Russia; workers are killed in St. Petersburg on "Bloody Sunday"; the first workers' soviet (council) is formed; sailors mutiny in the warship *Potemkin*; a general strike is called; in an "October Manifesto" Tsar Nikolai II agrees to an elected Duma (parliament) • Moroccan crisis: secret agreements by Britain, France and Spain to divide Morocco upset by visit of German Kaiser Wilhelm II to Tangier, where he declares support for the Moroccans • Norway becomes independent from Sweden • Alberta and Saskatchewan become Canadian provinces

Arts and Letters

PAINTING: Group of French painters is given nickname "Les Fauves" (the wild beasts); Edvard Munch (Nor), *The Bridge*; Paul Cézanne (Fr), *The Bathers*; John Singer Sargent (US), *The Marlborough Family*; MUSIC: Claude Debussy (Fr), tone-poem *La Mer*; Franz Lehár (Hung), opera *The Merry Widow*; Richard Strauss (Ger), opera *Salome*; LITERATURE: Baroness Orczy (UK), *The Scarlet Pimpernel*; H. G. Wells (UK), *Kipps*; Henry James (US), *The Golden Bowl*

Science and Discovery

Albert Einstein (Ger) publishes the theory of relativity

Politics and Wars

A French appeal court declares the innocence of army officer Alfred Dreyfus, wrongly convicted of treason 12 years earlier • Germany plans to build a fleet of battleships • The Liberal Party led by Henry Campbell-Bannerman obtains a large majority in British elections; it proceeds to introduce social reforms, including increased workmen's compensation • The Russian Duma (parliament) meets, but is quickly dissolved because its members criticize government of Tsar Nikolai II • US President Theodore Roosevelt intervenes in Cuba when Liberal Party revolts against government of president Tomás Palma • Transvaal and Orange Free State win self-government from Britain

Arts and Letters

PAINTING: André Derain (Fr), *The Port of London*; MUSIC: Sergei Rachmaninoff (Russ), opera *Francesca da Rimini*; Ethel Smyth (UK), opera *The Wreckers*; LITERATURE: John Galsworthy (UK) begins the "Forsyte Saga" with *The Man of Property*; Upton Sinclair (US), *The Jungle*; Jack London (US), *White Fang*; Edgar Wallace (UK), *The Four Just Men*

Science and Discovery

Frederick Hopkins (UK) discovers the existence of vitamins

Social and Economic

Alfred Binet (Fr) and Théodore Simon (Fr) devise a test for assessing intelligence and mental age • Drainage of the Zuider Zee begins in the Netherlands

Other Events

700 people die when earthquake rocks San Francisco

USA—**Theodore Roosevelt** ——————————————————————— □ **William H. Taft** —————————
UK—**Edward VII** ————————

Politics and Wars

Oklahoma becomes the 46th State of the USA • Russia's second Duma (parliament) meets but is dissolved after disagreement between radicals and reactionaries; new electoral laws are introduced to increase the representation of Russia's propertied classes; a third Duma embarks on the repression of revolutionary activities • Britain and Russia form an Entente • The Triple Alliance of Germany, Italy and Austria is renewed • The Korean emperor Kojong abdicates; Korea becomes a Japanese protectorate

Arts and Letters

PAINTING: Pablo Picasso (Sp), *The Young Ladies of Avignon*; Henri Rousseau (Fr), *Tne Snake Charmer*; first exhibition of Cubism in Paris; MUSIC: Gustav Mahler (Aus), 8th symphony ("Symphony of a Thousand"); LITERATURE: Edmund Gosse (UK), *Father and Son*; Maxim Gorki (Russ), *Mother*; J. M. Synge (UK), play *The Playboy of the Western World*; George Bernard Shaw (UK), play *Major Barbara*; OTHER: beginning of the Diaghilev ballet

Science and Discovery

Lee de Forest (US) invents a triode vacuum tube • The Lumière brothers (Fr) invent an autochrome plate for color photography

Social and Economic

British soldier Robert Baden-Powell founds the Boy Scout movement • Women obtain the vote in Norway

Other Events

1,000 die in an earthquake at Kingston, Jamaica

Politics and Wars

USA severs diplomatic relations with Venezuela • Portugal's King Carlos and Crown Prince Luis are assassinated; Carlos's second son succeeds as Manoel II • Bulgaria declares its independence from Turkey; Prince Ferdinand is made Tsar • The Balkan states of Bosnia and Herzegovina are annexed by Austria • Relations between Germany and Britain deteriorate as Germany builds more large warships • A South African constitutional convention agrees to create the Union of South Africa • Congo (now Zaïre) becomes a Belgian colony • Herbert Asquith (Liberal) becomes Prime Minister of Britain • William Howard Taft (Rep) is elected President of the USA

Arts and Letters

MUSIC: Edward Elgar (UK), 1st symphony; Maurice Ravel (Fr), suite *Mother Goose*; LITERATURE: E. M. Forster (UK), *A Room with a View*; Kenneth Grahame (UK), *The Wind in the Willows*; Arnold Bennett (UK), *The Old Wives' Tale*; G. K. Chesterton (UK), *The Man who was Thursday*

Science and Discovery

British explorer Ernest Shackleton gets to within 100 miles (160 km) of the South Pole

Religion and Philosophy

The Federal Council of Churches, forerunner of the National Council of Churches of Christ, is founded in USA

Other Events

Jack Johnson (US) becomes the first Negro to win the world heavyweight boxing championship • 150,000 people are killed in an earthquake which destroys Messina and Reggio, Sicily

Politics and Wars

William Howard Taft (Rep) becomes 26th President of the USA • Young Turks depose Sultan Abdul Hamid; Muhammad V succeeds him as ruler of Turkey • Turkey recognizes Bulgaria's independence and Austrian annexation of Bosnia • Japan imposes strict rule over Korea • Britain suffers a constitutional crisis when the House of Lords rejects Liberal government's budget, approved by the House of Commons • Parliament is dissolved • Belgium's king Leopold II dies; is succeeded by his nephew, Albert

Arts and Letters

PAINTING: Henri Matisse (Fr), *The Dance*; ARCHITECTURE: Frank Lloyd Wright (US), Robie House, Chicago; MUSIC: Richard Strauss (Ger), opera *Elektra*; Nikolai Rimsky-Korsakov (Russ), opera *The Golden Cockerel*; Gustav Mahler (Aus), 9th symphony; LITERATURE: H. G. Wells (UK), *Tono-Bungay* and *Ann Veronica*; André Gide (Fr), *Strait is the Gate*; Maurice Maeterlinck (Belg), *The Blue Bird*; G. M. Trevelyan (UK), *Garibaldi and the Thousand*

Science and Discovery

Leo H. Baekeland (US) invents Bakelite • Louis Blériot (Fr) makes the first powered airplane crossing of the English Channel • Explorer Robert E. Peary (US) reaches the North Pole

Social and Economic

The conditions of Russian peasants are improved by Land Laws • Old-age pensions are introduced in Britain • The first motion-picture newsreels are shown in North America and Europe

─□ George V ─

Politics and Wars
The Liberals win a British general election; the House of Lords passes the budget it previously vetoed • The House of Commons passes a Bill to curb the Lords' power and limit the period between elections to five years; the Lords veto the Bill, precipitating a new crisis; the Liberals win a second general election • Cape Colony, Natal, Transvaal and Orange Free State unite to form the Union of South Africa, an independent dominion under the British Crown • French railwaymen strike as part of long period of political unrest; Prime Minister Aristide Briand sends troops to quell them • Revolution breaks out in Portugal, and a republic is declared • Japan annexes Korea • Britain's king Edward VII dies; is succeeded by his son, George V

Arts and Letters
MUSIC: Giacomo Puccini (It), opera The Girl of the Golden West; Igor Stravinsky (Russ), ballet The Firebird; Ralph Vaughan Williams (UK), A Sea Symphony; LITERATURE: E. M. Forster (UK), Howard's End; Norman Angell (UK), The Great Illusion; H. G. Wells (UK), The History of Mr. Polly; J. M. Synge (UK), Deidre of the Sorrows

Science and Discovery
Bertrand Russell and A. N. Whitehead (UK) write the first volume of Principia Mathematica • Marie Curie (Fr) isolates radium • Arthur Evans (UK) excavates a Minoan palace at Knossos, Crete • Robert Falcon Scott (UK) and Roald Amundsen (Nor) begin separate expeditions to the South Pole

Politics and Wars
The USA and Japan sign a trade treaty • The Anglo-Japanese treaty is renewed • Britain's House of Lords, faced with a threat to create enough Liberal peers to ensure a majority, passes a Parliament Act curbing its own powers • Italy declares war on Turkey; annexes Tripoli and Cyrenaica in North Africa • International tension is caused by the arrival of a German warship, Panther, at Agadir, Morocco • France is given virtual control over Morocco • Russian premier Petr Stolypin is assassinated • China is torn by revolution; a republic is proclaimed; revolutionaries bomb Nanking; Sun Yat-sen is elected president of the United Provinces of China

Arts and Letters
PAINTING: Vassily Kandinsky (Russ) and Franz Marc (Ger) found the "Blue Rider" artists' group in Munich; MUSIC: Richard Strauss (Ger), opera Der Rosenkavalier; Frederick Delius (UK), tone poem On Hearing the First Cuckoo in Spring; Maurice Ravel (Fr), ballet Daphnis and Chloë; Igor Stravinsky (Russ), ballet Petrushka; Irving Berlin (US), song Alexander's Ragtime Band; LITERATURE: G. K. Chesterton (UK), The Innocence of Father Brown; D. H. Lawrence (UK), The White Peacock; H. G. Wells (UK), The New Machiavelli

Science and Discovery
Roald Amundsen (Nor) reaches the South Pole • Ernest Rutherford (UK) expounds a theory of atomic structure • Elmer Ambrose Sperry (US) develops a gyrocompass • Charles Franklin Kettering (US) invents an automobile self-starter

Politics and Wars
New Mexico becomes the 47th State of the USA • President Theodore Roosevelt (US) is wounded in an assassination attempt • US marines land in Cuba • In the Bàlkans, war breaks out between Turkey and an alliance of Bulgaria, Serbia, Montenegro and Greece • Greece refuses to sign the subsequent armistice • Albania becomes independent • Germany continues to increase its naval strength • Britain concentrates warships in the North Sea area, and France keeps its fleet in Mediterranean • Japan's emperor Mutsuhito dies; is succeeded by his son, Yoshihito • Woodrow Wilson (Dem) is elected President of the USA

Arts and Letters
PAINTING: Marcel Duchamp (Fr), Nude Descending a Staircase; Pablo Picasso (Sp), The Violin; LITERATURE: James Stephens (UK), The Crock of Gold; Rabindranath Tagore (Ind), Gitanjali

Science and Discovery
Robert Falcon Scott (UK) reaches the South Pole, but dies on the return journey • Frederick Soddy (UK) demonstrates the exitence of isotopes • The skull of Piltdown Man (later proved to be a hoax) is "discovered" in Sussex, England

Other Events
The British liner Titanic sinks on its maiden voyage; 1,500 people are drowned • The Girl Scouts movement is founded in the USA • The Royal Flying Corps is formed in Britain • Outstanding athlete Jim Thorpe (US) loses his two Olympic gold medals on account of "professionalism"

USA—**W. H. Taft** -☐ **Woodrow Wilson**

UK—**George V**

Politics and Wars

Woodrow Wilson (Dem) becomes 27th President of the USA • King George of Greece is assassinated • In a second Balkan War, Bulgarian troops capture Adrianople (Edirne, Turk); Turkey accepts the Great Powers' peace proposals and the war ends with a London Peace Treaty • In China, revolutionary forces capture Nanking, and their leader, Yuan Shih-kai, is elected president of the Chinese Republic • In India, Mahatma Gandhi, the nationalist leader, is arrested by British • British suffragettes demand the vote

Arts and Letters

PAINTING: John Singer Sargent (US), *Henry James*; MUSIC: Igor Stravinsky (Russ), ballet *The Rite of Spring*; Ralph Vaughan Williams (UK), *A London Symphony* and opera *Hugh the Drover*; LITERATURE: D. H. Lawrence (UK), *Sons and Lovers*; Marcel Proust (Fr), *Swann's Way*; Eleanor H. Porter (US), *Pollyanna*; Thomas Mann (Ger), *Death in Venice*; Robert Frost (US), poem *A Boy's Will*; George Bernard Shaw (UK), plays *Androcles and the Lion* and *Pygmalion*

Science and Discovery

Hans Geiger (Ger) invents a radiator-detector—the Geiger Counter • Richard Willstätter (Ger) discovers the existence of chlorophyll in plants

Social and Economic

The Federal Reserve Bank Act reforms the USA's banking system • The 17th Amendment to US Constitution introduces federal income tax

Other Events

The Panama Canal is opened to shipping

Politics and Wars

The assassination in Serbia of Austria's Archduke Franz-Ferdinand brings about World War I • Austria attacks Serbia • Germany declares war on Russia and France, and invades Belgium • Britain declares war on Germany • Italy and the USA declare their neutrality • German troops occupy Brussels • British and French armies retreat from Mons (Belg) • The Russians are defeated at Tannenburg, Prussia (now Stebark, Pol.) but force the Germans out of Poland • Turkey joins the war on Germany's side, and closes the Dardanelles Strait • The British navy wins victories in the Pacific and South Atlantic • Britain annexes Cyprus • Zeppelins carry out first air-raids on Britain • An Irish Home Rule Bill is passed by Britain's House of Commons despite opposition by Ulster Unionists, but is suspended for the duration of war

Arts and Letters

PAINTING: Augustus John (UK), portrait *George Bernard Shaw*; Oskar Kokoschka (Aus), *The Vortex*; LITERATURE: James Joyce (UK), *Dubliners*; Edgar Rice Burroughs (US), *Tarzan of the Apes*

Science and Discovery

Edward C. Kendall (US) isolates thyroxine, the active principle of the thyroid gland

Social and Economic

Construction of the Canadian Grand Trunk Railway from the Atlantic to the Pacific is completed

Other Events

St. Petersburg (Russ) is renamed Petrograd

Politics and Wars

World War I continues: Italy joins the Allies (France and Britain) • German troops use poison gas and flamethrowers on the Western Front • Battles are fought at Ypres (Belg), and Neuve Chapelle and Loos (Fr) • Allied soldiers land at Salonika, Greece, and Gallipoli, Turkey • British forces take Mesopotamia • Serbia is overrun by the Central Powers (Germany and Austria) • German armies enter Warsaw and capture Brest-Litovsk • The Russians take Przemysl, which is later retaken by Germans • German submarines inflict heavy losses on Allied merchant ships • US–German relations are strained when a German submarine sinks the British liner *Lusitania* • A German fleet is defeated by the British navy at Dogger Bank • Zeppelins drop bombs on London • US forces occupy Cuba • A Liberal–Conservative coalition government is formed in Britain, with Herbert Asquith as prime minister

Arts and Letters

PAINTING: Pablo Picasso (Sp), *Harlequin*; MUSIC: Manuel de Falla (Spain), ballet *Love the Magician*; Gustav Holst (UK), *The Planets*; LITERATURE: D. H. Lawrence (UK), *The Rainbow*; John Buchan, (UK), *The Thirty-Nine Steps*; W. Somerset Maugham (UK), *Of Human Bondage*; Ezra Pound (US), *Cathay*; FILM: D. W. Griffith (US), *The Birth of a Nation*

Science and Discovery

Albert Einstein (Ger) expounds his general theory of relativity

Social and Economic

The Women's Institute is introduced in Britain • The US Coast Guard is established

Politics and Wars

First woman member of the US Congress is elected—Miss Jeanette Rankin of Montana • USA purchases Virgin Islands from Denmark • World War I continues: the Battle of Verdun rages for 9 months; French and British armies launch offensives on the Somme and Marne rivers; tanks are in action for the first time; the Allies evacuate Gallipoli; but repel a Turkish attack on Egypt and begin a new offensive in Mesopotamia; the Russians mount an unsuccessful offensive on the Eastern Front; Romania enters the war against the Germans, who take Bucharest; British and German fleets fight the indecisive Battle of Jutland • Britain's war minister Lord Kitchener is drowned when the warship *Hampshire* is sunk • David Lloyd George (Lib) becomes prime minister of a British coalition government • Sinn Fein's "Easter Rebellion" in Dublin is suppressed by British troops • US troops quell disorders in the Dominican Republic • Woodrow Wilson (Dem) is reelected president of the USA

Arts and Letters

PAINTING: Henri Matisse (Fr), *The Three Sisters*; ARCHITECTURE: Frank Lloyd Wright (US), Imperial Hotel, Tokyo; MUSIC: Manuel de Falla (Sp), *Nights in the Garden of Spain*; LITERATURE: James Joyce (UK), *Portrait of the Artist as a Young Man*; John Buchan (UK), *Greenmantle*; Eugene O'Neill (US), *Bound East*; FILM: D. W. Griffith (US), *Intolerance*

Science and Discovery

US chemist Gilbert N. Lewis develops his electron theory of valancy, which explains how atoms are held together

Politics and Wars

USA declares war on Germany; US troops arrive in Europe • Bolshevik revolution breaks out in Russia: Allies Eastern Front collapses and German–Russian armistice is signed • On the Western Front the battles of Arras, Aisne, Messines, Passchendaele and Cambrai bring heavy casualties but few gains • Austrians defeat Italians at Caporetto • German submarine warfare intensifies • In the Middle East, the Allies win the Battle of Gaza and capture Jerusalem from the Turks • Britain's Foreign Secretary Arthur Balfour announces that the British favor the establishment of a national home for Jews in Palestine • Finland declares its independence from Russia

Arts and Letters

MUSIC: Maurice Ravel (Fr), *Le Tombeau de Couperin*; Serge Prokofiev (Russ), *Classical Symphony*; Salzburg Festival is started; LITERATURE: J. M. Barrie (UK), *Dear Brutus*; T. S. Eliot (US), *Prufrock and other Observations*; Norman Douglas (UK), *South Wind*; Paul Valéry (Fr), *La Jeune Parque*; Lion Feuchtwanger (Ger), *Jew Süss*

Science and Discovery

Carl Jung (Switz) writes *Psychology of the Unconscious* • The Germans develop a twin-engined biplane bomber

Social and Economic

Excess Profits Duty in Britain is increased to 80 per cent

Other Events

Britain's royal family drops the name of Saxe-Coburg-Gotha and adopts the surname Windsor

Politics and Wars

World War One ends after a major German offensive followed by Allied victories; Germany's war effort collapses; the German navy mutinies; revolution flares in Berlin; Kaiser Wilhelm II abdicates and a so-called "Popular" government assumes power; the German fleet surrenders • The Austrian emperor Karl abdicates; Austria becomes a republic • Lithuania and Latvia proclaim their independence from Russia • Poland is declared a republic • Turkey and Austria–Hungary surrender • Yugoslavia and Czechoslovakia become independent • Iceland becomes a sovereign state • President Woodrow Wilson (US) announces his Fourteen Points for peace settlement • Tsar Nikolai II and his family are executed in Russia • Labour ministers resign from Britain's coalition government; a new coalition government under David Lloyd George (Lib) is elected

Arts and Letters

PAINTING: Paul Nash (UK), pictures of the Western Front • Pierre Renoir (Fr), *Woman Tying her Shoe*; MUSIC: Béla Bartók (Hung), opera *Duke Bluebeard's Castle*; LITERATURE: Lytton Strachey (UK), *Eminent Victorians*; Gerard Manley Hopkins (UK), poems (published 29 years after his death); Pierre Benoit (Fr), *Koenigsmark*; Luigi Pirandello (It), *Six Characters in Search of an Author*; FILM: *Shoulder Arms*, with Charlie Chaplin

Social and Economic

Mme. Constance Georgine Markievicz is elected as Britain's first woman Member of Parliament (she does not take her seat) • Some women over 30 secure the vote in Britain

USA—**Woodrow Wilson** ————————————————— □ **Warren G. Harding** ——
UK—**George V** —————————————————————————————

Politics and Wars

The Treaty of Versailles imposes reparations and demilitarization on Germany • The USA begins a period of isolationism • The German fleet is scuttled at Scapa Flow (UK) • The National Socialist (Nazi) Party is formed in Germany • Eamon de Valera (UK) becomes president of the rebel Sinn Fein party in Ireland • In Russia, the Bolsheviks steadily overcome White Russian opposition, despite the help of British troops • Anti-British demonstrations occur in India: at Amritsar, troops fire on a mob, killing 379 people • Amendment 18 to the US Constitution is ratified; it prohibits the manufacture or sale of alcoholic liquor

Arts and Letters

PAINTING: Pablo Picasso (Sp), *Pierrot and Harlequin*; MUSIC: Manuel de Falla (Sp), ballet *The Three-Cornered Hat* (Picasso designs sets); ARCHITECTURE: Walter Gropius (Ger) founds the Bauhaus, a design school at Weimar (Ger); LITERATURE: Vicente Blasco Ibanez (Sp), *The Four Horsemen of the Apocalypse*; W. Somerset Maugham (UK), *The Moon and Sixpence*; Thomas Hardy (UK), *Collected Poems*

Science and Discovery

Francis William Aston (UK) devises the mass-spectograph • Bertrand Russell (UK) writes *Introduction to Mathematical Philosophy*

Other Events

British airforce officers John W. Alcock and Arthur W. Brown make the first non-stop Atlantic flight (Newfoundland–Ireland) • British airship R34 makes first lighter-than-air Atlantic crossing, and first double crossing

Politics and Wars

The League of Nations, brainchild of US President Woodrow Wilson, comes into being, but the US Senate votes against joining • Esthonia becomes independent of Russia • Danzig is made a free city under the League of Nations • Russia goes to war with Poland over disputed territory; Poland annexes Vilna • Civil war flares in Ireland over Home Rule: martial law is declared in Cork • Under the League of Nations, Mesopotamia and Palestine become British mandates, Syria and Lebanon become French mandates • Britain annexes Kenya • Warren G. Harding (Rep) is elected President of the USA

Arts and Letters

PAINTING: Stanley Spencer (UK), *The Last Supper*; Amadeo Modigliani (It), *Reclining Nude*; LITERATURE: Sinclair Lewis (US), *Main Street*; F. Scott Fitzgerald (US), *This Side of Paradise*; Sigrid Undset (Nor), *Kristin Lavransdatter*; John Galsworthy (UK), *In Chancery*; Agatha Christie (UK), *The Mysterious Affair at Styles*

Science and Discovery

Juan de la Cierva (Sp), designs an autogiro

Religion and Philosophy

French heroine Jeanne d'Arc (1412–1421) is canonized by the Roman Catholic Church

Social and Economic

Women are awarded degrees at Oxford University • By the 19th Amendment to the Constitution, US women secure the vote • The International Court of Justice is established at The Hague, Netherlands • Prohibition (of alcoholic liquor) comes into force in USA • Public radio broadcasting begins in Britain

Politics and Wars

Warren G. Harding becomes 29th President of the USA • The USA rejects trade overtures from Russia • The Immigration Act limits entry into the USA • Washington Naval Conference: Britain, France, Italy, Japan and the USA meet to agree on arms limitation • The Pacific Treaty, signed by the USA, Britain, France and Japan, confirms their interests in the Pacific area • The League of Nations settles a dispute between Poland and Germany over Upper Silesia: they agree on partition • Rebellion in Ireland ends with a treaty dividing the country: 26 southern counties become the Irish Free State with dominion status; 6 northern counties remain part of the United Kingdom • Greece declares war on Turkey, and is defeated at Sakkarya • Mackenzie King (Liberal) becomes Prime Minister of Canada

Arts and Letters

PAINTING: Paul Klee (Switz), *The Fish*; Pablo Picasso (Sp), *Three Musicians*; MUSIC: Sergei Prokofiev (USSR), opera *The Love of Three Oranges*; Arthur Honneger (Fr), oratorio *King David*; LITERATURE: D. H. Lawrence (UK), *Women in Love*; John Galsworthy (UK), *To Let* (part of Forsyte Saga); Aldous Huxley (UK), *Crome Yellow*; John Dos Passos (US), *Three Soldiers*; Eugene O'Neill (US), *The Emperor Jones*; Karel Capek (Czech), *The Insect Play*; George Bernard Shaw (UK), *Back to Methuselah*

Social and Economic

The British Legion for war veterans is formed • Britain and Russia agree a trade treaty • Germany suffers a financial crisis as the mark falls in value

□ Calvin Coolidge

1922

Politics and Wars
Egypt wins independence from British rule, with Fuad I as king • Sudan is under joint Anglo-Egyptian sovereignty • Ireland is torn by civil war: the Irish Free State is proclaimed; Northern Ireland votes against inclusion • Fascist chief Benito Mussolini leads "march on Rome" and takes over government • Washington Naval Treaty provides for a 10-year ban on building capital ships, and lays down proportionate sizes of the navies of USA, Britain, France and Japan • Independence leader Mohandas K. Gandhi is imprisoned by British authorities in India for civil disobedience • King Constantine of Greece abdicates; is succeeded by his eldest son, George II • Greece is defeated in war with Turkey • Turkish politician Mustapha Kemal proclaims a republic • Josef Stalin becomes secretary-general of the Communist Party in Russia

Arts and Letters
PAINTING: Paul Klee (Switz), *Twittering Machine*; Joan Miró (Sp), *The Farm*; MUSIC: Ralph Vaughan Williams (UK), *Pastoral symphony*; Arthur Bliss (UK), *Colour symphony*; LITERATURE: T. S. Eliot (US), *The Waste Land*; James Joyce (Ire), *Ulysses*; Sinclair Lewis (US), *Babbitt*; Katherine Mansfield (UK), *The Garden Party*; Edith Sitwell (UK), *Façade*; W. B. Yeats (Ire), *Later Poems*

Science and Discovery
Pharaoh Tutankhamun's tomb is discovered at Luxor, Egypt • Frederick Banting (Can) and Charles Best (Can) develop insulin treatment for diabetes

Religion and Philosophy
Pope Benedict XV dies; is succeeded by Pius XI

1923

Politics and Wars
US President Warren G. Harding dies; is succeeded by Vice-President Calvin Coolidge (Rep) as 30th President • Russia becomes the Union of Soviet Socialist Republics; USA refuses recognition • Gustav Stresemann becomes Chancellor of Germany • Nazi leader Adolf Hitler fails in an attempted *coup d'état* in Munich • Mustapha Kemal becomes president of the new Turkish republic • Independence for Transjordan is proclaimed • Stanley Baldwin (Con) becomes Britain's prime minister in succession to Arthur Bonar Law • Primo de Rivera becomes dictator of Spain • George II of Greece is deposed

Arts and Letters
PAINTING: Stanley Spencer (UK), *The Resurrection, Cookham*; MUSIC: William Walton (UK), *Façade*; Gustav Holst (UK), *The Perfect Fool*; LITERATURE: Colette (Fr), *The House of Claudine*; Adolf Hitler (Ger) begins *Mein Kampf* • D. H. Lawrence (UK), *Kangaroo*; George Bernard Shaw (UK), play *Saint Joan*; Karel Capek (Czech), play *R.U.R.*; Eugene O'Neill (US), *Anna Christie*; Elmer Rice (US), *The Adding Machine*; E. E. Cummings (US), *Enormous Room*

Science and Discovery
The first hot sheet steel continuous rolling mill opens at Ashland, Ky

Social and Economic
A commercial treaty is agreed by the USA and Canada • Inflation continues in Germany

Other Events
In Japan, more than 140,000 people die in an earthquake • The Wightman Cup tennis championship, for US and British women players begins

1924

Politics and Wars
Britain's first Labor government, under J. Ramsay Macdonald, lasts only nine months; following an election victory, the Conservatives under Stanley Baldwin take over • The Kuomintang (Nationalist party) in China admits Communists • China recognizes the USSR • Italy annexes Fiume • Giacomo Matteotti, socialist opponent of the Italian Fascist leader Benito Mussolini, is murdered • Albania becomes a republic • The "Teapot Dome" oil scandal in the USA leads to the resignations of Interior secretary Albert Fall and Navy secretary Edwin Denby • Calvin Coolidge (Rep) is elected to continue as US President

Arts and Letters
MUSIC: Giacomo Puccini (It), opera *Turandot*; Arthur Honneger (Fr) *Pacific* 231; George Gershwin (US), *Rhapsody in Blue*; LITERATURE: Margaret Kennedy (US), *The Constant Nymph*; Marc Connelly (US), *Green Pastures*; Noël Coward (UK), play *The Vortex*; E. M. Forster (UK), *A Passage to India*; Thomas Mann (Ger), *The Magic Mountain*; A. A. Milne (UK), *When We were Very Young*

Science and Discovery
Louis Victor de Broglie (Fr) investigates the wave nature of the electron • Arthur S. Eddington (UK) interprets Albert Einstein's theory of relativity in *The Mathematical Theory of Relativity*

Social and Economic
Japan adopts the metric system • The USA bans Japanese immigrants

Other Events
The Russian city of Petrograd is renamed Leningrad following the death of Vladimir Lenin

USA—**Calvin Coolidge**
UK—**George V**

Politics and Wars

President Sun Yat-sen of China dies • Paul von Hindenburg becomes German President on the death of Friedrich Ebert • The Locarco Treaties provide a system of guarantees for European frontiers • French occupation troops evacuate the Rhineland; British occupation troops leave Köln • The League of Nations settles a dispute between Greece and Bulgaria • Arabs revolt against the French in Syria; Damascus is bombarded • Reza Khan Pahlevi seizes Persian throne

Arts and Letters

PAINTING: Pablo Picasso (Sp), *Three Dancers*; SCULPTURE: Jacob Epstein (UK), *Rima*; MUSIC: Aaron Copland (US), 1st symphony; Alban Berg (Aus), opera *Wozzeck*; LITERATURE: F. Scott Fitzgerald (US), *The Great Gatsby*; Franz Kafka (Czech), *The Trial* (published anonymously); Theodore Dreiser (US), *An American Tragedy*; Anita Loos (US), *Gentlemen Prefer Blondes*; Noël Coward (UK), play *Hay Fever*; Sean O'Casey (Ire), play *Juno and the Paycock*; FILMS: *The Gold Rush* with Charlie Chaplin; *The Battleship Potemkin* (S. M. Eisenstein; Russ)

Science and Discovery

R. A. Millikan (US) discovers cosmic rays • E. V. Appleton (UK) identifies Vitamin B

Social and Economic

Britain returns to the gold standard • The USA's first woman state governor—Mrs Nellie Ross—is appointed in Wyoming • The teaching of Darwin's theory of human evolution is banned in Tennessee

Other Events

Norway's capital, Christiana, resumes its old name, Oslo

Politics and Wars

Hejaz becomes the Kingdom of Saudi Arabia, with Ibn Saud as king • Germany is admitted to the League of Nations • A preparatory disarmament conference, with the USA participating, begins in Geneva • The Riff rebels, led by Abd-el-Krim, are defeated in Morocco by the French • Lebanon becomes a republic • The Russian revolutionary leader Lev Trotsky is expelled from the Soviet Politburo • Civil war rages in China: the Nationalist leader Chiang Kai-shek establishes a provisional government in Hankow • US troops land in Nicaragua to restore order after a revolt

Arts and Letters

PAINTING: Marc Chagall (Russ), *Lovers' Bouquet*; Augustus John (UK), portrait *Lady Ottoline Morrell*; ARCHITECTURE: Le Corbusier (C. E. Jeanneret; Fr), book *The Coming Architecture*; LITERATURE: Louis Bromfield (US), *Early Autumn*; D. H. Lawrence (UK), *The Plumed Serpent*; T. E. Lawrence (UK), *The Seven Pillars of Wisdom*; A. A. Milne (UK), *Winnie the Pooh*; André Gide (Fr), *The Counterfeiters*; G. M. Trevelyan (UK), *History of England*

Science and Discovery

John Logie Baird (UK) demonstrates television in London • Raold Amundsen (Nor) flies by airship and Richard E. Byrd (US) by airplane over the North Pole

Social and Economic

A general strike in Britain is abandoned after nine days • Belgium and France suffer financial crises, and their currencies are devalued • The British economist John Maynard Keynes writes *The End of Laissez-Faire*

Politics and Wars

Allied military control ends in Germany and Hungary; the German president Paul von Hindenburg repudiates German responsibility for World War One, established in the Versailles Treaty • Josef Stalin secures political control in the Soviet Union; Lev Trotsky is expelled from the Russian Communist Party • The Chinese Kuomintang (Nationalists) set up government in Hankow but Nationalist leader Chiang Kai-shek breaks away and establishes a rival government in Nanking, which later displaces the Hankow government; Chiang purges communists from the Kuomintang

Arts and Letters

SCULPTURE: Jacob Epstein (UK), *Madonna and Child*; MUSIC: Jaromir Weinberger (Czech), opera *Schwanda, the Bagpiper*; Aaron Copland (US), 1st piano concerto; LITERATURE: Willa Cather (US), *Death Comes for the Archbishop*; Sinclair Lewis (US), *Elmer Gantry*; Virginia Woolf (UK), *To the Lighthouse*; Mazo de la Roche (Can), *Jalna*; Upton Sinclair (US), *Oil!*; Thornton Wilder (US), *Bridge of San Luis Rey*; Henry Williamson (UK), *Tarka the Otter*; American-born T. S. Eliot becomes a British citizen; films: *The Jazz Singer* (first full-length talkie); *Metropolis* (Fritz Lang)

Science and Discovery

Werner Heisenberg (Ger) develops the principle of indeterminacy in measuring electrons • John Logie Baird (UK) demonstrates early color television • Charles A. Lindbergh (US) makes the first solo airplane flight across the Atlantic

Social and Economic

The German economy collapses and the mark becomes worthless

□ Herbert C. Hoover ──────────────────▷

Politics and Wars

Britain recognizes the independence of Transjordan (later Jordan) • Chinese Nationalists led by Chiang Kai-shek capture Peking; Chiang is elected president of China • The Kellogg-Briand Pact, sponsored by US Secretary of State Frank B. Kellogg, denounces war and provides for pacific settlement of disputes; it is signed by 65 countries • Albania becomes a kingdom, with King Zog as monarch. • Italy enters into 20 year friendship treaty with Ethiopia • The Fascist Grand Council extends its political power in Italy • Newly-elected president Alvato Obregón of Mexico is assassinated • Herbert Hoover (Rep) is elected President of the USA

Arts and Letters

PAINTING: Edvard Munch (Nor), *Girl on a Sofa*; MUSIC: Kurt Weill (Ger), *The Threepenny Opera*; Maurice Ravel (Fr), *Bolero*; Igor Stravinsky (Russ), *Capriccio*; Jerome Kern (US) musical *Show Boat*; LITERATURE: Upton Sinclair (US), *Boston*; Evelyn Waugh (UK), *Decline and Fall*; Aldous Huxley (UK), *Point Counter Point*; FILM: first Mickey Mouse cartoon

Science and Discovery

Alexander Fleming (UK) discovers penicillin

Religion and Philosophy

Islam ceases to be the state religion of Turkey • George Bernard Shaw (UK) writes *The Intelligent Woman's Guide to Socialism and Capitalism*

Social and Economic

The Soviet Union launches its first Five-Year Economic Plan • Female suffrage from the age of 21 is approved in Britain • The economy of Brazil collapses

Politics and Wars

Herbert Hoover becomes 31st President of the USA • A second Labour government takes office in Britain • A world economic crisis begins with collapse of US Stock Exchange • The US ceases loans to Europe • The Young Plan, under which Germany pays reparations annually, is agreed by an international committee • Allied occupation troops begin to evacuate the Rhineland (Ger) • The revolutionary Lev Trotsky is expelled from Russia • King Amanullah is driven from Afghanistan • Riots occur in Palestine • In Italy, the Fascists monopolise parliament

Arts and Letters

PAINTING: Grant Wood (US), *Woman with Plants*; MUSIC: William Walton (UK), viola concerto; Constant Lambert (UK), *Rio Grande*; Noël Coward (UK), operetta *Bitter Sweet*; LITERATURE: William Faulkner (US), *The Sound and the Fury*; Ernest Hemingway (US), *A Farewell to Arms*; D. H. Lawrence (UK), *Lady Chatterley's Lover*; Virginia Woolf (UK), *Orlando*; Charles Morgan (UK), *Portrait in a Mirror*; Erich Remarque (Ger), *All Quiet on the Western Front*; J. B. Priestley (UK), *The Good Companions*; Robert Graves (UK), *Goodbye to All That*; Robert Bridges (UK), *The Testament of Beauty*

Science and Discovery

An experimental public television service begins in Britain

Religion and Philosophy

The Church of Scotland is formed • The Lateran Treaty between the Pope and the Italian government establishes the Vatican City as an independent state

Politics and Wars

In the USA, the Great Depression worsens and unemployment grows • In India, Mohandas K. Gandhi leads a civil disobedience campaign, seeking independence from British rule • The London naval disarmament treaty is signed by Britain, the USA, France and Japan • Statesman Ras Tafari becomes Emperor of Ethiopia as Haile Selassie • The Allied occupation of Germany (since World War One) finally ends • The National Socialists (Nazis) win one-third of the seats in the German Reichstag (parliament)

Arts and Letters

PAINTING: Grant Wood (US), *American Gothic*; ARCHITECRURE: Empire State Building, New York, NY; MUSIC: Igor Stravinsky (Russ), *Symphony of Psalms*; LITERATURE: T. S. Eliot (US), *Ash Wednesday*; John Dos Passos (US), *42nd Parallel*; W. Somerset Maugham (UK), *Cakes and Ale*; Victoria Sackville-West (UK), *The Edwardians*; Hugh Walpole (UK), *Rogue Herries*; George Bernard Shaw (UK), play *The Apple Cart*; Noël Coward (UK), play *Private Lives*; Elmer Rice (US), *Street Scene*

Science and Discovery

Clyde W. Tombaugh (US) discovers the plant Pluto • John Howard Northrop (US) makes a crystalline form of pepsin • Ernest O. Lawrence (US) invents the cyclotron

Other Events

A British airship, R101, crashes *en route* to India • Amy Johnson (UK) flies solo from London to Australia • Uruguay wins the first World Cup football final

USA—**Herbert C. Hoover** ———————————————— ☐ **Franklin D. Roosevelt** —
UK—**George V** —————————————————————————————————

Politics and Wars

In India, independence leaders suspend the civil disobedience campaign; Mohandas K. Gandhi is released from jail and attends an inconclusive Round Table Conference in London • In Britain, an economic crisis brings down the Labour government; a National Coalition is formed • A short-lived naval mutiny occurs at Invergordon (Scot) • Britain abandons the gold standard; Japan follows suit • By the Statute of Westminster, Dominions of the British Empire are recognized as sovereign states • Japan invades Manchuria, beginning a Sino–Japanese war • Revolution flares in Spain: King Alphonso XIII leaves the country and a republic is proclaimed

Arts and Letters

PAINTING: Edward Hopper (US), *Route 6, Eastham*; SCULPTURE: Jacob Epstein (UK), *Genesis*; MUSIC: William Walton (UK), *Belshazzar's Feast*; LITERATURE: Antoine de St. Exupery (Fr), *Vol de Nuit*; Pearl Buck (US), *The Good Earth*; Eugene O'Neill (US), *Mourning Becomes Electra*; FILMS *City Lights* (Charles Chaplain); *Le Million* (René Clair)

Science and Discovery

Physicist Auguste Piccard (Switz) ascends by balloon into the stratosphere • Chemist Paul Karrer (Switz) identifies Vitamin A • Geologist Douglas Mawson (Austral) explores the Antarctic coastline

Social and Economic

A collapse of the major Austrian, bank, Credit Anstalt, precipitates a financial crisis in Europe

Politics and Wars

Japan establishes a puppet state of Manchukuo in Manchuria, China • A World Disarmament Conference (in which USA and USSR join) opens in Geneva • The National Socialists (Nazis) become the largest party in the German Reichstag (parliament) • Former Labour politician Oswald Mosley forms the British Union of Fascists • War between Bolivia and Paraguay breaks out over the ownership of the Gran Chaco region • Peru and Colombia fight over Leticia harbor • Eamon de Valéra becomes president of the Irish Free State • Oliveira Salazar becomes premier of Portugal • Franklin Delano Roosevelt (Dem) is elected President of the USA

Arts and Letters

PAINTING: Grant Wood (US), *Daughters of the Revolution*; SCULPTURE: Pablo Picasso (Sp), *Head of a Woman*; MUSIC: Dmitri Shostakovich (USSR), opera *A Lady Macbeth of Mtsensk*; LITERATURE: Ernest Hemingway (US), *Death in the Afternoon*; Aldous Huxley (UK), *Brave New World*; Charles Morgan (UK), *The Fountain*; Erskine P. Caldwell (US), *Tobacco Road*; Damon Runyon (US), *Guys and Dolls*; J. B. Priestley (UK), play *Dangerous Corner*; Noël Coward (UK), play *Cavalcade*; FILM: *Red-Haired Alibi* (Shirley Temple's debut)

Science and Discovery

British physicist James Chadwick discovers the neutron and US physicist Carl D. Anderson discovers the positron • Chemist Harold C. Urey (US) discovers deuterium

Other Events

Sydney Harbor Bridge is opened in Australia

Politics and Wars

Franklin D. Roosevelt (Dem) becomes 32nd President of the USA, and announces a "New Deal" to cure the Depression, including help for farmers and the establishment of a Tennessee Valley Authority and Public Works Administration • Nazi leader Adolf Hitler becomes Chancellor of Germany; under his rule, open persecution of Jews begins, and trade unions are suppressed • German Reichstag (parliament) building destroyed by fire • Germany withdraws from the international disarmament conference and leaves the League of Nations • Japan also leaves the League • Nazis win an election in the free city of Danzig • Austrian Chancellor Engelbert Dollfuss suspends parliamentary government in Austria and dissolves the Nazi Party there

Arts and Letters

PAINTING: Henri Matisse (Fr), *The Dance*; MUSIC: Richard Strauss (Ger), opera *Arabella*; Roy Harris (US), 1st symphony; LITERATURE: James Hilton (UK), *Lost Horizon*; Ignazio Silone (It), *Fontamara*; Gertrude Stein (US), *The Autobiography of Alice B. Toklas*; Georges Duhamel (Fr), *The Pasquier Chronicles*; Maxwell Anderson (US), play *Mary of Scotland*

Science and Discovery

US aviator Wiley Post makes the first solo round-the-world flight—in 7 days, 18 hours, 49 minutes

Social and Economic

The USA and Canada abandon the gold standard; US banks close for four days to protect gold reserves • The 21st Amendment to the US Constitution repeals prohibition

Politics and Wars

President Paul von Hindenburg of Germany dies; Chancellor Adolf Hitler is given dictatorial powers as Führer (leader) • Some leading Nazis are murdered in a Munich Putsch ("Night of the Long Knives") • Austrian Chancellor Engelbert Dollfuss suppresses strikes, but is killed in an attempted Nazi *coup d'état*; Justice Minister Kurt von Schuschnigg succeeds him • King Alexander of Yugoslavia and French Foreign Minister Jean L. Barthou are assassinated in Marseilles (Fr) • A Balkan Entente is formed by Greece, Romania, Yugoslavia and Turkey • The USA decides the Philippines will have independence in 1945 • The USSR joins the League of Nations

Arts and Letters

PAINTING: Wassily Kandinsky (USSR), *Composition*; Paul Klee (Switz), *Temptation*; MUSIC: Paul Hindemith (Ger), opera *Mathis der Maler*; LITERATURE: F. Scott Fitzgerald (US), *Tender is the Night*; Mikhail Shokalov (USSR), *And Quiet Flows the Don*; Robert Graves (UK), *I Claudius*; A. J. A. Symons (UK), *The Quest for Corvo*; FILM: *The Thin Man* (W. S. Van Dyke)

Science and Discovery

Chemist Tadeus Reichstein (Switz) synthesizes Vitamin C (ascorbic acid) • US naturalist William Beebe descends over 3000 feet (900 meters) in the ocean in his bathysphere • Physicists Irene and Frederic Joliot-Curie (Fr), discover artificial radioactivity

Other Events

The Dionne Quintuplets are born near Callander, Ont • Two giant ocean liners, *Queen Mary* (UK) and *Normandie* (Fr), are launched

Politics and Wars

Germany repudiates the disarmament clauses of the Versailles Treaty (which ended World War One) and introduces conscription • In a plebiscite, the Saarland votes to return to Germany • Britain signs a naval treaty with Germany • German Jews are deprived of citizens' rights by the Nuremberg Laws • Abyssinian War: Italian troops invade Ethiopia (Abyssinia); the action is condemned by the League of Nations, which orders economic sanctions against Italy • Kurt von Schuschnigg tries to curb the growing Nazi strength in Austria • At the Stresa Conference, Britain, France and Italy denounce unilateral repudiation of treaties • Eduard Beneš becomes President of Czechoslovakia

Arts and Letters

MUSIC: George Gershwin (US), opera *Porgy and Bess*; Sergei Rachmaninov (USSR), *Rhapsody on a Theme of Paganini*; LITERATURE: T. S. Eliot (UK), play *Murder in the Cathedral*; Robert Sherwood (US), *The Petrified Forest*; Clifford Odets (US), *Waiting for Lefty*; John Steinbeck (US), *Tortilla Flat*; A. J. Cronin (UK), *The Stars Look Down*; Sinclair Lewis (US), *It Can't Happen Here*; FILM: *Anna Karenina* (Clarence Brown)

Science and Discovery

Physicist Robert Watson Watt (UK) devises radar

Social and Economic

The US Labor Relations Act encourages collective bargaining • Leaders of 8 labor unions form a Committee for Industrial Organization as part of the American Federation of Labor

Other Events

Persia changes its name to Iran

Politics and Wars

King George V of Britain dies; is succeeded by his eldest son, Edward VIII • German troops occupy the demilitarized Rhineland between Germany and France; an act which violates the Treaty of Versailles • The Abyssinian War ends when Italian troops occupy the Ethiopian capital, Addis Ababa; Emperor Haile Selassie goes into exile, and Italy annexes Ethiopia • In Spain, the left-wing Popular Front wins elections; a right-wing army revolt led by Emilio Mola and Francisco Franco starts a bloody civil war • Dictators Adolf Hitler (Ger) and Benito Mussolini (It) proclaim a Berlin–Rome "Axis" (alliance) • King Fuad of Egypt dies; is succeeded by his son, Farouk • In Britain, a romance between Edward VIII and an American divorcée, Mrs. Wallis Simpson, leads to a constitutional crisis; Edward abdicates and is succeeded by his brother, George VI • Franklin D. Roosevelt is elected to a second term as President of the USA

Arts and Letters

PAINTING: Maurice Utrillo (Fr), *Christmas in Montmartre*; MUSIC: Sergei Prokofiev (USSR), *Peter and the Wolf*; Dmitri Shostakovich (USSR), 4th symphony; LITERATURE: Margaret Mitchell (US), *Gone With the Wind*; Charles Morgan (UK), *Sparkenbroke*; Aldous Huxley (UK), *Eyeless in Gaza*; H. A. L. Fisher (UK), *History of Europe*; Robert Sherwood (US), play *Idiot's Delight*; Terence Rattigan (UK), play *French Without Tears*; Dale Carnegie (US), *How to Win Friends and Influence People*

Science and Discovery

A regular public television service begins in Britain

USA — **Franklin D. Roosevelt**
UK — **George VI**

Politics and Wars

Franklin D. Roosevelt begins a second term as President of the USA • In the Spanish Civil War, Germany and Italy give open military support to right-wing forces led by General Francisco Franco; the city of Guernica is bombed; Almeria is shelled; the Spanish Republic government withdraws to Barcelona • Britain's Prime Minister Stanley Baldwin (Con) retires; is succeeded by Neville Chamberlain • France and Britain adopt a policy of appeasement towards the Axis powers (Germany and Italy) • Italy withdraws from the League of Nations • The Irish Free State adopts a new constitution and becomes Eire

Arts and Letters

PAINTING: Pablo Picasso (Sp), *Guernica*; MUSIC: Carl Orff (Ger), *Carmina Burana*; Arthur Bliss (UK), ballet *Checkmate*; LITERATURE: Ernest Hemingway (US), *To Have and Have Not*; Jean Paul Sartre (Fr), *La Nausée*; George Orwell (UK), *The Road to Wigan Pier*; A. J. Cronin (UK), *The Citadel*; John Steinbeck (US), *Of Mice and Men*; FILMS: *Snow White and the Seven Dwarfs* (Walt Disney)

Science and Discovery

Physicist Carl D. Anderson (US) discovers mesons in solar radiation • Howard Aiken (US) begins work on digital computers • Frank Whittle (UK) pioneers jet engines • Airwoman Amelia Earhart (US) disappears when flying the Pacific Ocean

Other Events

The Golden Gate Bridge, San Francisco, is completed • A German airship, *Hindenburg*, is destroyed by fire at Lakehurst, N.J.

Politics and Wars

German Führer (leader) Adolf Hitler assumes command of Germany's armed forces • Hitler declares an Anschluss (union of Austria and Germany); Germans invade Austria • Demands for autonomy by Germans in Sudentenland causes a crisis in Czechoslovakia; Germany mobilizes; Britain's Prime Minister Neville Chamberlain meets Adolf Hitler at Berchtesgaden and Bad Godesberg, Germany: finally at Munich, Britain, France and Italy agree, without consulting the Czechs, to a German occupation of the Sudetenland; Czech President Edouard Beneš resigns; the Czechs cede Teschen to Poland and southern Slovakia to Hungary • Britain recognizes the Italian conquest of Ethiopia

Arts and Letters

PAINTING: Raoul Dufy (Fr), *The Regatta*; MUSIC: Aaron Copland (US), *Billy the Kid*; Richard Strauss (Ger), opera *Daphne*; LITERATURE: Rachel Lyman Field (US), *All This, and Heaven Too*; Graham Greene (UK), *Brighton Rock*; Christopher Isherwood (UK), *Goodbye to Berlin*; Thornton Wilder (US), *Our Town*; FILM: *Alexander Nevsky* (Sergei Eisenstein; USSR)

Science and Discovery

Georg Biro (Hung) introduces the ball-point pen

Social and Economic

A Wages and Hours Law provides for minimum wages and maximum hours of work in the USA • In Mexico, the government seizes US and British oil holdings • The US Committee for Industrial Organization changes its name to the Congress of Industrial Organizations (CIO), as a rival to the American Federation of Labor

Politics and Wars

The Spanish Civil War ends with victory for right-wing forces led by Francisco Franco • Spain leaves the League of Nations • German troops seize Bohemia and Moravia, completing their occupation of Czechoslovakia • Italian troops invade and conquer Albania • Germany annexes Memel from Lithuania • The USSR and Germany sign a non-aggression pact • German dictator Adolf Hitler demands access through Poland to the free city of Danzig and the province of East Prussia • The Poles refuse; Britain and France pledge support for Poland • German troops invade Poland; Britain and France declare war on Germany • Soviet forces invade Poland which is divided between Germany and the USSR • Russian armies invade Finland • A British expeditionary force lands in France • The USA amends its Neutrality Act to permit arms exports to belligerents

Arts and Letters

SCULPTURE: Jacob Epstein (UK), *Adam*; Henry Moore (UK), *Reclining Figure*; MUSIC: Béla Bartok (Hung), 6th string quartet; LITERATURE: James Joyce (Ire), *Finnegan's Wake*; John Steinbeck (US), *The Grapes of Wrath*; Richard Llewellyn (UK), *How Green Was My Valley*; C. S. Forester (UK), *Captain Hornblower*; Eric Ambler (UK), *The Mask of Dmitrios*; George S. Kaufman (US) and Moss Hart (US), play *The Man Who Came to Dinner*; FILMS: *Gone With the Wind* (Victor Fleming)

Science and Discovery

Swiss chemist Paul Müller develops the insecticide DDT • Physicists Otto Hahn (Ger) and Fritz Strassmann (Ger) achieve nuclear fission

Politics and Wars

World War Two continues: German troops invade Norway and Denmark; British forces land in Norway, but are later withdrawn • Neville Chamberlain resigns as British prime minister; is succeeded by Winston Churchill as head of an all-party coalition government • German armies overrun Belgium, the Netherlands and Luxembourg, and invade France; a trapped British army escapes across the Channel from Dunkirk • Italy enters the war on Germany's side • The Germans occupy Paris • French Premier Paul Reynaud resigns; is succeeded by World War One hero Marshal Philippe Pétain, who concludes an armistice with Germany; the southern part of France, ruled from Vichy, remains independent; Germans occupy the rest • Brigadier-General Charles de Gaulle establishes a Free French movement in London • British warships sink a French fleet at Oran in West Africa • German attempts to bomb Britain into surrender are foiled by the Royal Air Force in "The Battle of Britain" • The British navy wins a victory over Italian warships at Taranto • Russian forces invade Romania • The Russo-Finnish War ends with a Soviet victory

Arts and Letters

MUSIC: Igor Stravinsky (Fr), symphony in C major; LITERATURE; Ernest Hemingway (US), *For Whom the Bell Tolls*; Graham Greene (UK), *The Power and the Glory*; FILMS: *The Great Dictator* (Charles Chaplin); *Fantasia* (Walt Disney)

Science and Discovery

Pathologist Howard Florey (Austral) develops penicillin as an antibiotic

Politics and Wars

World War Two continues: British troops drive Italian forces out of Egypt, and back into Libya; the German Afrika Korps is sent to reinforce the Italians • British forces liberate Ethiopia from the Italians • German armies invade the USSR, overrunning Poland, the Ukraine and the Baltic states; the Soviet government moves to Kuibishev, and Russian armies mount a counteroffensive • Rudolf Hess, deputy to the German dictator Adolf Hitler, flies to Scotland on an abortive peace mission • Japan begins a campaign of conquest: without warning, Japanese planes bomb Pearl Harbor, Hawaii, inflicting heavy damage on the US fleet there; Britain and the USA declare war on Japan, and the USA declares war on Japan's allies, Germany and Italy • Japanese forces capture the Philippines and Hong Kong, and sink two British warships • The German air force renews its attacks on Britain

Arts and Letters

PAINTING: Paul Nash (UK), *Bombers over Berlin*; MUSIC: Dmitri Shostakovich (USSR), "Leningrad" symphony; Benjamin Britten (UK), violin concerto; LITERATURE: Ilya Ehrenburg (Russ), *The Fall of Paris*; John P. Marquand (US), *H.M. Pulham Esquire*; F. Scott Fitzgerald (US), *The Last Tycoon*; Noël Coward (UK), *Blithe Spirit*; FILM: *Citizen Kane* (Orsen Welles)

Science and Discovery

US and British scientists develop the first polyester fiber, Dacron (Terylene)

Social and Economic

The US Congress passes a Lease-Land Bill permitting aid to America's allies

Politics and Wars

World War Two continues: Japanese forces invade the Dutch East Indies and Burma; Singapore surrenders; the Japanese threaten India from Burma • US troops successfully defend Guadalcanal, and block the Japanese drive in the naval battles of the Coral Sea and Midway • In North Africa, German troops led by Erwin Rommel drive the British out of Libya and back into Egypt: at the Battle of Alamein, the British and their allies defeat the Germans and begin a fresh advance • American and British troops land in French North Africa • On the eastern European front, the Germans besiege Stalingrad (modern Volgograd) and are trapped in a Russian counteroffensive • British and American air raids on Germany and occupied France cause great destruction • British and Canadian troops raid Dieppe (Fr)

Arts and Letters

PAINTING: John Piper (UK), *Windsor Castle*; Graham Sutherland (UK) *Red Landscape*; MUSIC: Aaron Copland (US), *Lincoln Portrait*; LITERATURE: T. S. Eliot (UK), *Little Gidding*; C. S. Lewis (UK), *The Screwtape Letters*; Albert Camus (Fr), *The Stranger*; G. M. Trevelyan (UK), *English Social History*

Social and Economic

British economist William Beveridge publishes a *Report on Social Security and National Insurance* (the Beveridge Plan), foundation of Britain's welfare state

Other Events

Malta is awarded the George Cross by King George VI for its valor in resisting German air attacks

1943	1944	1945

USA—**Franklin D. Roosevelt** ——————————————— □ **Harry S. Truman** ——————
UK—**George VI** ———

Politics and Wars

World War Two continues: a German army at Stalingrad surrenders to the Russians, who recapture considerable territory • German/Italian forces are defeated in North Africa and surrender • US and British troops invade Sicily and the Italian mainland; the Italians depose their Fascist dictator Benito Mussolini, and Marshal Pietro Badoglio takes over the government: Mussolini is rescued by German commandos • Italy surrenders unconditionally and joins the war against Germany • German resistance in Italy continues • In Yugoslavia, Communist resistance forces led by Josip Broz ("Tito") open an offensive against the Germans • Heavy air attacks on Germany continue • US troops land in the Solomon and Gilbert Islands • A US fleet defeats a Japanese fleet in the Battle of the Bismarck Sea

Arts and Letters

SCULTURE: Henry Moore (UK), *Madonna and Child*; ARCHITECTURE: Frank Lloyd Wright (US), Guggenheim Museum, New York City; MUSIC: Dmitri Shostakovich (USSR), 8th symphony; Ralph Vaughan Williams (UK), 5th symphony; Richard Rodgers and Oscar Hammerstein II (US), musical *Oklahoma!*; LITERATURE: Noël Coward (UK), *This Happy Breed*; Dylan Thomas (UK), *New Poems*

Science and Discovery

Microbiologist Selman A. Waksman (US) discovers the drug streptomycin

Social and Economic

The United Nations Relief and Rehabilitation Administration is formed • The Germans massacre Jews in Warsaw

Politics and Wars

World War Two continues: US and British Commonwealth forces in Italy capture Monte Cassino monastery and Rome • "D-Day": US, British and allied forces land in Normandy; they liberate Antwerp, Brussels and Paris; airborne landings at Arnhem and Eindhoven (Neth) fail; German counteroffensive in the Ardennes region of Belgium also fails ("Battle of the Bulge") • Free French leader Charles de Gaulle sets up a provisional government in Paris • Allied forces from Italy land in southern France • On the eastern front, Russians enter Romania, Bulgaria, Yugoslavia, and Hungary • An attempt by German officers to assassinate German dictator Adolf Hitler fails • Germans launch rocket-bomb (V-1 and V-2) attacks on Britain • In Pacific theater, US and Allied forces land in northern New Guinea; US forces land on Guam and Peleliu islands and begin recapture of the Philippines; US fleets defeat Japanese fleets in Battles of the Philippine Sea and Leyte Gulf; British troops begin their reconquest of Burma • A conference of US, British and Russian delegates at Dumbarton Oaks, Washington, D.C., agrees to set up the United Nations • Franklin D. Roosevelt is reelected for a fourth term as President of the USA

Arts and Letters

PAINTING: Graham Sutherland (UK), *Christ on the Cross*; MUSIC: Aaron Copland (US), *Appalachian Spring*; Béla Bartók (Hung), violin concerto; LITERATURE: Tennessee Williams (US), play *The Glass Menagerie*; W. S. Maugham (UK), *The Razor's Edge*; T. S. Eliot (UK) *Four Quartets*

Politics and Wars

US President Franklin D. Roosevelt dies; is succeeded by Vice-President Harry S. Truman as 33rd President • World War Two continues; in Europe, a German counteroffensive in the Ardennes region of Belgium is broken; US, British and allied troops cross the Rhine River; Russian forces capture Warsaw, Cracow, Tilsit and Berlin; in Italy, Communist partisans capture and execute discredited dictator Benito Mussolini; two days later, on April 30, German dictator Adolf Hitler commits suicide in the ruins of Berlin; Germany surrenders unconditionally • May 8 is declared VE (Victory in Europe) Day • Potsdam Conference: Harry S. Truman (US), Josef Stalin (USSR), and Winston S. Churchill and Clement R. Attlee (UK)—meet to settle Germany's future • In Britain, landslide election brings Labour Party to power; Attlee replaces Churchill as prime minister • In the Pacific theater, US troops capture Okinawa; on August 6 and 9 US bombers drop atomic bombs on Hiroshima and Nagasaki, Japan; Japan surrenders; VJ (Victory over Japan) Day, August 14, marks end of World War Two • US troops occupy Japan • The United Nations Organization comes into formal existence (October 24) • Vietnam (part of French Indo-China) becomes independent, with Ho Chi Minh as president

Arts and Letters

PAINTING: Stuart Davis (US), *For Internal Use Only*; MUSIC: Dmitri Shostakovich (USSR), 9th symphony; Benjamin Britten (UK), opera *Peter Grimes*; LITERATURE: George Orwell (UK), *Animal Farm*; Kathleen Winsor (US), *Forever Amber*

Politics and Wars

The League of Nations is wound up • The United Nations General Assembly and Security Council meet in London; resume in New York, which becomes the UN's permanent headquarters; Trygve Lie (Norw), is elected secretary-general • Albania, Bulgaria, Yugoslavia and Czechoslovakia adopt Communist governments • Statesman Winston S. Churchill (UK) uses the phrase "Iron Curtain" in a speech at Fulton, Mo.; Transjordan becomes the kingdom of Jordan • Lebanon becomes independent • King Vittorio Emanuele III of Italy abdicates; is succeeded by son, Umberto II, who leaves Italy after referendum favoring a republic • Greek referendum favors the return of the monarchy • Juan Perón becomes president of Argentina • The Nuremburg Tribunal passes death sentences on 12 Nazi (German National Socialist) leaders for war crimes; others are jailed • The Philippines become an independent republic

Arts and Letters

PAINTING: Marc Chagall (Russ), *Cow with Umbrella*; MUSIC: Benjamin Britten (UK), opera *The Rape of Lucretia*; Gian Carlo Menotti (US), opera *The Medium*; LITERATURE: Robert Penn Warren (US), *All the King's Men*; Edmund Wilson (US), *Memoirs of Hecate County*; Jean Cocteau (Fr), play *The Two-headed Eagle*; Terence Rattigan (UK), play *The Winslow Boy*; Eugene O'Neill (US), *The Iceman Cometh*; FILM: *The Best Years of Our Lives* (William Wyler)

Social and Economic

US Supreme Court declares the segregation of Negroes on interstate buses unconstitutional

Politics and Wars

Arabs and Jews reject proposals for the partition of Palestine, currently under British mandate; Britain refers question to the UN, which approves a partition plan with an internationalized Jerusalem against strong Arab opposition • Fighting between Dutch and Indonesians is renewed; UN calls for ceasefire • Partition of India: Independence creates separate dominions of India (Hindu) and Pakistan (Muslim); riots in the Punjab follow; Indian absorption of Kashmir (which has Muslim population) creates crisis • Italy gives up its North African colonies and loses territory to Yugoslavia and Greece • Burma becomes an independent republic • Ceylon (Sri Lanka) gains independence as a dominion

Arts and Letters

PAINTING: Maurice de Vlaminck (Fr), *A Bunch of Flowers*; SCULPTURE: Albert Giacometti (Switz), *The Pointing Man*; ARCHITECTURE: Le Corbusier (Fr), Unité d'Habitation, Marseilles; MUSIC: Benjamin Britten (UK), opera *Albert Herring*; Gian Carlo Menotti (US), opera *The Telephone*; LITERATURE: Tennessee Williams (US), play *A Streetcar Named Desire*; *The Diary of Anne Frank* (Neth) is published posthumously; John Gunther (US), *Inside USA*

Social and Economic

General Agreement on Tariffs and Trades (GATT) is signed by 23 countries in Geneva (Switz) • Marshall Plan providing US aid for European recovery is introduced

Religion and Philosophy

A shepherd boy discovers the Dead Sea Scrolls at Qumran, Jordan

Politics and Wars

Indian religious leader Mohandas K. Gandhi is assassinated by a Hindu fanatic at Porbandar, India • The "Cold War" is at its height: Russians leave the Allied Control Commission in Germany and begin a blockade of West Berlin; Western Powers start a successful airlift in reply • British mandate in Palestine ends: Jews proclaim the State of Israel, which is immediately recognized by the USA; an Arab-Israeli war begins: UN orders ceasefire and appoints Count Bernadotte (Swe) as mediator, Bernadotte is assassinated by Jewish terrorists • Yugoslavia is expelled from the Cominform • Republic of Korea is established with Seoul as its capital • Communist North Korea is established as a rival republic • Harry S. Truman is reelected President of the USA

Arts and Letters

PAINTING: Jackson Pollock (US), *Composition No. 1*; Fernand Lèger (Fr), *Homage to David*; Ben Shahn (US), *Miners' Wives*; MUSIC: Bohuslav Martinů (Czech), 7th string quartet; Richard Strauss (Ger), *Four Last Songs*; Cole Porter (US), musical *Kiss Me, Kate*; LITERATURE: Norman Mailer (US), *The Naked and the Dead*; Graham Greene (UK), *The Heart of the Matter*; Alan Paton (S Afr), *Cry the Beloved Country*; Evelyn Waugh (UK), *The Loved One*; Christopher Fry (UK), play *The Lady's not for Burning*; FILMS: *The Fallen Idol* (Carol Reed); *Bicycle Thieves* (Vittorio de Sica)

Science and Discovery

John Bardeen, Walter Brattain and William Shockley (US) invent the transistor

USA—**Harry S. Truman** ───────────────────────────

UK—**George VI** ──────────────────────────────

Politics and Wars

Harry S. Truman begins a second term as president of the USA • Communist forces under Mao Tse-tung seize power in China; President Chiang Kai-shek and his Nationalist forces withdraw to Formosa • Belgium, Britain, Canada, Denmark, France, Iceland, Italy, Luxembourg, the Netherlands, Norway, Portugal and the USA pledge mutual assistance in the North Atlantic Treaty • The Council of Europe is established in Strasbourg • West Germany becomes the German Federal Republic, with Konrad Adenauer as Chancellor and Bonn as its capital • The USSR ends its blockade of Berlin • The East German Democratic Republic (a Communist state) is created • India becomes a republic within the British Commonwealth • The USA withdraws its occupying forces from South Korea • Siam changes its name to Thailand • Eire becomes the Republic of Ireland and leaves the British Commonwealth • Newfoundland becomes a Canadian province

Arts and Letters

PAINTING: Pablo Picasso (Sp), *Woman in a Fish Hat*; Graham Sutherland (UK), portrait *W. Somerset Maugham*; MUSIC: Arthur Bliss (UK), opera *The Olympians*; Richard Rodgers and Oscar Hammerstein II (US), musical *South Pacific*; Béla Bartók (Hung), viola concerto; LITERATURE: George Orwell (UK), *1984*; Simone de Beauvoir (Fr), *The Second Sex*; Arthur Miller (US), play *Death of a Salesman*; T. S. Eliot (UK), play *The Cocktail Party*; Kenneth Clark (UK), *Landscape into Art*; FILM: *The Third Man* (Carol Reed)

Science and Discovery

Philip S. Hench (US) and Edward C. Kendall (US) first use cortisone in the treatment of rheumatism • Russians test their first atomic bomb

Religion and Philosophy

The Vatican decrees excommunication for Roman Catholics who practice or preach Communism

Social and Economic

US president Harry S. Truman calls for a program of technical aid to underdeveloped countries • In Britain, clothes rationing ends and the iron and steel industries are nationalized

Other Events

US State Department official Alger Hiss is convicted of spying for the USSR

Politics and Wars

The USSR announces it has the atomic bomb • The US Atomic Energy Commission begins the development of a hydrogen bomb • The McCarthy Committee (named for its chairman, Senator Joseph McCarthy), begins a "witchhunt" of Communists in the USA • The UN transfers British trusteeship over Italian Somaliland to Italy for 10 years • The German Federal Republic becomes a member of the Council of Europe • West German Chancellor Konrad Adenauer proposes an economic union between Germany and France • The Korean War begins when North Korean troops invade South Korea; the UN sends troops under General Douglas MacArthur (US) to aid South Korea; after initial successes by North, UN forces recapture Seoul, South Korean capital, but are then forced to retreat • Chinese forces come to the aid of the North Koreans • Chinese troops invade Tibet

Arts and Letters

PAINTING: Marc Chagall (Fr), *King David*; SCULPTURE: Albert Giacometti (Switz), *Seven Figures and a Head*; MUSIC: Gian Carlo Menotti (US), opera *The Consul*; Frank Loesser and Abe Burrows (US), musical *Guys and Dolls*; LITERATURE: James Boswell (UK), *London Journal* (published 146 years after his death); Ezra Pound (US), *Seventy Cantos*; Ernest Hemingway (US), *Across the River and Into the Trees*; FILM: *La Ronde* (Max Ophuls, Ger), *Los Olvidados* (Luis Bunuel)

Science and Discovery
Chemist Glenn T. Seaborg (US) discovers the radioactive element californium • Explorer Thor Heyerdahl (Nor), publishes *The Kon-Tiki Expedition* • The Danish research ship *Galathea* investigates deep-sea organisms in the Pacific Ocean

Religion and Philosophy
The National Council of Churches is established in the USA • Pope Pius XII pronounces the dogma (official belief) of the bodily assumption of the Virgin Mary

Social and Economic
A European Coal and Steel Community plan is proposed

Other Events
The Stone of Scone, on which Scottish kings were crowned, is stolen from Westminster Abbey, London (Eng), by Scottish nationalists

Politics and Wars
The Korean War continues: with difficulty, UN forces supporting South Korea establish a front north of the border; General Douglas MacArthur (US), the UN commander, wants to attack China; President Harry S. Truman dismisses him; truce talks begin • The Labour Party is defeated in British elections: Winston S. Churchill returns as Prime Minister • Egypt abrogates treaties with Britain • In Iran, nationalist leader Muhammad Mosadeq becomes premier and nationalizes Iran's oil industry • The Japanese Peace Treaty is signed at San Francisco • India–Pakistan dispute over Kashmir continues; Prime Minister Ali Khan of Pakistan is assassinated • Leopold III of the Belgians abdicates; is succeeded by his son, Baudouin • King Abdullah of Jordan is assassinated in Jerusalem • British diplomats Guy Burgess and Donald Maclean, who were spying for the Russians, flee to the USSR

Arts and Letters
PAINTING: Pablo Picasso (Sp), *Massacre in Korea*; Salvador Dali (Sp), *Christ of St. John on the Cross*; MUSIC: Igor Stravinsky (US), opera *The Rake's Progress*; Benjamin Britten (UK), opera *Billy Budd*; Ralph Vaughan Williams (UK), opera *A Pilgrim's Progress*; Gian Carlo Menotti (US), TV opera *Amahl and the Night Visitors*; LITERATURE: C. P. Snow (UK), *The Masters*; Herman Wouk (US), *The Caine Mutiny*; Nicholas Monsarrat (UK), *The Cruel Sea*; J. D. Salinger (US), *The Catcher in the Rye*; Peter Ustinov (UK), play *The Love of Four Colonels*

Science and Discovery
Electricity is produced by atomic energy in the USA • The Comet, first jet airliner, is developed in Britain

Social and Economic
President Truman calls in troops during US railroad strike • The Colombo Plan for the development of South and Southeast Asian countries begins • The European Coal and Steel Community plan is agreed

Other Events
The Festival of Britain is held in London to mark the centenary of the Great Exhibition

USA—**Harry S. Truman** ————————————————— ☐ **Dwight D. Eisenhower** ——

UK—**George VI** ——————— ☐ **Elizabeth II** ————————————————

Politics and Wars

Vincent Massey becomes governor-general of Canada—first Canadian to hold the office • Britain's King George VI dies; is succeeded by his daughter, Elizabeth II • Korean war continues, and so do the armistice talks ; China accuses the USA of using germ warfare in Korea; USA denies the charges • Dispute between Britain and Iran after Iranian nationalization of oil continues • Coup d'etat in Egypt: army officers led by General Muhammad Neguib and Colonel Gamal Abdul Nasser seize power; King Farouk is forced to abdicate in favor of his baby son, Fuad II; Egyptian constituion of 1923 is abolished • In Kenya, activities of Mau-Mau terrorists lead to a state of emergency • In Jordan, King Talal is forced to abdicate on mental grounds; he is succeeded by his son, Hussein • President Chaim Weizzmann of Israel dies: is succeeded by Itzhak Ben-Zvi • Former president Fulgencio Batista of Cuba returns to power after army overthrow corrupt government of Carlos Socarrás; Batista establishes a brutal dictatorship • General Dwight D. Eisenhower resigns from post of Supreme Allied Commander in Europe and from US Army to fight election on Republican ticket; he is elected President of the USA in a landslide victory

Arts and Letters

PAINTING: Jackson Pollock (US), *Convergence*; Raoul Dufy (Fr), *The Pink Violin*; SCULPTURE: Barbara Hepworth (UK), *Statue* (abstract); Jacob Epstein (UK), *Madonna and Child*; MUSIC: Igor Stravinsky (US), opera *Babel*; Sergei Prokofiev (USSR), 7th symphony; Roy Harris (US), 7th symphony; Leonard Bernstein (US), opera

Trouble in Tahiti; Ralph Vaughan Williams (UK), *Romance* for harmonica and orchestra; LITERATURE: Ernest Hemingway (US), *The Old Man and the Sea*; Ray Bradbury (US), *The Illustrated Man*; Evelyn Waugh (UK), *Men at Arms*; Truman Capote (US), *The Grass Harp*; Edna Ferber (US), *Giant*; John Steinbeck (US), *East of Eden*; Samuel Beckett (Ire), play *Waiting for Godot*; Agatha Christie (UK), play *The Mousetrap*; FILMS *Limelight* (Charles Chaplin); *High Noon* (Fred Zinnemann)

Science and Discovery

Coelacanth fish, believed to be extinct since prehistoric times, is caught alive near South Africa • Building of first (US) atomic-powered submarine begins • First British atomic bomb tests take place • USA explodes first hydrogen bomb in the Pacific Ocean area

Religion and Philosophy

US theologian Reinhold Niebuhr writes *Christ and Culture*

Social and Economic

The European Coal and Steel community begins operations • Rhône Valley (Fr) hydroelectric power station is opened • Britain abolishes identity cards (a wartime measure)

Politics and Wars

Dwight D. Eisenhower becomes 34th President of the USA • Dag Hammarskjöld (Swe) becomes 2nd Secretary-general of the UN on retirement of Trygve Lie (Nor) • Egypt becomes a republic; General Muhammad Neguib as president is given dictatorial powers • In the USSR, death of dictator Josef Stalin leads to a struggle for power; main offices are held by Georgy M. Malenkov, as head of government, Nikita S. Khrushchev, First Secretary of the Communist Party, Nikolai Bulganin, defense minister, and Vyacheslav Molotov, foreign minister; police chief Lavrenty Beria is removed from office and shot • The Korean War ends with the signing of a peace treaty at Panmunjon; the USA and South Korea sign a mutual defense treaty • In Kenya, statesman Jomo Kenyatta, president of the Kenya African Union, is arrested for allegedly supporting Mau Mau terrorist activities • Israeli prime minister David Ben Gurion resigns; is succeeded by Mose Sharett • Britain sends troops to British Guiana to prevent a Communist take-over • The French government deposes the Sultan of Morocco • An attempted rising against the Communist government of East Berlin fails • Britain signs an alliance with Libya • The Kabaka of Buganda goes into exile • Former resistance leader Josip Tito becomes first president of Yugoslavia • Anti-British premier Mohammad Mosadeq falls from power in Iran; Britain and Iran resume diplomatic relations

Arts and Letters

PAINTING: Ben Nicholson (UK), *September 1953*; Georges Braque (Fr), *Apples*; SCULPTURE: Henry Moore (UK),

King and Queen; Reg Butler (UK), *The Unknown Political Prisoner*; MUSIC: Ralph Vaughan Williams (UK), 7th symphony; William Walton (UK), coronation march *Orb and Sceptre*; Dmitri Shostakovich (USSR), 10th symphony; Benjamin Britten (UK), opera *Gloriana*; Bohuslav Martinů (Czech), operas *What Men Live By* and *The Marriage*; Darius Milhaud (Fr), opera *David*; William Shuman (US), opera *Mighty Casey*; Karlheinz Stockhausen (Ger), *Electronic Study I*; Leonard Bernstein (US), musical *Wonderful Town*; LITERATURE: Saul Bellow (US), *The Adventures of Augie March*; Charles Morgan (UK), play *The Burning Glass*; Cecil Woodham Smith (UK), *The Reason Why*; Ian Fleming (UK), first "James Bond" novel *Casino Royale*; William Faulkner (US), *Requiem for a Nun*; T. S. Eliot (UK), play *The Confidential Clerk*; Arthur Miller (US), *The Crucible*

Science and Discovery
Myxamatosis epidemic almost destroys Britain's rabbit population • Edmund Hillary (NZ) and Sherpa Tenzing Norgay (Nepal), in British team led by Colonel John Hunt, make the first ascent of Mount Everest, world's highest mountain • An international nuclear research station is established at Meyrin (Switz) • USSR explodes a hydrogen bomb • An observatory to study cosmic rays is established at Mount Wrangell, Alaska • B. F. Skinner (US) writes *Science and Human Behavior*

Other Events
Flood disasters on the east coast of Britain and in the Netherlands claim over 2,000 victims

Politics and Wars
The USSR rejects Western Powers' proposals for the reunification of Germany • Theodor Heuss is elected president of the German Federal Republic • The occupation of West Germany ends • The Western European Union is formed • Trieste is divided between Italy and Yugoslavia • Colonel Gamel Abdul Nasser overthrows the régime of General Muhammad Neguib in Egypt and becomes premier and military governor; Egypt and Britain sign agreement for the evacuation of British troops from the Suez Canal Zone • Communist rebel forces in Indo-China take the towns of Hanoi and Dien Bien Phu from the French; under an armistice, France recognizes the independence of Laos, Cambodia, and Vietnam; the Communists are to evacuate South Vietnam and the French agree to leave North Vietnam • The South-East Asian Defence Treaty is signed by Australia, Britain, France, New Zealand, Pakistan, the Philippines, Thailand and the USA • The USA and Japan reach a mutual defense agreement • The French government sends 20,000 troops to Algeria to quell a nationalist revolt • Campaign in Cyprus (a British colony) for *enosis* (union with Greece) gets under way • Following elections in Gold Coast (Ghana), independence leader Dr. Kwame Nkrumah becomes the first prime minister of the British colony • The US Senate committee under Senator Joseph R. McCarthy continues its "witch-hunt" for Communists; eventually the Senate formally condemns McCarthy's activities

Arts and Letters
PAINTING: Pablo Picasso (Sp), *Sylvette*; Graham Sutherland (UK), portrait *Winston S. Churchill*; Marc Chagall (Fr), *The Red Roofs*; ARCHITECTURE: Basil Spence (UK), Coventry Cathedral; MUSIC: Quincy Porter (US), concerto for two pianos and orchestra; Roy Harris (US), *Symphonic Fantasy*; Edmund Rubbra (UK), 6th symphony; Aaron Copland (US), opera *The Tender Land*; Gian Carlo Menotti (US), opera *The Saint of Bleeker Street*; Benjamin Britten (UK), opera *The Turn of the Screw*; William Walton (UK), opera *Troilus and Cressida*; Arnold Schönberg (US), opera *Moses and Aaron*; LITERATURE: William Golding (UK), *Lord of the Flies*; John Masters (UK), *Bhowani Junction*; J. R. R. Tolkien (UK), *The Fellowship of the Ring*; C. P. Snow (UK), *The New Men*; John Steinbeck (US), *Sweet Thursday*; Françoise Sagan (Fr), *Bonjour Tristesse*; Dylan Thomas (UK), radio play *Under Milk Wood*; Tennessee Williams (US), play *Cat on a Hot Tin Roof*; John van Druten (US), play *I am a Camera*; Terence Rattigan (UK), play *Separate Tables*; FILMS: *The Seven Samurai* (Akira Kurosawa); *On the Waterfront* (Elia Kazan); *The Living Desert* (Walt Disney)

Science and Discovery
First vertical-take-off airplane ("Flying Bedstead") is developed in Britain

Social and Economic
Racial segregation in US schools is declared unconstitutional by the Supreme Court

Other Events
Medical student Roger Bannister (UK) runs the first under-4-minute mile in 3 min. 59.4 sec.

USA—**Dwight D. Eisenhower** ——————————————————————————
UK—**Elizabeth II** ——————————————————————————

Politics and Wars

British prime minister Winston S. Churchill (80) resigns; is succeeded by Foreign Secretary Anthony Eden • The USSR formally ends World War Two with Germany • West Germany becomes a member of the North Atlantic Treaty Organization (NATO) • The USSR creates the Warsaw Pact organization as rival to NATO • Britain, France, the USA and USSR end the military occupation of Austria and recognize its independence • The USSR and Yugoslavia sign a treaty of friendship • Georgy M. Malenkov resigns as premier of the USSR, and is succeeded by Nikolai Bulganin • At a "summit" conference at Geneva (Switz), the USSR refuses to discuss German reunification • UN accepts the principle of universal membership: 14 hitherto-excluded nations are admitted to membership; France withdraws temporarily because of criticisms of its Algerian policy • In Algeria, independence fighters protesting French rule carry out sabotage and killings • French settlers at Oved Zem, Morocco, are massacred • Violence breaks out in Cyprus over *enosis* (union with Greece); a state of emergency is declared; anti-Greek riots in Turkey follow • South Vietnam is proclaimed a republic • An uprising in Argentina results in the resignation and exile of president Juan Perón • In Hungary, moderate prime minister Imre Nagy is dismissed by the Communist Party following attempted reforms

Arts and Letters

PAINTING: Pietro Annigoni (It), portrait *Queen Elizabeth II*; John Bratby (UK), *Still Life with Chip-fryer*; Salvador Dali (Sp), *The Lord's Supper*; Oskar Kokoschka (UK), triptych *Thermopylae*; SCULPTURE: Lynn Chadwick (UK), *Winged Figures*; ARCHITECTURE: Eero Saarinen (US), General Motors Center, Warren, Mich; MUSIC: Michael Tippett (UK), opera *The Midsummer Marriage*; Rolf Liebermann (US), opera *School for Wives*; Sergei Prokofiev (USSR), opera *The Fiery Angel*; Walter Piston (US), 5th symphony; Darius Milhaud (Fr), 6th symphony; LITERATURE: Vladimir Nabokov (US), *Lolita*; John O'Hara (US), *Ten North Frederick*; Sloan Wilson (US), *The Man in the Grey Flannel Suit*; Richard Church (UK), *Over the Bridge*; Graham Greene (UK), *The Quiet American;* Evelyn Waugh (UK), *Officers and Gentlemen*; Joyce Cary (UK), *Not Honour More*; Arthur Miller (US), play *A View from the Bridge*; Stephen Spender (UK), *Collected Poems*; William Empson (UK), *Collected Poems*; FILMS: Richard III (Laurence Olivier); *The Seven Year Itch* (Billy Wilder); *Rebel Without a Cause* (Nicholas Ray)

Science and Discovery

The use of Ultra High Frequency (UHF) radio waves is developed at the Massachusetts Institute of Technology • Physician Jonas E. Salk (US) develops an anti-poliomyelitis vaccine • Astronomer B. F. Burk (US) discovers the emission of radio waves from the planet Jupiter

Social and Economic

Delegates from 72 countries discuss the peaceful uses of atomic energy at Geneva • The American Federation· of Labor and Congress of Industrial Organizations combine in one organization, the·A.F.L.– C.I.O.

Politics and Wars

The USA and Britain sign an atomic agreement • Colonel Gamel Abdul Nasser becomes president of Egypt • British troops evacuate the Suez Canal Zone • Nasser seizes the canal —largely owned by Britain and France, who refer the question to the United Nations; in the Security Council, the USSR vetoes a compromise solution • Israeli troops invade Egypt; France and Britain issue an ultimatum to both countries; Anglo-French forces invade Egypt to protect the canal; the USSR threatens to intervene • A US-backed resolution in the UN calls for a ceasefire and an international force is sent to Egypt to enforce it; British and French troops withdraw • Revolution breaks out in Hungary following installation of new Prime Minister E. Gero, who affirms strict Communist rule; a peaceful student procession in Budapest is fired on by police, and rebellion flares; Communist institutions are overthrown; moderate leader Imre Nagy is recalled to lead a coalition government; Soviet troops withdraw; Nagy takes Hungary out of the Warsaw Pact, and immediately Soviet forces with tanks invade Hungary; after savage fighting Communist rule is restored, Nagy is executed, and 150,000 refugees escape to the West • The UN censures the USSR for its intervention, but takes no action • Japan is admitted to the UN • France grants independence to Tunisia and Morocco • The French government decides to keep Algeria as part of France and sends 500,000 soldiers to Algeria to quell revolts • Pakistan adopts a new constitution making it an "Islamic republic" • India absorbs former French possessions in the country • Sudan becomes independent •

Dwight D. Eisenhower is re-elected President of the USA

Arts and Letters

SCULPTURE: Barbara Hepworth (UK), *Orpheus*; Richard Lippold (US), *Variation Within a Sphere, No 10: The Sun*; ARCHITECTURE: Eero Saarinen (US), US Embassy, London; Jøern Utzon (Den), Sydney Opera House (Austral); MUSIC: Humphrey Searle (UK), ballet *Noctambules*; Hans Werner Henze (Ger), opera *King Hirsch;* Ralph Vaughan Williams (UK), 8th symphony; Gian Carlo Menotti (US), opera *The Unicorn, the Gorgon and the Manticore*; Leonard Bernstein (US), musical *Candide*; Alan Jay Lerner and Frederick Loewe (US), musical *My Fair Lady*; LITERATURE: Winston S. Churchill (UK), *A History of the English-Speaking Peoples*; Angus Wilson (UK), *Anglo-Saxon Attitudes* and play *The Mulberry Bush*; Grace Metalious (US), *Peyton Place*; Rose Macaulay (UK), *The Towers of Trebizond*; Nicholas Montsarrat (UK), *The Tribe that Lost Its Head*; Colin Wilson (UK), *The Outsider*; Brendan Behan (Ire), play *The Quare Fellow*; Jean Anouilh (Fr), play *The Waltz of the Toreadors*; John Osborne (UK), play *Look Back in Anger*; FILMS: *The King and I*; *A Town Like Alice*; *Baby Doll* (Elia Kazan); *The Seventh Seal* (Ingmar Bergman)

Science and Discovery

F. W. Müller (Switz) develops the ion microscope, with $2\frac{3}{4}$ million magnification • US scientists at Los Alamos Laboratory, Cal., discover an atomic particle, the neutrino • A visual telephone is devised by US technicians

Politics and Wars

Dwight D. Eisenhower begins his second term as President of the USA • Britain's prime minister Anthony Eden resigns, seriously ill; he is succeeded by Harold Macmillan; later, Macmillan and Eisenhower meet at the Bermuda Conference to restore good Anglo–US relations, which were strained by British intervention in Egypt over the Suez Canal • Following the Suez dispute, Israeli forces withdraw from Sinai, and Egypt reopens the Suez Canal to shipping • Gold Coast, British West African colony, becomes independent as Ghana • Tunisia is declared a republic, with premier Habib Bourgiba as its first president • Internal crisis in Jordan: King Hussein proclaims martial law • Shake-up in government of the USSR: Andrei Gromyko becomes foreign minister; Vyacheslav Molotov, Georgy Malenkov, and Dmitri Shepilov are sacked from the Presidium of the Central Committee of the Communist Party • King Haakon of Norway dies; he is succeeded by his son Olav V • Dag Hammarskjöld (Swe), is re-elected UN Secretary-General for a second five-year term • Cuban dictator Fulgencio Batista suspends the constitution following a landing by Communist rebels headed by Fidel Castro; Castro's men fight a guerrilla campaign

Arts and Letters

PAINTING: Graham Sutherland (UK), portrait *Princess Gourielli*; SCULPTURE: Henry Moore (UK), *Seated Woman*; Jacob Epstein (UK), *Christ in Majesty*; ARCHITECTURE: Le Corbusier (Fr), Tokio Museum (Jap); MUSIC: William Walton (UK), cello concerto; Malcolm Arnold (UK), 3rd symphony; Elliott Carter (US), *Variations for Orchestra*; Jean Françaix

(Fr), opera *King Midas*; Paul Hindemith (Ger), opera *The Harmony of the World*; Igor Stravinsky (US), ballet *Agon*; Benjamin Britten (UK), ballet *The Prince of the Pagodas*; Leonard Bernstein (US), musical *West Side Story*; LITERATURE: John Braine (UK), *Room at the Top*; Lawrence Durrell (UK), *Bitter Lemons* and *Justine*; Iris Murdoch (UK), *The Sandcastle*; William Faulkner (US), *The Town*; Dr. Seuss (US), *The Cat in the Hat*; William Saroyan (US), *The Cave Dwellers*; Jack Kerouac (US), *On the Road*; Patrick White (Austral), *Voss*; Eugene O'Neill (US), posthumous play *A Long Day's Journey into Night*; John Osborne (UK), play *The Entertainer*; Samuel Beckett (Ire), play *Endgame*; Robert Bolt (UK), play *The Flowering Cherry*; FILMS: *Wild Strawberries* (Ingmar Bergman); *A King in New York* (Charles Chaplin), *The Bridge on the River Kwai* (David Lean)

Science and Discovery

The Space Age begins: Russians launch *Sputnik I*, the world's first unmanned space-craft, which orbits the Earth; *Sputnik 2* carries a dog

Social and Economic

US Civil Rights Act establishes a commission to investigate denials of civil rights • Schools segregation issue causes violence at Little Rock, Ark.: troops are used to restore order • Egypt and Iran give the vote to women • Britain abolishes the death penalty for all but a few offenses • The Treaty of Rome establishes the European Economic Community of Belgium, France, West Germany, Italy, Luxembourg and the Netherlands

USA—**Dwight D. Eisenhower** ————————————————————

UK—**Elizabeth II** ———————————————————————————————

Politics and Wars

The USA and Canada establish the North American Air Defense Command • Continuing war in Algeria leads to crisis in France; World War Two hero General Charles de Gaulle is called out of retirement to become prime minister, and forms a "government of national safety"; following a general election his party sweeps to power, pledged to introduce a new constituion • At the invitation of the Lebanese government, US troops land in Lebanon to restore order following disturbances; similarly, British troops are sent to Jordan at the request of King Hussein; both forces later withdraw • Egypt and Syria unite to form the United Arab Republic, with Egypt's president Gamal Abdul Nasser as head of state; Yemen later joins the UAR • Iraq and Jordan unite to form the Arab Federation, headed by King Feisal of Iraq; on his assassination, the federation is dissolved • The United Arab Republic breaks off diplomatic relations with Jordan • New shake-up in the USSR: Nikita Krushchev succeeds Nikolai Bulganin as chairman of the Council of Ministers (premier); Bulganin is dismissed from the Communist Party Presidium

Arts and Letters

PAINTING: James Brooks (US), *Acanda*; SCULPTURE: Henry Moore (UK), *Reclining Figure* (for the UNESCO Building, Paris); Alexander Calder (US), *Monumental Mobile*; ARCHITECTURE: Oscar Niemeyer (Braz), the Presidential Palace, Brasilia; Ludwig Mies van der Rohe (US), the Seagram Building, New York City; MUSIC: Dmĭtri Shostakovich (USSR), 11th symphony; Pierre Boulez (Fr), cantata *Le Visage nuptial*; Benjamin Britten (UK), *Noye's Fludde*; Ralph Vaughan Williams (UK), 9th symphony; Ildebrando Pizzetti (It), opera *Murder in the Cathedral*; Humphrey Searle (UK), opera *Diary of a Madman*; Gian Carlo Menotti (US), opera *Maria Golovin*; LITERATURE: Boris Pasternak (USSR), *Doctor Zhivago*; Iris Murdoch (UK), *The Bell*; Truman Capote (US), *Breakfast at Tiffany's*; Aldous Huxley (UK), *Brave New World Revisited*; J. G. Cozzens (US), *By Love Possessed*; T. H. White (UK), *The Sword in the Stone*; Mazo de la Roche (Can), *Centenary at Jalna*; J. Edgar Hoover (US), *Masters of Deceit*; Alberto Moravia (It), *Two Women*; Harold Pinter (UK), play *The Birthday Party*; T. S. Eliot (UK), play *The Elder Statesman*

Science and Discovery

Stereophonic phonograph recording is developed in Britain • The USA launches Earth satellite *Explorer I* and other spacecraft • A radiation belt around the Earth is discovered by James A. Van Allen (US) • The USSR launches *Sputnik 3*, an unmanned spacecraft • The US nuclear submarine *Nautilus* travels under the Arctic icecap

Religion and Philosophy

Pope Pius XII dies; is succeeded by John XXIII

Social and Economic

US unemployment rises to 5,000,000 • Race riots take place in London and Nottingham (UK) • Britain's parliament introduces life peerages—non-hereditary titles whose holders are entitled to seats in the House of Lords • The US Supreme Court orders admission of black children to school in Little Rock, Ark

Politics and Wars

Alaska becomes the 49th State of the USA, and Hawaii the 50th • In Cuba, Communist guerilla leader Fidel Castro, after a two-year campaign, overthrows the government of Fulgencio Batista, and becomes premier; Castro seizes American-owned sugar firms and introduces land reforms • In France, General Charles de Gaulle is proclaimed president of the 5th Republic • The Algerian crisis continues, with French settlers anxious to maintain union with France; but de Gaulle declares that Algerians should have the right to determine their own future • Tibetans rebel against occupying Chinese troops; when the rising fails their leader, the Dalai Lama, escapes to India • Anti-Belgian demonstrations break out in the Belgian Congo (Zaïre) • The USA joins the Baghdad Pact (alliance of Turkey, Iraq, Iran); alliance's name is changed to Central Treaty Organization (CENTO) • By agreement of Britain, Turkey and Greece; Cyprus becomes an independent republic, but the British retain military bases there; the exiled Greek-Cypriot leader Archbishop Makarios returns to the island • The French colonies of Senegal and Sudan unite to become the independent Federal State of Mali • Sean O'Kelly retires as president of the Irish Republic; is succeeded by Prime Minister Eamonn de Valera, former independence leader • Chinese troops invade north-eastern India • The UN votes not to admit Communist China to membership; China's UN seat continues to be occupied by the Nationalist Chinese of Formosa, led by Chiang Kai-shek

Arts and Letters
PAINTING: John Bratby (UK), *Coach-House Door*; Joan Miró (Sp), murals for UNESCO building, Paris; Ben Nicholson (UK), abstract *February 1959*; SCULPTURE: Barbara Hepworth (UK), *Meridian*; ARCHITECTURE: Frank Lloyd Wright (US), Guggenheim Art Museum, New York City; MUSIC: Francis Poulenc (Fr), opera *La Voix humaine*; Pierre Boulez (Fr), quartet *Livre du quattuor*; LITERATURE: William Faulkner (US), *The Mansion*; Saul Bellow (US), *Henderson the Rain King*; Norman Mailer (US), *Advertisement for Myself*; Robert L. Taylor (US), *The Travels of Jamie McPheeters*; Laurie Lee (UK), *Cider with Rosie*; John Braine (UK), *The Vodi*; Shelagh Delaney (UK), play *A Taste of Honey*; Eugene Ionesco (Fr), play *The Rhinoceros*; Jean Anouilh (Fr), play *Becket*; Brendan Behan (Ire), play *The Hostage*; Arnold Wesker (UK), play *Roots*; FILMS: *Our Man in Havana* (Carol Reed); *La Dolce Vita* (Federico Fellini); *Ben Hur* (William Wyler)

Science and Discovery
Christopher Cockerell (UK) invents the hovercraft • Russian spaceship *Lunik II* reaches the Moon • *Lunik III* photographs the "back" of the Moon

Social and Economic
The European Free Trade Association (EFTA) is created, providing trading links among Austria, Britain, Denmark, Norway, Portugal, Sweden and Switzerland • The UN General Assembly condemns apartheid and all forms of racial discrimination • The St. Lawrence Seaway (Canada/USA) is opened

Politics and Wars
British prime minister Harold Macmillan, in a speech to South African's parliament, declares that "a wind of change" is blowing through Africa • 14 African countries become independent: the Belgian Congo; British Somaliland, Nigeria and Togo; and former French colonies Cameroons, Central African Republic, Chad, Congo, Dahomey, Ivory Coast, the Malagasy Republic (Madagascar), Mauretania, Niger, Upper Volta; in addition British Cameroons joins with Cameroon, and British Somaliland with the former Italian colony of Somalia • Anti-apartheid demonstrations at Sharpeville, South Africa, lead to the shooting of 67 Africans • South African premier Hendrik Verwoerd survives assassination bid • Archbishop Makarios becomes first president of Cyprus republic • Marshal Kliment Voroshilov retires as president of the USSR; is succeeded by Leonid Brezhnev • Following independence of the former Belgian Congo, now Zaïre—the Congolese army mutinies; Belgium sends troops to restore order and Prime Minister Patrice Lumumba asks the UN for help; Moise Tshombe, premier of Congo's Katanga province, proclaims its independence; UN troops enter Katanga; Lumumba falls from power • The US government protests to Cuba over seizure of American property there; Cuba complains to the UN about alleged "US aggression" • Syngman Rhee resigns as premier of South Korea • An attempted revolt in Ethiopia fails • John F. Kennedy (Dem) is elected President of the USA

Arts and Letters
PAINTING: Arthur Boyd (Austral), *Half-Caste Bride*; John Bratby (UK), *Gloria with Sunflower*; MUSIC: Arthur Bliss (UK), *Tobias and the Angel*; Pierre Boulez (Fr), *Portrait of Mallarmé*; Benjamin Britten (UK), opera *A Midsummer Night's Dream*; Elliott Carter (US), 2nd string quartet; Hans Werner Henze (Ger), opera *The Prince of Homberg*; Karlheinz Stockhausen (Ger), electronic music *Kontakte*; Lionel Bart (UK), musical *Oliver!*; LITERATURE: John Updike (US), *Rabiit Run*; Lawrence Durrell (UK), *Clea*; Gavin Maxwell (UK), *Ring of Bright Water*; William L. Shirer (US), *The Rise and Fall of the Third Reich*; John O'Hara (US), *Ourselves to Know*; Harper Lee (US), *To Kill a Mockingbird*; Vance Packard (US), *The Waste Makers*; John Betjeman (UK), verse autobiography *Summoned by Bells*; Robert Bolt (UK), play *A Man for all Seasons*; Harold Pinter (UK), *The Caretaker*; Terence Rattigan (UK), play *Ross*; FILMS: *Exodus* (Otto Preminger); *Saturday Night and Sunday Morning* (Karel Reisz); *The Entertainer* (Laurence Olivier); *Psycho* (Alfred Hitchcock)

Science and Discovery
France explodes a nuclear bomb in the Sahara • American scientists develop laser beams • A US Navy bathyscaphe descends nearly 36,000 feet in the Pacific Ocean

Social and Economic
Mrs. Bandaranaike (Ceylon) becomes the world's first woman prime minister

Other Events
An earthquake at Agadir, Morocco, kills 12,000 people

USA—**Dwight D. Eisenhower**—□ **John F. Kennedy**

UK—**Elizabeth II**

Politics and Wars

John Fitzgerald Kennedy becomes 35th President of the USA • US-supported invasion of Cuba by Cuban exiles at the "Bay of Pigs" fails; Kennedy admits responsibility for the invasion • East Germans build the Berlin Wall, sealing off East Berlin from West Berlin • Albanian links with China lead to Albania's dismissal from the Soviet bloc • UN troops occupy breakaway Congo province of Katanga, and its secession ends; Katangese murder Congo's ex-premier Patrice Lumumba • UN Secretary-General Dag Hammarskjöld (Swe) is killed in airplane crash in Africa; U Thant (Burma) succeeds him • After a *coup d'état*, Syria withdraws from the United Arab Republic • British African colonies of Tanganyika and Sierra Leone become independent • Jamaica leaves the West Indies Federation • The Union of South Africa becomes a republic and leaves the Commonwealth • India annexes Portuguese possessions in the Indian sub-continent • Mongolia becomes a member of the UN, but Communist China is again denied entry • In Ghana leading members of the Opposition are detained • US Supreme Court rules that the US Communist Party is foreign-dominated • German Nazi leader Adolf Eichmann, kidnapped by Israelis in South America, is tried for war crimes in Israel and condemned to death • Raphael Trujillo, dictator of the Dominican Republic since 1930, is assassinated

Arts and Letters

ARCHITECTURE: Eero Saarinen (US), TWA Building, Idlewild (Kennedy) Airport; MUSIC: Hans Werner Henze (Ger), opera *Elegy for Young Lovers*;

Samuel Barber (US), opera *Vanessa*; Walter Piston (US), 7th symphony; LITERATURE: Iris Murdoch (UK), *A Severed Head*; Richard Hughes (UK), *The Fox in the Attic*; Graham Greene (UK), *A Burnt-out Case*; Muriel Spark (UK), *The Prime of Miss Jean Brodie*; J. D. Salinger (US), *Franny and Zooey*; Joseph Heller (US), *Catch-22*; John Osborne (UK), play *Luther*; Harold Pinter (UK), play *The Collection*; Tennessee Williams (US), play *The Night of the Iguana*; FILMS: *El Cid* (Anthony Mann); *Boccaccio '70* (Federico Fellini); *Jules et Jim* (François Truffeau)

Science and Discovery

The USSR sends the first man (Yuri Gagarin) into space in the spaceship *Vostok* • The USA follows with Alan B. Shepard • Astronomer Martin Ryle (UK) advances the theory that the Universe changes with time • Francis H. C. Crick (UK) and James Watson (US) construct a model of the structure of DNA (deoxyribonucleic acid) • British scientists reflect radio waves back to Earth from Venus • Excavations at Pompeii reveal further remains

Social and Economic

The Latin-American Free Trade Association is established • President Kennedy sets up the Young American Peace Corps • A wages pause is introduced in Britain

Other Events

After a volcanic eruption in Tristan da Cunha, the population is evacuated to Britain • A hurricane in British Honduras (Belize) causes many deaths

Politics and Wars

Western Samoa becomes independent • USSR and Cuba sign a trade agreement, and the Russians establish a fishing fleet base in the island • Fighting and unrest continue in Algeria, until a referendum shows that 99 percent of voters favor independence; France agrees, and ceasefire follows; Ferhat Abbas becomes president of the new country • Attempt to assassinate French president Charles de Gaulle fails • Chinese troops invade northern India, but subsequently withdraw • The West Indies Federation is dissolved: Jamaica and Trinidad and Tobago become independent • In Africa, Uganda becomes independent, and Tanganyika becomes a republic within the Commonwealth, with Julius Nyerere as president • The USA establishes a military command in South Vietnam • Cuban crisis: US President John F. Kennedy announces that the Russians have built missile bases in Cuba; US warships blockade Cuba; USSR agrees to dismantle its bases, and the blockade ends • Malta demands independence from Britain • Communist China again fails to secure membership of the UN • Kennedy agrees to supply Britain with Polaris atomic missiles • In Britain, Admiralty clerk William Vassal is jailed for spying

Arts and Letters

TAPESTRY: Graham Sutherland (UK), tapestry for Coventry Cathedral; MUSIC: Michael Tippett (UK), opera *King Priam*; Benjamin Britten (UK), *War Requiem*; Norman Dello Joio (US), opera *Blood Moon*; Dmitri Shostakovich (USSR), 12th symphony; Igor Stravinsky (US), opera *The Flood*; LITERATURE: Alexander Solzhenitsyn (USSR), *One Day in the Life of Ivan Denisovich*; Katherine Anne Porter (US), *Ship of Fools*; T. H. White (US), *The Making of the President*; Anthony Sampson (UK), *The Anatomy of Britain*; William Faulkner (US), *The Reivers* (published posthumously); Boris Pasternak (USSR), *In the Interlude*; Roy Fuller (UK), *Collected Poems*; Edward Albee (US), play *Who's Afraid of Virginia Woolf?*; Arnold Wesker (UK), play *Chips with Everything*; Ken Kesey (US), *One Flew Over the Cuckoo's Nest*

Science and Discovery
The USA launches a communications satellite, *Telstar*, and puts three astronauts into orbit round the Earth • An unmanned US *Ranger* spacecraft reaches the Moon • Scientists discover that the drug thalidomide causes deformities in babies • Alexander Moulton (UK) designs a new form of bicycle

Religion and Philosophy
Latin is confirmed as the language of the Roman Catholic Church • The Second Vatican Council meets in Rome

Social and Economic
Anglo-French agreement is reached to construct the *Concorde* supersonic aircraft • An Act to control immigration (Commonwealth Immigration Act) is passed in Britain • The US Congress passes the Trade Expansion Act

Other Events
An earthquake in Iran kills 12,000 people • In Peru, more than 3,000 people die in an avalanche

Politics and Wars
The USA, USSR and Britain sign a nuclear test ban treaty, outlawing the above-ground testing of atomic weapons • A "hot line" telephone is established between Moscow and Washington, D.C. • British Labour Party leader Hugh Gaitskell dies; is succeeded by Harold Wilson • France withdraws its naval forces from the North Atlantic Treaty Organization • The British colonies of Malaya, North Borneo, Sarawak and Singapore unite to form the Federation of Malaysia • Nigeria and Kenya become republics within the British Commonwealth • Zanzibar becomes independent • The Organization of African Unity is established at Addis Ababa, Ethiopia • Britain's Secretary for War John Profumo denies involvement in call-girl scandal; then admits he was involved, and resigns • Peerage Act brings about constitutional change in Britain: peers are allowed to disclaim hereditary titles for their own lifetime, thus enabling them to stand for election to the House of Commons • British prime minister Harold Macmillan resigns on health grounds; he is succeeded by Foreign Secretary the Earl of Home, who resigns his peerage and, as Sir Alex Douglas-Home, is elected to the Commons • Martial law in South Vietnam follows the assassination of President Ngo Dinh Diem • US President John F. Kennedy is assassinated in Dallas, Tex.; he is succeeded by Vice-President Lyndon B. Johnson as 36th President; Lee Harvey Oswald is accused of the assassination, but is himself murdered by nightclub owner Jack Ruby before trial • The UN condemns South Africa for repressive racial policies, and votes a partial embargo on arms to that

country • Fighting breaks out between Greeks and Turks in Cyprus; President Makarios asks for British troops to keep order; a neutral zone between the factions is agreed

Arts and Letters
PAINTING: A "Pop Art" exhibition is held at the Guggenheim Museum, New York City; ARCHITECTURE: Le Corbusier (Fr), Carpenter Center for the Visual Arts, Harvard University, Mass; MUSIC: Gian Carlo Menotti (US), opera *The Last Savage*; William Walton (UK), *Variations on a Theme by Hindemith*; Michael Tippett (UK), *Concerto for Orchestra*; Samuel Barber (US), 1st piano concerto; LITERATURE: Mary McCarthy (US), *The Group*; Iris Murdoch (UK), *The Unicorn*; Günter Grass (Ger), *Dog Years*; John Updike (US), *The Centaur*; John Robinson (UK), *Honest to God*; Louis Mac-Neice (UK), *The Burning Perch*; Rolf Huckhuth (Ger), play *The Representative*; Eugene Ionesco (Fr), *Exit the King*; FILMS: *Cleopatra* (Joseph L. Mankiewicz, costing $28,000,000/£12,000,000); *Tom Jones* (Tony Richardson); *Irma la Douce* (Billy Wilder)

Science and Discovery
Valentina Tereshkova (USSR) becomes the first woman cosmonaut to orbit the Earth

Religion and Philosophy
Pope John XXIII dies, and is succeeded by Paul VI

Other Events
In Britain, £2,500,000 is stolen in what becomes known as "The Great Train Robbery" • 2,000 people die in an earthquake at Skopje, Yugoslavia • Britain's "Beatles" pop group (John Lennon, Paul McCartney, George Harrison, and Ringo Starr), becomes internationally popular

USA—**Lyndon B. Johnson**
UK—**Elizabeth II**

Politics and Wars

Fighting is renewed in Cyprus between Greeks and Turks; a UN force takes over from the peace-keeping rôle of British troops • Greece withdraws its military units from the North Atlantic Treaty Organization • The British colony of Malta becomes independent • Tanganyika and Zanzibar unite as Tanzania • In the British colony of Southern Rhodesia, Prime Minister Winston Field resigns, and is succeeded by Ian Smith • Two more British colonies become independent: Zambia (formerly Northern Rhodesia) and Malawi (formerly Nyasaland); Southern Rhodesia adopts the name "Rhodesia" • Guerrilla warfare by the Communist Vietcong movement in South Vietnam increases in intensity; the USA becomes increasingly involved as a US destroyer is attacked by North Vietnamese forces and US aircraft attack bases in North Vietnam • The UN ends its military involvement in Congo (Zaïre); the country adopts Africa names for its cities and the capital, Léopoldville, becomes Kinshasa • A general election in Britain brings the Labour Party back to power; Harold Wilson becomes prime minister • In the USSR, Nikita Khrushchev falls from power; he is succeeded as First Secretary of the Communist Party by Leonid Brezhnev, and as premier by Alexei Kosygin • King Saud of Saudi Arabia is deposed, and is succeeded by Crown Prince Feisal • Lyndon B. Johnson is elected to continue as President of the USA

Arts and Letters

PAINTING: Allen Jones (UK), *Green Girl*; ARCHITECTURE: Basil Spence (UK), University of Sussex; MUSIC: Leonard Bernstein (US), 3rd symphony;

Richard Rodney Bennett (UK), *Aubade*; John Cage (US), *Atlas Elipticales with Winter Music* (electronic); Benjamin Britten (UK), *Curlew River*; Roger Sessions (US), *Montezuma*; Jerry Bock (US), musical *Fiddler on the Roof*; Jerry Herman (US), musical *Hello Dolly!*; LITERATURE: Saul Bellow (US), *Herzog*; Gore Vidal (US), *Julian*; C. P. Snow (UK), *The Corridors of Power*; Jean-Paul Sartre (Fr), *Les Mots*; Peter Shaffer (UK), play *The Royal Hunt of the Sun*; John Osborne (UK), play *Inadmissible Evidence*; Harold Pinter (UK), play *The Homecoming*; FILMS: *Lord of the Flies* (Peter Brook); *Dr. Strangelove* (Stanley Kubrick); *A Hard Day's Night* (Richard Lester)

Science and Discovery

An official US report links lung cancer with smoking • The US spacecraft *Ranger VII* photographs the Moon, and *Mariner IV* is launched to photograph Mars • China explodes its first nuclear bomb • Drilling begins for oil and natural gas in the North Sea • US scientists discover the fundamental atomic particle omega-minus

Religion and Philosophy

Pope Paul VI goes on a pilgrimage to the Holy Land • Britain's Roman Catholics are banned from using contraceptive pills

Social and Economic

Britain and France reach agreement on plans for a Channel Tunnel • President Johnson calls for War on Poverty • The Equal Opportunity Act is passed in the USA • Germany agrees to pay compensation to British victims of Nazi persecution

Politics and Wars

Lyndon B. Johnson begins his first full term as President of the USA • US involvement in the Vietnam war increases as North Vietnam-backed Vietcong Communist forces step up their attacks on South Vietnam; American planes attack North Vietnam; North Vietnamese premier Ho Chi Minh rejects an offer of negotiations • Rebellion flares in the Dominican Republic: US troops are sent in to restore order • The UN Security Council is enlarged from 11 to 15 members • Singapore secedes from the Federation of Malaysia and becomes an independent country • Indonesia withdraws from the UN and its troops attack Malaya; British forces go to Malaya to help defense • The British colony of Gambia gains independence • Charles de Gaulle is reelected as president of France • West Germany enters into diplomatic relations with Israel; as a result, the Arab countries sever their links with West Germany • A British Commonwealth Secretariat is established, with headquarters in London (UK) • Border clashes between Indian and Pakistani troops are followed by a ceasefire, but renewed fighting flares up over disputed province of Kashmir • Following abortive talks with the British government, Rhodesian premier Ian Smith issues a Unilateral Declaration of Independence (UDI); Britain declares the new régime illegal and imposes trade restrictions, including an oil embargo • Nikolai Podgorny replaces Anastas Mikoyan as president of the USSR

Arts and Letters

PAINTING: Pablo Picasso (Sp), *Self Portrait*; ARCHITECTURE: Eric Bedford (UK), Post Office Tower, London; MUSIC: Leonard Bernstein (US), *The Chichester Psalms*; Jean Françaix (Fr), opera *The Princess of Cleves*; Malcolm Williamson (UK), opera *Julius Caesar Jones*; LITERATURE: Norman Mailer (US), *An American Dream*; Muriel Spark (UK), *The Mandelbaum Gate*; John Le Carré (UK), *The Looking Glass War*; Iris Murdoch (UK), *The Red and the Green*; James Baldwin (US), play *The Amen Corner*; Frank Marcus (UK), play *The Killing of Sister George*; Arnold Wesker (UK), play *The Four Seasons*; Robert Lowell (US), poems *For the Union Dead*; FILMS: Doctor Zhivago (David Lean); *Othello* (Laurence Olivier); OTHER: A Commonwealth Festival of Arts is held in Britain

Science and Discovery
Photographs of Mars are transmitted from the US satellite *Mariner IV* • Soviet and American astronauts float and "walk" in Space • Oil and natural gas are found under the North Sea

Religion and Philosophy
Pope Paul VI addresses the UN General Assembly in New York • In Rome, Pope Paul formally exonerates Jews of blame for the death of Jesus

Social and Economic
The death penalty is abolished in Britain • India adopts Hindi as its official language • The Medicare Act provides medical care for old people in the USA

Other Events
A cyclone and floods kill 12,700 people in East Pakistan (now Bangladesh)

Politics and Wars
The USA and USSR agree terms of an international treaty governing Space • Four more British colonies gain independence: British Guiana, as Guyana; Barbados; Bechuanaland, as Botswana; and Basutoland, as Lesotho • South African prime minister Hendrik F. Verwoerd is assassinated; he is succeeded by justice minister Balthazar J. Vorster • President Kwame Nkrumah of Ghana is overthrown in a *coup d'état* • France announces withdrawal of its troops from NATO, and calls for removal of NATO bases from France • Talks on Rhodesian independence between British prime minister Harold Wilson and Rhodesian premier Ian Smith fail; UN votes sanctions against Rhodesia • Mrs. Indira Gandhi, daughter of Pandit Nehru, becomes prime minister of India • The Tashkent Declaration restores friendly relations between India and Pakistan • The prime minister of Nigeria and two regional premiers are murdered • China denounces Soviet collaboration with the West • Chinese leader Mao Tse-tung initiates the Red Guard movement to implement a "cultural revolution" • Vietnam War continues, interrupted only by a 48-hour truce at Christmas

Arts and Letters
PAINTING: Marc Chagall (Fr), mural *The Triumph of Music* (Metropolitan Opera House, New York City); MUSIC: Benjamin Britten (UK), opera *The Burning Fiery Furnace*; Michael Tippett (UK), *The Vision of Saint Augustine*; William Schuman (US), ballet *The Witch of Endor*; LITERATURE: Graham Greene (UK), *The Comedians*; Rebecca West (UK), *The Birds Fall Down*; Truman Capote

(US), *In Cold Blood*; William Manchester (US), *The Death of a President*; Jean Anouilh (Fr), *The Fighting Cock*; FILM: *The Countess from Hong Kong* (Charles Chaplin); OTHER: Floods damage art treasures in Florence, Italy

Science and Discovery
Soviet spacecraft *Luna 9* and *Luna 13* make unmanned "soft" landings on the Moon • Two US spaceships lock in orbit • The Volta River hydroelectric scheme is inaugurated in Ghana • US surgeons successfully use a plastic heart to help in surgery

Social and Economic
The USA's first Negro senator, Edward Brooke (Rep, Mass.) is elected • Race riots rage in American cities • Australia adapts to decimal currency • The European Economic Community adopts a common farm policy • A continuing serious economic situation in Britain leads to a "freeze" of wages and prices

Other Events
An earthquake kills 2,400 people in Turkey • At the Welsh village of Aberfan (UK), a coal-tip landslide kills 116 schoolchildren and 28 adults

USA—**Lyndon B. Johnson**
UK—**Elizabeth II**

Politics and Wars

Dispute over Rhodesia's declaration of independence continues; US President Lyndon B. Johnson bans trade with the former British colony as part of an international economic blockade ● The USA, USSR and Britain sign a pact barring the use of nuclear weapons in Space ● Right-wing army officers in Greece seize power; King ConstantineII flees to exile in Rome, Italy; George Papadopolous heads a new military government ● Tension mounts between Israel and its Arab neighbors; Egypt's president Gamal Abdul Nasser demands the withdrawal of the UN peacekeeping forces along the Egyptian–Israeli border, and closes the Gulf of Aqaba to Israeli shipping ● The "Six-Day War": fearing attack from the Arab countries, Israeli forces strike first, and inflict a humiliating defeat on the Arab forces; Israeli troops occupy the Sinai Peninsula and the Gaza strip (Egyptian), the Golan Heights (Syrian), and all Jordanian territory west of the Jordan River, including eastern Jerusalem; the fighting is ended by a UN ceasefire order ● Civil war breaks out in Nigeria when the province of Biafra (Eastern Nigeria) secedes from the Nigerian Federation ● USSR Communist Party chief Leonid Brezhnev attacks the policies of Chinese leader Mao Tse-tung as a threat to the world Communist movement ● Nguyen Van Thieu is elected president of South Vietnam ● A coup d'état in Indonesia deposes President Sukarno ● Riots break out in Hong Kong ● The people of Gibraltar (claimed by Spain) vote to remain in the British Commonwealth ● The People's republic of South Yemen is formed, with Aden as its capital ● French president

Charles de Gaulle visits Quebec, and causes a political storm by encouraging Canada's French-speaking separatists with a speech ending "Long live free Quebec"

Arts and Letters

PAINTING: Marc Chagall (Fr), The Blue Village; MUSIC: Willard Stright (US), opera Toyon of Alaska; William Walton (UK), one-act opera The Bear; LITERATURE: V. S. Naipaul (Trin), The Mimic Men; Thornton Wilder (US), The Eighth Day; Desmond Morris (UK), The Naked Ape; Ira Levin (US), Rosemary's Baby; Christopher Isherwood (US), A Meeting by the River; Alexei Arbuzov (Russ), play The Promise; Tom Stoppard (UK), play Rosencrantz and Guildenstern are Dead; FILMS: Bonnie and Clyde (Arthur Penn); The Jungle Book (Walt Disney), The Countess from Hong Kong (Charles Chaplin); Guess Who's Coming to Dinner (Stanley Kramer)

Science and Discovery

Surgeon Christiaan Barnard (S Afr) performs the world's first heart transplant operations ● China explodes a hydrogen bomb ● Europe's largest reflecting telescope is installed at the British Royal Observatory ● The US spacecraft Apollo 3 is destroyed by fire on its launching pad; three astronauts die ● A US rocket plane flies at 4,520 mph (7,232 kph) ● Yachtsman Francis Chichester (UK) sails singlehanded round the world and is knighted

Other Events

World fair "Expo 67" opens in Montreal (Can) ● A new British ocean liner, Queen Elizabeth 2, is launched, and the Queen Mary is withdrawn

Politics and Wars

The US Navy reconnaissance ship Pueblo is seized by North Vietnamese forces; its crew is released after months of argument ● The Vietnam War continues to escalate: more than 500,000 US troops are now involved; US planes bomb North Vietnamese infiltration routes into South Vietnam, and Vietcong (Communist) camps in Laos and Cambodia ● Pierre Trudeau becomes Prime Minister of Canada ● The USA, USSR, Britain and 58 other countries sign a treaty on the nonproliferation of nuclear weapons ● Students demonstrate in Mexico City, and violent incidents result when troops seize university buildings ● Alexander Dubček is named leader of the Communist Party in Czechoslovakia; he introduces a reform program relaxing restrictions and giving Press freedom; troops from the USSR and other Warsaw Pact countries invade Czechoslovakia; Soviet tanks patrol the streets of Prague, the capital; Dubček is arrested; a new Russian-backed régime reverses his reforms ● Two assassinations rock the USA: Preacher and Negro rights leader Martin Luther King Jr. is shot in Memphis, Tenn; Senator Robert L. Kennedy, former Attorney-General and brother of slain President John F. Kennedy, is killed in Los Angeles, Cal ● The British colonies of Mauritius and Swaziland become independent ● Civil War in Nigeria continues over the secession of Biafra (Eastern Nigeria); peace talks break down ● Arab terrorists hijack an Israeli airliner ● Jordan refuses to allow UN observers on the ceasefire line following the "Six-Day War" of 1967 ● Britain rejects a renewed claim by Argentina to the Falkland

─────────────── □ **Richard M. Nixon** ───────────────▷

Islands • Richard M. Nixon, former Vice-President (Rep), is elected President of the USA

Arts and Letters
SCULPTURE: Theodore Roszak (US), *Sentinel*; ARCHITECTURE: Ludwig Mies van der Rohe (Ger), National Gallery, West Berlin; MUSIC: Robin Orr (UK), opera *Full Circle*; Benjamin Britten (UK), opera *The Prodigal Son*; Gian Carlo Menotti (US), opera *Help! Help! the Glotolinks!*; LITERATURE: Alexander Solzhenitsyn (USSR), *Cancer Ward*; Gore Vidal (US), *Myra Breckinridge*; John Updike (US), *Couples*; Irish Murdoch (UK), *The Nice and the Good*; Michael Frayn (UK), *A Very Private Life*; John Osborne (UK), play *The Hotel in Amsterdam*; Arthur Miller (US), play *The Price*; FILMS: *Star!* (Robert Wise)

Science and Discovery
Astronomer Martin Ryle (UK) discovers pulsars (astronomical radio sources) • *Apollo 8*, crewed by three US astronauts, makes the first orbit of the Moon • Max Pertutz (UK) establishes the structure of the haemoglobin molecule • France explodes a hydrogen bomb

Social and Economic
In Britain a Race Relations Act, against racial discrimination, is passed, and a Commonwealth Immigration Act controls the immigration of Asian families expelled from Kenya

Other Events
An earthquake in Iran kills 12,000 people • Old London Bridge is sold to an American buyer, for re-erection at Lake Havasu City, Ariz

Politics and Wars
Richard M. Nixon takes office as 37th President of the USA • The Vietnam War continues, with the USA now fully involved; the war becomes unpopular with the US public, and there is nationwide unrest among students; Nixon orders some US troops to be withdrawn • Canada reduces its North Atlantic Treaty forces • Civil disturbances rage in Northern Ireland over the rights of Roman Catholic minority groups; IRA (Irish Republican Army) terrorist activities grow; troops from mainland Britain move in to restore order • Willy Brandt (Soc) is elected Chancellor of West Germany • In France, President Charles de Gaulle resigns following the defeat of his plans for reforming the administration; he is succeeded by Georges Pompidou • Mrs. Golda Meir becomes Israel's prime minister; she asks the USA for economic and military aid • Nigeria's civil war continues, with great suffering to the breakaway Biafrans • The "rebel" colony of Rhodesia breaks diplomatic links with Britain and declares itself a republic • Border clashes occur between Russian and Chinese troops • Aging Spanish dictator Francisco Franco names Prince Juan Carlos, of the former ruling royal family, as his eventual successor

Arts and Letters
SCULPTURE: Alexander Calder (US), *La Grande vitesse*; ARCHITECTURE: Gene Summers (US), McCormick Place, Chicago; MUSIC: Luciano Berio (It), *Sinfonia*; Karlheinz Stockhausen (Ger), vocal work *Stimmung*; Michael Tippett (UK), opera *The Knot Garden*; LITERATURE: James Gould Cozzens (US), *Morning, Noon and Night*; Britid Brophy (UK),

In Transit; Philip Roth (US), *Portnoy's Complaint*; Mario Puzo (US), *The Godfather*; Alexander Solzhenitsyn (USSR), *The First Circle*; FILMS: *Lock Up Your Daughters* (Peter Coe); *Satyricon* (Federico Fellini); *2001: A Space Odyssey* (Stanley Kubrick)

Science and Discovery
US astronaut Neil A. Armstrong becomes the first man to land on the Moon; Edwin E. Aldrin, Jr., also lands, while Michael Collins controls their orbiting Apollo 11 spacecraft; they return to Earth with samples of lunar soil • Apollo 12, four months later lands two more astronauts, who return with more lunar samples • The supersonic Anglo-French airliner Concorde makes its first flight from Toulon (Fr) • Oil is discovered in Alaska

Religion and Philosophy
Pope Paul VI names 33 new cardinals, including four Americans

Social and Economic
Voting age is reduced from 21 to 18 in Britain • Reform of British divorce laws makes breakdown of marriage sufficient justification for divorce • The British Post Office is made a public corporation • The US Supreme Court rules that segregation in schools must end immediately • Miss Angie Brooks of Liberia becomes first woman president of the UN General Assembly • The USA signs a cultural exchange agreement with Romania • French and English languages are given equal official status in Canada

USA—**Richard M. Nixon**
UK—**Elizabeth II**

Politics and Wars

The Vietnam War continues: US and South Vietnamese forces ' enter Cambodia, but withdraw after clearing Vietcong (Communist) troops from "sanctuary areas"; President Richard M. Nixon announces that 150,000 US troops will be withdrawn from Vietnam in 1971 • The USA and Spain renew a defense agreement for American use of Spanish bases • A British diplomat (later released) and a Quebec minister (murdered) are kidnapped by French-Canadian terrorists • Communist leader Salvador Allende becomes president of Chile, and makes closer ties with Communist countries; he announces plans to nationalize foreign banks and companies • In British elections Labour is surprisingly defeated and Edward Heath (Con) succeeds Harold Wilson as prime minister • Violence continues in Northern Ireland: the IRA (Irish Republican Army) makes further bomb attacks • The civil war in Nigeria ends with the collapse of the breakaway province of Biafra (Eastern Nigeria) • Israel alleges that Soviet pilots are flying for the Egyptian airforce; Israel withdraws from peace talks with Arab countries, claiming that Egypt is building missile bases during the ceasefire • Middle East tension increases when Palestinian guerrillas hijack 4 airliners—2 American, 1 British and 1 Swiss—and blow them up • Egypt's president Gamal Abdul Nasser dies, and is succeeded by Anwar Sadat

Arts and Letters

ARCHITECTURE: Kevin Roche (US), Knights of Columbus Building, New Haven, Conn; MUSIC: Dmitri Shostakovich (USSR), 14th symphony; Hans Werner Henze (Ger), opera *El Cimarron*; LITERATURE: John Updike (US), *Bech: A Book*; Henri Charriere (Fr), *Papillon*; Saul Bellow (US), *Mr. Sammler's Planet*; Nancy Mitford (UK), *Frederick the Great*; Muriel Spark (UK), *The Driver's Seat*; Robert Lowell (US), *Notebook*; Gore Vidal (US), *Two Sisters*; FILMS: *Anne of the Thousand Days* (Charles Jarrott); *Catch 22* (Mike Nichols); *Julius Caesar* (Stuart Burge); *Butch Cassidy and the Sundance Kid* (George Roy Hill)

Science and Discovery

The US *Apollo 13* Moon mission is checked by an explosion in midflight; using their lunar landing craft to steer the crippled spaceship, the crew orbit the Moon and return to Earth • China launches its first artificial satellite

Social and Economic

Five demonstrating students are killed at Kent State University, Ohio, when the National Guard opens fire • In Britain, industrial disputes cause serious cuts in electric power; the government intervenes to save the Rolls-Royce company from financial collapse; parliament rules that men and women should get equal pay for the same work • The USA and USSR sign an agreement widening their cultural relations

Other Events

East Pakistan is overwhelmed by a cyclone and tidal wave: at least 200,000 people die and 1,000,000 are left homeless • An earthquake destroys two towns in Peru: more than 50,000 people die and 800,000 are made homeless

Politics and Wars

East Pakistan breaks from West Pakistan and declares itself the independent republic of Bangladesh; the central government tries unsuccessfully to end the breakaway by force; India recognizes Bangladesh, and war between India and Pakistan ends with an unconditional Pakistani surrender • India signs a friendship treaty with the USSR • Several foreign diplomats are kidnapped by left-wing guerrillas in South America • The Vietnam War continues: South Vietnamese troops invade Laos, extending the area of conflict; demonstrators in Washington, D.C., protest against American involvement in the war; North Vietnamese forces capture the Plain of Jars in Laos • Congo (Kinshasa), is renamed the Zaïre Republic; Congo River is also renamed the Zaïre River • In a *coup d'état* in Uganda, General Idi Amin ousts president Milton Obote and seizes power • NATO moves its naval base from Malta to Naples (It), at the request of the Maltese premier Dom Mintoff • The UN finally admits Communist China as a member state; Taiwan (Formosa) ceases to occupy China's seat and leaves the UN • U Thant (Burma) resigns as UN Secretary-General, and is succeeded by Kurt Waldheim (Aus) • Violence in Northern Ireland continues: 172 people are killed there during the year

Arts and Letters

SCULPTURE: Armand Vaillancourt (Can) fountain at Embaradero Plaza, San Francisco, Cal; MUSIC: Leos Janacék (Czech), opera *The Makropolous Affair*; Krzystof Penderecki (Pol), symphony *Utrenja*; Robert Stigwood produces rock opera *Jesus Christ Superstar*; LITERATURE: V. S. Naipaul

(Trin), *In a Free State*; Graham Greene (UK), autobiography *A Sort of Life*; George Jackson (US), *Soledad Brother*; Mary McCarthy (US), *Birds of America*; Elizabeth Longford (UK), *Wellington: The Years of the Sword*; Nancy Mitford (UK), *Frederick the Great*; FILM: *A Clockwork Orange* (Stanley Kubrick)

Science and Discovery
A British Royal College of Physicians report recommends the banning of cigarette advertising and cigarette vending machines • Russian spacecraft *Soyuz 11* makes a successful docking with the orbiting spacestation *Salyut*; it returns safely to Earth but its three cosmonauts die when air pressure fails • The unmanned Soviet spaceship *Mars III* makes a "soft" landing on Mars • US *Mariner 9* orbits Mars • Two US astronauts land on the Moon from *Apollo 15*, and drive a lunar vehicle on the Moon's surface

Social and Economic
A financial crisis causes European currency markets to close; Austria and Switzerland revalue their currencies; West Germany and the Netherlands float theirs; the USA suspends the conversion of dollars into gold • Libya nationalizes British oil holdings • The Aswan High Dam, Egypt, is inaugurated

Other Events
An earthquake in Turkey kills more than 1,000 people • A tidal wave kills 15,000 people in Orissa, India • 66 people are crushed to death at a football match in Glasgow (UK) when a barrier collapses

Politics and Wars
President Richard M. Nixon (US) visits the USSR and China • The USA and the USSR agree a treaty to halt the nuclear arms race • Okinawa is returned by the USA to the Japanese • William Tolbert becomes president of Liberia • Bangladesh cuts all links with Pakistan, and signs a defense agreement with India • Bangladesh is recognized by the USSR, but China uses its veto to prevent Bangladesh becoming a member of the UN • Pakistan withdraws from British Commonwealth and SEATO • King Frederick IX of Denmark dies; is succeeded by his daughter, Margrethe • The USA lifts its ban on the importation of Rhodesian chrome and other metals • Violent disturbances continue in Northern Ireland; troops open fire on rioters in Londonderry, killing 13 — so-called "Bloody Sunday" incident; the British Government takes over direct rule of the province • The British Embassy in Dublin is destroyed by a mob • An army junta seizes power in Ecuador, deposing President José Ibarra for the fourth time • Border fighting occurs between Israel and Lebanon and Syria • The Vietnam War continues: North Vietnamese forces advance into South Vietnam; US aircraft bomb Hanoi and Haiphong; the US Navy blockades North Vietnamese ports • Egypt severs relations with Jordan • Egypt and Libya agree to merge into one state • Ceylon is renamed Sri Lanka • British reject an extension of Iceland's fishing limit to 50 miles, and the International Court rules against Iceland • Uganda expels 40,000 Asians, who claim British nationality; they flee to Britain • Ex-president Juan Perón returns to Argentina after 17 years' exile • Richard Nixon is reëlected President of the USA with a landslide majority

Arts and Letters
ARCHITECTURE: Minoru Yamasaki (Jap), World Trade Center, New York City; LITERATURE: Christopher Isherwood (US), *Kathleen and Frank*; P. G. Wodehouse (UK), *Thank You, Jeeves*; Herman Wouk (US), *Wind of War*; David Niven (UK), *The Moon's a Balloon*; Arthur Mizener (US), *The Saddest Story*; Frederick Forsyth (UK), *The Day of the Jackal*; Margaret Drabble (UK), *The Needle's Eye*; FILMS: *The Godfather* (Francis Ford Coppola); *Cabaret* (Bob Fosse)

Science and Discovery
US astronauts make two trips to the Moon (Apollo 16 and 17) and establish astronomical observatories there • An unmanned Soviet spacecraft brings Moon rocks back to Earth

Social and Economic
The US Supreme Court rules that the death penalty is contrary to the Constitution • Britain, the Republic of Ireland and Denmark join the European Economic Community; in a referendum, Norwegians vote against membership

Other Events
Earthquakes kill 5,000 people in Iran and 10,000 in Nicaragua • Floods in the eastern USA, kill 122 people and leave 27,000 homeless • An explosion at Wankie Colliery, Rhodesia, kills 427 miners • Arab terrorists kidnap Israeli competitors at the Olympic Games in Munich (Ger); 17 people, including 11 Israelis, are killed

USA—**Richard M. Nixon**
UK—**Elizabeth II**

Politics and Wars

The Watergate scandal: 7 men are accused of burgling Democratic Party headquarters in the Watergate Building, Washington D.C., and of trying to "bug" it; rumors that White House staff were involved are denied by President Richard M. Nixon; two of Nixon's advisers, John D. Ehrlichman and H. R. Haldeman, resign; former Attorney-General John N. Mitchell tells an inquiry there was a White House "cover-up" of the Watergate break-in • Eamon de Valera resigns as president of the Irish Republic at the age of 91; he is succeeded by Erskine H. Childers • Militant Indians protesting treaty grievances seize the hamlet of Wounded Knee, S. Dak, and hold it for 2 months • Violence continues in Northern Ireland, and Irish Republican Army terrorists set off bombs in London and other British cities; British, Northern Irish and Irish Republic leaders agree a plan for a joint Council of Ireland • Former president Juan Perón returns to power in Argentina, with his second wife Isabel as vice-president • President Salvador Allende of Chile commits suicide during an army *coup d'etat* • The USA and USSR sign an arms limitation and nuclear war pact • Libya takes 51 percent control of US oil interests in the country • Egyptian and Syrian troops invade Israel; Israeli forces cross the Suez Canal; Egyptians recapture part of Sinai; an uneasy cease-fire follows • As a result, Arab countries double the price of their oil, causing an energy crisis in Western countries • US Vice-President Spiro T. Agnew resigns in an income-tax-evasion scandal; Nixon nominates Congressman Gerald R. Ford to succeed Agnew

Arts and Letters

ARCHITECTURE: Bruce Graham (US), Sears Tower, Chicago, Ill; LITERATURE: Graham Greene (UK), *The Honorary Consul*; Harold Macmillan (UK), autobiography *At the End of the Day*; Elizabeth Longford (UK), *Wellington: Pillar of State*; Antonia Fraser (UK), *Cromwell: Our Chief of Men*; Richard Adams (UK), *Watership Down*; FILMS: *Last Tango in Paris* (Bernardo Bertolucchi); *Carnal Knowledge* (Mike Nichols)

Science and Discovery

Relays of American astronauts dock their vehicles with a space station, *Skylab* • USSR launches 4 unmanned spaceships to Mars • Japanese scientists investigate artificial tissue for use as substitute skin • German scientists invent an improved artificial kidney

Religion and Philosophy

Pope Paul VI reaffirms the doctrine of Papal infallibility

Social and Economic

The US dollar is devalued by 10 percent • A UK trade deficit leads to a state of emergency in Britain; the government orders cuts in the use of electric power and imposes a 3-day working week on "nonessential industries" • Serious drought in Ethiopia leads to more than 50,000 deaths

Other Events

Helgafell Volcano on Heimaey Island, Iceland, erupts, rendering 5,000 people homeless • A new London Bridge is opened • Crop failures cause famine and riots in India.

Politics and Wars

British miners vote to strike for more pay; Conservative prime minister Edward Heath rejects their demands and calls a general election in February; the Conservatives lose their overall majority; Heath resigns and is succeeded by Harold Wilson as head of a minority Labour government; a second general election in October gives Labour a narrow overall majority • The Watergate scandal grows in the USA: President Richard M. Nixon is implicated in a plot to cover up a White House-inspired burglary of the Watergate Building in Washington, D.C., during the 1972 election campaign; faced with the threat of impeachment, Nixon resigns; he is succeeded by Vice-President Gerald R. Ford as 38th President of the USA • Ford announces a pardon for Nixon • Ford nominates Nelson A. Rockefeller, former governor of New York, as Vice-President • Mrs. Golda Meir resigns as prime minister of Israel, and is succeeded by Yitzhak Rabin • President Georges Pompidou of France dies, and Valery Giscard d'Estaing is elected to succeed him • West German Chancellor Willy Brandt resigns when his personal aide, Gunter Guillaume, is unmasked as a Communist spy; Finance Minister Helmut Schmidt is elected to succeed Brandt • An army *coup d'etat* overthrows the dictatorial Portuguese government of Prime Minister Marcello Caetano • Fighting in the Portuguese colony of Mozambique marks the beginning of an independence struggle; meanwhile, the Portuguese colony of Guinea-Bisseau achieves independence • The USA and the USSR reach an agreement on limiting armaments • Violence continues in Northern Ireland, and

Ulster terrorists set off more bombs in mainland Britain • Following a series of demonstrations and riots, army officers in Ethiopia depose Emperor Haile Selassie, absolute ruler for 58 years • In a plebiscite, Greeks vote against the return of their exiled king, Constantine II

Arts and Letters

SCULPTURE: Alexander Calder (US), *Flàmingo*; MUSIC: Richard Rodney Bennet (UK), *Concerto for Orchestra*; William Schuman (US), *Concerto for Viola, Chorus and Orchestra*; musical *Over Here!* (US); LITERATURE: Graham Greene (UK), *Lord Rochester's Monkey*; Nicholas Montsarrat (UK), *The Kapillan of Malta*; John le Carré (UK), *Tinker, Tailor, Soldier, Spy*; Joseph Heller (US), *Something Happened*; James A. Michener (US), *Centennial;* FILMS: *The Exorcist* (William P. Blatty); *The Sting* (George R. Hill); *Scenes from a Marriage* (Ingmar Bergman)

Science and Discovery

A US spacecraft, *Mariner 10*, transmits pictures of the planet Mercury to Earth

Social and Economic

Inflation hits all parts of the world, especially Britain • Arab states lift their embargo on oil supplies to the USA

Other Events

More than 300 people are killed in North American tornadoes • A cyclone destroys most of Darwin, Northern Australia • A hurricane hits Honduras, leaving 8,000 dead and 300,000 homeless

Politics and Wars

US troops evacuate Cambodia • The Vietnam War ends as South Vietnamese resistance collapses; South Vietnam surrenders unconditionally to North Vietnam; a Communist provisional revolutionary government is established • Two women attempt to assassinate US President Gerald Ford • The Suez Canal, closed since 1973, is reopened to international shipping • The Portuguese colonies of Mozambique and Angola become independent; civil war breaks out between rival governments in Angola, supported by Cuban and South African troops • In India, a state of emergency is declared after prime minister Mrs. Indira Gandhi is found guilty of corrupt election practices; the conviction is quashed; Press restrictions are imposed • An army *coup d'etat* deposes president Yakubo Gowan of Nigeria • President Sheikh Mujibar Rahman of Bangladesh is assassinated; a series of coups and murders follows • King Faisal of Saudi Arabia is assassinated by a nephew; he is succeeded by his half-brother, Khalid • Fighting breaks out between Christians and Muslims in Lebanon • Violence continues in Northern Ireland, with more IRA (Irish Republican Army) bombing and kidnapping outrages in England and the Irish Republic • The Australian dependency of Papua–New Guinea becomes independent • Iceland extends its fishing limits from 50 to 200 miles (80–320 km); a so-called "Cod War" involving British trawlers and Icelandic gunboats results • Spanish dictator General Francisco Franco dies; the monarchy is restored with Prince Juan Carlos as king • Surinam (Dutch Guiana) gets independence

Arts and Letters

ARCHITECTURE: Welton Becket and Associates: Reunion Tower, Dallas, Tex; MUSIC: Georgy Ligeti (US), *San Francisco Polyphony*; Luigi Nono (It), opera *To the Great Sun Charged with Love*; LITERATURE: Vladimir Nabokov (US), *Tyrants Destroyed*; Saul Bellow (US), *Humboldt's Gift*; Patrick White (Austral), *The Cockatoo*; Susan Chitty (UK), *The Beast and the Monk*; P. G. Wodehouse (UK), *Aunts Aren't Gentlemen*; Agatha Christie (UK), *Curtain*; Anthony Powell (UK), *Hearing Secret Harmonies*; Wodehouse receives a knighthood a few weeks before his death; FILMS: *Jaws* (Stephen Spielberg); *Nashville* (Robert Altman)

Religion and Philosophy

The first American-born saint, Elizabeth Ann Bayley Seton (1774–1812), is canonized; so is Oliver Plunkett, Irish archbishop executed for treason in 1612.

Social and Economic

New York City, facing bankruptcy, is saved by a large federal loan • Britain's inflation crisis increases; the Trades Union Congress coöperates with the Labour government in a £6-a-week pay rise limit • Kuwait takes over British oil interests there • Britain obtains its first North Sea oil • The US Supreme Court rules against "closed shop" trade unions • In a referendum, the British people elect to stay in the European Economic Community

Other Events

An earthquake kills more than 2,000 people in Lice, Turkey

USA—**Gerald R. Ford**

UK—**Elizabeth II**

Politics and Wars

China loses its revolutionary leaders; premier Chou En-lai dies in January, and is succeeded by Hua Kuo-feng, one of the 12 vice-premiers; senior vice-premier Teng Hsiao-ping is dismissed from office; chairman Mao Tse-tung dies in September, and Hua succeeds him too; radical leaders, including Mao's widow Chiang Ching, are purged • A new "cod war" which flares between Britain and Iceland over fishing rights is settled after 5 months • British prime minister Harold Wilson resigns: is succeeded by Chancellor of the Exchequer James Callaghan • President María Estela (Isabel) Perón of Argentina is overthrown in a *coup d'état* • Civil war in Lebanon ends as neighboring Arab countries enforce a ceasefire • Spain gives up its African colony of Western Sahara, which is shared between Morocco and Mauretania • Civil war in Angola ends with victory for the communist M.P.L.A. (Popular Movement for the Liberation of Angola); guerrilla warfare continues • Palestinian hijackers seize a French plane with 103 passengers, mostly Israelis, and fly it to Entebbe, Uganda; in a daring raid Israeli commandos free the hostages • The USA and the USSR sign a treaty limiting underground nuclear explosions • In South Africa, racial riots break out in Soweto and other black townships: 400 die; meanwhile Transkei becomes an "independent" black homeland within South Africa • Vietnam is reunited under North Vietnamese (communist) control • Terrorism continues in Northern Ireland as attempts to establish a new government fail • Violence spills over into the Republic of Ireland, where British ambassador Christopher Ewart-Biggs is assassinated • Eire's president, Cearbhall O'Dalaigh, resigns in a dispute over antiterrorist laws; is succeeded by Patrick J. Hillery • James Earl ("Jimmy") Carter (Dem) is elected President of the USA • In Canada, the Parti Québécois, a separatist movement, wins control of Quebec's National Assembly

Arts and Letters

SCULPTURE: Alexander Calder (US), steel abstract for the Empire State Plaza, Albany, NY; ARCHITECTURE: Mitchell-Giurgola (US), Liberty Bell Pavilion, Philadelphia, Pa; Roger Taillibert (Fr), Velodrome, Olympic site, Montreal; MUSIC: Gian-Carlo Menotti (It), opera *The Hero*; John La Montaine (US), opera *Be Glad Then, America*; John Cage (US), *Renga with Apartment House 1776*; LITERATURE: Alice Walker (US), *Meridian*; Alex Haley (US), *Roots*; Gabriel Garcia Marquez (Colombia), *The Autumn of the Patriarch*; Robertson Davies (Can), *World of Wonders*; Anthony Powell (UK), *Hearing Secret Harmonies*; Alexander Solzhenitsyn (USSR), *Lenin in Zurich*; Muriel Spark (UK), *The Takeover*; Elizabeth Longford (UK), biography *Byron*; Bob Woodward and Carl Bernstein (US), *The Final Days*; Arthur Miller (US), play *The Archbishop's Ceiling*; Harold Pinter (UK), play *No Man's Land*

Science and Discovery

US spacecraft *Viking 1* lands on Mars and relays pictures back to Earth • Anglo-French supersonic airliner Concorde goes into service

Social and Economic

Inflation rates decline in most countries, but unemployment rises in Britain, France and Italy

Other Events

More than 655,000 people are reported dead in an earthquake centered on Tangshan, China • An earthquake flattens Guatemala City, killing 22,000 people • At Van, eastern Turkey, another 'quake kills 4,000 • Europe has its worst drought for more than 200 years; some crops are affected

———□ **James E. Carter** —————————————————▷
————————————————————————————————▷

Politics and Wars

James Earl ("Jimmy") Carter takes office as 39th President of the USA • Egypt and Syria end a year-long feud • Yitzhak Rabin resigns as Israeli prime minister following alleged violations of currency laws; in later elections Rabin's Labor party is defeated and the Likud ("Unity") coalition takes office, with Menachem Begin, 63, as prime minister • In South Africa, student riots continue in the black township of Soweto • Riots in Cairo, Egypt, over food prices last 2 days • In Britain, the Liberals agree to support the minority Labour government, to avert the danger of an early election • In Washington, D.C., Muslim terrorists hold 132 hostages for 36 hours, protesting against a movie about the prophet Muhammad • In India, a general election topples the 11-year-old government of Mrs. Indira Gandhi; she is succeeded as prime minister by 81-year-old Morarji Desai, of the Janata coalition • Britain and the USA lead year-long negotiations toward settling the future of Rhodesia (Zimbabwe) • Terrorist attacks in Northern Ireland continue, but at a much-reduced rate • Massacres and riots take place in Ethiopia • At Bovensmilde, Netherlands, South Moluccan terrorists seize a train and a school; after holding hostages for 20 days, they are overcome by marines in a commando-style raid • The government of prime minister Zulfikar Ali Bhutto is toppled in Pakistan following a coup by a group of military officers • Spain holds its first free parliamentary elections for 41 years • Eritreans rebel against the government of Ethiopia, seeking independence; they are supported by neighboring Somalia and by the USSR •

Months of tension between Egypt and Libya culminate in a short armed clash • Prime Minister Tanin Krai Vixien of Thailand is overthrown by a military coup • West German commandos storm a hijacked German jet airliner at Mogadishu, Somalia, rescuing 82 passengers and killing 3 terrorists; following the raid, 4 members of the Baader-Meinhof terrorist gang commit suicide in jail • South Africa clamps down on opposition to its apartheid policies, detaining many black leaders and banning *The World Newspaper* • In an unexpected peace move, President Sadat of Egypt visits Israel and addresses the Knesset (parliament) • Premier Ian Smith of Rhodesia announces acceptance of adult suffrage principle

Arts and Letters

SCULPTURE: Don Thibodeaux (US), *Muhammad Ali*; MUSIC: Leon Kirchner (US), opera *Lily*; George Crumb (US), *Star-child*; Keith Emerson (UK), *Abaddon's Bolero*; LITERATURE: Kingsley Amis (UK), *The Alteration*; Iris Murdoch (UK), *Henry and Cato*; Harry Patterson (US), *The Valhalla Exchange*; Carl Sagan (US), *The Dragons of Eden*; Richard Condon (US), *The Abandoned Woman*; Eric Ambler (UK), *The Siege of the Villa Lipp*; V. S. Naipaul (India), *India: A Wounded Civilization*; Louis Auchinloss (US), *The Dark Lady*; Paul Scott (US), *Staying On*; Evelyn Waugh (UK), *Diaries* (posthumous); Albert Innaurato (US), play *Gemini*; Bertha Egnos (S. Afr), play *Ipi-Tombi*; Tom Stoppard (UK), play *Dirty Linen*; Per Olov Enquist (Swe), play *The Night of the Tribades*; Hamilton Deane and John L. Balderston (US), play *Dracula*; FILMS: *Mohammad, Messenger of God* (Moustapha Akkad); *A Star is Born* (Frank Pierson); *Fellini's Casanova* (Federico Fellini); *Annie Hall* (Woody Allen); *Star Wars* (George Lucas); *A Bridge Too Far* (Richard Attenborough); *Equus* (Sidney Lumet); *Valentino* (Ken Russell)

Science and Discovery

A male birth-control pill is devised at the University of Washington medical school • US space scientists begin testing the "Space Shuttle" aircraft • Oil begins to flow through the Alaska pipeline

Social and Economic

11 oil-exporting countries raise prices by 15 percent • Following a world coffee shortage, Brazil, one of the world's leading exporters, has to import beans •. The pay policy of Britain's Labour government collapses; a wave of strikes follows as workers return to a form of "free collective bargaining," though still with limits • The Anglo-French *Concorde* aircraft wins landing rights at New York City's Kennedy Airport • Firemen in Britain strike for first time

Other Events

Earthquake rocks Romania: 20,000 homes are destroyed in Bucharest, more than 1,300 people die • The USA has its coldest spell for 100 years: severe snowstorms and bitter cold hit the northern states: Buffalo, NY, is buried under deep snowdrifts • Two jumbo jet airliners collide at Los Rodeos Airport, Tenerife, Canary Islands: more than 550 people die • Following violent thunderstorms, a power failure blacks out New York City and surrounding towns for 25 hours; widespread looting and other damage is estimated at $1,000 million

223

DATA BANK

PRESIDENTS OF THE UNITED STATES

No.	Name	Served	Party	Occupation	Vice-President
1	George Washington	1789–1797	Federalist	Planter	John Adams
2	John Adams	1797–1801	Federalist	Lawyer	Thomas Jefferson
3	Thomas Jefferson	1801–1809	Democratic-Republican	Planter	Aaron Burr George Clinton
4	James Madison	1809–1817	Democratic-Republican	Lawyer	George Clinton Elbridge Gerry
5	James Monroe	1817–1825	Democratic-Republican	Lawyer	Daniel D. Tompkins
6	John Quincy Adams	1825–1829	Democratic-Republican	Lawyer	John C. Calhoun
7	Andrew Jackson	1829–1837	Democrat	Lawyer	John C. Calhoun Martin Van Buren
8	Martin Van Buren	1837–1841	Democrat	Lawyer	Richard M. Johnson
9	William H. Harrison*	1841	Whig	Farmer	John Tyler
10	John Tyler	1841–1845	Whig	Lawyer	**
11	James K. Polk	1845–1849	Democrat	Lawyer	George M. Dallas
12	Zachary Taylor*	1849–1850	Whigier	Soldier	Millard Fillmore
13	Millard Fillmore	1850–1853	Whig	Lawyer	**
14	Franklin Pierce	1853–1857	Democrat	Lawyer	William R. King
15	James Buchanan	1857–1861	Democrat	Lawyer	John C. Breckinridge
16	Abraham Lincoln†	1861–1865	Republican	Lawyer	Hannibal Hamlin Andrew Johnson
17	Andrew Johnson	1865–1869	Democrat	Tailor	
18	Ulysses S. Grant	1869–1877	Republican	Soldier	Schuyler Colfax Henry Wilson
19	Rutherford B. Hayes	1877–1881	Republican	Lawyer	William A. Wheeler
20	James A. Garfield†	1881	Republican	Lawyer	Chester A. Arthur
21	Chester A. Arthur	1881–1885	Republican	Lawyer	**
22	Grover Cleveland	1885–1889	Democrat	Lawyer	Thomas A. Hendricks
23	Benjamin Harrison	1889–1893	Republican	Lawyer	Levi P. Morton
24	Grover Cleveland	1893–1897	Democrat	Lawyer	Adlai E. Stevenson
25	William McKinley†	1897–1901	Republican	Lawyer	Garret A. Hobart Theodore Roosevelt
26	Theodore Roosevelt	1901–1909	Republican	Writer	** Charles W. Fairbanks
27	William H. Taft	1909–1913	Republican	Lawyer	James S. Sherman
28	Woodrow Wilson	1913–1921	Democrat	Teacher	Thomas R. Marshall
29	Warren G. Harding*	1921–1923	Republican	Newspaperman	Calvin Coolidge
30	Calvin Coolidge	1923–1929	Republican	Lawyer	** Charles G. Dawes
31	Herbert C. Hoover	1929–1933	Republican	Engineer	Charles Curtis
32	Franklin D. Roosevelt*	1933–1945	Democrat	Lawyer	John N. Garner Henry A. Wallace Harry S. Truman
33	Harry S. Truman	1945–1953	Democrat	Businessman	** Alben W. Barkley
34	Dwight D. Eisenhower	1953–1961	Republican	Soldier	Richard M. Nixon
35	John F. Kennedy†	1961–1963	Democrat	Writer	Lyndon B. Johnson

continued overleaf

PRESIDENTS OF THE UNITED STATES
-continued-

No.	Name	Served	Party	Occupation	Vice-President
36	**Lyndon B. Johnson**	1963–1969	Democrat	Teacher	**
37	**Richard M. Nixon‡**	1969–1974	Republican	Lawyer	Hubert Humphrey / Spiro T. Agnew / Gerald R. Ford
38	**Gerald R. Ford**	1974–1977	Republican	Lawyer	Nelson A. Rockefeller
39	**James E. Carter**	1977–	Democrat	Farmer	Walter F. Mondale

*Died in office †Assassinated ‡Resigned
**Before 1967, a vice-president succeeding a president who had died had no vice-president for the remainder of that term of office

STATES OF THE U.S.A.

State	Abbreviation	Capital	Date Admitted to Union
Alabama	Ala.	Montgomery	1819
Alaska	Alaska	Juneau	1959
Arizona	Ariz.	Phoenix	1912
Arkansas	Ark.	Little Rock	1836
California	Calif.	Sacremento	1850
Colorado	Colo.	Denver	1876
Connecticut	Conn.	Hartford	1788
Delaware	Del.	Dover	1787
Florida	Fla.	Tallahassee	1845
Georgia	Ga.	Atlanta	1788
Hawaii	Hawaii	Honolulu	1959
Idaho	Ida.	Boise	1890
Illinois	Ill.	Springfield	1818
Indiana	Ind.	Indianpolis	1816
Iowa	Ia.	Des Moines	1846
Kansas	Kans. or Kan.	Topeka	1861
Kentucky	Ky. or Ken.	Frankfort	1792
Louisiana	La.	Baton Rouge	1812
Maine	Me.	Augusta	1820
Maryland	Md.	Annapolis	1788
Massachusetts	Mass.	Boston	1788
Michigan	Mich.	Lansing	1837
Minnesota	Minn.	St. Paul	1858
Mississippi	Miss.	Jackson	1817
Missouri	Mo.	Jefferson City	1821

STATES OF THE U.S.A.
─ continued ─

STATE	ABBREVIATION	CAPITAL	DATE ADMITTED TO UNION
Montana	Mont.	Helena	1889
Nebraska	Nebr. or Neb.	Lincoln	1867
Nevada	Nev.	Carson City	1864
New Hampshire	N.H.	Concord	1788
New Jersey	N.J.	Trenton	1787
New Mexico	N. Mex. or N.M.	Santa Fe	1912
New York	N.Y.	Albany	1788
North Carolina	N.C.	Raleigh	1798
North Dakota	N. Dak. or N.D.	Bismarck	1889
Ohio	O.	Columbus	1803
Oklahoma	Okla.	Oklahoma City	1907
Oregon	Ore. or Oreg.	Salem	1859
Pennsylvania	Pa. or Penn.	Harrisburg	1787
Rhode Island	R.I.	Providence	1790
South Carolina	S.C.	Columbia	1788
South Dakota	S. Dak. or S.D.	Pierre	1889
Tennessee	Tenn.	Nashville	1796
Texas	Tex.	Austin	1845
Utah	Ut.	Salt Lake City	1896
Vermont	Vt.	Montpelier	1791
Virginia	Va.	Richmond	1788
Washington	Wash.	Olympia	1889
West Virginia	W. Va	Charleston	1863
Wisconsin	Wis.	Madison	1848
Wyoming	Wyo.	Cheyenne	1890

GOVERNORS-GENERAL OF CANADA

Lord Monck	1867–1868	Lord Byng of Vimy	1921–1926
Lord Lisgar	1869–1872	Marquess of Willingdon	1926–1931
Marquess of Dufferin and Ava	1872–1878	Earl of Bessborough	1931–1935
Marquess of Lorne	1878–1883	Lord Tweedsmuir	1935–1940
Marquess of Lansdowne	1883–1888	Earl of Athlone	1940–1946
Lord Stanley of Preston	1888–1893	Viscount Alexander of Tunis	1946–1952
Earl of Aberdeen	1893–1898	Vincent Massey	1952–1959
Earl of Minto	1898–1904	Georges Philias Vanier	1959–1967
Earl Grey	1904–1911	Roland Michener	1967–1974
Duke of Connaught	1911–1916	Jules Léger	1974–
Duke of Devonshire	1916–1921		

IMPORTANT WARS

Abyssinian War	1935–1936	Mexican-American War	1846–1848
American War of Independence	1775–1783	Napoleonic Wars	1792–1815
Austrian Succession, War of the	1740–1748	October War	1973
Boer (South African) War	1899–1902	Peloponnesian War	431–404 BC
Chinese-Japanese Wars	1894–1895	Punic Wars	264–146 BC
	1931–1933	Russo-Japanese War	1904–1905
	1937–1945	Seven Years War	1756–1763
Civil War, American	1861–1865	Six-Day War	1967
Civil War, English	1642–1646	Spanish-American War	1898
Civil War, Nigerian	1967–1970	Spanish Succession, War of the	1701–1713
Civil War, Pakistan	1971	Thirty Years War	1618–1648
Civil War, Spanish	1936–1939	Vietnam War	1957–1975
Crimean War	1853–1856	War of 1812	1812–1814
Franco-Prussian War	1870–1871	Wars of the Roses	1455–1485
Hundred Years, War	1337–1453	World War One	1914–1918
Korean War	1950–1953	World War Two	1939–1945

BRITISH SOVEREIGNS

ENGLAND	
Egbert	827–839
Ethelwulf	839–858
Ethelbald	858–860
Ethelbert	860–865
Ethelred I	865–871
Alfred the Great	871–899
Edward the Elder	899–924
Athelstan	924–939
Edmund	939–946
Edred	946–955
Edwy	955–959
Edgar	959–975
Edward the Martyr	975–978
Ethelred II the Unready	978–1016
Edmund Ironside	1016
Canute	1016–1035
Harold I Harefoot	1035–1040
Hardicanute	1040–1042
Edward the Confessor	1042–1066
Harold II	1066
William I the Conqueror	1066–1087
William II	1087–1100
Henry I	1100–1135
Stephen	1135–1154
Henry II	1154–1189
Richard I	1189–1199
John	1199–1216
Henry III	1216–1272
Edward I	1272–1307
Edward II	1307–1327
Edward III	1327–1377
Richard II	1377–1399
Henry IV	1399–1413
Henry V	1413–1422
Henry VI	1422–1461
Edward IV	1461–1483
Edward V	1483
Richard III	1483–1485
Henry VII	1485–1509
Henry VIII	1509–1547
Edward VI	1547–1553
Mary I	1553–1558
Elizabeth I	1558–1603

SCOTLAND	
Malcolm II	1005–1034
Duncan I	1034–1040
Macbeth	1040–1057
Malcolm III Canmore	1058–1093
Donald Bane	1093–1094
Duncan II	1094
Donald Bane (restored)	1094–1097
Edgar	1097–1107
Alexander I	1107–1124
David I	1124–1153
Malcolm IV	1153–1165
William the Lion	1165–1214
Alexander II	1214–1249
Alexander III	1249–1286
Margaret of Norway	1286–1290
Interregnum	1290–1292
John Balliol	1292–1296
Interregnum	1296–1306
Robert I (Bruce)	1306–1329
David II	1329–1371
Robert II	1371–1390
Robert III	1390–1406
James I	1406–1437
James II	1437–1460
James III	1460–1488
James IV	1488–1513
James V	1513–1542
Mary	1542–1567
James VI*	1567–1625

*Became James I of England in 1603

GREAT BRITAIN	
James I	1603–1625
Charles I	1625–1649
Commonwealth	1649–1660
Charles II	1660–1685
James II	1685–1688
William III ⎫ jointly	1689–1702
Mary II ⎭	1689–1694
Anne	1702–1714
George I	1714–1727
George II	1727–1760
George III	1760–1820

UNITED KINGDOM	
George III	1760–1820
George IV	1820–1830
William IV	1830–1837
Victoria	1837–1901
Edward VII	1901–1910
George V	1910–1936
Edward VII	1936
George VI	1936–1952
Elizabeth II	1952–

BRITISH PRIME MINISTERS

Name	Political Party	Years in Office	Name	Political Party	Years in Office
Sir Robert Walpole	Whig	1721–1742	Earl of Derby	Conservative	1866–1868
Earl of Wilmington	Whig	1742–1743	Benjamin Disraeli	Conservative	1868
Henry Pelham	Whig	1743–1754	William E. Gladstone	Liveral	1868–1874
Duke of Newcastle	Whig	1754–1756	Benjamin Disraeli	Conservative	1874–1880
Duke of Devonshire	Whig	1756–1757	William E. Gladstone	Liberal	1880–1885
Duke of Newcastle	Whig	1757–1762	Marquess of Salisbury	Conservative	1885–1886
Earl of Bute	Tory	1762–1763	William E. Gladstone	Liberal	1886
George Grenville	Whig	1763–1765	Marquess of Salisbury	Conservative	1886–1892
Marquess of Rockingham	Whig	1765–1766	William E. Gladstone	Liberal	1892–1894
			Earl of Rosebery	Liberal	1894–1895
Earl of Chatham	Whig	1766–1767	Marquess of Salisbury	Conservative	1895–1902
Duke of Grafton	Whig	1767–1770	Arthur J. Balfour	Conservative	1902–1905
Lord North	Tory	1770–1782	Sir Henry Campbell-Bannerman	Liberal	1905–1908
Marquess of Rockingham	Whig	1782			
			Herbert Henry Asquith	Liberal	1908–1915
Earl of Shelburne	Whig	1782–1783			
Duke of Portland	Coalition	1783	Herbert Henry Asquith	Coalition	1915–1916
William Pitt	Tory	1783–1801			
Henry Addington	Tory	1801–1804	David Lloyd George	Coalition	1916–1922
William Pitt	Tory	1804–1806	Andrew Bonar Law	Conservative	1922–1923
Lord Grenville	Whig	1806–1807	Stanley Baldwin	Conservative	1923–1924
Duke of Portland	Tory	1807–1809	J. Ramsay MacDonald	Labour	1924
Spencer Perceval	Tory	1809–1812	Stanley Baldwin	Conservative	1924–1929
Earl of Liverpool	Tory	1812–1827	J. Ramsay MacDonald	Labour	1929–1931
George Canning	Tory	1827	J. Ramsay MacDonald	Coalition	1931–1935
Viscount Goderich	Tory	1827–1828	Stanley Baldwin	Coalition	1935–1937
Duke of Wellington	Tory	1828–1830	Neville Chamberlain	Coalition	1937–1940
Earl Grey	Whig	1830–1834	Winston S. Churchill	Coalition	1940–1945
Viscount Melbourne	Whig	1834	Winston S. Churchill	Conservative	1945
Sir Robert Peel	Tory	1834–1835	Clement R. Attlee	Labour	1945–1951
Viscount Melbourne	Whig	1835–1841	Winston S. Churchill	Conservative	1951–1955
Sir Robert Peel	Tory	1841–1846	Sir Anthony Eden	Conservative	1955–1957
Lord John Russell	Whig	1846–1852	Harold Macmillan	Conservative	1957–1963
Earl of Derby	Tory	1852	Sir Alec Douglas-Home	Conservative	1963–1964
Earl of Aberdeen	Peelite	1852–1855			
Viscount Palmerston	Liberal	1855–1858	Harold Wilson	Labour	1964–1970
Earl of Derby	Conservative	1858–1859	Edward Heath	Conservative	1970–1974
Viscount Palmerston	Liberal	1859–1865	Harold Wilson	Labour	1974–1976
Earl Russell	Liberal	1865–1866	James Callaghan	Labour	1976–

GOVERNORS-GENERAL OF AUSTRALIA

Earl of Hopetoun	1901–1903	Duke of Gloucester	1945–1947
Lord Tennyson	1903–1904	Sir William John McKell	1947–1953
Lord Northcote	1904–1908	Sir William Joseph Slim	1953–1960
Earl of Dudley	1908–1911	Viscount Dunrossil	1960–1961
Lord Denman	1911–1914	Viscount De L'Isle	1961–1965
Sir Ronald Craufurd Munro-Ferguson	1914–1920	Lord Casey	1965–1969
Lord Forster of Lepe	1920–1925	Sir Paul Hasluck	1969–1974
Lord Stonehaven	1925–1931	Sir John Kerr	1974–1977
Sir Isaac Alfred Isaacs	1931–1936	Sir Zelman Cowan	1977–
Lord Gowrie	1936–1945		

AUSTRALIAN STATE GOVERNORS

NEW SOUTH WALES	Took Office
Earl Beauchamp	1901
Sir Harry Holdsworth Rawson	1902
Lord Chelmsford	1909
Sir Gerald Strickland	1913
Sir Walter Edward Davidson	1918
Sir Dudley Rawson Stratford de Chair	1924
Sir Philip Woolcott Game	1930
Sir Alexander Gore Arkwright Hore-Ruthven	1935
Sir David Murray Anderson	1936
Lord Wakehurst	1937
Sir John Northcott	1946
Sir Eric Winslow Woodward	1957
Sir Arthur Roden Cutler	1966

QUEENSLAND	
Lord Lamington	1901
Sir Herbert Charles Chermside	1902
Lord Chelmsford	1905
Sir William MacGregor	1909
Sir Hamilton John Goold-Adams	1915
Sir Matthew Nathan	1920
Sir Thomas Herbert John Chapman Goodwin	1927
Sir Leslie Orme Wilson	1932
Sir John Dudley Lavarack	1946
Sir Henry Abel Smith	1958
Sir Alan Mansfield	1966
Sir Colin Thomas Hannah	1972

SOUTH AUSTRALIA	
Lord Tennyson	1901
Sir George Ruthven Le Hunte	1903
Sir Day Hort Bosanquet	1909
Sir Henry Lionel Galway	1914
Sir William Ernest George Archibald Weighal	1920
Sir George Tom Molesworth Bridges	1922
Sir Alexander Gore Arkwright Hore-Ruthven	1928
Sir Winston Joseph Dugan	1934
Sir Charles Malcolm Barclay-Harvey	1939
Sir Charles Willoughby Moke Norrie	1944
Sir Robert Allingham George	1953
Sir Edric Montague Bastyan	1961
Sir James William Harrison	1968
Sir Mark Laurence Elwin Oliphant	1971

TASMANIA	
Sir Arthur Elibank Havelock	1901
Sir Gerald Strickland	1904
Sir Harry Barron	1909
Sir William Grey Ellison-Macartney	1913
Sir Francis Alexander Newdigate Newdegate	1917
Sir William Lamond Allardyce	1920
Sir James O'Grady	1924
Sir Ernest Clark	1933
Sir Hugh Binney	1945
Sir Ronald Hibbert Cross	1951
Lord Rowallan	1959
Sir Charles Henry Gairdner	1963
Sir Edric Montague Bastyan	1968
Sir Charles Stanley Burbury	1973

AUSTRALIAN STATE GOVERNORS
continued

VICTORIA		WESTERN AUSTRALIA	
Sir George Sydenham Clarke	1901	Sir Arthur Lawley	1901
Sir Reginald Arthur James Talbot	1904	Sir Frederick George Denham Bedford	1903
Sir Thomas David Gibson Carmichael	1908	Sir Gerald Strickland	1909
Sir John Michael Fleetwood Fuller	1911	Sir Harry Barron	1913
Sir Arthur Lyulph Stanley	1914	Sir William Grey Ellison-Macartney	1917
Earl of Stradbroke	1921	Sir Francis Alexander Newdigate	
Lord Somers	1926	Newdegate	1920
Lord Huntingfield	1934	Sir William Robert Campion	1924
Sir Winston Joseph Dugan	1939	Sir James Mitchell	1948
Sir Reginald Alexander Dallas Brooks	1949	Sir Charles Henry Gairdner	1951
Sir Rohan Delacombe	1963	Sir Douglas Anthony Kendrew	1963
Sir Henry Arthur Winneke	1974	Hughie Edwal Edwards	1974
		Sir Wallace Kyle	1975

*

AUSTRALIAN PRIME MINISTERS

Edmund Barton	Liberal	1901–1903
Alfred Denkin	Liberal	1903–1904
John Watson	Labor	1904
George Reid	Coalition	1904–1905
Alfred Deakin	Liberal	1905–1908
Andrew Fisher	Labor	1908–1909
Alfred Deakin	Liberal	1909–1910
Andrew Fisher	Labor	1910–1913
Joseph Cook	Labor	1913–1914
Andrew Fisher	Labor	1914–1915
William Morris Hughes	Labor	1915–1916
William Morris Hughes	National	1916–1923
Stanley Melbourne Bruce	Coalition	1923–1929
James Soullin	Labor	1929–1931
Joseph Lyons	United Australia	1932–1939
Earle Page	United Australia	1939
Robert Menzies	United Australia	1939–1941
Arthur Fadden	United Australia	1941
John Curtin	Labor	1941–1945
Francis Forde	Labor	1945
Ben Chifley	Labor	1943–1949
Robert Menzies	Coalition	1949–1966
Harold Holt	Coalition	1966–1967
John Gorton	Coalition	1967–1971
William McMahon	Coalition	1971–1972
Edward Gough Whitlam	Labor	1972–1975
Malcolm Fraser	Coalition	1975–

NEW ZEALAND GOVERNORS-GENERAL

Lord Plunkett (Governor)	1907–1910	Lord Freyberg	1946–1952
Lord Islington (Governor)	1910–1912	Sir Charles Willoughby Moke Norrie	1952–1957
Earl of Liverpool†	1912–1920	Viscount Cobham	1957–1962
Viscount Jellicoe	1920–1924	Sir Bernard Edward Fergusson	1962–1967
Sir Charles Fergusson	1924–1930	Sir Arthur Porritt	1967–1972
Viscount Bledisloe	1930–1935	Sir Denis Blundell	1972–1977
Viscount Galway	1935–1941	Sir Keith Holyoake	1977–
Lord Newall	1941–1946		

†Governor until 1917; then Governor-General

NEW ZEALAND PRIME MINISTERS

Joseph Ward	Liberal	1907–1912	Peter Fraser	Labour	1940–1949
William Massey	Reform	1912–1915	Sydney Holland	National	1949–1957
William Massey	Coalition	1915–1925	Keith Holyoake	National	1957
Francis Bell	Reform	1925	Walter Nash	Labour	1957–1960
Gordon Coates	Reform	1925–1928	Keith Holyoake	National	1960–1972
Joseph Ward	United	1928–1930	John Marshall	National	1972
George Forbes	United	1930	Norman Kirk	Labour	1972–1974
George Forbes	Coalition	1931–1935	Wallace Rowling	Labour	1974–1975
Michael Savage	Labour	1935–1940	Robert Muldoon	National	1975–

FRENCH KINGS AND EMPERORS

Hugh Capet	987–996	Louis XII	1498–1515
Robert II, the Pious	996–1031	François I	1515–1547
Henri I	1031–1060	Henri II	1547–1559
Philip I	1060–1108	François II	1559–1560
Louis VI, the Fat	1108–1137	Charles IX	1560–1574
Louis VII, the Young	1137–1180	Henri III	1574–1589
Philip II Augustus	1180–1223	Henri IV	1589–1610
Louis VIII	1223–1226	Louis XIII	1610–1643
Louis IX, Saint	1226–1270	Louis XIV	1643–1715
Philip III, the Bold	1270–1285	Louis XV	1715–1774
Philip IV, the Fair	1285–1314	Louis XVI*	1774–1792
Louis X	1314–1316	The First Republic	1792–1804
John I	1316	Napoleon I (Emperor)	1804–1814
Philip V	1316–1322	Louis XVIII	1814–1824
Charles IV	1322–1328	Charles X	1824–1830
Philip VI	1328–1350	Louis Philippe	1830–1848
John II	1350–1364	The Second Republic	1848–1852
Charles V	1364–1380	Napoleon III (Emperor)	1852–1870
Charles VI	1380–1422	The Third Republic	1870–1947
Charles VII	1422–1461	The Fourth Republic	1947–1958
Louis XI	1461–1483	The Fifth Republic	1958–
Charles VIII	1483–1498		

*Louis XVI's heir, Louis-Charles, who died in prison at the age of 10, never became king of France, although when his father was beheaded in January 1793, French nobles in exile proclaimed the boy Louis XVII.

HOLY ROMAN EMPERORS

	Reigned
Charlemagne	800–814
Louis I, the Pious	814–840
Lothair I	840–855
Louis II	855–875
Charles (Karl) II, the Bald	875–877
Throne vacant	877–881
Charles (Karl) III, the Fat	881–887
Throne vacant	887–891
Guido of Spoleto	891–894
Lambert of Spoleto (co-emperor)	892–898
Arnulf (rival)	896–901
Louis III of Provence	901–905
Berengar	905–924
Conrad I of Franconia (rival)	911–918
Heinrich I, the Fowler	918–936
Otto I, the Great	936–973
Otto II	973–983
Otto III	983–1002
Heinrich II, the Saint	1002–1024
Konrad II, the Salian	1024–1039
Heinrich III, the Black	1039–1056
Heinrich IV	1056–1106
Rudolf of Swabia (rival)	1077–1080
Hermann of Luxenburg (rival)	1081–1093
Conrad of Franconia (rival)	1093–1101
Heinrich V	1106–1125
Lothair II	1125–1137
Conrad III	1138–1152
Friedrich I Barbarossa	1152–1190
Heinrich VI	1190–1197
Otto IV	1198–1215
Philipp of Swabia (rival)	1198–1208
Friedrich II	1215–1250
Heinrich Raspe (rival)	1246–1247
Willem of Holland (rival)	1247–1256
Konrad IV	1250–1254
The Great Interregnum	1254–1273
Rudolf I	1273–1291
Adolf I of Nassau	1292–1298
Albrecht I	1298–1308
Heinrich VII	1308–1313
Ludwig IV	1314–1347
Karl IV	1347–1378
Wenceslas	1378–1400
Friedrich III	1400
Rupert	1400–1410
Sigismund	1410–1437
Albrecht II	1438–1439
Friedrich III	1440–1493
Maximilian I	1493–1519
Karl V	1519–1558
Ferdinand I	1558–1564
Maximilian II	1564–1576
Rudolf II	1576–1612
Matthias	1612–1619
Ferdinand II	1619–1637
Ferdinand III	1637–1657
Leopold I	1658–1705
Josef	1705–1711
Karl VI	1711–1740
Karl VII of Bavaria	1742–1745
Franz I of Lorraine	1745–1765
Josef II	1765–1790
Leopold II	1790–1792
Franz II	1792–1806

ROMAN EMPERORS

From Augustus to the fall of Rome, A.D. 476

	Reigned
Augustus (Octavian)	27 BC–AD 14
Tiberius	14–37
Caligula (Gaius)	37–41
Claudius	41–54
Nero	54–68
Galba	68–69
Otho	69
Vitellius	69
Vespasian	69–79
Titus	79–81
Domitian	81–96
Nerva	96–98
Trajan	98–117
Hadrian	117–138
Antoninus Pius	138–161
Marcus Aurelius	161–180
Lucius Aurelius Verus	161–169
Commodus	180–192
Pertinax	193
Didius Julian	193
Septimius Severus	193–211
Caracalla	211–217
Macrinus	217–218
Elagabalus	218–222
Alexander Severus	222–235
Maximinus	235–238
Gordian I	238
Gordian II	238
Pupienus	238
Balbinus	238
Gordian III	238–244
Philip 'the Arab'	244–249
Decius	249–251
Gallus	251–253
Aemilian	253
Valerian	253–259
Gallienus	259–268
Claudius II	268–270
Aurelian	270–275
Tacitus	275–276

Florian	276
Probus	276–282
Carus	282–283
Numerian ⎱	283–284
Carinus ⎰	283–285
Diocletian	284–305
Maximian	286–305
Constantius I	305–306
Galerius	305–311
Constantine I, the Great	311–337
Constantine II	337–340
Constantius II	337–361
Constans	337–350
Julian, the Apostate	361–363
Jovian	363–364
Valentinian I (in the West)	364–375
Valens (in the East)	364–378
Gratian (in the West)	375–383
Valentinian II (in the West)	375–392
Theodosius, the Great (in the East, and after 394, in the West)	379–395
Maximus (in the West)	383–388
Eugenius (in the West)	392–394
Arcadius (in the East)	395–408
Honorius (in the West)	395–423
Constantius III (co-emperor in the West)	421
Theodosius II (in the East)	408–450
Valentinian III (in the West)	425–455
Marcian (in the East)	450–457
Petronius (in the West)	455
Avitus (in the West)	455–456
Majorian (in the West)	457–461
Leo I (in the East)	457–474
Severus (in the West)	461–465
Anthemius (in the West)	467–472
Olybrius (in the West)	472
Glycerius (in the West)	473
Julius Nepos (in the West)	473–475
Leo II (in the East)	473–474
Zeno (in the East)	474–491
Romulus Augustulus (in the West)	475–476

BYZANTINE RULERS

From the fall of Rome to the fall of Constantiniple, 1453

	Reigned		Reigned
		Michael IV (the Paphlagonian)	1034–1041
Zeno	474–491	Michael V (Kalaphates)	1041–1042
Basiliscus	475–476	Constantine IX (Monomachos)	1042–1055
Anastasius I	491–518	Theodora (empress)	1055–1056
Justin I	518–527	Michael VI (Stratioticos)	1056–1057
Justinian the Great	527–565	Isaac I (Komnenos)	1057–1059
Justin II	565–578	Constantine X (Dukas)	1059–1067
Tiberius II	578–582	Romanus IV (Diogenes)	1068–1071
Maurice (Maurikios)	582–602	Michael VII (Parapinakes)	1071–1078
Phocas I	602–610	Nicephorus III (Botaniates)	1078–1081
Heraclius I	610–641	Alexius I (Komnenos)	1081–1118
Constantine III (Constantinus)	641	John II (Komnenos)	1118–1143
Heracleon (Heracleonas)	641	Manuel I (Komnenos)	1143–1180
Constans II	641–668	Alexius II (Komnenos)	1180–1183
Constantine IV (Pogonatus)	668–685	Andronicus I (Komnenos)	1183–1185
Justinian II (Rhinotmetus)	685–695	Isaac II (Angelos)	1185–1195
Leontius	695–698	Alexius III (Angelos)	1195–1203
Tiberius II (Apsimar)	698–705	Isaac II (restored)	1203–1204
Justinian II (restored)	705–711	Alexius IV	1203–1204
Philippicus	711–713	Alexius V (Dukas)	1204
Anastasius II	713–715	Baldwin I	1204–1205
Theodosius III	715–717	Henry	1205–1216
Leo III (the Isaurian)	717–741	Peter of Courtenay	1216–1217
Constantine V (Kopronymos)	741–775	Yolande	1217–1219
Leo IV	775–780	Robert of Courtenay	1219–1228
Constantine VI (Porphyrogenetos)	780–797	Baldwin II	1228–1261
Irene (empress)	797–802	John of Brienne (co-emperor)	1231–1237
Nicephorus I	802–811	Theodore I (Lascaris)	1204–1222
Stauracius (Staurakios)	811	John III (Dukas Vatatzes)	1222–1254
Michael I (Rhangabe)	811–813	Theodore II (Lascaris)	1254–1258
Leo V (the Armenian)	813–820	John IV (Lascaris)	1258–1261
Michael II (Balbus)	820–829	Michael VIII (Paleologos)	1259–1261
Theophilus I	829–842	Michael VIII	1261–1282
Michael III	842–867	Andronicus II (the Elder)	1282–1328
Basil I (the Macedonian)	867–886	Michael IX (co-emperor)	1295–1320
Leo VI (the Wise)	886–912	Andronicus III (the Younger)	1328–1341
Alexander II	912–913	John V (Paleologos)	1341–1347
Constantine VII (Porphyrogenetos)	912–959	John VI (Kantakuzenos)	1347–1354
Romanus I (Lekapenos)	920–944	John V (restored)	1355–1376
Romanus II	959–963	Andronicus IV	1376–1379
Basil II (Bulgaroktonos)	963–1025	John V (restored)	1379–1391
Nicephorus II (Phocas)	963–969	John VII	1390
John I (Tzimisces)	969–976	Manuel II	1391–1425
Constantine VIII	1025–1028	John VIII	1425–1448
Zoe (empress)	1028–1050	Constantine XI	1448–1453
Romanus III (Argyropulos)	1028–1034		

POPES OF THE ROMAN CHURCH

This list includes those officially elected, and so entitled to be called popes, and also those illegally chosen, and generally described as 'antipopes'. The antipopes are set in italic type

Peter	33–c. 67	Celestine I	422–432
Linus	c. 67–c. 76	Sixtus III	432–440
Anacletus I	c. 76–c. 88	Leo I	440–461
Clement I	c. 88–c. 97	Hilarius	461–468
Evaristus	c. 97–c. 105	Simplicius	468–483
Alexander I	c. 105–c. 115	Felix III	483–492
Sixtus I	c. 115–c. 125	Gelasius I	492–496
Telesphorus	c. 125–c. 136	Anastasius II	496–498
Hyginus	c. 136–c. 140	Symmachus	498–514
Pius I	c. 140–c. 155	*Laurentius*	*498–505*
Anicetus	c. 155–c. 166	Hormisdas	514–523
Soter	c. 166–c. 175	John I	523–526
Eleuterus	c. 175–189	Felix IV	526–530
Victor I	189–199	Boniface II	530–532
Zephyrinus	199–217	*Dioscurus*	*530*
Calixtus I	217–222	John II	533–535
Urban I	222–230	Agapetus I	535–536
Hippolytus	*222–235*	Silverius	536–537
Pontian	230–235	Vigilius	537–555
Anterus	235–236	Pelagius I	556–561
Fabian	236–250	John III	561–574
(Vacancy)	250–251	Benedict I	575–579
Cornelius	251–253	Pelagius II	579–590
Novatian	*251–c. 258*	Gregory I	590–604
Lucius I	253–254	Sabinian	604–606
Stephen I	254–257	Boniface III	607
Sixtus II	257–258	Boniface IV	608–615
(Vacancy)	258–260	Deusdedit	615–618
Dionysius	260–268	Boniface V	619–625
Felix I	269–274	Honorius I	625–638
Eutychian	275–283	(Vacancy)	638–640
Caius	283–296	Severinus	640
Marcellinus	296–304	John IV	640–642
(Vacancy)	304–308	Theodore I	642–649
Marcellus I	308–309	Martin I	649–655
Eusebius	309–310	Eugene I	655–657
Miltiades	311–314	Vitalian	657–672
Sylvester I	314–335	Adeodatus	672–676
Marcus	335–336	Donus	676–678
Julius I	337–352	Agatho	678–681
Liberius	352–366	Leo II	681–683
Felix II	*353–365*	Benedict II	684–685
Damasus I	366–383	John V	685–686
Ursinus	*366–367*	Conon	686–687
Siricius	384–399	*Theodore II*	*687*
Anastasius I	399–401	*Paschal I*	*687–692*
Innocent I	401–417	Sergius I	687–701
Zosimus	417–418	John VI	701–705
Boniface I	418–422	John VII	705–707
Eulalius	*418–419*	Sisinnius	708

POPES OF THE ROMAN CHURCH
continued

Constantine	708–715	John XIV	983–984
Gregory II	715–731	Boniface VII	984–985
Gregory III	731–741	John XV	985–996
Zacharias	741–752	Gregory V	996–999
Stephen II	752–757	*John XVI*	*996–998*
Paul I	757–767	Sylvester II	999–1003
Constantine	*767*	John XVII	1003
Philip	*767*	John XVIII	1003–1008
Stephen III	767–772	Sergius IV	1009–1012
Adrian I	772–795	Benedict VIII	1012–1024
Leo III	795–816	*Gregory VI*	*1012*
Stephen IV	816–817	John XIX	1024–1033
Paschal I	817–824	Benedict IX	1033–1045
Eugene II	824–827	Sylvester III	1045
Valentine	827	Gregory VI	1045–1046
Gregory IV	827–844	Clement II	1046–1047
John VIII	*844*	Damasus II	1048
Sergius II	844–847	Leo IX	1049–1054
Leo IV	847–855	Victor II	1055–1057
Benedict III	855–858	Stephen IX	1057–1058
Anastasius III	*855*	Benedict X	1058
Nicholas I	858–867	Nicholas II	1058–1061
Adrian II	867–872	Alexander II	1061–1073
John VIII	872–882	*Honorius II*	*1061–1064*
Marinus I	882–884	Gregory VII	1073–1085
Adrian III	884–885	*Clement III*	*1080–1100*
Stephen V	885–891	Victor III	1086–1087
Formosus	891–896	Urban II	1088–1099
Boniface VI	896	Paschal II	1099–1118
Stephen VI	896–897	*Theodoric*	*1100–1102*
Romanus	897	*Albert*	*1102*
Theodore II	897	*Sylvester IV*	*1105*
John IX	898–900	Gelasius II	1118–1119
Benedict IV	900–903	*Gregory VIII*	*1118–1121*
Leo V	903	Calixtus II	1119–1124
Christopher	903–904	Honorius II	1124–1130
Sergius III	904–911	*Celestine II*	*1124*
Anastasius III	911–913	Innocent II	1130–1143
Lando	913–914	*Anacletus II*	*1130–1138*
John X	914–928	*Victor IV*	*1138*
Leo VI	928–929	Celestine II	1143–1144
Stephen VII	929–931	Lucius II	1144–1145
John XI	931–935	Eugene III	1145–1153
Leo VII	936–939	Anastasius IV	1153–1154
Stephen VIII	939–942	Adrian IV	1154–1159
Marinus II	942–946	Alexander III	1159–1181
Agapetus II	946–955	*Victor IV*	*1159–1164*
John XII	955–963	*Paschal III*	*1164–1168*
Leo VIII	963–964	*Calixtus III*	*1168–1178*
Benedict V	964	*Innocent III*	*1179–1180*
John XIII	965–972	Lucius III	1181–1185
Benedict VI	973–974	Urban III	1185–1187
Benedict VII	974–983	Gregory VIII	1187

POPES OF THE ROMAN CHURCH
continued

Clement III	1187–1191	Alexander VI	1492–1503
Celestine III	1191–1198	Pius III	1503
Innocent III	1198–1216	Julius II	1503–1513
Honorius III	1216–1227	Leo X	1513–1521
Gregory IX	1227–1241	Adrian VI	1522–1523
Celestine IV	1241	Clement VII	1523–1534
Innocent IV	1243–1254	Paul III	1534–1549
Alexander IV	1254–1261	Julius III	1550–1555
Urban IV	1261–1264	Marcellus II	1555
Clement IV	1265–1268	Paul IV	1555–1559
(Vacancy)	1268–1271	Pius IV	1559–1565
Gregory X	1271–1276	Pius V	1566–1572
Innocent V	1276	Gregory XIII	1572–1585
Adrian V	1276	Sixtus V	1585–1590
John XXI	1276–1277	Urban VII	1590
Nicholas III	1277–1280	Gregory XIV	1590–1591
Martin IV	1281–1285	Innocent IX	1591
Honorius IV	1285–1287	Clement VIII	1592–1605
Nicholas IV	1288–1292	Leo XI	1605
Celestine V	1294	Paul V	1605–1621
Boniface VIII	1294–1303	Gregory XV	1621–1623
Benedict XI	1303–1304	Urban VIII	1623–1644
Clement V	1305–1314	Innocent X	1644–1655
John XXII	1316–1334	Alexander VII	1655–1667
Nicholas V	*1328–1330*	Clement IX	1667–1669
Benedict XII	1334–1342	Clement X	1670–1676
Clement VI	1342–1352	Innocent XI	1676–1689
Innocent VI	1352–1362	Alexander VIII	1689–1691
Urban V	1362–1370	Innocent XII	1691–1700
Gregory XI	1370–1378	Clement XI	1700–1721
Urban VI	1378–1389	Innocent XIII	1721–1724
Clement VII	*1378–1394*	Benedict XIII	1724–1730
Boniface IX	1389–1404	Clement XII	1730–1740
Benedict XIII	*1394–1423*	Benedict XIV	1740–1758
Innocent VII	1404–1406	Clement XIII	1758–1769
Gregory XII	1406–1415	Clement XIV	1769–1774
Alexander V	*1409–1410*	Pius VI	1775–1799
John XXIII	*1410–1415*	Pius VII	1800–1823
(Vacancy)	1415–1417	Leo XII	1823–1829
Martin V	1417–1431	Pius VIII	1829–1830
Clement VIII	*1423–1429*	Gregory XVI	1831–1846
Benedict XIV	*1424*	Pius IX	1846–1878
Eugene IV	1431–1447	Leo XIII	1878–1903
Felix V	*1439–1449*	Pius X	1903–1914
Nicholas V	1447–1455	Benedict XV	1914–1922
Calixtus III	1455–1458	Pius XI	1922–1939
Pius II	1458–1464	Pius XII	1939–1958
Paul II	1464–1471	John XXIII	1958–1963
Sixtus IV	1471–1484	Paul VI	1963–
Innocent VIII	1484–1492		

INDEX

INDEX

A

Aachen 777, 786, 805
Abbas 724
Abbas, Ferhat 1962
Abbas Hilmi II, 1892
Abbas III (of Persia) 1731, 1736
Abbasid dynasty 747, 750, 754, 762, 905, 929, 932
Abdalmalik 685, 705
Abd-ar-Rahman I (caliph) 756
Abd-ar-Rahman II (caliph) 822
Abd-ar-Rahman III (caliph) 912, 929
Abd-el-Krim 1926
Abdullah (of Jordan) 1951
Abdul Hamid (of Turkey) 1909
Aberdeen 83
Aberdeen, Lord 1855
Aberfan 1966
Abö, Treaty of 1743
Abolition; see Slavery
Aboukir, Battle of 1799
Abruzzi 1706
Abu-al-Abbas 750
Abu Bakr (caliph) 632, 634
Abyssinia; see Ethiopia
Abyssinian War 1936
Académie Française 1635, 1694
Acadia 1707, 1710
Académie Royale de Danse 1661
Académie Royale des Sciences 1666
Academy at Athens 529
Academy of Painting (China) 1103
Accademia del Cimento 1657
acetylene gas 1836, 1862
Achaean League 280 BC, 197 BC, 146 BC
Achaeans 192 BC
Achaemenian 600 BC
achromatic lenses 1758
Acre 1104, 1191, 1271, 1291, 1799
Act of Grace 1690
Act of Uniformity 1662
Act of Union 1707
Act of Settlement 1701
actinium 1899
Actium, Battle of 31 BC
Adam brothers 1769
Adams, John 1776, 1796, 1797, 1800
Adams, John Quincy 1824, 1825
Adams, Richard 1973
Adams, Samuel 1772
adding machines 1642, 1885
Addis Ababa 1936, 1963
Addison, Joseph 1709, 1711, 1712
Addison, Thomas 1855

"Addled Parliament" 1614
Adelaide (Austr) 1836
Adelard of Bath 1126
Aden 1418
Adalbert, archbishop 1062
Adelheid 951
Adelphi, The 1769
Adena culture, 605 BC
Adenauer, Konrad 1949, 1950
Adolf Fredrick (of Sweden) 1751, 1771
Adolf of Nassau 1291, 1298
Adolphus (of Sweden) 1630, 1631, 1632
adrenalin 1901
Adrian I (Pope) 781
Adrian IV (Pope) 1154, 1155, 1159
Adrian VI (Pope) 1522, 1523
Adrianople 323, 378, 1362, 1713, 1878
Adrianople, Treaty of 1829
Adriatic 990
advertisements 1712
Aegina 489 BC, 458 BC
Aemilius Lepidus 78 BC, 77 BC
Aemilius Papinianus 205
Aeolians 1100 BC
Aequi 458 BC, 431 BC
Aëtius 436, 437, 451
Aetolian League 290 BC, 197 BC
Aetolians 219 BC, 192 BC
Afghanistan 787, 962, 997, 1001, 1030, 1151, 1187, 1193, 1206, 1387, 1738, 1747, 1929
Afghans 1451, 1556, 1709, 1722, 1730
Afghan Wars 1838, 1840, 1841, 1842, 1879
A.F.L-C.I.O. 1955
Afonso V (of Portugal) 1481
Afonso VI (of Portugal) 1656, 1667
Afonso de Albuquerque 1509
Afonso Henriques (of Portugal) 1112, 1128, 1139, 1143, 1185
African Company 1723
African Trading Company 1672
Afrika Korps 1941
Agadir (Morocco) 1911, 1960
Agassiz, Jean Louis 1840
Agathocles of Syracuse 311 BC
Aghlabid dynasty 801, 909
Aghlabid Muslims 827
Agincourt, Battle of 1415
Agilulf 590
Agnew, Spiro T. 1973
Agricola 77, 85

Agricola, Georg 1556
Agrippina 48, 54, 59
Ahmadabad 1411
Ahmad Shah of Gujarat 1411
Ahmed, Shah Durani 1747
Aidan 633
Aiken, Howard 1937
Ain Jalut 1260
Ainu territory 781
air 1654, 1777
airships 1898, 1919, 1930
Aisne, Battle of 1917
Aistulf 749
Aix-la-Chapelle; see Aachen
Aix-la-Chapelle, Treaties of 1668, 1748
Ajanta 51, 740
Akbar 1681
Akbar the Great (of India) 1556, 1562, 1573, 1582, 1605
Akhenaton 1379 BC
Akkadian empire 2360 BC, 2280 BC, 2400 BC, 2180 BC
Akko; see Acre
Akroinon, Anatolia 739
Alabama 1702, 1819, 1861, 1872
Alais, Peace of 1629
Alalia, Battle of 535 BC
Al-Amin 809
Alamanni 214, 235, 256, 276, 298, 355, 357, 496
Alamein, Battle of 1942
Alamo 1838
Alans 275, 372, 406, 409
Alarcón, Juan Ruiz de 1628
Alarcos 1195
Alaric 395, 396, 401, 402, 403, 409, 410
Alaska 1741, 1799, 1867, 1903, 1959, 1969, 1977
Al-Azhar university 970
Albania 1271, 1344, 1420, 1912, 1924, 1928, 1939, 1946, 1961
Albany Convention, The 1754
Albee, Edward 1962
Albert, the Bear 1138, 1150
Albert (of Belgium) 1909
Albert (of Saxe-Coburg-Gotha) 1840
Alberta 1905
Alberti, Leon 1446, 1452, 1470
Albigensians 1206, 1208
Alboin 568
Albrecht I (emperor) 1298, 1308
Albrecht II (emperor) 1438, 1439
Albrecht of Austria 1437

INDEX

INDEX

INDEX

INDEX

INDEX

INDEX

INDEX

INDEX

INDEX

INDEX

INDEX

INDEX

O

INDEX

INDEX

Q

R

INDEX

INDEX

INDEX

INDEX

INDEX

INDEX

X

Xanthippus 255 BC
Xavier, Francis 1549
xenon gas 1898
Xenophon 400 BC
Xerxes I (Persia) 486 BC
Xerxes II (Persia) 424 BC
"x-rays" 1895
"XYZ Affair" 1797

Y

Yale, Elihu 1718
Yale University 1701, 1718
Yamasaki Minoru 1972
Yamassee Indians 1715
Ya'qub (Afghanistan) 1879
Yaroslav 1019, 1036, 1054
Yashifusa 858
Yathrib 622
Ye (Anyang) 534–550
Year of Pacification 1135
"Year of Revolutions" 1848
Yeats, William Butler 1895, 1922
Yedigei 1408
yellow fever 1900
Yellow River (China) 1194
Yemen 1761, 1958
Yezdigird III: 634
Yomei (of Japan) 587
Yonge, Charlotte M. 1853
Yoritomo 1185, 1192
York 735, 766, 781, 866, 1437, 1440,
    1449, 1452, 1453, 1455, 1460, 1461,
    1468, 1644
York, Duke of 1664
York, House of 1461–1485
Yorkists 1448, 1455, 1459, 1460, 1461,
    1464, 1465
Yorkshire 1131, 1132
Yorktown (Va.) 1781
Yoruba 870, 1168
Yoshimasa (of Japan) 1449
Yoshihito (of Japan) 1912
Young, Edward 1742, 1762
Young American Peace Corps 1961
Young Men's Christian Association 1844
Young Plan 1929
"Young Pretender" (Charles Edward
    Stuart) 1745
Ypres, Battle of 1915
Yüan dynasty 1260, 1368
Yuan Shih-kai 1913
Yucatan 1517
Yueh State 334 BC
Yugoslavia 1918, 1943, 1946, 1947, 1948
Youngay, Battle of 1839
Yunnan uprising 1855

Z

Zaïre (see also Belgian Congo) 885, 1959,
    1960, 1971
Zaïre River 1875, 1877, 1884, 1971
Zallaka 1086
Zama, Africa 202 BC
Zamenhof, Ludovic Lagarno, 1887
Zambesi River 1430, 1616, 1852, 1855
Zambia (see also Northern Rhodesia)
    1964
Zangwill, Israel 1892
Zanj Revolt 883
Zanzibar 1885, 1890, 1963, 1964
Zeno (emperor) 476
Zenobia (of Palmyra) 267, 273
Zenta, Battle of 1697
Zeppelin, Ferdinand von 1898
Zeppelins 1914, 1915
zero (symbol) 600
Zeta (Montenegro) 1371
Zinnemann, Fred, 1952
Zionist Conference 1897
zirconium 1786
ziggurats 3000 BC, 2060 BC, 586 BC
zinc 500 BC
zodiac, signs of 2000 BC
Zoë (empress) 1028, 1034, 1042, 1050
Zoë (of Russia) 1472
Zog (of Albania) 1928
Zola, Emile 1880, 1885, 1892, 1898
Zollverein 1833
zoology 1599, 1771
Zorndof, Battle of 1758
Zubaran, Francisco de 1635
Zuider Zee 1906
Zululand 1837, 1838
Zulu war 1879
Zuravna, Treaty of 1676
Zürich (Switz) 1351, 1389, 1436, 1442,
    1443, 1444, 1450, 1531
Zürich, Battle of 1799
Zutphen, Battle of 1586
Zwingli, Huldrich 1531